AMERICAN PASSAGES

A HISTORY OF THE UNITED STATES

BRIEF EDITION

VOLUME I: TO 1877

EDWARD L. AYERS

University of Virginia

LEWIS L. GOULD

University of Texas at Austin, Emeritus

DAVID M. OSHINSKY

University of Texas at Austin

JEAN R. SODERLUND

Lehigh University

CANADA
PACIFIC OCEAN
Seattle
Olympia
WASHINGTON
Portland
Salem
OREGON
Helena
MONTANA
NORTH DAKOTA
Bismarck
Wounded Knee
Little Big Horn
SOUTH DAKOTA
Pierre
Boise
IDAHO
WYOMING
Promontory Point
Salt Lake City
NEBRASKA
Cheyenne
Omah
Lincoln
Reno
Carson City
Sacramento
San Francisco
NEVADA
UTAH
Boulder
Denver
COLORADO
Lecompton/Top
KANSAS
CALIFORNIA
Ronald Reagan's Ranch
Los Alamos
Santa Fe
Los Angeles
ARIZONA
Oklahoma City
Acoma
Albuquerque
OKLAHOM
San Diego
Phoenix
NEW MEXICO
Dallas
El Paso
TEXAS
MEXICO
Austin
Alamo
San Antonio
Brownsville
RUSSIA
Yukon
Fairbanks
ALASKA
CANADA
Anchorage
Bering Sea
Juneau
Gulf of Alaska
Aleutian Islands
Kauai
Lihue
Oahu
Honolulu
Lahaina
Maui
HAWAII
Kailua Kona
Hilo
Hawaii
PACIFIC OCEAN

CANADA
Lake Superior
Lake Michigan
Lake Huron
Lake Ontario
Lake Erie
ESOTA
MICHIGAN
WISCONSIN
ILLINOIS
INDIANA
OHIO
NEW YORK
PENNSYLVANIA
VERMONT
NEW HAMPSHIRE
MAINE
MASSACHUSETTS
RHODE ISLAND
CONNECTICUT
NEW JERSEY
MARYLAND
DELAWARE
WEST VIRGINIA
VIRGINIA
KENTUCKY
TENNESSEE
NORTH CAROLINA
SOUTH CAROLINA
GEORGIA
ALABAMA
MISSISSIPPI
LOUISIANA
ARKANSAS
MISSOURI
FLORIDA
WA
ATLANTIC OCEAN
Gulf of Mexico
BAHAMAS
St. Paul
Madison
Des Moines
Lansing
Detroit
Dearborn
Flint
Des Plaines
Chicago
Haymarket Square
Springfield
Indianapolis
Tippecanoe
Greenville
Gnadenhutten
Columbus
Dayton
Canton
Cleveland
Kent State University
Buffalo
Rochester
Seneca Falls
Saratoga
Albany
Woodstock
Hyde Park
Newburgh
New York
Statue of Liberty
Oyster Bay
Levittown
Hartford
Lawrence
Lowell
Lexington
Salem
Brook Farm
Boston
Plymouth
Pawtucket
Bethlehem
Princeton
Grovers Mill
Trenton
Harrisburg
Three-Mile Island
Philadelphia
Dover
Homestead
Pittsburgh
Gettysburg
Harpers Ferry
Washington, D.C.
Annapolis
Charleston
Richmond
Appomattox
Norfolk
Jamestown
Roanoke Island
Raleigh
Frankfort
Westminster College
Alton
St. Louis
East St. Louis
Jefferson City
White River
Nashville
Dayton
Memphis
Shiloh
Scottsboro
Little Rock
Hope
Atlanta
Columbia
Charleston
Stono
Port Royal
Jackson State University
Jackson
Selma
Montgomery
Mobile
Pensacola
Tallahassee
St. Augustine
Baton Rouge
New Orleans
Cape Canaveral
0 150 300 miles
0 150 300 kilometers
Important places in American Passages

Publisher/Executive Editor: Clark Baxter
Development Editor: Margaret McAndrew Beasley
Manuscript Editor: Carolyn Smith
Assistant Editor: Julie Iannacchino
Editorial Assistant: Jonathan Katz
Technology Project Manager: Jennifer Ellis
Marketing Manager: Caroline Croley
Marketing Assistant: Mary Ho
Advertising Project Manager: Stacey Purviance
Project Manager, Editorial Production: Ray A. K. Crawford
Print/Media Buyer: Karen Hunt
Permissions Editor: Stephanie Keough-Hedges
Production Service: Emily Bush, Carlisle Communications, Ltd.
Photo Researcher: Lili Weiner
Copy Editor: Sarah Greer Bush
Cover Designer: Lisa Mirski Devenish
Cover Image: Copyright Smithsonian American Art Museum, Washington, DC/Art Resource, NY
Cover Printer: Interglobe Printing, Transcontinental
Compositor: Carlisle Communications, Ltd.
Printer: Interglobe Printing, Transcontinental

Printed in Canada
1 2 3 4 5 6 7 06 05 04 03 02

For more information about our products, contact us at:
Thomson Learning Academic Resource Center
1-800-423-0563

For permission to use material from this text, contact us by:
Phone: 1-800-730-2214
Fax: 1-800-730-2215
Web: http://www.thomsonrights.com

Library of Congress Cataloging-in-Publication Data

American passages: a history of the United States/Edward L. Ayers . . . [et al.].—Brief ed.
p.cm.
Includes bibliographical references and index.
ISBN 0-15-505117-2 (alk. paper)
1. United States—History. I. Ayers, Edward L., 1953-

E178.1 .A4926 2002
973—dc21 2002024970

Wadsworth/Thomson Learning
10 Davis Drive
Belmont, CA 94002-3098
USA

Asia
Thomson Learning
5 Shenton Way #01-01
UIC Building
Singapore 068808

Australia
Nelson Thomson Learning
102 Dodds Street
South Melbourne, Victoria 3205
Australia

Canada
Nelson Thomson Learning
1120 Birchmount Road
Toronto, Ontario M1K 5G4
Canada

Europe/Middle East/Africa
Thomson Learning
High Holborn House
50/51 Bedford Row
London WC1R 4LR
United Kingdom

Latin America
Thomson Learning
Seneca, 53
Colonia Polanco
11560 Mexico D.F.
Mexico

Spain
Paraninfo Thomson Learning
Calle/Magallanes, 25
28015 Madrid, Spain

About the Authors

EDWARD L. AYERS Edward Ayers is the Hugh P. Kelly Professor of History at the University of Virginia. He was educated at the University of Tennessee and Yale University, where he received his Ph.D. in American Studies. He has written and edited five books. *The Promise of the New South: Life After Reconstruction* (1992) won prizes for the best book on the history of American race relations and on the history of the American South. It was a finalist for both the National Book Award and the Pulitzer Prize. He is the co-editor of *The Oxford Book of the American South* (1997) and *All Over the Map: Rethinking American Regions* (1996). Ayers has won a number of teaching awards, including the Outstanding Faculty Award from the State Council of Higher Education and the Distinguished Young Teacher Award from the Alumni Board of Trustees.

Ayers' current work is "The Valley of the Shadow: Two Communities in the American Civil War." The World Wide Web version of the project has been ranked as one of the top forty education sites in the world by the *Encyclopedia Britannica* and named as the best Civil War site by Yahoo! Ayers is Executive Director of the Center for Digital History, an institute at the University of Virginia dedicated to crafting and teaching history in new media, and is currently serving as Dean of the College and Graduate School of Arts and Sciences. Ayers is the author of Chapters 9–15.

LEWIS L. GOULD Lewis Gould is the Eugene C. Barker Centennial Professor Emeritus at the University of Texas at Austin. After receiving his Ph.D. from Yale University, he began a teaching career in which he had more than ten thousand students. He was recognized for outstanding undergraduate teaching in large lecture sections of the American History survey and for his excellent graduate teaching.

Gould is a nationally recognized authority on First Ladies and the presidency. His comments have appeared in numerous press accounts about presidential wives, including *The New York Times, The Washington Post,* and *The Los Angeles Times.* He has appeared on C-Span, *The CBS Morning News, Nightline, The ABC Evening News,* and a large number of nationally syndicated radio programs. He also participated in the PBS program on Lyndon Johnson and the A&E biography of Lady Bird Johnson. Among his important publications are *American First Ladies: Their Lives and Their Legacy* (2001); *1968: The Election That Changed America* (1993); *The Presidency of Theodore Roosevelt* (1991); *Lady Bird Johnson: Our Environmental First Lady* (1999); and *The Presidency of William McKinley* (1980). Gould is the author of Chapters 16–24, 31, and 32.

DAVID M. OSHINSKY David Oshinsky received his undergraduate degree from Cornell University and his doctorate from Brandeis. He has taught history for the past twenty-six years at Rutgers University, where he holds the Board of Governors Chair and is presently chairman of the History Department. Oshinsky is the author of four books, including *A Conspiracy So Immense: The World of Joe McCarthy* (1983), which was voted one of the year's "best books" by the "New York Sunday Times Book Review," and won the Hardeman Prize for the best work about the U.S. Congress. His latest book, *"Worse than Slavery": Parchman Farm and the Ordeal of Jim Crow Justice* (1996), won both the Robert Kennedy Book Award for the year's most distinguished contribution to the field of human rights, and the American Bar Association's Scribes Award for distinguished legal writing.

Oshinsky is a regular contributor to scholarly journals, to the "Washington Post Book World," "New York Sunday Times Book Review," "New York Times Op-Ed Page," and "New York Times Sunday Magazine." He was awarded a senior fellowship by the National Endowment for the Humanities and spent 1999–2000 as a Phi Beta Kappa Visiting Scholar. Oshinsky is the author of Chapters 25–30.

JEAN R. SODERLUND Jean Soderlund is Professor and Chair of the Department of History at Lehigh University and Co-Director of the Lawrence Henry Gipson Institute for Eighteenth-Century Studies. She received her Ph.D. from Temple University and was a post-doctoral fellow at the McNeil Center for Early American Studies at the University of Pennsylvania. Her book *Quakers and Slavery: A Divided Spirit* won the Alfred E. Driscoll Publication Prize of the New Jersey Historical Commission. Soderlund was an editor of three volumes of the Papers of William Penn (1981–1983) and co-authored *Freedom by Degrees: Emancipation in Pennsylvania and Its Aftermath* (1991).

She has written articles and chapters in books on the history of women, African Americans, Native Americans, Quakers, and the development of abolition in the British North American colonies and early United States. She is currently working on a study of the Lenape people within colonial New Jersey society. She is a council member of the McNeil Center for Early American Studies, and served as a committee chair for the American Historical Association. Soderlund is the author of Chapters 1–8.

IT'S ABOUT TIME . . . .

How do we get the past to stay still long enough to see it clearly? Textbooks on the history of the United States typically pursue one topic at a time—politics, culture, reform, or the economy. But people do not live one topic at a time. We encounter all the facets of history every day, our private lives interweaving with events and trends larger than ourselves.

People confront surprise every day, for history seldom follows a straight line. Every generation of Americans has seen history deal them unexpected challenges. No one could have predicted Bacon's Rebellion, John Brown's Raid, the Haymarket Riot, or the Watergate break-in. Nor could Americans have foreseen the emergence of Thomas Paine, Harriet Beecher Stowe, Henry Ford, or Martin Luther King, Jr. And who among us could know on the morning of September 11, 2001, how different life would seem just that afternoon and in the days and weeks following, as the story unfolded?

This book is built around the recognition that all people live in the flow of time. It shows the complicated and subtle ways that strands of history touched and connected. Each chapter carefully follows the contours of certain years, weaving politics, economics, and culture into an interrelated pattern.

American Passages offers several tools to help us see the past in connection. Its timelines and "passages" sections provide broad overviews that connect across chapters. Its illustrations and graphs are tightly woven into the narrative. Its rich Web site at http://ayersbrief.wadsworth.com amplifies the themes and materials of the book, offering hundreds of documents, maps, illustrations, and multimedia selections carefully matched to the text.

This brief edition preserves the key elements that help convey the excitement, drama, and importance of this nation's past. It achieves its brevity by careful editing, trimming words and phrases throughout rather than simply abandoning certain topics and events. We have kept many of the maps and images that help give this text its particular effectiveness and we have retained a carefully chosen primary document in each chapter.

SUPPLEMENTS

Test Manual
Janet Brantley, Texarkana College
0-15-505099-0
This test manual provides the instructor with a variety of question styles that emphasize critical thinking skills for the student. In addition to multiple-choice questions, there are identification questions, essay questions, and book report questions. This item is free to instructors.

Instructor's Manual
Barbara Stites, Los Angeles City College
0-15-505081-8
This guide is designed to support the instructor in preparing lectures and developing discussion questions and assignments. This manual contains chapter summaries and objectives; a "Making it Real" section that provides recommendations for assignments, lecture topic suggestions, and a "Further Resources" part that lists additional readings and audio and visual resources.

Overhead Transparency Acetates
Burt Rieff, University of North Alabama
0-15-506763-X
This full color transparency package contains over 180 transparencies comprising many outstanding maps, charts, and graphs from *American Passages.* Also included are a number of carefully selected images from the text. Provided for each acetate are teaching notes that offer the instructor a brief explanation of each acetate, features to note, and questions to facilitate classroom discussion.

American Passages: A History of the United States
Online Resources
http://ayersbrief.wadsworth.com
This innovative *American Passages* Web site provides access to many online resources for both instructors and students. On this site can be found the following:

- Chapters: All items are organized according to the same thirty-two chapters contained in the *American Passages* text. Within each chapter, the primary source materials are presented in modules organized around a particular event, place, time, or theme within the chapter's chronological structure.
- Exercises: Study questions, with answers, encourage students to think more deeply about the primary source materials, the issues and themes to which they connect, and the relevant parts of *American Passages* to which they relate. The exercises follow a variety of strategies: some focus on a particular document; others concentrate on several documents within one chapter, still others address themes and issues that connect items in different chapters and across time periods.
- Links: An annotated list of links directs students outside the *American Passages* Web site to especially useful and relevant content-rich sites on the Internet. The list is organized by chapter and is designed to complement material presented both on the Web site and in the text.
- Maps: Dynamic and animated interactive maps dramatically illustrate major developments and changes occurring over a period of time.
- Index: Several indices provide an archive of all primary source materials on the site. The indices point to summaries of the documents and to the documents themselves. Students may browse by subject, chapter, date, and type of item.

Study Guide, Volume I: To 1877;
Volume II: From 1863
Richard McMillan, Los Angeles Pierce College
Vol. I 0-15-505087-7 Vol. II 0-15-505093-1
This student resource guide is organized to assist the student in his or her comprehension of the material found in each chapter. It contains chapter outlines and summaries, essay questions, identification questions, and multiple-choice questions that provide aid in the student's understanding of the text. At the end of each chapter are map exercises, which reinforce the student's geographical knowledge as well.
Map Workbook Vol I (Rebhorn)
0-15-506758-3
Map Workbook Vol II (Rebhorn)
0-15-506759-1
Docs Workbook Vol I (Weise)
0-15-506760-5
Docs Workbook Vol II (Weise)
0-15-506761-3

American Passages Historical Geography Guide, Volume I: To 1877; Volume II: From 1863
Marlette Rebhorn, Austin Community College
This mapping workbook provides students with challenging and engaging exercises designed to test their geographical knowledge. In addition to labeling exercises, there are also fill-in questions to reinforce the student's comprehension.

United States History Documents Collection, Volume I: To 1877; Volume II: From 1863
Robert Weise, Eastern Kentucky University
This outstanding collection of documents includes over 100 primary source readings with introductory notes for each selection. This is available free to instructors and may be purchased by the student.

Second World War Photo CD-ROM
0-15-501957-0
The Second World War CD-ROM is a three-disc set that features selections from the National Archives. It includes more than 900 black and white images taken during the war that are accompanied by historically accurate captions. Adoption requirements apply.

ExamView
Windows 0-15-505075-3; Macintosh 0-15-508492-5
This fully integrated suite of test creation, delivery, and classroom management tools includes Thomson World Class Test, Test Online, and World Class Management software. Thomson World Class Testing Tools allows professors to deliver tests via print, floppy, hard drive, LAN, or Internet. With these tools, professors can create cross-platform exam files from publisher files or existing WESTest 3.2 test banks, edit questions, create questions, and provide their own feedback to objective test questions—enabling the system to work as a tutorial or an examination. In addition, professors can create tests that include multiple-choice, true/false, or matching questions; track the progress of an entire class or an individual student; integrate testing and tutorial results into the class management tool, which offers scoring, gradebook, and reporting capabilities. Call-in testing is also available.

InfoTrac College Edition
http://infotrac.thomsonlearning.com
Turn to *InfoTrac College Edition* for the latest news and research articles—online, updated daily, and spanning four years! Choose to package *InfoTrac College Edition* with any Wadsworth text and you and your students will have four months of free access to this easy-to-use online database of reliable, full-length articles (not abstracts) from hundreds of top academic journals and popular sources. Among the journals available twenty-four hours a day, seven days a week are *American History, Antiquity, Biography, History Today, Past & Present, Smithsonian,* and many more.

WebTutor on WebCT and Blackboard
http://e.thomsonlearning.com
"Out of the box" or customizable . . . *WebTutor* provides help when and where you need it most! *WebTutor* takes your course beyond classroom boundaries to an anywhere, anytime environment. This content-rich, Web-based teaching and learning tool is filled with preloaded, text-specific content and is ready to use as soon as you and your students log on. At the same time, you can customize the content in any way you choose, from uploading images and other resources, to adding Web links, to creating your own practice materials. For students *WebTutor* offers real-time access to a full array of study tools including flashcards (with audio), practice quizzes, online tutorials, and Web links. You can use *WebTutor* to provide virtual office hours, post your syllabi, set up threaded discussions, track student progress with quizzing material, and more. *WebTutor* provides rich communication tools, including a course calendar, asynchronous discussion, real-time chat, a whiteboard, and an integrated email system.

American HistoryLink
0-534-58715-1
This cross-platform digital library and presentation tool is available on one convenient multiplatform CD-ROM. With its easy-to-use interface, you can take advantage of Wadsworth's already-created text-specific presentations, which consist of map images, slides of art and architecture photos,

interactive map and timeline images, and much more. You can even customize your own presentation by importing your personal lecture slides or other material you choose. The result is an interactive and fluid lecture that truly engages your students.

American Heritage Reader

In partnership with *American Heritage*, the preeminent magazine of the American experience, Thomson Custom Publishing is offering you the opportunity to build your own Custom American Heritage reader. The process is simple, contact our Custom group at 1-800-335-9983 or ask your Thomson sales representative for details. Then we can share with you a list of articles available for your reader. For nearly half a century, American Heritage has been the nation's memory, telling our shared story with verve, humor, passion, and, above all, authority. Our wars and our songs, our heroes and our villains, our art and our technology—all are brought to vivid and immediate life through incisive prose and a wealth of original images.

American History Atlas

0-15-505919-x

An invaluable collection of more than fifty clear and colorful historical maps covering all major periods in American history. Please contact your local sales representative for information.

Historic Times: Wadsworth History Resource Center

http://history.wadsworth.com

Both instructors and students will enjoy our Historic Times Web Page. From this full-service site, instructors and students can access many selections, such as a career center, lessons on surfing the Web, and links to great history-related Web sites. Students can also take advantage of the online Student Guide to InfoTrac College Edition, featuring lists of article titles with discussion and critical thinking questions linked to the articles to invite deeper examination of the material. Instructors can visit book-specific sites to learn more about our texts and supplements, and students can access chapter-by-chapter resources for the book, including interactive quizzes.

American Journey Online

The landmark events of American history recorded by eye-witnesses . . . the great themes of the American experience according to those who lived it . . . these are captured in the 15 primary source collections that make up American Journey Online. Each key topic in American history and culture addressed by the series encompasses hundreds of carefully selected, rare documents, pictures, and archival audio and video. Essays, headnotes, and captions by scholars set the sources in context.

Full text searchability and extensive hyperlinking provide fast and easy access and cross-referencing. The scope of the collections and the power of online delivery make American Journey Online a unique and unprecedented tool for historical inquiry for today's researchers.

Acknowledgments

I would like to thank my students and colleagues at the University of Virginia who have helped me struggle with the tough questions of American history. I am grateful, too, to the diligent editors such as Margaret Beasley for their patience, good will, and good advice in the creation of this book. Finally, I am very appreciative of my co-authors, who have been engaged scholars, thoughtful critics, devoted teachers, and good friends throughout the years it took us to write *American Passages.*

EDWARD L. AYERS

I would like to acknowledge the help of the following former students who contributed in constructive ways to the completion of the textbook: Martin Ansell, Christie Bourgeois, Thomas Clarkin, Stacy Cordery, Debbie Cottrell, Patrick Cox, Scott Harris, Byron Hulsey, Jonathan Lee, John Leffler, Mark Young, and Nancy Beck Young. Karen Gould gave indispensable support and encouragement throughout the process of writing the text. I am grateful as well to the readers of my chapters who made so many useful and timely criticisms.

LEWIS L. GOULD

I would like to thank my colleagues and students at Rutgers for allowing me to test out an endless stream of ideas and issues relating to modern American history, and also for their thoughts on how a good college textbook should "read" and what it should contain. As always, the support and love of my family—Matt, Efrem, Ari, and Jane—was unshakable. Above all, I must commend my co-authors and my editors for their remarkable patience and professionalism during this long collaborative process.

DAVID M. OSHINSKY

I am grateful to my husband, Rudolf Soderlund, and my family for their support throughout this project. They have provided valuable feedback on the text. Many scholars in the colonial and early national periods shared their ideas orally and through publications. I received very helpful comments from James S. Saeger, Roger D. Simon, Marianne S. Wokeck, my co-authors of this text, and the anonymous readers for the press.

JEAN R. SODERLUND

Reviewers

The authors wish to thank the following professors who have provided comments and suggestions on manuscript at various stages in the writing of *American Passages.*

Joseph Adams — St. Louis Community College at Meramec
Dawn Alexander — Abilene Christian University
Charles Allbee — Burlington Community College
Julius Amin — University of Dayton
Melodie Andrews — Mankato State University
Robert Becker — Louisiana State University
Peter Bergstrom — Illinois State University
John Brooke — Tufts University
Neil Brooks — Essex Community College
Linda D. Brown — Odessa College
Colin Calloway — Dartmouth University
Milton Cantor — University of Massachusetts
Kay Carr — Southern Illinois University
Paul Chardoul — Grand Rapids Junior College
Myles Clowers — San Diego City College
William Cobb — Utah Valley State College
David Coon — Washington State University
Stacey Cordery — Monmouth College
Debbie Cottrell — Smith College
A. Glenn Crothers — Indiana University Southeast
David Cullen — Collin County Community College
Christine Daniels — Michigan State University
Ronnie Day — East Tennessee State University
Matthew Dennis — University of Oregon
Robert Downtain — Tarrant County Junior College, Northeast Campus
Robert Elam — Modesto Junior College
Monte S. Finkelstein — Tallahassee Community College
Linda Foutch — Walter State Community College
Robert G. Fricke — West Valley College
David Hamilton — University of Kentucky
Beatriz Hardy — Coastal Carolina University
Peter M. G. Harris — Temple University
Thomas Hartshorne — Cleveland State University
Ron Hatzenbuehler — Idaho State University
Robert Hawkes — George Mason University
William L. Hewitt — West Chester University
James Houston — Oklahoma State University
Raymond Hyser — James Madison University
Lillian Jones — Santa Monica College
Jim Kluger — Pima Community College
James Lacy — Contra Costa College
Alton Lee — University of South Dakota
Liston Leyendecker — Colorado State University
Robert Marcom — San Antonio College
Greg Massey — Freed-Hardeman University
Michael Mayer — University of Montana
Loyce B. Miles — Hinds Community College
Elsa Nystrom — Kennesaw State
David O'Neill — Rutgers University
Elizabeth R. Osborn — Indiana University—Purdue University, Indianapolis
Betty Owens — Greenville Technical College
Mark Parillo — Kansas State University
J'Nell Pate — Tarrant County Junior College, Northeast Campus
Louis Potts — University of Missouri at Kansas City
Noel Pugach — University of New Mexico
Alice Reagan — Northern Virginia Community College
Marlette Rebhorn — Austin Community College, Rio Grande Campus
David Reimers — New York University
Hal Rothman — Wichita State University
John G. Selby — Roanoke College
Ralph Shaffer — California Polytechnic University
Kenneth Smemo — Morehead State University
Jack Smith — Great Basin College
Thaddeus Smith — Middle Tennessee State University
Phillip E. Stebbins — Pennsylvania State University
Marshall Stevenson — Ohio State University
William Stockton — Johnson County Community College
Frank Towers — Clarion University
Daniel Usner — Cornell University
Daniel Vogt — Jackson State University
Stephen Webre — Louisiana Technical College
John C. Willis — University of the South
Harold Wilson — Old Dominion University
Nan Woodruff — Pennsylvania State University
Bertram Wyatt-Brown — University of Florida
Sherri Yeager — Chabot College
Robert Zeidel — University of Wisconsin

List of Documents

List of Maps

Brief Table of Contents

Detailed Table of Contents

Passages Prehistory to 1763 2

Chapter 1 Contact, Conflict, and Exchange in the Atlantic World to 1590 8

Chapter 2 Colonization of North America, 1590–1675 32

CHAPTER 3 CRISIS AND CHANGE, 1675–1720 56

CHAPTER 4 THE EXPANSION OF COLONIAL BRITISH AMERICA, 1720–1763 78

PASSAGES 1764 TO 1814 102

CHAPTER 5 WARS FOR INDEPENDENCE, 1764–1783 106

Chapter 8 The New Republic Faces a New Century, 1800–1814 179

Passages 1815 to 1855 204

Chapter 9 Exploded Boundaries, 1815–1826 208

Chapter 10 The Years of Andrew Jackson, 1827–1836 231

CHAPTER 11 PANIC AND BOOM, 1837–1845 251

CHAPTER 12 EXPANSION AND REACTION, 1846–1854 272

PASSAGES 1855 TO 1877 294

CHAPTER 13 BROKEN BONDS, 1855–1861 300

CHAPTER 14 DESCENT INTO WAR, 1861–1862 321

CHAPTER 15 BLOOD AND FREEDOM, 1863–1867 346

CHAPTER 16 RECONSTRUCTION ABANDONED, 1867–1877 373

APPENDIX A-1

INDEX I-1

PASSAGES

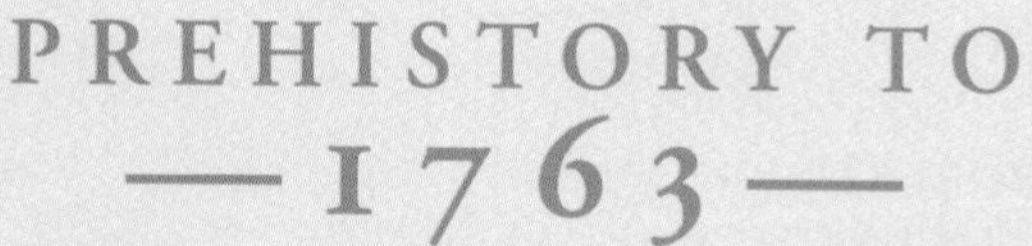

And so we journeyed for seventeen days, at the end of which we crossed the river [Rio Grande] and traveled for seventeen more. At sunset, on plains between some very tall mountains, we found some people who eat nothing but powdered straw for a third of the year. Since it was that season of the year, we had to eat it too. At the end of our journey we found a permanent settlement where there was abundant corn. The people gave us a large quantity of it and of cornmeal, squash, beans, and cotton blankets. . . . From here we traveled [to where people] gave me five emeralds made into arrowheads. . . . Since they seemed very fine to me, I asked them where they had gotten them. They told me that they brought them from some very high mountains to the North.

—Cabeza de Vaca, 1542*

FROM 1534 TO 1536, the Spanish explorer, Álvar Núñez Cabeza de Vaca, and three others, including a black man, Esteban, traveled through Texas and northern Mexico, trying to reach Mexico City. They had been part of an expedition to Florida that ran afoul of Apalachee Indians, escaped across the Gulf of Mexico in makeshift boats, then were enslaved in Texas by Karankawa Indians. In his *Relación,* Cabeza de Vaca described their adventures, including the harrowing passage across the gulf, long journeys without food, and sojourns among Texas Indians.

Warpaths, ocean voyages, hunting trails, trade routes, death, communication and exchange among people—creating societies in America embodied passages of every kind. Asians moved across the Bering land bridge more than 14,000 years ago, settling throughout North and South America. Over time, they created distinct cultures in every part of the hemisphere, from the Aztecs of Mexico to the Algonquians of eastern North America. Over thousands of years, American civilizations rose and fell, as empires built pyramids and temple mounds, developed cities and cultures, and competed for territory and trade.

In the fifteenth century A.D., Western Europeans came to America to fish, trade, and establish colonies, bringing new technology, lust for wealth, and destructive microbes that spelled death for millions of Native Americans. The

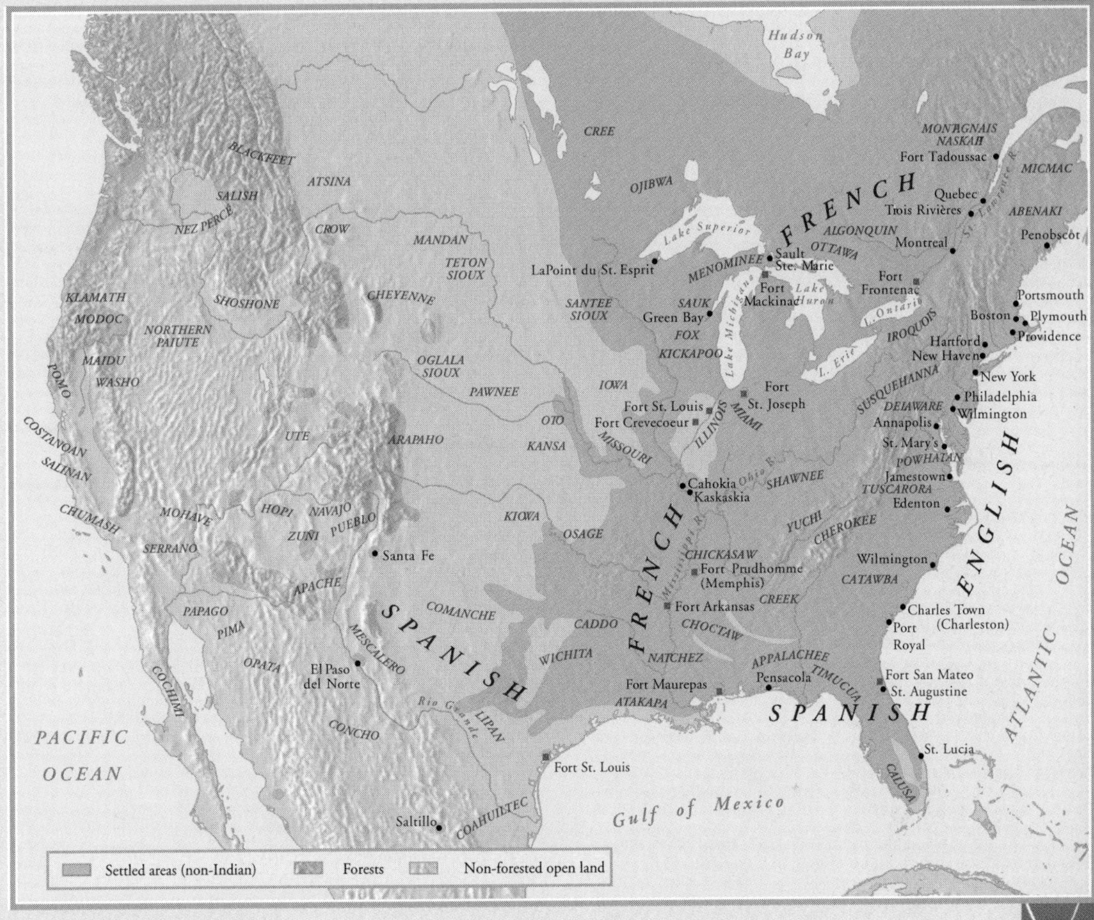

North America in 1700

Europeans adapted their traditions and goals to exploit the abundant resources of the New World. The Spanish struck it rich with the Potosí and Zacatecas silver mines that financed their religious wars in Europe and became the envy of other nations. Privateers from France, England, and the Netherlands attacked the Spanish silver fleets, while explorers searched unsuccessfully for mines in North America. Instead, they found treasures in furs, sugar, tobacco, and rice.

To reap fortunes from the earth, the colonizers first exploited Native Americans, who died in such numbers from disease and harsh treatment that Europeans turned to another continent, Africa, for laborers. Portugal developed the Atlantic slave trade during the fifteenth century, initially buying slaves to toil on sugar islands near Africa. With the development of sugar, and later tobacco

and rice, in America, the Portuguese and other Europeans purchased millions of people from African merchants for transport across the Atlantic. For more than 350 years, the cultures, sweat, and blood of enslaved Africans enriched the New World societies.

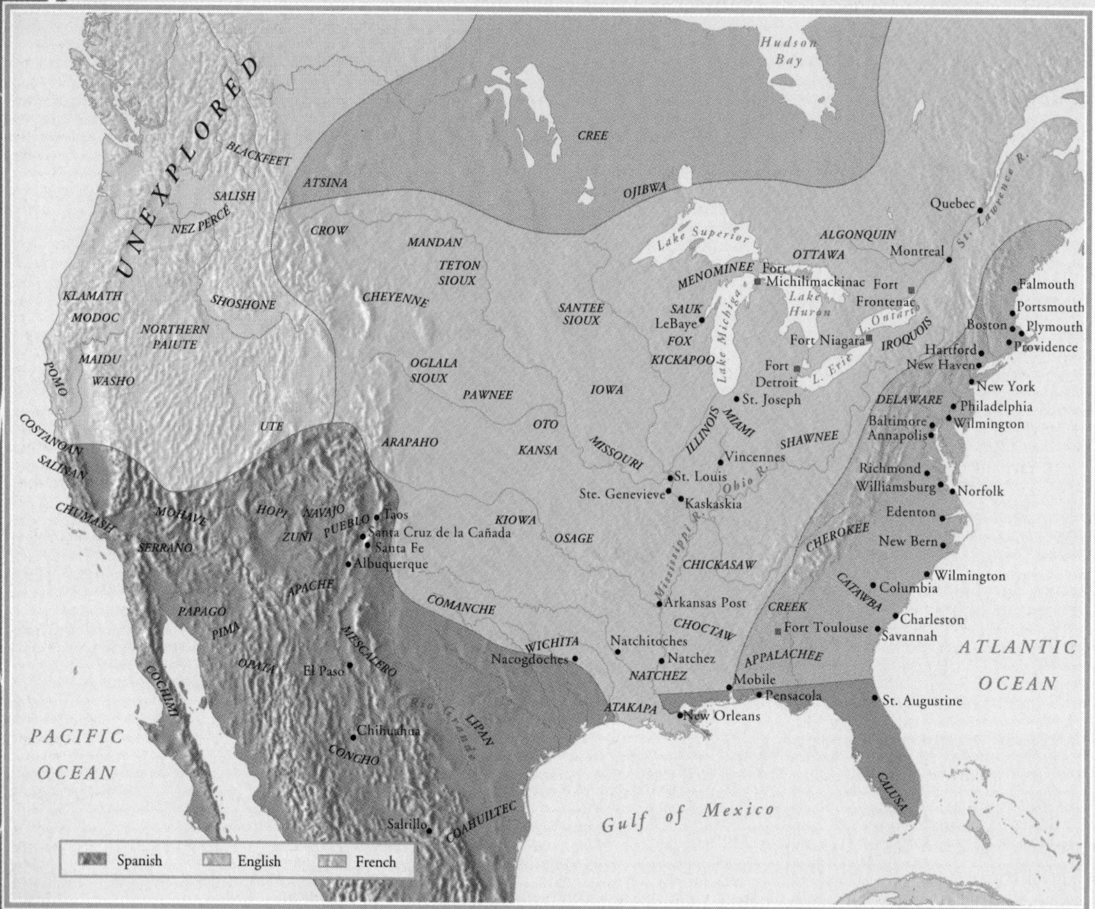

North America in 1750

Population Growth of the Thirteen British Mainland Colonies, 1630–1760

1630	*1640*	*1650*	*1660*	*1670*	*1680*	*1690*
4,646	26,634	50,368	75,058	111,935	151,507	210,372

From the sixteenth century on, Europeans battled for North America with Native Americans and among themselves. The French settled Canada and the Mississippi Valley, primarily for furs. Spain held Florida, Texas, and New Mexico as outposts to protect its silver mines and fleets. The English founded colonies in New England, the Chesapeake, and Carolinas for economic opportunity and religious freedom. In 1664, they pushed the Dutch out of New Netherland, thus connecting their chain of colonies along the Atlantic. Throughout America, Europeans hoped for a new chance in the New World.

The thirteen mainland British colonies had various beginnings, charters, provincial governments, economic bases, peoples, and religions. Yet they all had ties with England in language, imperial government and laws, culture, and commerce. During the eighteenth century, the colonies forged closer bonds with the English—with greater participation in imperial wars, increased trade, and better communication. At the same time, the British provinces also became more distinctly American, as people from Africa, Ireland, and the European continent diversified the population and its culture. With natural population growth and swelling immigration, the British colonies expanded across the continent.

Native Americans responded to depopulation, defeat, and white expansion by creating new worlds of their own. Despite some military successes, they ultimately reshaped their communities and cultures, as disease worked its tragic course and European-American societies grew. The surviving members of Indian nations often merged to forge new ethnic identities, or lived together in multi-ethnic communities, often with whites and escaped slaves. Some retained remnants of their land within white settlements, whereas the majority moved to the frontier for political autonomy.

Three centuries passed from the time Western European fishermen first camped on North American shores until Great Britain and its colonies expelled France from the continent with the French and Indian War. By 1763, the land and people of America had permanently changed.

For additional information and resources pertaining to this period in American history, please visit the American Passages Web Site at:

http://ayersbrief.wadsworth.com

*Martin A. Favata and José B. Fernandez, *The Account: Álvar Núñez Cabeza de Vaca's Relación* (1993), p.103.

1700	1710	1720	1730	1740	1750	1760
250,888	331,711	466,185	629,445	905,563	1,170,760	1,593,625

	38,000 B.C. – 1000 A.D.	1000 A.D. – 1300	1400 – 1500
POLITICS & DIPLOMACY	**38,000–12,000 B.C.:** Ancient hunters migrate to America **300–1600 A.D.:** Ghana, Mali, and Songhay empires in West Africa **700–1450 A.D.:** Cahokia and other Mississippian centers in North America	**c. 1000 A.D.:** Leif Eriksson's colony on Newfoundland **c. 1300 A.D.:** Aztecs settle in Valley of Mexico	**1420:** Prince Henry of Portugal begins exploration **1492:** Christopher Columbus crosses Atlantic Ocean **1513:** Juan Ponce de León explores Florida for Spain **1519:** Magellan's expedition to circumnavigate world **1521:** Hernán Cortés conquers Aztecs **1528:** Cabeza de Vaca to Florida and Texas **1540:** Coronado explores American Southwest
SOCIAL & CULTURAL EVENTS		**1324:** Gonga-Mussa's pilgrimage to Mecca	**1507:** Martin Waldseemüller names New World after Amerigo Vespucci **1517:** Martin Luther challenges the Church of Rome **1534:** English Act of Supremacy **1536:** John Calvin's *Institutes of the Christian Religion* **1542:** Bartolomé de las Casas' *A Short Account of the Destruction of the Indies*
ECONOMICS & TECHNOLOGY	**Pre-2500 B.C.:** Corn developed as staple crop in central Mexico **c. 1200 B.C.:** Corn produced in American Southwest		**1440s:** Portuguese mariners take Africans as slaves **c. 1450:** European fishermen at Grand Banks off Newfoundland **c. 1452:** Portugal begins sugar production on Madeira **c. 1460:** European improvements in navigation and ships **1478:** Abraham Zacuto calculates latitude using sun **1502:** Enslaved Africans imported in Spanish America **1503:** Spanish Casa de Contratación to supervise trade **1540s:** Silver mines at Zacatecas and Potosí

1550 1600 1650 1700 1750

c. 1550: Iroquois form confederacy
1565: Spanish found St. Augustine, Florida
1585: English colony at Roanoke Island
1599: Spanish destroy Ácoma
1607: English colony at Jamestown
1608: French establish Quebec
1620: Separatists found Plymouth
1630: Puritans establish Massachusetts Bay colony
1634: The *Ark* and the *Dove* arrive in Maryland
1642: English Civil War begins

1643: New England Confederation
1663: Carolina proprietors receive charter
1664: English forces conquer New Netherland
1675: Metacom's War Bacon's Rebellion
1680: Popé's Rebellion
1681: William Penn receives Pennsylvania charter
1688: Glorious Revolution in England
1689: Massachusetts, New York, and Maryland revolutions
1691: Salem witchcraft hysteria

1699: French establish Louisiana
1712: Slave revolt in New York City
1732: Founding of Georgia
1739: Stono Uprising in South Carolina
1754: Albany Congress
1754–1763: French and Indian War
1763: Pan-Indian war in Ohio Valley and Great Lakes

1585: John White's drawings of Roanoke
1590: Theodor de Bry's *America*
1636: Harvard College established Roger Williams' exile to Rhode Island
1637: Anne Hutchinson tried for heresy
1638: First printing press in the English colonies
1639: French establish first hospital in North America
1647: Massachusetts requires town schools
1649: Maryland's act for religious toleration

1650: Anne Bradstreet's *The Tenth Muse Lately Sprung Up in America*
c. 1661: Henri Couturier's portrait of Peter Stuyvesant
1662: Halfway Covenant
1663: John Eliot's Bible in Massachusetts Indian language
c. 1674: *Mrs. Freake with Baby Mary* by unknown artist
1682: Publication of *The Narrative of the Captivity and Restoration of Mrs. Mary Rowlandson*
1687: Isaac Newton's *Principia Mathematica*
1688: Germantown, Pennsylvania, Quakers issue antislavery protest
1690: John Locke's *Essay concerning Human Understanding*
1693: College of William and Mary founded
1695: Jews worship openly in New York

1704: First regular newspaper in Anglo-America, *The Boston News-Letter*
1716: Theater built in Williamsburg, Virginia
1720: Theodore Jacob Frelinghuysen's revivals in New Jersey
1721: Smallpox inoculation in Boston
1731: Benjamin Franklin's circulating library in Philadelphia
1739: George Whitefield tours northern colonies
1751: Benjamin Franklin's reports on electricity
1752: Adoption of Gregorian Calendar in Anglo-America
1761: John Winthrop observes the transit of Venus
1763: Rise of Delaware prophet Neolin

1562: John Hawkins interlopes in slave trade
c. 1585: Growth of Amsterdam as mercantile center
1602: Dutch East India Company
1617: Tobacco successful staple crop in Virginia
c. 1619: Africans arrive in Virginia
1621: Dutch West India Company
1640s: Sugar production in English West Indies
1642: French found Montreal for fur trade

1651: First English Navigation Act
1672: Royal African Company
1673: Regular postal route between Boston and New York
1670s: Shift to slaves in Chesapeake
1698: Royal African Company loses slave trade monopoly
1699: Woolen Act

1700s: Adoption of rice in South Carolina
1720s: Expansion of German and Scots-Irish immigration
1732: Hat Act
1733: Molasses Act
1740s: Eliza Pinckney cultivates indigo in South Carolina
1750: Iron Act Georgia legalizes slavery
1750s: British colonial trade expands with Southern Europe "Consumer revolution" in British colonies
early 1760s: Economic slump in British colonies

Chapter 1

Contact, Conflict, and Exchange in the Atlantic World to 1590

On October 12, 1492, the *Santa Maria, Pinta,* and *Niña,* under command of the Italian navigator Christopher Columbus, sighted an island in the Caribbean Sea he called San Salvador. Columbus had spent years trying to obtain support from the rulers of England, France, Portugal, and Spain for a voyage westward across the Atlantic Ocean to find Asia. Finally he convinced Isabella and Ferdinand of Spain to provide funds. If he found a transatlantic route to Asia, Columbus argued, Spain would have the competitive edge over Portugal.

Sailing from one Caribbean island to another, Columbus met many Native Americans, whom he called "*Indios,*" or Indians, because he thought he had reached islands in the Far East. What he actually had done was initiate the conquest and settlement of two continents—the Americas—whose vast extent and riches were previously unknown to Europeans.

Columbus' arrival had momentous consequences. For Native Americans, white men and sailing ships spelled demographic catastrophe. Within 150 years, the pre-contact Indian population was reduced by 90 percent, their cities conquered and destroyed, and, for many, their lands appropriated for farming and grazing livestock. For Europeans, Columbus unexpected "discovery" represented new challenges and opportunities. For sub-Saharan Africans, the navigator's landfall half a world away signaled the burgeoning slave trade, which over the next four centuries transported at least 10 million Africans across the Atlantic. To exploit the riches of America, Europeans used the labor of both Native Americans and Africans.

Yet contact among Native Americans, Europeans, and Africans involved more than conquest, enslavement, and death. Together the three major cultural groups created new traditions and societies in the New World. Although the Europeans must be declared winners in the contest for power, the American colonies were shaped by exchange of knowledge, culture, and work among all participants. Three major cultural traditions came together in the Western Hemisphere. The patterns of annihilation, exploitation, resistance, accommodation, and trade created new cultures and social systems throughout the hemisphere.

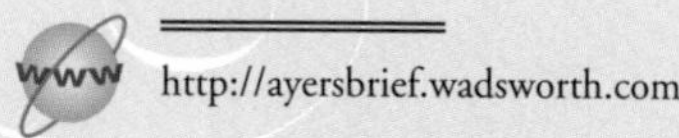

http://ayersbrief.wadsworth.com

CHRONOLOGY

38,000–12,000 B.C. Migration of ancient hunters to the Americas

300–900 A.D. Height of Mayan civilization in Yucatán

300–1600 A.D. Succession of empires, Ghana, Mali, and Songhay, in West Africa

700–1450 A.D. Mississippian people build Cahokia and other urban centers in North America

c. 1000 A.D. Leif Eriksson establishes Viking colony on Newfoundland

c. 1300 A.D. Aztecs settle in Valley of Mexico

1420 Prince Henry of Portugal initiates search for ocean route to Asia

1440s Portuguese mariners take Africans as slaves

c. 1452 Portugal begins sugar production on Madeira

c. 1460–1500 European improvements in navigation and ships

1487 Bartholomeu Dias of Portugal rounds Cape of Good Hope

1492 Christopher Columbus crosses Atlantic Ocean

1494 Treaty of Tordesillas establishes Line of Demarcation

1497–1498 Vasco da Gama reaches India for Portugal

1517 Martin Luther challenges the Church of Rome

1519–1521 Hernán Cortés conquers the Aztecs

1519–1522 Magellan's expedition circumnavigates the world

1528–1536 Cabeza de Vaca's adventures in Florida and Texas

1534 Act of Supremacy separates England from the Church of Rome

1539–1542 Hernando de Soto explores the region from Florida to the Mississippi River

1540–1542 Coronado explores the American Southwest

1541 Cartier establishes Charlesbourg-Royal in Canada

1556 Philip II of Spain takes the throne

1558 Elizabeth I becomes queen of England

1564 French Huguenots build Fort Caroline in northern Florida

1577–1580 Sir Francis Drake circumnavigates the globe

1585 English attempt colonization at Roanoke Island

1588 English defeat the Spanish Armada

THE FIRST AMERICANS

In 1492, an estimated 70 million Native Americans lived in North and South America. They possessed widely divergent cultures. In the geographic area that now encompasses the United States, they included mound-building farmers of the Mississippi valley, the pueblo-dwelling Hopi and Zuñi Indians and nomadic Apaches of the southwest, and the Iroquois and Algonquians of the eastern woodlands.

Native American Societies Before Contact

These diverse peoples were descendants of small bands of hunters who crossed the Bering land bridge from Siberia to Alaska some time between

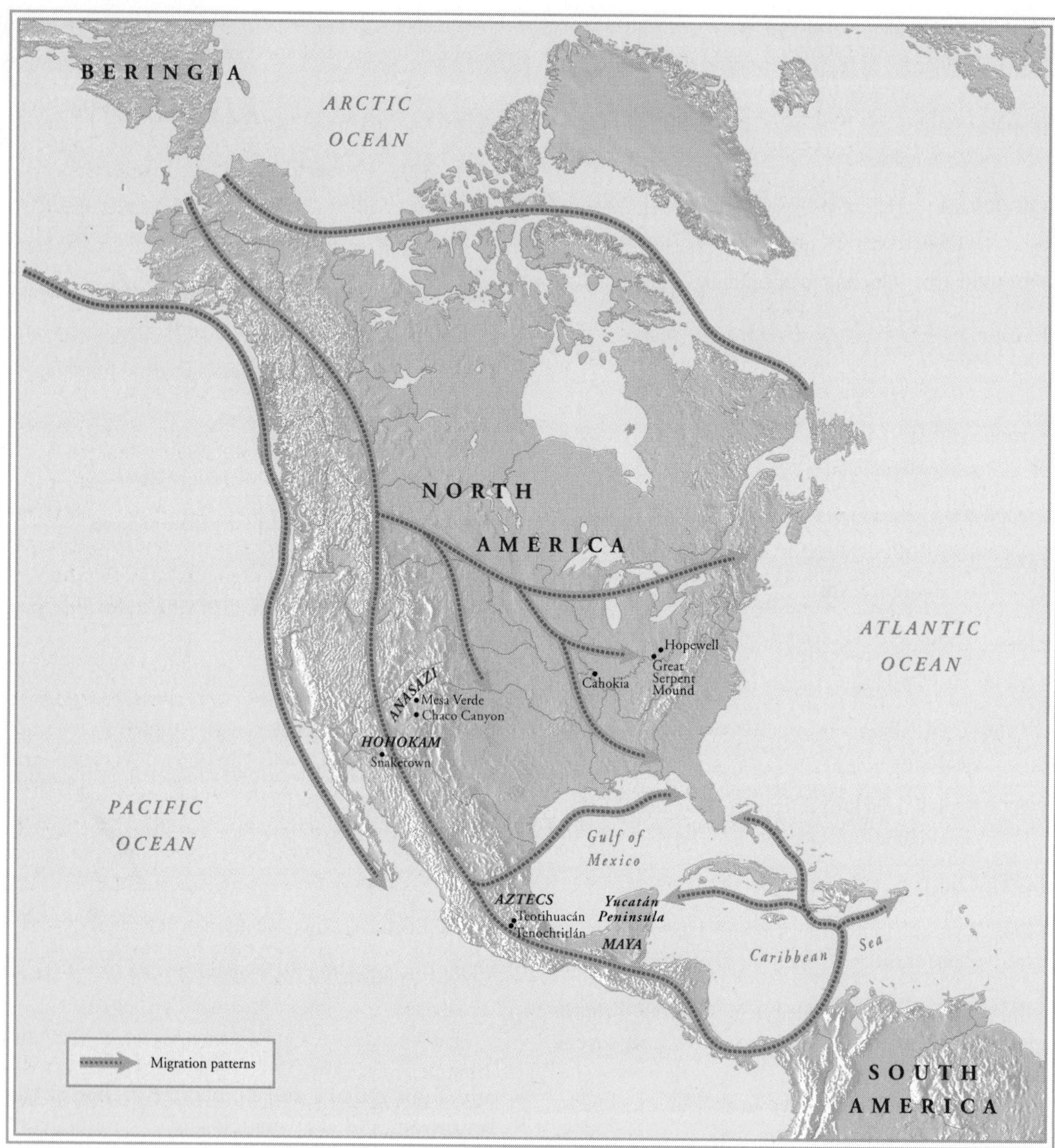

MAP 1.1 | AMERICA BEFORE COLUMBUS

40,000 and 14,000 years ago. When the glacier covering much of Canada receded, they followed big game south to the Great Plains. Among the earliest evidence of their arrival, dating from about 12,000 B.C., are sites containing human remains and the skeletons of animals with the stone spearheads used to slay them. As the climate of North America became warmer, and perhaps as a result of overhunting, several species of large animals disappeared. Buffalo remained plentiful on the Great Plains, but elsewhere Indians hunted smaller game, fished, and collected berries, seeds, and nuts. As groups migrated throughout North and South America and adapted to their environments, their cultures and languages diverged.

When ancient Americans began cultivating crops, they laid the foundation for more densely populated societies. Of greatest importance to Indians of North America was the development of maize, or Indian corn, probably from the grass *teosinte,* which grew in dry areas of Mexico and Guatemala. In addition to maize, early Mexicans domesticated beans, squash, chili peppers, and avocado. Agriculture proved revolutionary for some ancient American societies, as higher yields spurred population growth and a greater division of labor.

Between 1500 B.C. and Columbus' arrival, civilizations rose and declined throughout the Americas. Ancient Americans built empires, much like their counterparts in Egypt, Greece, and Rome, with cities, extensive trade networks, systems of religion and knowledge, art, architecture, and hierarchical social classes. Two of the best-known civilizations of pre-contact America were the Mayan, located on the Yucatán peninsula, and the Mexican. The Maya, at their height from 300 to 900 A.D., built cities of stone pyramids, temples, and palaces, with populations ranging to more than 60,000. Mayan kings, considered divine, extended their empire to over fifty different states and maintained trade with distant peoples. The Maya had a numeral system based on units of twenty, hieroglyphics, a knowledge of astronomy, and several calendars.

The Mexicans, who lived in the Valley of Mexico, built the city of Teotihuacán east of Lake Texcoco. Its population of about 200,000 depended on intensive farming of nearby irrigated lands. The grid-patterned Teotihuacán held at its core the Pyramid of the Sun and the Pyramid of the Moon. Even after the city's decline it retained religious significance for later Mexicans.

The Aztecs settled in the Valley of Mexico in the fourteenth century, building their capital, Tenochtitlán, on an island in Lake Texcoco, which they connected to the shore by causeways. They cultivated intensively the marshlands surrounding their island and built a militaristic state. By the time the Spanish *conquistadores* arrived in 1519, the Aztecs controlled territory from the Pacific to the Gulf Coast. The Aztecs required tribute from the people they conquered—gold, feathers, turquoise, food, cotton, and human beings for sacrifice. They believed that every day they had to feed human hearts to the sun god, Huitzilpochtli, to prevent the world from coming to an end.

To the north of the Valley of Mexico, Indians also developed distinctive cultures. The Hohokam occupied desert lands in Arizona and northern Sonora, where, with irrigation, they cultivated Indian corn, cotton, squash, and beans. When Athabaskan raiders from the north attacked Hohokam towns, they tried to protect themselves by building high adobe walls, then after 1400 A.D. simply abandoned many of their villages.

Enemy attacks and crop failures from lack of rain forced other Indians of the southwest to leave their towns. The Anasazi farmers of northern Arizona and New Mexico, Colorado, and Utah relied on rain and floods to water their crops. One of their settlements was Pueblo Bonito in Chaco Canyon, which housed perhaps 1,000 people in 800 rooms surrounded by high walls. Descendants of the Anasazi—the Hopi and Zuñi Indians—were called "Pueblo" Indians by the Spanish for the adobe villages with large apartment dwellings in which they lived.

Farther east, in a large area drained by the Mississippi River, by 1000 B.C. early Americans developed civilizations characterized by large earthen burial mounds, some sixty feet high. These mounds entombed corpses and such grave goods as copper spoons and beads made from seashells. These Mississippian people lived in small villages along rivers, hunted game, fished, and raised squash, Indian corn, sunflowers, and gourds. As evidenced by the grave goods, their trading network extended from the Gulf Coast (shells) to Lake Superior (copper). By 700 A.D., the Mississippian people constructed large towns. At the center of these towns were large rectangular mounds topped by temples and mortuaries in which members of the upper class were buried. By 1450, the region's population declined, perhaps as a result of illness spread by urban crowding.

People of the Eastern Woodlands

Along the Atlantic seaboard extending inland to the Appalachian Mountains lived Native Americans of two major language groups, the Algonquian and the Iroquois. The eastern woodlands incorporated a wide variety of habitats. In most parts, decent soil and moderate rainfall and temperatures supported agriculture and many kinds of game, fish, and wild plants. Algonquian-speaking people dominated the Atlantic coast from Canada to Florida; they included the Pokanokets, Narragansetts, and Pequots in New England; the Delawares of the middle Atlantic region; and members of the Powhatan confederacy in what became Virginia. Many of the Iroquois lived in the Finger Lakes area of central New York. They belonged to five tribes: the Mohawks, Oneidas, Onondagas, Cayugas, and Senecas, from east to west, who banded together in the Iroquois confederacy.

Although important cultural differences existed between the two language groups and even among bands within each group, Indians of the eastern woodlands had much in common. They held land cooperatively: the tribe as a whole claimed ownership rights, not individual members or families. Except in far northern New England, Indians had a mixed economy of agriculture, gathering, fishing, and hunting. Women were responsible for raising corn, squash, beans, and (where possible) tobacco. They also gathered nuts and fruit, built houses, made clothing, took care of the children, and prepared meals, while men cleared land, hunted, fished, and protected the village from enemies. The combination of corn, squash, and beans enriched the soil, providing high yields from small plots of land; eaten together these foods were high in protein. The Native Americans cleared land by girdling the large

Woman and girl of Pomeioc, watercolor by John White, 1585. Algonquian women cared for children and raised crops, including corn and tobacco. (© British Museum)

trees (removing a strip of bark around the trees about three feet from the ground). When the trees died, the Indians removed them, burned the underbrush, and sowed crops among the stumps. Eastern woodlands people used nets and weirs to catch fish and, to assure good hunting, they periodically burned underbrush from sections of forest. The burning stimulated the growth of lush grass, providing fodder for deer and other game. The fires allowed some sunlight to penetrate the forest, promoting the growth of strawberries, raspberries, and blackberries.

Indian religions, though widely diverse in many ways, incorporated a common worldview. The people of the eastern woodlands believed that the earth and sky formed a spiritual realm of which they were a part, not the masters. Spirits inhabited the earth and could be found in plants, animals, rocks, or clouds. Each spirit, or *manitou,* could become the guardian of a young Indian man (less often a young woman), who, in search of a manitou, went into the woods alone, without eating or sleeping perhaps for days. If the spirit made itself known, it would provide help and counsel to the individual for the rest of his or he life. These Native Americans also believed in a Master Spirit or Creator, who was all-powerful and all-knowing, but whose presence was rarely felt. Religious leaders were *shamans,* who performed rituals to influence weather conditions or ward off danger. They were usually men, but in some communities were women. Indians believed that shamans could cure illness, interpret dreams, bring good weather, and predict the future.

The kinship group, or extended family, formed the basis of Native American society. The heads of kinship groups chose the band's chief leaders, called *sachems,* who with advice assigned fields for planting, decided where and when to hunt, managed trade and diplomacy with other Indians and Europeans, and judged whether or not to go to war. Among Algonquian-speaking natives, the heads of extended families were men, as were the sachems they chose. But Iroquois society was matrilineal, with family membership passing from mother to children; and matrilocal, as the husband left his family to live with his wife's. Women elders could not speak publicly at tribal councils or serve as sachems, but they chose these political leaders and advised them on such matters as waging war.

Thus, in 1492 highly complex and differentiated societies existed in North and South America. Dense populations inhabited parts of South, Central, and North America. Throughout the hemisphere, Indian people had distinctive cultures tied to the resources of their environment. Despite this wide variety of languages and cultures, most Europeans adopted the single name that Columbus mistakenly employed—Indians. An alternative the colonists used was "savages." The view that Native Americans had undifferentiated, uncivilized societies justified conquest and expropriation of their lands.

Beginning of European Overseas Expansion

The Europeans who invaded the Americas after 1492 had more in common with Native Americans than they liked to admit; nevertheless, in important ways, their cultures were distinct. Europeans spent most of their energy producing or gathering food. They farmed, raised livestock, and gathered nuts and berries. In the south and west of England, for example, farmers engaged in intensive cultivation of wheat, rye, and other crops. In most of England and Wales, however, farmers planted just an acre or two and spent more time gathering. In contrast to Native Americans, Europeans believed that individuals could own land and thus had the right to sell, fence, plant, erect buildings, hunt, cut lumber, and exclude others from use.

The societies from which most colonizers came were patriarchal, meaning that descent followed the father's line and political power was nearly always in the hands of men. Though women occasionally took the throne, for instance, Isabella of Spain and Elizabeth I of England, men controlled government, the church, and the military. Married women were considered subordinate to their husbands. Under English common law, a married woman was a *feme covert,* or covered woman, who could not own or manage property, make a contract, write a will, take custody of her children, own a business, or sue in court, without her husband's permission. An unmarried woman or widow, in legal terms a *feme sole,* was not subject to these restrictions.

In the fifteenth century, the pope headed a united Christian church in western and central Europe. At the same time, monarchs consolidated power in Portugal, Spain, France, and England, providing financial support and a greater sense of national identity to fuel European expansion. In turn, wealth from distant empires and trade funded wars among these emerging nations.

Trade with the East

When Columbus sailed out into the Atlantic Ocean in 1492, he expected to establish a new trade route with Asia. In the fifteenth century, eastern trade was a chief source of riches, for affluent Europeans wanted spices for preserving and flavoring their food. The spices would not grow in Europe, so merchants commanded high prices for transporting them from India, the East Indies, and other parts of East Asia.

Before 1500, Arab and Italian merchants dominated the eastern trade. Arabs controlled eastern trading centers and carried goods across the Arabian Sea to the Red Sea and Persian Gulf. From there, caravans took cargoes to Mediterranean ports for purchase by Italian merchants. The Italians then distributed the spices and other goods throughout Europe by way of pack train and coastal shipping. European cities developed to handle the exchange of valued eastern products in return for silver, gold, woolen and linen cloth, furs, and leather. Centers of trade and banking included Paris, Lyons, Amsterdam, London, Hamburg, Danzig, Barcelona, Cadiz, Lisbon, Venice, and Genoa. The rise of great cities accompanied the growth of unified political states. Merchants provided funding for kings to consolidate small feudal states into nations. In Portugal, Spain, France, and England, commercial interests supported unification to obtain social order, monopolistic privileges, and standardized codes of law.

Portugal Explores the West African Coast

Early in the fifteenth century, Prince Henry of Portugal, called "the Navigator," decided to challenge the Arab and Italian hold on eastern commerce. Henry brought together men interested in overseas trade and exploration. Beginning in 1420, he sent ships down the western coast of Africa. He had four goals: to increase the power of Portugal by adding territorial possessions; to benefit economically from commerce with the African coast; to reach Asia and take a share of that trade; and to spread Christianity.

Headway down the African coast was slow because European sailors knew nothing of the ocean beyond Cape Bojador. In 1420, cartographers knew a great deal about the Mediterranean Sea and constructed highly accurate charts, called *portolano,* of its shorelines and harbors. Such maps did not exist for the West African coast, so one task of Prince Henry's explorers was to chart their progress. From ancient mathematicians and geographers, most notably Ptolemy, mapmakers knew that the world was round, but they also adopted Ptolemy's belief that a southern continent joined Africa to China, thus eliminating the possibility of a sea route from the Atlantic to the Indian Ocean. Prince Henry challenged current wisdom by sending ships down Africa's coast to find a route to the east.

New Technology

In the early and mid-fifteenth century, the lack of adequate instruments hampered navigation. Compasses had been in use since at least the thirteenth century, but not until about 1460 did Europeans develop the means of determining latitude (distance north or south from the equator). In the Northern Hemisphere, sea captains calculated the height of the Pole Star from the horizon to determine their latitude. The Pole Star cannot

Engraving by Stradunuse of an early sixteenth-century cosmographer working in his study with contemporary instruments, including dividers, rule, compass, quadrant, and sand glass. (National Maritime Museum)

be seen south of the equator, however, so navigators there measured the altitude of the sun at midday. In making these calculations, they used the astrolabe or the quadrant to determine the angle of the sun from the horizon, then consulted astronomical tables that Abraham Zacuto, a Jewish astronomer, compiled in 1478.

Improvements in ships and gunnery during the fifteenth century also aided exploration and conquest. The first European oceangoing ships were square-rigged. Their broad sails could power large vessels, but they required a favorable tailwind to proceed from one point to another. To increase maneuverability, Portuguese seafarers designed the caravel with lateen (triangular) sails. The most successful Portuguese ship for long voyages was the *caravela redondo,* the square-rigged caravel, developed late in the fifteenth century. This ship combined the speed of square rigging with the more responsive handling of lateen sails. The Portuguese mounted artillery on the caravels and by 1500 introduced the practice of broadside fire. They changed nautical warfare by sinking enemy vessels with gunfire instead of boarding them with foot soldiers.

Despite these improvements in the design of ships, they remained uncomfortable places in which to live. Except for senior officers, none of the seamen had regular sleeping quarters—they slept on deck, or below in bad weather. When it rained, everything got wet, including the cooking fire built in a sandbox on deck. The mariners ate ship's hardtack, beans, and salt pork and beef, and drank mostly wine, since their casked water quickly became foul.

Africa and the Atlantic Slave Trade

Despite their limited technology, the Portuguese explorers ventured farther and farther down the West African coast. In 1434, Gil Eannes sailed past Cape Bojador. Subsequent voyages established a lucrative coastal trade in slaves, gold, and malaguetta pepper in the Senegal region and farther south and east to the Gold Coast and Benin. Merchants now began investing in expeditions. Between the 1440s and 1505, Portuguese traders transported 40,000 Africans to perform domestic labor in Portugal and Spain, and to work on the sugar plantations of the Azores, Madeira, and Canary Islands.

West African Cultures

From before 300 A.D. to 1600, a succession of empires—Ghana, Mali, and Songhay—dominated Western Africa. They had large armies, collected tribute over vast distances, and traded with Europeans and Arabs. West Africans were predominantly agricultural people. Ghana declined by 1100 as a result of droughts that dried up several rivers. Mali then took control, as its monarchs regulated the gold trade. The Mali kings were followers of Islam: one of the most famous, Gonga-Mussa, made a pilgrimage to Mecca in 1324 to fulfill his religious duty as a Muslim.

Mali provided stable government over a wide area until the fifteenth century, when Songhay successfully challenged its dominance. Songhay was centered at Gao. Under Sonni Ali, who ruled from 1468 to 1492, Songhay captured Timbuktu, an important trading and cultural center of Mali. Askia Mohammed, who ruled from 1493 to 1528, expanded the empire even farther. He strengthened ties with other Muslims and reformed government, banking, and education. He adopted Islamic law and encouraged intellectual growth at Timbuktu and Gao. After his reign, Songhay declined; Moroccans conquered Timbuktu in 1593.

Beyond these empires, along the West African coast lay smaller states with highly developed cultures. Although influenced by Islam, they retained much of their traditional religions. Divine kings governed many of the coastal states. Like Native Americans and Europeans, the people of Africa kept religion central to their lives and endowed their leaders with both political and religious authority.

Most important in traditional African religions was a single all-powerful God, the Creator. The Creator provided lesser gods, including gods of rain, thunder, and lightning; of rivers and lakes; of animals, trees, and hills. These gods could be benevolent or harmful, so people had to seek positive relationships through rituals, sacrifice, and prayer. Africans also believed that their ancestors watched over the extended family. When the eldest father, or patriarch, of a kinship group died, his spirit became a god. Elaborate funeral rites demonstrated the importance of the dead to the living. Before his death, the patriarch had been the extended family's priest; he communicated with its ancestors through prayer and sacrifice. The patriarch also served as political leader. Thus in many African societies, the state, religion, and family united under a single hierarchical structure.

Kinship in West Africa varied from one culture to another, as extended families could be either patrilineal or matrilineal. In all cases, however, a child belonged to only one kin group. If the system was patrilineal, then descent flowed from father to child. If it was matrilineal, descent pro-

A Fula town in West Africa, drawn by a European. West Africans, like Europeans but not Native Americans, kept domestic livestock. (Reproduced from the collections of the Library of Congress)

ceeded from mother to child, but the mother's brother, not the mother, assumed responsibility. When a woman married, she usually went to live with her husband's family. The husband compensated her family for the loss of her services with a payment called bridewealth. *Polygyny,* or having more than one wife, was generally reserved to men of high status. When men had more than one wife, each woman lived with her children in a separate house.

The extended family held land in common and assigned plots to individual families. Women and men worked in fields growing crops such as rice, cassava, wheat, millet, cotton, fruits, and vegetables. They had livestock, including cattle, sheep, goats, and chickens. Families produced food for their own use and for the market, where women were the primary traders. Artisans were skilled in textile weaving, pottery, basketry, and woodwork. They also made tools and art objects of copper, bronze, iron, silver, and gold.

The Atlantic Slave Trade Begins

Over the course of four centuries, West Africa lost to the Atlantic slave trade at least 20 million people, of whom 10 million actually survived. Slavery had existed in Africa and throughout the Mediterranean for centuries before the Portuguese arrived on the West African coast. African slavery was different, however, from the institution that developed in America. Most African slaves were prisoners of war; others had committed some offense that caused their kinfolk to banish them. All were considered "outsiders." The primary function of slavery in West Africa was social rather than economic—to provide a place in society for people cut off from their families. Trans-Saharan traders transported some African slaves for sale to wealthy European households. Because this trade was limited, most slaves remained in West Africa, where they achieved status as a member of a household, married, and had children. Enslaved Africans could be transferred from one owner to another at will, but their children could not be sold and were frequently emancipated.

The plantation slave system that became dominant in America began near Africa. Portugal began growing sugar as early as 1452 on the island of Madeira, off West Africa. Sugar cane required large amounts of menial, unpleasant labor in a hot climate. To supply Madeira, Portuguese merchants purchased black slaves from Muslim trans-Saharan traders and from Africans along the coast. When sugar production could expand no farther in Madeira, the Portuguese colonized the small islands in the Gulf of Guinea. Sugar production was successful, but mortality was high and the demand for laborers great, spurring growth of the slave trade on the Gold Coast. By the end of the fifteenth century, Portugal developed both the plantation system and the commercial mechanism for purchasing human beings. The growth of slavery and the slave trade in America after 1500 represented an expansion of these earlier developments.

SPAIN AND PORTUGAL DIVIDE THE GLOBE

Once Portugal had established trade on the West African coast, Spanish merchants tried to participate. Prince Henry appealed to the pope, who in 1455 gave Portugal sole possession of lands to the south and east toward India. The pope's decision gave Portugal a monopoly on the Atlantic slave trade. Spain and Portugal affirmed the decision with the Treaty of Alcaçovas (1479), in which Spain recognized Portugal's sphere of interest in Africa, and Portugal acknowledged Spain's claim to the Canary Islands.

As the Portuguese sailed south, they came to recognize the vastness of the African continent. They made rapid progress only after 1482, when King John II of Portugal stepped up the program of discovery. In 1483, Diogo Cão reached the Congo River and in 1487 Bartholomeu Dias rounded the Cape of Good Hope. The Portuguese now knew that a sea route to India existed.

Columbus Sails West

The Spanish had to find another course if they were going to trade with the Far East. Thus, Isabella and Ferdinand funded Columbus, despite their skepticism of his calculation of the distance to Asia. In August 1492, Columbus sailed west from the Canaries, taking advantage of the favorable current and trade winds. The ships reached San Salvador in October, but Columbus thought they had located the East Indies. Hoping to establish trade, Columbus sailed southward to Cuba, then touched Hispaniola. When the Spanish lost their flagship *Santa Maria* on a coral reef, they built a small fort with its timbers.

Columbus set out for home in January 1493, but encountered a violent storm and sought shelter in Portugal. King John II refused to believe that Columbus located Asia. The lands he had found, the king claimed, lay within Portugal's sphere.

Spanish and Portuguese "Spheres"

Isabella and Ferdinand rejected Portugal's argument, petitioning Pope Alexander VI to grant them dominion over the newly discovered lands. After negotiations with John II, the pope established a Line of Demarcation, giving all lands "discovered or to be discovered" west of the line to Spain and all lands east of the line to Portugal. The Treaty of Tordesillas (1494) located the line 370 leagues (about 1,000 miles) west of the Azores and expanded the principle of "spheres of influence." Portugal retained its rights to the Atlantic slave trade and the sea route around Africa to India. Spain received permission to explore, conquer, and Christianize all lands and people to the west.

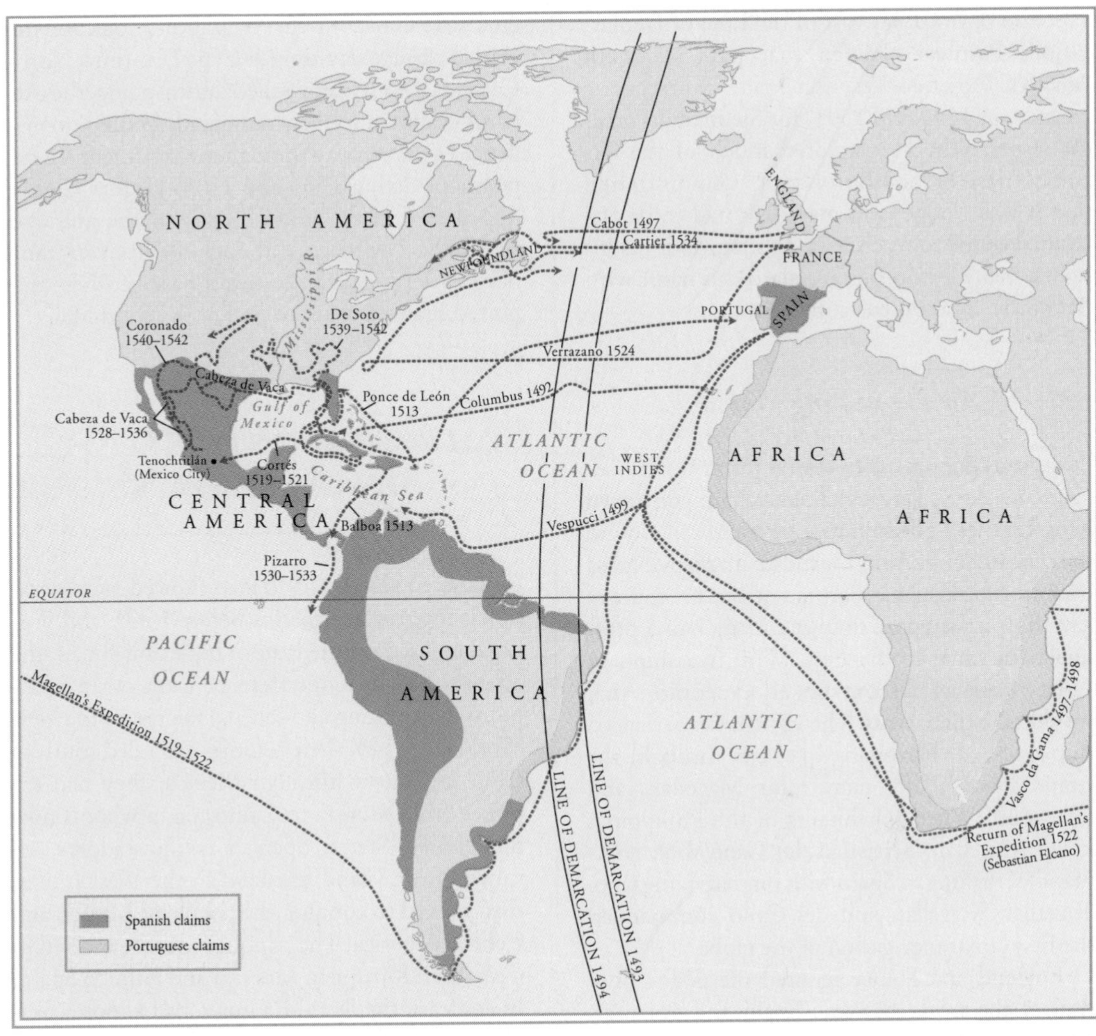

Map 1.2 | European Explorations, 1492–1542

Between 1494 and 1529, Portugal and Spain sent out expeditions to explore their spheres. Columbus made three more voyages to the west: in November 1493 he sailed with seventeen ships to the Lesser Antilles, Puerto Rico, and Hispaniola. Later he explored the shores of South and Central America. Meanwhile, Columbus' claim that he had found a passage to the East by sailing west prodded the Portuguese to complete their efforts to reach India. In 1497–1498, Vasco da Gama rounded the Cape of Good Hope and sailed across the Indian Ocean, returning to Portugal with a cargo of pepper and cinnamon. In 1500, Portugal instructed Pedro Álvares Cabral to find the Cape of Good Hope by sailing west. Instead, he touched the coast of Brazil, further convincing the Portuguese that this was not Asia. On the basis of Cabral's expedition and because a section of Brazil lay east of the Line of Demarcation, Portugal claimed that part of South America. Amerigo Vespucci made two separate voyages, in 1499 and 1501, for Spain and Portugal respectively. He explored much of the Atlantic coast of South America, demonstrating that it was a huge land mass that had to be circumnavigated to reach Asia. In reward for his insights, many Europeans associated his name with the newly "discovered" continents.

An Expanding World

Europeans continued to search for a western sea route to Asia. Ferdinand Magellan convinced King Charles I of Spain that he could sail around the cape of South America and claim the Molucca Islands. Magellan was Portuguese but his country gave him no support since it already had a profitable sea route to the East. With five ships, in 1519 Magellan set out on an expedition that would take three years. The voyagers experienced shipwreck, a harrowing passage through the straits subsequently named for Magellan, and starvation. When inhabitants of the Philippines killed Magellan, Sebastian del Cano took command, returning to Spain with one surviving ship. Together, Magellan and del Cano commanded the first circumnavigation of the globe.

England and France ignored the pope's division of the world between Spain and Portugal. They sought a northwest passage to the East. During the fifteenth century (before Columbus' landfall), seafarers from England and France had caught fish in the Newfoundland Banks. Some sailors had camped ashore, where they traded with Native Americans. When King Henry VII of England sent John Cabot in search of a northwest passage in 1497, the expedition reached Newfoundland. Cabot sailed again the next year, but most of his ships were lost and he died at sea. Although the English were discouraged by Cabot's failure to find a passage, his efforts supported England's later claim to land in North America.

A generation after Cabot, the French entered the search for a route to Asia. In 1524, King Francis I sent Giovanni da Verrazano to look for the elusive passage. Landing at Cape Fear (now North Carolina), Verrazano sailed north along the Atlantic seaboard to Newfoundland, finding no evidence of a waterway through the continent. In expeditions dating 1534 and 1535, Jacques Cartier hoped to find the route by way of the gulf and river of St. Lawrence. Although neither Verrazano nor Cartier found a northwest passage, they supported France's claim to part of the continent.

THE SPANISH EMPIRE IN AMERICA

Because England and France showed only occasional interest in America before 1560, and Portugal focused on the eastern trade and Brazil, the Spanish had little interference from other Europeans in exploring and settling the rest of the New World. By 1543, their colonies extended south to Chile and north through Mexico; they had explored from Florida to California in what is now the United States. Spanish conquistadores advanced from island to island in the West Indies, then moved to conquer the people of Mexico and Central America. The conquistadores expected to make their fortune in America and retire to Spain. In contrast, the Spanish Crown had a more complicated set of goals in colonizing America: to enhance its power among European nations; to exploit the wealth of these lands; and to convert the conquered Americans to Christianity. While in many ways the goals of the Spanish monarchy and its settlers overlapped, sometimes their interests diverged, especially when it came to the welfare of Native Americans.

Spanish Conquest

When they found little gold on Hispaniola, the Spanish exploited the labor of its inhabitants and the land. The natives died when the Spanish enslaved them to work on plantations and tend livestock. European diseases took their toll, as did cruel treatment. As a result, the colonists sent slave-raiding parties to other islands and to the mainland. The conquistadores who first explored Cuba in 1508 were seeking slaves and gold. For the same reasons, they colonized Puerto Rico in 1509. Juan Ponce de León, known for his search in 1513 for the legendary "fountain of youth," sought Indian slaves. The same year Vasco Núñez de Balboa led explorers across the Isthmus of Panama, becoming the first Europeans to see the Pacific Ocean.

As the Spanish explorers became aware of the vastness of the Americas, they organized militarily to subdue the Americans. Despite the small size of their armies, the Spanish prevailed over large empires, in part because of superior technology and in part because they made alliances with the enemies of the Indian emperors. They also had help from disease. The most famous of the conquerors is Hernán Cortés who, in 1519, launched an expedition against the Aztecs. With an army of only 500 troops, Cortés persuaded the Totonacs of Cempoala, who were dominated by the Aztecs, to join him. Then defeating the Tlaxcalans and gaining their support as well, he marched to Tenochtitlán, the Aztec capital. He entered the city without opposition and seized Moctezuma, the emperor. When Cortés outlawed human sacrifice and made incessant demands for gold, the Aztecs rebelled. In the heat of battle, they killed Moctezuma and forced the Spanish and their allies to retreat, slaying many as they tried to escape across the causeways linking Tenochtitlán with the shore of Lake Texcoco. Cortés was not finished, however, and in 1521 with reinforcements advanced on the Aztec capital. This time the Spanish built small ships to cross Lake Texcoco, took control of all causeways, and destroyed Tenochtitlán building by building. A smallpox epidemic killed many Aztecs. The conquerors rebuilt the city as Mexico City, the capital of New Spain.

Having defeated the Aztecs, Cortés sent troops to take Guatemala; in 1524 rival conquistadores took control of Honduras. Then they advanced to the south, as Francisco Pizarro vanquished the Incas of Peru in 1531–1534, and others expanded into Argentina and Chile. Alonso Álvarez de Pineda in 1519–1520 sailed the coastline of the Gulf of Mexico from Florida to Mexico.

Exploration of Florida and the American Southwest

In 1528, Pánfilo de Narváez led an expedition to Florida. His venture led to later exploration of territories that became the southern United States. Narváez and his men landed at Tampa Bay where they met Native Americans who warned them to return to the sea. When the Europeans refused, and spoke of their search for silver and gold, the Indians directed them to "Apalachen," near the present site of Tallahassee. The Spanish marched northward through insect- and snake-infested terrain. Soon discouraged, they made the mistake of kidnapping a chief of the Apalachees. The Indians attacked, convincing the Spanish to return to New Spain immediately. The soldiers constructed barges to carry them across the Gulf of Mexico. When storms separated the craft, most of the explorers, including Narváez, were lost at sea.

Two barges crossed the gulf intact, beaching their occupants on the Texas coast. The native Karankawas enslaved the survivors. After several years, one of the Spaniards, Álvar Núñez Cabeza de Vaca, escaped with three others, including Esteban, a black slave. They hoped to reach New Spain, but lacked maps or instruments to find their way. For several years they sojourned with a series of Native American peoples, learning their languages and customs. The Spanish earned the Indians' friendship and respect with seemingly miraculous cures. When they finally reached Mexico City in 1536, Cabeza de Vaca told the Spanish viceroy about their journey.

Cabeza de Vaca's report excited interest in exploring lands north of Mexico. When Cabeza de Vaca refused to head an expedition, the viceroy sent Esteban with a Franciscan monk, Fray Marcos de Niza, along with several Indians. When Esteban was killed by Zuñis, Fray Marcos returned to Mexico City with extravagant claims that the land flowed with riches.

An Aztec Report of the Fall of Tenochtitlán 1521

The Aztecs fought the Spanish and their Indian allies for months before the invaders, led by Hernán Cortés, prevailed. This document gives an Aztec view of the surrender and shows the immediate impact of the conquest on ordinary men, women, and children.

And when night had fallen, then it rained and sprinkled at intervals. Late at night the flame became visible; just so was it seen, just so it emerged as if it came from the heavens. Like a whirlwind it went spinning around and revolving; it was as if embers burst out of it—some very large, some very small, some like sparks. . . .

None shouted; none spoke aloud.

And on the next day, nothing more happened. All remained quiet, and also our foes [so] remained.

But the Captain [Cortés] was watching from a roof-top at Amaxac—from the roof-top of [the house of] Aztauatzin—under a canopy. It was a many-colored canopy. He looked toward [us] common folk; the Spaniards crowded about him and took counsel among themselves.

And [on our side] were Quauhtemoc and the other noblemen—the vice ruler Tlacotzin, the lords' judge Petlauhtzin, the captain of the armies Motelchiuhtzin. . . . All of these noblemen were assembled

In 1540, an army of 336 Spanish and about 1,000 Indians marched north under command of Francisco Vásquez de Coronado, with Fray Marcos as their guide. The explorers intended to conquer the cities of gold (the so-called "Seven Cities of Cibola") but were disappointed. The "golden" city that Fray Marcos had spotted was actually a Zuñi Indian pueblo, Hawikúh, made of adobe. The Zuñis resisted the intruders but were conquered, then informed the Spanish that the cities of gold lay to the west. Another Indian told stories about great wealth in the country to the east. Over the next year, Coronado's troops explored in both directions. They encountered the Hopi of northeastern Arizona and buffalo-hunting Indians of the Great Plains and traveled as far east as Kansas. They found no gold or silver but left descriptions of a substantial part of the American Southwest.

To reinforce Coronado's army, the viceroy in 1540 sent Hernando de Alarcón by ship up the western coast of Mexico. Though the two explorers failed to make contact, Alarcón sailed into the Colorado River. Two years later, Juan Rodríguez Cabrillo sailed with two ships up the coast of Baja California. They were the first Europeans to visit what is now California. After Cabrillo died in January 1543, his deputy Bartolomé Ferrelo sailed almost as far north as Oregon.

at Tolmayecan; they appeared to consult among themselves how to do that which we were to undertake and how we should yield to [the Spaniards].

Thereafter only two [men] took Quauhtemoc in a boat. . . .

And when they carried Quauhtemoc off, then there was weeping among all the common folk. They said: "Now goeth the young lord Quauhtemoc; now he goeth to deliver himself to the gods, the Spaniards!"

And when they had betaken themselves to bring and disembark him thereupon all the Spaniards came to see. They drew him along; the Spaniards took him by the hand. After that they took him up to the roof-top, where they went to stand him before the Captain, the war leader. And when they had proceeded to stand him before [Cortés], they looked at Quauhtemoc, made much of him, and stroked his hair. Then they seated him with [Cortés] and fired the guns. They hit no one with them, but only made them go off above, [so that] they passed over the heads of the common folk. Then [some Mexicans] only fled. With this the war reached its end. . . .

And everywhere the Spaniards were seizing and robbing the people. They sought gold. . . .

And [the Spaniards] seized and set apart the pretty women—those of light bodies, the fair[-skinned] ones. And some women, when they were robbed, covered their face with mud and put on old, mended shirts and rags for their shifts. They put all rags on themselves.

And also some of us men were singled out—those who were strong, grown to manhood, and next the young boys, of whom they would make messengers, who would be their runners, and who were known as their servers. And on some they burned [brand marks] on their cheeks; on some they put paint on their cheeks; on some they put paint on their lips.

And when the shield was laid down, when we gave way, it was the year count Three House and the day count was One Serpent.

Unknown to Coronado, an expedition led by Hernando de Soto, governor of Cuba, came within a few hundred miles of his own company at about the same time. In 1539, De Soto and about 600 troops landed in Tampa Bay. Over the next three years they trekked through the southeast, exploring lands hitherto unknown to the Spanish. They plundered the towns of the Apalachees and other Florida Indians who were part of the Mississippian cultures. Stealing food, taking Indians as slaves, and killing those who resisted, De Soto's men marched north from the Florida peninsula, through central Georgia to the Carolinas, then west across the Appalachians into the Tennessee River valley. They followed the river south into Alabama, then traveled west toward the Mississippi. Despite heavy losses when Chickasaws burned their camp and supplies, De Soto crossed into Arkansas. After he died of a fever in 1542, the 300 survivors of his expedition safely reached New Spain by boat.

In 1542, the initial period of Spanish expansion came to a close throughout America. Without discovery of precious metals, they had little immediate reason to push farther into North America. During the half century since Columbus sailed west, contact and exchange among Native Americans, Europeans, and Africans created new political and social systems. Although the Spanish expected to create a society much like the one at home, the results of colonization proved different than planned.

Spanish Patterns of Colonization

As conquest of the Americas progressed, Spain established a colonial government whose purposes were to convert Native Americans and bring them under control of the Spanish monarchy, and to exploit their labor and the wealth of the New World. The Spanish were only partly successful in imposing their rule over the Indians. The colonial government was most effective in central Mexico and the Andes, where the Europeans substituted their own imperial rule for that of the Aztecs and Incas. Native Americans in northern Mexico, Florida, Arizona, New Mexico, and central Chile, who had never been subject to empires, evaded Spanish rule. Many in the fringe areas, such as the Apaches, avoided Spanish domination altogether.

The Spanish colonial administration was hierarchical. Sovereignty, or supreme political power, rested in the monarch. The Spanish believed that God vested such power in the Crown. Neither Spanish colonists nor Indians had much say in making and enforcing laws. The right of subjects to appeal official decisions to the king, however, along with delays caused by distance, corruption, and inefficiency, introduced flexibility into the governmental structure.

Directly below the monarch was the Council of the Indies, located in Spain and composed of men who knew little about the New World. The council regulated trade, appointed officials, made laws, and determined who should be allowed to emigrate. The highest officials residing in America were the viceroys. In the sixteenth and seventeenth centuries the Spanish empire consisted of two viceroyalties: New Spain, with its capital in Mexico City, and Peru, with its capital in Lima. The viceroyalties were divided into provinces, ruled by governors and *audiencias,* which advised the governors and functioned as courts. The audiencias could appeal all decisions to the king, thus limiting the wide powers of the viceroys and governors. So did the *residencia,* which investigated these officials at the end of their terms and reported any corruption to Spain.

In central Mexico and Peru, the Spanish viceroys, governors, and audiencias took the place of the ruling native elite. At the local level, native leaders often retained their positions. Called *caciques,* they headed the Indian towns, collected tribute from every household, and recruited forced laborers upon the demand of the colonial authorities.

Spanish Mercantilism

The Crown regulated commerce through the *Casa de la Contratación,* a trading house founded in 1503 in Seville. Thus Spain elaborated its economic policy of mercantilism, which held that nations had monopolistic rights to trade with their colonies. With tight governmental control, the primary goal of economic activity under mercantilism was to achieve a favorable balance of trade. Colonies were expected to serve as markets for goods from the home country and provide raw materials, gold, and silver to increase its wealth. All merchants desiring to send ships to Spanish America needed permission from the Casa. To the monarch, a crucial function of the Casa was registration of precious metals, because the king received one-fifth, called the "royal fifth," of all silver and gold. Colonists had to obtain permission to build plantations and mines. In return they paid taxes to the king and, if they found precious metals, the royal fifth.

When Columbus obtained gold from the inhabitants of Hispaniola, he raised expectations of great wealth. However, the explorers at first met disappointment. Even the Aztecs failed to satisfy the Spanish thirst for gold, so most colonists turned to agriculture to make their fortunes. Then, in the 1540s, the Europeans located two immensely rich silver mines, one at Potosí in present-day Bolivia and the other at Zacatecas in Mexico. Between 1500 and 1650 about 16,000 tons of silver officially reached Europe from

America. Production of silver expanded greatly in the 1570s with the introduction of mercury to the refining process.

The Spanish organized their silver trade to outwit privateers of other nations, especially France and England. In 1565, the Spanish founded St. Augustine in Florida as a base to fight the buccaneers. St. Augustine also reinforced Spain's claim to North America (as discussed later in this chapter). The Spanish devised a convoy system to protect their fleets. Two convoys left Seville each year, carrying goods such as wine, books, clothing, and other luxuries: One left in May headed for Mexico, and the other departed in August for the Isthmus of Panama, from which mules carried the goods to Peru. Both convoys stayed the winter with the intention of meeting in Cuba by early summer so they could return to Spain before the onset of hurricanes. The Panama fleet sometimes ran into trouble when the mule train carrying Potosí silver arrived late.

For the Spanish monarchy, the discovery of rich mines fulfilled their dreams in the New World. The king used the bullion to pay for his European wars. American silver and gold helped to create inflation throughout Europe. With the immense supply of the metals, their value declined and the prices of other goods increased. Merchants depended on the bullion to pay for luxuries from the East. Goods worth about one-half the value of the metals were returned to the colonies.

New World Societies

If some European settlers hoped to duplicate Spanish society and have millions of Christianized Indian workers do their bidding, they were disappointed. For a number of reasons, including the lack of women among Spanish immigrants, the catastrophic level of native deaths, and the resistance of Indians to conversion, the developing New World societies diverged from what both the Spanish and Native Americans had previously known.

Despite rapid demographic decline among the Native Americans, the Spanish colonists remained a small percentage of the population. In 1550 about 100,000 whites lived in the Spanish colonies. By comparison, the population of the Aztec empire before the conquest had been an estimated 25 million. With the devastating effects of diseases that Europeans brought to the Western Hemisphere, by 1570 the number of natives in central Mexico was only 2.6 million.

In conquering the Native Americans, the chief ally of the Spanish was disease, of which smallpox was most lethal. Other killers included measles, chicken pox, influenza, whooping cough, and diphtheria. The Indians had no immunity to these diseases. Disease spread from one native population to another. As the native population of the Americas declined by an estimated 90 percent, whole tribes were eliminated and others weakened severely.

Most surviving Native Americans resisted assimilation to Spanish culture. The degree to which they blocked acculturation depended largely on class. The Spanish focused much attention on the caciques and their sons. Many caciques learned to speak Spanish, converted to Christianity, and adopted Hispanic clothing. Their sons attended schools where they learned Latin and other advanced subjects. The common Indians avoided

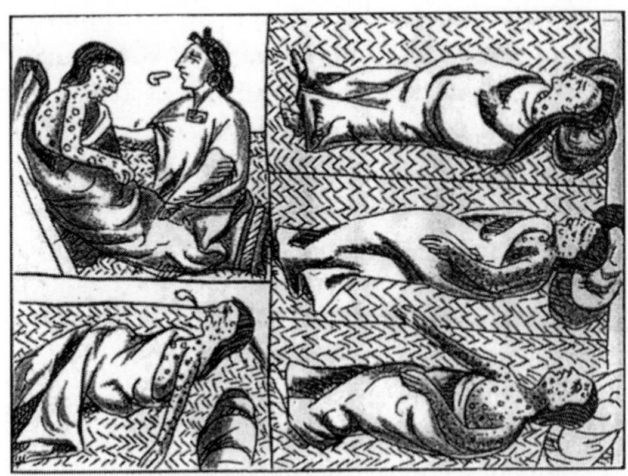

Sixteenth-century drawings of Aztecs suffering from smallpox when the Spanish invaded. (Reproduced from the Collections of the Library of Congress)

some Spanish ways of living and accepted others. They raised and ate chickens, but grew wheat primarily to pay as tribute. They abhorred cattle, but groups like the Apaches quickly accepted the horse. Natives favored their digging-sticks over the European plow, which would have required alteration in the assignment of fields.

The "Columbian exchange," as the transfer of culture among Americans, Europeans, and Africans has been called, did not proceed in just one direction. While the Europeans introduced deadly diseases, European wheat, firearms, and Christianity to the Indians, the Native Americans in turn provided crops that had a major impact on the growth of world populations. The white potato of South America became a major staple in northern Europe; the sweet potato, cassava, and Indian corn were important throughout the world.

The complexity of interaction between the Spanish and Native Americans can be seen most vividly in religion. The Europeans had a mandate from the pope to convert the "pagans" of America to Christianity. The missionaries believed that it was an act of humanity to introduce the Indians to Catholicism. The Spanish eliminated human sacrifice and destroyed temples and relics, but for the most part avoided forced conversion. At first, the missionaries expected most Native Americans to accept Spanish religious practice without change. But most Indians merged the European faith with rituals and beliefs of their traditional religions, resulting in *syncretism,* the blending of two faiths. For example, some natives added the Christian God to their polytheistic system; others focused on the saints or the Trinity rather than the supreme God. Indians organized *cofradías,* which were societies to raise money for church functions and festivals. The natives controlled the cofradías and at times asserted independence from the Spanish church authority.

The retention of native beliefs and practices disappointed many Spanish priests. Nevertheless, missionaries worked for humane treatment of Indians. Colonists often justified enslaving Indians because they had "inferior" cultures and religion. A number of priests, of whom Bartolomé de las Casas is best known, condemned the cruelty and enslavement. In his *Short Account of the Destruction of the Indies,* written in 1542, las Casas argued for more enlightened policies. He informed the king of "the excesses which this New World has witnessed, all of them surpassing anything that men hitherto have imagined even in their wildest dreams."

Forced Labor Systems

In 1500, the Spanish Crown ruled that only Indians captured in a "just war" could be forced into perpetual bondage. This judgment had little impact because conquistadores could define as hostile any natives who resisted capture. In 1513, the government drew up a document called the *Requerimiento* (or Requirement), which explorers read when they entered an Indian town for the first time. The requerimiento informed the natives that they must accept the sovereignty of the Catholic church and the Spanish monarchy. If they did, they would become Spanish subjects in peace; if they did not, they would be captured and enslaved. By the time the king outlawed most Native American slavery in 1542, the Arawaks of the West Indies had been destroyed. The Spanish had expropriated their lands for sugar plantations, replacing the Indians with enslaved Africans. On the mainland, the Spanish government established two forms of forced Indian labor. With the *encomienda,* Indians living on specified lands had to pay tribute to individual colonists and sometimes provide labor for which they received minimal wages. At first, the encomienda system included no transfer of land to the colonists, but as the numbers of Native Americans declined and Spanish increased, the colonists took Indian property for farms and ranches. By the seventeenth century, grazing livestock replaced Indian farms on vast stretches of Spanish America.

In 1600, about 1 million Indians survived in central Mexico, down from 25 million a century before. This severe decline caused problems for the Spanish who depended upon the natives for food and labor. Thus, the government devised the *repartimiento* system. Indians could be forced to work in mines, agriculture, or public works for several weeks, months, or even a year. For example, natives labored for yearlong stints at the Potosí silver mines in Bolivia. At Potosí, workers assigned as carriers climbed some 600 feet through tunnels about as wide as a man's body with heavy loads of silver ore on their backs. Those who worked in refining were exposed to mercury poisoning. As the Indian population declined, the Spanish had difficulty in finding enough workers. When they attempted to increase the length and frequency of work periods, Indians resisted the changes, sometimes successfully.

As early as 1502, on West Indies plantations, the Spanish turned to the people of Africa to meet their insatiable labor demands. They had already purchased Africans from Portuguese traders to work in Spain and on the sugar plantations of the Canary Islands. The government set up a system of licenses, or *asientos,* for merchants to supply certain numbers of slaves. During the sixteenth century, ships transported approximately 75,000 Africans to Spanish America, with perhaps an equal number dying en route. The Spanish imported Africans to work on sugar plantations in the West Indies and coastal areas of the mainland where most Native Americans had died. Severe work regimes and rampant disease also resulted in high death rates among imported blacks.

An exterior view of Potosí, the Spanish silver mine in what is now Bolivia. The mine yielded immense wealth, but with a dreadful toll as laborers worked in harsh conditions deep underground. (The John Carter Brown Library at Brown University)

PROTESTANT NORTHERN EUROPEANS CHALLENGE CATHOLIC SPAIN

Until 1560, French and English activity in America remained much more tentative and sporadic than Spain's. Although fishing expeditions regularly visited the North American coast, initiatives for permanent colonies gained little support. But religious and political change in Northern Europe provided the impetus to test Spain's domination of the New World. In the age of Reformation and religious wars, America became both a refuge for religious dissidents and a battlefield on which European nations fought for wealth, glory, and national sovereignty.

The Protestant Reformation

When the German priest Martin Luther in 1517 circulated his ninety-five theses against the sale of indulgences, the Church of Rome was the sovereign faith of western and central Europe. Luther believed the church was corrupt. The sale of indulgences, which were supposed to reduce the amount of time a deceased person spent in purgatory, was an example of its waywardness. Luther believed that people received salvation as a gift from God in return for faith rather than for good works. They could not earn salvation by taking pilgrimages, giving money to the church, hearing masses, or going on crusades against the Muslims. Luther also challenged the authority of priests; he argued that Christians should seek the word of God in the Bible. Luther contended that the Bible recognized only two sacraments, baptism and communion, not the seven authorized by the Catholic church. He also opposed the requirement of celibacy for priests.

Luther's teachings led to many divisions in western Christianity. In Germany, which was composed of many individual states, some princes accepted Lutheranism and others remained Catholic. Lutheranism spread through northern Germany and into Scandinavia. Luther inspired other critics of Catholicism to offer variant Protestant doctrines, including the Mennonites, Hutterites, and Swiss Brethren, all called Anabaptists because they required adult baptism.

The most influential of the systems of belief that Lutheranism spawned was that of John Calvin, a native of France, who attempted to create a model society at Geneva, Switzerland. Followers of Calvin established churches in the Reformed tradition: they were known variously as French Huguenots, English Puritans, Scottish Presbyterians, and Dutch and German Reformed. Calvin argued that humans could do nothing to save themselves. This concept of predestination meant that God alone determined who would be saved (the "elect"). Through communion with God, the elect learned that they were saved; they strove to live blamelessly to reflect their status.

Calvin and his followers convinced the city council and churches of Geneva to adopt many Reformed doctrines. The Bible became the basis for law. The civil government punished moral offenders and nonbelievers identified by the church elders. The Calvinists disciplined individuals for dancing, wearing fancy clothes, and insubordination. They forced one man to walk through the city wearing only a shirt because he criticized Calvin. Although Calvin failed to obtain all of his demands from the Geneva council, he came close to establishing a theocracy, in which the church fathers ruled in the name of God.

Protestant ideas spread to France and England quickly. In France, Calvin attracted many adherents, called Huguenots, among the nobles and prosperous commoners. The French monarchy considered Protestants a threat to its monopoly of power. Even after the Edict of Nantes of 1598, which offered freedom to worship, Huguenots faced serious discrimination.

In England, years before Luther, opposition had existed to the Catholic hierarchy. Thus Henry VIII found sympathy for his break with Rome when the pope refused to allow an annulment of his marriage to Catherine of Aragon. Henry wanted to marry Anne Boleyn, who he hoped would provide a male heir. Parliament passed the Act of Supremacy (1534), mandating that the king be "taken, accepted, and reputed the only supreme head on earth of the Church of England." Henry was no Lutheran, however, for the Six Articles (1539) that formed the theological basis of Anglicanism confirmed Catholic beliefs on priestly celibacy, the mass, confession, and sacraments. But because the Six Articles were ambiguous on many points, the Church of England from its inception allowed a fairly wide range of doctrine. In 1552, the revised Anglican prayer book incorporated many Protestant beliefs. Soon after, Henry's daughter Mary I attempted to force England back to the Church of Rome; her persecution of Protestants earned her the name "Bloody Mary." When Mary died in 1558, her half-sister, Elizabeth I, became queen, ending the immediate threat that England would return to Catholicism.

In the religious struggles of the late sixteenth century, England became a dominant Protestant power, supported the Dutch revolt against Philip II of Spain, and challenged Spain's monopolistic claims to the New World. Elizabeth confirmed England's break with the pope and approved earlier moderate Protestant reforms. The Act of Uniformity (1559) required adherence to the Anglican Book of Prayer. The queen suppressed resistance from both Calvinists, who wanted further reforms, and the supporters of Rome. Some Catholics turned to Elizabeth's cousin, Mary, Queen of Scots, a Roman Catholic and heir to the English throne. In 1587, after several unsuccessful plots on Elizabeth's life, Mary was tried as a conspirator and beheaded.

One of Mary, Queen of Scots' most fervent supporters was Spain's Philip II. Throughout Europe he strove to wipe out the Protestant heresy. He considered Elizabeth a dangerous foe, not least for her support of the revolt in the Netherlands. When many Dutch adopted Calvinism, Philip retaliated with his Inquisition, executing thousands. The Dutch rebelled. In 1581, the northern part of the Netherlands, composed of seven provinces, including Holland, declared its independence as the United Provinces. The southern region, called the Spanish Netherlands (now Belgium), remained under Philip's control. When Elizabeth sent aid to the United Provinces in 1585, she in effect declared a war on Spain. The most important battle occurred in 1588, when Philip sent his mighty Armada of 130 ships and 30,000 men to invade England. The English defeated the Armada, thus preserving their national sovereignty and religion.

French Huguenots and English Sea Dogs

In France, persecution led some Protestant Huguenots to look to America as a refuge. In 1555, a group of wealthy Frenchmen sent Huguenot settlers to Brazil. When disputes occurred among the colonists, some returned to France; the Portuguese, who claimed Brazil, killed or enslaved the majority who remained. In 1562, Huguenots tried again, establishing Charlesfort on the South Carolina coast, in part to attack the Spanish silver fleet as it headed home. When the Spaniards moved against the small French colony in 1564, they found it already abandoned. But the Huguenots attempted another settlement that year, this one at Fort Caroline on the St. Johns River in northern Florida. The Spanish quickly destroyed it, murdering most of the settlers.

The English "sea dogs" learned a great deal about the New World from the Huguenots. With Elizabeth I's ascension to the throne in 1558, seafarers and colonizers like John Hawkins, Francis Drake, Humphrey Gilbert, and Walter Raleigh gained favor and support. Hawkins visited Fort Caroline in 1565; other Englishmen gained knowledge of the North American coast from the French.

The English took their time before attempting an American colony. The Spanish remained a serious threat. Thus for two decades, until the 1580s, English adventurers sought wealth by sea. In 1562, John Hawkins took 300 Africans to Hispaniola without a license. The local Spanish officials allowed him to exchange the slaves for sugar and hides because the colony needed labor. Hawkins made a second voyage, earning another handsome profit, this time mostly in silver. When the Spanish authorities protested, Elizabeth forbade further expeditions, but reversed her decision in 1567. On his third voyage, Hawkins was conducting business in the harbor of San Juan de Ulúa, Mexico, when the annual fleet arrived from Spain several weeks early, destroying three of his ships. Hawkins and his cousin Francis Drake escaped with two badly damaged vessels.

Hawkins stopped interloping in Spanish trade, but other English privateers followed. The most famous was Francis Drake, who in 1572 intercepted the mule train carrying Potosí silver across Panama. Five years later he set out to circumnavigate the globe. Following Magellan's route through the straits, he attacked Spanish towns along the Pacific coast, explored the North American coast, and returned to England in 1580 by way of Asia and the Cape of Good Hope. Six years later, when England and Spain were formally at war, Drake attacked Spanish ports in America, including St. Augustine in Florida.

While Drake was making his fortune through piracy, other sea dogs hoped to make their mark by starting colonies. On the basis of Cabot's voyage of 1497, Elizabeth granted a charter to Humphrey Gilbert, who sailed to Newfoundland in 1583. He assumed ownership for the English Crown. Nothing came of Gilbert's colony, however, as he was lost at sea on his return to England.

Walter Raleigh then attempted a settlement farther south, in the land named for the "virgin" Queen Elizabeth. In 1585, the first group of settlers arrived at Roanoke Island. After their ships returned home leaving them with short supplies, the colonists tried to force neighboring Indians to provide food. Quickly a pattern of hostility emerged between the English and Native Americans. Francis Drake saved the Roanoke colonists from starvation, carrying them home in 1586. A year later, Raleigh sent out another expedition. This time the war with Spain prevented ships from returning to Roanoke until 1590, when all that was left of the colony was the word "Croatoan" carved on a tree. The colonists may have moved to nearby Croatoan Island, or farther inland to live with Native Americans, but the fate of the "Lost Colony" has never been determined. The English did not colonize successfully in North America until the founding of Jamestown in 1607.

CONCLUSION

By 1590, the Spanish had created an empire that extended from South America through the West Indies and Mexico. They funded their European wars to extinguish Protestantism with American silver and gold. The Portuguese, united under the Spanish Crown in 1580, had developed the Atlantic slave trading system that sent enslaved Africans to Brazil and New Spain.

The irony of colonization in America was that European nations at war in the Old World emulated one another in the New. The Spanish and Portuguese provided the model for later colonizers in expropriating land and labor from Indians and Africans. Europeans justified their behavior toward the people of America and Africa by emphasizing religious and cultural differences, ignoring much that they had in common. Although European nations organized colonization in various ways, all sought mercantilistic ends. In the early seventeenth century, when the English, French, and Dutch settled in North America, their goals were very similar to those of Spain. They hoped to locate precious metals, find the elusive northwest passage, exploit Indian labor, extend Christianity to America, and expand the power of the state.

Recommended Readings

Bethell, Leslie, ed. *Colonial Spanish America* (1987). Essays provide useful syntheses on the development of the Spanish colonies.

Casas, Bartolomé de las. *A Short Account of the Destruction of the Indies.* Ed. and trans., Nigel Griffin (1992). A priest's sharp denunciation of Spanish colonization, written in 1542.

Davidson, Basil. *The Search for Africa: History, Culture, Politics* (1994). A recent, readable history by a veteran historian of the continent.

Kupperman, Karen Ordahl. *Roanoke: The Abandoned Colony* (1984). A lively account of the early English attempt to settle in North America.

Meinig, D. W. *The Shaping of America: A Geographical Perspective on 500 Years of History, Vol. 1: Atlantic America, 1492–1800* (1986). Provides a broad cultural view of European expansion.

Nash, Gary B. *Red, White, and Black: The Peoples of Early North America,* 3d ed. (1992). An excellent introduction to the meeting of cultures in the New World.

Parry, J. H. *The Establishment of the European Hegemony, 1415–1715: Trade and Exploration in the Age of the Renaissance,* 3d ed. (1966). A short, interesting introduction to the European explorations.

Quinn, David B. *North America from Earliest Discovery to First Settlements: The Norse Voyages to 1612* (1977). A comprehensive source on early European explorations.

Weber, David J. *The Spanish Frontier in North America* (1992). The best synthesis on Spanish exploration and colonization north of Mexico.

American Journey Online and InfoTrac College Edition

Visit the source collections at www.americanjourney.psmedia.com and infotrac.thomsonlearning.com and use the Search function with the following key terms to explore documents, images, audio and video clips, articles, and commentary related to the material in this chapter.

Maya
Aztecs
Atlantic slave trade
Spanish empire
Iroquois
Algonquian
Anasazi
Christopher Columbus
Protestant Reformation
Martin Luther
Hernán Cortés
Francis Drake

Chapter 2

Colonization of North America, 1590–1675

IN 1590, the only permanent European settlement in what is now the United States was St. Augustine. Spain was much more concerned with its silver mines and West Indies plantations than in colonizing along the Atlantic coast, yet wanted to prevent intrusion by other nations, for good reason. In the late sixteenth century, buccaneers from France and England thought the best way to get rich was by looting the Spanish silver fleet and ports.

By 1675, however, the major European nations had planted colonies in America. The West Indies became a magnet, with colonizers vying for tiny islands as sugar boomed. In North America, the Spanish held Florida and New Mexico, the French occupied Canada, and the English had a string of settlements along the Atlantic coast. English colonization proceeded with little regulation from the Crown, resulting in a variety of social, economic, and political structures.

The expansion of European settlement changed the countryside forever. Cheap, even free land and developing commerce offered opportunity to men and women of all economic classes who were willing to risk their lives by crossing the Atlantic. Their farms eliminated Indian hunting lands, altering the ecological balance of plants and animals. Though many Native Americans resisted the European invasions, disease seriously undermined their power. The fur trade also changed the cultural values of many Indians, drawing them into Atlantic commerce and tempting them to overhunt.

The Spanish in North America

After Coronado and de Soto failed to locate cities of gold, Spain abandoned further exploration in North America. Then, Francis Drake's voyage along the Pacific coast raised alarms of foreign interest in the region north of Mexico. In 1581, the viceroy of New Spain gave Franciscan priests permission to establish missions among the Pueblo Indians of the Rio Grande Valley. The friars named the area San Felipe del Nuevo México. The missionaries described the Pueblos as friendly and numerous: thousands could be made Christian and forced to labor for Hispanic colonists. But by the time a party arrived in 1582 to escort the Franciscans back to Mexico, the missionaries had been killed by the Native Americans.

Chronology

1598 Spanish expedition into New Mexico

1599 Destruction of Ácoma by the Spanish

1603 James I takes the English throne

1605 French establish Port Royal

1607 English found colony at Jamestown

1608 French establish Quebec

1609 Henry Hudson explores for the Dutch East India Company

1609–1614 Anglo-Powhatan War in Virginia

1616–1618 Plague epidemic decimates eastern New England natives

1619 Africans arrive in Virginia

Virginia Company establishes a representative assembly

1620 Separatists found the Plymouth colony

1622 Native Americans attack the Virginia colony

1624 Virginia Company loses charter; Virginia becomes a royal colony

Dutch West India Company establishes New Netherland

1625 Charles I becomes king of England

1630 Massachusetts Bay colony founded by Puritans

1634 The *Ark* and the *Dove* arrive in Maryland

1636 Founding of Connecticut and Rhode Island

1637 Massachusetts and Connecticut troops destroy the Pequots

Anne Hutchinson is tried for heresy

1642–1648 English Civil War

1649 Charles I of England is beheaded

1651 English Parliament passes first Navigation Act

1660 Charles II of England becomes king

1663 Carolina proprietors receive charter

1664 English forces conquer New Netherland; New York and New Jersey are founded

1673 Dutch recapture New York, then return the colony to England with the Treaty of Westminster (1674)

Settlement of New Mexico

Despite this setback, Spaniards remained interested in the region. Conquistadores needed permission from the Crown to invade new lands, however, for the king had issued Orders for New Discoveries (1573), which more strictly regulated colonization. When one would-be conqueror led an illegal expedition into New Mexico in 1590, he was arrested and returned to Mexico City in chains.

The Spanish government delayed appointing a governor of New Mexico until 1595, when the viceroy authorized Juan de Oñate to undertake settlement with his own funds. Oñate, a native of Mexico, inherited great wealth and obtained even more by marrying Isabel Tolosa Cortés Moctezuma, a descendant of both Cortés and the Aztec emperor. The expedition proved expensive as delays increased costs. Finally, in 1598, 129 soldiers, their families, servants, and slaves, and 7,000 livestock headed north. Ten Franciscan missionaries accompanied the colonists. Oñate expected his investment to yield an empire. The governor envisioned mines of silver and gold and a water passage through the continent.

Upon arrival in New Mexico, Oñate declared Spanish sovereignty over Pueblo lands. In a ritual complete with trumpets and High Mass, he promised peace and prosperity to those who cooperated.

Navajo wall art in the Canyon del Muerto, Arizona, showing the arrival of a Spanish missionary and soldiers in the late sixteenth or early seventeenth century. (© Jerry Jacka)

According to the Spanish, the Pueblos acquiesced "of their own accord." The Franciscans founded missions in the largest pueblos and supervised construction of a church in the Tewa pueblo, Yungé, which the Spanish designated as their capital, San Gabriel.

For some months, the Spanish and the Indians coexisted without serious incident. The colonists moved into the Pueblos' apartments in San Gabriel, forcing the inhabitants to depart. Soon the Indians tired of providing food. The soldiers resorted to murder and rape to obtain supplies. The crisis came in December 1598, when a Spanish troop demanded provisions from the people of Ácoma, a pueblo high atop a mesa west of the Rio Grande. The Pueblos refused to give flour to the soldiers and killed eleven men when they attempted to take the food by force. Oñate swiftly punished the village so others would not join in revolt. His small army laid siege to Ácoma with several cannons; men and women defended the town with arrows and stones. The Spanish killed approximately 500 men and 300 women and children; they captured the survivors. The town was leveled. Everyone was sentenced to servitude, and each man over age twenty-five had one foot cut off.

With this harsh action, Oñate only temporarily prevented further resistance among the Pueblos, for another town rebelled the following year. The colonists also complained of food shortages and the governor's mismanagement; many returned to Mexico. The Franciscans charged that Oñate's cruelty to the Indians made conversion difficult. Oñate was removed as governor, tried, and found guilty of mistreating the Native Americans and some of his settlers. He was banished from New Mexico, but sailed to Spain, where he received a knighthood and position as the Crown's chief inspector of mines.

After Oñate's departure, New Mexico became a royal province. Pedro de Peralta, the next governor, established a new capital at Santa Fe in 1610. As late as 1670 only 2,800 Spanish colonists lived in the Rio Grande valley. The Hispanics lived on farms and ranches along the river, exploiting the

Pueblos' labor through the encomienda system (see Chapter 1) to produce hides, blankets, sheep, wool, and pinenuts for sale in Mexico.

Spanish Missions in New Mexico and Florida

The Franciscan missionaries, who assumed a major role in colonizing the Spanish borderlands, were members of the Catholic religious order that Francis Bernardone of Assisi had founded (in Italy) in 1209. The friars vowed not to engage in sexual relations or acquire property, living on the gifts of others. Unlike other religious brotherhoods, the Franciscans operated in the world among ordinary Christians. The Orders for New Discoveries of 1573 gave primary responsibility to the monks for "pacifying" the Indians of New Mexico and Florida.

During the first part of the seventeenth century, many Pueblos seemed to accept the Franciscans' message. The friars offered gifts of food, metal tools, beads, and clothing. Placing some confidence in the priests, the natives agreed to build convents and churches. Women built the walls, while men did carpentry. The priests decorated the sanctuaries with paintings, statues, and silver chalices. They created missions by imposing their influence over existing Indian towns, backed by threat of military force. In New Mexico, the Spanish started more than fifty churches by 1629; in Florida, missions extended west from St. Augustine to the Gulf Coast and north into Georgia (or Guale, as the region was called).

The Native Americans who came under Spanish control could, in theory, choose whether or not to accept Christian baptism, but recognized that soldiers supported the priests. The Franciscans expected the natives to learn the catechism and enough of the Castilian (Spanish) language to communicate, and to adopt European dress, food, and farming methods. Many Indians embraced Catholicism but in doing so, modified the religion. Even in the twentieth century, the Pueblos preserved both native and Catholic religious practices.

In merging Indian gods with the Christian Trinity and adding Catholic holidays to native celebrations, Native Americans altered Spanish Catholicism. With the "Lady in Blue," they created a religious tradition that both the Indians and Spaniards accepted. In the 1620s, Plains Indians reported that a nun appeared to them, telling them in their language to become Christians. Though the woman remained invisible to the missionaries, they believed the stories. On a trip to Spain, one priest discovered that a Franciscan nun, María de Jesús de Agreda, claimed to have made flights to America with the help of angels. María de Agreda's claims and the Indians' visions together created the resilient legend of the Lady in Blue.

THE ENGLISH INVADE VIRGINIA

New Mexico and Florida remained marginal outposts in the Spanish empire. In the aftermath of the Spanish Armada's failure to conquer England, Philip II's government proved incapable of preventing other European nations from settling in North America. During the first decade of the seventeenth century, the English, French, and Dutch sent expeditions to fish, search for a northern passage to the East, trade for furs, and establish colonies.

English Context of Colonization

Seventeenth-century England was a society undergoing turmoil and change. Elizabeth I's successor was her cousin, James I, who governed from 1603 until 1625, when he died and his son, Charles I, took the throne. Both James and Charles had strife-torn reigns marked by power struggles with Parliament, culminating in Charles' loss of the English Civil War and his beheading in 1649. Parliament was composed of two houses: the House of Lords, made up of nobles and high church officials; and the House of Commons, who were elected representatives from the counties and boroughs. The Commons normally comprised country gentry, government officials, and lawyers; the electorate included male landowners, or an estimated 15 to 30 percent of all Englishmen. By imposing levies without Parliament's consent, James I and Charles I challenged its prerogative to approve or reject new taxes. For their part, the legislators tried to whittle away at royal powers. The fundamental issue concerning how the powers of the king versus property holders, as represented in Parliament, should be balanced remained unsettled until 1688.

Economic developments loosened English society, giving individuals greater opportunity to change from one social class or occupation to another. Many found it necessary to move geographically as the woolen industry expanded, causing landowners to raise more sheep. In what has been called the "enclosure movement," landlords ended leases for tenant farmers living on their lands, confiscating common fields that peasant communities had shared for grazing their livestock and raising crops. The landowners enclosed the commons with fences and hedges. Thus many tenants were forced from the land.

A developing economy meant dislocation for poor tenants; it spelled opportunity for merchants. They found it first in the woolen trade with Antwerp, in what is now Belgium. When this trade declined after 1550, they looked for alternative investments, which they found as war with Spain brought demand for coal, lead, glass, ships, salt, iron, and steel. Investors formed joint-stock companies to explore trade routes and establish new markets. The companies obtained capital by selling stocks. These investments were risky, for shareholders were liable for all company debts. The stocks could also be immensely profitable, as in the case of Francis Drake's circumnavigation of the globe, which brought a 4,600 percent profit.

Joint-stock companies provided capital for the first permanent English colonies in America. Unlike the Spanish monarchy, the English Crown had little role in funding, or even governing, its first New World settlements. In 1606, James I granted a charter to the Virginia Company with rights to settle colonies in North America. The Virginia Company included two groups, one in London and the other in Plymouth, in the west of England. The groups received overlapping claims, with the Plymouth group obtaining lands from what is now Maine to Virginia and the London group receiving Connecticut to the Carolinas.

Jamestown

In 1607, the Virginia Company of London funded the first permanent English colony at Jamestown. When the first 104 settlers arrived in May 1607, they had endured a long winter crossing. The native inhabitants watched the invaders select a site on the James River, chosen for safety from Spanish attack, but next to malarial swamps. The Native Americans were Algonquian-speaking Indians; most belonged to a confederacy that Powhatan, head sachem of the Pamunkey tribe, had forged in eastern Virginia. Before the arrival of the English, the chief unifying force among the bands of the Powhatan confederacy was the threat from powerful enemies, the Manahoacs and the Monacans, who controlled lands to the west. The leaders of tribes subject to Powhatan were supposed to pay tribute and provide military assistance, but they sometimes refused.

One of Powhatan's brothers was Opechancanough. Historical evidence suggests that he was born around 1544 and, at about age sixteen, was taken by a Spanish ship to Spain, where he received instruction in the Castilian language and adopted the name Don Luis de Velasco. The new Don Luis stayed with the Spanish until 1570, when he accompanied several missionaries to his homeland on Chesapeake Bay. He broke with the priests when they criticized him for taking several wives, and murdered the priests the next year. If Opechancanough and Don Luis were the same man, as seems likely, he was well prepared with

In this conjectural view of Jamestown c. 1614, the fortified wall shows concerns for defense against the Spanish and the Powhatan confederacy. (Colonial Williamsburg Foundation)

knowledge of the Europeans when the Jamestown settlers arrived.

The English colony's first decade was a struggle. The company ran Virginia as a business enterprise, keeping control of government, land, and trade. To satisfy investors, the company instructed the colonists to search for gold and silver mines, find a passage to Asia, and establish industries and trade that would offer handsome returns. Among the first Jamestown settlers were many gentlemen who expected to strike it rich and return to England. The rest of the first colonists included the gentlemen's personal servants, a jeweler, goldsmith, perfumer, carpenters, blacksmiths, and some laborers. No one described himself as a farmer.

When the colonists failed to locate mines or a passage to the East, their lives became aimless. Rather than plant crops or even hunt and fish, they expected the company and neighboring Indians to provide food. When sufficient provisions failed to arrive, the settlers starved. One of the leaders, a young officer named John Smith, took control in 1608, stabilizing the colony briefly by making everyone work. When criticism of his strict discipline reached company officials the next year, they removed him from command. During the particularly bitter winter of 1609–1610, some of the colonists dug up graves to eat the corpses. By spring 1610, only sixty colonists remained of at least 600 who had come to Jamestown in three years. Though some had returned to England or escaped to live with the Indians, the majority died of starvation and disease.

In 1609, without gold mines or a trade route to Asia, the company hoped to salvage its investment by exploiting the land. To recruit farmers, the company offered each emigrant one share of stock and a parcel of land after seven years of service. The settlers remained employees of the company in the meantime, with assigned tasks and the obligation to buy all supplies and ship all products through the company store.

Still, the Jamestown settlers refused to work. When Sir Thomas Dale arrived as governor in May 1611, he found nothing but a few gardens planted. He established his *Laws Divine, Morall and Martiall,* which were mostly martial. The men received military ranks, were divided into work gangs, and proceeded from home to work—and to church twice daily—at the beat of a drum. Laws prescribed death for a variety of crimes, including rape, adultery, theft, lying, and blasphemy. For the first offense of failing to work regular hours, an idler was tied neck to heels all night. The punishment for a second offense was whipping and for a third offense, death. Though the required hours of work were reasonable—five to eight hours per day in the summer and three to six in the winter—the punishments specified in "Dale's Laws" became a scandal in England, discouraging prospective emigrants.

The Struggle for Virginia

The Jamestown adventurers had expected to put the Indians to work in mines and fields, as in Mexico, but the inhabitants proved too few in number for an adequate workforce, yet too powerful for the wretched gang of settlers to conquer. During the early years at Jamestown, the English seemed irrational in their dealings with the Native Americans. To many colonists, the natives were barbarians. While some settlers attempted to trade for food, others burned Indian villages and crops.

In 1608–1609, Captain John Smith tried to force the sachems to provide food. His life had been spared by the Indians several times, including one occasion when Powhatan's daughter Pocahontas intervened on his behalf. Nevertheless, he kidnapped two men, obligating Opechancanough to beg for their release. Next, he entered the Pamunkey village with soldiers demanding food, which the Indians refused to give, and again humiliated the tall sachem: in Smith's words, he did "take this murdering Opechancanough . . . by the long lock of his head; and with my pistol at his breast, I led him [out of his house] amongst his greatest forces, and before we parted made him [agree to] fill our bark with twenty tuns of corn."

Between 1609 and 1614, full-scale war existed between the Virginia colonists and the Powhatan confederacy. The English defeated Powhatan, taking control of the James River. Powhatan faced another disappointment when Pocahontas married John Rolfe, accompanying him to England, where she died. The colonists had less success against Opechancanough.

In contrast to Spain, the English Crown failed to take responsibility for protecting any rights of Native Americans. When colonists had sufficient power, they enslaved Indians. The English justified expropriation of native lands with the belief that the king of England, as the Christian monarch, received sovereignty over North America from God. Thus, the Virginia Company obtained rights to land from the Crown, not the Indians. Another basis for taking native territory was the legal concept, *vacuum domicilium,* which meant that lands not occupied could be taken. To the English, "occupation" meant improving the land with buildings, fences, and crops; they did not recognize Indian sovereignty over the vast stretches of hunting lands that extended beyond small villages and fields. Even when the English purchased land from the Indians, their contrasting concepts of ownership caused grave misunderstanding. Whereas the colonists believed in private property, the natives thought they were selling the rights to use lands for hunting, fishing, and communal farming. They expected to continue using the territory they had "sold" for these purposes. Conflicts resulted when, for example, a settler's cattle trampled Indian crops, or when a native killed a colonist's cow, mistaking it for a deer.

Tobacco Boom

Demand for land became paramount in Virginia after 1617, when the colonists discovered tobacco as a staple crop. The mercantilist advantages were

Earliest known illustration of an American tobacco factory, c. 1670. (© Corbis-Bettmann)

clear. With production in Virginia, the English could acquire tobacco from its own colony, rather than pay premium prices to foreign countries, and could generate an industry to process the leaves. For Virginians, the tobacco trade meant capital to purchase manufactures from home. Tobacco became the first staple crop in England's colonial mercantilist system.

In 1619, the Virginia Company updated the land policy, granting "headrights" of one hundred acres of land to those who came before 1616 and fifty acres to those who came after. Settlers who paid their own way received land immediately; those who immigrated at the company's expense received land after seven years of service. Virginia settlers thus fell into two categories: freeholders who paid for their own transportation; and servants, whose way the Virginia Company or someone else financed. Recipients of headrights did not pay for the land, but owed quitrents, annual payments to the company, of one shilling per year for each fifty acres. Also in 1619, the Virginia Company relaxed its hold on the government of Virginia by establishing an assembly of elected delegates. The governor, who was appointed by the company, retained the right to veto all laws; the company's General Court in London could also disallow any decision.

While the revised land policy and the assembly gave settlers a greater stake in society, the adoption of tobacco assured Virginia's ultimate success. During the 1620s, tobacco drew high prices. Virginia became the first North American "boom town." Between 1617 and 1623, approximately 5,000 new immigrants arrived. Because the amount of the crop a planter could grow depended largely on the number of workers, those with capital eagerly paid for transporting servants. The Virginia Company imported workers too, but still failed to show a profit, partly because company officials diverted many servants to their own plantations.

Africans in Early Virginia

To strike it rich from tobacco, Virginia planters also purchased Africans. Though some of these Africans became servants, others probably were slaves. Although, over the years, slave traders brought more Africans to Virginia, English servants provided most of the labor in the colony until late in the seventeenth century. In 1625, Africans numbered twenty-three of 1,200 Virginia colonists. In 1660, about 900 blacks and 24,000 Europeans lived in the Chesapeake Bay area.

In contrast, by that same year, Africans outnumbered whites in Barbados, the richest of the English West Indies. Founded in 1627, Barbados quickly turned to sugar production, importing Africans to raise and process the crop. The white islanders forced the rapidly growing black population to perform hard, repetitive labor.

Until the 1660s, conditions for Africans remained less rigid in Virginia than in the West Indies. Some Virginia blacks achieved freedom, married, and a few acquired land. Even so, other Africans remained in bondage, as Virginians adopted the practice by example from the Portuguese, Spanish, and Dutch.

Early Virginia documents distinguished consistently between white servants and blacks, always with the suggestion that Africans were subordinate. Censuses of the 1620s, for example, point to the lower regard for Africans: English settlers were listed with full names while most Africans were enumerated simply with a first name or designated as "negar" or "Negro." The Virginia tax law of 1643 further demonstrated that the colonists viewed Africans as different from themselves. Everyone who worked in the field was to be taxed—all men and black women. White women apparently were not expected to tend tobacco. Virginia also excepted blacks, but not white servants, from the obligation to bear arms.

The Colony Expands

The colonists had found the way to success—by growing tobacco—but Virginia experienced difficulty for many years. Because mortality remained high and settlers had few children, the population grew slowly despite immigration that averaged about 1,000 people per year. From 1619 to 1640, the population rose from 700 to about 8,000, though approximately 20,000 immigrants had arrived during that time. Young men and women who left England to become servants in Virginia gambled with their lives to obtain land, which they could not gain at home. Dysentery, typhoid fever, and malaria took their toll on new settlers. Men were much more likely to migrate to the colonies than women. A 1625 census indicated that more than three-quarters of the Virginia colonists were male and less than one-fifth were children. Many people came as servants, which meant that they could not legally marry and have children for years, until their terms expired. The census also provided ample evidence of mortality and disrupted families, as many of the married couples were childless, in part because of high infant and childhood mortality. And with short life expectancy for adults, more than one-half of the colony's children had lost one parent, and one-fifth apparently had no relatives in Virginia at all.

By 1621, Opechancanough and a prophet Nemattanew recognized the threat of increased immigration. Now that the English had tobacco, they were not going to leave. Nemattanew inspired a nativist religious revival among the Powhatans, rejecting Christianity and European customs. Opechancanough organized a military offensive to push the English back into the sea. At the same time, he used diplomacy to convince the settlers to lower their guard. When several whites killed Nemattanew in 1622, Opechancanough rallied his troops, slaying one-fourth of the settlers before the colony could react. A ten-year war followed, in which each side tried to annihilate the other, but failed, and in 1632 agreed to peace.

Though the bankrupt Virginia Company lost its charter in 1624, immigration to the colony continued. Its economic promise helped convince the English Crown to claim it as a royal colony. Desire for new tobacco lands placed constant pressure on the Powhatans, so in 1644, Opechancanough launched another attack. After two years of war, the Powhatans submitted and Opechancanough was captured and murdered by a guard. The 1646 treaty required the Native Americans to live on lands north of the York River and to pay an annual tribute of twenty beaver skins. Colonists expanded rapidly north and south of the James River and to the eastern shore.

Fishing, Furs, and Settlements in the North

While settlers and Native Americans struggled for Virginia, French, Dutch, and English adventurers explored and colonized the region to the north. French and English sailors had fished the Newfoundland Banks since the fifteenth century. By 1600, groups monopolized specific waters. The beaver furs that Europeans obtained in petty trade with Native Americans became popular in Europe for making felt hats, exciting merchants in France, the Netherlands, and England to seek more permanent arrangements. All three nations claimed the northern territories as their own.

New France

In North America, French traders focused on furs. When a ship sent to North America in 1582 returned to France with a cargo of furs earning a 1,500 percent profit, merchants enthusiastically organized more voyages. Samuel de Champlain established the first successful French colony in the New World. Working for Pierre du Gua de Monts, who had received a charter from the French king, in 1605 Champlain planted a temporary base at Port Royal on the Bay of Fundy in Canada. He sailed south to Cape Cod looking for a permanent site, but decided in 1608 to retain Port Royal and establish a main settlement on the St. Lawrence River. The French chose Quebec, an ideal location for controlling the Canadian interior.

For two decades, both Port Royal and Quebec remained little more than trading posts. The French had already traded with the Micmacs of the coastal region and Algonquins of the St. Lawrence Valley. Champlain strengthened these ties, and made new alliances with several groups: the Montagnais, who lived in the region north of the St. Lawrence River and spoke Algonquian languages; and the Hurons, who were Iroquoian and lived north of Lake Ontario. In 1609, to demonstrate allegiance to his allies, Champlain helped them fight a group of Iroquois from what is now New York, thus making the Five Nations enemies of New France. He also explored the watershed of the St. Lawrence River and lands as far west as Lake Huron.

In 1627, Quebec was still essentially a trading post with about 100 French inhabitants. Cardinal Richelieu organized the Company of One Hundred Associates to spur colonization. The company received a charter for territory from the Arctic Circle to Florida and from the Atlantic to the Pacific, with a monopoly on the fur trade. The company also pledged to send missionaries to the Indians and grant them the status of "natural French" when they were baptized. The priests established missions in Indian villages and learned their languages, looking for similarities between the two cultures in an effort to make the Indians part of French society.

Because the company focused on the fur trade and considered transporting settlers too expensive, in 1663 just 3,000 French settlers lived in the colony. The Crown revoked the company's charter, making New France a royal province. Nevertheless, population growth remained slow. From the beginning, the government refused to allow Protestants to settle there. Further, New France developed under feudal land tenure, in which wealthy lords received large manors, or *seigniories,* along the St. Lawrence River. Ordinary settlers on these manors became tenants rather than independent farmers. Lacking the opportunity to improve their status in the New World, French peasants were reluctant to make the dangerous transatlantic voyage.

The fur trade and small population made French relations with the Native Americans different from those of New Spain and Virginia. The most efficient way to obtain furs was to offer desirable products from Europe, including textiles, guns, and alcohol, not drive trading partners from the land or exploit their labor.

Nevertheless, the French arrival had tragic effects for the Indians of Canada, who succumbed to disease in large numbers. The demand for furs altered cultural attitudes and intensified hostility among nations. In keeping with their religion,

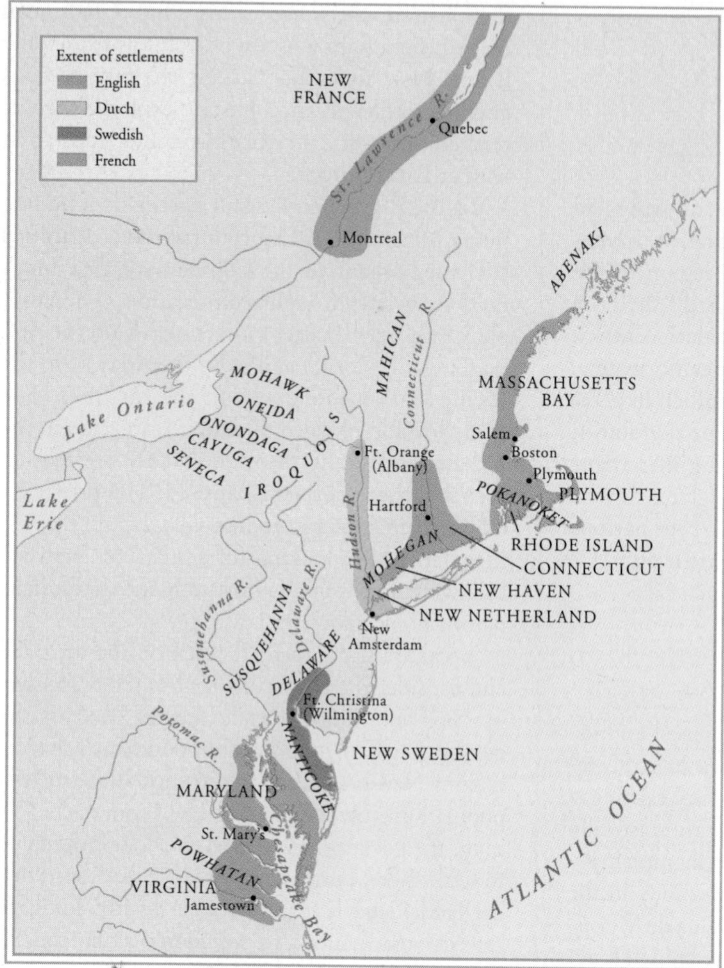

Map 2.1 French, English, Dutch, and Swedish Colonies in Eastern North America, 1650

Indians had taken only what they needed from nature and little more; they generally used entire animals, the meat as well as the skins. With the fur trade, natives killed animals just for their furs and in numbers far greater than before. As a result, the balance of nature that the Native Americans had maintained was broken. They had to reach farther and farther back into the continent as they exterminated the deer, beaver, and other fur-bearing animals.

New Netherland

In the first decade of the seventeenth century, the Dutch, too, challenged the dominance of Spain in the New World. The seven northern United Provinces had declared independence from Spain in 1581 and remained at war until 1609, when they signed a twelve-year truce. With its expiration, the war resumed and continued as part of the Thirty Years' War, which ended in 1648 with the Treaty of Münster, recognizing Dutch independence.

Despite this ongoing struggle, Dutch commerce flourished. Because land was scarce and high priced in the Netherlands, and agriculture insufficient, affluent individuals put their capital into trade. In 1602, merchants formed the United East India Company, which six years later had 160 ships around the globe. In 1609, the company sent out Henry Hudson, an Englishman, to search for the long-sought northwest passage through North America. He sailed up the river that later bore his name, trading for furs with the Native Americans. The pelts brought a good return in Holland, so the company dispatched traders who set up a post near the present site of Albany and explored Long Island Sound and the Connecticut River. In 1621, the Dutch government chartered another group, the West India Company, to establish commerce and colonies in America. Like the East India Company, it received broad powers, including the rights to make war and sign treaties. During the seventeenth century, the Dutch muscled their way to control a large part of international commerce, including the Atlantic slave trade and routes to Asia.

To provide a base for trade in the Hudson River region, in 1624 the Dutch West India Company appointed Cornelius Jacobsen May to found New Netherland; the first colonists were mostly Protestant refugees from the Spanish Netherlands. They established their primary settlement, called New Amsterdam, on Manhattan Island, and maintained trading posts at Fort Orange (near Albany), and on the Delaware and Connecticut rivers. As in Jamestown, the first settlers were employees of the company, which paid for their transportation, tools, livestock, and two years' worth of supplies, assigning them company land on which to plant. The colonists were expected to trade only with the company. The government consisted of appointed company officers headed by a director-general, or governor, with wide powers.

With good soil, the lucrative fur trade, and lumbering, the colony prospered economically, though its population grew slowly. Brewing became the second most important industry. People of many nationalities and religions arrived to take advantage of the Dutch policy of religious freedom. In 1629, the company attempted to spur population growth by offering huge manors, called patroonships, to any member of the company who transported fifty persons to work his land. On the Hudson River, each patroonship extended for miles along one bank or both banks. Similar to New France, the settlers were tenants of the manor. This arrangement attracted few settlers: In fact it discouraged immigration because the manors tied up large tracts that might otherwise go to small farmers.

At first, New Netherland had good relations with the Indians because the colony grew slowly

An early view, with two residents, of New Amsterdam. The Dutch port later became New York City. (Rare Books Division, The New York Public Library. Astor, Lenox and Tilden Foundations)

and depended on the fur trade. In the famous 1626 purchase, Director-general Peter Minuit exchanged goods worth about 60 guilders for Manhattan Island. Upriver, the Dutch bought furs from the Iroquois, the enemies of the Algonquians and Hurons who supplied the French, thus contributing to the devastating warfare among tribes. By the late 1640s, the Iroquois, with help from epidemics, destroyed the Hurons, a nation of about 20,000 people. At the same time, constant warfare and disease seriously debilitated the Iroquois as well.

In the region surrounding New Amsterdam, relations deteriorated between the whites and the Indians after 1638. As with the English, the Dutch and natives had different conceptions of land ownership. Although the Indians understood that they had sold rights to share the land and intended to continue using it themselves, the Dutch believed they had bought exclusive rights. Violence erupted as the settlers' cattle trampled the Indians' corn, and dogs belonging to Native Americans attacked Dutch livestock. Beginning in 1640, the Dutch and Indians of the lower Hudson Valley fought a series of damaging wars that ended only in 1664, when the English took control of New Netherland and made peace with the Native Americans.

New England Before the Pilgrims

Along the coast of New England, relations between the Indians and English were rocky from the start. Before the Pilgrims established Plymouth in 1620, a number of expeditions explored the region, traded, and tried to colonize. In 1602, Bartholomew Gosnold and thirty-two men sailed the *Concord* to Maine and continued south to Martha's Vineyard, where they traded for furs. When they alienated the natives and one of their men was wounded, Gosnold and his crew returned to England. In 1607, the Plymouth group of the Virginia Company sent an expedition to the Kennebec River in Maine, but the colony lasted only one year. The company abandoned efforts to establish a permanent base, instead funding voyages for fish and furs. Like the Dutch and French, the English set up commercial networks with tribes who had contested land and resources before the Europeans arrived, thereby intensifying these rivalries.

Even before the founding of Plymouth, then, the natives of New England had considerable experience with the English. This contact had catastrophic effects on the Indian population. A plague epidemic brought by Europeans swept eastern New England during 1616–1618, killing thousands. Large areas along the coast were depopulated. The Massachusetts natives were initially friendly and interested in trade, but good relations proved elusive. The English shot some Native Americans and set dogs on others. A few they kidnapped, then expected them to serve as diplomats to their people. The English also made trade agreements, then failed to honor them. By the time the Pilgrims arrived in 1620, the surviving Indians along the coast were understandably wary of the newcomers.

RELIGIOUS EXILES FROM ENGLAND

While the colonizers of Virginia, New France, and New Netherland had primarily economic motives, the English founders of Plymouth, Massachusetts Bay, and Maryland sought a place where they could practice their religion free from persecution and at the same time earn a decent living. Seventeenth-century England was rife with religious controversy. The government required attendance at Anglican worship and financial support of ministers. When dissenters refused to obey, holding separate services, they could be imprisoned and fined. Roman Catholics could also be stripped of their property and jailed for life if they refused to take the oath of supremacy to the king, which denied the authority of the pope. The search for freedom of worship became a major impetus for crossing the Atlantic.

English Calvinists

By 1603, when James I took the throne, two strains of English Calvinism, or Puritanism, had developed. One group included the Separatists, or Pilgrims, who founded Plymouth in 1620; the others, known as Puritans, established the Massachusetts Bay colony ten years later. Both groups charged that the Anglican church needed to be "purified" of its rituals, vestments, statues, and bishops. They rejected the church hierarchy, believing each congregation should govern itself. The Separatists started their own congregations, abandoning all hope that the church could be reformed. The Pilgrims' decision to begin a colony in America was the ultimate expression of this separatism. The Puritans, on the other hand, hoped to reform the Church of England from within. Their purpose in founding Massachusetts Bay was to develop a moral government that they hoped the people of England would someday make their own.

The Plymouth Colony

The Pilgrims were a small band who had originated in Scrooby, England, where they established a separate congregation. In 1607, when some were jailed as nonconformists, they decided to leave England for the Netherlands, which offered freedom of worship. The Pilgrims settled in Leyden, but were unhappy there, too. They therefor made an agreement with a group of London merchants who obtained a patent for land from the Virginia Company. In exchange for funding to go to America, the Pilgrims promised to send back fish, furs, and lumber for seven years.

Thirty-five of the Leyden congregation chose to emigrate. Sailing first to England, they joined sixty-seven others, of whom many were not Separatists. In September 1620, the *Mayflower* departed Plymouth, England, crowded with 102 passengers, about twenty crew members, and assorted pigs, chickens, and goats. Headed for Virginia, the ship reached Cape Cod on November 9th. In shallow waters, fearing shipwreck, the exhausted travelers built their colony at Plymouth, even though they were outside the jurisdiction of the Virginia Company. They now lacked a legal basis for governing themselves or for claiming land. The first problem was most urgent because some of the colonists questioned the authority of the Pilgrim leaders. The group avoided a revolt by drafting and signing the "Mayflower Compact," a social compact by which they agreed to form a government and obey its laws. The London merchants eventually solved the second problem by obtaining title to the land.

Plymouth's first years were difficult. Over the first winter the settlers built houses, but one-half of the colonists died of disease and exposure to the cold. In the spring of 1621, they planted corn and other crops.

The natives helped the Plymouth colony, despite earlier problems with Englishmen. In 1614, Squanto and about twenty other Patuxets had been kidnapped by an English sea captain, who intended to sell them as slaves in Spain. Saved from bondage by Spanish priests, Squanto made his way to England, where he learned the language, then to Newfoundland, and finally back to Patuxet in 1619. There he found unburied bodies of many of his people who had perished in an epidemic.

At harvest in 1621, the Indians and colonists celebrated together for three days. Soon after their feast, the ship *Fortune* arrived with thirty-five new settlers, for whom no food was available until the next year's crop. When the colonists filled the *Fortune* with furs and lumber in hopes of starting to repay their debt to the London merchants, the French captured the ship.

By 1623, though, the Plymouth colony was well established and growing. The community solved the problem of food supply by assigning individual plots to families. Still, the hard-working colonists had trouble fulfilling their bargain with the merchants. During a trading voyage, the crew mutinied. On one fishing trip, the ship sank; when it was raised and sent out again, the Spanish captured it. The London merchants gave up and in 1626 agreed to sell the land to the colonists for a large sum, which they paid by 1645, receiving a patent of ownership. Although Plymouth's economic fortunes improved, the colony remained small and self-consciously separate from the larger group of English dissenters who streamed into New England.

The Great Puritan Migration

The Puritan migration to Massachusetts Bay was much larger than that to Plymouth. During 1630, 700 women, men, and children arrived in eleven ships. Though at least 200 died during the first winter, the colony grew quickly. The Massachusetts Bay Company organized the "great migration" of about 12,000 people who came to Massachusetts during the 1630s. From King Charles I, the company obtained a charter specifying its government and the colony's boundaries. When most of the company officials emigrated,

THE MAYFLOWER COMPACT 1620

When the *Mayflower* reached land at Cape Cod (in what is now Massachusetts) and the colonists decided to settle there instead of prolonging their difficult journey, they lacked the legal basis (a charter) to establish a government. Thus, the adult males of the colony signed a mutual agreement for ordering their society, what John Locke called, decades later, a "social compact."

In the name of God Amen. We whose names are underwriten, the loyall subjects of our dread soveraigne Lord King James by the grace of God, of great Britaine, Franc, & Ireland king, defender of the faith, &c.

Haveing undertaken, for the glorie of God, and advancements of the Christian faith and honour of our king & countrie, a voyage to plant the first colonie in the Northerne parts of Virginia, doe by these presents solemnly & mutualy in the presence of God, and one of another, covenant & combine our selves togeather into a civill body politick; for our better ordering, & preservation & furtherance of the ends aforesaid; and by vertue hearof to enacte, constitute, and frame shuch just & equall lawes, ordinances, Acts, constitutions, & offices, from time to time, as shall be thought most meete & convenient for the generall good of the Colonie: unto which we promise all due submission and obedience.

In witnes whereof we have hereunder subscribed our names at Cap-Codd the · 11 · of November, in the year the raigne of our soveraigne Lord King James of England, France, & Ireland the eighteenth and of Scotland the fiftie fourth. An°: Dom. 1620.

John Carver
William Bradford
Edward Winslow
William Brewster
Isaac Allerton
Myles Standish
John Alden
Samuel Fuller
Christopher Martin
William Mullins
William White
Richard Warren
John Howland
Stephen Hopkins
Edward Tilley
John Tilley
Francis Cooke
Thomas Rogers
Thomas Tinker
John Rigdale
Edward Fuller
John Turner
Francis Eaton
James Chilton
John Crakston
John Billington
Moses Fletcher
John Goodman
Degory Priest
Thomas Williams
Gilbert Winslow
Edmund Margeson
Peter Brown
Richard Britterige
George Soule
Richard Clarke
Richard Gardiner
John Allerton
Thomas English
Edward Doty
Edward Leister

taking the charter with them, they greatly enhanced the colony's independence from the Crown and the Anglican church.

Thus the Massachusetts Bay colonists did not answer to London merchants who expected handsome profits. The Puritans themselves financed colonization; they included wealthy investors as well as many middling families who could pay their own way. As a result, the founders devoted much of their energy to creating a model society. In the words of leader John Winthrop, the colony would be "as a Citty upon a Hill, the Eyes of all people are uppon us; soe that if wee shall deale falsely with our god in this worke wee have undertaken and soe cause him to withdrawe this present help from us, wee shall be made a story and a by-word through the world." The Puritans believed that they had a covenant with God that bound them to create a moral community. They held that individuals were saved from eternal damnation by faith, rather than by good works. Men and women could seek to avoid sin throughout their lives, but unless they were among God's chosen, or the "elect," they would go to hell. Under the covenant, the elect were responsible for the behavior of unsaved members of their community. The Puritan leaders were responsible to God. They thought that if they maintained a moral society, the Lord would help it prosper.

In Massachusetts, the Puritans restructured the company government. According to the Massachusetts Bay charter, the company officials included a governor, deputy governor, and executive board of eighteen "assistants," to be elected by "freemen" (stockholders) who would meet in a general assembly, called the General Court. These officers could make laws and regulations, appoint lower officials, grant lands, and punish lawbreakers. The colony's leaders changed the rules to allow all male church members (the male elect), not just stockholders in the company, to become freemen.

With the governor and assistants, the General Court drew up a law code for the colony, which after several revisions was published as the *Laws and Liberties of Massachusetts* (1648). The code protected the liberties of individuals by upholding trial by jury and due process of law, including the rights of the accused to a prompt public trial and to call witnesses. It also prohibited feudal tenure of lands and outlawed slavery, "unlesse it be lawfull captives, taken in just warrs, and such strangers as willingly sell themselves or are solde to us." This provision limited the possibility that whites would be enslaved, but had little effect on black bondage. The *Laws and Liberties* included as capital offenses blasphemy and adultery (in cases where the woman was married), which under the English common law were lesser crimes. Children could be put to death for failing to respect their parents, while fornicators were required to marry and be whipped or fined. Although these terms may seem harsh, the colony did not actually impose the death penalty for blasphemy or abuse of parents by children, and executed only two people for adultery. The magistrates evidently wanted to instill fear in the hearts of potential offenders rather than to exact harsh punishments.

The Puritans attempted to create a theocracy, a government operated according to God's will, as determined by the colony's patriarchs. The Puritan government was composed of members of the elect; ministers advised the magistrates but could not serve officially. The government required all inhabitants to attend Puritan churches. Persons who disagreed with orthodox doctrines could be expelled, whipped, fined, and even executed. The church was the center of each town, with all property owners paying taxes for its support. Though the Puritans had suffered persecution for their beliefs in England, they refused to allow freedom of worship in Massachusetts.

Massachusetts Society

Unlike the Jamestown settlers, a large proportion of Puritan immigrants came in families. Many originated from Norfolk, Suffolk, and Essex (together called East Anglia). East Anglia, located directly across the North Sea from the Netherlands, was the center of both the wool trade and Puritanism. By

1630, its residents had kept contact with European Calvinists for almost a century. Entire congregations, ostensibly part of the Church of England, adopted Puritan ways. For decades they had worshipped freely, protected by the local Puritan gentry. Then during the 1620s and 1630s, the Puritans faced a series of hardships, including a depressed market for woolen cloth, poor harvests, and bubonic plague. Charles I enforced laws against nonconformists, removing Puritan ministers from their pulpits. Many families migrated to Massachusetts, where they could make a new start under a congenial government.

In Massachusetts, the migrants created towns that often resembled the ones they had left. When a group arrived, its leaders petitioned the General Court for a place to settle and permission to establish a church and town government. The town meeting elected a board of selectmen who administered town business. It also divided the town lands. The amount of land a family received depended upon its wealth and social status. Typically, a town followed one of two patterns of land distribution. Emigrants from East Anglia generally chose the *closed field* system, in which families received individual farms, with house lot and land for planting, grazing livestock, and cutting lumber. These settlers also created commercial towns. In contrast, emigrants from Yorkshire, in northern England, chose the *open field* system, designating town lands for different purposes—house lots lined up in compact rows, fields, meadows, and wood lots. In Rowley, Massachusetts, for example, families received strips in the fields, where they grew crops in cooperation with their neighbors. Together they made many decisions, including which fields to plant and which to leave fallow. Families also received "stinting rights," or permission to pasture animals on common lands. The number of cattle and sheep a family could pasture depended upon the size of their lands.

If the model society were to succeed, everyone had to have a place in the family, church, and commonwealth. In the family, the husband was superior to the wife, but together they ruled the children and servants. In the church, the minister and elders dominated the congregation. In the commonwealth, the officials led the people. Ideally, this hierarchy required little coercion, when people saw themselves as part of the community and worked for the common good, or "weal" (hence "commonwealth"), rather than for their own benefit. They understood that all humans were equal spiritually but accepted social inequality as the will of God.

Most Puritan women accepted a subordinate place in their society without complaint. They viewed themselves as part of a community and a family, with duties determined by their sex and age, not as individuals with equal rights. Women raised children; kept the house and garden; preserved fruits and vegetables; made beer, cider, cheese, and butter; tended livestock and poultry; spun and wove cloth; sewed clothing, cared for the sick, and supervised the training of daughters and servants. Men had responsibility for raising grain such as wheat, Indian corn, and rye; cutting firewood; and maintaining the fences, buildings, and fields. In addition to farming, many followed a trade or profession such as fishing, carpentry, shopkeeping, overseas trade, medicine, or the ministry. Only men could vote in church and town meetings, serve as government officials, or become ministers. Only when a man became incapacitated, or was away from home, was his wife expected to take his place at work or to represent the family in legal matters or disputes. She temporarily assumed the role of "deputy husband," then yielded it when he became well or returned.

The role of Puritan women in the church was indicative of their place in society. On the one hand, women were the spiritual equals of men and held responsibility for the religious education of their children. On the other hand, women were expected to keep quiet in the church. They could not preach or vote on church business, though they could exert informal influence on their husbands. The Puritans believed that by nature women were morally and intellectually weak. The pain of childbirth was God's punishment of all women for Eve's seduction of Adam. Although a few rebelled against the injunction to keep quiet, most Puritan women and girls accepted their subordination to men.

In this patriarchal society, children deferred to their fathers, assuming a subservient role until they were able to establish households of their own. Families on average had five children who reached adulthood. They worked for their parents until marriage—longer in the case of sons who inherited the family farm. Living conditions in Massachusetts promoted patriarchy, for life expectancy was long. Persons who survived childhood diseases often lived past age sixty or even seventy. Thus, eldest sons could be middle-aged before their fathers died and willed them control of the family homestead. On the other hand, younger sons who had little hope of receiving the farm often moved away from their parents. Parents usually attempted to give all of their children a start in life, with a farm, apprenticeship, money, or college tuition to sons, and personal property or cash to daughters.

Connecticut and New Haven

An early destination for emigrants looking for good land was Connecticut. The first Puritans went there to trade with Native Americans, but when news of attractive land in the Connecticut Valley arrived in Massachusetts, many settlers decided to move. The Earl of Warwick owned the rights to the land at the mouth of the Connecticut River, which he ceded to a group of Puritan noblemen. To build a trading post and settlement they sent John Winthrop, Jr., who convinced Thomas Hooker, the minister of Newtown, Massachusetts, to lead some of his congregation there. Another group left from Dorchester. They founded Connecticut in 1636. Though they had no charter from the king, the founders agreed upon the *Fundamental Orders of Connecticut,* which created a General Assembly of representatives from each town. In most respects, the Connecticut government resembled that of Massachusetts, with the exception that freemen, or voters, did not have to be church members. The assembly elected a governor, who could serve only one year at a time, and a group of magistrates who functioned as the upper house of the assembly. As in Massachusetts, Puritanism was the only recognized religion.

As white settlement expanded, relations between the Puritans and Native Americans deteriorated. Like other English, the Puritans believed that the Indians worshipped the devil. They considered the Indians "strangers," who could have no role in building the model society. They were dispensable and dangerous, presenting a dual threat because their customs could corrupt the holy commonwealth and they resented their loss of lands.

The 1637 war against the Pequots of eastern Connecticut showed the lengths to which the New England settlers could go. The Pequots, a powerful tribe, attempted to unite New England Indians against the English. In May 1637, troops from Massachusetts and Connecticut, with their Indian allies, the Narragansetts, attacked a Pequot village on the Mystic River before dawn, killing hundreds of sleeping women, children, and old men. The Pequots who escaped this massacre, mostly young men absent from the town, were later executed or enslaved. The Treaty of Hartford (1638) declared their nation dissolved.

Shortly after the Pequot War, in 1638, a group of staunch Puritans established New Haven, on the Long Island Sound west of the Connecticut colony. Persecuted in England, Reverend John Davenport took his flock first to Boston, but decided to move on. They had no charter for New Haven, so the freemen made the Bible their law, eliminating trial by jury, for example, because it had no scriptural basis. Only male church members could vote. The colony grew as the settlers built towns farther west along the sound and on Long Island. Together, the towns agreed upon a government comprised of a governor, magistrates, and a representative assembly.

Exiles to Rhode Island

The founding of Rhode Island resulted from another kind of emigration from Massachusetts, that of persons who refused to subordinate their own beliefs to those of the Puritan magistrates. The first was Roger Williams, a minister who challenged Massachusetts Bay's policy toward the Indians and its theocratic laws. Williams had studied divinity at Cambridge University, where he became a vocal Separatist. He immigrated to Massachusetts Bay in 1631, arousing the colony when he refused the pulpit in a Boston church because its members had not renounced the Church of England.

Williams then accused Massachusetts of holding fraudulent title to its territory because the king had no authority to give away Indian lands. The colony should send the charter back to the king for correction; the settlers should return to England if they could not obtain rights from the true owners of the land. Williams raised a troublesome issue that the Puritan officials refused to recognize, so they ordered him to be still. He would not be quiet, soon broaching the issues of religious freedom and separation of church and state. He attacked the laws requiring church attendance and tax support of Puritan churches. Williams feared that government would pollute the church, not that giving legal preference to one religion was unfair. He opposed laws regulating religion to protect the church from state interference.

The General Court banished Williams from Massachusetts for challenging the government; in 1636 he went to Narragansett Bay. There he purchased land from the Narragansett Indians, establishing Providence Plantation at the Great Salt River. With the sympathizers who joined him, he created a society based on religious toleration, separation of church and state, and participation in government by all male property owners. Williams welcomed people of all religions to Providence Plantation, as long as they accepted the right of others to worship freely. Williams himself became wealthy through trade with the Native Americans and the Dutch. In 1638, he transferred ownership of Providence to a group of thirteen associates, of whom he was one.

Another exile from Massachusetts was Anne Hutchinson, a midwife and nurse, who in 1634 arrived in Boston with her husband, merchant William Hutchinson, and children. As Hutchinson assisted women in childbirth and sickness, she became convinced that Bostonians placed too much emphasis on good works and not enough on faith. She was a follower of one of Boston's ministers, the influential John Cotton, who stressed the importance of the individual's relationship with God over the obligation to obey laws. Hutchinson went further than Cotton, nearly saying that if a person were saved it did not matter how she or he behaved, a belief known as the Antinomian heresy.

To the orthodox Puritan faction led by Governor John Winthrop, Hutchinson was a threat for several reasons. She emphasized individual judgment over the community's. She told the Puritan patriarchs that God spoke to her directly, that she did not need the assistance of magistrates and ministers in interpreting God's will. Further, Hutchinson went outside the accepted role of women by taking a public stand on religion. But most seriously, she became the standard bearer for a group who contested power with the Winthrop faction. In 1637, Winthrop's government put Hutchinson on trial for defaming ministers and exiled her from the colony. With her family and supporters she founded a colony at Portsmouth on Narragansett Bay.

Following the settlement of Williams and Hutchinson on Narragansett Bay, several other dissenters established colonies there. William Coddington, a supporter of Hutchinson, started the town of Newport; and Samuel Gorton founded Warwick. The four leaders had trouble cooperating, but knew they needed a charter from the English government to avoid annexation by Massachusetts. Roger Williams went to England for that purpose. The 1644 Rhode Island charter, which Parliament granted, united the four settlements under one representative assembly, which could pass statutes consistent with the laws of

England. The Rhode Island colonists based their government on Williams's principles of freedom of worship, separation of church and state, and wide participation in government.

The Proprietary Colony of Maryland

In 1632, Charles I granted a charter for Maryland. George Calvert, the first Lord Baltimore, had served in high office until he converted to Catholicism. Forced to resign, but still a royal favorite, Calvert requested a grant in America to build a haven for Catholics. He also expected to support his family by selling the land. He died before obtaining the charter, so his son, Cecilius Calvert, the second Lord Baltimore, became lord proprietor of Maryland. The colony was carved out of the northern part of Virginia. Calvert received ownership of the soil and was sovereign in government, subject only to the king.

Calvert spent £40,000 for two ships, the *Ark* and the *Dove,* with supplies to send the first 150 settlers, who arrived in Maryland in 1634. The proprietor planned a feudal system in which manorial lords held large tracts, which they rented to tenants. For example, a person who transported five laborers at a total cost of £20 received a manor of 2,000 acres.

Though Maryland settlers suffered no "starving time" as in Virginia and had a cash crop in tobacco, the colony grew slowly. Mortality was high and immigration sluggish. By 1642, Calvert had granted rights for only sixteen manors, mostly to wealthy Catholic friends. To improve his income, Calvert distributed farms to more ordinary immigrants, who had to pay annual quitrents.

The extension of land ownership beyond Calvert's circle of loyal supporters created problems for the lord proprietor. Under the charter, he was obligated to call together an assembly of freemen, or landowners, to enact laws. Calvert interpreted this to mean that they should approve legislation he prepared, while the freemen, meeting first in 1635, claimed the right to draft the code of laws. Calvert refused to accept their draft,

Cecilius Calvert, the second Lord Baltimore, with his grandson and an enslaved African. Calvert was proprietor of Maryland until 1675 when he died and the boy's father, Charles, succeeded him. (Courtesy Enoch Pratt Free Library, Baltimore)

so for three years the colony operated without a code. In 1638, they reached a compromise, with the proprietor and assembly each drafting some of the bills.

But the struggle for power between the proprietor and freemen continued. The ordinary planters, who formed the majority of freemen and were mostly Protestant, resented the power of the Catholic elite and had little sympathy for Calvert's vision of a society in which all Christians could worship freely. Religious and political strife became most acute in Maryland during the English Civil War and the Puritan Commonwealth, from 1642 to 1660.

The Impact of the English Civil War

For two decades, the English Civil War altered the political situation in England. The war resulted from a contest for power between Parliament and Charles I. Charles imprisoned opponents without due process, and launched a crusade to force all his subjects, even those in Presbyterian Scotland and Catholic Ireland, to conform to the Anglican church. In 1642, war broke out between the "Cavaliers," or royalists, and the "Roundheads," or parliamentary forces, of whom many were Puritans. Oliver Cromwell led the Roundheads to victory in 1648; the following year they beheaded the king.

The revolutionaries attempted to rule through an elected Parliament, but conflicting factions of Puritans and radical sects undermined their plans. Some radical theorists wanted an entire restructuring of society. They called for extension of the vote to all men and redistribution of land. The gentry and wealthy merchants who had led Parliament to victory considered these ideas anathema. In 1653 they named Cromwell the Lord Protector of the Commonwealth of England, Scotland, and Ireland. Cromwell ruled alone, backed by the army, until his death in 1658. An attempt failed to make his son Richard the successor, and two years later, the monarchy was restored. The accession of Charles II did not mean a complete reversal to the time of his father. The king confirmed Parliament's right to approve taxes and abolished the royal courts that had punished opponents of the Crown. But the Restoration brought the Cavaliers back into power, making the Anglican church the state religion once again.

The struggle for power during the Civil War and its aftermath had repercussions in the colonies. Initially, the rebellion of English Puritans against the king raised hopes among New Englanders that English society would be reformed. Of more practical importance to the colonies was the lack of military protection from England. Plymouth, Massachusetts, Connecticut, and New Haven counted among their enemies the French, Dutch, Native Americans, and Rhode Island. In 1643, they joined together to form the New England Confederation. The confederation agreed to share the cost of war, provide soldiers in proportion to population, and make no treaties without each colony's consent. The New England Confederation was the first league of colonies in English North America. In assuming power to conduct war and make treaties, it went beyond colonial rights. The English government, in the midst of Civil War, was too preoccupied to react.

In the Chesapeake colonies, the Civil War and its aftermath were more disruptive. In 1652, the English Commonwealth removed the royalist Virginia governor, William Berkeley, because he had proclaimed Charles II the king upon his father's execution. In Maryland, the parliamentary revolt weakened the position of Lord Baltimore, whose authority came directly from the king. Protestants, especially Puritans, constituted an antiproprietary force. Ironically, the proprietor had encouraged Puritans to migrate from Virginia, where they had suffered Governor Berkeley's persecution. Calvert had approved the "Act Concerning Religion" (1649), which guaranteed freedom of religion to all Christians. Nevertheless, in 1654, the Maryland Puritans established a commonwealth. Their assembly deposed the proprietor's government, restricted the right of Catholics to worship, and created a Puritan code of behavior. Calvert appealed to Oliver Cromwell, who confirmed his proprietorship, but Lord Baltimore regained control of the colony only in 1657, after a period of local civil war.

ENGLISH COLONIZATION AFTER 1660

The accession of Charles II in 1660 initiated a new phase of colonization, in which the English government paid more attention to its colonies than it had before the Civil War. In 1662, the

Crown granted Connecticut a charter, and the following year confirmed the charter Rhode Island had received from Parliament. To tighten colonial administration, the king and Parliament approved a series of navigation acts that formed the basis of a mercantilist colonial policy.

Navigation Acts

The Navigation Act of 1651 required that goods brought to England or its colonies from Asia, Africa, or America be carried on English ships (including those of its colonies). Goods from European nations had to be transported on either English ships or those of the country of origin. The chief purposes of the act were to encourage growth of England's merchant marine and to challenge Dutch ascendancy on the seas and in colonial ports. The Commonwealth went further in 1652–1654, with the first Anglo-Dutch War, by attacking Dutch vessels in the English Channel and North Sea.

The Navigation Acts of 1660, 1663, and 1673 created a list of "enumerated articles"—major colonial products including tobacco, sugar, indigo, cotton, ginger, and dyewoods—which could be shipped only to England or another English colony. The "articles" first went to England, where they were taxed and reexported by English merchants, who benefited from the business. Conversely, with some exceptions, goods shipped from other nations to the English colonies had to go to England first. The colonists considered these laws detrimental because English middlemen added charges to products going in both directions. The English government created a colonial administration to enforce the acts, but the results were complicated and inefficient. Colonial governors lacked the resources (and in many cases the will) to eliminate smuggling.

Carolina

Charles II was penniless when he ascended the throne and owed substantial debts to his supporters. Expansion of the colonial empire permitted him to repay these creditors and at the same time advance England's commerce and national power. Carolina, named for the king, was the first post-Restoration colony on the North American mainland. In 1663, the area between Virginia and Spanish Florida was unoccupied by Europeans, but Spain had better title to the land than England. With the Treaty of Madrid (1670), the English obtained Spain's concession of lands north of present-day Charleston. The chief promoters of Carolina were Anthony Ashley Cooper, Governor William Berkeley of Virginia, and John Colleton, a West Indies planter. They obtained help from five men who were close to the king; together the eight associates became proprietors of Carolina. They obtained a charter like Maryland's and received wide latitude in matters of religion. They drew up the "Fundamental Constitutions of Carolina," creating a complicated feudal society with nobles and lords, a scheme the ordinary settlers of Carolina refused to accept.

Two colonies developed in Carolina. Small planters from Virginia built the first, which later became North Carolina. As early as 1653, people had settled on the shores of Albemarle Sound, where they raised tobacco, corn, and livestock. In 1664, Berkeley sent William Drummond to organize a council and assembly. The Albemarle settlement remained poor and difficult to govern. In 1691, the Carolina proprietors effectively established North Carolina by appointing a separate governor.

The second Carolina colony was located at Charles Town, in the future South Carolina. After two unsuccessful attempts, Anthony Ashley Cooper in 1670 organized a permanent settlement. Many of its early settlers came from the West Indies island of Barbados, which had run out of vacant land. The Barbadian planters had money to develop plantations in Carolina and owned African slaves to do the work. The proprietors offered generous acreages to household heads for each person brought to the colony. A planter, with his own family and several enslaved blacks, could qualify for hundreds of acres. From the colony's founding, a large proportion of South Carolinians were African slaves. They produced food, livestock, firewood, and barrel staves for Barbados.

New York and New Jersey

To control North America, the English next had to seize New Netherland. With a series of outposts, the Dutch held the region between Connecticut and Maryland. The English justified their attack in 1664 against New Netherland on several grounds, including John Cabot's 1497 voyage to the region and Dutch illegal trade with English colonies. Settlers from New England living under Dutch jurisdiction reported that Dutch military defenses could not withstand attack. James, the duke of York, Lord High Admiral of the Navy, urged his brother, Charles II, to send a fleet. The king granted James a proprietary charter for lands between the Connecticut and Delaware Rivers, as well as Long Island, Nantucket, Martha's Vineyard, and part of present-day Maine. The charter gave the duke wide governmental powers, even dispensing with an assembly. The duke could write his own legal code as long as it conformed to the laws of England.

With charter in hand, James forced out the Dutch. In 1664, his deputy governor, Richard Nicolls, took New Amsterdam without a fight. The second Anglo-Dutch War (1665–1667) in part resulted from this action. Assuming ownership, James called his colony New York, but granted the land between the Delaware and lower Hudson Rivers to John Lord Berkeley and Sir George Carteret, who named the area New Jersey.

Despite his extensive powers, James realized that he had to make New York attractive to inhabitants if his colony was to prosper. He gave residents the choice of keeping their Dutch citizenship or becoming naturalized as English subjects. In 1665, he issued a legal code, called the "Duke's Laws," which guaranteed freedom of religion, recognized preexisting titles to land, and allowed New Englanders living in towns on Long Island to choose selectmen. The New York government consisted of a governor and council appointed by the duke, but no legislature.

When England and the Netherlands continued their rivalry in the third Anglo-Dutch War (1672–1674), the Dutch easily recaptured New York. After sixteen months they returned the colony to England as part of the Treaty of Westminster (1674). Receiving a new charter, James resumed possession of New York and reconfirmed his grants to New Jersey. The territory had by then been divided into two colonies, West New Jersey and East New Jersey. Berkeley had sold West Jersey to a Quaker, Edward Byllinge, who then transferred title to a group of coreligionists, including William Penn. The duke confirmed Carteret's right to East Jersey immediately, but waited until 1680 to approve the Quaker proprietorship of West Jersey.

CONCLUSION

During the first three-quarters of the seventeenth century, the English, French, and Dutch ended Spain's mastery of the New World. By 1675, the English held colonies along the Atlantic coast from New England to the Carolinas. The French controlled Canada and had explored the Great Lakes and the upper Mississippi Valley. The Dutch established, but lost, New Netherland. Spain retained its borderland outposts in New Mexico and Florida. Everywhere the Europeans colonized, the Indians died from epidemic disease. Their relations with the white invaders depended a great deal on the numbers of Europeans who arrived, their attitudes, and goals of settlement.

From the beginning, the English colonies were diverse. The Crown fostered this variety by granting charters to an assortment of companies and individuals, including Puritan and Catholic opponents of the established church. Virginia and Maryland prospered from tobacco, but battled persistent high mortality. Most New Englanders came primarily to start a model society based on their Calvinist beliefs. They enjoyed a healthier climate than the people of the Chesapeake, but inferior soil. They supported themselves modestly by fishing and mixed farming, developing trade with the West Indies to pay for English imports. In New Mexico, Hispanic colonists exploited the Pueblos' labor to support their trade with Mexico, while Catholic missionaries tried to claim the Indians' souls. In all three areas—New England, the Chesapeake, and New Mexico—pressures between Europeans and Native Americans, and within the colonial societies, would soon erupt in war.

RECOMMENDED READINGS

Anderson, Virginia D. *New England's Generation: The Great Migration and the Formation of Society and Culture in the Seventeenth Century* (1991). Compares the motivations and experiences of Puritan settlers with succeeding generations.

Berkin, Carol. *First Generations: Women in Colonial America* (1996). A balanced survey of women of different backgrounds.

Breen, T. H., and Innes, Stephen. *"Myne Owne Ground": Race and Freedom on Virginia's Eastern Shore, 1640–1676* (1980). Focuses on opportunities of free blacks before the onslaught of rigid racial slavery.

Cronon, William. *Changes in the Land: Indians, Colonists, and the Ecology of New England* (1983). Contrasts Native American and settler use of the environment.

Dunn, Richard S. *Sugar and Slaves: The Rise of the Planter Class in the English West Indies, 1624–1713* (1972). An insightful history of the creation of slave regimes in the English Caribbean.

Greene, Jack P. *Pursuits of Happiness: The Social Development of Early Modern British Colonies and the Formation of American Culture* (1988). Provides a useful framework for understanding the various ways in which British settlements evolved.

Gutiérrez, Ramón A. *When Jesus Came, the Corn Mothers Went Away: Marriage, Sexuality, and Power in New Mexico, 1500–1846* (1991). Provocative evaluation of Spanish settlement, focusing particularly on women's status.

Morgan, Edmund S. *American Slavery, American Freedom: The Ordeal of Colonial Virginia* (1975). A detailed, stimulating account of English settlement and the transition to slavery.

Ulrich, Laurel Thatcher. *Good Wives: Image and Reality in the Lives of Women in Northern New England, 1650–1750* (1982). Considers the various roles of colonial women.

Wood, Peter H. *Black Majority: Negroes in Colonial South Carolina from 1670 Through the Stono Rebellion* (1974). Demonstrates the impact of rice culture on blacks in the Lower South.

AMERICAN JOURNEY ONLINE AND INFOTRAC COLLEGE EDITION

Visit the source collections at www.americanjourney.psmedia.com and infotrac.thomsonlearning.com and use the Search function with the following key terms to explore documents, images, audio and video clips, articles, and commentary related to the material in this chapter.

Jamestown
Plymouth colony
Puritans
Massachusetts Bay colony
Spanish missions
Virginia Company
Anne Hutchinson

Chapter 3

CRISIS AND CHANGE, 1675–1720

IN FEBRUARY 1676, Narragansett Indians burned Lancaster, Massachusetts, killing many of the English settlers and taking others prisoner, including Mary White Rowlandson, a minister's wife, and her three children. The Narragansetts had joined the Wampanoags, led by the sachem Metacom, to destroy the European settlements. In the Indians' words, according to Rowlandson, "they would knock all the Rogues in the head, or drive them into the Sea, or make them flie the Country."

Though Rowlandson began her captivity with hatred toward the Indians, she came to respect some as individuals and to appreciate aspects of their culture. She was most impressed, she said, that while the Algonquians had little corn, "I did not see (all the time I was among them) one Man, or Woman, or Child, die with Hunger." They ate "Ground-nuts . . . also Nuts and Acorns, Harty-choaks, Lilly-roots, Groundbeans, and several other weeds and roots that I know not." Desperately hungry, Rowlandson ate unfamiliar foods too, surviving to rejoin her husband in Boston.

Metacom's War was just one of the crises that afflicted colonial America in the years 1675 to 1680. In the Chesapeake, a comparatively minor skirmish between Indians and whites escalated into serious warfare, resulting in Bacon's Rebellion, a civil war among the English settlers of Virginia. In 1680, the Pueblos expelled their Spanish taskmasters from New Mexico for thirteen years. During the 1680s, an unstable English government disrupted politics in the colonies. Charles II died just a few years after granting a charter for Pennsylvania. His brother, James II, a Roman Catholic, succeeded him and attempted to make sweeping changes in both the home and colonial governments. James' efforts met strong resistance: The Glorious Revolution quickly ended his reign. In 1689, settlers in Massachusetts, New York, and Maryland overthrew his provincial governments, declaring allegiance to the new king and queen, William and Mary. In Massachusetts, the impact of years of political uncertainty helped spread witchcraft hysteria from Salem to other towns.

From 1689 to 1713, European wars spilled into North America, fueling conflicts in Florida and Canada among Native Americans, English, French, and Spanish. The French moved south through the Mississippi Valley and founded Louisiana, while the English pushed south into Florida, west across the Appalachian Mountains, and north into Maine. As the English colonies expanded and matured, their economies and labor

CHRONOLOGY

1675 Appointment of English Lords of Trade

1675–1676 Metacom's War

Bacon's Rebellion

1678 Charles II demands renegotiation of Massachusetts charter

1680 Popé's Rebellion

1681 William Penn receives Pennsylvania charter

1682 La Salle claims the Mississippi Valley for France

1683 Iroquois of New York defeat New France

1684 Revocation of Massachusetts charter

1685 James II becomes king of England

Dominion of New England created

1688–1689 Glorious Revolution in England

William and Mary ascend throne

1689 Revolutions in Massachusetts, New York, and Maryland

1689–1697 King William's War

1690 Spanish settlements in Texas

1691 Massachusetts receives its new charter

1691–1692 Salem witchcraft hysteria

1693 Spanish regain control of New Mexico

1696 Board of Trade and Plantations replaces Lords of Trade

1698 Royal African Company loses slave trade monopoly

1699 French establish Louisiana

1701 Iroquois treaty of neutrality

1702–1713 Queen Anne's War

1704 South Carolina defeats Spanish Florida

1712 Slave revolt in New York City

1715 Calverts regain Maryland government

Yamassee War in South Carolina

systems diverged, particularly with the entrenchment of slavery in the south. Even with so much conflict during the late seventeenth century, planters built successful staple crop economies in the southern colonies, while northerners profited from networks of trade with England, Europe, and the slave regimes of the Caribbean, Carolina, and the Chesapeake.

REBELLIONS AND WAR

The wars of 1675 to 1680 in New England, Virginia, and New Mexico resulted from pressures that had been building for decades. In Massachusetts, the spread of settlement forced Native Americans to defend their homes. In Virginia, demands of ex-servants for good land precipitated a civil war, while in New Mexico, severe droughts deepened opposition to forced labor, impelling the Pueblos to rid themselves of Spanish overlords. After the upheavals, elites in each settlement made changes that avoided further serious revolt.

The Decline of New England Orthodoxy

In 1675, Massachusetts seemed to have lost sight of the goals of its first settlers. When the Indians attacked, Puritan ministers warned the sons and daughters of the founding generation that God was punishing them for their faithlessness and sin.

In fact, Puritan church membership had declined since 1650, especially among men. The ministers believed that men were becoming more worldly, thus undermining the church's social and political authority. A related problem was that the children of nonchurch members could not be baptized. In 1662, the clergy devised an alternative to full church membership, the Half-Way Covenant. The covenant permitted adults who had been baptized but who were not yet saved to be "half-way" members. In congregations that accepted this innovation, people could assume partial status by showing that they understood Christian principles and would strive to obey God. As unconverted members, they were not entitled to take communion, but could have their children baptized.

The growth of competing religions in New England also proved to Puritan ministers that the model society had failed. Believing theirs to be the only true religion, Puritans rooted out dissent. After 1650, though, the Quakers and Baptists threatened religious unity. The Society of Friends, or Quakers, was a radical Protestant sect. Like the Puritans, they were reformers who believed that the Church of England was corrupt and should be purified of its rituals, decorations, and hierarchy. But the Quakers went even further. They claimed that the Puritans also practiced false doctrine by paying ministers to preach, relying too much on the Bible as the word of God, and retaining the sacraments of baptism and communion. The Friends believed that God communicated directly with individuals through the "Spirit" or "Light." They worshipped by gathering in plain meetinghouses to "wait upon the Lord." In worship services, they had no Bible reading, prepared sermon, music, or ritual. Rather, they waited in silence for the Spirit to inspire one or several of the congregation to communicate God's message. Those to whom the Spirit manifested itself regularly were ministers, including women as well as men.

Appalled by these Quaker teachings, Puritan leaders tried to prevent their spread by deporting the traveling English missionaries who arrived on their shores. The ministers were stubborn, however, repeatedly returning to Massachusetts. They interrupted Puritan church services, preached in the streets, and made some converts among the people. The Puritan magistrates arrested and whipped them, even cropping their ears. In 1658, the General Court prescribed the death penalty for Quakers who returned after banishment.

The hangings of several Quaker missionaries caused consternation on both sides of the Atlantic. When Charles II demanded an explanation, the Puritans ended the executions. The magistrates continued to persecute nonconformers, but over the decades following 1660 realized that their policy of intolerance had failed. Rhode Island served as a base for Quaker missionaries to evangelize in the Puritan colonies. The Baptists also increased in numbers after approval of the Half-Way Covenant, which they vehemently opposed. They believed that a church should include only the saved. Despite persecution, dissenters successfully formed congregations throughout New England.

Metacom's War

The unceasing expansion of white settlers into the frontier destroyed the relative peace between the Algonquians and the settlers of New England. By 1675, more than 50,000 whites inhabited the region. The colonists had large families of sons and daughters who desired farms of their own. These settlers occupied more and more of the hunting, fishing, and agricultural lands of the Indians.

Since the massacre of the Pequots in 1637, the Puritans and Native Americans of New England had managed an uneasy peace. The colonists traded for furs with local nations and with the Mohawks, the closest nation of Iroquois in New York. Some Puritan ministers, of whom John Eliot is best known, convinced several local tribes who were greatly diminished by disease and loss of lands to dwell in "praying towns." In these villages, the Indians were supposed to adopt English customs and learn the fundamentals of Puritan religion. By 1674, Eliot had organized fourteen praying towns of Native Americans who took the first steps toward giving up their traditional ways.

Metacom, the Wampanoag leader, who in 1676 tried to drive the New England settlers back "into the Sea."
(Courtesy, American Antiquarian Society)

Many New England Indians kept their autonomy, although they remained allies of the Puritan governments for many years. Trouble began in 1671, when the Plymouth government attempted to force the Wampanoags to surrender their firearms and obtain permission to sell land. Metacom built a league with neighboring tribes. When John Sassamon, an Indian educated at Harvard College, informed the Plymouth government of impending attack and was murdered, the white authorities hanged three Wampanoags for the deed.

Metacom mobilized Algonquians throughout New England, attacking fifty-two English towns. White refugees fled to Boston. But by the end of summer 1676, with the help of the Mohawks, the colonial governments turned back the attack, as disease, hunger, and a weapons shortage weakened Metacom's troops. The war took a heavy toll on both sides, for the Algonquians destroyed twelve towns and killed many colonists.

For the Indians of southern New England, the war was calamitous. Even bands who supported the English lost autonomy. At the outbreak of war, the colonists had forced residents of the praying towns to live on desolate Deer Island in Boston Harbor, where they suffered from lack of food and shelter. Some of the Indian men later fought in the colonial militia against Metacom, but when the war was over, all Native Americans in southern New England had to live in praying towns, where they worked as servants or tenant farmers for neighboring whites. Metacom was killed; his wife and son were sold as slaves.

War in the Chesapeake

Just as New England struggled over land in Metacom's War, Virginia faced a similar crisis in Bacon's Rebellion. The Chesapeake uprising involved civil war among the English as well as Indian-white conflict. But at its root, the chief issue was land. Since the 1640s, the white population of Virginia and Maryland had grown quickly with the arrival of immigrants. By 1670, approximately 40,000 colonists lived in the Chesapeake, including native-born sons and daughters of early settlers as well as the more recent arrivals. In the 1670s, however, many Virginians discovered that the combination of low tobacco prices and high land prices blocked their dream of obtaining plantations. They received headrights, but could find no good vacant tobacco land to claim.

Part of the problem, these landless freemen believed, was that the Indians held too much territory. Specifically, the 1646 treaty between the Virginia government and the Powhatans designated the area north of the York River for Native Americans. This agreement had been acceptable to whites in the 1640s when space south of the York seemed ample, but was unsatisfactory thirty years later, when white settlement was pushing north.

A reconstruction of a typical Chesapeake colonist's house at the Godiah Spray tobacco plantation at Historic St. Mary's City, Maryland. (Courtesy of Historic St. Mary's City)

The first flames of war occurred in July 1675, when some Doeg Indians attempted to take hogs as payment for a settler's unpaid debt. After people on both sides were killed, the Susquehannocks got involved. When the Susquehannocks attacked frontier settlements, a thousand-man army of Virginia and Maryland colonists marched against their village on the Potomac River. Vastly outnumbered, several sachems agreed to negotiate, but when they left their stockade, the colonists murdered them. During the winter of 1675–1676, the Susquehannocks retaliated. Discontented and vengeful colonists responded indiscriminately, killing friendly neighboring Indians rather than those who were actually attacking the frontier.

The landless freemen found a leader in Nathaniel Bacon. Only twenty-nine years old, Bacon had come to Virginia with enough money to purchase a large plantation. Governor Berkeley nominated him to the Virginia council, despite his youth. Nevertheless, Bacon evidently saw his opportunity to challenge Berkeley for leadership of the colony by mobilizing freemen and small planters against the Indians. Although Berkeley wanted peace with the Susquehannocks, Bacon's forces intended to annihilate all of the natives. The settlers knew that the natives were weak, with just a fraction of their pre-1607 population. Bacon's supporters also demanded a greater voice in the Virginia government.

Governor Berkeley declared Bacon a traitor and sent troops to end his forays against the Indians. He also called new elections that brought many Bacon supporters into the House of Burgesses. The delegates passed measures that extended suffrage to landless freemen, taxed provincial councilors, required the election of local representatives for assessing taxes, and placed limits on the terms and fees of local officials. These efforts failed to end the rebellion. For months, Virginians plundered the plantations of neighbors who took the other side. Few white fatalities resulted from this depredation, however. The rebellion finally ceased with Bacon's death, probably of dysentery, in October 1676. The war marked a serious defeat for the Indians of the Chesapeake, who lost the protection of the 1646 treaty.

Bacon's Rebellion awakened the Virginia elites to the dangers of a large class of landless freemen, but resulted in no substantive political change. A new assembly in 1677 reversed the reform acts of the 1676 House of Burgesses. A commission appointed by the Crown to end the rebellion also opposed expanding popular power. The commission did call for taxing "the greate Ingrossers of Lands," but nothing was done. Rather than create a society in which power and wealth were distributed more evenly, the planter elite began importing more enslaved Africans. Bound for life and restricted by laws, black slaves could not demand farms or a voice in government. With settlement in New Jersey, Carolina, and Pennsylvania during the 1670s and 1680s, immigrants had better options than Virginia.

Popé's Rebellion

Four years after Bacon's Rebellion, across the continent in New Mexico, the Pueblos drove out the Spanish—and kept them out for thirteen years. The Pueblos had the advantage of a much smaller white population in New Mexico—2,800—than in New England or the Chesapeake. The Spanish hold over the missions was tenuous. Nevertheless, the Hispanic settlers and priests demanded forced labor and strict adherence to Christianity. A number of Indian towns had rebelled during the previous half century, but most failed to win autonomy.

The Pueblos became more desperate during the 1670s, when New Mexico endured severe drought. As famine persisted, Apaches and Navajos attacked the Pueblos. The Pueblos became convinced that the root of their troubles lay in their rejection of ancient gods, the *katsina.* To bring rain and renewed prosperity, some presented gifts to the katsina and performed dances that the Spanish had outlawed. When punished for abandoning Catholicism, the Indians felt even greater resentment, leading to revolt.

The leader of the 1680 rebellion was Popé, a medicine man of the village of San Juan, north of Santa Fe. When the katsina told him that the Spanish must be driven from the land, he organized a general insurrection. On August 10, 1680, the Pueblos launched a full-scale attack, killing 400 colonists and twenty-one priests. When Santa Fe fell to the rebels on September 21, the whites escaped south, settling in the area of present-day Ciudad Juárez, Mexico. Some Spaniards explained the revolt as God's punishment for their sins, whereas others blamed the harsh labor and efforts to repress native religions. As Popé supervised, the Pueblos destroyed churches, broke up church bells, and burned images of Christ and the saints.

Several times during the next few years, the Spanish attempted without success to retake New Mexico. The rebellion spread south into northern Mexico, where Native Americans demolished settlements and missions. But by 1692, as famine continued, the Pueblo alliance fell into disarray. The new Spanish governor of New Mexico, Don Diego de Vargas, marched north to Santa Fe with 160 troops. Though many Indians resisted, the Spanish reestablished control over the province. In December 1693, after a three-day siege, Vargas troops took Santa Fe, killing all of the Indian men and making slaves of the women and children. The Spanish subsequently retained a foothold in New Mexico, but not without further struggle. The Pueblos rejected the Franciscan missionaries, revolting once again in 1696. Some Pueblos fled from New Mexico while others submitted as Vargas systematically conquered the Indian towns once again. After 1696, the Spanish and Pueblos lived together in relative peace, but only because the Hispanics eased requirements for tribute, forced labor, and adherence to Christianity.

William Penn's "Holy Experiment"

In England, the Quaker leader William Penn approached Charles II with a petition to establish a new colony in America, one that would avoid bloodshed by dealing justly with the Indians. While the Pueblos had not yet driven out the Spanish, Penn knew of Metacom's War and Bacon's Rebellion. He was determined to do things differently in Pennsylvania.

Plans for Pennsylvania

William Penn had inherited a £16,000 debt owed to his father by the king, but had little hope for repayment in cash, so he requested a colony on the west bank of the Delaware River. The king approved Penn's request in 1681, granting him a charter for Pennsylvania that was more restrictive than Lord Baltimore's, in part because the English government was attempting to assert greater control over its colonies, in part because Penn was a Quaker. The new proprietor received the right to enact laws and impose taxes with the consent of the freemen, but was required to submit all laws for approval to the home government within five years of passage. And to protect the status of the Church of England, the charter stipulated that twenty Anglican inhabitants could request a minister from the bishop of London.

In establishing Pennsylvania, Penn hoped to provide a haven for Quakers. Like New England Quakers, those in England confronted persecution as an outlaw sect. English Friends refused to pay tithes for church support or attend Anglican services. Even more, Quakers refused to give oaths, so they could not legally pledge allegiance to the king. Friends also professed to live according to the doctrine that all were equal in the eyes of God; they refused to follow certain customs, such as removing one's hat in the presence of superiors. For practicing their faith, they were jailed and fined, and when they refused to pay, local English officials took their property.

William Penn conceived of his colony as a "holy experiment," a place where Quakers could exercise their beliefs without interference and the government would operate like a Quaker meeting, acting in unison as it followed God's will. Penn also intended to pay the Delaware Indians for tracts of land and set up arbitration panels of Native Americans and colonists to resolve conflicts peacefully. He paid the Delawares a much lower price than he in turn charged the settlers, however, and assumed the Indians would leave after they sold their land.

Like Lord Baltimore, Penn intended to make a fortune from Pennsylvania. Despite his strong Quaker convictions, which for some suggested a simple life, he appreciated fine food, drink, and accommodations. He possessed large landholdings in southern England and Ireland, retained many servants, and enjoyed such delicacies as salmon, partridges, saffron, and chocolate. Urgently needing money, he thought the sale of millions of acres in America would solve his financial problems.

Penn spent a great deal of time planning the colony. His scheme of government established an assembly with two houses, both elected by the

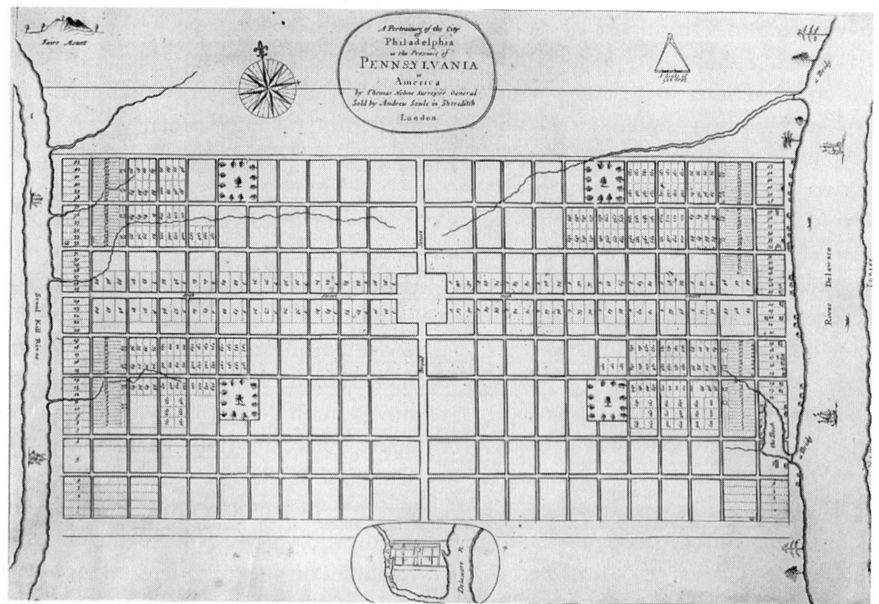

William Penn's plan of Philadelphia, which his surveyor-general Thomas Holme rendered in 1683 as A Portraiture of the City of Philadelphia. *During the colonial period, the city developed along the Delaware River (to the right), not on the Schuylkill River (to the left).* (The Library Company of Philadelphia)

freemen. Freemen included adult males who owned at least fifty acres of land or paid taxes on other property. During the early decades, when servants received fifty acres at the end of their terms, nearly every man in Pennsylvania could vote. Penn did not extend that right to women. Though women Friends took an active role in their meetings, their legal status in the Quaker commonwealth was similar to that in other colonies. Penn's laws stood out in another respect, however, requiring capital punishment for just two offenses, treason and murder.

The proprietor's planning went beyond politics, for he also drew up specifications for his capital city. In designing Philadelphia, Penn conceived the city as a large "green country town," with wide streets in a grid pattern, public parks, ample lots, and brick houses. He failed to fulfill his plan completely because he could not obtain enough acreage to build Philadelphia as he wanted. Dutch and Swedish residents already owned the land along the Delaware River, so Penn decided to buy a site of just 1,200 acres between the Delaware and Schuylkill Rivers. His plan remained orderly, with the grid design and parks, but with lots of one-half to one acre instead of one hundred acres for those who purchased "proprietary shares" of 5,000 acres. To maintain a constant income from the colony, landowners would pay annual quitrents.

A Diverse Society

Penn sold land briskly, as 600 people bought 700,000 acres within four years. Most of the buyers were Quaker farmers, merchants, artisans, and shopkeepers from England, though many also originated from Scotland, Ireland, Wales, Europe, the West Indies, Maryland, and New York.

Penn's settlers moved into an area inhabited by the Delaware, or Lenape, Indians, who were peaceful, sedentary Algonquians, and by Swedes, Finns, and Dutch, who served as intermediaries with the Indians. The Delawares, who farmed, hunted, and fished, had welcomed trade with the Dutch as early as 1610 and yielded land to the whites. Because Dutch and Swedish settlements remained small, relatively few violent incidents occurred. By the time Penn arrived with thousands of colonists, the Lenape had declined significantly from disease, so they had little choice but to sell their lands and move away if they wanted to remain autonomous. In deeds negotiated between 1682 and 1684, the Delaware sachems sold tracts along the Delaware River from Christiana Creek in northern Delaware to the falls of the river in Bucks County, Pennsylvania.

The European "old residents" integrated with the new arrivals, though not without friction. Some earned money by selling land and provisions, or serving as guides and interpreters. One local Swede, Captain Lasse Cock, in 1682 translated for the Indians and English and traveled to the Susquehanna and Lehigh Rivers as Penn's emissary. The Swedish, Dutch, and Finns continued to worship in their own congregations, but became naturalized as English subjects. The old residents made up a large part of the population in the Lower Counties (later Delaware), leading to conflict as the different interests of the Lower Counties and Pennsylvania became clear. In 1704, after two decades of wrangling, the three southern counties obtained their own separate Delaware assembly.

Pennsylvania got a boost from its late arrival on the colonial scene because its merchants could tap existing networks in the Atlantic economy. Substantial traders came from New York, the Chesapeake, and the West Indies, bringing their connections and capital to build breweries, tanneries, warehouses, wharves, and ships. Farmers found a market for wheat, livestock, and lumber in the West Indies trade. By 1700, Philadelphia became a thriving port town, with 700 houses and more than 3,000 people.

But for William Penn, his colony was deeply disappointing, as land sales reaped smaller profits than he had hoped and the costs of administering the colony soared. When purchasers refused to send him quitrents, he went more seriously into debt. Penn traveled to his colony twice, but stayed a total of only four years. Although the province became prosperous and quite successful as a tolerant, diverse society, he reckoned it a failure.

THE GLORIOUS REVOLUTION AND ITS AFTERMATH

The founding of Pennsylvania coincided with the English government's effort to tighten colonial administration. Compared to the Spanish empire, English administration was a hodgepodge. The Privy Council at first appointed temporary committees to address colonial concerns, then in 1675 formed a permanent committee, the Lords of Trade, which met sporadically. Even after 1696, when the more formalized Board of Trade and Plantations was established, this body could gather information and give advice, but lacked authority to appoint colonial officials or enforce laws. These powers belonged to a host of governmental offices, including the secretary of state, the Treasury, and the War Office.

Dominion of New England

While experimenting with these committees, the Crown made other efforts to rein in the colonies. Most vulnerable was the Massachusetts Bay colony. In 1678, Charles II required Massachusetts to send agents empowered to renegotiate the charter. He specifically wanted the New Englanders to comply with the Navigation Acts and apologize for having coined their own money. The colonists delayed action, though they sent regrets for having passed laws contrary to the laws of England. They offered to renounce any "except such as the repealling whereof will make us to renounce the professed cause of our first coming hither."

Impressed by neither the Puritans' arguments nor the speed of their response, the English government brought legal proceedings against the Massachusetts Bay Company for "usurping to be a body Politick," and revoked the charter in 1684. The colony's assembly, the General Court, was prohibited from meeting. In February 1685, before a royal governor could be appointed, Charles died and his brother James became king. James II quickly took advantage of events to move toward centralizing the colonies. With the Privy Council's consent, in 1685, he combined Massachusetts, New Hampshire, and Maine under the Dominion of New England, added Plymouth, Rhode Island, and Connecticut in 1686, and New York and New Jersey in 1688. Apparently, James' plan for the colonies was to create two large dominions, one north of the fortieth degree of latitude (the approximate location of Philadelphia) and one to the south. These dominions would supersede colonial charters, eliminating the confusing diversity of laws and political structures. Representative government would end.

For Massachusetts Puritans, the Dominion of New England was a disaster. James' governor-general, Sir Edmund Andros, made sweeping changes that undercut the Puritan notion of a covenanted community. He levied taxes without the approval of a representative assembly, restricted the power of town meetings, mandated religious toleration, and confiscated a Boston church for use by Anglicans. Andros enforced the Navigation Acts, required landowners to obtain new land titles from the Crown, demanded payment of quitrents, and took control of common lands. A number of colonists rebelled, refusing to pay taxes without a voice in their passage, but were jailed and fined.

Revolutions of 1689

Governor Andros managed to avoid serious revolt until the spring of 1689, when news of James' removal from the throne reached Massachusetts. A Roman Catholic, James had installed his friends in office and defied Parliament. Protestants feared he would make England a Catholic nation under authoritarian rule. Thus, parliamentary leaders forced him into exile in France, inviting his Protestant daughter Mary and her husband William of Orange, the leader of the Dutch, to take the throne. The Glorious Revolution, though bloodless, had long-lasting results in England: it permanently limited the king's power by establishing parliamentary control of taxation, supremacy of law, and autonomy of the courts.

In the morning of April 18, 1689, many of Boston's populace formed companies with the militia. The rebels arrested Andros and his supporters and deposed the dominion government. They interpreted the revocation of the charter and James' illegal taxation and expropriation of lands as part of a "popish plot" that Protestant New England must help destroy.

With the dominion gone, Plymouth, Rhode Island, and Connecticut reactivated their charters, but Massachusetts, which had lost its charter under Charles II, had to negotiate a new one. The resulting 1691 Massachusetts charter, which annexed Plymouth to the Bay colony, established a royal province with an elected assembly and a governor appointed by the king. The charter required freedom of worship and forbade religious restrictions on voting.

Revolutions also took place in New York and Maryland in the wake of James II's fall. New York fell into turmoil with news of William and Mary's ascent to the throne in England and Andros' arrest in Boston. The reports unleashed opposition to Lieutenant Governor Francis Nicholson, who headed the dominion's government in New York. Again, the struggle was defined in religious terms, as a crusade to destroy the "papist" threat.

In the city of New York, insurgents included merchants and artisans who had been denied economic privileges to trade and mill flour under James' government. In 1689, with Jacob Leisler, a German-born merchant and militia captain, in the lead, they forced Nicholson back to England and elected a Committee of Safety to replace James' council. When Henry Sloughter, the new governor appointed by William and Mary, arrived in 1691, however, he reinstalled James' councilors, executing Leisler for treason.

In Maryland, simmering resentment of Protestants against the Roman Catholic proprietor erupted in the summer of 1689. Charles, Lord Baltimore, had departed the province in 1684 to defend at Court his northern boundary against William Penn. Baltimore's troubles intensified when his nephew, George Talbot, president of the provincial council, murdered the king's customs collector. This event rocked the colony, so Baltimore sent a man he thought would provide strong leadership as governor, William Joseph, a Roman Catholic and adherent of James II. Upon arriving in 1688, Joseph proceeded to alienate Maryland's assemblymen, calling them adulterers and drunks. When he required them to renew their oaths of fidelity to the proprietor, they refused.

In July 1689, a handful of Maryland leaders formed the Protestant Association. Aroused by rumors that Catholics were plotting with the Indians to destroy the Protestants, the Association raised troops, defeating the proprietary government without a shot. The rebels obtained articles of surrender that banned Catholics from provincial offices; sent a message to William and Mary informing them of the takeover and requesting a Protestant government; and elected an assembly—the "Associators' Convention"—which ruled Maryland for the next two and one-half years.

The three provincial revolutions of 1689, in Massachusetts, New York, and Maryland, failed to bring about permanent change in the constitutional relationship between England and its colonies. The provincials, lacking delegates in Parliament, continued to endure taxation and mercantilist regulation without their assent. The colonial revolts of 1689 resembled Bacon's Rebellion of 1676, as they mobilized out-of-power elites against those who controlled the colonial governments. In 1676, in Virginia, the insurgents had manipulated landless discontents by appealing to hatred against Native Americans as well as grievances against Berkeley's government. In 1689, the leading rebels employed the twin specters of authoritarianism and Catholicism, with rumors of impending French and Indian attack, to gain support from the populace.

Witchcraft in New England

In May 1692, Governor William Phips arrived in Boston harbor with the new Massachusetts charter in hand. He found the colony in disarray. Symptomatic of the state of affairs was the witchcraft hysteria that had erupted months earlier in Salem Village, a farming community north of

THE TRIAL OF BRIDGET BISHOP, AN ACCUSED WITCH, SALEM 1692

This report of Bridget Bishop's trial, published by Cotton Mather in *Wonders of the Invisible World*, shows the grounds on which Massachusetts courts convicted women and men of practicing witchcraft, including spectral evidence. In Goody Bishop's case, her accusers said her "shape" had attacked them. They also testified that Bishop's specter had tried to compel them to sign the devil's "book."

I. She was indicted for bewitching of several persons in the neighborhood, the indictment being drawn up, according to the form in such cases usual. And pleading, not guilty, there were brought in several persons, who had long undergone many kinds of miseries, which were preternaturally inflicted, and generally ascribed unto a horrible witchcraft. There was little occasion to prove the witchcraft; it being evident and notorious to all beholders. Now to fix the witchcraft on the prisoner at the bar, the first thing used was, the testimony of the bewitched; whereof, several testified, that the shape of the prisoner did oftentimes very grievously pinch them, choke them, bite them, and afflict them; urging them to write their names in a book, which the said specter called, ours. One of them did further testify, that it was the shape of this prisoner, with another, which one day took her from her wheel, and carrying her to the riverside, threatened there to drown her, if she did not sign to the book mentioned; which yet she refused. Others of them did also testify, that the said shape, did in her threats, brag to them, that she had been the death of sundry persons, then by her named; that she had ridden a man, then likewise named. . . .

II. It was testified, that at the examination of the prisoner, before the magistrates, the bewitched were extremely tortured. If she did but cast her eyes on them, they were presently struck down; and this in such a manner as there could be no collusion in the business. But upon the touch of her hand upon them, when they lay in their swoons, they would immediately revive; and not upon the touch of anyone's else. Moreover, upon some special actions of her body, as the shaking of her head, or the turning of her eyes, they presently and painfully fell into the like postures. . . .

III. There was testimony likewise brought in, that a man striking once at the place, where a bewitched person said, the shape of this Bishop stood, the bewitched cried out, that he had tore her coat, in the place then particularly specified; and the woman's coat, was found to be torn in that very place.

IV. One Deliverance Hobbs, who had confessed her being a witch, was now tormented by the specters, for her confession. And she now testified, that this Bishop, tempted her to sign the book again, and to deny what she had confessed. She affirmed, that it was the shape of this prisoner, which whipped her with iron rods, to compel her thereunto. And she affirmed, that this Bishop was at a general meeting of the witches, in a field at Salem Village and there partook of a diabolical sacrament, in bread and wine then administered!

Boston. Since 1675, the Bay colony had one crisis after another—Metacom's War, loss of the charter, Andros' dominion, the Revolution of 1689. Accompanying this turmoil were structural changes in the society, as traditional religious authority yielded to elites whose power rested on mercantile wealth. The Salem witch mania was a tragic holdover from a passing culture. Its fury was aggravated by the psychological reaction of traditionally minded folk to the new, more commercial, secular society of turn-of-century New England.

Belief in witchcraft was embedded in European and Anglo-American culture. The colonists believed that both God and Satan influenced everyday events. When something bad happened that they could not explain, people turned to supernatural explanations, including the possibility that an individual had compacted with the devil to do evil deeds. In England, witchcraft had been a capital offense since the time of Henry VIII in the early sixteenth century; colonial governments followed suit. Over the seventeenth century, the Puritan governments charged many more men and women with witchcraft than did other English colonies: 350 New Englanders were accused during the years 1620 to 1725. Of this number, the Salem episode accounted for almost 200.

The witchcraft cases of Salem in 1691–1692 at first resembled those in other places and times. Several girls experimented with magic, aided by a slave woman Tituba and her husband John. The girls, who included nine-year-old Betty Parris, the daughter of Salem Village's minister, started having fits, presumably caused by witches. According to one report, the girls began "getting into holes, and creeping under chairs and stools, and to use sundry odd postures and antic gestures, uttering foolish, ridiculous speeches." Possession spread to other village girls, leading to the arrest of three women as witches—Tituba; a poor beggar, Sarah Good; and an ailing elderly woman, Sarah Osborne.

These three alleged witches were the sort of people traditionally prosecuted for the crime. Generally, in witchcraft cases, the accused were women past menopause, who in various ways deviated from expected roles. Lacking sons, a significant number were heirs or potential heirs of estates, with greater

Hanging of witches in England c. 1650. No similar image exists of the Salem hangings. (Courtesy, Peabody Museum, Salem, Mass.)

economic autonomy than most New England women. Some accused witches claimed the power of a "cunning woman" to heal and foretell the future; and they often were involved in conflict within their families and neighborhoods. Revealingly, men of the same age group and troublesome character were much less likely to be identified as witches. These assertive old women went beyond the accepted bounds of female behavior.

The Salem craze commenced in the timeworn pattern, soon engulfing people of all social levels. Accusations descended upon prosperous church members, a minister, a wealthy shipowner, and several town officials. Over three-quarters of the alleged witches were women; half of the accused men were their relations. Of those executed, fourteen women and five men were hanged on "Witches Hill" and another man was crushed to death with stones. Only one of the dead was of high status—the Puritan minister George Burroughs. Governor Phips, supported by influential clergymen, had allowed the prosecutions to proceed after his arrival, but put a stop to them when the accusers pointed to people at the highest levels of society, most significantly to his own wife, Mary Phips. It had become clear, to many besides the governor, that the situation was out of control, that the evidence presented by the possessed was unreliable and quite likely the work of the devil.

WARS AND RIVALRY FOR NORTH AMERICA

From 1680 to 1713, the Spanish, English, French, and many Indian nations battled for control of territory in North America. Despite the political and social turmoil of the 1680s and early 1690s, the English settlements were the largest and most dynamic European colonies on the continent. By the mid-1680s, New France had approximately 10,000 settlers, compared with more than 70,000 in New England alone. Spanish Florida was comprised chiefly of missions, run by forty Franciscan priests, and the fortified town of St. Augustine, which held about 1,400 Hispanic, African, and Indian residents. Despite declining populations, many Native American peoples remained powerful in eastern North America.

In the late seventeenth century, the three primary areas of dispute on the continent were Florida and Guale (later Georgia), Louisiana and Texas, and Canada. Conflict occurred against the backdrop of two long European wars, the War of the League of Augsburg, 1689–1697, and the War of the Spanish Succession, 1702–1713 (respectively known as King William's War and Queen Anne's War to the English colonists).

Florida and Guale

Beginning in 1680, the English colonists of South Carolina decided to take advantage of smoldering unrest among the mission Indians of Guale and Florida to attack the Spanish colony. The Native Americans had rebelled against forced labor and efforts to stamp out their traditional religions. The Carolinians raided Guale and Florida from no humanitarian motives to assist the Indians. In

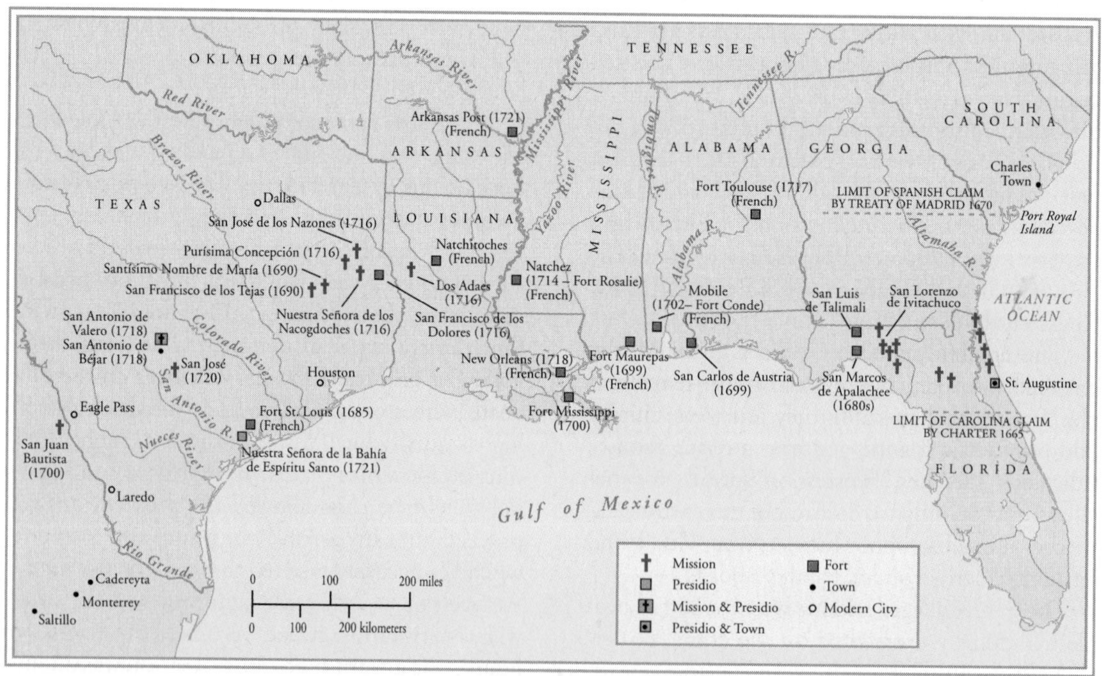

MAP 3.1 | SOUTHEASTERN NORTH AMERICA IN THE EARLY 18TH CENTURY

fact, a chief reason for attacking the Spanish missions was to capture Native Americans to sell as slaves in the West Indies.

By 1686, the Carolinians thrust the missionaries out of Guale. Then in 1704, during Queen Anne's War, an army under former Carolina governor James Moore crushed the missions in Apalachee. The Carolinians obtained help from their trading partners, the Yamassees, and from many of the mission Indians, who resented Spanish oppression. Moore's troops inflicted brutal torture, burning people alive. The surviving Apalachees dispersed, losing their identity as a nation. The Spanish retained St. Augustine and a fort they built at Pensacola in 1698, but lost control of Guale and most of Florida.

Louisiana and Texas

The Spanish erected their fort at Pensacola Bay in response to French efforts to establish a colony in Louisiana. In 1682, René Robert Cavelier, Sieur de La Salle, had explored the Mississippi River from New France to the gulf, naming the territory Louisiana in honor of King Louis XIV. La Salle sailed to France, then returned to set up a colony. However, he miscalculated the location of the Mississippi, instead building Fort St. Louis in Texas, near Matagorda Bay. The colony quickly dissolved from disease, loss of ships, and attacks by Karankawa Indians; in 1687, La Salle was murdered by his men.

The French incursion in the Gulf of Mexico inspired the Spanish to expand its settlements in the borderlands. In 1690, they founded missions among the Caddo people of eastern Texas and western Louisiana, from whom they took the Caddo word, Tejas or Texas, meaning "friends." Three years later, when the Caddos blamed the friars for bringing smallpox, they escaped. The Spanish abandoned Texas until the French once again entered the area.

In 1699, Pierre LeMoyne, Sieur d'Iberville, resumed the French search for an opening to the Mississippi River, which was difficult to locate in the muddy Mississippi Delta. Iberville found the river's mouth by accident, then built forts at Biloxi Bay and on the Mississippi to establish French possession. Spain might have forced the French out of Louisiana with quick action, but in 1700, the grandson of French King Louis XIV took the Spanish throne; the two nations became allies against the English, Dutch, and Austrians in the War of the Spanish Succession.

Although the French-Spanish alliance gave Louisiana a chance to develop without interference from New Spain, the colony grew slowly. In 1708, about one hundred white soldiers and settlers lived in Louisiana. They obtained food, deerskins, and the right to occupy the land from local Native Americans by exchanging firearms and other goods. Relations between the French and Indians were not trouble-free, however. In 1715, for example, after Natchez Indians killed four French traders, the colonists literally demanded the assassins' heads. When the Natchez failed to execute all of the perpetrators, the French murdered Indian hostages and required the Natchez to accept a fortified trading post on their land.

Canada

Conflict developed in the north when the Iroquois confederation attacked New France to stop French fur trading in the Ohio Valley and Illinois. The Iroquois defeated New France in 1683, but war continued as the English, French, and Native Americans struggled over trade routes and territory. The outbreak of King William's War in 1689 fueled the contest, as the Five Nations attacked settlements in Canada, while the French and their Indian allies destroyed English frontier outposts from New York to Maine. New England troops took Port Royal in Acadia, but failed to conquer Quebec. Though the European belligerents agreed in the Peace of Ryswick (1697) to return to prewar status in North America, the Canadians won an important victory over the Iroquois and their English allies. The Five Nations signed a neutrality treaty in 1701. Frustrated by New York's failure to provide reinforcements, they ended their alliance with the English. New France then developed trade in the Great Lakes and Illinois Territory.

The renewal of hostilities between the English and French in 1702, with Queen Anne's War, again brought raids on the New England frontier. In 1704, the Canadians and Native Americans attacked Deerfield, Massachusetts, burning houses and barns, killing inhabitants, and taking many captives. The English once again took Port Royal, but called off an attack on Quebec when they lost 900 men in storms on the St. Lawrence River. This time, however, the peace treaty gave the victory to England, (which had joined with Scotland in 1707 to form Great Britain). In North America, the Treaty of Utrecht (1713) ceded Nova Scotia (formerly Acadia), Newfoundland, and control of the Hudson Bay territory to the British. Yet they had failed to oust France from North America.

THE ENTRENCHMENT OF SLAVERY IN BRITISH AMERICA

The most significant development in British North America during the late seventeenth and early eighteenth century was large-scale investment in enslaved Africans. The slave buyers could not foretell the monumental effects of their actions. They responded to economic conditions: their need for workers, the declining availability of white servants, and the developing Atlantic slave trade.

Adopting Slavery

How could people who increasingly prized their own freedom deprive other human beings of liberty, and often life itself? The answer lies in traditional English culture and the colonists' perceived economic needs.

The English, like other Europeans, believed that hierarchies existed in human society and, indeed, all of nature. Humans were superior to animals; Christians superior to "heathens." English language and culture also differentiated sharply between white and black, with whiteness suggesting purity and good, blackness imbued with filth and sin. The English compared their light skin with the Africans' darker brown color, judging the latter to be inferior. In African religion, social customs, dress, and political organization, the Europeans found serious deficiencies. The people of sub-Saharan Africa, the English thought, were lower on the scale of humanity and could justifiably be enslaved. The example of the Portuguese, Spanish, and—most recently—the Dutch made the decision to buy Africans seem natural. The mainland English colonists could also look to their countrymen in the West Indies, where thousands of African slaves toiled in sugar fields, outnumbering whites.

Despite this cultural context, colonists viewed their investment in slaves as an economic decision. In Virginia and Maryland, planters purchased Africans because they needed large numbers of workers to grow tobacco. Chesapeake settlers had learned that Native Americans, who easily escaped enslavement and died in catastrophic numbers, would not fill their labor needs. White servants filled the gap until about 1675. In the last quarter of the century, however, the supply of English servants declined. Economic conditions improved in England, while good tobacco land became scarce. With the founding of the Carolinas, New Jersey, and Pennsylvania, where land was plentiful, servants had a wider range of options.

Chesapeake planters searching for an alternative labor supply turned to African slaves. Population figures for Virginia and Maryland demonstrate graphically the result of individual decisions. In 1660, only 900 blacks resided in the Chesapeake, some of whom had come as servants and were free. Two decades later, their number had grown to 4,300; by 1720, blacks comprised one-fifth of the population.

The Slave Trade

English entry into the Atlantic slave trade helped spur the transition to an African workforce. Though smugglers like John Hawkins had interloped earlier in the Spanish trade, England officially became involved in selling human beings in 1663. Charles II granted a monopoly to supply captives to the English colonies first to the Company of Royal Adventurers, then in 1672 to the Royal African Company. When the companies could not meet the demand of labor-hungry colonists, smugglers got involved, so in 1698, the Crown abandoned the monopoly, opening the slave trade to any English merchant who wanted to participate.

The experience of enslavement and transport across the Atlantic Ocean was dehumanizing and perilous. Probably one-half of the persons sold into slavery died before reaching the New World. Approximately three-quarters of those taken to English North America came from the area of West Africa between Senegambia and the Bight of Biafra, with the remainder coming mostly from Angola. As European sea captains made successive trips to the coast, African traders had to reach farther and farther into the continent to find enough people to enslave. Some captives marched 500 miles or more to the sea in "coffles," the term given to the files of shackled prisoners. On the coast, they were confined in enclosures called barracoons. When a ship arrived, according to a Dutch trader, Willem Bosman, in 1700, the Africans were lined up on shore,

> where, by our surgeons . . . they are thoroughly examined, even to the smallest member, and that naked both men and women, without the least distinction or modesty. Those that are approved as good, are set on one side; and the lame or faulty are set by as invalids, which are here called *mackrons:* these are such as are above five and thirty years old, or are maimed in the arms, legs or feet; have lost a tooth, are grey-haired, or have films over their eyes; as well as all those which are affected with any venereal distemper, or several other diseases.

For the Africans chosen for transport, the horror had only begun. The Europeans branded them

Theodor de Bry's illustration of a Dutch ship trading on the coast of West Africa. The people in the canoe, indicated with "B," represent African merchants who traded human beings to the Europeans for goods such as cloth, rum, and firearms. (Rare Books Division, The New York Public Library. Astor, Lenox and Tilden Foundations)

with the insignia of the company. Then followed the voyage across the Atlantic, called the "middle passage," which could take from three weeks to more than three months. Ships normally carried rations for three months, so bad storms could mean starvation. Weather permitting, the captives spent their days on deck, the men in chains, the women and children unrestrained. At night, and around the clock if weather was bad, slaves occupied spaces about the size of coffins in the hold of the ship, where temperatures could reach extremely high levels. Disease was often rampant. Some slaves attempted suicide by jumping overboard or refusing to eat: the latter was so common that traders invested in a tool called the *speculum oris* to force open a person's mouth.

Africans also rebelled violently, attacking the white captain and crew, occasionally taking over the ship. Because they were unfamiliar with ocean navigation, mutineers had the best hope for success when the ship was still in African waters and large numbers could carry out the revolt, escaping to shore. When rebels failed, punishment was swift and brutal.

Upon arrival in America, the Africans faced the ordeal of sale by auction or prearranged contract. They were stripped naked once again and examined for disease and physical defects. Because the greatest need was for strong field hands who would provide years of labor, plantation owners paid the highest prices for healthy young men in their prime. Buyers paid less for women, children, and older men. For both the Africans and their owners, the year following debarkation was most critical. During this period of seasoning, Africans endured serious illness and high mortality from the new disease environment.

Systems of Slavery in British North America

As more and more Africans arrived, colonial assemblies instituted black codes to define slavery and control the black population. Before 1660, Maryland had officially sanctioned perpetual bondage, but Virginia moved more slowly. Enough flexibility existed in Virginia society to allow black servants to gain freedom, earn their livelihoods, and in some cases acquire land. In the 1660s, however, Virginia joined Maryland in enacting laws that recognized differences in the terms of white servants and African slaves. By law, slavery lasted a person's entire lifetime, descended from mother to child, and was the normal status of blacks, but never whites.

In the late seventeenth and early eighteenth century, both Virginia and Maryland created clearly articulated caste systems. A person's skin color denoted status: all Africans and their descendants encountered severe discrimination, whether enslaved or free. The Virginia assembly ruled that any master who killed a slave during punishment was not guilty of a felony. Conversely, no black person, slave or free, could strike a white, even in self-defense. Virginia lawmakers made emancipation difficult to obtain. Evolving black codes banned interracial marriage, forbade owners from releasing their slaves except in special cases, and restricted enslaved blacks from traveling without permission, marrying legally, holding property, testifying against whites, or congregating in groups. Over the course of the eighteenth century, other British colonies passed similar codes that ranged from fairly moderate New England laws to a harsh regime in Carolina.

In the life of an African slave, these laws had force, but more direct was the power of the master over work and family. To be a slave meant that someone else possessed your body and could command your daily activities. The owner chose your job; he or she decided whether your children would stay with you or be sold away. During off-hours, Africans generally maintained autonomy in religion, social customs, and family life.

The work Africans and native-born African Americans performed varied from one region to another. In the Chesapeake and the Carolinas, most slaves spent long hours planting, weeding, and harvesting tobacco, corn, and rice. A farm's production depended largely upon the number of workers tending the crop. Over time, as the southern black population increased naturally and importation continued, the supply of labor became more plentiful. Plantation owners assigned slaves to different tasks, though most still raised the staple crop. Some men became drivers and artisans; some women served as nurses, cooks, and spinners. Both women and men performed domestic service.

Agricultural production in the middle colonies and New England centered on grains and livestock, which demanded less labor than tobacco or rice, so most parts of the northern countryside had relatively few slaves. Exceptions included New York and neighboring eastern New Jersey, which had difficulty attracting European immigrants; thus, well-to-do farmers purchased large numbers of Africans to work their land. In Rhode Island's Narragansett region, some plantation owners held as many as fifty blacks. Most northern slaves lived in the port towns, however, where women worked as cooks and household servants, and men labored at crafts, domestic service, and as shipbuilders and sailors. In New York City, blacks were about one-fifth of the population; in Boston and Philadelphia, they comprised about one-tenth.

A source of comfort to slaves who had lost their African homelands and kin was to establish new families in America. All knew, however, that owners could destroy loving relationships by selling away spouses, children, brothers, and sisters. The ability of blacks to form families changed over time and varied from one region to another. High mortality and a skewed sex ratio prevented many African-born men from marrying and having children. In northern cities like Philadelphia, mortality was so high that colonists had to keep importing Africans to avoid population decline. In the Chesapeake colonies, however, natural population growth began with the first generation of native-born slaves. African American women had more children than their African mothers, creating communities of slaves on large plantations. Whereas most of the first Africans dwelled in white households with just a few blacks, their offspring, known as "country-born" slaves, lived with parents, brothers, and sisters. The third generation lived with grandparents and cousins as well.

Resistance and Rebellion

Although for many slaves family and kin helped to reduce their feelings of despair, for others nothing relieved the pain of lifetime bondage. Many resisted their masters' power by staging slowdowns, pretending illness, destroying crops and tools, committing theft, arson, assault, and murder. Newly arrived Africans were especially likely to rebel against their new status, often running away. Slaves who were sold away from their families frequently escaped to join them once again. Men ran away in greater numbers than women, who, as mothers, found it difficult to escape with children in tow.

Although slaves in the English West Indies often rebelled, blacks in the mainland colonies rarely took the ultimate step of armed insurgency, primarily because they were so outnumbered by whites. Before 1713, West Indian blacks staged seven full-scale revolts; their large population made success seem possible. On the mainland, just one slave revolt occurred by the early 1700s. In New York City, in 1712, about twenty slaves set fire to a building, attacking the white men who came to extinguish it. Nine whites were killed; terror spread up and down the Atlantic coast. As in the case of later slave revolts and conspiracies, the revenge wreaked upon the black community surpassed any violence the rebels had committed. In the wake of the New York revolt, thirteen slaves were hanged, three burned at the stake, one tortured on the wheel (an instrument used to stretch and disjoint its victims), and another starved to death in chains; six committed suicide to avoid such treatment.

Early Abolitionists

As slavery became entrenched in the American colonies, a few white colonists questioned its morality. Slavery was morally repugnant, they believed, because all humans are equal in the eyes of God. One of the American opponents of perpetual bondage was Samuel Sewall, a Boston judge, who wrote in 1700, "It is most certain that all

Men, as they are the Sons of Adam . . . have equal Right unto Liberty, and all other outward Comforts of Life."

Quakers also spoke out publicly against the institution. Certainly not all Friends were abolitionists, but a few interpreted Quaker ideals to mean that human bondage reeked with sin. According to John Hepburn of New Jersey, for example, slavery violated the Golden Rule to do unto others as you wish others to do unto you. Whereas owners got rich without physical labor, wore fine-powdered wigs and greatcoats, and their wives and children similarly lived well, slaves endured beatings, wore rags, and slept in the ashes of the fire. In the context of rising importation throughout the colonies, however, the protests of Sewall, Hepburn, and a few other critics had little effect.

Economic Development in the British Colonies

Despite differences in agriculture, labor, and commerce from one region to another, the mainland colonies were all part of the Atlantic economy, dominated by the staple crops—sugar, tobacco, and rice. The developing mercantile economies of New England and the mid-Atlantic region depended heavily upon the slave system, because their chief market was providing food for the multitudes of blacks laboring on West Indies sugar plantations.

Northern Economies

Family farms and dependence on the sea characterized New England's economy. When its agriculture failed to provide a lucrative staple crop, traders turned to fishing and shipping. With rocky, generally poor soil and a cool climate, the region could not grow a profitable commercial crop like tobacco or sugar, so rural New England families raised livestock, wheat, rye, Indian corn, peas, other vegetables, and fruit. They ate most of what they produced within their families and communities.

Fishing and shipping developed as important industries during the seventeenth century. The New England fishers initially sold their catch, in return for manufactured goods such as shoes, textiles, glass, and metal products, to London merchants, who sent the fish to Spain, Portugal, and the Wine Islands, off the coast of Africa.

The fishing industry spurred the growth of maritime trade. New England merchants formed partnerships among themselves and with English merchants, encouraging a local shipbuilding industry. The New Englanders exported fish, barrels, and other wood products. They imported wine, fruit, and salt from the Wine Islands, and rum, molasses, sugar, dyes, and other goods from the Caribbean. Soon, aided by the Navigation Acts, they were the chief carriers of goods along the North American coast, exchanging enslaved Africans and rum distilled from West Indies molasses for Pennsylvania wheat and livestock, Chesapeake tobacco, North Carolina tar and turpentine, and South Carolina rice.

The economy of the Middle Colonies resembled New England's in a number of ways, but was much more prosperous agriculturally. With plenty of good land, farmers raised wheat and livestock commercially, purchasing servants and some slaves to supplement family labor. The region had two ports: one at New York City and the other at Philadelphia. Though neither city matched Boston in population or commercial importance before 1750, both quickly surpassed the Massachusetts seaport after that date. New York merchants maintained links with Amsterdam, the Dutch West Indies, and New Spain even after the English takeover in 1664. Philadelphia Quakers exploited their connections with Friends in other ports, especially in England and the West Indies.

Life in the Seaports

Maritime trade encouraged the development of port cities in the British provinces. Until 1750, merchants of Boston and other seaport towns in Massachusetts and Rhode Island dominated colonial trade. The ports thrived because they forged commercial links between farmers and external dealers, housing the markets through which imports and exports flowed. The maritime industry itself created demand for shipbuilders, suppliers of provisions, rope and sailmakers, carters, dockworkers, and sailors.

Commercial growth brought social change. Some merchants became fabulously wealthy. They spent their income conspicuously, building costly mansions, purchasing enslaved Africans as household servants, and wearing expensive clothes. Other city dwellers were much less fortunate, because they earned minimal wages or lacked employment. Port cities stimulated both affluence and dire poverty. They attracted many people who hoped to make their fortunes, or at least a decent living, but died with little more than the clothes on their backs. Maritime commerce frequently suffered disruption from war, bad weather, and economic downturns. Seamen and artisans could expect little work during the winter. City folk were also at greater risk of death than those who lived in the country, as some arriving ships spread smallpox and other diseases to the dense urban populations. The towns lacked adequate sanitation facilities, so garbage and waste cluttered streets, polluting the water supply.

As trade expanded, sailors became an important segment of the labor force. They were a varied lot. Some went to sea only part-time to supplement the income of their farms. Others chose seafaring as a career. Some had no choice in the matter at all, for they were enslaved Africans whose masters purchased them to man the ships. Sailors led a difficult and dangerous life. Crews on ordinary merchant ships were small, so seamen worked long hours loading and unloading the ship, maintaining the rigging and sails, and pumping water from the bilge. The organization of labor on board was hierarchical, with power descending from the captain to mate, to specialists like ship carpenter and surgeon, to seamen. Discipline could be harsh. The crewmen had little hope of moving up through the ranks, for captains were generally from affluent families, often merchants and part-owners of their ships. Instead, the more common fate of an ordinary "Jack Tar" was early death or disability from shipwreck, combat with enemies or pirates, and such occupational hazards as falling overboard, broken bones, scurvy, rheumatism, and hernia, or the "bursted belly" as they called it.

When conditions on the ship became insufferable, the seamen rebelled, sometimes deserting the ship at the next port. Most radically, men mutinied and, if successful, sometimes became pirates. They plundered merchant vessels and port towns, sharing the proceeds evenly among themselves, electing officers, and recruiting much larger crews than could be found on merchant ships. With eighty or more men on a pirate ship of average size, compared with fifteen on a comparable merchant vessel, each had much less work to do.

Plantation Economies in the Chesapeake and South Carolina

From 1675 to 1720, tobacco remained king in Maryland and Virginia. The wealth of plantation owners grew with each child born to a slave mother. The wealthiest man in early eighteenth-century Virginia was Robert Carter of Lancaster County, called "King" Carter. As a slave trader and land speculator, he parlayed his inheritance of £1,000 and 1,000 acres into an estate of £10,000 in cash, 300,000 acres of land, and over 700 slaves. Carter, with his relatives and friends, formed a tightly knit group of Chesapeake gentry.

In 1720, and throughout the eighteenth century, Chesapeake society was hierarchical. At the bottom of the social structure were slaves. Above them were the non-landholding whites, perhaps 40 to 50 percent of white families, who rented land, owned a horse or two, some cows, a few pigs, tools, and some household goods, but rarely held bound servants or slaves. Their incomes from tobacco were so meager that they had trouble paying taxes and rent. Often they were in debt to the local merchant-planter for needed manufactured goods, such as ammunition, fabric, shoes, and tools. Next higher were small landholders whose incomes allowed them to live more comfortably, with pottery, more furniture, and nicer (though still quite small) homes.

In the upper 5 percent were the gentry, who owned many slaves, large acreages, and usually acted as merchants as well. They served as intermediaries for smaller planters, selling tobacco abroad and importing manufactured goods. In Maryland and Virginia, the merchant-planters conducted trade without the development of port cities. Ships docked at their plantations along the many tributaries of the Chesapeake Bay to load casks of tobacco and unload imported goods. Tobacco required little processing: planters dried the leaves in sheds and packed them in casks made by local coopers. Merchant-planters and rural artisans, including slaves, provided goods and services for the community without centralizing their activities in towns.

Situated in a semitropical climate, South Carolina developed a plantation economy that was linked to, and in many ways resembled, the West Indies. Most early settlers, both black and white, came from the English colony of Barbados. White planters claimed Carolina headrights, then sold corn, salt beef, salt pork, barrel staves, firewood, and Native American slaves to the islands. South Carolinians enslaved the Indians they captured in raids throughout the American Southeast and also obtained them in exchange for guns, ammunition, and cloth from native traders.

As with the northern fur trade between Europeans and Indians, the Carolinians used English trade goods to establish alliances with native groups. However, such major trading partners as the Yamassees quickly discovered that white merchants used theft, violence, rum, and false weights to gain unfair advantage. In 1715, in league with the Creeks, the Yamassees attacked white settlements, nearly destroying the colony. The whites saved themselves by getting help from the Cherokees. The Yamassees and Creeks were defeated, their people killed, enslaved, or forced to migrate from the coastal area. White South Carolinians then expropriated their lands.

The settlers wanted the new territory because they had found a lucrative export. Planters had experimented with a variety of crops—tobacco, cotton, sugar, silk, wine grapes, and ginger—but rice proved most successful in the wet lowlands of the Carolina coast. Also significant were the skills in rice production that many Africans brought to America. The chief markets for rice were Europe and the West Indies. Carolinians first sent their crop directly to Portugal, but in 1705 Parliament added rice to the list of enumerated products that had to be shipped to England first, taxes paid, and then reexported to Europe. The colonists argued that, in the case of southern Europe, this detour made their crop arrive too late for Lent, when much of it was consumed. In response, Parliament allowed South Carolina after 1731 to trade directly with Spain, Portugal, and Mediterranean Europe, but the larger share of the rice crop, which went to northern Europe, still required transit through Britain.

Before planters adopted full-scale rice production, slaves had performed a variety of jobs in crafts, timber, livestock, and agriculture. Their workloads were moderate, especially in comparison with the West Indies. Rice monoculture changed this situation altogether, as planters imported thousands of Africans. In the coastal areas north and south of Charleston, blacks reached 70 percent of the population in the 1720s. With high importation and harsher working conditions, death rates surged. As in the Chesapeake, wealthy planters bought up neighboring farms while investing heavily in slaves. They created large rice plantations, worked by growing numbers of African slaves. Small planters moved to the periphery, where they raised grain and livestock for the rice district and the Caribbean. The rice planters found the Carolina lowlands isolated and unhealthy, so they left their plantations part of the year. However, the Carolinians supervised their plantations directly—unlike British West Indian sugar planters who fled to England, leaving management in the care of overseers.

CONCLUSION

Between 1675 and 1720, the people of North America shed their blood over territory, trade, and political autonomy. As English, French, and Spanish settlers expanded into new regions, they established commerce, but also spread smallpox and fostered conflict among the Indians. Despite ardent defense of homelands, Native Americans throughout the continent, weakened by disease and war, yielded to the Europeans.

By the turn of the eighteenth century, the Spanish reconquered New Mexico and infiltrated Texas, France had started Louisiana, and the English were pushing out in many directions. To develop their economies, the British colonists imported Africans in large numbers. With the growth of plantation slave economies in the South and maritime commerce in the North, British North America developed distinctive regional characteristics. Yet in 1720, the Atlantic seaboard colonies had much in common: their settlement by enterprising men and women, regard for English rights of property and representation, and governance within the British imperial system. During the next half century, the importance of these commonalities would become clear.

RECOMMENDED READINGS

The sources listed for Chapter 2 are useful for the period from 1675 to 1720 as well.

Demos, John. *The Unredeemed Captive: A Family Story from Early America* (1994). The evocative tale of a Puritan minister's daughter who was held captive by the Mohawks and refused to return home.

Dunn, Mary Maples, et al., eds. *The Papers of William Penn,* 5 vols. (1981–1987). Basic documents, with scholarly introductions, on the founding and early development of Pennsylvania.

Innes, Stephen, ed. *Work and Labor in Early America* (1988). Insightful essays that demonstrate the range of labor systems and working conditions in the British colonies.

Jordan, Winthrop D. *White over Black: American Attitudes Toward the Negro, 1550–1812* (1968). Basic source on the construction of ideas about race in Anglo-America.

Karlsen, Carol F. *The Devil in the Shape of a Woman: Witchcraft in Colonial New England* (1987). Convincing argument about the significance of gender in witchcraft trials.

Lovejoy, David S. *The Glorious Revolution in America* (1972). The best introduction to the colonial revolutions of 1689.

McCusker, John J., and Menard, Russell R. *The Economy of British America, 1607–1789, With Supplementary Bibliography* (1991). An excellent survey of economic and demographic development.

Pestana, Carla Gardina. *Quakers and Baptists in Colonial Massachusetts* (1991). Contrasts the experience of two persecuted sects in early New England.

Usner, Daniel H., Jr. *Indians, Settlers, and Slaves in a Frontier Exchange Economy: The Lower Mississippi Valley Before 1783* (1992). A history of colonial Louisiana and West Florida, focusing on relations between Europeans and Native Americans.

AMERICAN JOURNEY ONLINE AND INFOTRAC COLLEGE EDITION

Visit the source collections at www.americanjourney.psmedia.com and infotrac.thomsonlearning.com and use the Search function with the following key terms to explore documents, images, audio and video clips, articles, and commentary related to the material in this chapter.

Metacom
Metacom's War
William Penn
Bacon's Rebellion
Glorious Revolution
Salem witch trials

Chapter 4

The Expansion of Colonial British America, 1720–1763

In 1721, smallpox hit Boston viciously. Business stopped for several months, as almost every family battled the contagion. In many respects, this epidemic was unremarkable in the British American colonies. But this time, one Puritan minister took an unprecedented step. Cotton Mather, who thirty years earlier had helped aggravate the Salem witch hysteria, encouraged a Boston doctor, Zabdiel Boylston, to test inoculation. Mather had learned from Onesimus, his African slave, and from English scientific papers that inoculation was used in Africa and Turkey to prevent smallpox epidemics. An experiment would be risky, for the procedure involved introducing the smallpox virus into the body, thereby giving the person what was usually (but not always) a mild case of the disease. Many doctors, as well as much of Boston's populace, condemned the proposal. Nevertheless, Dr. Boylston inoculated about 250 persons over the course of a year. Those who submitted to the procedure had a much lower death rate than Bostonians who contracted the disease naturally.

Mather was far ahead of his time in advancing the theory that disease was caused by an invasion of the body by viruses. Significantly, it was a minister, rather than a physician or scientist, who advanced this hypothesis. During the eighteenth century, science lacked the rigid boundaries of complexity and specialization that would later separate it from other fields of intellectual endeavor. American theologians and philosophers, as well as doctors, naturalists, and astronomers, read the latest scientific literature from England and Europe. The great divide between science and religion did not yet exist. Like many other theologians, Mather understood epidemics as God's punishment for sin. But he also believed inoculation was a divine gift, that people should use any means available to combat disease.

Mather's support for inoculation has been called the greatest contribution to medicine by an American during the colonial period. Certainly it represented change. During the years 1720 to 1763, the British provinces experienced intellectual, religious, and social ferment as they continued to expand through North America. As new knowledge, beliefs, and consumer goods arrived from Europe, colonists from Maine to Georgia (founded in 1732) increasingly lived within a common cultural framework. This common culture had important ties to England, yet was not altogether English, for immigrants from Scotland, Ireland, and the continent of Europe, and slaves from Africa brought ideas and practices from their native lands.

CHRONOLOGY

1720 Theodore Jacob Frelinghuysen begins revivals in New Jersey

1721–1722 Smallpox inoculation in Boston

1732 Founding of Georgia

Hat Act

1733 Molasses Act

1734 Jonathan Edwards starts revivals in Northampton, Massachusetts

1737 Walking Purchase in eastern Pennsylvania

1739 Stono Uprising in South Carolina

1739–1740 George Whitefield tours northern colonies

1739–1744 War of Jenkins' Ear

1740 James Oglethorpe leads invasion of Florida

1741 British attack on Cartagena

1744–1748 King George's War

1745 New Englanders conquer Louisbourg

1747 Boston riot against impressment

1750 Iron Act

1754 Defeat of Virginia militia at Fort Necessity

Albany Congress proposes plan for colonial unity

1754–1763 French and Indian War

1755 Braddock's defeat near Fort Duquesne

1758 British capture Louisbourg

1760 British conquer Montreal, seizing control of Canada

1763 Pan-Indian war begins in Ohio Valley and Great Lakes region

Proclamation of 1763 outlaws white settlement west of the Appalachians

Paxton Boys revolt in Pennsylvania

The Europeans came looking for land: when they set up farms in contested territory, they provoked conflicts with the Native Americans, French, and Spanish, resulting in a series of wars that lasted a quarter century. When the French and Indian War ended in 1763, the British colonies took a great deal of pride in their contribution to the victory, offering it as evidence of their economic and political maturity within the empire.

INTELLECTUAL TRENDS IN THE EIGHTEENTH CENTURY

The willingness of Mather and Boylston to try inoculation showed important changes in the way people viewed their world. The Puritan clergyman's personal journey from witch hunter in 1692 to medical investigator in 1721 reflected the growing inclination to find natural rather than supernatural causes for unexplained events. Though primarily intellectual, the Enlightenment had far-reaching effects, inspiring new technology as well as concepts of human freedom. For Americans, its greatest significance lay in the acceptance of natural rights philosophy, which paved the way for independence and republican government.

Newton and Locke

In the late seventeenth century, two English theorists, Sir Isaac Newton and John Locke, had challenged traditional notions that humans had no role in determining their fate, that they could only trust in God to rule the universe. They confronted

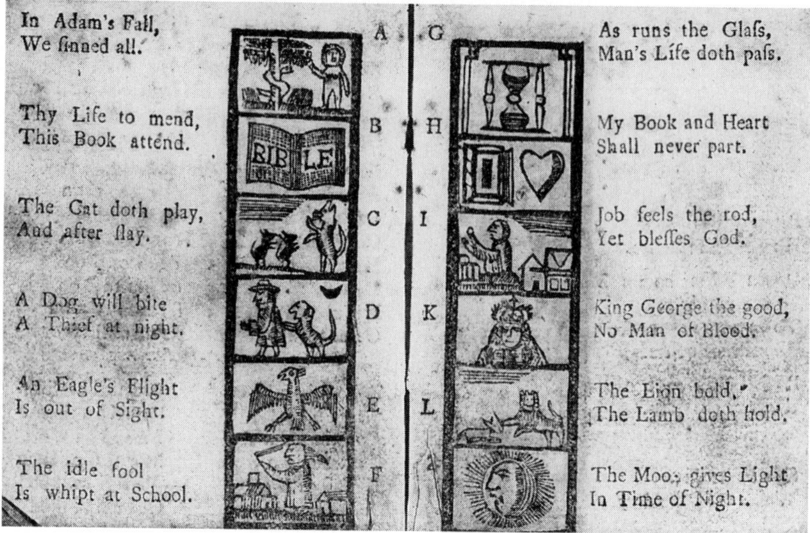

In Adam's Fall,
We ſinned all.
A

Thy Life to mend,
This Book attend.
B

The Cat doth play,
And after ſlay.
C

A Dog will bite
A Thief at night.
D

An Eagle's Flight
Is out of Sight.
E

The idle fool
Is whipt at School.
F

G
As runs the Glaſs,
Man's Life doth paſs.

H
My Book and Heart
Shall never part.

I
Job feels the rod,
Yet bleſſes God.

K
King George the good,
No Man of Blood.

L
The Lion bold,
The Lamb doth hold.

The Moon gives Light
In Time of Night.

The New England Primer, *first published in the 1680s, taught children moral lessons along with their alphabet and spelling.* (Courtesy, American Antiquarian Society)

this older view without denying the existence of God. Newton discovered universal laws that predictably govern the motion of planets, moons, and comets, the motion of falling bodies on earth (gravity), and the ebb and flow of tides. Locke built upon Newton's breakthrough in his *Essay Concerning Human Understanding* (1690). Locke argued against the accepted belief that infants are born with ideas implanted by God in their minds. He contended that all knowledge is gained by experience.

Locke, and the Enlightenment thinkers he inspired, believed in freedom and the right of people to improve the conditions in which they live. Science, of course, was an important means of such improvement. The English philosopher also had a major impact upon eighteenth-century politics, in particular providing a theoretical basis for the American Revolution and the Constitution. In *Two Treatises on Civil Government* (1690), he argued that humans, according to natural law, had rights to life, liberty, and property. By social contract, they formed governments to guarantee those rights. If a state failed in its obligation, the people had the duty to rebel and establish a new government.

Education in the British Colonies

Throughout British North America, formal education beyond basic reading, writing, and arithmetic was rare, so few read the works of Locke and Newton directly. After 1720, however, as newspapers became more available and reprinted articles from London, provincial readers gained greater familiarity with Enlightenment thought. Many colonists learned to read, though boys and girls spent much of their time learning the occupations they would pursue as adults. The availability of formal schooling varied widely by region, class, and gender. Nowhere did a system of universal, free, public education exist. Everywhere, schools emphasized moral behavior.

New England made the greatest effort of the British colonies to educate its populace. In 1642, the Massachusetts legislature required parents and ministers to teach all children to read. In 1647, the assemblymen ordered towns with at least fifty families to establish petty (elementary) schools, and those with one hundred families to maintain Latin grammar (secondary) schools. Connecticut and Plymouth passed similar legislation. Though some towns ignored the laws, most New England children learned to read, whether from their parents, at the town school, or at dame schools, where women in their homes taught young girls and boys for a fee. Writing was considered a separate skill, less crucial for girls to learn. The percentage of New England females who could write and do arithmetic was significantly lower than for males. Girls, on the other hand, commonly learned sewing and knitting. Boys who planned to enter college attended grammar school from about age seven to fourteen, studying Latin, elementary Greek, and sometimes Hebrew. Latin was necessary for the professions, including law, medicine, and the ministry.

In the Middle Colonies, churches and private teachers offered instruction. Affluent Quaker and Anglican boys were most likely to obtain formal education, though after 1750 girls and poor boys, including African Americans, had better access to schools. As in Massachusetts, females were much less likely to learn to write than males. In the Chesapeake, with dispersed settlement, neither Maryland nor Virginia had many schools. Upper-class boys and girls had private tutors, whereas middling families in some localities pooled their resources to establish schools. Overall, sons received much more instruction than daughters, and large numbers of poor whites obtained no education at all. Very few slaves learned to read and write.

New England also surpassed other regions in higher education, as the Puritans established Harvard College in Massachusetts in 1636, and Yale College in Connecticut in 1701. William and Mary, founded in Virginia in 1693, was the only other college in the British colonies before the 1740s. None of the colonial colleges admitted women. The Puritans intended Harvard to preserve classical learning and civilization, provide liberal education, and ensure a supply of well-educated ministers. Harvard offered a curriculum of ethics, religion, logic, mathematics, Greek, Hebrew, rhetoric, and natural history (biology and geology). Most early graduates became clergymen, while others went into medicine, public service, teaching, commerce, and agriculture.

Harvard alumni in Connecticut established Yale to provide advanced education closer to home. Yale had a tentative beginning, but gained more stability by 1720, after receiving funds from Elihu Yale and about 800 volumes for its library. The College of William and Mary also struggled at first. Chartered by the Crown to train Anglican clergy, educate young men in religion, and convert Native Americans, the school failed to offer college-level courses until the 1720s. Many elite families in the southern provinces continued to depend upon private tutors, trips to Britain, and northern colleges to educate their sons.

The Growth of Science

After 1720, influenced by Scottish universities, American colleges expanded their coursework to include French, English literature, philosophy, and science. They offered mathematics and what was then called natural philosophy—astronomy, physics, and chemistry. The colleges purchased scientific apparatus, including telescopes, sextants, clocks, and orreries, which demonstrate the motion of planets and moons within the solar system.

American professors of natural philosophy were part of a larger community of scholars centered in the prestigious Royal Society of London. This transatlantic community included academics like John Winthrop of Harvard College, as well as largely self-taught men like Benjamin Franklin and John Bartram. Scientists took from the Enlightenment a commitment to experiment and observe natural phenomena to obtain information that would lead to human progress. John Winthrop was the most renowned professor of natural philosophy in British America, with research interests in such wide-ranging subjects as sunspots, mathematics, earthquakes, and the weather. In 1761, Winthrop participated in an important international scientific effort to calculate the distance between the earth and sun, made possible by the transit of the planet Venus across the face of the sun. Venus had last crossed

Benjamin Franklin Describes His Experiments on Electricity 1755

In this letter, Franklin answers some queries from John Lining of Charleston, South Carolina, a physician who had published his own scientific work. Franklin's description of his experiments and explanation of how he came to the conclusion that lightning was electrical exemplify the scientific method. His use of men as guinea pigs in one experiment, however, is shocking in more ways than one.

Philadelphia, March 18, 1755

Sir, . . .

In answer to your several enquiries. The tubes and globes we use here, are chiefly made here. The glass has a greenish cast, but is clear and hard, and, I think, better for electrical experiments than the white glass of London, which is not so hard. . . .

As to the difference of conductors, there is not only this, that some will conduct Electricity in small quantities, and yet do not conduct it fast enough to produce the shock; but even among those that will

the sun in 1639, when no useful measurements had been made. Winthrop journeyed to Newfoundland to observe the transit. His data, combined with observations from the Cape of Good Hope, were inexact, but eight years later, scientists—including Winthrop—had another chance. This time, at least part of the transit could be viewed in the mainland British colonies. The stakes were high, because another transit would not occur for 105 years. The data were again imprecise, but when combined with measurements from around the globe, yielded results very close to the accepted distance of 93 million miles between the earth and sun.

Other colonists contributed to understanding the physical world. Perhaps best known for his diplomacy and political leadership during the Revolutionary era, Benjamin Franklin has become a symbol of the American Enlightenment. Franklin was born in Boston, ran away at age seventeen from an apprenticeship with his older brother, and arrived in Philadelphia nearly penniless. He built a highly successful printing business, publishing a newspaper, books, and *Poor Richard's Almanack,* which gained a readership throughout the colonies. Throughout his life, Franklin put the Enlightenment ideal of human progress into action. He founded a debating club conduct a shock, there are some that do it better than others. Mr. Kinnersley has found, by a very good experiment, that when the charge of a bottle hath an opportunity of passing two ways, i.e. strait through a trough of water ten feet long, and six inches square; or round about through twenty feet of wire, it passes through the wire, and not through the water, though that is the shortest course; the wire being the better conductor. When the wire is taken away, it passes through the water, as may be felt by a hand plunged in the water; but it cannot be felt in the water when the wire is used at the same time. . . .

Your question, how I came first to think of proposing the experiment of drawing down the lightning, in order to ascertain its sameness with the electric fluid, I cannot answer better than by giving you an extract from the minutes I used to keep of the experiments I made. . . .

"Nov. 7, 1749. Electrical fluid agrees with lightning in these particulars: 1. Giving light. 2. Colour of the light. 3. Crooked direction. 4. Swift motion. 5. Being conducted by metals. 6. Crack or noise in exploding. 7. Subsisting in water or ice. 8. Rending bodies it passes through. 9. Destroying animals. 10. Melting metals. 11. Firing inflammable substances. 12. Sulphureous smell. The electric fluid is attracted by points. We do not know whether this property is in lightning. But since they agree in all the particulars wherein we can already compare them, is it not probable they agree likewise in this? Let the experiment be made." . . .

The knocking down of the six men was performed with two of my large jarrs not fully charged. I laid one end of my discharging rod upon the head of the first; he laid his hand on the head of the second; the second his hand on the head of the third, and so to the last, who held, in his hand, the chain that was connected with the outside of the jarrs. When they were thus placed, I applied the other end of my rod to the prime-conductor, and they all dropt together. When they got up, they all declared they had not felt any stroke, and wondered how they came to fall; nor did any of them either hear the crack, or see the light of it. . . .

to discuss politics, morals, and natural philosophy, and helped establish the first American lending library, a hospital, and the College of Philadelphia. Franklin's experiments in electricity yielded information about its properties. His inventions included bifocal eyeglasses, the lightning rod, and an iron stove that was more efficient than colonial fireplaces.

John Bartram, also of Pennsylvania, was the most energetic of American naturalists, whose chief contribution to science was collecting specimens of New World plant life. In return for a yearly pension from the king and payment for seeds he sent to wealthy collectors in England, Bartram traveled all over the eastern seaboard searching for new plants and animals. His efforts greatly expanded botanical knowledge of the Western Hemisphere.

Another prominent American naturalist was Cadwallader Colden, a Scot who immigrated to the colonies after receiving his medical degree. While serving as surveyor-general and lieutenant-governor of New York, he collected and classified plants in the neighborhood of his estate. He corresponded with European botanists, sending them specimens and descriptions. Colden also ventured into the field of physics, publishing a pamphlet in which he attempted unsuccessfully to explain the causes of gravity.

Changes in Medical Practice

Just as Colden and other university-trained doctors were interested in many scientific fields, the practice of medicine itself attracted people of widely different backgrounds. During the colonial period, men with formal medical education comprised a small proportion of the people who provided care for disease, physical injury, and childbirth. Having completed formal coursework abroad, educated physicians were at the top of their profession, and charged the highest fees. Consequently, they practiced primarily in the cities. Below them were men who learned their craft as apprentices; though they assumed the title of doctor in the colonies, they were actually akin to the surgeon-apothecaries of Great Britain. As surgeons, they performed emergency procedures such as setting bones, amputating limbs, and removing superficial tumors, but no major surgery. As apothecaries, they prepared and prescribed drugs for a variety of illnesses.

Female midwives traditionally attended childbirth, treated the ill, and prescribed herbal remedies, having learned their skills through informal apprenticeships and from witnessing the childbirths of neighbors and relatives. During the colonial period, childbirth was the province of women. As an expectant mother's labor began, she called together a group of women, presided over by the midwife, who assisted in the birth. In the early stages of her labor, the woman provided special refreshments, called "groaning beer" and "groaning cakes." The attendants helped her walk around and offered herbal teas or liquor to relieve the pain. In normal deliveries, the mother squatted on a "midwife's stool" or remained standing while supported by several women. If complications occurred, the midwife manipulated the infant manually, but would not perform a Caesarean section. Without modern antibiotics, women constantly faced the threat of infection during pregnancy and in the weeks following delivery.

In the last half of the eighteenth century, the practice of obstetrics changed. In 1762, Dr. William Shippen, Jr., returned from studying medicine in England and Scotland to give lectures in anatomy to Philadelphia midwives and doctors. Soon he accepted only male students. Shippen established an obstetrical practice of his own, quickly attracting well-to-do patients who expected a more elevated level of care than they received from midwives. Affluent urban women were convinced that the male physicians offered a better chance for a safe, less painful delivery. The doctors' obstetrical training, their use of opiates and instruments such as forceps, spelled progress to these women. That the new obstetrics brought improvement is doubtful. The male doctors attended their clients in darkened rooms, with the woman lying in bed under covers. The physicians also lacked the means to prevent infection; their use of blood-letting and opium could impede safe delivery. In any case, midwives continued to attend the great majority of women, those who lived in rural areas and the poor.

The Great Awakening

As Enlightenment ideas gained sway, many Protestant ministers embraced Christian rationalism, a theology that stressed moral, rational behavior and the free will of individuals to lead their lives and achieve salvation. Some rationalists spoke of an impersonal God who had long ago created the universe to operate according to natural laws, rather than a loving or angry God who controlled a person's daily life. For many, the rationalist religion was comforting, because it included in the church all who tried to live decent Christian lives. To others, however, Christian rationalism was heretical, for it rejected the Calvinist belief that people must be saved to be full members of the church.

From the 1720s to the 1760s, ministers from various denominations called for the renewal of these beliefs in a series of revivals, known as the Great Awakening. Religious ferment convulsed British North America, spreading from the churches to threaten social and political authority.

Religious Diversity Before the Great Awakening

In 1720, the British provinces varied widely in religious and ethnic makeup. New England was the most homogeneous, for Massachusetts, New Hampshire, and Connecticut remained predominantly Puritan. The established Puritan churches received tax support, but Anglicans, Baptists, and Quakers could also worship freely. Rhode Island, which still embraced the principles of religious liberty and separation of church and state, was home to various denominations, including Quakers, Baptists, and Separatists.

From their founding, the Middle Colonies offered an open door to people of various backgrounds. In the late seventeenth century, according to one report, residents of New York City spoke eighteen different languages. In eastern New Jersey, Scottish Presbyterians, Dutch Reformed, New England Puritans, Baptists, and Quakers settled towns and plantations, and farther south, on both sides of the Delaware River, Native Americans, Dutch, Swedes, and Finns met the Quakers who accompanied William Penn. Philadelphia and its environs in the 1720s boasted organized meetings of Swedish Lutherans, Quakers, Mennonites, Baptists, Anglicans, Presbyterians, Dunkards, German Reformed, Dutch Reformed, German Lutherans, and Roman Catholics.

With few towns in the Chesapeake, the established Anglican church suffered from southern rural conditions. Ministers in Virginia faced serious obstacles in meeting the spiritual needs of their scattered congregations. Only half of the Anglican churches had regular preachers. Few planters were interested in converting their African slaves. The colony's laws against nonconformity prevented most dissent, so only a few Presbyterians and Quakers worshipped openly. In Maryland, many Quakers and Roman Catholics retained their faith, but suffered legal disabilities.

The established Church of England in South Carolina was in better condition than in Virginia. Even so, Presbyterians, Baptists, Huguenots, and Quakers worshipped freely, for the proprietors had actively recruited dissenters from England, Scotland, and France to increase population and obtain their political support.

The Great Awakening shattered the existing church structure of the colonies, as congregations wakened to the teachings and vigorous preaching style of revivalist, or New Light, ministers. Religious diversity grew in provinces where established churches, with government support, dominated religious life—especially Puritan churches in Connecticut and Massachusetts, and the Anglican establishment in Virginia. As a result of the revivals, these colonies became more like Rhode Island, New York, New Jersey, Pennsylvania, and South Carolina.

Early Revivals in the Middle Colonies and New England

In 1720, New Jersey felt the first stirrings of the Great Awakening, when Theodore Jacob Frelinghuysen emigrated from Holland to serve four churches in the Raritan Valley. He had been educated in Dutch Reformed pietism, which emphasized the importance of conversion and personal religious experience (or piety). Using an emotional, revivalist preaching style, he led many people to experience salvation. But Frelinghuysen created a split in the Dutch Reformed churches of New Jersey between his followers, who believed a person must experience God's saving grace before participating in church sacraments, and his opponents, who thought that a commitment to living a godly life was sufficient.

Next, revivals engulfed Presbyterian churches in New Jersey, as they adopted doctrines preached by Gilbert and John Tennent, the sons of William Tennent, a Scots-Irish immigrant and Presbyterian minister. The younger Tennents took pulpits in New Brunswick and Freehold, close to Frelinghuysen's congregations. Impressed by the Dutch Reformed pastor's style of preaching, they inspired revivals of their own. Meanwhile, in Neshaminy, Pennsylvania, the elder Tennent established a seminary, called the "Log College" by his critics, where many New Light ministers received training.

Reverend Gilbert Tennent, son of the founder of the "Log College," was an avid New Light minister during the Great Awakening. (Collection of the New York Historical Society)

In Massachusetts, revivals began in 1734, when minister Jonathan Edwards of Northampton preached a series of sermons on salvation, inclining many of his parishioners to believe they were saved. They went through the process of self-judgment—first feeling despair as sinners who were damned to hell, then rejoicing in the conviction that God rescued them from this fate. Edwards wrote to a colleague that "this town never was so full of Love, nor so full of Joy, nor so full of distress as it has lately been."

Revivalism Takes Fire

Beginning in 1739, the Great Awakening spread throughout the British mainland colonies after a young Anglican minister, George Whitefield, arrived from England to tour the Middle Colonies. Called the Grand Itinerant, he had a magnificent voice, ranging from a whisper to a roar, that could be heard by large crowds in fields and city streets. Benjamin Franklin calculated that 25,000 people could easily hear the spectacular preacher at one time.

Whitefield found adherents across denominational lines and among native-born Americans and immigrants alike. In 1740, Jonathan Edwards invited Whitefield to Northampton, prompting the itinerant to travel through New England, where he attracted crowds as large as 8,000 in Boston. Other New Light ministers followed, including Gilbert Tennent and James Davenport, a Puritan preacher of Southold, Long Island. Davenport took the Awakening to extremes, harshly attacking other pastors as "unconverted."

The full force of the Awakening hit the south later than New England and the Middle Atlantic. During the 1740s, Presbyterian missionaries set up churches on the southern frontier. The new settlements were a fertile field for the revivalists because few regular clergy had migrated west. The more explosive Baptist revivals began in the 1750s, when itinerants traveled through Virginia and North Carolina making converts and forming churches. The Baptists believed that individuals should be saved before they are baptized. With their emotional religious style, they appealed particularly to ordinary white farmers and enslaved African Americans. Followers called each other "Sister" and "Brother," whether slave or free, affluent or poor. They refused to attend their local parish services and met in fields and homes. The ministry was open to all, even women and slaves, with no requirement for college training.

The Awakening's Impact

The revivals proved to be socially divisive, as many communities split into two groups, the "New Lights" and the "Old Lights." The style of most New Light preachers was to give impassioned, extemporaneous sermons that contrasted dramatically with the closely reasoned sermons of their opponents, the rationalist Old Light ministers. New Lights believed that salvation was more important than religious training; they required a "saved" ministry, with a dynamic preaching style. Congregations responded by fainting, shrieking, and shedding tears. Old Light clergymen, who defended their advanced education, resented accusations that they were unsaved. In turn, they charged the revivalists with being unlearned.

As congregations broke apart, bitter disputes ensued over church property and tax support. Where strong established churches existed—as in Massachusetts, Connecticut, and Virginia—the New Lights challenged political as well as religious authority. In response, the Connecticut Assembly, for example, passed an Anti-Itinerancy Act, which made it illegal for a clergyman to preach in another's parish without his permission and repealed the 1708 law permitting religious dissent.

Higher education in the British colonies also felt the flames of revivalistic fervor. Yale College was at the center of the intense religious and political battles in Connecticut. When the New Haven church separated, a large number of students, many of them studying for the ministry, followed the New Lights. They skipped classes to attend revivals and questioned whether their teachers were saved. Thomas Clap, head of the college, obtained permission from the Connecticut Assembly to expel any student who attended New Light services. Clap's opposition to the Awakening was not permanent, however, for by 1753 he himself had become a New Light. As in many congregations, people eventually found ways to heal the bitterness and division that the Great Awakening had caused.

A more lasting effect of the revivals was the founding of new colleges. Until the mid-1740s, only Harvard, William and Mary, and Yale existed in the British colonies. The revivals created a need for ministerial training. Between 1746 and 1769, the revivalists founded the College of New Jersey (now Princeton), the College of Rhode Island (Brown), Queen's College (Rutgers) in New Jersey, and Dartmouth College in New Hampshire. Anglicans established King's College (Columbia) in New York City, while a group of civic leaders, headed by Benjamin Franklin, started the College of Philadelphia (University of Pennsylvania). Though each of these new schools except the College of Philadelphia was tied to a specific religious denomination, they all accepted young men of various faiths. These new colleges taught traditional subjects but also adopted the new curricula in mathematics, science, and modern languages.

IMMIGRATION AND EXPANSION

Between 1720 and 1760, the population of British North America grew from 472,000 to 1,600,000. Much of this growth came from natural increase, but new arrivals also spurred population growth, as thousands of Germans and Scots-Irish immigrated, and slave traders continued to import blacks.

The newcomers brought ideas, religious beliefs, skills, and ways of life that significantly altered the cultural mix of the British colonies. The immigrants from the European continent and the British Isles sought a new beginning in "the best poor man's country": many disembarked in the Middle Colonies, traveling west to settle the backcountry from Pennsylvania south through the Shenandoah Valley to the Carolinas. Others went directly to Georgia, which reformers started in 1732 as a haven for the poor. The population explosion and demand for new lands brought the British colonists face to face with the Spanish in Florida, the French in Canada and the Ohio Valley, and Native Americans all along the frontier.

German and Scots-Irish Immigrants

More than 100,000 Germans left their homelands for America during the century after 1683. Some were forced out by religious persecution and war; others sought economic opportunity. Promoters called "newlanders" told Germans of cheap fertile land and mild government in the British colonies. Many immigrants paid their own passage. Those who could not signed on as "redemptioners," the equivalent of indentured servants, whose labor would be sold for a number of years upon arrival. Immigrants went to ports from New York to Georgia, with most entering the Delaware Valley. Some Germans remained in Philadelphia, but the majority headed for the Pennsylvania hinterland and south through the backcountry of Maryland, Virginia, and the Carolinas.

German-speaking immigrants found the freedom they sought in North America, congregating in distinct communities, building separate churches and schools, and maintaining German language and culture. Pennsylvania was the heart of German America, as the colony's religious freedom allowed a multitude of sects and churches to flourish—the Mennonites, Amish, Brethren, Moravians, Schwenkfelders, Lutherans, and Reformed.

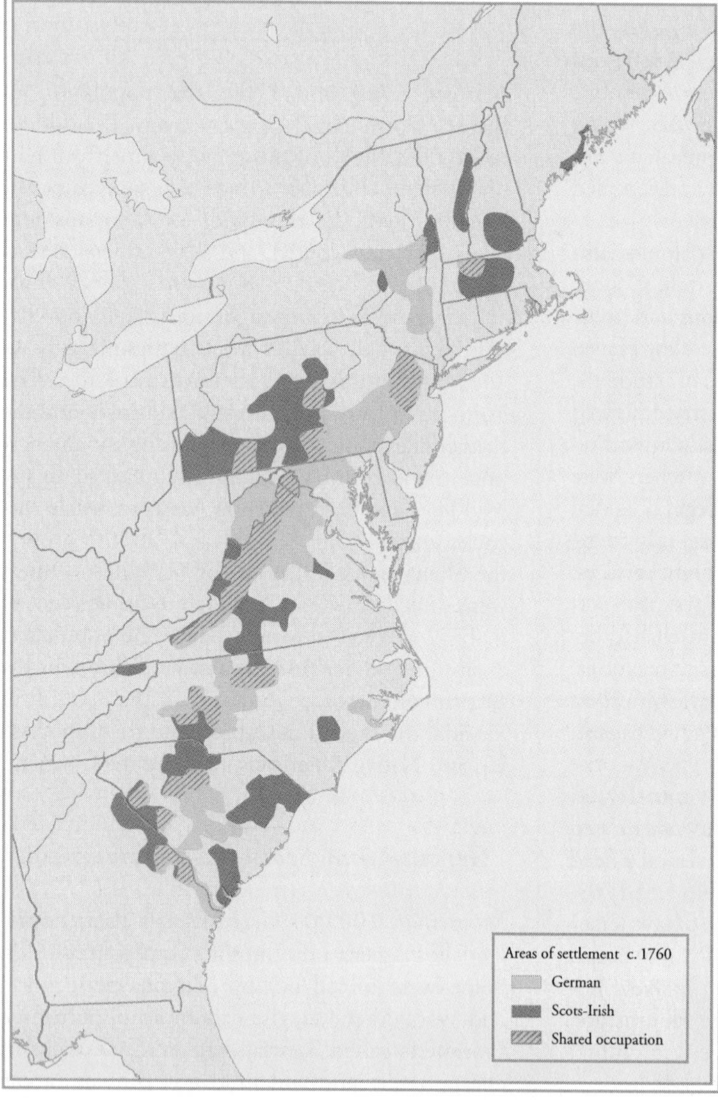

Map 4.1 | German and Scots-Irish Settlements in Colonial British America, c. 1760

Cultural exchange between the Germans and English enriched American society. German churches introduced the sophisticated choral music of their homelands. The printer, Christopher Saur, reprinted German hymnals along with his German-language newspaper and almanac. Congregations founded schools in which children learned both German and English. Immigrants retained the old tongue in their churches and homes, but used English in business, the courts, and politics. German American decorative arts proliferated by the 1740s, in house ornaments, furniture, and elaborately illustrated documents, such as marriage certificates, with gothic *Fraktur* lettering.

German farm women did much heavier fieldwork than most English wives, but otherwise played a similar role in maintaining domestic culture. Germans favored the more efficient European stoves over English fireplaces, and pewter over tinware. In diet, they ate relatively little meat, and preferred coffee to tea. But like their English neighbors, German women served as midwives and dispensed herbal remedies.

Though some German immigrants engaged in politics and law, most remained uninvolved in government. As non-British immigrants with little wealth, they needed time to become naturalized, learn the language and political culture, and establish themselves economically.

Large numbers of Scots, Scots-Irish, and Irish Catholics also came during the eighteenth century, settling in New York, Pennsylvania, Delaware, western Maryland, and the southern backcountry. Most were Ulster Scots (or Scots-Irish as they were called in America), Presbyterians whose families had migrated during the 1600s from Scotland to northern Ireland in search of economic opportunity. There they had combined tenant farming and weaving until the early eighteenth century, when their leases expired. Because landlords raised rents exorbitantly, many Ulster Scots left with their families for the colonies. The first large wave of immigrants departed during 1717–1718; poor harvests and downturns in the linen industry impelled successive groups toward America.

In the colonies, the Scots-Irish achieved a reputation as tough defenders of the frontier. As relatively late arrivals, they had to stake out farms on the edges of existing white settlements. The combination of agriculture and linen manufacture was a distinctive contribution of the Ulster Scots to the colonial economy. As frontier inhabitants, the Scots-Irish came into frequent contact with Native Americans, often with tragic results. The new settlers often marked out their farms on Indian hunting lands without negotiating a sale. One Pennsylvania frontiersman, not recognizing the Indians' rights, echoed the early Puritans when he argued that it was contrary to "the laws of God and nature, that so much land should be idle, while so many Christians wanted it to labor on, and to raise their bread."

The Founding of Georgia

The last of the British mainland colonies, Georgia, lured many German and Scots-Irish immigrants, as well as Scots and English. Animated by Enlightenment ideals of human progress and freedom, James Oglethorpe and John Viscount Percival, members of the Associates of the Late Doctor Bray, a philanthropic society, sought a charter for the colony. They were convinced that something had to be done to help the poor. They also argued that the settlement could serve as a buffer between Spanish Florida and South Carolina. George II granted the charter, placing control of the colony in the hands of trustees, or proprietors, who could neither receive financial benefits from the province nor own land within its bounds.

The double function of Georgia as a haven for the poor and a military outpost shaped the terms under which settlers immigrated. The trustees intended to create a peaceful, moral society of small farmers in which everyone, except indentured servants, worked for themselves. The Georgia Trustees, led by Oglethorpe, set three significant policies: they prohibited importation of hard liquor, banned slaveholding, and limited land ownership to 500 acres or less. Each free male immigrant was granted land at no charge, but no one could buy or sell real estate, and only men could inherit land. The trustees hoped to keep Georgia as a refuge for small farmers who, coincidentally, would defend the southern frontier. The rule that only men could inherit land meant that each farm must be owned by a man who, at least ideally, could fight.

In February 1733, the ship *Anne* with approximately one hundred passengers arrived at a site on the Savannah River. Here they built the first town, Savannah, on a high bluff overlooking the river. Oglethorpe purchased land from the Native Americans and established alliances with Lower Creeks, Cherokees, and Chickasaws against Spanish Florida, not least because English traders offered better merchandise than their rivals.

But many settlers in Georgia believed that the prohibitions on liquor, land sales, and slavery were unreasonable. The embargo on rum, a major Caribbean commodity, prevented expansion of trade with the West Indies, a ready market for their abundant lumber. The bans on slavery and large landholdings were also unpopular with many settlers, who coveted the grander lifestyle of planters north of the Savannah River, in South Carolina.

In consequence, Georgia grew slowly, as some settlers left almost immediately. The trustees gradually recognized their failure, allowing the importation of rum in 1742, and land sales and slavery in 1750. Preparing to turn the colony over to the Crown, in 1751 they called together Georgia's first elected assembly, which obtained legislative powers three years later when the royal government took control. The Georgia population swelled as South Carolinians migrated across the Savannah River, transforming Georgia into a slave society.

Despite its halting start before 1750, Georgia attracted settlers of a variety of nationalities and religions. The colony tapped the eighteenth-century flow of European immigrants, including Spanish and German Jews and German-speaking Lutherans. One of the Lutheran ministers described their satisfaction with the new land: "Every year God gives them what they need. And since they have been able to earn something apart from agriculture, through the mills which have been built and in many other ways, they have managed rather well with God's blessing, and have led a calm and quiet life of blessedness and honesty." Another group of German Protestants, the Moravians, were less content in Georgia. They arrived in 1735 and were gone five years later, because as pacifists, Moravian men could not serve in the militia. When the threat of Spanish invasion intensified in the late 1730s, most of the Moravians departed for Pennsylvania, which required no military service.

The Growth of the African American Population

The failure of the trustees to create a free society in Georgia was symptomatic of the entrenchment of slavery in America. Nowhere did significant abolitionism exist before 1750. Like the Germans and Scots-Irish, Africans helped diversify the American population and shape its culture. Though the number of African Americans grew naturally in many places, slave traders imported over 200,000 people between 1720 and the Revolution, most from West and Central Africa. In 1750, blacks comprised one-fifth of the population of the mainland colonies, including about 40 percent in the Chesapeake and the Lower South.

As the number of African Americans increased and slave societies matured, blacks created patterns of community, work, and culture. Extended kinship networks structured community life on large plantations, and even in places where slaves lived in small numbers, family ties remained paramount. Blacks were most successful in perpetuating African language and customs in regions where they were most numerous, particularly the South Carolina low country and, later, Georgia. Because they came from hundreds of societies in Africa, with many different cultural attributes, they had difficulty keeping traditional ways intact. They melded African and European forms together, and in the process, influenced evolving mainstream cultures, especially in the south.

The opportunity of slaves to engage in independent activities varied with the amount of time they had to spend working for their master. In South Carolina, each slave received a certain amount of work to perform each day—a field to hoe, thread to spin, a fence to build. Those who completed their assignments quickly had time to raise their own crops and livestock. Consequently, Carolina slaves participated in trade, selling their production at the "Negro market" in Charleston on Sundays. In the Chesapeake, most slaves on plantations labored for a specified number of hours rather than by the task. They planted, weeded, or harvested in gangs until the overseer told them to stop. As a result, they had little time to work for themselves.

The persistence of African culture was conspicuous in language, food, music, dance, and religion. Some newly arrived Africans knew Dutch, Spanish, Portuguese, French, or English from former contacts in Africa or the West Indies, but to communicate with other slaves and with Europeans, most adopted creole speech, a combina-

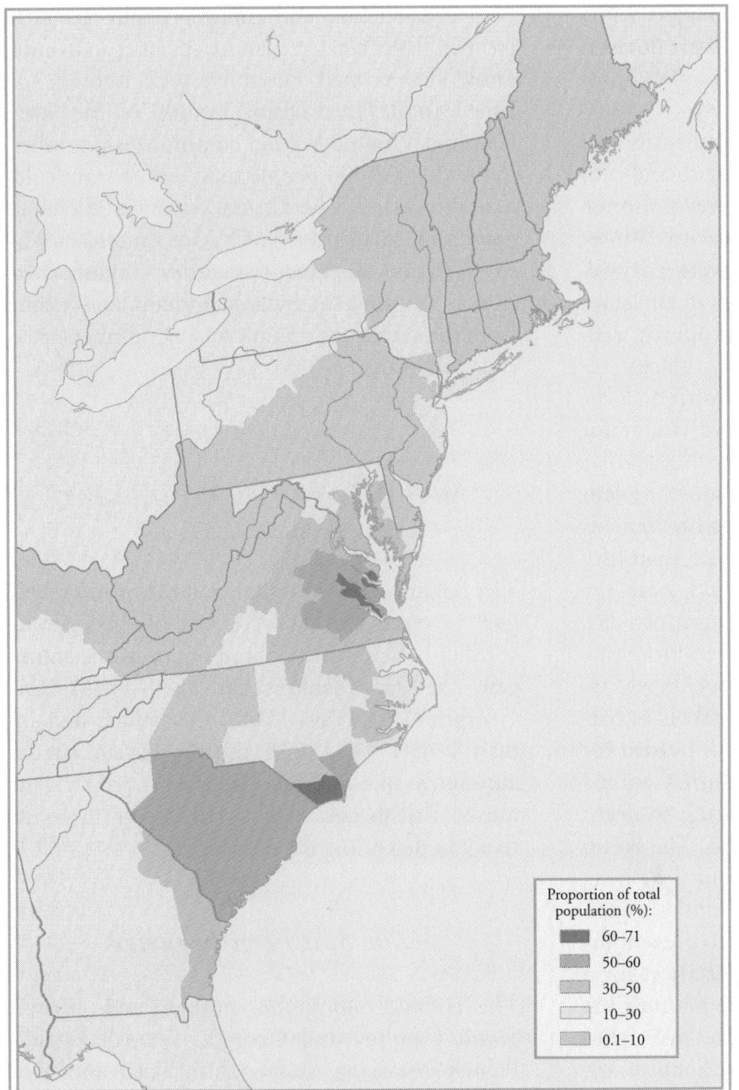

MAP 4.2 AFRICAN AMERICAN POPULATION IN COLONIAL BRITISH AMERICA, C. 1760

tion of English and African languages. In the Lower South, for instance, the creole tongue known as Gullah evolved from English and various languages from southern Nigeria, the Gold Coast, Angola, and Senegambia. African Americans retained black dialect from creole. For example, most blacks used the word *buckra,* from the African word meaning "he who governs," to refer to white men. Africans also influenced white speech patterns, when white children and immigrants sometimes adopted African American dialect. Some African words became part of American vocabulary, including cola, yam, goober (peanut), and toting (carrying) a package.

Blacks contributed to the food and material culture of British America, popularizing new foods such as okra, melons, and bananas. They made clay pipes, pottery, and baskets with African designs, and carved eating utensils, chairs, and other useful objects from wood. They built houses on African models rather than European. In music, they introduced the use of percussion instruments—cymbals, tambourines, and drums—to British military bands. They also helped create the Virginia "jig," a fusion of African and European elements, accompanied by banjos and fiddles.

Along with whites, during the Great Awakening, Africans shaped the forms of worship in southern Baptist churches. Blacks retained traditional African concepts of the hereafter, where the deceased reunited with ancestors, combining these beliefs with European views of heaven. Funerals remained important to African Americans throughout the colonies, as mourners buried the dead facing Africa, with traditional rituals, music, and dance. Blacks also passed down African medical practice, a combination of physical and psychological treatment including magic. More African American women than men were doctors, practicing midwifery as well as nursing and providing cures.

Despite cultural exchange and indications of human understanding, the antagonism and economic exploitation inherent in slavery poisoned relationships among whites and blacks. Whites believed that African Americans were an inferior race; masters used their power in the slave system to control their human property with harsh punishments. Nevertheless, blacks refused to accept their subordinate position, as increasing numbers ran away or were truant for weeks at a time.

Some enslaved Africans took more violent means, killing their masters or setting fire to fields and homes. In 1739, a group of more than fifty bondmen mounted an armed revolt near the Stono River in South Carolina. For most of a day, they marched with drums and banners from one plantation to another, killing about twenty whites. When armed planters defeated the rebels in battle, some of the slaves regrouped and headed for St. Augustine, Florida. But the South Carolina militia pursued the insurgents, putting to death everyone suspected of being involved. The Stono Uprising sent shock waves throughout the American colonies. The South Carolina legislature enacted a harsh slave code in an effort to prevent future revolts and limited slave importation for a decade. Most of the core group who planned the Stono Rebellion were African-born slaves, who hoped to escape to Florida, where Spanish authorities offered them religious sanctuary and freedom. By 1740, about one hundred former Carolina slaves had built the village of Gracia Real de Santa Teresa de Mose, called Mose, two miles north of St. Augustine.

During the eighteenth century, newly arrived Africans, often called "salt-water Negroes," were more likely to rebel or run away than creole, or "country-born" slaves. Predominantly male, imported Africans often lacked wives and children to root them to a plantation. Finding slavery intolerable, some fled as soon as they arrived. With Native Americans and runaway white servants, escaped slaves created maroon societies in frontier areas. They farmed, raised livestock, hunted, and fished. In the Great Dismal Swamp, on the North Carolina-Virginia border, communities numbering perhaps 2,000 people took refuge from colonial authorities. The Dismal Swamp settlements grew from small groups of Native Americans who survived the seventeenth-century English invasion of Virginia to include Indians and whites from the Carolinas, and increasing numbers of escaped Africans.

WARS FOR EMPIRE

The Spanish offer of refuge and the Stono rebels' goal to reach Florida were part of the ongoing conflict between Britain and Spain in the southeast. The War of Jenkins' Ear (1739–1744), King George's War (1744–1748), the French and Indian War (1754–1763), and the Indian war for autonomy in the Ohio Valley (1763–1765) required British colonists to participate more actively in defending the empire.

The Southern Frontier

The colonies along the southern tier—British South Carolina and Georgia, Spanish Florida, French Louisiana, and Spanish Texas and New Mexico—competed for trade with Native Americans and control of territory. Except for war between Georgia and Florida in the early 1740s, the most important battles along the southern rim were commercial, a competition the British traders often won because they had more plentiful and cheaper goods. They exchanged tools, clothing, scissors, guns, ammunition, and rum in return for slaves, deerskins, and furs from the Indians. In comparison with the English provinces, the Spanish and French colonies remained small. In 1760, Florida had approximately 3,000 Hispanic settlers, Texas had 1,200, and New Mexico about 9,000, while Louisiana counted 4,000 whites and 5,000 enslaved Africans.

Governor James Oglethorpe of Georgia tried to use the outbreak of the War of Jenkins' Ear to eject the Spanish from Florida. As part of the 1713 Treaty of Utrecht, Britain had obtained the right to sell a specified number of African slaves and commodities to the Spanish provinces. This opening led to British smuggling, which the Spanish countered with heavy-handed searches of British ships. Accounts of Spanish brutality inflamed the British public, especially when Captain Robert Jenkins displayed one of his ears, which he claimed the Spanish cut off when they caught him smuggling. In 1740, Oglethorpe attacked Florida with seven ships and 2,000 troops. They captured several Spanish forts and Mose, the village of escaped Carolina blacks, but failed to conquer Fort San Marcos, where the residents of St. Augustine and Mose took cover. When Hispanic and black soldiers slipped out of the fort and recaptured Mose, and then the fort was resupplied by Cuba, Oglethorpe retreated.

In 1741, a force of 3,600 colonists participated in the British expedition against the Spanish fort at Cartagena, in what is now Colombia. The campaign ended bitterly, with heavy losses from battle and smallpox. The following year, the Spanish took revenge for the invasion of Florida by attacking St. Simon's Island, Georgia, but withdrew before conquering it. After some minor skirmishes, both sides gave up, bringing calm to the Georgia-Florida border.

King George's War

The British avoided further conflict with Florida because in 1744, they began hostilities with France in the War of the Austrian Succession, known to the colonists as King George's War. The war began in Europe, but spilled into North America when, provoked by French attacks on Nova Scotia, Governor William Shirley of Massachusetts organized an offensive against the French fort at Louisbourg, which controlled access to the St. Lawrence River. In April 1745, 4,000 New England farmers and fishermen assaulted Louisbourg. The French garrison held out against the badly organized offensive until June, then surrendered. The war then degenerated into a series of debilitating border raids. The Canadians and their Indian allies ravaged Saratoga, New York, and northern New England. In spring 1746, a fleet of seventy-six ships left France to retake Louisbourg, but after fighting disease and Atlantic storms for three months they returned to France empty-handed.

Despite this reprieve, New Englanders had little to celebrate, for they faced another threat—from their own imperial navy. During the war, Parliament permitted naval officers to impress sailors without the permission of colonial authorities. The Royal Navy used impressment, or involuntary recruitment, because many seamen fled the harsh conditions on naval vessels. In 1747, several thousand Bostonians protested when a British press gang from the fleet of Admiral Charles Knowles swept up men along the waterfront. The mob surrounded the governor's house and burned a British barge in his courtyard. When the governor called up the militia, the troops refused to move. Knowles threatened to shell the town, but after negotiations lasting several days, he released the impressed men instead.

As the colonists became more involved in imperial politics, they learned that their interests held little sway. To their shock, the British government restored Louisbourg to the French in the Treaty of Aix-la-Chapelle (1748), as the combatants agreed to return all North American territories seized during the war. Despite heavy human and financial costs, the war brought no change in the power balance between Great Britain and France in North America.

Native American Worlds in the Mid-Eighteenth Century

The peace of 1748 did not end conflict between the European colonists and Native Americans.

With bulging population growth and immigration, the British settlements pushed into the Appalachians, forcing Native Americans once again to rearrange their lives.

Some Indian survivors of earlier struggles remained within the British provinces. They worked as servants, slaves, day laborers, artisans, and tenant farmers, assimilating some parts of English culture. Some continued to hunt, peddling venison and turkeys to the colonists. Dr. Alexander Hamilton, a recent immigrant from Scotland, recorded many encounters with Indians in 1744 as he traveled through the settlements from Maryland to Maine. The Native Americans he met varied greatly in status, from an Indian sachem who had established himself as a wealthy planter, to those on the margins, who tried to hold on to native traditions within an alien culture.

During worship in a Boston church, Hamilton sat near several Native Americans. But he also met natives who retained at least some of their customs. In New York, Hamilton watched "about ten Indians fishing for oysters . . . stark naked" near his tavern. Although most Indians who stayed in white settled areas had given up political autonomy, they had not surrendered all of their traditions. Many spoke English in addition to their native language, but did not learn to read and write. The Great Awakening converted many settlement Indians who had long resisted Christianity. The dynamic preaching of New Light ministers was attractive to Native Americans who had retained traditional rituals and dance.

Many Indians tried to preserve their political independence by moving west. From 1660 to the 1740s, for example, Iroquois, Shawnees, and Delawares moved into the eastern part of the Ohio Valley. Wyandots inhabited the lands to the west, at Sandusky and near the French fort at Detroit. Some of the Delawares migrated as a result of the "Walking Purchase" of 1737, when two of William Penn's sons, the proprietors, used an alleged 1686 deed to cheat the Indians out of their last stronghold on the Pennsylvania side of the Delaware River. The deed, of which only a copy survived, ceded lands as far as a man could walk in one and a half days. Coerced by an alliance between the Penns and the Iroquois, the Delawares agreed to comply. The Penns sent runners to cover more than sixty miles in a day and a half, a deception the Delawares could not fail to remember; with the outbreak of war in 1754, they sought revenge.

The Ohio Valley became the focus of conflict in the 1740s as the British and French competed for trade. The valley, as one Indian leader said, was "a country in between" the English and the French. From 1754 to 1814, the Native Americans fought the British and Americans to keep their lands and native religions, forging pan-Indian alliances to meet the Anglo threat.

The French and Indian War

During King George's War, the British and Iroquois had evicted French traders from the Ohio Valley. The Canadians returned, however, backed by a government that was determined to force out the British. The French built forts to stop the incursion of Anglo-American traders and to block Virginia's claim to the territory, which dated from its charter. In 1754, after the British government granted half a million acres to the Ohio Company, the Virginia governor sent a young militia officer, George Washington, with 160 troops to expel the French. The Virginians were defeated at Fort Necessity by a superior force of French and Indians.

Recognizing that war was imminent, seven colonies sent delegates to a congress at Albany, New York, where they negotiated unsuccessfully with the Iroquois for an alliance against the French. The Albany Congress also supported a plan devised by Benjamin Franklin to unite the colonies for common defense. When the delegates returned home with the proposal for an intercolonial government empowered to tax, pass laws, and supervise military defense, not one of the assemblies approved.

The British decided to destroy French forts in what they considered their territory. In early

1755, Major General Edward Braddock landed in the colonies with two British regiments. Joined by hundreds of provincial soldiers, the army of 1,400 marched through the Virginia backcountry to capture Fort Duquesne, the French outpost near the site of present-day Pittsburgh. Ten miles short of the fort, however, the French and allied Indians ambushed Braddock's army, killing or wounding two-thirds of the British force. The general himself lay dead. George Washington, his uniform ripped by bullets, led the retreat.

The 650 Native Americans who fought with the French included their traditional allies and some Delawares and Iroquois of the Ohio Valley who had previously supported the British. By 1754, some Ohio Indians were convinced that Britain and its colonies posed the greatest threat to their lands; with the defeat of Braddock, many more joined the French. Between 1755 and 1757, Delawares, Shawnees, Iroquois, and many others attacked the white frontier from Pennsylvania to Virginia, burning settlements and killing or capturing thousands of colonists.

Help for the westerners was slow in coming. In 1756, the struggle in North America became part of the larger European conflict known as the Seven Years' War, in which Great Britain supported Prussia against Austria, Russia, and France. Through 1757 and half of 1758, in America, the British and provincials lost one battle after another. The French penetrated into New York, seizing Fort William Henry and 2,000 soldiers at Lake George. The tide changed after the British statesman William Pitt took command of the war effort. He poured money and men into the American theater. The new generals Jeffery Amherst and James Wolfe, with an army of almost 10,000 men, captured Louisbourg in July 1758. The French then pulled their troops out of the Ohio Valley to protect Quebec and Montreal, allowing the British to take control of the west. Without French supplies and devastated by smallpox, the Native Americans ended their war on the frontier.

In 1759, the British and provincial armies had even greater success, leading some of the Iroquois of New York to abandon neutrality to join their side. The British reestablished control of New York, while from Louisbourg, General Wolfe sailed up the St. Lawrence to Quebec, where after several months he finally pierced the defenses of the well-fortified city. The next year, Amherst's army seized Montreal, thus ending French control of Canada.

During the French and Indian War, thousands of colonists joined the British army, and many more served in the provincial forces. The experience brought ordinary settlers into close contact with the imperial authorities. The British army contained professional soldiers drilled rigorously in military tactics, cleanliness, and order. British officers, from the upper classes, maintained discipline with punishments of death for major offenses such as desertion, and up to 1,000 lashes—which could also kill—for lesser crimes. The British officers disdained the colonial units, which submitted to much lighter discipline and sometimes elected their superiors. Because the provincials failed to keep their camps and clothing clean, many died from disease. For their part, many colonial soldiers thought the British regulars were immoral, profane men who needed to be controlled with brutal discipline.

The British colonists welcomed the Treaty of Paris in 1763, which finally ended the war. Under the treaty, France lost all of its territory in North America. Spain relinquished Florida to get back Cuba and the Philippines and acquired French territory west of the Mississippi and New Orleans, located on the east side of the river. The Treaty of Paris gave the British colonists security from France and Spain, whereas the home government received two unprofitable colonies, Canada and Florida. The provincials celebrated the victory with patriotic fervor. Many viewed it as a sign that God favored Britain and its colonies.

The Indians Renew War in the Ohio Valley

For Native Americans, the Treaty of Paris was a disaster. The agreement ended the conflict among

European powers, but not for them. Indeed, the defeat of France worsened their situation in the Ohio Valley, for they could no longer play one European nation off the other. East of the Mississippi, the British alone supplied European goods, so they could set prices and the terms of trade. Further, with the end of the French and Indian War, white settlers streamed west into Indian lands, as wealthy land speculators and poor squatters alike ignored treaties that colonial governments had made with the Native Americans.

Chief Pontiac, *by Jerry Farnsworth. When whites streamed west at the end of the Seven Years' War, Indians allied under Pontiac's leadership to attack British forts and settlements in the Ohio Valley and Great Lakes region.* (Courtesy of the National Museum of the American Indian, Smithsonian Institution)

The altered British trade policies and land grabbing drove many Delawares, Shawnees, Iroquois, and others to renew the fighting. They gained spiritual unity from the Delaware prophet Neolin, who preached that Indians must reject Christianity and European goods, particularly rum, and revitalize their ancient culture. Neolin called on Native Americans to drive the Europeans out. He warned his followers, "if you suffer the English among you, you are dead men. Sickness, smallpox, and their poison will destroy you entirely."

Many Indians throughout the Ohio Valley adopted Neolin's strategy, boycotting the fur trade by hunting only for their own food and personal needs. In 1763, Indians from western Pennsylvania through the Great Lakes region launched a pan-Indian assault on British garrisons, often called Pontiac's War. A follower of Neolin and leader of the Ottawas, Pontiac laid siege unsuccessfully to the British fort at Detroit. Other Indians defeated thirteen British outposts. Although the British army established military dominance in the Ohio Valley by the end of 1763, after the Native Americans ran short of ammunition and succumbed to smallpox, fighting continued for two more years.

In addition to armed force, the British government tried to end the war by keeping white settlers out of the Ohio Valley. The king issued the Proclamation of 1763, which drew a line along the crest of the Appalachian Mountains from Maine to Georgia, requiring colonists to move east of the line. Colonial governors were instructed to prohibit surveys or land grants west of the Proclamation line; only authorized agents of the Crown could buy lands from the Indians. The proclamation failed in its purpose, however, as land speculators continued their operations and immigrants demanded farms. The British government failed to supply manpower to enforce the law. The government withdrew troops from the Ohio Valley and Great Lakes region, while provincial governments ignored encroachment on Indian lands.

The British Provinces in 1763

The end of the French and Indian War brought pivotal changes in British North America. For over a century and a half, Europeans had crossed the ocean to trade with the Native Americans, build farms and businesses, and develop networks of Atlantic commerce. The colonies had dealt with crises, from economic slumps to rebellions, becoming ever more confident of their position as semi-independent societies. During the last quarter century, with greater involvement in imperial affairs and rising importation of consumer goods, the provincials felt more a part of the British empire—more English—even as they created a separate identity as Americans. Most importantly, they believed that they were equal to the residents of Great Britain, that they possessed the rights of English people.

The Economy

In 1763, the mainland provinces still operated within the system of British mercantilism, which consisted of regulations on colonial trade and manufactures. For mercantilism to work to Britain's benefit, the colonies had to produce raw materials and agricultural staples needed by the home economy and serve as a market for its manufactured goods. Such colonial products as sugar, molasses, tobacco, cotton, certain wood products, copper, and furs were "enumerated," meaning that they could be shipped only to Britain or British colonial ports, not to foreign countries such as France and Spain. The basic laws establishing the British mercantilist system were the seventeenth-century Navigation Acts, which Parliament supplemented from time to time. Though most colonial trade conformed to the law by the eighteenth century, smuggling occurred often. Colonial shippers bribed customs officials to ignore the Molasses Act (1733), which levied prohibitive duties on foreign sugar products. If the Molasses Act had been enforced, it would have severely damaged the economies of New England and the Middle Colonies, who traded with the French, Spanish, and Dutch West Indies as well as the British islands.

Other laws passed by Parliament prior to 1763 had a significant but uneven impact on colonial economic growth. The Woolen Act (1699) and the Hat Act (1732) banned the export of American-produced woolen products and hats from one colony to another. The Iron Act (1750) allowed duty-free import of colonial bar iron into Britain, but forbade fabrication of iron goods in the colonies. Nevertheless, crude iron production received substantial investment, as did shipbuilding and rum distilling.

Despite these laws, the wealth of the British colonies increased between the 1720s and 1760, as trade flourished with the West Indies and, after 1750, with southern Europe. The Middle Colonies were well situated to supply new markets. Philadelphia became the largest city in the British colonies: its wealthy merchants invested in ships, built mansions, purchased coaches and other luxuries, and speculated in western lands from the profits of trade. Artisans, shopkeepers, and farmers prospered. To the south, large planters in the Chesapeake and Carolinas accumulated great estates, while ordinary farmers more modestly improved their standard of living. All along the eastern seaboard, after 1750, white families indulged in what has been called a "consumer revolution." Not only could they purchase cloth, clothing, carpets, paper, gloves, mirrors, clocks, silverware, china tea sets, pottery, and books, but they had more choices in the specific kind of cloth or paper or gloves they could buy. In New York City in the 1750s, for instance, merchants advertised gloves of various colors—purple, orange, white, and flowered—as well as different sizes and materials.

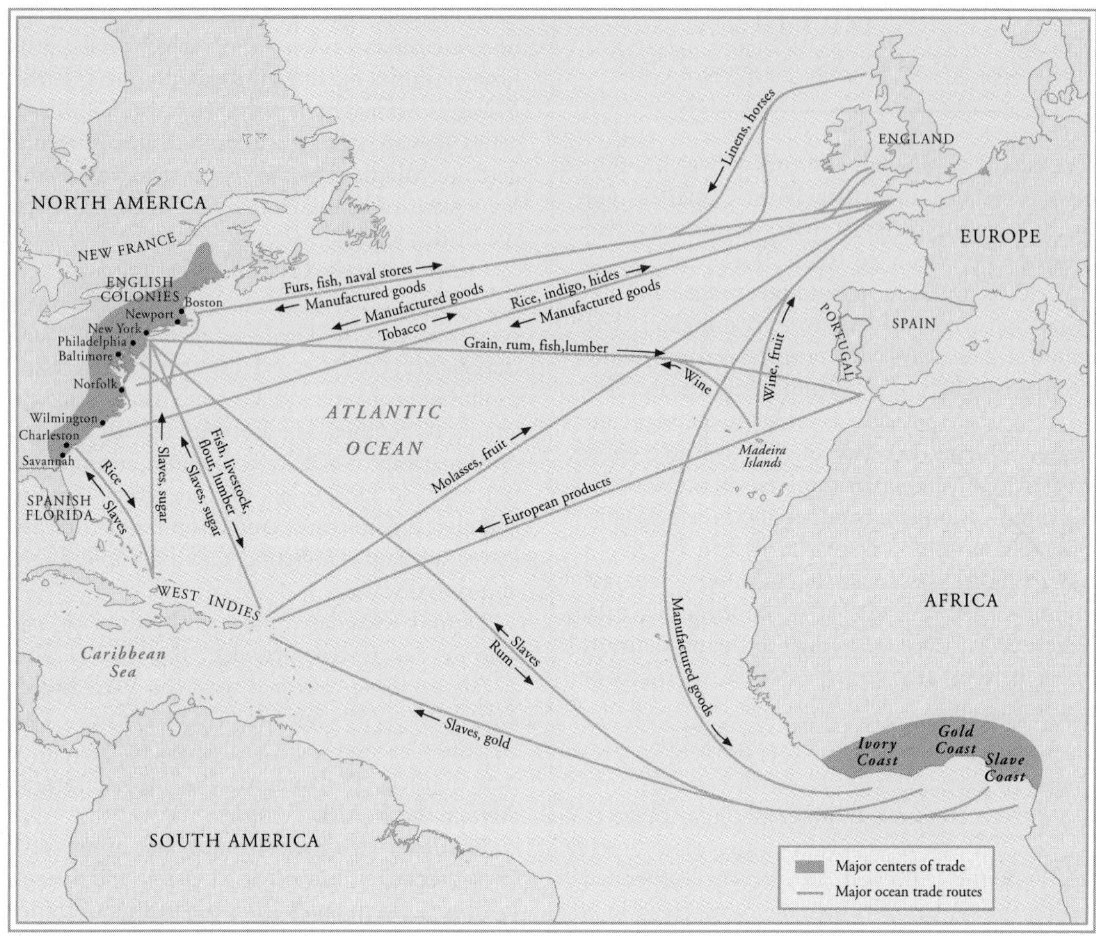

Map 4.3 | Colonial Overseas Trade

The colonies became major markets for textiles, metalware, and other items, which under the Navigation Acts they could import only from Britain. The consumer revolution made the British more attentive to their North American provinces, while at the same time, the imports helped to create in America a more standardized English culture.

The economic upswing of the 1750s gave way to a depression after 1760, as the Seven Years' War moved to the Caribbean and military spending dropped. The seaport towns, having attracted workers during the wartime boom, faced deepening poverty and rising demands for relief. With depressed wages and long periods of unemployment, families found survival difficult. The resumption of immigration from Europe after the war intensified economic hardships and contributed to unrest on the frontier.

Politics

In late 1763, after months of Indian attacks in the Ohio country, a band of western Scots-Irish Pennsylvanians used violence to force the

Quaker-dominated assembly to provide military protection. The "Paxton Boys" of Lancaster County murdered a number of Christian Indians at Conestoga, then marched on Philadelphia. By the time the rebels reached the capital, the legislature had passed a bill raising 1,000 troops to defend the frontier. The westerners returned home without attacking the city. At the heart of their revolt was the belief that they were poorly represented in the provincial government. As the backcountry population exploded, eastern politicians guarded their power by allotting fewer assembly seats to outlying counties than they deserved.

The Paxton Boys revolt signaled the end of an era of political stability, which had prevailed since the late 1720s in the British mainland provinces. As part of Britain's empire, the eighteenth-century colonists believed themselves among the most fortunate people on earth. The Glorious Revolution of 1688–1689, which removed James II, had ended the long, bitter contest between king and Parliament. The monarch's power was subsequently limited by the national legislature, comprised of the House of Lords, which represented the aristocracy, and the House of Commons, which in theory represented everyone else. As a result of the 1689 settlement, Parliament's consent was necessary for taxes, new courts, raising an army in peacetime, and foreign invasions. The balance of powers, political theorists argued, prevented domination by a single segment of society, the monarch, aristocracy, or common people. In their provincial governments, the British colonists expected to find a similar balance, one that would protect their rights. Indeed, the prevailing structure of governor, appointed council, and elected lower house of assembly reflected the English model. The British provinces were the only European settlements in North America where ordinary people had representative legislatures. Further, an estimated 50 to 75 percent of white men were qualified to vote in the British colonies. According to English political theory, a person needed a "stake in society," a certain amount of property, to vote or hold office. Servants, slaves, children, and unpropertied men were beholden to someone else, so could not make independent decisions. Giving them suffrage would award their owner, father, or employer another vote, the theorists claimed. By tradition, women also lacked the franchise, whether or not they owned property or were married. Denial of the vote to all females arose from the general belief that they were intellectually and morally inferior to men and thus should have no formal role in government.

Beyond suffrage, English political theory also recognized the right of common people to resort to crowd action to withstand tyranny and require authorities to protect them from harm. At various times, colonial mobs protested to prevent grain from being exported when food was in short supply, destroy houses of prostitution, and stop the British navy from impressing men into the king's service.

King George III, at the time of his coronation in 1760, by Allan Ramsay. (Colonial Williamsburg Foundation)

The most important and sustained political development in British America during the first half of the eighteenth century was the rise of the elected lower houses of assembly. The legislatures acquired greater power and assumed more functions, most significantly, the right to initiate bills to raise taxes and disburse public funds—the "power of the purse." They also gained the authority to initiate other legislation, choose their own leadership, and settle disputed elections.

The political stability and rise of the assemblies that marked the mid-eighteenth century resulted from a number of factors, including the long period of economic growth that began in the 1720s. Prosperity supported the formation of cohesive elites. They formed a class of skilled politicians. Economic prosperity inclined ordinary whites to defer to the elites as long as opportunity was good and they had crops to tend or other work to do. Their deference to social and economic superiors became most visible after 1725, when participation at the polls declined among eligible voters, and incumbent assemblymen won re-election year after year.

The provincial elites also benefited after 1720 from the British decision to administer the colonies with a light touch, allowing royal governors to accommodate the assemblies. And while riots occurred during the 1740s and 1750s over land claims and impressment, none threatened social disorder on the level of the seventeenth-century rebellions. Indeed, most ordinary whites feared attacks by Native Americans and slave revolts more than misuse of governmental power by elites.

CONCLUSION

By the end of 1763, the British colonists of North America had reason to be optimistic about their future. After a quarter century of war, they celebrated the withdrawal of Spain and France east of the Mississippi, and looked forward to peace and semi-autonomy within the empire. Free colonists appreciated the benefits of being British—their liberties and right to participate in government as well as access to advanced learning and consumer goods. At the same time, the Americans were creating societies quite different from the English, with greater ethnic and religious diversity, dependence on enslaved labor, and wider opportunity to acquire land (even if it meant pushing out the Indians). After 1763, the London government shocked the American colonists with its effort to rein in the empire. In turn, the British were unprepared for the coordinated fury with which the thirteen mainland provinces greeted their "reforms."

RECOMMENDED READINGS

Anderson, Fred. *A People's Army: Massachusetts Soldiers and Society in the Seven Years' War* (1984). An influential study of the origins and motives of ordinary soldiers.

Bailyn, Bernard, and Morgan, Philip D., eds. *Strangers Within the Realm: Cultural Margins of the First British Empire* (1991). Important essays on specific groups, including Native Americans, Scots-Irish, African Americans, Germans, and Dutch.

Carson, Cary, et al., eds. *Of Consuming Interests: The Style of Life in the Eighteenth Century* (1994). Excellent essays on topics ranging from housing and art to consumer behavior.

Isaac, Rhys. *The Transformation of Virginia, 1740–1790* (1982). Uses anthropological methods to explore cultural and political change in eighteenth-century Virginia.

Jedrey, Christopher M. *The World of John Cleaveland: Family and Community in Eighteenth-Century New England* (1979). Shows continuity of family strategies over the colonial period.

Merrell, James H. *The Indians' New World: Catawbas and Their Neighbors from European Contact Through the Era of Removal* (1989). Shows how South Carolina Indians created a new nation and identity in the wake of European settlement.

Morgan, Philip D. *Slave Counterpoint: Black Culture in the Eighteenth-Century Chesapeake and Lowcountry* (1998). A comprehensive study of African American work and culture in the South.

Steele, Ian K. *Warpaths: Invasions of North America* (1994). Examines the Seven Years' War as one of a series of European invasions of Indian territory during the colonial period.

Ulrich, Laurel Thatcher. *A Midwife's Tale: The Life of Martha Ballard, Based on Her Diary, 1785–1812* (1990). The prize-winning account of a Maine midwife within the context of eighteenth-century society.

American Journey Online and InfoTrac College Edition

Visit the source collections at www.americanjourney.psmedia.com and infotrac.thomsonlearning.com and use the Search function with the following key terms to explore documents, images, audio and video clips, articles, and commentary related to the material in this chapter.

Benjamin Franklin
Great Awakening
French and Indian War
Seven Years' War
Proclamation of 1763

PASSAGES

—1764 TO 1814—

DURING the American Revolution, sixteen-year-old Dicey Langston of the South Carolina frontier left home in the middle of the night, by herself, to warn her brother's unit about tory troop movements. As a historian later described Langston's journey,

> Many miles were to be traversed, and the road lay through woods, and crossed marshes and creeks where the conveniences of bridges and foot-logs were wanting. She walked rapidly on, heedless of slight difficulties; but her heart almost failed her when she came to the banks of the Tyger—a deep and rapid stream, rendered more dangerous by the rains that had lately fallen. . . . But the energy of a resolute will, under the care of Providence, sustained her.*

Dicey Langston's effort, like those of thousands of Americans, was emblematic of her country's passage from a collection of British provinces in 1764, to a stable republic with some international standing a half century later. The thirteen mainland colonies, proud of their contribution to victory in the French and Indian War, were stunned by Britain's program to curtail their rights. Stretching from the mountains of northern New England to the rice fields of coastal Georgia, diverse in economics, religion, ethnicity, and politics, they mustered enough unity to organize a revolutionary Congress, stop British imports, raise an army, obtain help from France, and win the war.

The states refused to create a unified nation, however, and instead established, under the Articles of Confederation, thirteen separate republics joined loosely by a representative Congress. Without power to tax or raise troops, the Congress faced severe postwar problems in demobilizing the army, paying the war debt, protecting the frontiers, and unifying a populace divided by war. In the wake of bankruptcy and insurrection in 1787, nationalists called together a constitutional convention. Through a series of compromises, the framers drafted the new Constitution, which gave more authority to the central government yet retained considerable power in the states.

After the first national elections, the Constitution's proponents, the Federalists, controlled the new government, with George Washington as president. Having agreed upon the frame of government, they were unprepared for the bitter factionalism that forged political parties in the 1790s. Nor were they ready for the foreign entanglements that resulted from two decades of war between Great Britain and post-revolutionary France. Only after the United States declared war on the British in 1812 and held its own as the conflict ended in a stalemate, did the nation finally demonstrate its independence. By 1814, most of the men who led the American Revolution had passed from power—though James Madison would remain president for several years—and a new generation was taking control.

The heroic story of the young nation surmounting difficulties—two wars against Great Britain, a constitutional crisis, several internal rebellions, an undeclared conflict with France, and constant fighting on the frontier—masks other

*Elizabeth F. Ellet, *Domestic History of the American Revolution* (1850), p. 234.

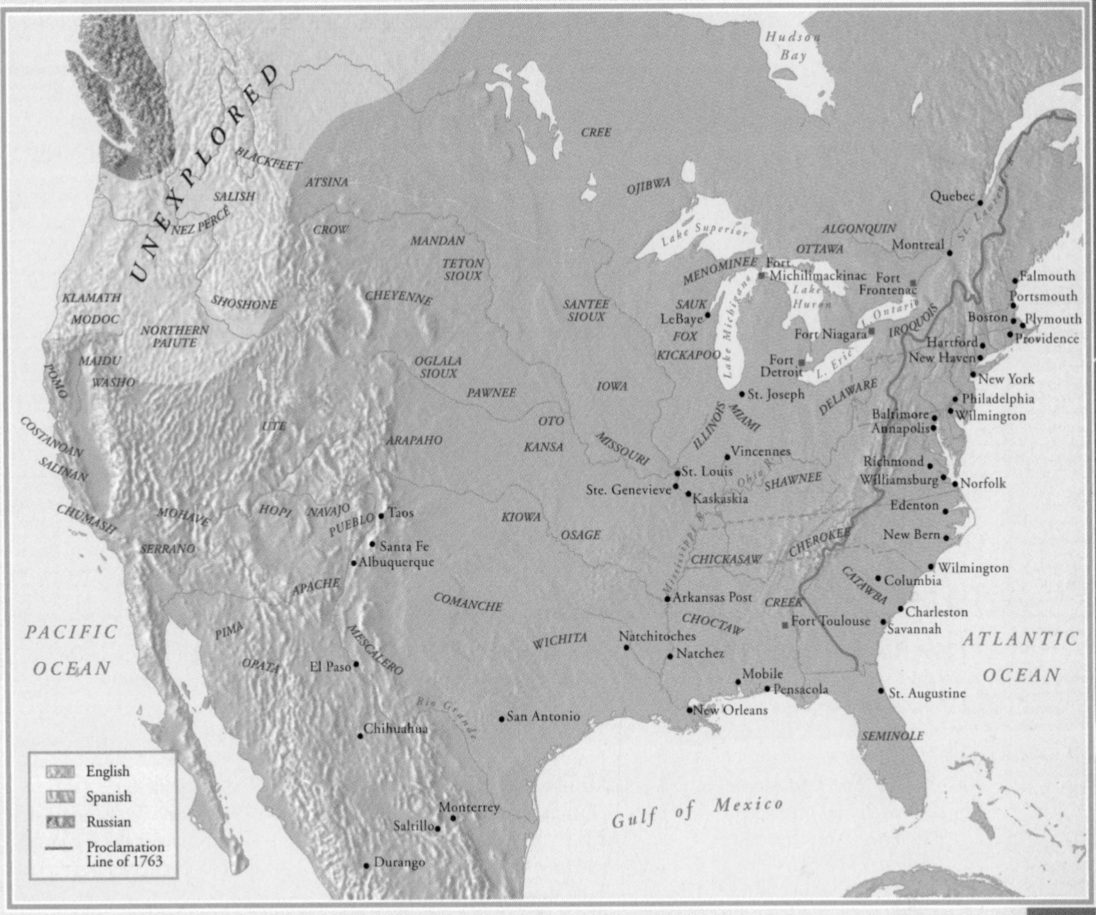

North America in 1764

narratives, those of women, African Americans, and Native Americans, who failed to achieve autonomy. Though Dicey Langston was just one of thousands of sisters, mothers, and wives who risked their lives during the Revolution, women still lacked basic legal and political rights to hold property after marriage, vote, and take part in government. And while revolutionary rhetoric against slavery resulted in abolition in the north, most African Americans remained enslaved, a condition perpetuated by the new Constitution and development of cotton.

For Native Americans, the success and growth of the new nation meant their decline. Despite revitalization movements to restore traditional cultures led by Neolin, Handsome Lake, and others, and destructive wars to defend their homelands in Alabama, Tennessee, Kentucky, and Ohio, by 1814 the United States dominated most of the territory east of the Mississippi River. Native Americans tried various routes to survive and retain as much of their autonomy as possible—adoption of white culture, alliances with Great Britain and Spain, and pan-Indian war. In the face of unremitting westward settlement and continuing disease, the Indian peoples of eastern North America became remnants of formerly powerful nations.

For additional information and resources pertaining to this period in American History, please visit the American Passages Web Site at:

www http://ayersbrief.wadsworth.com

	1764	1775	1780	1785	1790

POLITICS & DIPLOMACY

1765: Stamp Act protest
1766–1771: Regulator movements in North and South Carolina
1767: John Dickinson's "Farmer" letters against Townshend Act
1768: Non-importation movement
1769: Spanish colonize California
1770: Boston Massacre
1772: Committees of Correspondence
1773: Boston Tea Party
1774: Coercive Acts; port of Boston closed
First Continental Congress
1775: Battles of Lexington and Concord
Lord Dunmore's proclamation to servants and slaves

1776: Thomas Paine's *Common Sense*
Declaration of Independence
1777: Burgoyne surrenders to Americans at Saratoga
1778: Alliance with France
Iroquois attacks in New York and Pennsylvania
1780: Pennsylvania law for gradual abolition of slavery
1781: Articles of Confederation ratified
Surrender of Cornwallis at Yorktown
1783: Treaty of Paris

1787: Shaysites attack Springfield, Massachusetts, arsenal
Northwest Ordinance
Constitution sent to states for ratification
1789: Inauguration of President George Washington
1791: Bill of Rights ratified
1794: Whiskey Rebellion

SOCIAL & CULTURAL EVENTS

1765: First American medical school
1766: Queens College (Rutgers)
New Southwark Theatre in Philadelphia
1769: *The American Magazine* (Philadelphia) published
Benjamin West's *Death of General Wolfe*
American scientists observe transit of Venus
1770: Equestrian statue of George III installed in New York
1771: Benjamin Franklin starts *Autobiography*
c. 1772: John Singleton Copley's portrait of Samuel Adams
1773: Phillis Wheatley's *Poems on Various Subjects, Religious and Moral*

1776: Jemima Wilkinson becomes Public Universal Friend
1779: John Murray's American Universalist Church
1780s: Northern black separate churches and societies
1783: Noah Webster's American spelling book
First daily newspaper, *Pennsylvania Evening Post*
1784: Judith Sargent Murray begins essays on women's status

1786: Virginia statute for religious liberty
Gilbert Stuart's portrait of Joseph Brant
1791: Charles Willson Peale's *Thomas Jefferson*
c. 1793: Mary Wollstonecraft's *Vindication of the Rights of Women* circulates in the U.S.

ECONOMICS & TECHNOLOGY

1760s: British American traders cross Mississippi River
1764: Sugar and Currency Acts
1776: Adam Smith's *An Inquiry into the Nature and Causes of the Wealth of Nations*
1778: Captain James Cook explores the Pacific Northwest
1779: Continental money becomes nearly worthless

1780s: Rapid settlement of Kentucky and Tennessee
Oliver Evans automates grist mills
1781: Bank of North America in Philadelphia
1783: Great Britain closes West Indies to American ships
1784: Spain closes port of New Orleans to Americans
Debt crisis spurs protests in U.S.

1788: Pennsylvania Society for the Encouragement of Manufactures and the Useful Arts introduces spinning jennies
1790: Samuel Slater builds first U.S. water-powered textile mill
Congress passes patent law
1791: Bank of the United States
Excise tax on whiskey
Alexander Hamilton's plan for promoting manufactures
1793: British blockade of French West Indies
Eli Whitney's cotton gin

1795 | 1800 | 1810 | 1814

1795: Jay Treaty
1798: Allen and Sedition Acts Quasi-war with France
1799: Fries Rebellion

1800: Washington, D.C., becomes national capital
Gabriel's Rebellion
Jefferson elected President
1803: *Marbury v. Madison* case
Louisiana Purchase
1804: Lewis and Clark expedition
1809: Tecumseh organizes pan-Indian confederacy

1812: U.S. war with Great Britain
1814: Treaty of Ghent

1795: Philadelphia Quaker women establish first female benevolent society in U.S.
1797: Second Great Awakening begins in New England
1799: Rise of Handsome Lake as Seneca prophet
Charles Brockden Brown's *Wieland*

1800s: Tenskwatawa, the Shawnee Prophet, inspires following
1800: Library of Congress
1801: Cane Ridge, Kentucky, camp meeting
1805: Pennsylvania Academy of Fine Arts

1795: Great Britain opens West Indies to U.S. trade
1796: Spain opens navigation on Mississippi River
Alexander Hamilton's industrial town in New Jersey fails
1798: Eli Whitney attempts to manufacture guns with interchangeable parts
1790s: U.S. international trade soars with European conflict
Cotton expands Southern slavery
Northern cities become magnets for African Americans

1802: Oliver Evans' high pressure steam engine
1806: Non-Importation Act
1807: Embargo Act
1808: Federal ban on international slave trade
1809: Giles' Enforcement Act
Embargo repealed; replaced with Non-Intercourse Act

1811: Charter of national bank expires

Chapter 5

Wars for Independence, 1764–1783

THE TREATY OF 1763, forced Spain and Great Britain to reassess their North American colonies. For the Spanish, the borderlands in North America were of secondary importance, serving as a buffer to protect the Mexican silver mines. For Britain, however, the mainland provinces had become increasingly significant as a source of revenue and market for consumer goods.

The Seven Years' War marked Britain's ascendancy to world power, but resulted in a national debt of £130 million. When Parliament imposed levies on the American colonies to help pay expenses, the colonists protested vehemently that they should not be taxed without their consent. Beginning in 1764, the Americans petitioned, rioted, and boycotted British goods. The colonists' belief that they possessed the same rights as the English was something for which many were willing to fight.

Nevertheless, the consensus to declare independence did not come quickly. Americans who disagreed that the British actions warranted insurrection remained loyal to the king. These loyalists, also called tories, tried to subvert the revolutionary governments and formed loyalist militia units to fight alongside British troops. Other colonists remained neutral, whether from principled opposition to violence or from sheer indifference. The Revolution touched everyone, Native Americans, women, and enslaved blacks, as well as the white men who served as military and civilian leaders and comprised most of the armed forces. The cause of the patriots—or whigs, as the American revolutionaries called themselves—depended upon the efforts of many people, those who supplied and supported the troops, as well as those who fought.

Realignments in the Spanish Borderlands

The peace of 1763 required Spain to withdraw from Florida, assume the government of Louisiana, and rethink its defenses in Texas and New Mexico. With Britain's enhanced power, safeguarding the Mexican silver mines took high priority. The Spanish also considered the soaring population of the British colonies a threat to their American empire.

CHRONOLOGY

1764 Sugar and Currency Acts

St. Louis founded

1765 Stamp Act provokes widespread colonial protest

Stamp Act Congress

1766 Parliament repeals Stamp Act, passes Declaratory Act

Spanish governor arrives in Louisiana

1766–1771 North Carolina Regulator movement

1767 Passage of Townshend Act

John Dickinson publishes "Farmer" letters

1767–1769 South Carolina Regulator movement

1768 Massachusetts assembly sends "circular letter"

Non-importation movement against Townshend duties

British troops stationed in Boston

Louisianans expel Spanish governor

1769 Spanish reestablish control of Louisiana

1770 Boston Massacre

Partial repeal of Townshend Act

1772 Burning of *Gaspée*

1772–1773 Committees of Correspondence established

1773 Boston Tea Party

1774 Passage of Coercive Acts; port of Boston closed

Quebec Act

First Continental Congress

Congress organizes Continental Association

1775 Battles of Lexington and Concord

Second Continental Congress

Battle of Bunker Hill

Congress authorizes invasion of Canada

Lord Dunmore's proclamation to servants and slaves

1776 Thomas Paine publishes *Common Sense*

British evacuation of Boston

Declaration of Independence

Cherokee War on the southern frontier

Americans defeated on Long Island; British occupation of New York City

Battle of Trenton

1777 Battle of Princeton

British occupy Philadelphia after defeating Washington at Brandywine

Battle of Germantown

Burgoyne surrenders to Americans at Saratoga

Congress approves Articles of Confederation; sends document to states for ratification

1778 Alliance with France

Iroquois and loyalist attacks in New York and Pennsylvania

British withdraw from Philadelphia

Whig frontiersmen take settlements in the Illinois country

British invade Georgia

1780 Americans surrender at Charleston

Battle of Camden

1781 Battle of Cowpens

Articles of Confederation ratified

Battle of Guilford Courthouse

Southern army reconquers most of South Carolina and Georgia

Surrender of Cornwallis at Yorktown

1782 Massacre at Gnadenhutten

1783 Signing of Treaty of Paris

Florida and Louisiana

Spain ordered all of its subjects to leave Florida when Britain took control. Though the British promised religious freedom to the Catholic Floridians, some 200 Christian Indians, 79 free African Americans, 350 slaves, and nearly all of the 3,000 Hispanics departed. They sold their property at a loss to British bargain hunters. The free blacks of Mose, near St. Augustine, could expect enslavement by the English, so took Spain's offer of homesteads in Cuba. They received some tools and money from the government, but never received adequate compensation for their property in Florida.

Acquisition of Louisiana, including all French territory west of the Mississippi River and New Orleans, on the east bank, gave Spain an extensive region to administer. Spain needed to win the loyalties of French inhabitants and Native Americans, and hoped to keep the British colonists out. The concern about British expansion became all too real as interlopers spanned the Mississippi River to trade with Indians on the Great Plains. British colonists moved quickly to the Gulf Coast and eastern shore of the Mississippi, where, within a decade, 4,000 whites and 1,500 African American slaves were living.

The more immediate challenge for Spanish authorities in Louisiana, however, was asserting political control of the province. For several years, French government remained; even after the first Spanish governor, Antonio de Ulloa, arrived in 1766, he tried to govern jointly with the last French governor. Ulloa left the French administration and legal system intact, even allowing the French flag to fly over the capital.

Ulloa did not extend this leniency to commerce, however. He tried to stop business with France and Great Britain and restricted the Native American trade to certain dealers. New Orleans merchants feared loss of markets and lower prices for their tobacco, indigo, sugar, deerskins, and lumber. They protested the new restrictions, then in October 1768 issued a declaration of loyalty to the king of France. With few Spanish troops at his disposal, Governor Ulloa left for Cuba. When the French refused to intervene, the colony became independent, but only for a year.

The Spanish regained Louisiana when General Alexander O'Reilly arrived in 1769 with more than 2,000 soldiers. An Irishman with a successful career in the Spanish army, O'Reilly arrested the rebels, put five of them to death, but pardoned most who had participated in the uprising. He raised the Spanish flag and within a year ended French government, changed the legal system, made Castilian the official language, and outlawed trade with other nations. Despite the merchants' fears, the economy flourished. St. Louis, established in 1764, became the thriving center of trade for beaver, buffalo, and deerskins. Louisiana remained culturally French, as the numbers of French settlers far surpassed the Spanish.

Fortifying the Southwest

By the 1760s, the most immediate danger in Texas and New Mexico came from the Apaches and Comanches, who defended their freedom from Hispanic slave catchers and attempted to drive the Spanish back into Mexico. Skillfully adopting the European horse and gun, they refused to submit to Spanish rule or Christianity. Spain gave up trying to convert them through missions, emphasizing military defense instead. The Apaches and Comanches raided settlements and pack trains, stole horses, mules, cattle, and supplies, killing Pueblos and white settlers alike.

During the 1760s and 1770s, in the face of constant Indian assaults, Spain tried to reform administration and improve defense. From 1766 to 1768, the Marqués de Rubí, a high-level military official from Spain, inspected the fortifications and missions of the southwest. He discovered badly located presidios (or forts) and soldiers suffering from lack of food and clothes. He recommended building new presidios and relocating others to create an orderly cordon of military bases situated about a hundred miles apart. The presidios would extend from the Gulf of California to the Gulf of Mexico, along a line that was close to the present boundary between the United States and Mexico. Small numbers of Spanish troops would hold garrisons at Santa Fe and San Antonio, north of the cordon, to help defend Hispanics and allied Indians in New Mexico and Texas. The borderlands officials also received more autonomy to deal with local problems, but lacked sufficient troops to conquer the Apaches and Comanches.

The British Colonies Resist Imperial Reform

In Britain's colonies, which experienced few restrictions before 1763, trouble began when George III appointed George Grenville as first minister, with responsibility for solving the debt crisis. Grenville decided that Americans should pay more taxes because they benefited from the Seven Years' War and continued to drain the government's budget for administrative and military costs. Because the British at home were highly taxed, Grenville's plan to make the colonies pay their way seemed reasonable to many. The Americans saw it differently, however, and quickly moved to the brink of revolt.

The Sugar and Currency Acts

Grenville began his program in 1764 with the Sugar Act, which initiated a new policy of charging duties primarily to raise revenue rather than to regulate trade. It reduced the duty on foreign molasses from sixpence to threepence per gallon, which was further reduced to one penny in 1766. Grenville assumed merchants would pay the lower tariff rather than go to the risk of smuggling and bribery. The law also added timber, iron, and hides to the list of enumerated goods. To make smuggling more hazardous, the act gave increased powers to the vice-admiralty courts. Because these courts lacked juries, the government expected easy convictions for smuggling. Parliament also passed the Currency Act (1764), which had the potential to cause further hardship by forbidding colonies from issuing paper money, thus creating a shortage of currency.

Coming in the midst of an economic depression, this legislation stirred up colonial protest. Provincial assemblies sent petitions to England requesting relief. Most urgently, merchants feared that if imports of foreign molasses were cut off, their provision trade to the Spanish and French West Indies would be lost. Without foreign credits, they could not pay for British manufactures. The Americans slowed down their orders from Britain and encouraged home industry, arousing opposition to Grenville's policies from English businessmen. One colonial merchant wrote to associates in England that if the government deprived Americans of paper currency, "we shall not be able to export Provisions &c. in the same Degree as formerly, and if we are not on any Terms allow'd a Trade to get Money from abroad, we shall have none to pay you for Goods, and then unless you will send them Gratis our Dealings must end."

The Stamp Act

Passed by Parliament in 1765, the Stamp Act provoked an even greater storm of protest. The act required individuals to purchase stamps for official documents and published papers, including deeds, liquor licenses, bills of lading, court documents, wills, passports, playing cards, newspapers, and pamphlets. All publications and official transactions were to be subject to this special tax, which increased with the value of a land sale or the size of a pamphlet. The tax could be paid only in specie, an onerous requirement because colonists generally used paper money and credit instead of the scarce gold and silver.

Colonists of all walks of life found the Stamp Act offensive. Everyone who engaged in public business, whether to buy a newspaper or sell property, would have to pay the tax. Because Parliament, not their provincial assemblies, passed the act, Americans considered it a violation of their rights as British subjects. As they understood the British constitution, the people must consent to taxes through their representatives. The provinces could not send delegates to Parliament, so that body should not tax them to raise revenue. Only tariffs to regulate trade, many colonists believed, were constitutionally valid.

Recognizing Parliament's attack on their powers, provincial assemblies protested the Stamp Act. In the Virginia House of Burgesses, the newly elected Patrick Henry introduced fourteen resolves against the tax. The Virginia assembly refused to accept all of Henry's proposals, but in June 1765, approved the more moderate resolutions that defended the colonists' right to tax themselves.

When newspapers spread word of Virginia's action, other provinces responded. Rhode Island instructed its officials to ignore the stamp tax; Massachusetts, Connecticut, New York, New Jersey, Pennsylvania, Maryland, and South Carolina passed resolves similar to Virginia's. In October 1765, representatives from nine colonies traveled to New York City to attend the Stamp Act Congress. In resolutions and petitions to Parliament, the congress upheld the power of representative assemblies, not Parliament, to tax the colonists. By issuing resolves and organizing the Stamp Act Congress, the colonial elite challenged British efforts to assert control.

Paul Revere's engraving of the hanging in effigy of an American-born member of Parliament, John Huske, an alleged Stamp Act supporter. (Courtesy, American Antiquarian Society)

Ordinary colonists joined the challenge. They drew upon the tradition of the mob to protest what they considered tyranny. The anti-Stamp Act riots began in Boston on August 14, 1765, when a group who called themselves the Loyal Nine organized a demonstration to hang in effigy the appointed stamp collector for Massachusetts, Andrew Oliver. The crowd destroyed a partially constructed building they thought he intended as his stamp office, then damaged his home. Oliver resigned his commission. Twelve days later, a Boston mob attacked the houses of several other officials.

Protesters all along the Atlantic seaboard mobilized to prevent stamp distribution, scheduled to begin November 1. News of Oliver's resignation prompted anti-Stamp Act mobs in other cities to demand the same from their appointed stampmen. In some colonies, rioters forced stamp officials to relinquish their commissions. In others, just the threat of disorder was effective. By the end of 1765, distributors in every colony except Georgia had resigned.

The men who led the crowds called themselves Sons of Liberty. They were mostly propertied men—small merchants, shopkeepers, and craftsmen. The activists were people who needed documents to conduct business, who would regularly feel the pinch of the stamp tax. The Sons of Liberty also established networks to organize boycotts

Virginia Resolves against the Stamp Act 1765

When news arrived in 1765 that Parliament had passed the Stamp Act, the colonists protested the internal tax. In the Virginia assembly, Patrick Henry introduced resolutions defending the right of "taxation of the people by themselves, or by persons chosen by themselves to represent them" and accusing Parliament of attempting to destroy "American freedom." Newspapers published seven resolutions, of which the Virginia legislators passed the first four listed below, which were more moderate than the rest.

Resolved, That the first adventurers and settlers of this His Majesty's Colony and Dominion of Virginia brought with them, and transmitted to their posterity, and all other of His Majesty's subjects since inhabiting this His Majesty's said Colony, all the liberties, privileges, franchises, and immunities, that have at any time been held, enjoyed, and possessed, by the people of Great Britain.

Resolved, That by two royal charters, granted by King James the First, the colonists aforesaid are declared entitled to all liberties, privileges, and immunities of denizens and natural subjects, to all intents and purposes, as if they had been abiding and born within the realm of England.

Resolved, That the taxation of the people by themselves, or by persons chosen by themselves to represent them, who can only know what taxes the people are able to bear, or the easiest method of raising them, and must themselves be affected by every tax laid on the people, is the only security against a burthensome taxation, and the distinguishing characteristick of British freedom, without which the ancient constitution cannot exist.

Resolved, That His Majesty's liege people of this his most ancient and loyal Colony have without interruption enjoyed the inestimable right of being governed by such laws, respecting their internal polity and taxation, as are derived from their own consent, with the approbation of their sovereign, or his substitute; and that the same hath never been forfeited or yielded up, but hath been constantly recognized by the kings and people of Great Britain.

Resolved therefore, That the General Assembly of this Colony have the only and sole exclusive right and power to lay taxes and impositions upon the inhabitants of this Colony, and that every attempt to vest such power in any person or persons whatsoever other than the General Assembly aforesaid has a manifest tendency to destroy British as well as American freedom.

Resolved, That His Majesty's liege people, the inhabitants of this Colony are not bound to yield obedience to any law or ordinance whatever, designed to impose any taxation whatsoever upon them other than the laws or ordinances of the General Assembly aforesaid.

Resolved, That any person who shall, by speaking or writing, assert or maintain that any person or persons other than the General Assembly of this Colony, have any right or power to impose or lay any taxation on the people here, shall be deemed an enemy to His Majesty's Colony.

of British goods. By early 1766, the Sons of Liberty coerced customs officials and judges to open the ports and resume court business without stamps. Later that year, Parliament repealed the Stamp Act after British businessmen from more than twenty cities petitioned for relief. Suffering from postwar economic depression and unemployment, the British textile industry faced even worse times with an American boycott.

Protest Widens in the Lower South

In the Carolinas, the Stamp Act resistance spawned revolts against colonial elites. To blacks, the radicals' oft-spoken argument that the English government intended to deprive white Americans of freedom—to make them slaves—seemed ironic. Yet such statements also gave hope, for the revolutionary movement spotlighted the institution of slavery and its immorality and injustice. In January 1766, in Charleston, 1,400 seamen and a group of black slaves threatened serious disorder. The sailors became restless because the customs agents refused to release ships from port without stamped documents. The people of Charleston were even more concerned, however, when a group of enslaved men marched through the town shouting "Liberty!" The city armed itself against a slave revolt, while the South Carolina assembly became so frightened that it restricted slave imports for three years.

The North Carolina Regulator movement also began in 1766, inspired by the uproar against the Stamp Act, but targeted the colonial elite, not Britain. Six thousand western farmers demanded confirmation of land titles and the end of speculators' monopoly of the best land. The Regulators also protested corrupt local officials, excessive court fees and taxes, and lack of adequate representation for ordinary backcountry farmers in the North Carolina legislature. The North Carolina Regulators refused to pay taxes and closed several courts. In 1771, when the government sent the eastern militia, 2,000 Regulators met them at Alamance Creek but were dispersed.

Most of the grievances of the South Carolina Regulators were different. There, the Regulators were planters who wanted to bring order, "to regulate" the backcountry. The legislature had failed to create local government for the westerners, so they had no courts or jails. Everyone had to travel to Charleston to conduct legal business, but even worse, bandits roamed freely, stealing horses and cattle, destroying property, and sometimes torturing and killing their victims. The frontier robbers were mostly propertyless whites and some free blacks and escaped slaves. The Regulators resorted to vigilante "justice," capturing and whipping suspected felons, taking some to jail in Charleston, and evicting others from the colony. They finally ceased their activities in 1769 when the legislature established a circuit court system for the entire province.

The Townshend Revenue Act

In other British mainland colonies, attention focused on imperial tensions rather than regional disputes. The British government and American radicals emerged from the Stamp Act crisis with conflicting views: although the Americans celebrated the Stamp Act's repeal, the British yielded no authority. In the Declaratory Act, passed with the repeal in March 1766, Parliament affirmed its power "to make laws and statutes of sufficient force and validity to bind the colonies and people of America, subjects of the crown of Great Britain, in all cases whatsoever." The act generated little response in the colonies, but should have, for it laid the basis for subsequent restrictions.

In June 1767, Parliament passed three more laws affecting the Americans: an act establishing the American Board of Customs Commissioners to enforce legislation against illegal trade, the New York Restraining Act, and the Townshend Revenue Act. The Restraining Act would have dissolved the New York Assembly for refusing adequate supplies to British soldiers stationed in the province. Instead, the New York legislators gave in, pledging additional funds for the troops. The Townshend Revenue Act was conceived by Charles Townshend, the British chancellor of the exchequer, who wanted the Americans to contribute, over time, an increasing percentage of imperial expenses in North America. The Townshend Act, which placed duties on tea, glass, paper, and paint would be just the beginning. The revenues would pay the salaries of governors and judges, thus removing their dependence upon the provincial legislatures.

To American whigs, the Townshend Act was dangerous for two reasons: it raised revenue without the approval of colonial assemblies and it removed royal officials from the lawmakers' control. If the king rather than the legislatures paid provincial governors, the colonies lost a powerful negotiating tool for obtaining consent to the laws they wanted. Although the British saw the Townshend Act as an appropriate way to force the Americans to begin paying their share, the colonists believed it was a step towards tyranny.

At first, colonial reaction to the Townshend Act was restrained. Then, in December 1767, a few weeks after the Townshend Act went into effect, John Dickinson, a Philadelphia lawyer and owner of a Delaware plantation, began publishing a series of twelve letters signed "A Farmer." Soon reprinted by newspapers throughout the thirteen colonies and published in pamphlet form as *Letters from a Farmer in Pennsylvania* (1768), Dickinson's arguments galvanized opposition to the Townshend duties. He rejected the position that the colonists should accept external taxes (duties) but not internal taxes (like the stamp tax), stating that only elected representatives could legally impose *any* revenue tax. He believed that Parliament could collect duties in the colonies if the purpose was to regulate trade (as with the Molasses Act of 1733), but not to raise revenue. Further, the purpose of the funds collected under the Townshend Act was oppressive, for it eliminated the power of the colonial legislatures over Crown officials. Dickinson predicted that if the Americans failed to have this act repealed, harsher measures would be forthcoming. Dickinson urged the thirteen colonies to petition for repeal; if that failed, they should once again boycott British goods.

Massachusetts responded first. In early 1768, its assembly petitioned George III for redress, then dispatched a "circular letter" to the other twelve colonies suggesting they do the same. The new English secretary of state for the colonies, Lord Hillsborough, realized that the circular letter was a call to unified resistance. Denouncing Dickinson's pamphlet as "extremely wild," he ordered the Massachusetts assemblymen to rescind their circular letter. They refused. When he directed colonial governors to dissolve assemblies that responded to the letter, most legislatures sent petitions and were disbanded. Simultaneously, Hillsborough reassigned military units from the Ohio Valley to Florida, Nova Scotia, Quebec, and the mid-Atlantic region where they could be called upon to control the defiant provinces.

In June 1768, when Massachusetts remained unbowed and the customs commissioners demanded protection against rioters, Hillsborough sent British regiments to Boston. When troops disembarked in Boston in October 1768, they heard cries of protest but met no armed resistance. As months passed, however, the presence of the redcoats created tensions that would eventually erupt in bloodshed.

Between the time Lord Hillsborough ordered the regiments to Boston and their arrival four months later, city residents had signed a non-importation agreement against the Townshend Act. Most Boston merchants pledged to stop importing goods from Great Britain after January 1, 1769, unless the Townshend duties were repealed. The non-importation movement soon spread to New York City, where artisans supported the merchants by agreeing to boycott any retailer who imported British goods. Traders in Philadelphia, New Haven, and other northern ports delayed action, however. They waited until 1769 for the imperial government to respond to their petitions, then approved non-importation. In Virginia, George Washington kindled the boycott. He wrote, "At a time when our lordly masters in Great Britain will be satisfied with nothing less than the deprivation of American freedom, it seems highly necessary that some thing should be done to avert the stroke and maintain the liberty which we have derived from our Ancestors."

The boycotts met uneven success. Between 1768 and 1769, American imports from England declined fairly substantially. As the months passed, however, importers wavered as their incomes fell. In contrast, craftsmen—beyond their concern for liberty—often benefited from the boycott because it created a demand for their products. Some artisans organized into street groups to threaten merchants and customs officials who tried to undermine the non-importation pacts.

Women participated both as purchasers of goods and as producers. Many "Daughters of Liberty" gave up imported tea and clothing. The *Boston News-Letter* reported that "a large circle of very agreeable ladies in this town . . . unanimously agreed" not to purchase ribbons and other imports. In Boston, some impoverished women profited from the temporary demand for American-made cloth, when William Molineaux, a merchant and radical whig, contracted with local artisans to build 400 spinning wheels, which he distributed to women to spin yarn in their homes. With this "putting-out" system, Molineaux and the spinners responded to both their patriotism and economic needs.

Crisis in Boston

During the years 1769 to 1775, Boston became the powder keg of the Revolution. Violence broke out in the summer of 1769 between the Bostonians and British redcoats, whose chief responsibilities were to protect the despised customs commissioners and help them collect duties. The first serious incident occurred in July 1769, when a redcoat, John Riley, was jailed for hitting a local butcher who had insulted him. A near riot followed as twenty of Riley's comrades tried to rescue him from jail.

Such episodes continued into early 1770. On March 2, the violence escalated when soldiers seeking revenge for an insult attacked workers at John Gray's ropeworks. Street fights intensified over the next few days. On March 5, the bloodiest incident occurred, the so-called Boston Massacre. A young apprentice taunted the British sentry at the Customs House, who hit the boy with his gun. When a crowd gathered, shouting at the sentry, "Kill him, kill him, knock him down," Captain Thomas Preston led seven soldiers to assist him. The crowd grew larger, throwing snowballs, ice, and sticks at the soldiers, and threatening them with clubs. Then someone hit a redcoat with a club, knocking the gun out of his hands. Preston's men fired, killing five townspeople and wounding six. The dead became martyrs, with March 5 commemorated as "Massacre Day" in the years ahead. The incident crystallized the colonists' opposition to standing armies. Nevertheless, when Captain Preston and six soldiers were tried for murder, the jury found two soldiers guilty of manslaughter and cleared the others. The radical whig lawyer John Adams defended them, saying that all Englishmen should have a fair trial.

Just as the crisis in Boston reached its head in spring 1770, the British government decided on partial repeal of the Townshend Act, removing its duties except on tea. The duties had raised under £21,000 in revenues, but cost hundreds of thousands of pounds sterling in trade as a result of the non-importation movement. As in the case of the Stamp Act, British officials backed away from a specific revenue measure without abandoning their right to levy taxes. Following Parliament's action, merchants in New York City and other colonial ports, eager to resume trade, cancelled their boycotts except on tea. Imports into the thirteen colonies from England rebounded over the next several years.

The Gaspée Incident

For two years, the conflict between Great Britain and the colonies abated, then flared again in 1772. Trouble began this time in Rhode Island,

Burning of Gaspée, *by Charles De Wolf Brownell. The seizure and burning of the British customs ship* Gaspée *by Rhode Island merchants in June 1772 moved the colonies closer to revolution.* (Courtesy of the Rhode Island Historical Society)

when more than one hundred men burned the British schooner *Gaspée.* Avidly enforcing the Sugar Act, the *Gaspée* had harassed merchant vessels sailing through Narragansett Bay. The Crown named a Commission of Inquiry to locate the perpetrators and send them to England to be tried for high treason. Though the commission identified none of the *Gaspée's* attackers, colonists viewed the policy of taking defendants to England for trial as a serious threat to their constitutional rights.

In response, the Virginia assembly appointed a Committee of Correspondence to monitor British policy and recommended to other colonies that they do the same. Within a year, Committees of Correspondence in all thirteen provinces coordinated opposition to Britain's restraints.

The Boston Tea Party

The final showdown began in 1773, when Parliament passed the Tea Act to bail out the nearly bankrupt East India Company. Though some colonists purchased British tea, the boycott on the product was still in effect. To sell the company's huge surplus, the government dropped a heavy import duty into England on tea headed for America, but retained the Townshend duty, which Lord North insisted on keeping to uphold Parliament's power to tax. The company also received a monopoly in the colonies, with the right to choose certain provincial merchants as agents. The company selected consignees in the ports of Charleston, Philadelphia, New York, and Boston, to whom it promptly dispatched nearly 600,000 pounds of tea.

The Tea Act was doubly offensive to American whigs as it renewed opposition to the duty and caused outrage over favoritism and privilege. Before the tea ships arrived in Charleston, Philadelphia, and New York, militants convinced the East India Company's agents to resign. In Boston, the consignees declined to quit. When three ships arrived, members of the Boston Committee of Correspondence, led by Samuel Adams, prevented them from unloading. Adams had been the chief agitator in Boston since the Stamp Act. A skilled politician and writer, he kept the pot simmering against British policies. Now, with the Boston committee, he brought matters to a head: in a series of meetings, thousands of residents of Boston and surrounding towns met to refuse the tea. On December 16, 1773, when customs officials denied the ships clearance to leave port, radicals ill-disguised as Mohawks boarded the ships, broke open the tea chests, and dumped them overboard.

For the British, the Boston Tea Party required stern action. London decided that steps must "be taken to secure the Dependence of the Colonies," and in particular, "to mark out Boston and separate that Town from the rest of the Delinquents." In 1774, Parliament passed four Coercive Acts that closed the port of Boston until residents of the city paid for the destroyed tea; altered the provincial charter to limit the power of town meetings and make the council the appointees of the Crown instead of elected officials; expanded the governor's control over the courts; provided that trials of royal officials could be moved to England or to another colony; and permitted quartering of troops in private buildings if a colony failed to provide suitable barracks. Americans called these the Intolerable Acts.

The First Continental Congress

Though the British government expected the Coercive Acts to isolate Boston and convince other provinces to be obedient, the policies actually pushed Americans toward more unified resistance. After the port of Boston closed, residents faced severe unemployment and food shortages. Neighboring towns provided supplies and harbored refugees looking for work. When Sam Adams and the Boston Committee of Correspondence requested an immediate boycott of British trade, instead the other provinces favored a Continental Congress to consider what action to take. The Massachusetts assembly proposed a meeting in Philadelphia on September 1, 1774, to which all of the thirteen colonies except Georgia sent delegates.

The primary purpose of the First Continental Congress was to obtain repeal of the Coercive Acts and other restrictions. The Congress wanted Parliament to recognize the rights of Americans, but was not ready to declare independence. Some of its leadership argued for a moderate course, but the Congress was committed to action. It confirmed the Suffolk County Resolves forwarded to Philadelphia by a local Massachusetts convention. The Resolves blasted the Coercive Acts as "gross infractions of those rights to which we are justly entitled by the laws of nature, the British constitution and the charter of this province." The laws should "be rejected as the attempts of a wicked administration to enslave America." Everyone qualified to fight should learn "the art of war as soon as possible, and . . . appear under arms at least once a week." By endorsing these Resolves, the Congress took a militant stance.

Further, the Continental Congress passed non-importation, non-exportation, and non-consumption resolutions, ending all trade with Great Britain and Ireland, and exports to the West Indies. If the British had hoped to divide the colonies by closing Boston, expecting other cities to pick up its trade, the plan backfired when all of the colonies closed their ports. The boycott would continue until repeal of the Coercive Acts. Congress set up the Continental Association to enforce the ban on trade through elected local committees, called Committees of Observation and Inspection, or Committees of Safety. The groups would expose violators of the boycott as "enemies of American liberty," publicizing their names and interrupting their business. Almost every town and county in the thirteen colonies elected these committees, which soon took on other functions of local government, including raising militias and collecting taxes. This transfer of authority from colonial governments to the Committees of Observation was revolutionary, for Americans were vesting sovereignty in themselves rather than in Parliament.

Resistance Becomes a War for Independence

Over the winter of 1774–1775, the rift widened between the thirteen colonies and Great Britain. George III and his ministers considered the colonies in rebellion, yet the colonists themselves were unprepared to declare independence.

Lexington and Concord

The British instructed General Thomas Gage to take forceful action. Headquartered in Boston, he decided to seize the patriots' stores of food and ammunition at Concord, which he had learned about from an informer. Militant Bostonians discovered Gage's plan from their own spies, so were ready to spread the alarm on the night of April 18, 1775, when 700 redcoats mustered on Boston Common. Paul Revere and William Dawes escaped the city to raise the colonial militia and alert leaders Sam Adams and John Hancock, who were staying at Lexington, on the route to Concord.

As the British marched the sixteen miles to Concord, they heard church bells and saw lights in windows. Soon after sunrise on April 19th they reached Lexington, where they met about seventy armed militia, nearly half of the town's adult males. The Lexington company, led by Captain John Parker, had formed only a few weeks earlier, so their training was incomplete. In the face of six companies of British infantry, Captain Parker attempted to disperse his troops. The British officer, Major John Pitcairn, wanted to disarm the Americans, not engage in battle. As the British advanced, a shot rang out, then several shots, and a British volley. Pitcairn tried to stop his troops, but the carnage continued for fifteen to twenty minutes, leaving eight Lexington men dead and ten wounded. Only one British soldier was wounded and none killed.

The British reached Concord at about eight o'clock in the morning. Following a brief skirmish in which the Americans inflicted more casualties than the British, the redcoats headed back to Boston. The march became a harrowing escape for their lives. Hundreds of colonial militia from throughout the Massachusetts countryside rushed to battle. These farmers used guerrila tactics, shooting from behind trees, walls, rocks, and buildings. The British countered the guerrilas by sending advance parties to clear houses along the route. Using their famed skills with the bayonet, the redcoats killed the occupants and set fire to the homes. By the end of the day, British losses totaled seventy-three dead and 200 wounded or missing, while Massachusetts counted forty-nine killed and forty-three wounded and missing.

In the days that followed the battles of April 19, New England went to arms. Over 20,000 volunteers streamed to Cambridge. A large proportion of these soldiers soon returned home, but many stayed, expecting their wives, mothers, and sisters to work the family farms and defend the towns.

Troops from throughout New England besieged Gage's redcoats in Boston. Nathanael Greene, a young ex-Quaker, led 1,500 troops from Rhode Island. Connecticut promised 6,000 men and New Hampshire sent 2,000. Without a unified army, each colony separately raised troops, selected officers, and secured provisions. By May 1775, the New England forces surrounding Boston numbered about 17,000. Ethan Allen and his Green Mountain Boys of Vermont captured Fort Ticonderoga, the British garrison on Lake Champlain in northern New York.

The Second Continental Congress

On May 10, 1775, the day after Allen's victory at Ticonderoga, the Second Continental Congress met in Philadelphia. Although the delegates remained

George Washington, *by James Peale. In choosing Washington as commander-in-chief, the Continental Congress selected a revolutionary dedicated to republican government. His perseverance and leadership kept the army together despite battlefield reverses and lack of supplies.* (Independence National Historical Park)

unwilling to support independence, they were disappointed by Parliament's refusal to change its course. They faced the prospect of executing a war already in progress, convinced that British troops had fired the first shots. To ensure that all the colonies backed the war and to place the military under the control of Congress, they appointed George Washington of Virginia as commander-in-chief of the Continental army. Designating a southerner to head the military, which in June 1775 consisted of New Englanders, broadened the appeal of the Massachusetts cause. At the same time, Washington was himself a delegate to Congress and steadfastly committed to civilian control of the armed forces. Despite his limited military experience, Washington proved to be an excellent choice. His military bearing, determination, dignity, physical stamina, and ability to learn from his mistakes suited his role as commander-in-chief.

To serve under Washington, Congress appointed thirteen generals. Its four major generals were Artemas Ward of Massachusetts; Philip Schuyler of New York; Israel Putnam of Connecticut; and Charles Lee, a veteran officer of the British army and recent immigrant to Virginia. The adjutant general was Horatio Gates, also a veteran British officer and Virginia planter.

"An Open and Avowed Rebellion"

Before Washington could arrive in Massachusetts, his troops engaged in the Battle of Bunker Hill. Learning that the British planned to seize the hills overlooking Boston, a detachment of the patriot army began to fortify the Charlestown heights. By mistake, the men built defenses on Breed's Hill rather than on the higher and less exposed Bunker Hill. This lapse might have isolated the detachment from the rest of the army had the British moved more quickly. Instead of attacking immediately, however, they foolishly allowed the Americans to complete their fortifications and obtain reinforcements. The British regulars lined up in proper European formation to storm Breed's Hill. While the redcoats shot as they advanced up the hill—to little effect—the patriots waited until the enemy was within range of their guns. The redcoats failed on their first two assaults, losing many officers and troops, then with reinforcements took the hill when the Americans' ammunition gave out. The patriots retreated, pounded by artillery from British ships. Although the British won the battle, over 40 percent of their combatants were killed or wounded.

During the year following Bunker Hill, many colonists became whigs. The lives lost on battlefields in eastern Massachusetts undercut advocates of restraint. Still, given opposition from many delegates, the Continental Congress could not declare independence. During the summer of 1775, Congress asked the king for peace while preparing for war. In July, it approved a petition to George III, called the Olive Branch Petition, asking that he resolve their dispute with Parliament. Upon receipt of the petition in August, outraged by the colonists' armed resistance, the king proclaimed the thirteen provinces in "an open and avowed rebellion." In December, Parliament cut off all trade with the colonies, making American ships and any vessels engaging in commerce with the mutinous provinces subject to confiscation. For many Americans, these actions proved that the British government meant to crush the colonies militarily and economically.

The Continental Congress further alienated the British by ordering General Philip Schuyler to invade Canada. The congressmen hoped to make Canada the fourteenth British colony in rebellion. They expected to obtain help from French Canadians and perhaps even France itself, but even more, they wanted to prevent a northern attack. The American invasion of Canada was a failure from the start. Schuyler, suffering from illness and indecision, assembled troops and provisions too slowly, wasting valuable summer days. In September, much too late, Brigadier General Richard Montgomery took charge and moved the army north via Lake Champlain, but as Montgomery said, a "winter Campaign in Canada! Posterity won't believe it!"

Concurrently, Washington dispatched a small army under Benedict Arnold and Daniel Morgan over a rugged route through Maine. Their march took so much longer than predicted that the men had to eat their dogs and soap. When the combined American forces finally attacked Quebec in a blinding December snowstorm, they were defeated with heavy casualties. The army remained in Canada until May 1776 when British reinforcements arrived, pushing the patriots back into New York. For Congress, the campaign was a tragic error. The thirteen colonies lost 5,000 troops to battle, desertion, and disease and an enormous amount of supplies.

Taking Sides

The deepening conflict forced colonists to decide whether or not to support the revolutionary whigs. Some people remained neutral, either because they cared little about the issues involved or because they were opposed to violence on religious grounds. Loyalists rejected the Revolution for a variety of motives. Some believed that the king and Parliament were right, or at least had reason to expect the colonists to pay their share toward imperial administration. During the course of the war, about 80,000 loyalists departed for Britain or other British colonies. Many more, numbering perhaps several hundred thousand, continued to live among their patriot neighbors. Tories included Crown officials, Anglican clergy, and merchants with close ties to Britain. Some of the best known loyalists were wealthy gentlemen and officeholders: Governor Thomas Hutchinson and Chief Justice Peter Oliver of Massachusetts; Joseph Galloway, speaker of the Pennsylvania Assembly; and Frederick Philipse, landlord of a 50,000-acre manor in New York.

Many tories were not rich or intimately tied to Great Britain, for the Revolution became a power struggle within American society, not just one between the colonies and London. The tenants of New York manors, for example, took the opposite side of their landlords. Thus, residents of Frederick Philipse's manors became whigs, while tenants of the patriot Livingstons and Schuylers supported the British. In Maryland, the loyalists gained widespread backing in Eastern Shore counties where farmers, suffering from economic decline and lack of political power, regarded the patriot elite as their enemies. The South Carolina backcountry divided along lines drawn during the 1760s, with the more affluent former Regulators supporting the whigs, and their opponents, the "lower sort," casting their lot with the British.

Of considerable concern to white Americans were the loyalties of enslaved African Americans. Of the 2.5 million people in the thirteen colonies in 1775, about 500,000 were blacks. As the rhetoric of revolution reached African American slaves, increasing numbers escaped.

A chief source of unrest, the patriots believed, was the November 1775 proclamation of Lord Dunmore, royal governor of Virginia, declaring "all indented [sic] servants, Negroes, or others [owned by rebels] free, that are able and willing to bear arms, they joining His Majesty's Troops." Whigs considered this proclamation foul play, an attempt to start an insurrection. They increased slave patrols and warned of harsh punishments to those who ran away or took up arms against their masters. The penalty for slave rebellion, of course, was death. Nevertheless, African Americans aided the British by joining the army and employing their firsthand knowledge of Chesapeake Bay. Some served as pilots along its tributaries, while others delivered fresh provisions to the British ships by foraging plantations at night.

African Americans also supported the Revolution, but received little welcome from the whigs. As the Americans created an army from volunteer forces besieging Boston, they excluded slaves and even free blacks from participating. From 1775 through much of 1776, when white enlistments seemed adequate, the patriot leaders, many of them slaveowners, were unwilling to exchange freedom for military service. By 1777, however, when recruiters found it difficult to fill their quotas, the states north of Virginia began accepting free blacks and slaves. Officially, Virginia took only free African Americans, but some masters sent slaves as substitutes for themselves. An estimated 5,000 African Americans served in the Continental army and state militias or at sea on American privateers. At the end of their service, many but not all of the enslaved African Americans who fought for independence received freedom. Some masters who had pledged liberty to their slaves if they served as substitutes broke the promises after the war.

Estimates of the total number of Americans who joined the whig forces range from 100,000 to 250,000. Most signed up for tours of duty lasting several months or a year, not for the duration of the war. Thus, Washington and his generals constantly faced the problem of expiring enlistments, a condition that severely hampered execution of the war. The inability of Congress to pay

Baron Ludwig von Closen's sketch of American army uniforms reflects the military role of African Americans. (Anne S. K. Brown Military Collection, Brown University Library)

soldiers adequately also hindered recruitment and retention of troops. As time went on, the American troops became better trained and disciplined, but originated from less privileged rungs of society. By 1778, most of the states had to adopt conscription to fill their quotas. Men were drafted by lottery, but could pay a fine or hire a substitute, loopholes that contributed to disproportionate service by the poor.

Women took part in the American war effort by operating farms and businesses in their husbands' absence, defending their homes and families against marauding enemy soldiers, supplying food and clothing for the troops, and joining the army. Perhaps several hundred women put on uniforms to become soldiers. These troops included Deborah Sampson of Massachusetts, who enlisted under the name Robert Shurtleff. She fought in battle, but was discovered when she received a wound; after the war she collected an army pension. Others performed unofficial short-term service as spies. The most substantial contribution of women to the American military was that of the Women of the Army, as George Washington called them. Numbering perhaps 20,000 over the course of the war, they served as nurses, cooks, laundresses, and water carriers. They were regular members of the army who drew rations and were subject to military discipline. Some saw action in battle, particularly women in artillery crews who carried water to swab out the cannon after each firing. The story of "Molly Pitcher" evolved from women like Mary Hayes of Carlisle, Pennsylvania, who took the place of fallen soldiers.

Independence and Confederation

During the winter and spring of 1776, fighting continued between Great Britain and the thirteen colonies. Though the Canada campaign was a disaster, the Americans gained success in their siege of Boston. They sledged the heavy guns from Fort Ticonderoga about 300 miles, installing them in March 1776 on the Dorchester Heights. Instead of storming the artillery, the British withdrew from the city, sailing to Nova Scotia in preparation for an invasion of New York City.

In 1776, London undertook a huge effort to put down the revolt. It sent across the Atlantic Ocean 370 transports with supplies and 32,000 troops, of whom many were German mercenaries. The British intended these soldiers to join General William Howe's 10,000 troops from Nova Scotia, take New York City, and destroy Washington's army. The British navy, with seventy-three warships and 13,000 sailors in American waters, would bombard seaports and wreak havoc on colonial shipping.

As the British military descended upon New York in midsummer 1776, the Continental Congress finally declared independence. The force of events propelled most moderate delegates to cast their vote for a complete break. In January 1776, Thomas Paine had published *Common Sense.* Though his arguments were familiar to Congress and readers of political tracts, Paine convinced the American public of the need for independence. *Common Sense* sold over 100,000 copies within a few months, reaching hundreds of thousands of people as copies changed hands and nonreaders listened to Paine's words read aloud. Paine used language that appealed to ordinary Protestant Americans, employing biblical arguments that churchgoing farmers and craftspeople could appreciate, and avoiding Latin phrases and classical references. He wanted to demonstrate that the time for compromise had passed, that the proper course was to shed the British monarchy and aristocracy to create an American republic. "We have it in our power to begin the world over again . . . ," he wrote. The bloodshed that began at Lexington justified rejection of the king: "No man was a warmer wisher for a reconciliation than myself, before the fatal nineteenth of April, 1775, but the moment the event of that day was made known, I rejected the hardened, sullen-tempered Pharaoh of England for ever." Pragmatically, Paine argued that the colonists must break their ties with London if they expected aid from France and Spain. He pointed out the importance of American exports, which "will always have a market while eating is the custom in Europe."

Through the spring of 1776, sentiment for independence increased. The provincial assemblies of Georgia, South Carolina, and North Carolina gave their delegates in Congress permission to support the break, while Rhode Island declared independence on its own. Virginia proposed that Congress separate from Britain, taking measures "for forming foreign alliances and a confederation of the colonies." But in June, the New York, Pennsylvania, Delaware, and Maryland assemblies, controlled by moderate factions, were still not ready to condone a split. Nevertheless, Congress appointed a committee to draft the Declaration of Independence, of which Thomas Jefferson, a wealthy Virginia planter and lawyer, was the principal author.

The Declaration set forth Congress's reasons for separating from the government of George III. It held "these truths to be self-evident: That all men are created equal; that they are endowed by their Creator with certain unalienable rights; that among these are life, liberty, and the pursuit of happiness." (See the Appendix for full text.) Employing the philosophy of John Locke and other Enlightenment writers, Jefferson continued, "that, to secure these rights, governments are instituted among men, deriving their just powers from the consent of the governed; that whenever any form of government becomes destructive of these ends, it is the right of the people to alter or to abolish it, and to institute new government." Congress placed the blame for the breach on the king, listing his misdeeds: refusing to approve necessary laws passed by the colonial assemblies, dissolving legislatures and courts, stationing a standing army, interrupting trade, and imposing taxes without colonial consent. Most recently, Congress announced to the world, George III had declared "us out of his protection and wag[ed] war against us. He has plundered our seas, ravaged our coasts, burned our towns, and destroyed the lives of our people." For these reasons and

In this painting, The Declaration of Independence *by John Trumbull, the drafting committee stands at center: from left to right, John Adams, Roger Sherman, Robert Livingston, Thomas Jefferson, and Benjamin Franklin.* (Yale University Art Gallery, Trumbull Collection. Copyright Yale University Art Gallery)

more, Congress declared the thirteen colonies, now to be called the United States of America, "free and independent states" having "full power to levy war, conclude peace, contract alliances, establish commerce, and do all other acts and things which independent states may of right do."

On July 2, 1776, all delegations to Congress approved independence except New York's, which had not received new instructions so was forced to abstain. Completing revisions two days later, Congress adopted the Declaration. For many Americans, independence ended the problem of fighting a government that they continued to recognize as sovereign. When the Continental troops heard the Declaration read on July 9, they cheered, as did civilians throughout the states. However, the battles to defend this independence still lay ahead.

To mount sufficient military force to win the war, the states needed unity. In mid-July 1776, Congress began debating the Articles of Confederation, a plan for permanent union, which it approved and sent to the states for ratification over a year later. The chief disagreement among the congressmen was one that remained central to American politics for two centuries, the power of the national government versus that of individual states. The Articles permitted less centralized authority than would the Constitution, which was drafted a decade later. Under the Articles, Congress had responsibility to conduct foreign affairs, make war and peace, deal with Native Americans residing outside the states, coin and borrow money, supervise the post office, and negotiate boundary disputes between states. The "United States" meant thirteen sovereign states joined together by a Congress with specific functions. Article 1 established the "confederacy" to be called the United States of America, not a sovereign nation. Article 2 held that "each State retains its sovereignty, freedom and independence, and every power, jurisdiction, and right, which is not by this confederation expressly delegated to the United States, in Congress assembled." The Congress could neither tax nor raise troops, but could only assess quotas on the states, a serious disadvantage in time of war. Even so, the Articles failed ratification until 1781, when the last of the thirteen states finally approved.

War in the North, 1776–1779

For the American patriots, the Revolution was a defensive war. It lasted eight years, from 1775 to 1783. The Continental army was often outmatched, for it remained smaller than General Washington wanted; his troops constantly needed training as veterans left and new recruits arrived. But as the theater of war moved from one region to another, American generals obtained reinforcements from state militias and local volunteers. The British, despite considerable assistance from tories, lacked enough reserves to subdue the rebellious North American seaboard. The sheer expanse of the thirteen states and the 3,000-mile distance from England made the British army's task extremely difficult.

Invasions of New York

To conquer New York, and thus divide New England from the rest of the states, in July 1776, British troops landed on Staten Island. In August, they attacked Washington's army at Brooklyn Heights. The redcoats defeated the Americans badly, pushing them back to Manhattan Island, and then to White Plains. But they failed to take advantage of Washington's mistakes, which could have allowed them to surround his troops. In November, however, the British did hand Washington a humiliating defeat by capturing the 2,900 defenders of Manhattan's Fort Washington.

The Continental army retreated across New Jersey with the British and German allies at its heels. The patriots crossed the Delaware River into Pennsylvania, allowing the British to occupy New Jersey towns. The British gathered tory support by

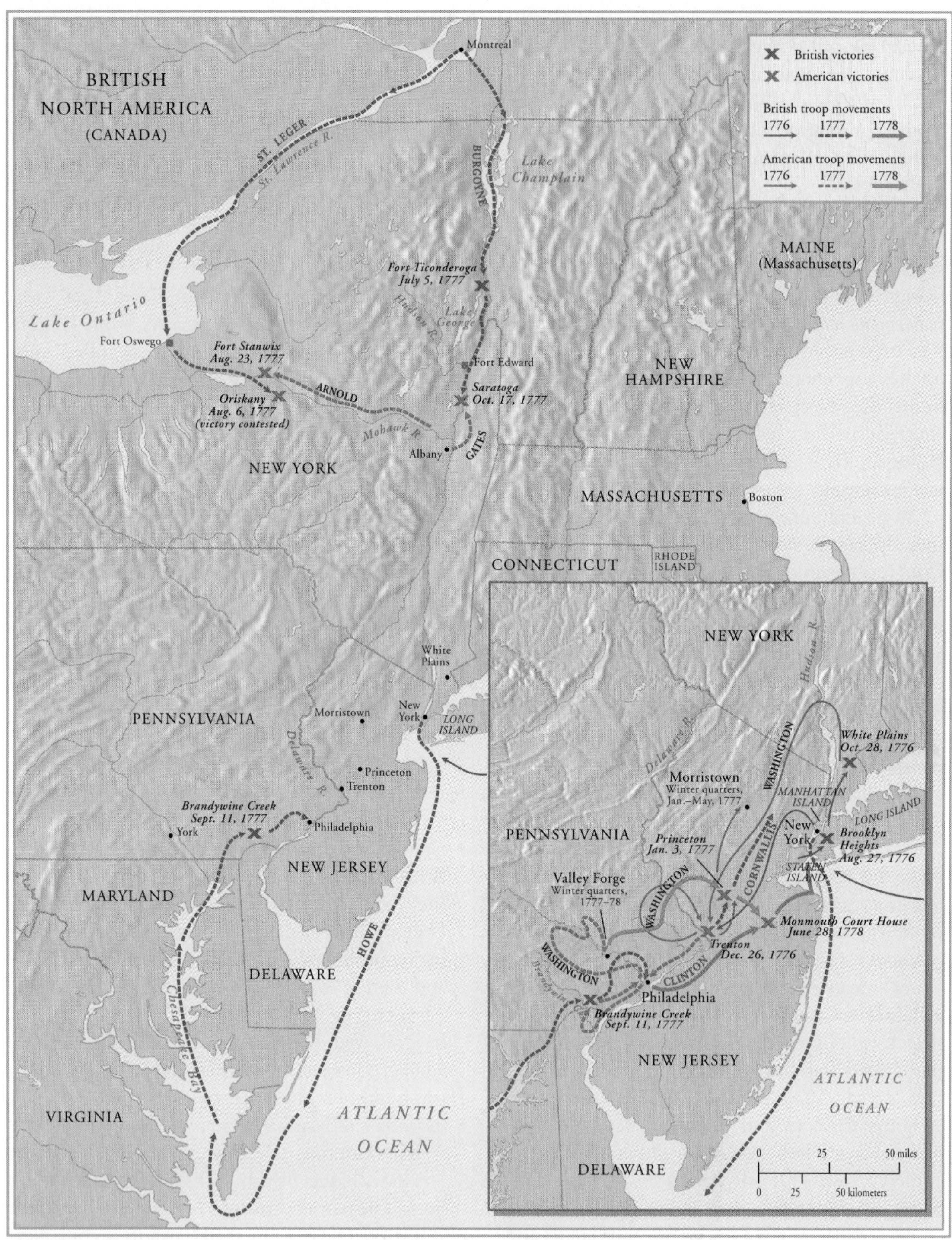

Map 5.1 | Northern Campaigns, 1776–1778

offering a pardon to anyone who would take a loyalty oath within sixty days. For the whigs, as Thomas Paine wrote, these were "times that try men's souls." The army was in retreat, the New Jersey government had dispersed, and citizens who were skeptical of Washington's abilities rallied to the British.

Before the end of the year, however, fortunes changed. British plundering across New Jersey turned indifferent farmers into radical whigs, who became guerrilas, ambushing the enemy and stealing supplies. Meanwhile, Washington devised a plan that bought him time, acting before the enlistments of a large proportion of his army would expire on December 31. He attacked 1,400 German mercenaries at Trenton on Christmas night, in the midst of a winter storm. Taking the enemy by surprise, the Americans captured more than 900 men. In early January, Washington took the offensive once again, having convinced many of his soldiers to extend their terms for six weeks. Pennsylvania and New Jersey militia, inspired by the victory at Trenton, reinforced his troops. Washington eluded a superior British army under Lord Cornwallis, then defeated a smaller force at Princeton. General William Howe withdrew most of the British army to New York. In the words of one British officer, the Americans had "become a formidable enemy."

In 1777, as the British made plans to suppress the rebellion once and for all, their strategy for the upcoming campaign became confused. General Howe intended to take Philadelphia, not by crossing New Jersey, but by means of his brother Admiral Richard Howe's fleet. At the same time, London organized an invasion from Canada, to win back Fort Ticonderoga and divide the states. The campaigns were not coordinated and neither commenced before June, when British General "Gentleman Johnny" Burgoyne led his force of over 7,000 British regulars, German mercenaries, Native Americans, and Canadians by boat down Lake Champlain. Burgoyne easily took Fort Ticonderoga, then headed for Albany. The American forces under Philip Schuyler felled trees and rolled boulders into the path of Burgoyne's heavy column. Covering twenty-three miles of terrain that was difficult even without American sabotage took the British army twenty-four days. Short on supplies and horses, Burgoyne sent 800 troops to Bennington, Vermont, where General John Stark and his militia ambushed them by pretending to be tories. Reinforcements under British officer Barry St. Leger returned to Canada when they heard that Benedict Arnold was headed west to intercept them. The rebel forces, on the other hand, burgeoned with volunteers as British soldiers pillaged the countryside. In September, near Saratoga, Burgoyne encountered the American army under General Horatio Gates, who had replaced Schuyler. The Americans surrounded the enemy, firing upon them day and night. Burgoyne sent for help from New York City, but Howe had long since sailed with most of his troops to Philadelphia. Burgoyne's 5,800-man army thus surrendered at Saratoga on October 17, 1777.

The British Occupy Philadelphia

As Burgoyne marched toward disaster in New York, General Howe more successfully reached Philadelphia. In July, his 13,000 soldiers departed from New York City aboard a fleet of 260 ships, but instead of disembarking within a week along the Delaware River, they sailed south to the Virginia capes, then up the Chesapeake Bay to Head of Elk. Their voyage lasted over a month, costing Howe valuable time that might have permitted him to assist Burgoyne. Washington tried unsuccessfully, with an army of 11,000 at Brandywine, to block Howe's advance through southeastern Pennsylvania. The British occupied Philadelphia, dividing their forces between Germantown and the capital. On October 4, 1777, Washington attacked the British encampment at Germantown, inflicting serious damage though he was once again defeated. Elizabeth Drinker, a Quaker resident of Philadelphia, in her diary reported significant losses on both sides. She recorded news of the Continental army's movements, fearing that the troops would carry the battle to her city. But

Washington did not attack Philadelphia, so the enemy retained control of the capital until they withdrew the next June.

Even so, in 1777, the British had failed to put down the American rebellion during yet another season of war. Upon hearing that Burgoyne's army had surrendered, the Howe brothers resigned. General Henry Clinton became the new commander of British forces in North America. The redcoats wintered in relative comfort at Philadelphia while Washington's troops nearly starved and froze to death at Valley Forge, to the west of the city. In February 1778, Continental soldiers lacked adequate clothing and received just three pounds of bread and three ounces of meat to last a week. Nevertheless, they became a disciplined army at Valley Forge, under the Prussian officer Baron von Steuben, who rigorously trained the Americans in the European art of war.

Alliance with France

While February 1778 brought despair to the Americans, it also brought hope—in the form of an alliance with France. Convinced by the victory at Saratoga that the former colonies could win the war, the French signed two pacts with the United States. The first was the Treaty of Amity and Commerce, in which France recognized American independence and both nations pledged "a firm, inviolable and universal peace." The second was the military Treaty of Alliance, in which they agreed to fight Great Britain jointly until the Americans had won independence, pledged not to negotiate a separate peace, and confirmed their defensive alliance "forever." France renounced claims to its former colonies in North America, but could retain any of the British West Indies that it conquered.

In supporting the Americans, the French renewed their long struggle with Great Britain that had been suspended in 1763. The following year, Spain allied with France, but refused to recognize or assist the American insurgents beyond providing limited financial aid. Unlike France, which denied interest in North America, the Spanish viewed the Americans as potentially dangerous competitors.

The Wartime Economy

Despite France's economic assistance, the United States had grave economic problems during the war. The loss of British markets devastated farmers, merchants, and fishermen, as the embargo closed crucial ports in the West Indies and British Isles. The Royal Navy attacked and blockaded American harbors and ravaged ships at sea. On land, the armies laid waste to farms and towns.

For Congress, the chief economic problem was paying for the war. Without the power to tax, it printed money, a total of almost $200 million in paper bills by 1779. The states printed a similar amount, despite their ability to tax, primarily because printing money was easier than trying to collect revenues from a financially strapped populace. Unfortunately, as the war continued year after year, the demand for military equipment, food, medical supplies, clothing, and soldiers' wages persisted. This extraordinary demand for provisions coupled with the continuing emission of paper money sent prices soaring. By 1779, the paper money was nearly worthless.

The depreciation of currency resulted in popular unrest, as a group of Philadelphia militia in 1779 demanded a more equitable military draft and regulation of food prices. They were angry that the burden of militia service fell disproportionately on the poor because others could pay fines to avoid the draft. At the same time, the prices of food and firewood skyrocketed. In just two months, August and September 1779, the price of beef, flour, and molasses rose by more than 80 percent.

In what has been called the "Fort Wilson Incident," armed members of the Philadelphia militia met at Burns' Tavern on October 4, planning to capture and exile from the city four suspected tories. Several hundred militiamen marched their prisoners through the streets. When rumors raced through the capital that the militia planned to arrest others, about thirty gentlemen who thought they might be targets armed themselves and gathered at the house of lawyer James Wilson. Though a member of Congress, Wilson was suspect because he opposed price regulation. The militia marched past "Fort Wilson," gave three cheers, then shots rang out. Though it is unknown who shot first, both sides subsequently exchanged fire. After cavalry broke up the battle, six people lay dead and seventeen wounded, the majority of them militia.

The Fort Wilson Incident terrified many people because lower-class patriots had directed armed force against the whig elite. Henry Laurens, a wealthy South Carolina merchant and member of the Continental Congress, wrote, "we are at this moment on a precipice, and what I have long dreaded and often intimated to my friends, seems to be breaking forth—a convulsion among the people."

The War Moves West and South

The failure of the British army to defeat Washington's troops and the entry of France into the war led the imperial government to rethink its military strategy. Protection of Caribbean sugar islands from the French navy gained top priority. With redeployment of forces to the West Indies, British General Clinton had to consolidate his army, so in June 1778, he pulled his occupation forces out of Philadelphia, marching across New Jersey toward New York. Washington's army caught up with Clinton at Monmouth Courthouse, where the battle, fought in traditional European style, was indecisive. The British escaped to New York.

The Frontier War

In the west, from New York to Georgia, fighting devastated the backcountry. When the Revolution broke out, many Indians supported the British, who still held garrisons in the west and had more gunpowder and provisions than the patriots. Yet Native Americans responded in various ways to "this dispute between two brothers," as neutral Iroquois called the Revolution in 1775. Just as colonists divided among radical whigs, tories, and neutrals, so did the Native Americans, even within some tribes, separate into factions who favored the British or the Americans, or wanted to avoid any involvement. The militant Indians who sided with Great Britain considered the threat of white settlers crossing the Appalachians as most dangerous to their future. Many attempted to form pan-Indian alliances to fight their own wars of independence against land grabbers from the east.

Beginning in 1776, Indians attacked Anglo-Americans from the Georgia frontier to the Great Lakes. The Cherokees raided the southern backcountry and planned a major assault on Tennessee, but ran short of gunpowder and were defeated by whig militia in fall 1776. Many Cherokees, Choctaws, Creeks, Shawnees, Iroquois, and others did not give up, however, but rather planned in 1779 "a general invasion of the Frontiers" coordinated by Henry Hamilton, the British lieutenant governor of the Illinois country. George Rogers Clark, a surveyor, heard of plans for the Indian and British offensive. To Patrick Henry, he wrote, "the Case is Desperate but Sir we must Either Quit the Country or attack Mr. Hamilton." In 1779, with a small force, Clark assaulted Fort Vincennes and obtained the British surrender, thus ending the pan-Indian campaign.

Despite Clark's victory at Vincennes, the Kentucky-Ohio frontier remained embattled throughout the war. The same was true of Pennsylvania and New York, where after 1777 most Iroquois and Delawares abandoned their neutrality to ally with the British. In 1778 and 1779, Major John Butler, his son Captain Walter Butler, and the Mohawk leader Theyendanegea, also known as Joseph Brant, led tory and Native American forces against white settlements. The loyalists and Iroquois burned houses, barns, fields, and orchards, ran off livestock, and killed or captured settlers over a swath of frontier ranging from fifty to a hundred miles wide. In summer 1779, General Washington sent General John Sullivan with 4,000 troops, who retaliated by burning Iroquois villages, orchards, and fields of corn. At Newtown, New York, Sullivan defeated a contingent of about 700 loyalists and Indians. His scorched-earth policy seriously damaged most of the Iroquois towns; displaced Indians suffered through the winter of 1779–1780 on short rations. But the next spring, they renewed their raids.

Because many Anglo-Americans had trouble distinguishing between Indian friends and foes, Native Americans who allied with the United States or remained neutral throughout the war fared little better with the whigs than those who sided with the British. In March 1782, frontier militia massacred ninety-six pacifist Indian men, women, and children at the Moravian mission of Gnadenhutten. Another group, the Catawbas of South Carolina, performed extensive service for the patriots. They searched for loyalists and escaped slaves, supplied food to the rebels, fought the Cherokees in 1776, and battled the British, who destroyed their village in retaliation. The Mahicans of Stockbridge in western Massachusetts who fought in the American army returned home to find that whites had taken over their town.

The Southern Campaigns

Although the Revolution ravaged the frontier, the main theater of war remained east of the Appalachians, where in 1778, the British inaugurated a new strategy. Retaining troops in New York City, they invaded the south, counting on loyalist support in Georgia, the Carolinas, and Virginia to restore colonial governments to the Crown. In November 1778, General Clinton sent 3,500 troops under Lieutenant Colonel Archibald Campbell to Georgia, where they joined 2,000 soldiers from Florida. They captured Savannah and Augusta. Then, with 10,000 troops, they turned to Charleston, where in May 1780 they compelled the American general Benjamin Lincoln to surrender 5,500 men. The British fanned out through South Carolina, as many residents pledged their loyalty to the king. In July 1780, General Horatio Gates arrived to build a new southern army. Disaster struck once again, when Gates placed too much responsibility on untrained militia in action against Lord Cornwallis at Camden. The battle was a rout; even the regular Continentals were dispersed.

The tide turned after General Nathanael Greene replaced Gates as commander of the southern army. The British contributed to the turnaround, as they became more insistent in demanding oaths of allegiance from Carolinians who preferred to keep out of the fray. This provoked a backlash. The redcoats and tories also plundered, outraging many southerners and pushing them into the American camp. Most notorious was Banastre Tarleton's Tory Legion, which executed prisoners of war and destroyed houses and fields, leaving many families homeless. "Bloody" Tarleton created new revolutionaries, who joined Greene's army or the smaller irregular brigades led by Thomas "The Gamecock" Sumter, Colonel Andrew Pickens, and Francis Marion, "the Swamp Fox."

Although not welcome as soldiers in South Carolina and Georgia, African American slaves played an important role in the southern campaigns, acting as spies and counterspies for each side. Throughout the south, African Americans provided much of the supporting labor for both armies, as they built fortifications, worked in lead mines, constructed and repaired roads, produced arms and ammunition, and drove wagons. American officers complained about the chronic shortage of black laborers, because whig slaveowners jealously guarded their strongest and most talented slaves to work on their plantations. Further, thousands of African Americans took advantage of General Clinton's 1779 proclamation offering freedom to those who joined the king's service.

One practice of rebel leaders that highlighted their ability to dissociate their own fight for lib-

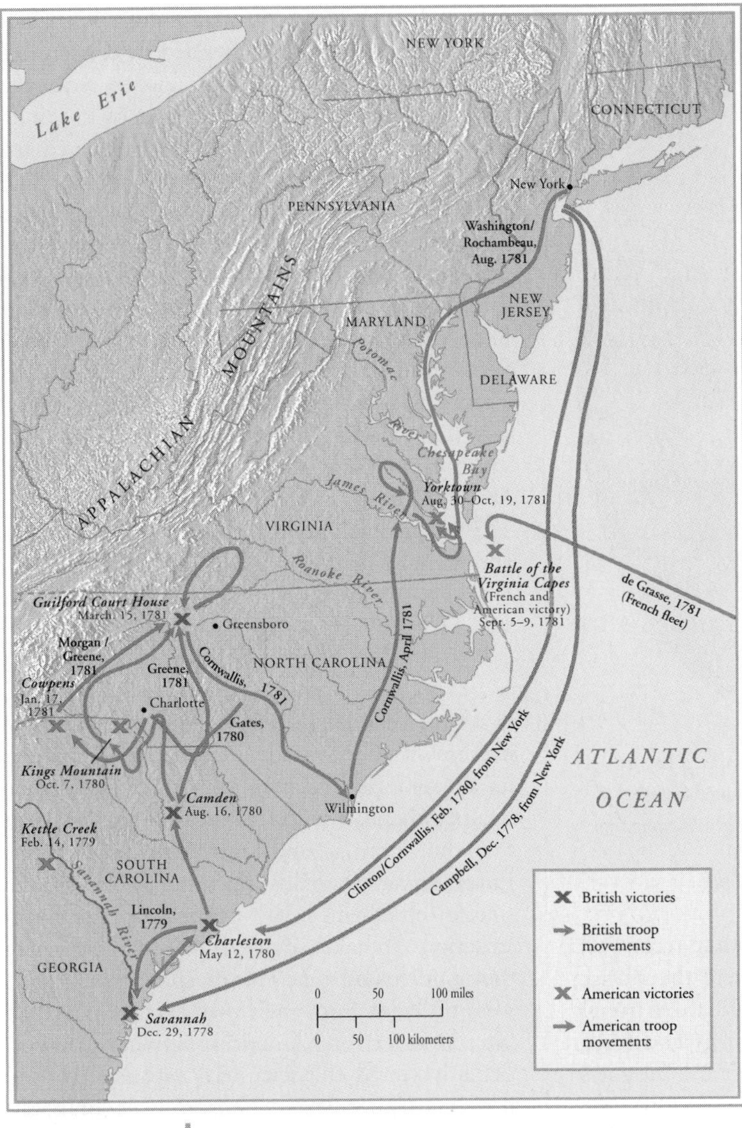

MAP 5.2 | SOUTHERN CAMPAIGNS, 1778–1781

erty from the plight of enslaved African Americans was to offer recruits enlistment "bounties" in slaves. In South Carolina, Thomas Sumter offered one African American bondman or woman to each private who would enlist for ten months. A colonel would receive three mature blacks and one child. The practice was adopted by Andrew Pickens as well, and supported by General Greene, who expected to pay the bounties from slaves confiscated from loyalist estates.

In fall 1780, Lord Cornwallis decided to head north, for while the British had destroyed two American armies and taken control of South Carolina and Georgia, the time had come to conquer the entire south. As his forces marched toward North Carolina, however, they met heavy resistance. In several battles, the conflict became a civil war, as Americans fought on both sides. In October 1780, just to the south of the state line at King's Mountain, whig frontier units defeated an enemy force, of which only Patrick Ferguson, the commander of the loyalists, was British. In January 1781, at Cowpens, General Daniel Morgan crushed Tarleton's Tory Legion by making the most of his sharpshooting frontiersmen. Morgan lined up the riflemen in front of his disciplined Continentals. The sharpshooters fired several volleys at Tarleton's troops, then withdrew to back up the regulars, who took the brunt of the fighting.

When Cornwallis learned that Tarleton's legion was lost, he chased the Americans into North Carolina, abandoning most of his equipment and supplies to move quickly. In March, Cornwallis met Greene at Guilford Courthouse. Though the battle ended indecisively, one-fourth of Cornwallis' troops lay wounded or dead. Having discarded tents, medical equipment, and food—and cut off from his base in South Carolina—the British general withdrew to the North Carolina coast.

Nathanael Greene, *by Charles Willson Peale. A former Quaker, Greene used both guerrila tactics and formal military methods to wage his successful southern campaign.* (Independence National Historical Park)

Meanwhile, Greene moved south to reconquer South Carolina and Georgia, where the British still had 8,000 men in arms. Because these troops were spread out in numerous towns and forts, Greene's 1,500 Continental soldiers and the guerrila brigades of Sumter, Pickens, and Marion could pick off the garrisons one by one. By July, the Americans had pushed the redcoats and tories back to a narrow strip of territory between Charleston and Savannah. Despite initial disastrous defeats, the whigs prevailed in the Carolinas and Georgia by recruiting irregular forces and employing them strategically.

The surrender of Cornwallis at Yorktown in October 1781 effectively ended the war. The general had moved into Virginia, replacing Benedict Arnold as commander of the British forces there. Arnold, the former American officer, had turned traitor, joined the British army, and most recently captured Richmond. With an army of about 8,000 men, Cornwallis intended to concentrate British military efforts in Virginia, so requested more troops from New York. General Clinton refused. Their squabbling and delay allowed the Americans and French to surround by land and sea Cornwallis' camp on the Virginia peninsula. Several times before, the French forces had collaborated with the Americans, but their joint efforts had resulted in failure. This time, soldiers under the Comte de Rochambeau and French fleets commanded by the Comte de Grasse and Comte de Barras played a decisive role in defeating Cornwallis. Washington's army marched south from New York to join American and French troops assembled in Virginia. With 17,000 men and heavy artillery, the American and French forces won the British surrender.

The Peace Settlement

In negotiating the peace, the United States had to reckon with both its adversary Great Britain and its ally France, which in turn was beholden to Spain. American peace commissioners Benjamin Franklin, John Jay, and John Adams worked one European nation against the other to obtain a desirable settlement. They ignored Congress's instructions to take advice from France because they understood that French and Spanish goals were different from their own. France had little interest in a strong American nation; Spain particularly feared the territorial expansion of the fledgling United States. Thus, in violation of the 1778 treaty with France, the American diplomats negotiated separately with the British, obtaining recognition of independence and most other provisions they requested.

The British and American peacemakers approved preliminary articles of peace on November 30, 1782; the Treaty of Paris signed on September 3, 1783 was essentially unchanged. The new nation would extend from approximately the present United States—Canada boundary on the north, to the Mississippi River on the west, to the thirty-first parallel on the south. The British agreed to evacuate their troops promptly from the United States "without causing any destruction or carrying away any Negroes or other property of the American inhabitants." For its part, Congress would urge state governments to return confiscated property to the loyalists. Prewar debts owed by citizens of each country to citizens of the other would be honored.

The treaty was a success on paper for the United States, but left France and Spain dissatisfied and pro-British Native Americans "Thunder Struck." In coming decades, the Americans would struggle to enforce its provisions. The French gained little from the war except the separation of the mainland colonies from Great Britain. The Spanish had wanted to keep the Americans out of the Mississippi Valley and hoped to obtain the return of Gibraltar from the British. They instead accepted East and West Florida and the Mediterranean island of Minorca. Native Americans were furious that their British allies had signed away their lands.

Although U.S. possession of the trans-Appalachian region remained disputed for decades, the provision that most immediately caused trouble was the one dealing with enslaved African Americans. Even before the final treaty was signed, American slaveowners claimed that the British military forces were taking their "property." The British ruled that blacks who sought refuge before the signing of the provisional treaty in November 1782 could not be considered the property of Americans because they were already free, but slaves who escaped after that date would be returned to their masters. General Washington, Congress, and state governments tried but failed to convince the British to return all blacks to their former masters. At least 20,000 African Americans left with the British military. Some went to Nova Scotia, whereas many others were transported to Florida and the West Indies. In the sugar islands most of the newly freed blacks were quickly re-enslaved.

CONCLUSION

The War for Independence was a success as American whigs cast off a monarchy to create a new republic. They rejected the British government's efforts to restrict representative government, calling the "reforms" tyranny. Against many odds and with the help of France, the thirteen British colonies won independence, created a confederation of sovereign states, and obtained rights to the vast trans-Appalachian territories. They avoided military dictatorship, preserved individual rights for white Americans, and established the framework for a future democratic society. Yet the changes of the revolutionary era were less than promised by the ideals of the Declaration of Independence. Though some African Americans attained freedom, the vast majority remained enslaved, and women's political and legal status was essentially the same. The Treaty of Paris ignored the territorial rights of Native Americans. As state governments retained property requirements for voting and holding office, political power stayed in the hands of affluent white men. The War for Independence had given birth to a new republic, but failed to extend the rights of "life, liberty, and the pursuit of happiness" to large numbers of Americans.

RECOMMENDED READINGS

Buel, Joy Day, and Buel, Richard, Jr., *The Way of Duty: A Woman and Her Family in Revolutionary America* (1984). The detailed biography of a Connecticut woman from the colonial period through the Revolution.

Foner, Eric. *Tom Paine and Revolutionary America* (1976). A readable "life and times" of the author of *Common Sense.*

Gross, Robert A. *The Minutemen and Their World* (1976). An interesting study of how revolutionary fervor developed in Concord, Massachusetts.

Higginbotham, Don. *The War of American Independence: Military Attitudes, Policies, and Practice, 1763–1789* (1971). Straightforward military history of the Revolution.

Hoffman, Ronald, and Albert, Peter J., eds. *Women in the Age of the Revolution* (1989). Very good essays on women's status and contributions to the War for Independence.

In Search of Early America: The William and Mary Quarterly, 1943–1993, comp. Michael McGiffert (1993). Compilation of classic essays published in the foremost journal of early American history.

Morgan, Edmund S., and Morgan, Helen M. *The Stamp Act Crisis: Prologue to Revolution,* 2d ed. (1996). A close examination of a crucial episode in the prerevolutionary decade.

Nash, Gary B. *The Urban Crucible: Social Change, Political Consciousness, and the Origins of the American Revolution* (1979). Evaluates the role of urban unrest in leading to the Revolution.

Quarles, Benjamin. *The Negro in the American Revolution,* 2d ed. (1996). The classic text on African Americans during the war.

Young, Alfred F., ed. *The American Revolution: Explorations in the History of American Radicalism* (1976). Important essays on the role of ordinary Americans in the Revolution.

AMERICAN JOURNEY ONLINE AND INFOTRAC COLLEGE EDITION

Visit the source collections at www.americanjourney.psmedia.com and infotrac.thomsonlearning.com and use the Search function with the following key terms to explore documents, images, audio and video clips, articles, and commentary related to the material in this chapter.

Stamp Act
Boston Tea Party
Boston Massacre
Battle of Lexington
Battle of Concord
Declaration of Independence
Thomas Paine

Chapter 6

Toward a More Perfect Union, 1783–1788

THE AMERICAN PATRIOTS had won victory on the battlefield and, at least on paper, in negotiating the peace. The new country soon discovered, though, that independence brought severe challenges as well as opportunities. In 1786, Dr. Benjamin Rush of Philadelphia summarized in a pamphlet the tasks facing the United States:

> There is nothing more common than to confound the terms of *the American revolution* with those of *the late American war.* The American war is over: but this is far from being the case with the American revolution. On the contrary, nothing but the first act of the great drama is closed. It remains yet to establish and perfect our forms of government; and to prepare the principles, morals, and manners of our citizens, for those forms of government. . . .

Having fought for liberty and self-government, Americans now had to create an effective political framework to protect those rights. Their first government was a confederation of small republics in which property-holding white men elected representatives. But questions remained about how to avoid the opposite evils of tyranny and anarchy, questions that inspired fiery debates.

American leaders had understood since 1776 that the task of creating a workable government lay before them. They were less prepared for other problems that arose soon after the peace. With limited powers under the Articles of Confederation, the Congress faced challenges in demobilizing the army, conducting trade, paying the war debt, dealing with Native Americans, and supervising white settlement in the west. The need for a more powerful central government quickly became clear. Just four years after the conclusion of peace, delegates from the states met in Philadelphia to draft the new Constitution, which became law upon ratification in 1788. This Constitution has endured, with relatively few amendments, for over two centuries.

The Limits of Revolutionary Change

In contrasting "the American revolution" with "the late American war," Rush made a distinction that many people have debated since the

http://ayersbrief.wadsworth.com

CHRONOLOGY

1783 Protest of Continental army officers at Newburgh, New York

Great Britain closes British West Indies to American ships

Massachusetts Supreme Court finds slavery unconstitutional

1784 Rhode Island and Connecticut pass gradual abolition laws

Spain closes port of New Orleans to Americans

Spain signs treaty of alliance with the Creeks

United States forces Iroquois to cede rights in Northwest Territory with Treaty of Fort Stanwix

1785 Native Americans yield lands in Ohio with Treaty of Fort McIntosh

Congress passes land ordinance for the Northwest Territory

1786 Shawnees sign Treaty of Fort Finney

Country Party takes control of Rhode Island assembly

Virginia statute for religious liberty

Annapolis Convention fails

Western Confederacy rejects treaties ceding lands in the Northwest Territory

Massachusetts farmers close county courts

1787 Shaysites attack the federal arsenal at Springfield, Massachusetts

Constitutional Convention meets in Philadelphia

Congress passes Northwest Ordinance

Constitution signed and sent to the states for ratification

1787–1788 Publication of *The Federalist* essays

Ratification of the Constitution by eleven states

1780s. Rush thought the Revolution had to continue because the government was not yet "perfect"—the states had too much power, leading to disunity and inertia. Others have framed the question in a different way: to what extent did the War of Independence bring about basic changes in politics and society? The war was revolutionary for propertied white men, but less so for women, African Americans, religious minorities, and the poor.

Republican Politics

Under the Articles of Confederation, the United States consisted of thirteen sovereign states rather than one nation. In framing the Confederation, representatives from the states had refused to transfer sovereignty to a central government. Only state assemblies, elected by the voters, could impose taxes; the central government, or Congress, would be an agent of the states. The states feared that a too-powerful national government would be dominated by factions whose interests conflicted with their own. Thus, the Articles formed a confederacy of sovereign states, with a weak Congress as the only organ of national government. Comprised of delegates from each of the states, "appointed in such manner as the legislature of each State shall direct," Congress had responsibility to conduct foreign affairs, declare war and peace, and coin money, but could not levy taxes or raise troops. Each state had an equal vote in Congress. During the 1780s, its dependence on the states for funds brought the Confederation to a standstill.

The structure of the state governments reflected their framers' concept of republicanism. Most of the state constitutions resembled the old colonial governments but incorporated changes that made them more responsible to the people. Most had two-house legislatures and a governor, but gave the largest share of power to the lower house of assembly, elected annually by the voters. The radical Pennsylvania constitution of 1776 dropped the office of governor and the upper house of assembly, or senate, which was designed to represent the wealthier segment of society. Georgia also excluded the upper house and denied its governor any power. Even states that retained the governor prevented him from appointing many officials or dissolving the assembly. They eliminated the governor's veto over legislation or allowed the assembly to override with a two-thirds vote.

During the late 1770s and 1780s, as Americans formulated and revised state constitutions, they also developed the method by which frames of government were written and approved, the constitutional convention. Pennsylvania radicals called the first state convention in 1776, explaining that its members would be "invested with powers to form a plan of government only, and not to execute it after it is framed." Then, in 1780, Massachusetts voters demanded a convention to write a new constitution rather than accept a document that assemblymen had prepared. The constitution was ratified by the people (voters), who thus claimed to be sovereign—the ultimate source of political power—because the frame of government originated with them. Within a few years, other states adopted the same process, recognizing that a constitution should not be written by a governmental body—the legislature—that the constitution created. Remarkably, in Massachusetts in 1780, every free man, even those without property, could vote for or against the new constitution. The document they approved limited suffrage to propertied men.

State constitutions also provided some protection for the liberties many Americans had defended in the Revolution. Virginia included a model Declaration of Rights that other states copied loosely. Most state constitutions offered freedom of worship, required search warrants, and banned excessive fines and quartering of troops in private dwellings. Only some of the states, however, guaranteed trial by jury and the rights of free speech, press, and assembly. A few opposed monopolies and imprisonment for debt.

Although the state constitutions were radical in the context of eighteenth-century politics, the definition of who was qualified to cast ballots and hold office remained traditional. John Adams spoke for most politicians of his time when he wrote that only property holders should be counted among the sovereign people who could choose and serve as magistrates. Voters, according to republican theory, must have a stake in society. Wives, slaves, servants, and unpropertied laboring men were dependent on others and thus unqualified for suffrage. Yet in most places, women and free African Americans who owned property were also barred from voting, by law or by informal pressure. One exception was New Jersey, where the 1776 state constitution extended the vote to "all free inhabitants" who held sufficient property; in 1807, the legislature fell into line with other states by disenfranchising all women and blacks.

Women's Rights

Republican politics brought little change to women's lives. A married woman was still subject to the English common law that gave control of her property and earnings to her husband and denied her the right, without his permission, to make a will, sign contracts, sue in court, or act as a guardian. Despite independence, the American lawmakers refused to cast off this English tradition. Women were also barred from positions of high status. They could serve as ministers among Quakers and some Baptists but in no other churches; they taught school only at the primary

"Keep Within Compass," published during the era of the new republic (c. 1785–1805), warned young women to remain within traditional female roles despite the revolutionary change in government. (Courtesy, Winterthur Museum)

level. None were lawyers or wealthy merchants, though some became successful shopkeepers. Women also lost ground in medicine. As medical courses at the college level became available to men, doctors with formal training displaced lay practitioners, including some midwives.

In the post-revolutionary years, increased support for female education marked the most positive alteration in women's lives. This change accompanied the more general perception that a republic needed an educated people. Though women were denied entrance to all colleges, a number of academies opened their doors to provide secondary-level education to well-to-do girls. The school curricula included the three R's, English composition and grammar, geography, music, dancing, and needlework. The young women did not receive instruction in Latin, Greek, or advanced science and mathematics.

Discussion of the need for better female education became intertwined with ideas about women's roles in the new nation. Beginning in 1784, Massachusetts writer Judith Sargent Murray published a series of essays, later compiled in a book titled *The Gleaner,* in which she argued that young women should prepare to support themselves in case they found no suitable husband or their spouse died. Murray believed that young women should learn a vocation for independence but also justified advanced female education on the grounds that girls with developed minds would become better wives and mothers. Dr. Benjamin Rush pointed out that improved schooling would help women fulfill their duties in running households and preparing sons to be virtuous, wise leaders of the republic. Nurturing incorruptible future leaders, or "republican motherhood," he claimed, was women's principal responsibility under the new government, not voting or holding office.

The Question of Abolishing Slavery

The revolutionary rhetoric of freedom and self-determination unleashed a public debate over the legitimacy of slavery. African Americans fueled the discussion by escaping to the British and serving in the American army. In doing so, African Americans made whites more aware of the hypocrisy of fighting a war of independence while they kept other human beings in chains. In petitions, Massachusetts blacks made the connection explicit during the war, writing that as long as whigs failed to emancipate slaves, they were "chargeable with the inconsistency of acting . . . the part which they condemn & oppose in others."

In the north, the first significant opposition to slavery had developed among Pennsylvania and New Jersey Quakers well before the Revolution. Since the seventeenth century, individual members of the Society of Friends had argued that black bondage violated basic Christian concepts, particularly the belief that all humans are equal in the eyes of God. For decades, these Quaker abolitionists failed to convince their meetings that slavery was wrong because many wealthy, powerful Friends held slaves. But after 1750, the Society of Friends became the first American religion to denounce perpetual bondage as a sin and to prohibit members from holding slaves. The Quakers then spearheaded an emancipation movement that gained strength among other whites in the 1770s and 1780s. In addition, by the 1780s, slavery was less important economically in northern states than in the south, thus the combination of religious conviction, natural rights concepts of liberty and equality, and pressure by African Americans could undercut its viability. Prospective owners, already sensitized by guilt, grew wary of purchasing slaves, who were likely to demand emancipation or run away. Instead, northern employers hired workers from among the growing numbers of free laborers.

In Pennsylvania and New England, state governments acted against slavery by the mid-1780s. The Pennsylvania assembly passed the first abolition law in 1780, its preamble reflecting the ideas that inspired many abolitionists of the revolutionary era:

> When we contemplate our abhorrence of that condition to which the arms and tyranny of Great Britain were exerted to reduce us, when we look back on the variety of dangers to which we have been exposed, [we are grateful for] the manifold blessings which we have undeservedly received. . . . We conceive that it is our duty, and we rejoice that it is in our power, to extend a portion of that freedom to others.

The act was less comprehensive than its heartiest supporters wished. As a result of compromises required for passage, the Pennsylvania act abolished slavery gradually—so gradually that under its provisions no black Pennsylvanian would achieve freedom until 1808. The law provided that children born to slave mothers after March 1780 would be freed when they reached the age of twenty-eight. Slaves who had been born before that date would remain in bondage.

Nevertheless, the Pennsylvania act was more effective than expected, as many enslaved blacks, exasperated that the law failed to free them, escaped their masters, and hundreds of slaveholders conformed to the spirit of the law by manumitting their slaves, regardless of birth date, at about age twenty-eight. Though these owners benefited from the labor of African Americans during their prime years, still, the manumissions helped to bring about the early end of slavery in the state. Also significant was the work of the Pennsylvania Abolition Society, which tested the limits of the 1780 abolition act by providing legal counsel to African Americans to defend their liberty.

Elsewhere in the north, the Massachusetts supreme court in 1783 decided that slavery was

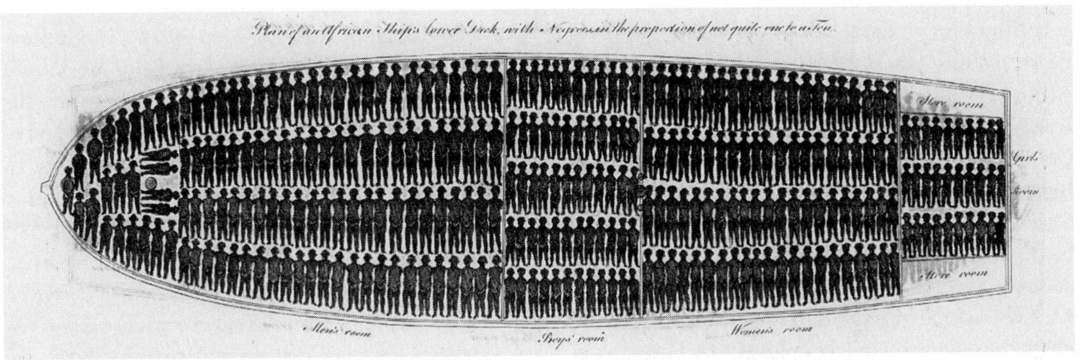

One of the goals of the Pennsylvania Abolition Society was to end the international slave trade. The text of this 1789 tract states that enslaved Africans on slave ships were "packed, side by side, almost like herrings in a barrel, and reduced to the state of being buried alive." (The Library Company of Philadelphia)

incompatible with the state's 1780 constitution, which said all men are free and equal, though it did not specifically outlaw perpetual bondage. As blacks sued for freedom, the courts ruled on their behalf, and so by 1790, Massachusetts reported no slaves on the federal census. The Connecticut and Rhode Island legislatures in 1784 followed Pennsylvania's example by passing gradual abolition laws, and Vermont and New Hampshire also banned the institution. New York and New Jersey passed gradual abolition acts in 1799 and 1804 respectively.

Southern states, like their northern counterparts, continued the First Continental Congress's prohibition of the slave trade. Some people expected cessation of the trade to result in the gradual death of slavery in Virginia and Maryland—a mistake because the African American population there grew naturally by reproduction. Involuntary bondage would persist without positive action for abolition.

Thomas Jefferson exemplified the troubled and confused state of mind of many white Americans about slavery. Though he remained a slaveholder throughout his life and held racist beliefs, Jefferson claimed to support a strategy for gradual abolition in Virginia. The plan, never considered by the assembly, would have freed and educated African American children born after the law went into effect and, when adults, remove them to a separate territory. Relocation to a new land was one suggestion for abolishing slavery yet maintaining white power.

Efforts for general abolition failed south of Pennsylvania, yet some progress occurred when Virginia (in 1782), Delaware (in 1787), and Maryland (in 1790) made private emancipation easier. New manumission laws permitted slaveholders who were inspired by antislavery beliefs to free their slaves. A private abolition movement took fire in areas of the Upper South where Quakers and Methodists were numerous and planters were changing from tobacco to wheat as their chief crop, thus requiring fewer field hands. Though declining demand for labor played a role in their decision, still, slaveholders had the choice of whether to emancipate or sell their bondpeople.

The rise in the number of free African Americans in the Upper South was a measure of opposition to slavery. The free black population in Delaware rose to 8,000 by the end of the century; in Maryland to 20,000, and in Virginia to nearly 13,000. Even with impressive numbers of manumissions, however, in 1800 emancipated blacks were just 8 percent of all African Americans in the region.

Defining Religious Liberty

Another question that faced the architects of the new state governments was religious freedom. Revolutionary ideals led many to challenge laws that forced people to attend and financially support an established church. Before the Revolution, the colonies had varied widely in the relationship of church and state. Congregational churches were tax-supported in Massachusetts, New Hampshire, and Connecticut, whereas the Church of England (Anglican) was established in the Carolinas, Virginia, Maryland, and New York. In contrast, Rhode Island, New Jersey, and Pennsylvania protected a great diversity of religions, giving none of them public funds. All of the colonies, however, placed limits on who could serve in political office.

The break with Great Britain had the greatest impact on the established Church of England. With independence, some of its parishes dissolved. Many Anglican clergymen and laypeople in New England and the Mid-Atlantic region became loyalists, helping to fuel the whig movement for disestablishment. All of the states in which the Anglican church was established promptly ended government support except Virginia. Virginia finally acted in 1786, when the assembly passed Thomas Jefferson's statute for religious liberty, which stated,

> no man shall be compelled to frequent or support any religious worship, place or ministry whatsoever, nor shall be enforced, restrained, molested, or burthened in his body or goods, nor shall otherwise suffer on account of his religious opinions or belief.

Petition of Philadelphia Jews for Equal Rights, 1783

Though Pennsylvania was renowned for religious liberty, its constitution limited election to the state assembly to Christians. As other states broadened religious liberty during the revolutionary era, Philadelphia Jews called for redress of this inequity. The new Pennsylvania constitution adopted in 1790 removed this religious test.

To the honourable the Council of Censors, assembled agreeable to the Constitution of the State of Pennsylvania. The Memorial of . . . the Synagogue of the Jews at Philadelphia, . . .

Most respectfully showeth,

That by the tenth section of the Frame of Government of this Commonwealth, it is ordered that each member of the general assembly of representatives of the freemen of Pennsylvania, before he takes his seat, shall make and subscribe a declaration, which ends in these words, "I do acknowledge the Scriptures of the old and new Testament to be given by divine inspiration. . . ."

Your memorialists beg leave to observe, that this clause seems to limit the civil rights of your citizens to one very special article of the creed; whereas by the second paragraph of the declaration of the rights of the inhabitants, it is asserted without any other limitation than the professing the existence of God, in plain words, "that no man who acknowledges the being of a God can be justly deprived or abridged of any civil rights as a citizen on account of his religious sentiments." But certainly this religious test deprives the Jews of the most eminent rights of freemen, solemnly ascertained to all men who are not professed Atheists.

May it please your Honors, . . .

Your memorialists cannot say that the Jews are particularly fond of being representatives of the people in assembly or civil officers and magistrates in the State; but with great submission they apprehend that a clause in the constitution, which disables them to be elected by their fellow citizens to represent them in assembly, is a stigma upon their nation and religion. . . .

The Jews of Pennsylvania in proportion to the number of their members, can count with any religious society whatsoever, the Whigs among either of them; they have served some of them in the Continental army; some went out in the militia to fight the common enemy; all of them have cheerfully contributed to the support of the militia, and of the government of this State; they have no inconsiderable property in lands and tenements, but particularly in the way of trade, some more, some less, for which they pay taxes; they have, upon every plan formed for public utility, been forward to contribute as much as their circumstances would admit of; and as a nation or a religious society, they stand unimpeached of any matter whatsoever, against the safety and happiness of the people. . . .

One of the chief causes of the Revolution had been the peacetime quartering in New York and Boston of the British army. But now the United States faced threats from the Spanish in Florida and Louisiana, the British in Canada, and Native Americans everywhere along the frontier. In April 1783, Congress appointed a committee to consult Washington and other generals on military requirements. The commander-in-chief argued that the United States had to be prepared against its enemies. He suggested retaining 2,600 Continentals in one artillery and four infantry regiments. He also advised Congress to organize a national citizens' militia that would stay in training for ready defense. In 1784, Congress dismissed Washington's plan, stationing a total of eighty men at two forts in New York and Pennsylvania. For reasons of principle and finances, the Confederation government virtually disbanded the army during an interval of peace, a pattern the nation would follow well into the twentieth century.

Economic Troubles

The Confederation Congress failed to solve the problem of its war debt, which by 1790 amounted to an estimated $10 million owed to other countries and $40 million owed to Americans. During the war, the government had issued paper currency to pay for goods and services. It abandoned this policy because of rampant inflation. Congress turned to the states, which refused to contribute sufficient funds, then borrowed from France and from American merchants and farmers for military provisions. It also deferred payment on soldiers' wages. As the principal and interest mounted on these promissory notes and bonds, Congress requested an amendment to the Articles to permit a national duty of 5 percent on all imports. Unanimous agreement of the states was necessary. The legislators tried for five years, but failed on each attempt.

One long-lasting consequence of the war's inflationary crisis was conflict between urban and rural interests over public finance. The spiraling cost of food and fuel in the late 1770s had hurt city residents much more than farmers. Farmers wanted access to government loans based on the value of their land and its production. Merchants and urban artisans believed that paper currency based on real estate would send prices sky-high. At the same time, merchants knew that the economy would stagnate if specie (gold and silver) were required for every transaction, so they embraced an alternative method of generating paper currency, the bank.

The first bank in the United States was the Bank of North America, created in 1781 in Philadelphia. Robert Morris proposed the institution, based on the Bank of England, as a way to help solve the wartime fiscal crisis. Morris obtained support from Alexander Hamilton, Thomas Paine, and a committee of Congress for his plan; both the Congress and state of Pennsylvania chartered the institution. Instead of issuing paper currency through a land office, the bank issued currency in the form of short-term loans to merchants. These bank notes were backed by gold and silver plate and coins that investors deposited in return for a share of the bank's profits. If people doubted the security of the bank, they could redeem their bank notes. Bank advocates believed that once a few people tested its soundness and received specie, others would trust the bank and accept the bank notes as currency.

In fact, the Bank of North America followed a conservative course that kept it solvent financially but made it unpopular with many people. The bank's manager, Thomas Willing, lent money only to good credit risks in the mercantile community, thus angering artisans and farmers. Also, Willing refused to liberalize the bank's loan policy by taking advantage of confidence in the bank's strength. Instead of expanding the money supply as later banks did, the Bank of North America made loans only up to the amount of specie in its vaults.

The Bank of North America helped the mercantile community through a time of uncertainty. Commerce had suffered during the revolution as merchants lost connections with trading partners in Great Britain and the British West Indies. In 1783, Americans expected to reestablish those ties as well as enter new markets in Europe and the French and Spanish colonies. With their newly won independence, they gained release from the restrictions of British mercantilism.

But being part of the mercantilist system had brought advantages as well as constraints. The British closed the ports of the British West Indies to American ships, a sharp blow for New England and the Middle Atlantic states. To Great Britain and its colonies, the United States was now a foreign country. Americans could sell provisions in the islands and purchase rum, sugar, and molasses, but everything had to be carried on British ships. West Indies planters complained because this resulted in higher prices; American shipowners had to find new routes. On the other hand, Britain was eager to purchase tobacco from the Chesapeake and sell to Americans all the manufactures they would buy. U.S. merchants had access by treaty to ports in France and the French colonies, but were barred from trading in New Spain. Gradually, Americans developed trade with Germany, the Netherlands, Scandinavia, and even China. By the end of the 1780s, U.S. exports recovered to approximately their prerevolutionary level.

The road to recovery was rocky, however, because in the immediate postwar years American demand for British manufactures far outstripped exports. During the Revolution, American artisans had attempted to supply metal goods and textiles, but had been unable to match British quality and prices. With peace, British manufacturers extended generous credit to American consumers for clocks, watches, furniture, textiles, clothing, mirrors, and other goods. When depression hit in fall 1783 because of the loss of the West Indies market, American farmers, merchants, and shopkeepers found themselves seriously in debt. Although the economy improved after mid-1785, many farmers had difficulty escaping from debt.

Indeed, estimates of the gross national product suggest that the Revolution had an extended negative impact on the American economy. Data available for 1774 and 1790 indicate that income declined by over 40 percent, close to the decrease Americans experienced during the Great Depression of the 1930s.

Foreign Affairs

Though the United States had won both the war and the peace, its leaders soon learned that they received little respect among European nations. Despite the boundary provisions of the Treaty of 1783, Spain and Great Britain took advantage of the Confederation's weakness to trespass on territory in the west. The Spanish and English gained allies among Native Americans who were losing their lands to the steady stream of white settlers crossing the Appalachians.

During the 1780s, the Spanish tried to restrict expansion of the United States. The Spanish government had refused to accept the treaty boundaries granting the region between the Appalachians and the Mississippi River to the United States. With settlers rapidly filling the area, Spain feared for its control of Louisiana and East and West Florida; it wanted to extend its territory north from West Florida to the Ohio River. The Spanish pursued this objective in a number of ways. They retained forts north of the 31st parallel, which the United States claimed as its southern border. Then, in 1784, the Spanish government closed the port of New Orleans to Americans, apparently hoping to detach from the United States the region that later became Kentucky and Tennessee. Settlers in the trans-Appalachian region protested vigorously because they needed access to the New Orleans market for their goods. Some threatened to secede from the United States unless Congress convinced Spain to reverse its decision.

Congress directed John Jay, the secretary of foreign affairs, to negotiate with Spain to reopen the port. The Spanish diplomat, Diego de Gardoqui, refused to budge, instead offering to open other Spanish ports to U.S. commerce if Americans would relinquish demands for free navigation on the lower Mississippi. With the permis-

MAP 6.1 | WESTERN LAND CESSIONS, 1782–1802

sion of Congress, Jay agreed to a treaty that provided commercial advantages for eastern merchants but closed New Orleans to westerners for a generation. The west and south erupted in opposition, blocking approval of the Jay-Gardoqui Treaty. The lower Mississippi River remained closed until 1788.

The Spanish government also cooperated with Native Americans to slow the influx of Anglo-American settlers into contested territory. Spanish colonists in the Floridas remained few, so they depended upon good relations with the Creeks, Choctaws, and Chickasaws who controlled the region. Contrary to Spain's traditional policy of considering Native Americans as subjects to the Crown, its colonial officials in 1784 signed written treaties of alliance with the Indians.

Most threatening of these pacts to the United States was the one with the Creeks, which their leader Alexander McGillivray arranged. The son of a Scottish trader and a French-Creek woman, McGillivray could negotiate his way in both European and Indian societies. To protect Creek lands from settlers streaming in from Georgia, he offered the Spanish "a powerful barrier in these parts against the ambitious and encroaching Americans" in return for an alliance and weapons. With Cherokees and Shawnees to the north, the Creeks battled Anglo-Americans through the 1780s.

The Confederation government also had difficulty establishing its claims against the British and the Indians of the Ohio Valley. In the treaty of 1783, the British had promised to remove their troops from forts in the Great Lakes region. Through the 1780s, however, they refused to withdraw, hoping for return of the territory. They barred American ships from the Great Lakes and allied with Native Americans who wanted to halt white settlement. British diplomats justified these actions with the excuse that Americans had failed to pay prewar debts to British creditors and return confiscated loyalist property.

Great Britain's neglect of its Indian allies in negotiating the peace led the U.S. government to treat them as a conquered people. American commissioners said to the Ohio Indians, "You are mistaken in supposing that . . . you are become a free and independent nation, and may make what terms you please. . . . You are a subdued people." Under threat of arms, a group of Iroquois yielded rights in the Northwest with the Treaty of Fort Stanwix (1784); Wyandots, Delawares, and others ceded Ohio lands in the Treaty of Fort McIntosh (1785); and Shawnees gave up territory in the Treaty of Fort Finney (1786). Many Native Americans refused to recognize these treaties because the Indian negotiators lacked authority and had been forced to sign. Soon, frontier warfare made U.S. officials realize that they were the ones who were "mistaken" in presuming that the Indians had been "subdued." Theyendanegea (Joseph Brant), the pro-British Mohawk leader, rallied Indians against white settlement in the Northwest. Their resistance convinced Secretary of War Henry Knox that the United States must change its tactics or risk a general Indian war. He suggested that Congress return to the policy of purchasing lands, instead of demanding them by conquest. The congressmen agreed, incorporating into the Northwest Ordinance of 1787 the futile promise that the Indians' land "shall never be taken from them without their consent."

The Northwest Ordinances

Despite the presence of British troops, the Confederation Congress moved forward with legislation to create the Northwest Territory. The issue of western lands had divided the thirteen states even during the Revolution. Some states claimed territories from their colonial charters, whereas others had never possessed such claims. Titles stood in conflict with one another, as in the case of the region north of the Ohio River, which Virginia claimed in its entirety and Connecticut and Massachusetts claimed in part. States lacking rights to western lands believed that all should be ceded to the Confederation because together the states had won the trans-Appalachian territory in the Revolution. Virginia, whose charter rights were oldest, resolved the issue in 1781 by agreeing to transfer to the United States the region north and west of the Ohio River, the area that later became the states of Ohio, Indiana, Illinois, Michigan, and Wisconsin. Virginia offered cession on the condition that the territory eventually be divided into states that would join the Confederation on an equal basis with the original thirteen. The trans-Appalachian lands south of the Ohio River remained temporarily under the control of Virginia, North Carolina, and Georgia.

Congress passed three ordinances to establish guidelines for distributing land and governing the Northwest Territory. Thomas Jefferson was principal author of the first ordinance, which passed Congress in 1784. The Northwest would be divided into seven districts, with the settlers of each to gov-

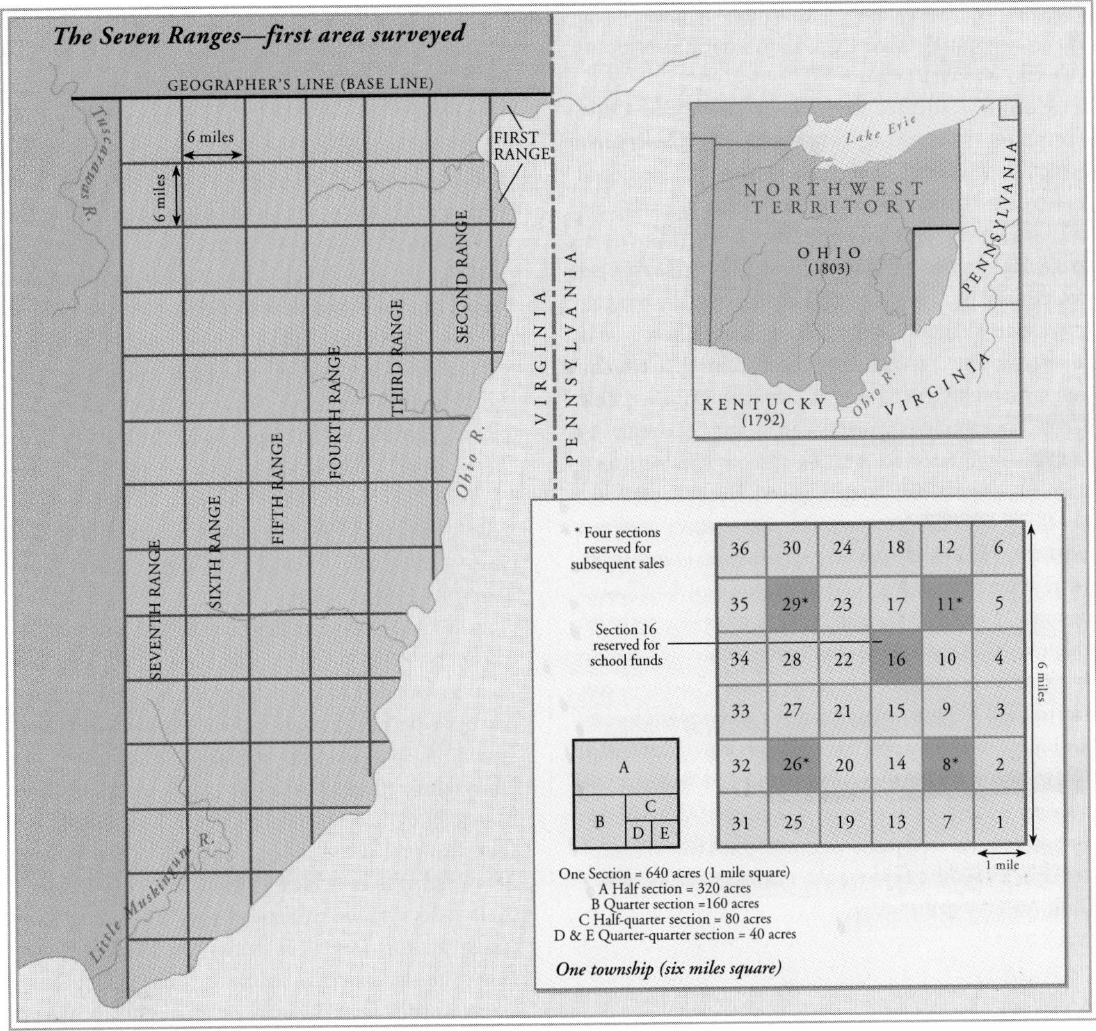

Map 6.2 | Land Ordinance of 1785

ern themselves by choosing a constitution and laws from any of the existing states. When any district reached the population of the smallest of the original thirteen states, it would be admitted as a state to the Confederation on equal terms. Congress retained responsibility for selling the public lands.

The second ordinance, passed in 1785, set the rules for distributing lands. The influence of speculators was apparent, for the minimum price of a lot was $640, payable in specie or its equivalent, a sum far beyond the means of many potential settlers. All property would be surveyed before sale, laid out in townships six miles square. Each lot would contain 640 acres sold at a minimum of one dollar per acre, with better land offered at a higher price. The government retained lots for public schools and for distribution to Revolutionary War veterans. Because of the relatively high cost, Congress found few individual buyers. So it accepted a deal offered by a group of New England speculators, the Ohio Company, agreeing to sell them 1.5 million acres for $500,000 in depreciated bonds, or less than ten cents per acre in hard money. Given the Confederation's debt, the sale was welcome.

Congress further cooperated with the Ohio Company in drafting the Northwest Ordinance of 1787. The law established firmer congressional control over the territory, providing settlers less self-government than under the 1784 ordinance. Initially, a governor, secretary, and three judges appointed by Congress would administer the government. When 5,000 adult males resided in the territory, they could elect an assembly, but the governor held a veto over its actions. Men were eligible to vote if they owned at least fifty acres of land. Three to five states would be created from the Northwest Territory, with each state qualified to enter the union when its population reached 60,000. New states would have equal status with the original thirteen. The ordinance of 1787 also protected private contracts, religious liberty, trial by jury, and habeas corpus (protection against illegal imprisonment). It prohibited slavery from the region forever. Thus, while catering to the interests of speculators, the Northwest Ordinance also extended rights won during the Revolution to new settlers in the west. Further, it limited the spread of slavery, and determined that western territories would achieve the status of states rather than remain colonies.

Political and Economic Turmoil

Political strife under the Articles of Confederation disappointed Americans who had high hopes for their republic. Instead of harmony, economic interests clashed; the states failed to satisfy everybody. Many elites thought the United States was becoming too democratic and anarchic, as farmers revolted, government failed to control the violence, and some legislatures approved the insurgents' demands.

Creditors Versus Debtors

As a result of the postwar depression, farmers throughout the United States faced economic hardship. Many had eagerly purchased British manufactures, expecting to pay for the new clothes and consumer goods by selling their grain and livestock to the West Indies. The house of cards collapsed when the British government closed the West Indies to American ships. English mercantile houses called in their debts in specie only. Americans lacked the gold and silver that the British demanded, but merchants refused to accept payment in farm products. In many places, the number of debt cases rose dramatically. For example, in Hampshire County, Massachusetts, from 1784 to 1786, the court heard 3,000 debt cases: almost one-third of the county's adult males were prosecuted for insolvency.

State governments aggravated the situation by imposing taxes to repay war bonds in full, a policy that worked to the advantage of wealthy speculators who had bought up the bonds from farmers and artisans at a large discount. The Massachusetts government particularly favored mercantile interests, levying on farmers high taxes that also had to be paid in specie. When farmers defaulted, the courts sold their land and cattle. If their assets failed to cover the debts and back taxes, the farmers were imprisoned until they or someone else paid the sum. Ordinary folk became angry as they feared imprisonment and the loss of their farms.

Farmers Demand Reform

Protesters mobilized, meeting in county conventions to draw up petitions to the state assembly. In Massachusetts, they demanded changes in the state constitution to make the government more responsive to their needs and less costly to run. They wanted abolition of the state senate, which represented the commercial elite; lowering of property qualifications to hold office; and transfer of the capital from Boston to a more central location. The farmers also demanded paper money and tender laws, the latter enabling them to settle debts and taxes with goods rather than specie. During the Revolution, the yeomen had benefited from the inflation that resulted from government issued paper money because they received high prices for their produce and were able to pay off prewar debts with cheap dollars. Although the farmers stopped short of demanding a return to high inflation, they hoped for a gentle upswing in prices and a larger money supply to help them pay their debts.

When state legislatures emitted paper money or passed tender laws, as in Rhode Island, North Carolina, New York, and Georgia, little unrest ensued. In Rhode Island, political parties channeled conflict, for after the Country party ousted the Mercantile party in spring 1786, the new assembly issued paper money with stiff fines for creditors who refused to accept it.

In other states, mercantile factions maintained control of the government. They detested paper money because debtors would pay in depreciated bills; they opposed tender laws because of the lack of a market for grain and livestock. Merchants argued that paper currency issued as loans on farm property (rather than as notes based on gold and silver deposited in banks) was immoral because it would lose value, allowing debtors to violate contracts by paying back less than they had borrowed. Creditors asserted that their property rights were at risk.

Shays' Rebellion

When state governments failed to help, debtors in New England, New Jersey, Pennsylvania, Maryland, Virginia, and South Carolina protested militantly. Events moved furthest in Massachusetts. In fall 1786, armed Massachusetts farmers closed down county courts to prevent further hearings for debt. Perhaps one-fourth of potential soldiers in the state were involved, calling themselves the "Regulators," after the Carolina insurgents of the 1760s. Their opponents first labeled the rebels

Daniel Shays and Job Shattuck, from the cover of a pamphlet supporting Shays' Rebellion. (The Granger Collection)

"Green Bushers" because they wore a sprig of evergreen—the Massachusetts symbol for liberty—then called them Shaysites when Daniel Shays, a forty-year-old veteran of Bunker Hill and Saratoga, emerged as leader. The government frantically requested aid from Congress, which complied by requisitioning $530,000 and 1,340 soldiers from the states. When the states failed to cooperate, the powerlessness of the Confederation was clear.

The Massachusetts government acted on its own, taking measures that further alienated angry farmers. The assembly passed the Riot Act, which prohibited armed groups from gathering in public and permitted sheriffs to kill rioters who refused to disband. The legislature also suspended habeas corpus, allowing officials to jail suspected insurgents without showing cause. The farmers refused to back down. They protested that the suspension of habeas corpus was "dangerous if not absolutely destructive to a Republican government." Nevertheless, in November 1786, the state government sent 300 soldiers to arrest rebel leaders; when that failed to stop the farmers from closing the courts, Boston merchants raised private funds to outfit 4,400 troops. Revolutionary general Benjamin Lincoln commanded the army; in January 1787, they marched to Worcester to protect the county court.

Lincoln's army forced the Shaysites to choose between submission and armed rebellion, for a middle ground of petitions and court closings was no longer viable. The farmers amassed their own troops, estimated at 2,500 men, with Shays in charge of one regiment. They unsuccessfully attacked the federal arsenal at Springfield for weapons to assault Boston, then regrouped to await the merchants' army. Lincoln attacked Shays by surprise in a blizzard, dispersing the rebels within half an hour.

The aftermath of Shays' defeat was more divisive and bloody than the engagements between the armies. The assembly declared a state of "open, unnatural, unprovoked, and wicked rebellion," giving the governor the power to treat the Shaysites as enemies of the state. The legislators passed the Disqualification Act, which barred people implicated in the revolt from voting and holding office for three years, teaching school, or keeping inns and taverns. Many of the insurgents escaped to New York and Vermont. Others were imprisoned. Militant Shaysites prolonged the conflict by kidnapping people who had sided with the government. As a result of the uprising and repression, voter turnout skyrocketed in the April 1787 election. A much greater number of western Massachusetts towns sent delegates to the legislature than they had in previous years, making the new assembly somewhat more responsive to rural debtors. Although refusing to approve paper money, it enacted a tender law and quickly restored the civil rights of the insurgents.

The Movement for Constitutional Reform

The Confederation's helplessness in response to spreading armed rebellion strengthened the hand of nationalists who had been arguing for a more powerful central government. By 1787, Congress had lost much of its authority. Because it had failed to obtain a national tax and could not force the states to send requisitioned funds, the Confederation was broke.

The Philadelphia Convention

In September 1786, representatives gathered for a convention in Annapolis, Maryland, to discuss amending the Articles to give Congress power to regulate trade. The convention failed when only five state delegations arrived on time. Several of the delegates called for another convention to meet in May 1787 at Philadelphia to consider a more thorough revision of the Articles. By early 1787, the disorder in Massachusetts and the growing concern about state emission of paper money built support for constitutional reform. In February, Congress endorsed a change. Twelve states—all but Rhode Island where farmers controlled the legislature—sent delegates to Philadelphia.

Though the appointed day was May 14, 1787, the convention failed to start until May 25 when enough representatives finally arrived. State legislatures had delayed choosing their delegations and travel was slow. Among the first were Virginia's representatives, who used the extra time for planning. James Madison, a thirty-six-year-old planter, slaveholder, and intellectual who had served in the Virginia assembly and Congress, came to the convention well prepared. Madison wanted to reform the Confederation to create a stronger central government. He believed that state constitutions with powerful assemblies were too democratic, giving too much influence to the common people. As a consequence, these legislatures collaborated with debtors by circulating paper money, which Madison considered an attack on property. The people should be represented adequately, Madison thought, but their power must be constrained. The United States needed a new constitution that would place authority in the hands of well-educated, propertied men.

A total of fifty-five men served at the Constitutional Convention between opening day and adjournment four months later. Twenty-one were practicing lawyers, another thirteen had been educated in the law, seven were merchants, and eighteen were farmers or planters; nineteen owned African American slaves. Many had served in the Revolution and had held political office. Benjamin Franklin, now eighty-one years old and ailing, was a member of the Pennsylvania delegation. Several heroes of the revolution were absent, including Thomas Jefferson and John Adams, who were ambassadors abroad; Samuel Adams, who was not chosen as a delegate; and Patrick Henry, who refused to serve because he "smelt a rat."

The Great Compromise

The convention can be divided into two periods. During the first seven weeks, the matter overshadowing all discussion was the power of "large" versus "small" states. After this issue was resolved, delegations formed blocs in new ways, according to concerns about the executive, slavery, and commerce. The basic question that the convention avoided debating at length was whether to amend the Articles of Confederation or write an entirely new constitution. Madison, who thought the Confederation beyond repair, moved the convention along with a document he had drafted in advance, called the Virginia Plan, which scrapped the Articles.

The Virginia Plan proposed a powerful central government, dominated by a National Legislature of two houses (bicameral). The lower house would be elected by qualified voters and would choose the members of the upper house from nominations by state legislatures. The number of delegates from each state depended upon population. This bicameral National Legislature was empowered to appoint the executive and judicial branches of the central government and to veto state laws.

Several states opposed the Virginia Plan because it gave greater representation in the National Legislature to states with large populations. If the Virginia Plan were adopted, just four states could dominate the legislature. In dividing on this issue, states considered the possibility of future population expansion as well as present size. Thus states with unsettled territories mostly sided with the large states, while those without room for growth chose the opposite camp.

The small states preferred a constitution that retained the structure of the Confederation Congress, but expanded its powers. In mid-June, William Paterson introduced the New Jersey Plan, which proposed a one-house, or unicameral, Congress in which the states had equal representation. Congress would appoint an executive council, which in turn would choose a supreme court. As in the Virginia Plan, the authority of Congress was much enlarged, with powers to tax, regulate commerce, and compel states to obey its laws. The large states objected to this plan, arguing that Delaware (population 59,000) should not have as much power as Virginia (population 748,000).

The debate over representation in Congress brought the convention to an impasse. The large states had the votes in the convention but knew they could never get the constitution ratified if the Virginia Plan prevailed. The Delaware delegation threatened to walk out until Connecticut put forward its proposal, allowing debate to continue. The "great compromise," as Connecticut's plan became known, established a bicameral Congress, with representation in the lower house based upon population. This house, called the House of Representatives, would be elected directly by the voters and have the sole right to initiate revenue bills. Thus, the idea that people with a stake in society should elect the representatives who taxed them was incorporated into the document. In the upper house, called the Senate, states would have equal representation; each state legislature chose two senators to serve six-year terms. The House of Representatives would be elected every two years. The bicameral Congress resolved the division between the small and large states and also satisfied those who wanted to limit the influence of ordinary voters. Senators were expected to come from the wealthier, more established segments of society; their long terms

This painting of the Constitutional Convention of 1787 by an unknown artist shows George Washington presiding. Because the convention met in secrecy, the artist used his imagination to paint the scene. (Independence National Historical Park)

and appointment by state legislators would shield them from public opinion. Both houses of Congress had to approve legislation.

The compromise between the large and small states created a government that was both national and federal. It was *national* because the House of Representatives was popularly elected, with not more than one representative per 30,000 people. Upon ratification, the United States would become a single nation rather than a confederacy of states. By expanding legislative powers, the sovereign people vested more authority in the central government. Congress received the powers to tax, coin and borrow money, regulate commerce, establish courts, declare war, and raise armed forces. States were specifically forbidden from keeping troops without the permission of Congress, making treaties, coining money, and issuing paper currency. At the same time, the new Constitution established a *federal* government, one in which the states retained rights, including equal representation in the Senate. Congress was forbidden from giving one state preference over another when levying taxes and regulating trade, nor could it impose export duties, prohibit the slave trade until 1808, or carve a new state from any state's territory without permission. Approval by three-fourths of the states would be necessary to amend the Constitution. But despite these provisions, many Americans believed that the states had lost too much power. The struggle for ratification revolved in large part around this issue.

The Executive, Slavery, and Commerce

Once the question of state representation was solved with the "great compromise," the convention made greater headway. Factions within the convention shifted from one debate to the next.

The power of the executive was a concern to people living in a world dominated by kings and princes. Delegates wanted to ensure that their government remained a republic. At the same time, they believed that the executive branch should serve as a check on the legislature. The convention debated several questions affecting the executive's power. Should there be a single president or an executive board? Although some argued that a plural executive could prevent one person from usurping power, the convention chose a single president. Length of term also stimulated discussion, for the longer the term, the greater a president's autonomy. The convention reached agreement on a four-year term.

The question of how the president would be chosen was divisive, between those who preferred direct election by the people and those who wanted Congress or the state legislatures to make the choice. A committee appointed by the convention devised an ingenious but complicated formula to satisfy all sides—the electoral college. The electoral college was empowered to elect the president and vice president, with each state allotted as many votes as it had representatives and senators. Thus, even the smallest state received three votes and the large states were represented according to population. The state legislatures could determine how to choose the electors. The electoral college would never meet together as a group. The electors of each state gathered within their states to cast votes, which they sent to Congress for counting. If no candidate received a majority, the House of Representatives made the selection from among the five candidates with the most votes.

Of the Philadelphia convention's decisions on the executive most crucial to the endurance of the Constitution was the balance of power between the executive and legislative branches. The convention gave the president a veto over laws passed by Congress. The legislators could override the veto if two-thirds of both houses approved. Congress also had authority to remove the president by impeachment and trial for treason, bribery, and "other high Crimes and Misdemeanors." Whereas Congress received power to declare war and raise troops, the president served as commander-in-chief. Only with the "advice and consent" of the Senate could the chief executive negotiate treaties and appoint ambassadors, Supreme Court justices, and other officials.

Slavery was a major factor in the convention's deliberations, though the words "slavery," "slave," and "slave trade" appeared nowhere in the 1787 Constitution. The southern states wanted to include slaves in a state's population when computing delegates to the House of Representatives and votes in the electoral college. Northerners protested that this gave white southerners an unfair advantage (illustrated in Table 6.1) because enslaved people could not vote. As part of the "great compromise," the convention decided that five enslaved Americans would count as three free persons for apportioning representation and direct taxes among the states. Since three-fifths of slaves living in the Chesapeake and Lower South numbered 380,000 people, the power of white voters south of Pennsylvania was significantly magnified.

Table 6.1 United States Population, 1790

	Total (all whites and free African Americans)	*Slaves*
New England	1,009,206	3,763
Middle Atlantic	1,017,087	45,210
Maryland and Virginia	1,067,338	395,663
Lower South	726,626	237,141

Political bargaining resulted in additional provisions that furthered slavery. The convention approved a fugitive slave clause, which prevented free states from emancipating slaves who had escaped from masters in other states. The delegates also adopted a provision that forbade Congress from prohibiting slave importation for twenty years. North and South Carolina and Georgia demanded the option of importing people from Africa because they expected settlement to continue into western Georgia and the present states of Alabama, Mississippi, and Tennessee. Northern delegates, who might have pushed the convention toward the abolition of slavery, did almost nothing to promote that end.

Instead of trying to eliminate slavery under the new government, the northerners made the regulation of commerce their priority. The southern states suspected that the national government, if dominated by northerners in the future, would place heavy taxes on tobacco, rice, and indigo—the south's main exports. Southerners thought that navigation laws could also work to their detriment, because northern merchants owned most American shipping. If Congress passed legislation requiring that all exports be transported in American ships, southerners would lose the choice of using a foreign, perhaps cheaper, carrier. Northerners, on the other hand, wanted Congress to have the authority to negotiate trade agreements on an equal basis with other nations. Congress could then retaliate if a country imposed restrictions such as closing ports. The convention settled these matters, first by forbidding Congress from imposing export duties, then with a deal that empowered Congress to regulate commerce. In return for South Carolina's vote for the latter provision, New England agreed to extend the slave trade for twenty years.

The Philadelphia convention created a Constitution that shifted important powers to a national government, but still vested a great deal of authority in the states. The framers painstakingly created checks and balances among the branches of government. They required direct popular election of only the House of Representatives, giving that body the right to initiate taxes. The convention incorporated flexibility into the document by permitting amendment with approval of two-thirds of both houses of Congress and three-fourths of the states. The document shielded some individual rights. It protected trial by jury in criminal cases and habeas corpus. It banned religious tests for holding office under the United States, ex post facto (retroactive) laws, and bills of attainder, which extinguished a person's civil rights upon sentence of death or as an outlaw. While codifying the principles of self-government and individual liberties, however, the convention denied them to almost one-fifth of the American population by embedding slavery within the fabric of the new government.

Ratification

After the delegates to the Philadelphia convention signed the Constitution on September 17, 1787, they quickly sent it to the Confederation Congress in New York City. Article 7 of the document required ratification by nine state conventions. States refusing to ratify could remain independent or unite together under another frame of government. The majority of Congress had approved the Constitution as members of the Philadelphia convention, so they forwarded it to the states after little debate.

The group favoring ratification was not particularly well organized but had two advantages over its opponents. One came from the choice of a name, the Federalists. James Madison, Alexander Hamilton, John Jay, and other supporters of the Constitution argued in favor of the federalist provisions that reserved powers to the states as well as the nationalist elements of the prospective government. While others denounced the Constitution because it transferred too much power to the national government from the states, the Federalists claimed the document provided balance. The critics were obliged to take the negative name of Antifederalists, which misrepresented their position in favor of states' rights.

Most newspapers supported the Constitution. For example, in New York, where the ratification battle became intense, Hamilton, Madison, and Jay published in the newspapers a series of eighty-five essays that provided a detailed argument in favor of the Constitution. The essays also gained wide attention outside New York, and in spring 1788, the authors published them in book form as *The Federalist.*

Most Federalists gained their livelihoods as merchants, shopkeepers, professionals, artisans, and commercial farmers. As creditors and consumers, many favored the Constitution because it stopped state emission of paper currency. Federalists desired a government that would foster the growth of a market economy and facilitate trade with other countries. They believed a national government would provide the stability and strength that were lacking under the Confederation. Some frontier settlers, seeking military defense against Native Americans, also supported the Constitution.

The Federalists thought the purpose of government was to arbitrate among opposing interests. They considered elusive the republican ideal of a community in which everyone could reach consensus because they had similar needs. Madison argued in *Federalist* #10 that people possess different interests because they have unequal abilities and thus varying success in accumulating property. People by nature also have "different opinions concerning religion, concerning government, and many other points." In a free society, they form factions. He wrote:

> A landed interest, a manufacturing interest, a mercantile interest, a moneyed interest, with many lesser interests, grow up of necessity in civilized nations, and divide them into different classes, actuated by different sentiments and views. The regulation of these various and interfering interests forms the principal task of modern legislation, and involves the spirit of party and faction in the necessary and ordinary operations of the government.

Madison claimed that the Constitution would be beneficial because a large republic contained more safeguards than a small one. In an extended polity, so many factions exist that the ability of a single interest to monopolize power is reduced. With the national government, "you take in a greater variety of parties and interests; you make it less probable that a majority of the whole will have a common motive to invade the rights of other citizens."

Antifederalists disagreed with this analysis. Small farmers, many of them debtors who considered the mercantile elite their enemies, wanted nothing to do with this Constitution. At the core of their opposition was the belief that power should remain in the states. The Antifederalists argued that a republic must be geographically small with a homogeneous population in order to meet the needs of its people. They believed the new central government would be too large and too remote, that the interests of citizens of the thirteen states were too diverse. A congressman could never know the will of 30,000 constituents; with so few persons elected to Congress and such large electoral districts, affluent well-known candidates would have the advantage over ordinary men who ran for office. Thus, even the House of Representatives, the branch of government closest to the people, would become the domain of the rich. To the Antifederalists, the Constitution lacked sufficient barriers against corruption and abuse of power.

Antifederalists also pointed to the omission of a bill of rights as cause for rejecting the Constitution. They advocated freedom of speech, press, assembly, and religion; jury trials for civil cases; judicial safeguards such as the right to a speedy trial and to confront accusers and witnesses; and prohibitions against unwarranted searches and seizures. The Federalists answered that a bill of rights would be superfluous because state constitutions offered these protections (some did, but in no case was protection comprehensive), and because a bill of rights was needed against a powerful king, not when the people themselves were sovereign. This latter argument ignored the vulnerability of the individual to the will of the majority. The Federalists used poor judgment in failing to incorporate a bill of rights into the 1787 Constitution. Omitting these rights, for which the patriots had fought, turned many Americans against the proposed frame of government.

Nevertheless, ratification proceeded rapidly at first as state legislatures called elections for the state ratifying conventions. Delaware was the first to ratify when its convention approved the Constitution unanimously on December 7, 1787. In Pennsylvania, where resistance was potentially heavy in the backcountry, Federalists moved quickly, securing approval by a two-to-one margin. New Jersey and Georgia then ratified unanimously. When Connecticut accepted the new government in January 1788 by a three-to-one vote, five states had joined the union.

Then the conventions became more acrimonious. North Carolina and Rhode Island rejected the document outright and New Hampshire put off its decision. Maryland and South Carolina ratified easily, but the vote in Massachusetts was close. Turnout for the Massachusetts convention was huge, as farmers in the central and western regions of the state believed the Constitution represented the interests of the eastern elite. The convention barely ratified the document by a vote of 187 to 168, recommending a series of amendments to protect individual rights and limit the powers of Congress. In June 1788, New Hampshire finally acted, becoming the ninth state to ratify, the number required to establish the new government. Nevertheless, two states remained crucial, Virginia and New York, whose size and economic importance made their approval necessary if the Constitution was to succeed. Virginia ratified in late June after a fierce debate, recommending to the first Congress a series of amendments, including a bill of rights. New York approved in late July, also with recommended changes, after New York City threatened to secede from the rest of the state if rural districts failed to accept the document.

CONCLUSION

With ratification by eleven states, the United States began a new experiment in republican government. The Articles of Confederation had failed to inspire the thirteen states to work together to solve the Confederation's most pressing problems—the national debt, trade, and protection of U.S. borders against Spain and Great Britain. Even Congress's chief success, the legislation for governing and distributing land in the Northwest Territory, was marred by high land prices, favoritism toward speculators, and conflict with Native Americans. Of course, not all Americans thought the Articles were an utter failure. The Antifederalists preferred a confederacy of sovereign states in which governments stood ready to respond to local needs. But to the Federalists, this had led to paper money and armed rebellion. They demanded a new Constitution, one in which educated, propertied men like themselves would determine national economic policy and foreign affairs. The next challenge for the young United States was to put this new frame of government into effect.

RECOMMENDED READINGS

Beeman, Richard, Botein, Stephen, and Carter, Edward C., eds. *Beyond Confederation: Origins of the Constitution and American National Identity* (1987). These essays provide an excellent introduction to the Confederation period and the making of the Constitution.

Berlin, Ira, and Hoffman, Ronald, eds. *Slavery and Freedom in the Age of the American Revolution* (1983). Important essays on change, or lack thereof, in the status of African Americans during the revolutionary era.

Doerflinger, Thomas M. *A Vigorous Spirit of Enterprise: Merchants and Economic Development in Revolutionary Philadelphia* (1986). A very good study of Philadelphia merchants and their impact on economic growth in the emergent United States.

Equiano, Olaudah. *The Interesting Narrative of the Life of Olaudah Equiano,* in Henry Louis Gates, Jr., ed., *The Classic Slave Narratives* (1987). Autobiography of a kidnapped African who was enslaved in America, then eventually gained freedom.

Greene, Jack P. *Peripheries and Center: Constitutional Development in the Extended Polities of the British Empire and the United States, 1607–1788* (1986). Links the constitutional structure of Britain and its colonies to the Constitution of 1787.

Hamilton, Alexander, Jay, John, and Madison, James. *The Federalist Papers* (1788). Defense of the Constitution of 1787; seminal treatise of American political thought.

Kenyon, Cecilia M. "Men of Little Faith: The Anti-Federalists on the Nature of Representative Government," *William and Mary Quarterly*, 3d ser., 12 (1955): 3–43. Insightful essay on the men who opposed ratification of the Constitution of 1787.

Kerber, Linda K. *Women of the Republic: Intellect and Ideology in Revolutionary America* (1980). Evaluates the impact of the revolution on attitudes toward women.

Szatmary, David P. *Shays' Rebellion: The Making of an Agrarian Insurrection* (1980). A detailed study of the western Massachusetts revolt.

American Journey Online and InfoTrac College Edition

Visit the source collections at www.americanjourney.psmedia.com and infotrac.thomsonlearning.com and use the Search function with the following key terms to explore documents, images, audio and video clips, articles, and commentary related to the material in this chapter.

Shays' Rebellion
Constitutional Convention
James Madison
The Federalist essays
Northwest Ordinance

Chapter 7

The Federalist Republic, 1789–1799

After ratification, the Federalists took leadership in creating the new government. Everyone expected George Washington to become president. The three authors of *The Federalist,* Alexander Hamilton, James Madison, and John Jay, who had been so important in achieving the Constitution, went on to play a central role in making it work. John Adams and Thomas Jefferson, who were serving as ambassadors in Europe during the convention, returned home to become, respectively, vice president and secretary of state.

Though many Federalists disagreed with specific parts of the Constitution, they accepted compromise. In the flush of victory over the Antifederalists, they set to the task of remedying the nation's ills. Differences soon became clear, however, between Hamilton on the one side, and Madison and Jefferson on the other. As a result of their conflict over policy, varying interpretations of the Constitution, and competition for power, the nation's first political parties developed.

The New Government

The first national elections went well, from the Federalist point of view. The great majority of representatives and senators in the first Congress were Federalists. Many had served in the Constitutional Convention and had signed the document. Most had military or political experience during the Revolution and Confederation period. While the first congressmen were revolutionaries, they were also elites who believed that the country's interests coincided with their own. They wanted a stable government to foster economic growth.

George Washington Becomes President

The choice of George Washington as president was a foregone conclusion. In February 1789,

http://ayersbrief.wadsworth.com

CHRONOLOGY

1789 First Congress meets

Inauguration of George Washington as president

French Revolution begins

Judiciary Act of 1789

1790 Site on Potomac River chosen for permanent capital

Congress approves the funding and assumption plans

Samuel Slater builds first water-powered textile mill in the United States

First national census

Nootka Convention

1791 Bank of the United States is established

Native Americans of the Ohio Valley destroy Arthur St. Clair's army

Ratification of Bill of Rights

1793 France declares war on Great Britain and Spain

Washington begins second term

Proclamation of Neutrality

Genêt Affair

Britain seizes U.S. merchant fleet

Eli Whitney invents cotton gin

1794 Battle of Fallen Timbers

Whiskey Rebellion

1795 Senate approves the Jay Treaty

Treaty of Greenville

Treaty of San Lorenzo

1797 John Adams becomes second president

1798 XYZ Affair becomes public

Congress passes Alien and Sedition Acts

Kentucky and Virginia Resolutions

1798–1800 Quasi-War with France

1799 The Fries Rebellion

Napoleon takes power in France

members of the electoral college met in their state capitals to cast unanimous votes for the former commander-in-chief. Washington's leadership during the war, his dignity and character, and his support for republican government made him the obvious choice. He might have tried to grasp power during the shaky Confederation, but he did not. The first president's commitment to the success of the Constitution ensured the nation's survival during the early years. John Adams, elected vice president, received fewer than half as many votes as Washington.

The president-elect's trip from Mount Vernon to New York City, the temporary federal capital, became an eight-day triumphal march. In large and small towns along his way, crowds of people, troops of infantry and cavalry, and local officials feted him with ceremonies and banquets.

George Washington arrived in New York City for his inauguration as president to the cheers of thousands. (The Granger Collection)

Philadelphia citizens erected a Roman arch, crowning the revolutionary hero with a laurel wreath. In New Jersey, throngs saluted his military victories at Trenton and Princeton. On April 23, 1789, Washington crossed into Manhattan on a festooned barge, welcomed by thousands of cheering New Yorkers. He took the oath of office a week later.

The president and Congress, aware that they were setting precedent, initially placed a great deal of emphasis on titles and the comportment of officials. In this republic, in a world of monarchies, how should they be addressed? Should the president keep his door open, or should he remain detached? Although the questions may seem trivial, they indicate the novelty of this republican experiment. Adams, with diplomatic experience in Europe, urged Congress to adopt titles like those of other nations. A Senate committee suggested, for example, that Washington be called "His Highness the President of the United States of America, and Protector of their Liberties." After much debate, Congress dropped the notion of titles. Washington and his successors have been addressed simply as "Mr. President."

For his part, the president wondered how to dignify his office. He could easily have spent all of his time meeting with visitors, entertaining, and dining out. On the other hand, he did not want complete separation from the people. Washington's personality tended toward aloofness. He decided to hold a one-hour reception once a week, invite a few visitors to dinner, and sometimes attend the theater.

Washington also developed, by trial and error, the way in which the chief executive would deal with Congress. Early in his administration, in advance of negotiating a treaty with the Creek Indians, he attended the Senate to request their "advice and consent," as the Constitution seemed to direct. The senators were unprepared to discuss Washington's proposal, leading to embarrassment on both sides. The president resolved never to consult in formal session again. Instead, he set the precedent of private informal meetings with members of Congress. Heads of executive departments would attend congressional hearings, not the president. And in the case of treaties, the executive would seek the Senate's consent *after* negotiations were complete, not advice—at least formally—beforehand.

Beyond titles and modes of operating, Congress and the president needed to establish executive departments and courts, and draw up a bill of rights. In creating executive departments, which included War, Treasury, State (foreign affairs), and the attorney general, the most crucial constitutional question concerned who would be able to remove the heads of departments from office. Some senators hoped to restrict the president's power by requiring Senate approval before office-holders could be fired, thus making them more accountable to the legislature. In rejecting this proposal, Congress clarified one aspect of the Constitution's balance of powers.

With the Judiciary Act of 1789, Congress put some flesh on the skeleton outlined in Article III of the Constitution, which stated that the "judicial power of the United States shall be vested in one Supreme Court, and in such inferior courts as the Congress may from time to time ordain and establish." Congress might have created a full-blown national court system, but supporters of states' rights opposed such enhancement of national power. Thus, the Judiciary Act, the result of compromise, established a Supreme Court of six justices and a system of federal inferior courts, which were few in number and restricted primarily to consideration of federal crimes. State courts retained original jurisdiction in most civil and criminal cases, with the U.S. Supreme Court taking appeals from the highest state courts.

The Bill of Rights

During its first months, Congress took up the question of amending the Constitution to satisfy criticisms voiced during ratification. More than the original document, the first ten amendments, called the Bill of Rights, represented the will of the American people.

The ratification campaign had elicited a mountain of proposals for amending the Constitution. Opponents offered two major grounds for altering the document or abandoning it altogether. Antifederalist leaders believed it took too much power from the states, whereas popular opinion feared the loss of personal freedoms to a strong national government.

James Madison became the chief proponent of the Bill of Rights in Congress. In order to get elected to the House of Representatives, he had promised his Virginia constituents to obtain the safeguards. Madison took his vow seriously, pushing his reluctant Federalist colleagues to the task. Antifederalist leaders, who wanted to scrap the Constitution entirely, now denied support to the Bill of Rights because they knew protection of individual freedoms would garner popular support.

After much negotiation between the Senate and the House, on September 25, 1789, Congress sent to the states for ratification a total of twelve amendments. By December 15, 1791, three-quarters of the states approved the ten amendments known as the Bill of Rights, thus putting them into effect. Of the two amendments not approved at the time, one was a rule concerning congressional salaries that was not ratified for two centuries, until 1992, and the other was a complicated formula for computing representation in Congress that was never adopted. Of the Bill of Rights, Articles 1 through 8 enumerated basic individual rights, while the intention of Article 9 was to protect any personal freedoms omitted from this list. Article 10 directed that "powers not delegated to the United States by the Constitution, nor prohibited by it to the States, are reserved to the States respectively, or to the people." Passage of the Bill of Rights by Congress attracted enough support to bring in the two remaining states; North Carolina ratified the Constitution in November 1789, and Rhode Island followed suit in May 1790.

The First Census

Congress also promptly ordered a census of the American population, which the Constitution required within three years of Congress's first meeting and every ten years subsequently. It set August 1790 as the date for the first census, appointing marshals to complete their work within nine months, which actually stretched to eighteen. The first census was less complicated than later ones, with just six questions: name of head of household,

THE BILL OF RIGHTS, 1791

During the debates over ratification of the Constitution, many people argued for increased protection of individual rights, including freedom of religion, speech, the press, assembly, and petition, and judicial safeguards such as the right to a speedy trial and prohibition of cruel punishments. The Bill of Rights, or Amendments 1 through 10, added such provisions to the Constitution.

Amendment I

Congress shall make no law respecting an establishment of religion, or prohibiting the free exercise thereof; or abridging the freedom of speech, or of the press; or the right of the people peaceably to assemble, and to petition the government for a redress of grievances.

Amendment II

A well-regulated militia being necessary to the security of a free State, the right of the people to keep and bear arms shall not be infringed.

Amendment III

No soldier shall, in time of peace, be quartered in any house without the consent of the owner, nor in time of war, but in a manner to be prescribed by law.

Amendment IV

The right of the people to be secure in their persons, houses, papers, and effects, against unreasonable searches and seizures, shall not be violated, and no warrants shall issue but upon probable cause, supported by oath or affirmation, and particularly describing the place to be searched, and the persons or things to be seized.

Amendment V

No person shall be held to answer for a capital, or otherwise infamous crime, unless on a presentment or indictment of a grand jury, except in cases arising in the land or naval forces, or in the militia, when

number of free white males aged sixteen years and over, number of free white males under sixteen, number of free white females, number of other free persons, and number of slaves. The separate listing of enslaved persons was required by the clause of the Constitution that counted three-fifths of slaves for representation and taxes. The distinction between free whites and blacks came from cultural values rather than some practical use. The census did not include Native Americans who lived outside areas settled by whites.

Although sketchy and incomplete, the 1790 census served as a baseline for measuring the growth of a dynamic, expanding people. President Washington reported to Congress a total of 3.9 million people, of whom 60,000 were free in actual service in time of war or public danger; nor shall any person be subject for the same offense to be twice put in jeopardy of life or limb; nor shall be compelled in any criminal case to be a witness against himself, nor be deprived of life, liberty, or property, without due process of law; nor shall private property be taken for public use without just compensation.

Amendment VI
In all criminal prosecutions, the accused shall enjoy the right to a speedy and public trial, by an impartial jury of the State and district wherein the crime shall have been committed, which district shall have been previously ascertained by law, and to be informed of the nature and cause of the accusation; to be confronted with the witnesses against him; to have compulsory process for obtaining witnesses in his favor, and to have the assistance of counsel for his defense.

Amendment VII
In suits at common law, where the value in controversy shall exceed twenty dollars, the right of trial by jury shall be preserved, and no fact tried by a jury shall be otherwise reexamined in any court of the United States, than according to the rules of the common law.

Amendment VIII
Excessive bail shall not be required, nor excessive fines imposed, nor cruel and unusual punishments inflicted.

Amendment IX
The enumeration in the Constitution, of certain rights, shall not be construed to deny or disparage others retained by the people.

Amendment X
The powers not delegated to the United States by the Constitution, nor prohibited by it to the States, are reserved to the States respectively, or to the people.

African Americans and almost 700,000 were slaves. The census covered the territory included in the thirteen original states, and also Vermont, Kentucky, and Tennessee, which became states respectively in 1791, 1792, and 1796.

During the 1780s, the white population of the country had swelled by an extraordinary 44 percent, mostly through reproduction; in the 1790s, the increase remained high at 36 percent. After the Treaty of Paris, European immigrants had once again begun crossing the Atlantic Ocean, with the majority coming from Ireland. The African American population also grew quickly during the 1780s and 1790s, at a rate of 32 percent per decade.

Especially striking in the 1790 census are the small numbers of enslaved African Americans in

New England and Pennsylvania compared with Maryland, Virginia, and the Carolinas, the result in part of northern abolition. This sectional difference would grow in the nineteenth century as the north focused more on commerce whereas the south cast its fate with agriculture.

Opposing Visions of America

Almost immediately during Washington's first administration, political divisions arose between sides favoring commerce versus agriculture. Two divergent conceptions of the nation's future emerged, and two political parties developed. As events unfolded in foreign and domestic affairs, the two parties contested one issue after another.

Hamilton Versus Jefferson

Alexander Hamilton, appointed by Washington as secretary of the treasury, saw the future greatness of the United States in commerce and manufacturing. Born in the West Indies, Hamilton attended King's College in New York City, then served as Washington's aide-de-camp during the Revolution. He was a major proponent of the new Constitution. Appointment to the treasury allowed him to promote his concept of a strong nation, modeled on Great Britain, but his efforts to foster commerce and manufacturing aroused resistance among former allies, particularly Madison and Jefferson, leading to bitter partisan disputes.

Hamilton's party, which embraced the name Federalist though it was really nationalist, favored commercial development, a national bank, high tariffs to spur manufacturing, and a strong central government. The Federalists favored the British, abhorred the French Revolution after 1792, and were generally suspicious of power wielded by ordinary folk. They were somewhat critical of slavery, however, and gained the allegiance of free blacks. Because their power base lay in New England and the Middle States, the Federalists could generate little enthusiasm for western expansion.

Alexander Hamilton, *1792, by John Trumbull. The first secretary of the treasury saw Great Britain, with its strong central government and expanding industrial economy, as a model for the new United States.* (Corbis-Bettmann)

The Republican party, in contrast, opposed a strong central government and federal privileges for manufacturing and commerce. They thought Hamilton's plans for funding the national debt, the bank, and protective tariffs infringed upon states' rights. They disdained the British model and charged Hamilton with advocating a return to monarchy. With their power base in the south, west, and northern cities, the Republicans rejected efforts to abolish slavery and were ardent expansionists on the frontier.

Thomas Jefferson became the chief spokesman for the Republican party. Jefferson, author of the Declaration of Independence, former ambassador to France, and now Washington's secretary of state, argued that Hamilton wanted too much national power. He believed the root of Britain's effort to destroy American liberty in the 1760s and 1770s had been commercial speculation and greed. Manufacturing in cities created poverty, dependency, and political corruption. Instead, the United States, with limitless land, should foster an agrarian society. A virtuous republic was one made up of small farmers whose goal was to produce enough to support their families. Commerce should exist primarily to allow them to sell their surplus in Europe and purchase manufactured goods in return. The farmers should be educated to participate wisely in republican government.

Paradoxically, a large proportion of the Republicans were not small farmers. Many of the leaders were southern plantation gentry or old Antifederalist elites. The party drew together people who had opposed ratification of the Constitution as well as those who favored it but abhorred the government's direction under Washington and Hamilton. The Republicans received solid backing from farmers, especially in the south and west, and from urban craftsmen and small traders.

Funding the National Debt

In becoming secretary of the treasury, Alexander Hamilton's primary challenge was the Revolutionary War debt. A strong nationalist, he viewed the debt more as an opportunity to enlarge national power than as a financial hurdle. The United States owed $10 million to foreigners, particularly the French, and $40 million to Americans. The states also owed $25 million in domestic debts. To continue the War for Independence when funds were depleted, Congress and the states had issued certificates to merchants, artisans, and farmers for supplies and to soldiers for wages. After the war, many ordinary folks could not wait for the government to pay—or lost hope that the money was forthcoming—so they sold their certificates to wealthy speculators for a fraction of face value.

In his Report on the Public Credit of January 1790, Hamilton formulated a plan by which the U.S. government would honor at face value all Revolutionary War debts, including those of the states. His "funding" proposal involved the exchange of new federal securities for the old debt certificates. He planned to pay off foreign creditors as soon as possible, but retain the domestic debt, paying only interest and a small amount of the principal each year. A customs duty on imports and an excise tax on whiskey would cover the interest; Post Office income would gradually reduce the principal. Hamilton's funding plan would tie wealthy Americans to the new government through their continuing investment. His "assumption" plan, by which the federal government assumed state war debts, expanded this strategy by reorienting the loyalty of investors from the states to the nation.

Congress eventually passed Hamilton's proposal, though with great opposition. Many people, including Madison, thought that repaying the domestic debt at face value was unfair, that speculators received a windfall at the expense of the poor. The split between Hamilton and Madison began over this issue. Critics argued that funding allowed the "few" to benefit from the hardships of the "many," who had lost money when they sold their war bonds and would pay again through import duties and the excise tax. Opponents feared the expansion of national power, and became convinced that the treasury secretary was upsetting the balance between the central government and the states. Assumption raised additional questions because some states had more debt remaining than others. Despite these divisions, the funding and assumption program passed Congress in July 1790, as part of a bargain struck by Hamilton, Jefferson, and Madison to situate the nation's permanent capital on the Potomac River, in Maryland and Virginia.

Planning Washington, D.C.

The choice of the Potomac for the nation's capital was controversial. Although everyone agreed that a central location was necessary, regional interests surfaced as congressmen recognized the economic and political benefits that the seat of government could bestow. They also debated the question of the temporary capital. Should New York City or Philadelphia host the federal government until the permanent site was ready? The complicated negotiations over funding and assumption resulted in moving the temporary capital from New York to Philadelphia as well as locating the new city on the Potomac.

President Washington and his fellow Virginians supervised the development of the capital. The Residence Act of 1790 gave the president authority to select a ten-mile-square location somewhere along the Potomac; he chose the land on both sides of the river that included Alexandria, Virginia, and Georgetown, Maryland. The federal city would not be built in either of those towns, but on open land on the east bank of the river. Washington appointed a surveyor, three commissioners to manage the project, and Pierre Charles L'Enfant to design the layout of the capital and its major buildings. L'Enfant's grandiose street plan and Greek and Roman architecture expressed an exalted vision of the republic. The commissioners named the federal city "Washington" and the entire district "Columbia."

The president expected to finance construction by selling lots in the capital, thinking that land prices would skyrocket. Instead, land sold poorly and lack of money undermined the project. When the commissioners suspended construction temporarily for insufficient funds, L'Enfant protested and was fired. His plan for grand boulevards, public squares, fountains, and imposing buildings was retained, but its execution would wait. For a decade the enterprise limped along, saved by grants from Maryland and Virginia. In 1800, when the government moved to Washington, the president's mansion was still unfinished and only one wing of the Capitol had been built.

The National Bank

The cornerstone of Hamilton's new commercial order was a national bank. The Bank of the United States and its branches, established in selected cities, would hold the federal government's funds and regulate state banks. The chief purpose of the national bank was to expand the money supply, thereby encouraging commercial growth.

The Bank of the United States, which Congress chartered in 1791 for a minimum of twenty years, would have assets of $10 million, including $2 million in government deposits. Private investors could purchase the remaining $8 million in stock. As the bank prospered, stockholders would receive dividends on their funds. Thus, Hamilton created a way for wealthy Americans, who had just profited from funding the Revolutionary War debt, to benefit further. Because the government was a major stockholder, it also received dividends that could be used to pay off the national debt. The bank made loans to merchants beyond the value of its stock of gold and silver (specie), thus increasing the supply of money. The bank notes circulated as currency; the federal government supported their value by accepting them for taxes. To Hamilton and his commercial backers, the Bank of the United States was essential for economic growth. The majority of the House of Representatives agreed, by a vote of thirty-nine to twenty.

The plan had many opponents, who variously considered the bank immoral, monopolistic, or unconstitutional. Some believed that all paper money should be based on gold and silver. "Every dollar of a bank bill that is issued beyond the quantity of gold and silver in the vaults," John Adams said, "represents nothing, and is therefore a cheat upon somebody." The wild frenzy to purchase the bank's stock, in which 25,000 shares sold in two hours, reinforced fears that the national bank would undermine republican virtue. Some charged the bank with monopoly, complaining that merchants could secure short-term loans to finance their commercial ventures, but farmers and artisans could not obtain mortgages for purchasing property or making improvements.

In Congress, Madison opposed the national bank on the constitutional grounds that the federal government lacked the power to create corporations, a strict interpretation of the Constitution. In particular, Madison said, the Tenth Amendment denied the central government any power not expressly given. Hamilton and his supporters countered with a loose interpretation, that some powers of the federal government are implied. In the case of the bank, for example, the Constitution delegated to Congress and the president the power to lay and collect taxes, pay debts, regulate commerce, and coin and regulate money. It also provided the authority to "make all laws which shall be necessary and proper for carrying into execution the foregoing powers. . . ." Hamilton argued that the bank was a method by which the United States could fulfill its functions, and because some means was necessary, the power to establish the bank was implied. Though President Washington was initially unsure, he accepted Hamilton's reasoning and approved the bill.

Jefferson, like Madison, was convinced the national bank was unconstitutional. By 1791, the secretary of state realized the political and economic consequences of the funding act—channeling more power to the federal government and more money to the rich—and thought the bank could only further these trends. He now believed that the treasury secretary's program was "calculated to undermine and demolish the republic." For his part, Hamilton chafed at this criticism, stating "that Mr. Madison, cooperating with Mr. Jefferson, is at the head of a faction decidedly hostile to me and my administration; and actuated by views, in my judgment, subversive of the principles of good government and dangerous to the Union, peace, and happiness of the country."

Encouragement of Manufacturing

Although the treasury secretary won congressional support for the bank and funding the national debt, he was much less successful in his plan for industry. In 1791, the United States lacked a solid manufacturing base. Hamilton proposed high protective tariffs on certain goods to discourage Americans from buying imports and thus spur U.S. production. He also advocated bounties, or subsidies, on selected products to encourage entrepreneurs. Hamilton believed that a strong nation needed self-sufficiency in manufactures, especially for military defense, but failed to obtain congressional support. Madison contended that granting bounties would expand the power of Congress, whereas others argued that they were like monopolies and too expensive.

In the 1790s, U.S. manufacturing remained on a small scale. Americans appreciated the quality of British imports; what they did not import, they produced themselves or purchased from neighboring artisans. Industry could not be stimulated overnight, for it required technology and the willingness of businessmen to invest time as well as capital for the long term. Mechanized factories with mass production still lay in the future.

During the colonial and revolutionary periods, urban entrepreneurs had attempted large-scale textile manufacturing, but these efforts were short-lived and not mechanized. The "factories" had consisted of workhouses, in which large numbers of impoverished widows produced thread and yarn at traditional spinning wheels. Other businessmen used a "putting-out" system, whereby they distributed flax and wool for spinning at home.

In 1788, the Pennsylvania Society for the Encouragement of Manufactures and the Useful Arts introduced spinning jennies to their textile factory in Philadelphia. The jennies threatened to displace home spinners by producing cheaper yarn and thread. In 1790, however, the factory and its wooden jennies went up in flames, as did other early textile mills in the Delaware Valley. Although the promoters believed that home spinners were sabotaging the factories, the fires may well have been accidental because the mills were highly flammable.

Samuel Slater, a twenty-two-year-old millworker and recent immigrant from Great Britain, in 1790 instituted a new phase in American cloth production by building a textile mill in Pawtucket, Rhode Island, using water power to run the spinning machines. From memory he constructed a spinning frame, a machine that produced stronger

Until after 1815, households performed one or more steps in textile manufacturing. Here a family works together, with the wife spinning thread, which the husband then wove on his loom. Women also wove cloth, but men rarely—if ever—used a spinning wheel. (Rare Books Division, The New York Public Library: Astor, Lenox and Tilden Foundations)

threads than the jenny. No satisfactory power loom yet existed, so Slater's mill performed only the first two steps of cloth production: carding, or preparing the cotton fibers for spinning, and spinning the thread. Slater then used the putting-out system of distributing the thread to families, who produced the cloth at home. Though Slater established additional mills in Rhode Island and Massachusetts, his workforce stayed fairly small, with about a hundred millworkers in 1800.

Alexander Hamilton tried an ambitious industrial program in Paterson, New Jersey, with the Society for Establishing Useful Manufactures. The society hoped to create an industrial town on the Passaic River where skilled craftsmen recruited from Britain would produce a variety of cloth and clothing, blankets, carpets, shoes, hats, pottery, metal wire, and paper. After obtaining a state charter from New Jersey, the society sold stock. As in the case of the national bank, the stock sold quickly and appreciated in value. The project lost capital, however, when major stockholders sold their shares to make a fast profit. The managers failed to obtain reliable machinery and workers, closing shop in 1796.

Although the results of Hamilton's plans were disappointing, the United States did make progress during the 1790s toward industrialization. In 1790, Congress passed patent legislation, giving inventors exclusive rights to their work for seventeen years, and Slater initiated water-powered textile manufacture. Then, in 1793, Eli Whitney invented the cotton engine, or gin. The device, which separated cotton fibers from husks and seeds, greatly increased the productivity of cotton cultivation, swelling the demand for African American slaves and fertile land in the southwest, and spurring cloth production in the north. Because the gin could be duplicated easily, though, Whitney failed to make a fortune from his invention. In 1798, he further laid the basis for industrial growth by attempting to manufacture guns with interchangeable parts. After receiving a government contract for 10,000 weapons, he specified that each part be made identical to its counterparts so that it could be exchanged from one rifle to another. At this early date, however, such rigid standards were impossible to meet, and as a result, parts needed filing to fit together smoothly.

An inventor who would have benefited from Hamilton's proposed bounties was the Delaware-born artisan Oliver Evans, who apprenticed as a wagonmaker and became fascinated by machines. In 1772, at age seventeen, he heard that the Scottish inventor James Watt had improved the steam engine a few years earlier. Evans began building his own model, but thirty years passed before he actually installed a high pressure steam engine in his gypsum fertilizer factory in Philadelphia. This was the first such application of steam power to an industrial setting. In the meantime, in the 1780s, Evans also developed the idea of automating mills. He devised water-powered machinery for large grist mills that allowed one worker instead of three to supervise all the steps of producing flour. Evans obtained exclusive rights from the states of Pennsylvania and Maryland to his system of automated elevators, conveyors, and hoppers.

Expansion and Conflict in the West

While Alexander Hamilton's financial policies aided commerce in the east, dynamic growth also occurred in the west. The expansion of settlers from east to west challenged the ability of the new government to keep their loyalty. In particular, Hamilton's excise tax on whiskey weighed heavily on westerners. The young nation also contended with the Native Americans, whose lands the settlers were taking; the British military, who kept forts in the northwest; and the Spanish, who contested U.S. territorial claims and rights to navigate the Mississippi.

Kentucky and Tennessee

During the 1780s, the region west of the Appalachians and south of the Ohio River developed quickly. Even before the Revolution ended, settlers crossed the mountains in large numbers: Kentucky swelled from 150 settlers in 1775 to 61,000 whites and 12,500 enslaved blacks in 1790; Tennessee reported 32,000 whites and 3,500 slaves in the latter year.

White settlement of Kentucky and Tennessee proceeded quickly as state governments, speculators, and frontiersmen defeated the Cherokees, who claimed ancestral rights to the territory. Understanding that they were renting the land rather than selling it, in 1775 a group of Cherokee leaders traded 27,000 square miles to Richard Henderson and his associates for a cabin of consumer goods. Called Henderson's Purchase, the sale involved most of Kentucky and was illegal in Indian and English law. With the outbreak of the Revolution, most Cherokees joined the British, fighting for return of their lands. Receiving little help from Britain, the Cherokees were defeated in 1777 and forced to sign away even more territory.

Young militants led by Dragging Canoe, Bloody Fellow, and others, assisted by loyalist whites who intermarried and became members of the tribe, rejected these land cessions. In the 1780s and early 1790s, the militant Cherokees, called Chickamaugas, allied with Creeks and Shawnees against settlers along the frontier from Kentucky to Georgia. On both sides, fighting was vicious, and, as in so many cases, the whites failed to distinguish between enemy Indians and those who wanted peace.

The Washington administration attempted to end the hostilities with the Treaty of Holston in 1791, but gave responsibility for negotiating with the Cherokees to Governor William Blount of the Tennessee Territory. Blount ignored Washington's promise to the Cherokees that if they ceded territory on which the whites had settled, the United States would guarantee their remaining lands. Instead, Blount required a cession of over 4,000 square miles in return for an annual payment of $1,000 and no guarantee. When Blount surveyed the border without Cherokee witnesses, the treaty fell apart and war continued. In 1794, after Dragging Canoe died and the Spanish stopped supplying the Indians because of war in Europe, the Chickamaugas met defeat.

By the end of the war, parts of Kentucky and Tennessee had passed the initial stages of settlement. Early on, groups of settlers had gathered in frontier stations consisting of two-story log houses connected by a high wall to create a fort against Indian attack. As the population grew and the threat from Native Americans declined, families moved away from the stations. In the early years, all family members worked to provide food, clothing, shelter, and a few amenities such as soap and rough-hewn furniture. The settlers used skills they had learned at home: they grew corn, tobacco, hemp, cotton, vegetables, and fruits; raised cattle, sheep, horses, and pigs; hunted and fished. Soon the settlers produced a surplus to trade for necessities they could not make themselves, such as nails, rifles, ammunition, needles, tools, and salt, as well as to pay taxes and fees. They sold furs, ginseng, agricultural produce, and livestock. As fertile lands such as Kentucky's Bluegrass region yielded bountiful crops, farmers sought markets by way of the Mississippi River and the port of New Orleans. Because transporting crops overland through the mountains was much more difficult and expensive than sending them downstream, southwestern farmers demanded that the federal government convince Spain to end its restrictions on lower Mississippi shipping.

The trans-Appalachian region had few schools or church buildings. Most children, if taught at all, learned reading and arithmetic at home. In towns where schools existed, boys might attend for a few months but girls stayed at home. The exception were the children of wealthy families who attended academies with secondary school curricula. One man remembered the experience of most residents of Kentucky in the 1790s: "Our preachers and teachers were, in general, almost as destitute as the people at large, many of whom could neither read nor write, did not send their children to school, and of course, kept no books in the house."

Religion was the frontier's chief cultural institution. Throughout the region, Presbyterian, Baptist, and Methodist ministers held services in private homes. Baptist lay ministers farmed beside their neighbors through the week, then led services on Sunday. Methodist circuit riders traveled from one congregation to another, conducting worship services, baptisms, marriages, and prayer meetings. The churches expected members to avoid sin, including fighting, excessive drinking, and adultery. If members committed offenses and failed to express sorrow, they were expelled, a serious consequence for people who had few social outlets. In addition to church, social activities included barn raisings, corn huskings, and log rollings.

The Ohio Country

White settlement moved more slowly north of the Ohio River than in Kentucky and Tennessee, partly because the U.S. government kept tighter control in the Northwest Territory, but more because Native Americans resisted strongly. Delawares, Shawnees, Iroquois, and many others refused to cede lands that the federal government wanted to sell to land-hungry easterners. In the 1780s, the United States obtained a series of cessions, but from just some of the people who owned the land. Indians who were not party to the agreements rejected them. Forming a confederacy to withstand U.S. invasion, Ohio Indians attacked whites who risked settling in the region. This northern Indian confederacy allied with the Chickamaugas and Creeks in the south, establishing a pan-Indian defensive that gained help from the Spanish in the south and the British in the north.

In the early 1790s, President Washington challenged the northern confederacy by sending two expeditions, both of them unsuccessful. Arthur St. Clair, governor of the Northwest Territory, led the second invasion in 1791, in which 600 of his 1,400 men died. Washington believed that the disaster resulted from the use of militia, so instructed General Anthony Wayne to raise 5,000 regulars. Wayne trained the troops for two years, then marched west against the Indian confederacy. On August 20, 1794, the U.S. army defeated the Native Americans decisively at the Battle of Fallen Timbers. Though the British had customarily given aid to the Ohio tribes, this time they did not. A year later, when it became clear to the Native Americans that their alliance with the British had ended, they signed the Treaty of Greenville ceding to the United States most of the land in present-day Ohio.

The Whiskey Rebellion

In the same year, 1794, the Washington administration also sent troops against western Pennsylvania farmers, who since 1791 had resisted the whiskey tax. Farmers throughout the west resented the tax on spirits, for distilling whiskey from grain made their produce less bulky, thus less expensive to transport to eastern markets. They also used the whiskey instead of cash and consumed a good portion of it themselves. In much of the trans-Appalachian region, officials failed to collect the excise at all.

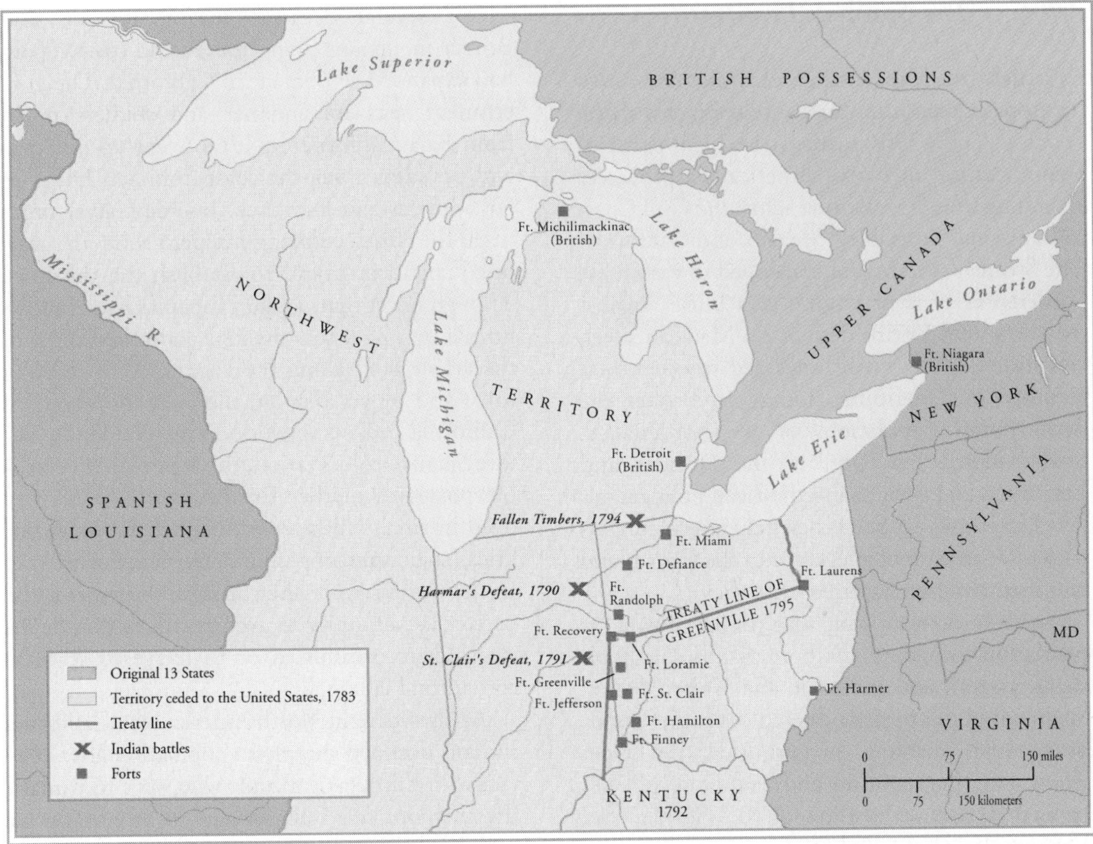

Map 7.1 | Conflict in the Northwest Territory, 1790–1796

The administration found willing officials in western Pennsylvania, however, and proceeded to enforce the law. The Pittsburgh area farmers held protest meetings and refused cooperation with the collectors. They tarred and feathered collaborators, burned barns, and destroyed stills of people who paid the tax. The farmers charged that the tax favored large distillers and was collected unevenly. Rebels left notes signed "Tom the Tinker" to warn distillers who registered for the tax that their stills would be "fixed" (that is, ruined) unless they joined the revolt.

Events came to a climax in July 1794. When officials continued to collect the tax and arrest resisters, 500 men surrounded the excise inspector's home, exchanged gunfire that killed several people, and burned the house. The official and his family escaped. In the days that followed, rebels set more buildings on fire, attacked collectors, and rumored secession. The uprising spread to central Pennsylvania, Virginia, Maryland, and Ohio. Washington sent commissioners to obtain oaths of submission, but the insurrection continued. Hamilton, as acting secretary of war, called up 13,000 eastern troops, who marched west with the president briefly in command. By the time the soldiers reached western Pennsylvania, the revolt was over, as the show of force intimidated the rebels. The administration had demonstrated that armed resistance to federal policies would not be tolerated.

The Spanish Frontier

As settlers from the United States migrated across the Appalachians, they came into contact with the Spanish. The 1790s marked the high point of Spain's control in North America, its provinces extending from East Florida across the Gulf Coast to Louisiana, Texas, New Mexico, and California. The Spanish government continued to view these borderlands of their empire as a buffer against American and British designs on Mexican silver. Nevertheless, the Spanish decided to open their territory to Americans, hoping to bolster the small settler populations of the borderlands. Spain offered free land in the Floridas and Louisiana, and even changed official policy to allow Protestants to keep their religion as long as they took an oath of allegiance to the Crown and had their children baptized Catholic.

Spanish mercantilism also broke down, as plantation owners in the borderlands sold their sugar, cotton, and indigo in the United States. Spain could not provide desired consumer goods or adequate markets, so permitted this trade. These new immigration and economic policies facilitated later acquisition of the Floridas and Louisiana by the United States.

Farther west, in New Mexico, the Spanish finally achieved peace with Native Americans during these years. Abandoning their attempt to integrate Comanches and Apaches as subjects of the Crown, Spain signed a treaty recognizing them as sovereign people. The Indians, through military prowess and endurance, had forced the Spanish to set aside the goal of complete domination and to provide such gifts as guns, ammunition, clothing, mirrors, paint, tobacco, and sugar. Still, the Spanish sent prisoners of war to Cuba as forced laborers and settled other Apaches on reservations called *establecimientos de paz,* or peace establishments. Many Apaches refused to live on the reservations, however, steadfastly maintaining their independence. But the fighting stopped, making Texas, New Mexico, and Arizona safer for travel and economic development. Finally, settlers could journey directly between San Antonio, Santa Fe, and Tucson without fear of attack.

For several decades, fearing Russian and British incursions along the Pacific coast, Spain had expanded settlement in California. The government sent missionaries and soldiers north from Baja California in 1769 to set up missions and presidios along the coast from San Diego as far north as San Francisco. José de Gálvez organized the effort, enlisting Junípero Serra, the zealous Franciscan priest, to establish the missions. Though fewer than 1,000 Hispanics lived in California by 1790, the missions controlled most of the arable land along the Pacific. With military force and by conversion, they put thousands of California Indians to work on mission lands. Before Spanish colonization, the region's native people possessed neither firearms nor horses; they lived in small villages with neither elaborate political structures nor much experience with war. In the earliest years after Spanish settlement, the natives lacked unity to avenge crimes that Spanish soldiers committed or to refuse to serve as agricultural laborers.

As elsewhere in North America, the California Indians declined sharply in population after contact with Europeans. People who went to work in the missions lived an average of ten to twelve years; their high death rate probably resulted from close quarters and exposure to disease. The native population in the mission region along the Pacific coast declined from approximately 60,000 in 1769 to 35,000 at the end of the century.

The Spanish also looked to the Pacific Northwest, which they investigated in 1774, four years earlier than the British explorer Captain James Cook. After Cook publicized the trade for sea otter furs, however, British and American merchants sailed to Nootka Sound, at Vancouver Island, challenging the Spanish claim to the area north of San Francisco. The traders made huge profits by purchasing the silky black otter pelts from the Tlingit, Haida, Nootka, and Chinook peoples to sell in China for tea, porcelain, and silk. The Spanish attempted to enforce their rights to the Northwest coast by seizing two British ships. When England threatened war, Spain signed the Nootka Convention (1790), yielding its sole claim to the area and returning the confiscated vessels. Over

This sketch by José Cardero in 1791 shows Native Americans and soldiers working outside the presidio of Monterey, California. (The Bancroft Library, University of California, Berkeley, CA)

the next several years, the two countries tried but failed to negotiate a northern boundary of California. Of more concern to Spain, Great Britain, and the United States during the 1790s was the outbreak of war in Europe and the Atlantic, in the wake of revolution in France.

Foreign Entanglements

In 1789, the United States rejoiced when the French abolished noble privileges and formed a constitutional monarchy. Americans believed that France had followed their example, for during the first phase of the French Revolution, its moderate leaders included friends of the United States, notably the Revolutionary War hero, the Marquis de Lafayette. In 1792, however, radicals took control. The international situation became perilous when the French Republic declared war on Britain and Spain. The king's execution and thousands of deaths by guillotine during the second phase of the revolution cost the French support in the United States, particularly among Federalists. Republicans remained sympathetic toward France because they hated monarchical Britain more.

Neutrality

The European war presented Americans with a tricky situation, for they had connections with both France and Britain that were potentially dangerous. The U.S.-France commercial and military alliance of 1778 remained in force. Although it did not require the United States to enter the war, the French Republic expected favorable trade policies and informal military assistance. Though Secretary of State Jefferson favored France and hated Britain, he agreed that neutrality was essential. American commerce was closely tied with Britain, whose navy could sweep U.S. ships from the sea. Hamilton was particularly concerned that British imports remain high because tariffs paid the lion's share of interest on the national debt. With all of this in mind, President Washington made the only reasonable decision, issuing his Proclamation of Neutrality in April 1793. The message warned citizens to avoid hostile acts against either side, including sale of weapons and privateering.

American neutrality quickly hit shoals when the activities of the new French ambassador, Edmond Genêt, became known. Citizen Genêt, as he was called in republican France, had arrived in Charleston several weeks before Washington proclaimed neutrality. He enlisted American mercenaries to man privateers and obtained ships to sail under the French flag against British shipping. The privateers, with largely American crews, seized British vessels, towing them to U.S. ports. There the French consuls sold the ships and their cargoes, paying the mercenaries with part of the proceeds. The French claimed this right under the 1778 alliance. The Washington administration, fearful of British reprisals, closed the ports to Genêt's privateers and requested his recall. The government prohibited foreign belligerents from arming vessels in U.S. ports and recruiting U.S. citizens in American territory; set the limit of U.S. territorial waters at three miles; and forbade foreign consuls from holding admiralty courts in U.S. cities to auction confiscated ships.

The Washington administration had greater success protecting the nation's sovereignty from French designs than from the British. The American republic's weakness became all too clear when the Royal Navy began impressing—recruiting by force—U.S. citizens from merchant ships. Although the navy's official goal was to reclaim British deserters, the commanders often failed to distinguish among deserters, British immigrants who had become U.S. citizens, and native-born Americans.

Then, in November 1793, the British ordered a total blockade of the French West Indies. The blockade was time to coincide with their invasion of St. Domingue, or Haiti, where enslaved blacks had risen up against their French masters in 1791. The British kept the blockade a secret until after U.S. ships headed for the Caribbean. Over the winter, their navy seized more than 250 American vessels, whether they were aimed for French, British, or neutral ports. The British impounded ships, cargoes, and even the sailors' possessions. Because international correspondence was so slow, Washington received no intelligence of the blockade and confiscations until March 1794.

The United States and Britain seemed headed for war. Exacerbating the crisis was the British refusal to vacate their forts in the Ohio country, as they had agreed to do in the 1783 Treaty of Paris. Britain also helped Native Americans resist settlement in the west. In fact, in 1794, the governor of Canada, Lord Dorchester, told a group of Indians that they could expect war to break out between the United States and Britain within a year. With British victory, Dorchester promised, the Native Americans could reclaim the lands they had lost north of the Ohio River.

The Jay Treaty

The crisis abated when the British ended their total blockade of the French islands, now permitting Americans to trade foodstuffs and consumer goods but not war material. Rather than take retaliatory action, the president nominated John Jay, the chief justice of the Supreme Court, to serve as special envoy to the British. Jay's instructions were to convince them to evacuate their forts in the west, pay for African American slaves who had left with the British army after the Revolution, end impressment, open British West Indies trade to American ships, and compensate recent shipping losses in the Caribbean.

Jay completed his negotiations in England in November 1794. He was unable to secure compensation for slaves who departed with the British army over a decade earlier; nor did he convince the British to stop impressment or to recognize all of the neutral rights that Americans demanded. But he obtained British withdrawal from the western forts by June 1, 1796, payment for confiscated ships in the Caribbean, and the opening of trade in the British West Indies to American vessels of 70 tons or less. He agreed, however, that American shippers would not export from the United States certain tropical products, including cotton, molasses, sugar, coffee, and cocoa.

Washington received Jay's treaty in March 1795, keeping its contents secret until the Senate debate in June. Twenty Federalist senators voted to ratify while ten Republicans refused. The Federalists struck the provision forbidding U.S. merchants from exporting tropical crops. If they had agreed to this section, American trade would have faced a serious obstacle, particularly with the development of cotton. Thus, the Senate approved the treaty by exactly the two-thirds needed and sent it to the president, who signed the treaty as amended.

When the Jay Treaty became public, Republicans flew into a rage. They abhorred *any* treaty with the British and complained about Jay's failures on impressment, neutral rights, and compensation for slaves. The Jay Treaty greatly hastened the growth of political parties. While Hamilton defended the treaty, opponents roared that it surrendered American independence to the former imperial tyrant. Mass meetings, petitions, and demonstrations protested the treaty throughout the country.

By spring 1796, however, the tumolt was over, in part because news arrived that Thomas Pinckney had concluded an agreement with Spain the previous October. The Treaty of San Lorenzo opened the Mississippi River to free navigation, allowed Americans to use the port of New Orleans without charge, and fixed the boundary between the United States and West Florida at the 31st parallel as specified in the Treaty of Paris.

Washington Retires

With the threat of war temporarily eased, the west open for settlement and trade, and a flourishing economy, the success of the republic seemed more certain. General Wayne's defeat of the Ohio Indians, the Jay Treaty, and Pinckney's diplomatic success gave westerners resolution of their major problems. Eastern merchants and farmers benefited from the lifting of trade restrictions in the British West Indies. Wartime demand for provisions in Europe and the Caribbean drove up farm prices and stimulated production. By the end of the century, American exports and shipping profits were almost five times their 1793 level. With increased transportation profits, merchants invested more heavily in ships. The shipbuilding boom created demand for lumber, rope, and other supplies; wages for craftsmen and laborers rose. Americans took advantage of their newfound prosperity to buy British imports, which in turn paid tariff income toward the national debt. Hamilton's funding plan was a success.

As the election of 1796 approached, George Washington announced his retirement. In his Farewell Address, he surveyed the accomplishments of his administration and gave the nation advice. The United States should avoid as much as possible becoming entwined in international affairs, he counseled. The European war demonstrated how perilous such involvement could be, and how difficult it was to escape. "The great rule of conduct for us in regard to foreign nations is, in extending our commercial relations to have with them as little *political* connection as possible," Washington urged. His other major argument concerned factions. The outgoing president warned against parties based on sectional differences—North against South or East against West. And he cautioned against parties more generally, that the "disorders and miseries which result [from factionalism] gradually incline the minds of men to seek security and repose in the absolute power of an individual."

THE ADAMS PRESIDENCY

Though Washington's successors appreciated the wisdom of his "great rule" of foreign policy, they had less enthusiasm for his advice on factions. In 1796, the parties yet lacked full-scale national organization, and candidates did not campaign. But the contest was very much alive, as Federalists supported the policies of Hamilton and Washington, while Republicans opposed them.

The Election of 1796

In the third presidential election under the Constitution, both parties had sufficient cohesion to offer national tickets: the Federalist candidates were John Adams for president and Thomas Pinckney for vice president; the Republicans put up Thomas Jefferson for president and Aaron Burr, a senator from New York, for the second spot. The results of the electoral college vote were close: Adams 71, Jefferson 68, Pinckney 59, Burr 30, and a number of other candidates totalling 48. As specified by the Constitution, Adams became president and Jefferson, vice president. Americans quickly realized the problem of this procedure for electing the executive, as the president represented one party and the vice president the other. In any event, the Federalists kept control of the presidency, though barely, and they increased their votes in Congress by a small margin, to 64 Federalists versus 53 Republicans.

John Adams had contributed to prerevolutionary agitation in Boston, served as a delegate to the Continental Congress, promoted the Continental navy, and assisted Jefferson in drafting the Declaration of Independence. He had helped negotiate the 1783 Treaty of Paris, and in 1785, became the first U.S. ambassador to Great Britain. Although Adams was a skilled diplomat and entirely honest, he lacked Washington's charisma, military bearing, and understanding of executive leadership. As a lawyer, Adams' style was more intellectual and independent; he had no experience as an executive.

Like Washington, Adams denounced parties. He began his administration with the hope, soon abandoned, that he might bridge the gulf between Federalists and Republicans. Jefferson rebuffed the chief executive's peace overture and directed the Republican opposition from his post as vice president. After the first few days of the Adams administration, the president and vice president never consulted one another.

John Adams, elected second president of the United States, had been involved in the revolutionary movement since the 1760s. He was the sole non-Virginian and the only president to serve a single term among the first five chief executives. (Independence National Historical Park)

"Quasi-War" with France

The second president inherited an international situation that had worsened by the time he assumed office in March 1797. The French, now ruled by a dictatorial executive board called the Directory, declared that the Jay Treaty revoked the 1778 alliance. They confiscated American merchant ships and cut off diplomatic relations. Once again, the United States seemed destined for war.

Called by Adams into special session in May 1797, Congress authorized the mobilization of 80,000 militia, completion of three war vessels,

The Constellation *capturing the* Insurgente, *February 9, 1799. In the Quasi-War, the U.S. Navy, with British help, quickly outperformed the French.* (Courtesy, Peabody Essex Museum, Salem, MA)

and fortification of harbors. Adams also appointed a commission of three men to negotiate with France: John Marshall of Virginia, Elbridge Gerry of Massachusetts, and Charles Cotesworth Pinckney of South Carolina. Their assignment was to prevent war, stop the confiscation of American ships carrying nonmilitary cargoes, and obtain compensation for recent losses. In France, the commission corresponded with French Foreign Minister Talleyrand through three intermediaries, who later became known to the American public as X, Y, and Z. The French agents told the commissioners that, like other petitioners to the Directory, they must pay a bribe even to be heard. The amount specified in this case was $250,000. The Directory also required an apology from Adams for criticizing France, a huge loan, and assumption by the U.S. government of any unpaid debts owed by France to American citizens. The commission refused these conditions and returned home. Their experience became known as the XYZ Affair.

In spring 1798, Adams received delayed correspondence that his envoys had been rebuffed. When he called for additional troops and warships, Congress responded by giving him more than he requested. When Republicans demanded to see evidence of France's treachery, Adams made the commission's dispatches public. War fever engulfed the nation. Congress expanded the regular army and war fleet, established the Department of the Navy, authorized naval vessels to protect American merchant ships, suspended commerce with France, and revoked the French alliance. George Washington assumed command of the army, with Alexander Hamilton in charge of field operations. To pay for all of this, Congress levied a direct tax of $2 million on dwelling houses, land, and slaves.

Without declaring war, the United States engaged France in hostilities from 1798 to 1800. In what was known as the Quasi-War, the U.S. navy dominated the French, defeating their warships and sinking privateers. The British navy helped by protecting U.S. carriers. Although some congressmen feared a French invasion and thereby justified further military preparations, French naval losses to Great Britain and the United States quickly removed that threat.

The Alien and Sedition Acts

The Federalists rode the crest of patriotism in 1798, using their majority in Congress to pass a series of acts that limited the rights of immigrants and critics of the administration. Congressional sponsors argued that the laws were necessary wartime measures. Their practical purpose, however, sought to destroy the Republicans by undermining their support and closing newspapers. The Federalists tried to take advantage of the Quasi-War to link their opponents with the enemy. This strategy worked in the short term, as the pro-French Republicans lost votes in the 1798 congressional election, but proved suicidal for Adams' party after the fear of invasion had passed.

This Federalist design resulted in four restrictive laws. The Naturalization Act of 1798 lengthened the period of residence needed for citizenship from five to fourteen years. The legislation was intended to stop the flow of Irish immigrants who, because they were anti-British and pro-French, swelled the number of Republican voters. The Alien Enemies Act established procedures in the event of declared war or invasion for jailing and deporting citizens of the enemy nation who were considered likely to spy or commit sabotage.

Two additional laws gave wide powers to the president during peacetime as well as in war. The Alien Act, which had a term of two years, allowed the president to deport any non–U.S. citizens "he shall judge dangerous to the peace and safety of the United States, or shall have reasonable grounds to suspect are concerned in any treasonable or secret machinations against the government thereof." Like the Naturalization Act, this law potentially threatened Irish immigrants. But because Adams refrained from using it, the Alien Act's importance was more symbolic than real.

The Federalists did enforce the fourth law, the Sedition Act, with serious results. Its term lasted until March 3, 1801, the day before the next president would be inaugurated. Thus the Federalists ensured that if the next chief executive were a Republican, he would not be able to retaliate without obtaining a new statute. The Sedition Act made it illegal for "any persons [to] unlawfully combine or conspire together, with intent to oppose any measure or measures of the government of the United States" or to interfere with the execution of a law. Nor could a person "write, print, utter or publish . . . any false, scandalous and malicious writing or writings against the government of the United States, or either house of the Congress . . . or the President." In effect, this law permitted imprisonment and fines for criticizing the government. It was an obvious infringement upon freedom of speech and freedom of the press.

Nevertheless, the administration enforced the law. The prime targets for prosecution were Republican newspapers. Among the indicted was Benjamin Bache, the grandson of Benjamin Franklin and editor of the Philadelphia *Aurora,* who was one of Adams's most powerful critics. The official authorized to administer the act was Secretary of State Timothy Pickering, a staunch Federalist, who methodically reviewed the Republican papers for actionable offenses. Under the law, the Federalists indicted and tried at least seventeen people for sedition. They timed cases to reach court in the fall of 1799 or the following spring, with the goal of silencing the Republican press during the 1800 election. Some papers folded and others closed temporarily while their editors were imprisoned.

The Republican Opposition Grows

Passage of the Alien and Sedition Acts and the jailing of Republican spokesmen shifted the political winds. In late 1798, the Kentucky and Virginia legislatures approved resolutions that protested the Alien and Sedition Acts on the grounds that they were unconstitutional. The resolutions argued that these laws violated the First Amendment and granted powers to the national government not delegated by the Constitution. The Virginia assembly resolved that "in case of a deliberate, palpable, and dangerous exercise of other powers, not granted by the [Constitution], the states . . . have the right, and are in duty bound, to interpose, for arresting the progress of the evil." Virginia and Kentucky sent their resolutions to other legislatures, none of which agreed that states could declare a federal law unconstitutional. Nevertheless, the resolutions contributed toward a theory of "nullification," the idea that a state had the right to veto a federal law it considered unconstitutional.

With the Alien and Sedition Acts, the Federalists made a strategic error. Where formerly the Republicans could be branded as a faction creating animosity and disunity, they now became legitimate defenders of revolutionary principles. The Republican party justified its opposition by warning that the Federalists were on the road to tyranny. The Sedition Act, the Virginia Resolutions argued, impeded free investigation of the actions of government officials and "free communication among the people thereon, which has ever been justly deemed the only effectual guardian of every other right." The administration's effort to destroy its adversaries backfired as the Republicans gained respectability among Americans who had formerly supported the Federalists.

The administration fanned the flames of indignation with its heavy-handed reaction to a tax rebellion among Germans of rural eastern Pennsylvania. The Republicans took advantage of the Pennsylvanians' aversion to the 1798 federal property tax to win their votes in the congressional election. They circulated petitions against the tax, the defense buildup, and the Alien and Sedition laws, petitions that Congress ignored. By early 1799, the people of Northampton and Bucks counties held public meetings and stopped tax assessors from doing their work. In March, after the U.S. marshal jailed eighteen suspected tax resisters in Bethlehem's Sun Tavern, John Fries, a fifty-year-old auctioneer of upper Bucks County, led a band of 140 armed men to release the prisoners.

The Fries Rebellion ended quickly, as the rebels considered the magnitude of their offense. Fries announced that he would pay the tax and would even welcome the assessor to his house for dinner. Nevertheless, the president decided to make an example of the episode. He dispatched troops that failed to march until almost four weeks after the resistance had ceased. The army descended upon Northampton and Bucks counties, entering houses and arresting sixty men. Contrary to the Judiciary Act of 1789, the prisoners were taken to Philadelphia for trial. Fries and two others were found guilty of treason by a Federalist court and sentenced to hang, but were subsequently pardoned by the president. The Republicans added the administration's unwarranted use of force to their arsenal of charges against the Federalists.

CONCLUSION

George Washington had warned in his Farewell Address that "the spirit of part . . . agitates the community with ill-founded jealousies and false alarms; kindles the animosity of one part against another; foments occasionally riot and insurrection." He invoked the ideal of consensual community, challenging his fellow citizens to work together for the good of their country. The flaw of this conception was that Americans could not agree on which policies were best for everyone. The interests of farmers, merchants, and artisans, of residents of the north, south, and west, often diverged. The Federalist and Republican parties grew out of different visions of the nation's future. During the 1790s, the Federalists retained control of the central government. They denounced parties, identifying their government with the republic as a whole. When they tried to eliminate factions by silencing their adversaries with the Sedition Act, ironically they legitimized the party system in the eyes of many Americans.

RECOMMENDED READINGS

Anderson, Margo J. *The American Census: A Social History* (1988). A very good source on the first federal census of 1790.

Charles, Joseph. *The Origins of the American Party System* (1956). Insightful examination of the development of parties in the 1790s.

Cochran, Thomas C. *Frontiers of Change: Early Industrialism in America* (1981). A good introduction to industrialization in the early republic.

Elkins, Stanley, and McKitrick, Eric. *The Age of Federalism* (1993). Detailed narrative of the Washington and Adams administrations.

North, Douglass C. *The Economic Growth of the United States, 1790–1860* (1966). Includes a useful analysis of U.S. trade amid international conflict.

Onuf, Peter S., ed. *Jeffersonian Legacies* (1993). Wide-ranging essays on Thomas Jefferson's character and politics.

Slaughter, Thomas P. *The Whiskey Rebellion: Frontier Epilogue to the American Revolution* (1986). An excellent book on the struggle between Alexander Hamilton and western Pennsylvania farmers over excise taxes.

Smith, James Morton. *Freedom's Fetters: The Alien and Sedition Laws and American Civil Liberties* (1956). Focuses on the Federalists' attempt to curtail civil rights.

White, Richard. *The Middle Ground: Indians, Empires, and Republics in the Great Lakes Region, 1650–1815* (1991). Influential study of Indian-white relations from New France through the War of 1812.

Young, James Sterling. *The Washington Community, 1800–1828* (1966). Interesting work on the development and growth of the new federal capital.

AMERICAN JOURNEY ONLINE AND INFOTRAC COLLEGE EDITION

Visit the source collections at www.americanjourney.psmedia.com and infotrac.thomsonlearning.com and use the Search function with the following key terms to explore documents, images, audio and video clips, articles, and commentary related to the material in this chapter.

George Washington
Alexander Hamilton
John Adams
Abigail Adams
Eli Whitney
Whiskey Rebellion
XYZ Affair

Chapter 8

The New Republic Faces a New Century, 1800–1814

Americans confronted the nineteenth century with a variety of fears. For the Federalists, the growing Republican opposition warned that the evils of democracy and anarchy stood ready to take control. For the Republicans, the Alien and Sedition Acts and Federalist repression of the whiskey rebels and John Fries underscored the need for change. Both parties thought in terms of the ideals for which they had fought against the British. They also measured events against what was transpiring elsewhere in the world. By 1800, the French Revolution and Napoleon Bonaparte's rise to power dismayed Americans. The never-ending European war threatened to involve the United States for twenty years, and finally did in 1812.

Though Thomas Jefferson's presidency proved to be less revolutionary than many Federalists expected, the new century brought indelible changes to American politics and society. The Federalist party shriveled and died, the Louisiana Purchase expanded the nation's territory to the Rocky Mountains and beyond, slavery became more firmly embedded in the southern economy, and the republic fought once more against Great Britain. The Second Great Awakening, the series of religious revivals that gained steam after the turn of the century, influenced the ways in which many people interpreted these events.

Religion in American Society

During the first decade of the nineteenth century, religion absorbed the energies of many different groups: frontier settlers and Native Americans caught up in revivals, organizations to provide welfare relief in towns and cities, new sects like the Shakers, and free African Americans. Many people believed that renewed emphasis on religion would transform the nation through individual faith and communal action.

The Second Great Awakening

As the century began, people throughout the country sought spiritual renewal. Among New England Congregationalists, the revivals spread from one town to another between 1797 and 1801. The national Methodist conference of

CHRONOLOGY

1800 Washington, D.C., becomes national capital

Gabriel's Rebellion

Convention of 1800 with France

Jefferson's election as president

Rise of Handsome Lake as a Seneca prophet

1801 Adams' "midnight appointments"

John Marshall becomes chief justice
Tripolitan War

Cane Ridge, Kentucky, camp meeting

1802 Judiciary Act of 1801 repealed

1803 *Marbury v. Madison* case

Great Britain and France resume war

Louisiana Purchase

1804 Lewis and Clark expedition departs from St. Louis

Aaron Burr kills Alexander Hamilton

Twelfth Amendment ratified

Haiti founded

Reelection of Jefferson as president

1805 *Essex* decision in Britain

1806 Non-Importation Act

1807 Burr tried for treason

Leopard-Chesapeake Affair

Embargo Act

1808 Federal ban on importation of slaves

Madison elected as president

1809 Giles' Enforcement Act

Embargo repealed; replaced with Non-Intercourse Act

Treaty of Fort Wayne

1810 Annexation of West Florida

1811 Charter of national bank expires

Tecumseh organizes pan-Indian resistance to land cessions

Battle of Tippecanoe

1812 U.S. declares war on Great Britain

Hull surrenders Detroit

Madison elected to second term

1813 Perry defeats British navy on Lake Erie

Battle of the Thames

1814 Battle of Horseshoe Bend

British burn public buildings in Washington, D.C.

Americans repel invasion on Lake Champlain

Hartford Convention

Treaty of Ghent

1800 held in Baltimore witnessed an outpouring of religious fervor. These flames heralded a series of revivals—the Second Great Awakening—which lasted into the 1830s. In accepting the message of revival, large numbers of Americans embraced evangelicalism—the belief that they must take their message of salvation to others. They expected to create a more godly nation through conversion and good works.

In particular, eastern clergy worried that people on the frontier, with few churches, would let sin take control of their lives. The clerics expressed their dread in terms of millennialism, the belief that the millennium—Christ's second coming—was at hand, as foretold in Revelation, the last book of the Bible. Pastors urged their congregations to prepare for the millennium by supporting missionary efforts in the west. They believed Americans throughout the country must embrace Christianity and convert Native Americans and the people of other lands.

Circuit preachers and missionaries traveled throughout the frontier; the churches they started were often the first social organizations in new communities. The great western revivals of 1800–1815, which built upon this work, began when several Presbyterians summoned the first camp meeting, a religious gathering held outside

Methodist Camp Meeting, engraving by E. Clay. During the Second Great Awakening, itinerant preachers held outdoor revivals that often lasted for several days. (Collection of the New-York Historical Society)

over the course of several days. People came together to hear revivalist preachers. The most famous of the early camp meetings took place in August 1801 at Cane Ridge, Kentucky, where Presbyterian, Methodist, and Baptist clergy preached for about a week to a throng numbering about 20,000. From wagons and crude tents, the crowds listened to the spiritual message that Jesus Christ could save all people from their sins. People reacted emotionally and physically to this message, some jerking their heads or entire bodies, others falling to the ground in a faint.

Reminiscent of the Great Awakening in the South during the 1750s and 1760s (see Chapter 4), the camp meetings spread through Kentucky, Tennessee, and southern Ohio, gathering new congregations. The Methodist and Baptist churches, which placed less importance on the fine points of religious doctrine than the Presbyterians, benefited most from the revivals. The Methodists and Baptists saw extraordinary growth among ordinary people, especially in the South. As one minister wrote, "the illiterate Methodist preachers actually set the world on fire, (the American world at least,) while [pastors of other denominations] were lighting their matches!"

Religion was important to black Americans, whether they remained enslaved or had achieved freedom. In the South, African Americans responded enthusiastically to revivalist preachers. The Methodists and Baptists welcomed free and enslaved blacks into their congregations as equals in spirit though not in governing the church. In hostile northern cities, free black communities depended upon separate churches for leadership and communal fellowship.

Growth of Sects

The period around 1800 witnessed the expansion of several dissenting sects: the Shakers, the Society of the Public Universal Friend, and the Universalists. They are called sects, rather than denominations, because they were new and fairly small. They held distinctive beliefs that set them apart from mainstream religions, yet had a significant influence on intellectual and social movements of their times.

The Shakers, whose official name was the United Society of Believers in Christ's Second Coming (the Millennial church), came to America in 1774, when Mother Ann Lee arrived from Britain with eight disciples. The group grew slowly at first, but expanded after Lee's death in 1784, as it reaped followers from revivals, especially Baptists. The sect offered an avenue for people who had been spiritually reborn in the Awakening and sought a distinctive way to represent that rebirth in their lives.

From visions, Mother Lee believed that she embodied Christ's Second Coming, that the millennium had already arrived. As Christ had appeared as a man, and Lee came as a woman, God had both male and female elements. The Shakers believed in salvation by confession of sin, equality regardless of sex or race, opposition to slavery and war, and assistance to the poor. They abstained from sexual relations. In Shaker communities, which by 1809 existed from Maine to Kentucky, men and women ate, slept, and worked separately. They followed a strict discipline and aspired to economic self-sufficiency. Shakers sat on straight-backed chairs, cut their food into square pieces, and walked along paths laid out in right angles. But in religious worship, they abandoned this right-angle order. In a large open space without pulpit or pews, worshippers danced, shouted, and sang.

A similar but smaller sect was the Society of the Public Universal Friend, founded by Jemima Wilkinson of Rhode Island. Disowned by Quakers in 1776 for joining the Baptists, Wilkinson became ill, believed that she died, and then returned to life as the Public Universal Friend. Her mission was to convince others to repent their sins and prepare for the millennium. Like Mother Lee, Wilkinson preached celibacy, peace, and opposition to slavery. She traveled sidesaddle on horseback, attracting a coterie of believers in New England and Pennsylvania. In 1788, upon gathering over 200 Universal Friends, she organized a community called Jerusalem in western New York. The Universal Friends neither organized a communal economy like the Shakers nor continued to seek new members. Nevertheless, the community survived well past Wilkinson's death in 1819.

Another sect, the Universalists, rejected the Calvinist belief that only a minority of people, the elect, could attain salvation. They preached that "it is the purpose of God, through the grace revealed in our Lord Jesus Christ, to save every member of the human race from sin." The American Universalist Church, established in 1779 by an Englishman, John Murray, found a sympathetic audience among ordinary people caught up in the Second Great Awakening in New England and on the frontier.

Revivalism among Native Americans

While the Second Great Awakening and dissenting sects claimed the imagination and souls of white and black Americans, a new wave of revivals drew together Native Americans. Among the Iroquois living on reservations in western New York and the Shawnees, Creeks, Cherokees, and other nations retaining lands in the trans-Appalachian region, prophets warned of imminent doom unless people changed their ways. Native Americans had continued to lose lands to whites throughout the area from the Appalachians to the Mississippi. Decline in the numbers of fur-bearing animals caused economic hardship, while conflict over whether to cooperate with the United States created political factions within tribes.

Like the Delaware prophet Neolin in the 1760s (see Chapter 4), the new nativists blamed loss of land and power on the Indians' failure to maintain traditional rituals and on their adoption of wicked practices from the whites. Among many prophets, Handsome Lake of the Senecas (a nation of the Iroquois) and Tenskwatawa of the Shawnees wielded the greatest influence in the first decade of the nineteenth century.

Handsome Lake, a respected warrior and leader of the Allegany Senecas, fell ill in 1799, seemed to die, then came back to life saying that he had a vision in which messengers told him to become a prophet. In a series of revelations over several years, Handsome Lake received a message of impending catastrophe and a means to salvation. He told his people to stop drinking alcohol and practicing witchcraft; instead, they should perform their ancestral rituals.

Handsome Lake also advocated peace. He embraced the U.S. acculturation policy by which Quakers tried to convince the Iroquois to adopt white farming methods and gender roles, but he opposed further large-scale land cessions, the whiskey trade, social dancing in couples, and gambling with cards. Other Indians opposed acculturation, which required women to leave the fields and take up spinning, and men to farm rather than hunt. They viewed the policy, accurately, as a way to justify further expropriation of hunting lands.

Handsome Lake served as political leader of the Iroquois only briefly, from 1801 to 1803, but his spiritual message remained strong in the years that followed. Most influential was his drive against liquor. Many Iroquois abstained from hard drink. One Quaker visitor "noted with satisfaction that in the course of our travels among all the Indians on the Allegheny River . . . we have not seen a Single individual the least intoxicated with Liquor—which perhaps would be a Singular Circumstance to Observe in traveling among the same number of white Inhabitants."

Handsome Lake was one of the most influential Indian prophets of the late eighteenth and early nineteenth century. Another was Tenskwatawa, called the Shawnee Prophet, who became prominent among the people of the Great Lakes and Ohio Valley. With his brother, Tecumseh, he inspired a nativist movement to resist the U.S. government's acculturation policy and land grabbing. To avoid fiery destruction, he warned, Indians must revitalize their traditional ceremonies, avoid liquor, and reject the new gender roles.

AFRICAN AMERICANS

As slavery ended in the north, blacks faced discriminatory practices that kept the racial caste system in place, including segregation in churches and schools, and restriction from politics and many occupations. Despite this racism, northern blacks created new lives, institutions, and communities that offered a potent draw to African Americans in the south. Southern blacks also considered more violent means to end bondage, as in the case of Gabriel's revolt in Virginia.

Free Blacks in the North

By 1800, Pennsylvania, New York, and all of New England had passed gradual abolition acts or ended slavery outright. New Jersey in 1804 became the last northern state to pass a law for gradual emancipation, which, like those of other states, freed children henceforth born to slave mothers, but retained slaves born before that date in perpetual bondage. The black children who benefited from the law would be required to serve their mother's owner until a certain age.

Despite the gradual nature of these emancipation laws, slavery declined rapidly in the northern states. Responding to their slaves' requests for freedom and to the spirit of the abolition acts, owners freed people whom the laws left in bonds. Masters usually required some additional years of service for the promise of freedom. Frequently, blacks negotiated agreements for themselves or family members. A New Jersey man promised to pay his owner $50 per year for four years in return for his release. When masters proved recalcitrant, blacks often forced the issue by running away.

The northern cities became magnets for escaped slaves. In addition, humanitarian concerns touched some southern masters, including George Washington, who freed his slaves in his will. Some owners in Delaware and the Chesapeake region, who held more slaves than they needed, emancipated their slaves, then sold them as indentured servants in the north.

TABLE 8.1 NUMBER OF ENSLAVED AFRICAN AMERICANS, 1800 AND 1810

	1800	*1810*
New England	1,339	418
New York	20,903	15,017
New Jersey	12,422	10,851
Pennsylvania	1,706	795
Delaware	6,153	4,177
Maryland & District of Columbia	107,707	115,056
Virginia	346,968	394,357
North Carolina	133,296	168,824
South Carolina	146,151	196,365
Georgia	59,406	105,218
Kentucky	40,343	80,561
Tennessee	13,584	44,535
Mississippi Territory	3,489	17,088

Philadelphia and New York City became centers of free African American culture. In Philadelphia, responding to hostility, freed men and women organized separate congregations in the 1780s and 1790s. Reverend Richard Allen, for example, led black worshippers from St. George's Methodist Episcopal Church when whites insisted on segregated seating. Allen purchased a blacksmith's shop and converted it into a church, calling it Bethel. By 1803, the black Methodist church had 457 members, the result of revivals and Allen's fervent preaching. But although the evangelical message of Methodism appealed to African Americans, and "Mother" Bethel grew, the congregation found relations with the hierarchy of the white Methodist church difficult. In the early decades of the nineteenth century, black Methodists in Philadelphia, Baltimore, Wilmington, and New York struggled against white control, finally seceding to form separate denominations. In 1816, Philadelphia's Bethel became the first congregation of the African Methodist Episcopal church.

Reverend Richard Allen, a former slave, was founder of the African Methodist Episcopal Church and a leader of the Philadelphia black community. (Moorland-Spingarn Research Center, Howard University)

Urban black churches provided mutual aid, fellowship, and avenues for leadership. One benefit of belonging to a New York congregation became obvious to an eighty-year-old woman after a fire destroyed her home. When asked where she would find shelter, she answered, "O a sister in the church has promised to take me in." Shunned by white organizations, effectively barred from politics, and lacking equal opportunity for employment, African Americans created alternatives through the church.

Like white urban residents, freed men and women formed mutual benefit societies. The names African Americans chose for these organizations demonstrated pride in their African heritage. Philadelphians, for example, formed the Free African Society, Daughters of Ethiopia, Angola Society, Sons of Africa, and many others. The official purpose of these societies was to collect dues to provide relief to poor widows and children, but, just as important, the groups facilitated community involvement.

With little money or access to capital, few African Americans, perhaps one in ten, scraped together the funds to purchase a house, shop, or farm. In the first decades of the nineteenth century, many blacks were still completing terms of servitude, while others, though free, lived and worked in white households as domestic servants. Even if they established their own households, women generally washed clothes or performed domestic service for others. Most men were mariners or hired as common laborers. The African American community provided additional opportunity by employing its own. Residents supported black shoemakers, carpenters, food retailers, hucksters, barbers, hairdressers, seamstresses, tailors, cooks, bakers, schoolteachers, and ministers. In Philadelphia, a few African Americans achieved considerable wealth and fame. By 1807, James Forten employed thirty men—blacks and whites—to produce sails for the city's shipbuilders. Robert Bogle developed the idea of catering parties, weddings, and funerals, while Frank Johnson became the city's premier musician.

Northern blacks faced daily challenges in their quest for economic success and equal status. But they revered their African roots. The word African in the name of most mutual aid societies and churches testified to their pride of origins, though many of the founders were two, three, even four generations removed from ancestral lands.

African Americans in northern cities also knew of recent struggles by slaves in St. Domingue and elsewhere. During the 1790s, blacks on St. Domingue led by Toussaint L'Ouverture, a former slave, defeated local whites and the French, Spanish, and British armies. In 1802, Napoleon tried once again to take control of the island, but failed when disease decimated his forces. In 1804, the victorious rebels of St. Domingue established Haiti as an independent nation. Most white Americans dreaded the importation of black revolt.

Slave Rebellion in the South

With more than 850,000 enslaved blacks in the American south in 1800, whites had reason to be concerned about slave insurgency. After St. Domingue erupted, Georgia and the Carolinas declared black emigrés from the West Indies a threat, prohibiting their entry. South Carolina, in reopening its international slave trade in 1803, made every effort to avoid admitting rebels. The state excluded blacks from the West Indies and South America, and any who had ever lived in the French West Indies.

In August 1800, the worst fears of white southerners were nearly realized when an enslaved blacksmith named Gabriel organized an armed march against the capital of Virginia. With about 600 supporters from Richmond and surrounding counties, Gabriel planned a full-scale insurrection. His strategy included seizing guns from an arsenal, taking Governor James Monroe hostage, and forcing concessions from town officials. Gabriel expected poor whites to join him because they, like slaves, lacked political power. The attack failed when a torrential rainstorm washed out bridges, making travel impossible. Efforts to try again another day collapsed when two informers passed word of the conspiracy to authorities who rounded up suspects. Though Gabriel eluded capture for more than three weeks, he was arrested and hanged, as were twenty-six others implicated in the plot.

White Americans still held the revolutionary belief that all men and women desired freedom; masters took seriously the threat of slave revolt. In 1802, Virginians discovered additional conspiracies, with rumors of more violence heightening tensions. In 1805, after four whites had been poisoned in North Carolina, officials burned a slave woman alive, hanged three other slaves, and whipped and cut off the ears of another. Gabriel's plot, the St. Domingue uprising, and what appeared to be an upsurge of murders and arson by blacks convinced southern lawmakers to enact more stringent slave codes. South Carolina and Georgia tightened requirements for slave patrols and defined as treason any collaboration in slave rebellion. Hardening attitudes toward slavery snuffed out southern antislavery societies that were already faltering. On a more positive note, as the twenty-year constitutional restriction on prohibiting the slave trade expired (see Chapter 6), Congress officially banned the importation of slaves after January 1, 1808.

JEFFERSON'S REPUBLIC

In 1800, the federal government moved to an unfinished village on the Potomac: Washington, D.C. The ruling party also changed, as voters voiced their dissatisfaction with the Federalists by electing Thomas Jefferson and a Republican Congress. Jefferson's promise of reduced government and taxes appealed to a populace concerned about other things besides national politics. Events prevented the young nation from wrapping itself in isolation, however, for its economic prosperity depended a great deal upon international commerce, a trade severely hampered by the ongoing European war.

The Election of 1800

Most recently, the United States had been involved in the Quasi-War with France, in which the French navy ravaged the American merchant fleet. Congress had expanded the army, authorized the U.S. Navy to protect commercial ships, and revoked unilaterally the American-French treaty of 1778. The Federalists had swept the congressional elections of 1798 on the crest of anti-French fervor; they tried to use war fever against the Republicans through the Alien and Sedition Acts. Instead, the backlash of concern about civil liberties swelled the opposition.

As the 1800 election approached, many Federalists expected to paint the Jeffersonian Republicans as pro-French, hence un-American. Nevertheless, President John Adams moved to end hostilities. He nominated a three-man commission, including William Vans Murray (ambassador to the Netherlands), Chief Justice Oliver Ellsworth, and Governor William R. Davie of North Carolina, to make peace with France. Its mission was to obtain French agreement that the 1778 alliance had ended and indemnities for confiscated American ships. In March 1800, Murray, Ellsworth, and Davie met with Napoleon, who had no intention of paying compensation. The commissioners reached an accord only by ignoring their instructions. The Convention of 1800, signed in France in October and ratified reluctantly by the U.S. Senate in February 1801, echoed provisions of the 1778 commercial treaty in calling for "a firm, inviolable, and universal peace." The Convention voided the defensive alliance of 1778, however, thus eliminating the French claim to U.S. support against Great Britain. The pact also included a vague confirmation by the French of neutral rights in international trade, but provided no restitution to American shippers, a failing that opponents said made the convention worthless. In fact, it had value in normalizing relations between the two countries.

The chief beneficiary of reduced tensions with France was Thomas Jefferson, named in May 1800 as Republican nominee for president, with Aaron Burr of New York for vice president. John Adams received the Federalist nomination for reelection, with Charles Cotesworth Pinckney of South Carolina as his running mate. Many Federalists opposed Adams for making peace with France. When the electoral votes were tallied, Jefferson and Burr each received 73 votes, Adams had 65, Pinckney 64, and John Jay 1. In lining up votes in the electoral college, the Republicans had failed to take account of the constitutional election procedures that lacked provision for party slates. The Constitution directed that each elector cast two votes, with the candidate receiving the highest number elected president and the runner-up vice president. The electors had no way of designating which candidate they supported for president and which for vice president. The Federalists avoided the difficulty by having one elector vote for John Jay, thus giving Pinckney one less vote than Adams. But the Republicans all cast one vote for Jefferson and one for Burr, resulting in the tie.

If Burr had simply yielded to Jefferson in 1800, the problem would have been resolved without complication. But the New Yorker reached for the presidency, thereby earning the enmity of Jefferson and his party. The tie sent the election to the House of Representatives, which had a Federalist majority. Each state delegation received one vote. Some of the Federalists hatched a plan to support Burr, thinking that they might be able to control him as president. Hamilton opposed the plot vigorously. The former secretary of the treasury advised his party to make a deal with Jefferson to keep the system of public credit and the navy, retain Federalist appointees in office, and remain neutral in the war between Britain and France. The House of Representatives required thirty-six ballots over six days before the Federalist delegate from Delaware, James A. Bayard, shifted his position to break the tie.

Jefferson's "Revolution"

On March 4, 1801, Jefferson delivered his inaugural address to the new Congress, which the Republicans dominated in the House by 69 votes to

36, and in the Senate by an 18–13 majority. The speech reflected his Republican beliefs: emphasis on the power of state governments, freedom of religion and the press, majority rule but protection of minority rights, low government expenditures, and reduction of the federal debt. Jefferson upheld the Convention of 1800 with France implicitly by stating that he desired amity and trade with foreign nations and "entangling alliances with none." His most famous statement, "We are all republicans, we are all federalists," attempted to get beyond the partisan battles that had bedeviled his two predecessors. He later described his election as "the revolution of 1800" that "was as real a revolution in the principles of our government as that of 1776 was in its form." Despite bitter political enmity, American leaders had created a party system by which power could be contested in elections rather than through bloodshed. With the election of 1800, the Constitution passed a crucial test, with peaceful transfer of power from one party to its opponents.

The new president worked to put his principles into action, to create an agrarian republic in which the federal government kept its role to a minimum. The location in Washington, D.C., seemed the ideal setting for a weak government. In 1800, the town had fewer than 400 dwellings. The Capitol was incomplete, with wings for the Senate and House but no center. The president's house was not yet finished in 1814 when the British burned it. Construction materials littered the grounds during Jefferson's administration to the extent that, according to one guest, "in a dark night instead of finding your way to the house, you may, perchance, fall into a pit, or stumble over a heap of rubbish." Cows grazed on what later became the Mall; hogs ran through the city's streets.

Washington, D.C., remained a village in part because the federal government was small. In 1802, federal personnel throughout the country numbered under 10,000, of whom 6,500 served in military posts. Of the nonuniformed officials, fewer than 300 worked in the capital. The president and Supreme Court each had one clerk, Congress employed thirteen, and the attorney general none. The central government had relatively little to do, for state and local governments or voluntary associations took primary responsibility for keeping law and order, maintaining roads and bridges, supervising the militia, and providing welfare relief and schools.

Thomas Jefferson, 1791, by Charles Willson Peale. The third president called his election "the revolution of 1800," effected not by violence "but by the rational and peaceable instrument of reform, the suffrage of the people." (Independence National Historical Park)

Jefferson's lack of attention to building Washington, D.C., revealed his approach to the presidency. In contrast to Federalist efforts to reflect the grandeur of European courts and capitals, he adopted informality and frugality. Jefferson dealt with members of Congress and foreign diplomats personally, inviting small groups for dinner and conversation. He avoided making speeches, sending written messages to Congress.

The change of political power from the Federalists to the Republicans raised questions about officeholding and political spoils. At the highest level of executive appointments, the cabinet, Jefferson assumed his right to appoint trusted supporters. He named James Madison of Virginia, his closest ally, as secretary of state, and Albert Gallatin of Pennsylvania as secretary of the treasury. Other members of the cabinet included Levi Lincoln of Massachusetts as attorney general, Henry Dearborn of Massachusetts as secretary of war, and Robert Smith of Maryland as secretary of the navy.

The question of whether or not to retain bureaucrats was more difficult. Jefferson supported the idea of a civil service in which public officers held their positions on the basis of merit; during the election crisis he suggested that he would allow officeholders to keep their jobs. When he learned that Washington and Adams had appointed only six Republicans to about 600 positions, however, the new president replaced about one-half of the Federalists with Republicans. Most infuriating were the "midnight appointments," as Jefferson called them—the appointments Adams made as a lame duck after he knew that the election was lost.

Jefferson and Gallatin placed high priority in decreasing government expenditures, taxes, and the national debt. Gallatin opposed all spending by the federal government, including military. With support of the Republican Congress, the administration cut the defense budget in half and eliminated several ambassadorships in Europe. It repealed all excise taxes, including that on whiskey, relying primarily on import duties for income.

Jefferson's plan to reduce the navy and remain clear of international conflicts hit a snag when Yusuf Karamanli, the leader of Tripoli in North Africa, declared war on the United States. Karamanli demanded payments from the United States to "protect" American merchant carriers from pirates. To end this extortion, in 1801 Jefferson sent naval vessels to blockade Tripoli and protect shipping. When a small force of U.S. Marines and Arab mercenaries seized Derna, the Tripolitans agreed to peace. The war had propelled military expenditures upward, however, and convinced Jefferson of the navy's value, thus hindering somewhat the administration's plans for reduced government spending.

The Judiciary

Although the Republicans had captured the presidency and Congress in 1800, the judiciary remained firmly in the hands of the Federalists. Adams and the outgoing Congress had tried to solidify their party's power in the courts with the Judiciary Act of 1801, which amended the act of 1789. By appointing additional federal judges, the new law ended the onerous requirement for Supreme Court justices to ride from state to state holding circuit courts twice a year. The Republican Congress, in early 1802, repealed this law, reinstating the Judiciary Act of 1789, thus forcing some federal judges out of their jobs and the Supreme Court back to the circuit.

Jefferson's bitter relationship with the Supreme Court resulted in part from his antipathy toward Chief Justice John Marshall, his distant cousin, whom Adams had named to the bench in early 1801. Like Jefferson, Marshall was tall, informal in manner, and a native of Virginia. He had joined the patriot forces in 1775, serving until 1781. He began a successful law practice after the war, served as a Virginia assemblyman, supported ratification of the Federal Constitution, then became the leading Federalist in his state. In the legal environment of the new republic, many colleagues appreciated his originality in building cases on logic and natural law rather than depending upon English precedent. On the Supreme Court, too, Marshall followed his own lights, creating the legal basis on which the power of the Court rests. During his long, illustrious career, which lasted until 1835, Marshall solidified the authority of the judicial branch of the federal government.

Marshall's most important decision, *Marbury v. Madison* (1803), commenced in a suit by William Marbury, nominated by Adams as a justice of the peace but not commissioned by the Jefferson administration. Marbury sued under the Judiciary Act of 1789, which granted the Supreme Court the power to require Secretary of State Madison to hand over Marbury's commission. Given the partisanship involved, most observers expected Marshall and his Federalist court to direct Madison to comply. Instead, the Chief Justice said that he could not remedy Marbury's situation, though he wished to do so, because the Congress had erred in giving the Court such authority. Marshall declared the provision of the 1789 Judiciary Act unconstitutional, thus establishing the Supreme Court's power of judicial review.

Jefferson decided that the federal judiciary, still dominated by Federalists and growing in power under Marshall, had to be controlled. Because federal judges constitutionally held their seats for life, "during good behavior," the president suggested to congressional Republicans that they start impeachment proceedings against objectionable Federalists. The Republicans impeached John Pickering, an official of the federal district court of New Hampshire, who was an alcoholic and insane, but who had not to anyone's knowledge committed any high crimes. The Senate found him guilty anyway and removed him from his position. Next, in January 1805, the House of Representatives impeached Samuel Chase of Maryland, an associate justice of the Supreme Court and extreme Federalist who castigated Jefferson's administration. But the prosecution failed to convince two-thirds of the Senate that Chase should be expelled from office for misconduct and other charges. Some moderate Republicans refused to adopt Jefferson's strategy to eject troublesome opponents. Thus ended Congress's attempt to remove Federalists from the bench by impeachment.

Domestic Politics

Jefferson and the Republicans gained in popularity as they steered a course more moderate than the "revolution" of 1800 had promised. The president had reduced taxes and attempted to limit the judiciary, but did not dismantle the Federalist edifice of national power, including the military and the national bank. His policies, combined with booming exports, steadily increased Republican support, as many Federalist voters switched parties. In the election of 1802, the Republicans won 102 seats to the Federalists' 39 in the House of Representatives; the Republican margin in the Senate was 25 to 9.

Looking forward to the next presidential election, Congress acted promptly to avoid the deadlock that had occurred in 1800. The Republicans wanted a formal way to keep the Federalists from conspiring once again to elevate the Republican candidate for vice president to the presidency. The Twelfth Amendment to the Constitution, which required the electors to draw up distinct lists for president and vice president, was ratified by September 1804.

The election of 1804 demonstrated the demise of the Federalists as a national party. Jefferson defeated the Federalist presidential candidate, Charles Cotesworth Pinckney, by 162 electoral votes to 14.

Jefferson had replaced Aaron Burr as his running mate with George Clinton, also of New York, thus keeping the ticket balanced geographically. For his part, Burr ran for governor of New York against the Republican candidate, Morgan Lewis, but lost by a landslide. Alexander Hamilton played a decisive role in the defeat by publicly denouncing his longtime enemy. Burr challenged Hamilton to a duel. When the two faced each other at Weehawken, New Jersey, in July 1804, Burr shot Hamilton to death. In doing so, the vice president ended his own political career as well as the life of one of the architects of the American nation-state.

The Louisiana Purchase

Jefferson had boosted his popularity prior to the 1804 election with the Louisiana Purchase. Long interested in the west, he scored a diplomatic coup that doubled the size of the United States and reduced Spain's dominance west of the Mississippi River.

The Bargain with Napoleon

The chain of events leading to the Louisiana Purchase began in 1800, when France signed a secret treaty with Spain for lands in western North America. France would get back the territory it had ceded to Spain in 1763. When Jefferson and Madison heard in 1801 of the impending transfer, they sent the new U.S. ambassador to France, Robert R. Livingston, with instructions to prevent the exchange or at least obtain West Florida. The Americans wanted to prevent France from controlling the Mississippi Valley; the dilapidated Spanish empire caused trouble enough. In October 1802, the Spanish suspended once again the right of Americans to deposit goods for export at New Orleans. The Americans thought, incorrectly, that Napoleon was behind the ban. Many wanted to take New Orleans by force. Jefferson pushed for negotiations, however, not war.

In response to Livingston's overtures, Napoleon decided to sell the entire Louisiana Territory to the United States. The French leader's zeal to construct an American empire had cooled with the loss of his army in St. Domingue; moreover, he needed money, as he was at war with Great Britain once again. In documents dated April 30, 1803, the United States agreed to pay France $15 million, to respect the rights of the French and Native Americans living in the territory, and to recognize the French residents as American citizens. Spain was furious because Napoleon had promised not to sell the region to the British or the Americans. Jefferson ignored the Spanish objections, but worried that the Louisiana Purchase was unconstitutional because the federal government had no specific power to acquire territory. He put aside these concerns, confident that it was right to avoid war and add vast lands for expansion of the American republic. "By enlarging the empire of liberty," the president argued, the nation could maintain its agrarian foundations. A successful republic was dependent upon broad property holding, for virtuous, independent, middling farmers made ideal citizens. Although some Federalists disagreed, most Americans celebrated the end of friction over the Mississippi River and New Orleans. Western farmers could get their products to market; eastern merchants prospered from the trade.

Disputes with Spain

When U.S. officials gained formal possession of Louisiana in December 1803, the Spanish had only recently transferred control to the French. The ceremonies took place in New Orleans, a city of 8,000 that had been reconstructed in Spanish style since several great fires a decade earlier. New Orleans served as the cultural and economic center of the lower Mississippi Valley. In population, it was larger than other towns of the Spanish borderlands. The entire white population of the Louisiana Territory was approximately 50,000, including French, Spanish, Germans, English, and Americans.

Beyond Spain's objection to the U.S. purchase of Louisiana, the two nations also disputed the territory's boundaries. Jefferson demanded West Florida, with an eastern boundary at the Perdido River, the present boundary between Alabama and the Florida panhandle. The president also thought his new acquisition extended in the southwest to the Rio Grande, incorporating all of Texas and part of New Mexico, and in the northwest to the Rocky Mountains. Spain, on the other hand, said the Louisiana Territory included only a constricted region along the west bank of the Mississippi from northern Missouri to the Gulf of Mexico.

The Lewis and Clark Expedition

To strengthen U.S. claims to the west, Jefferson sponsored an exploratory mission to the Pacific Ocean. Several times since 1783, he had tried to organize expeditions for scientific knowledge and to promote American interests in the region. As president, he now had the authority and financial resources to support this major undertaking. By the early nineteenth century, however, others had surveyed parts of the territory. In 1792, an American sea captain, Robert Gray, explored the Columbia River, and George Vancouver, a British naval officer, sailed the northwest coast.

Even before buying Louisiana, the president had decided to send an expedition west; the purchase gave the project greater urgency. He appointed his private secretary, Meriwether Lewis, as captain of the enterprise. Lewis chose his friend

Map 8.1 | Western Exploration, 1803–1807

William Clark to be his partner. Lewis and Clark had served in the army together in the old Northwest, so both were familiar with frontier conditions. Jefferson selected Lewis for his scientific interests as well as his wilderness experience. The president wanted "a person who to courage, prudence, habits & health adapted to the woods, & some familiarity with the Indian character, joins a perfect knoledge of botany, natural history, mineralogy & astronomy."

Jefferson had a long list of goals for his explorers. They were to travel to the source of the Missouri River to find the elusive Northwest Passage, fill in huge blanks in geographic knowledge of the West, and bring back descriptions of unknown species of plants and animals. Lewis and Clark more than fulfilled their assignment, keeping daily journals of their experiences, including descriptions of Indian societies and culture, systematic weather records, and observations of flora and fauna, as well as a detailed map of their journey.

Lewis and Clark received commissions as army officers to lead the Corps of Discovery of about forty men who departed from St. Louis in May 1804. During that summer and fall they traveled up the Missouri River, using poles and tow ropes against the current. They battled the hot sun, diarrhea, and mosquitoes; several men deserted and one died. The adventurers met with the leaders of Indian nations along the way, telling them that the United States had taken possession of the territory from the Spanish. They arrived in the Mandan and Hidatsa villages of what is now North Dakota, where they spent the winter of 1804–1805.

In April 1805, the Lewis and Clark expedition set out with their guide Sacagawea, a Shoshone woman. They proceeded up the Missouri River, made an arduous crossing of the Rockies, and reached the mouth of the Columbia River before winter. On the way back, the corps divided in two, with Clark leading a party southeast along the Yellowstone River and Lewis taking a northern route through Montana. They joined forces once again in North Dakota, then returned to St. Louis by September 1806. They had been away so long that many assumed they had been killed by the Spanish or Native Americans.

Spies and Infiltrators

Spanish officials in fact had tried to intercept Lewis and Clark, whom they correctly suspected of making allies for the United States among the western Indians. General James Wilkinson, commander of U.S. troops in the west, governor of the Louisiana Territory, and a double agent known to the Spanish as "Agent 13," had tipped off New Spain about the expedition. The governor of New Mexico sent out search parties but failed to find Lewis and Clark. They did stop the mission of Thomas Freeman and Peter Custis, who in 1806 set out from Louisiana to find the source of the Red River. Another Spanish party nearly intercepted Zebulon Pike, whom Wilkinson had dispatched to explore and spy in the region that is now Kansas, Colorado, and New Mexico. Pike became lost in the southern Rockies, was rescued by Spanish soldiers, arrested, then released.

Both the United States and Spain knew they were playing for high stakes. The United States could use exploration of the west and alliances with Native Americans to help confirm its claims to broad boundaries of the Louisiana Territory. The Spanish had by far superior documentation for Texas, New Mexico, Arizona, California, and western Colorado. But they also denied American rights to what is now western Louisiana. Jefferson sent General Wilkinson with troops to the undefined boundary between Louisiana and Texas; the Spanish dispatched Lt. Col. Simón de Herrera to defend eastern Texas. The two officers avoided fighting by establishing a neutral zone until diplomats could negotiate the border.

Still concerned about protecting their silver mines in Mexico, the Spanish took steps to increase settlement in Texas. They welcomed Indian exiles from lands overrun by American settlers east of the Mississippi, but the Hispanic population failed to grow significantly. New Spain officials specifically

THE JOURNAL OF MERIWETHER LEWIS 1805

During their journey through the northwest, explorers Meriwether Lewis and William Clark used diaries to record information about the Native Americans they met as well as the plants, animals, weather, and landscape along their route. In the entries below, Lewis describes the birth of a son to Sacagawea, the expedition's Shoshone interpreter and guide, and the challenges the Corps of Discovery faced in mid-winter 1805.

[Lewis] *11th February Monday 1805.*

The party that were ordered last evening set out early this morning. the weather was fair and could wind N. W. about five oclock this evening one of the wives of Charbono was delivered of a fine boy. It is worthy of remark that this was the first child which this woman had boarn and as is common in such cases her labour was tedious and the pain violent; Mr. Jessome informed me that he had freequently administered a small portion of the rattle of the rattle-snake, which he assured me had never failed to produce the desired effect, that of hastening the birth of the child; having the rattle of a snake by me I gave

barred U.S. citizens from Texas. Anglo-American traders continued to infiltrate Texas, however, to trap animals and bargain for horses with Comanches and other Indians.

The Burr Conspiracy

While Lewis and Clark were reconnoitering the far Northwest, Aaron Burr conceived a plot to create a separate nation in the west. He contacted the double agent James Wilkinson, various unhappy politicians, and representatives of foreign governments. Burr suggested a variety of plans to those who would listen, including an invasion of New Spain, an attack on Washington, D.C., and secession of the west. Wilkinson cooperated with Burr at first, then turned informer when the conspiracy became public knowledge. Jefferson ordered Burr's arrest for treason. Burr tried to escape to Europe, but was captured and taken to Richmond, Virginia, where he was tried in 1807.

The Burr conspiracy case, presided over by Chief Justice Marshall, might have been called the trial of the century. An unbiased jury could not be found; one juror said before the case was heard that Burr should be hanged. The principal actors in the trial were Marshall, who ignored his responsibility as an impartial judge to favor the defense, and Jefferson, who directed the prosecution from afar. Because Marshall upheld a definition of treason that required actual gathering of troops, not just conspiracy, the case against Burr collapsed.

it to him and he administered two rings of it to the woman broken in small pieces with the fingers and added to a small quantity of water. Whether this medicine was truly the cause or not I shall not undertake to determine, but I was informed that she had not taken it more than ten minutes before she brought forth. . . .

[Lewis] *12th February Tuesday 1805.*

The morning was fair tho' could, thermometer at 14° below naught wind S. E. . . I directed some meal brands given [to the horses] moisened with a little water but to my astonishment found that they would not eat it but prefered the bark of the cotton wood which forms the principall article of food usually given them by their Indian masters in the winter season; for this purpose they cause the trees to be felled by their women and the horses feed on the boughs and bark of their tender branches. . . . The Indians are invariably severe riders, and frequently have occasion for many days together through the whole course of the day to employ their horses in pursuing the Buffaloe or transporting meat to their vilages during which time they are seldom suffered to tast food; at night the Horse returned to his stall where his food is what seems to me a scanty allowance of wood. under these circumstances it would seem that their horses could not long exist or at least could not retain their flesh and strength, but the contrary is the fact, this valuable anamall under all those disadvantages is seldom seen meager or unfit for service.—A little after dark this evening Capt. Clark arrived with the hunting party—since they set out they have killed forty Deer, three buffaloe bulls, & sixteen Elk, most of them were so meager that they were unfit for uce, particularly the Buffaloes and male Elk—the wolves also which are here extremely numerous heped themselves to a considerable proportion of the hunt—if an anamal is killed and lyes only one night exposed to the wolves it is almost invariably devoured by them.

More Foreign Entanglements

While the renewal of war in 1803 between Great Britain and France had impelled Napoleon to sell Louisiana, it also portended trouble for the United States. American merchants flourished, but their ships became vulnerable to the British navy and French privateers.

A Perilous Neutrality

The British intended to stop American traders from carrying foreign sugar, coffee, and other tropical products to Europe, even though the merchants conformed technically to British guidelines by taking the goods first to U.S. ports, then reexporting. In the *Essex* case of 1805, British courts stiffened their rules, stating that merely carrying Spanish and French goods to U.S. soil for reexport was insufficient, that only commodities originally meant for sale in the United States, then subsequently redirected to Europe, would be considered exempt from seizure. Few reexported cargoes met the new guidelines. Then, in 1806 and 1807, the British and French established blockades of each other's harbors, in combination eliminating neutral trade with Europe and the British Isles.

After the British destroyed the French and Spanish navies in 1805 at Trafalgar, off the coast of Spain, the British restrictions and impressment of sailors were by far the most troublesome to Americans. Many Federalists and some Republicans cried for war. But Jefferson and the congressional majority looked for ways to avoid hostilities. With a trimmed federal budget and small military, the Republicans were unprepared for war, so looked for alternatives. Congress passed a Non-Importation Act (1806) banning specified British goods, while the president opened negotiations with Great Britain to end impressment and recognize neutral trading rights. No agreement satisfactory to both sides could be reached. Then, in June 1807, the British ship *Leopard* fired upon the American frigate *Chesapeake* for refusing to submit to a search for British deserters. The *Chesapeake,* hit twenty-two times, managed to respond with only one shot. The *Leopard* boarded her, impressing four alleged deserters.

The Embargo of 1807

Jefferson closed U.S. ports to the British navy and recalled ships from the Mediterranean. The British refused to stop impressing American sailors, arguing that they only seized British deserters. They challenged Jefferson's port closure by firing on coastal towns in Maine and sailing in Chesapeake Bay. The president resisted a declaration of war, but placed military posts and gunboats on alert.

At the urging of President Jefferson and Secretary of State Madison, Congress passed the Embargo Act in December 1807. The law prohibited exportation to all other countries. The administration hoped in particular to defang the former parent country by withholding provisions to the British Isles and West Indies. A by-product of non-exportation would be a severe drop in imports of British manufactures, of which the United States purchased about one-third of total production. Jefferson and Madison argued that the boycott would hurt all warring parties, but Britain worst. During 1808, the administration faced difficulty enforcing the embargo because ships, especially from New England, left harbor pretending to sail to American coastal ports but headed for foreign destinations instead. The trade with the British West Indies continued illegally. Federal agents also had little success in preventing smuggling into Canada. In January 1809, the government resorted to an extreme measure, Giles' Enforcement Act, which empowered the president to use the militia against smugglers.

The embargo had considerable impact on the U.S. economy. Agricultural prices declined, leading to farm foreclosures. According to official records, exports declined by 80 percent in 1808, though smuggling certainly lessened the effect. The U.S. Treasury suffered a loss in customs revenue, its chief source of income.

With stern enforcement under Giles' Act, New Englanders became more strident in their demands for termination of the embargo. Jefferson refused to support repeal at a time when the embargo was starting to work. Republicans in Congress moved anyway, on March 1, 1809, replacing the embargo with a Non-Intercourse Act, which reopened trade with all countries except Great Britain and France. If either of the two belligerents changed its policy to favor neutral rights, the United States would resume commerce with that nation as well.

Congress made this shift just days before the close of Jefferson's presidency. Jefferson thus ended his administration without solving the nation's international troubles, which Americans increasingly defined as an effort by Britain to subjugate its former colonies. As he returned to Monticello, however, the president could reflect favorably upon the goals he had achieved—lower taxes and national debt, smaller government, open doors to immigrants, and peace. He also took pride in an accomplishment he had not foreseen in 1801, the purchase of the Louisiana Territory. Jefferson's administration was remarkable for what it did—and for what it did not do, considering his opposition to Hamiltonian policies in the 1790s. Under Jefferson, the Republicans left intact the national bank, the federal administrative structure, and armed forces. However, the

Republican commitment to minimal government left the United States militarily unprepared.

Madison and the War of 1812

When Britain continued to impress American sailors and seize ships, Jefferson's successor had two choices: accept humiliation or declare war on Great Britain. The British argued that they acted from necessity, as Napoleon conquered Europe. Americans upheld their rights as neutrals to sell provisions to both sides. They considered British impressment of 6,000 seamen as a violation of national sovereignty and human rights. Between 1809 and 1812, these conflicts developed into war.

The Election of 1808

Despite the embargo, Jefferson retained enough popularity to win a third term, had he chosen to run. When he withdrew, he designated James Madison as his successor. James Monroe, who had served as governor of Virginia and ambassador to Britain, challenged Jefferson's choice; but congressional Republicans endorsed Madison. Dissenting Republicans, called the Quids, gave Monroe some support, but his candidacy died quickly. George Clinton accepted renomination for vice president. The Federalists put up Charles C. Pinckney and Rufus King.

The Federalists improved upon their performance in 1804 and 1806, gaining twenty-four seats in Congress, but still had much less than a majority. The electoral vote for president was 122 for Madison and 47 for Pinckney. Although Americans suffered from the embargo, most were unprepared to desert the Republicans. In electing the new president, citizens ratified Jefferson's political philosophy and policies, which Madison had helped formulate. The country could expect a continuation of Jeffersonian policies.

James Madison, *painted by Gilbert Stuart, a few years before he became the fourth U.S. president. Called the "Father of the Constitution," Madison also helped develop the two-party system through opposition to the Federalists in the 1790s.* (Colonial Williamsburg Foundation)

In another way, however, the new administration presented a real departure. Madison brought his elegant wife Dolley Payne Madison with him to the executive mansion. The first lady transformed the president's house into a proper executive mansion. She served as hostess to frequent teas and dinner parties, inviting Federalists and Republicans to socialize together.

Heading for War

After Madison's election, the European struggle continued to embroil the United States. While both Britain and France were hostile to free trade, the British dominated the seas, and as a consequence had substantial impact on U.S. commerce. Over the period to 1812, as Napoleon pushed across Europe, invaded Russia, and met defeat, he became inconsequential as a threat to the Americans. Indeed, his attempt to install his brother Joseph Bonaparte as king of Spain in 1808 undermined Spanish control in the New World. In West Florida, Anglo-Americans who had earlier pledged allegiance to Spain, in 1810 commandeered the Spanish fort at Baton Rouge, declared independence, and petitioned Madison for annexation by the United States. The president promptly claimed West Florida as part of the Louisiana Purchase, and American troops occupied Baton Rouge. When Louisiana became a state in 1812, it included the western part of West Florida from Baton Rouge to the Pearl River.

In 1811, Madison appointed James Monroe, his former rival for the presidency, as secretary of state. Monroe took office hoping to reach an accord with the British, but soon decided that they wanted nothing less than to put the United States back into its colonial yoke. The Royal Navy continued to impress American seamen. When Napoleon partially lifted his blockade in 1811, the United States resumed trade with France. Madison tried to convince the British to drop their restrictions as well, but instead they pounced on American ships headed for French ports.

Tecumseh in 1811 attempted to unite northern and southern Indians to defend their remaining lands east of the Mississippi River. Portrait from Benjamin Lossing's Pictorial Field Book of the War of 1812 *(1869).* (Smithsonian Institution, Bureau of American Ethnology)

Events in the west also intensified anger toward Britain, because Anglo-Americans believed that the British in Canada were stirring up Native American discontent. In fact, while some Indians traded with the British, many natives distrusted the whites of both Canada and the United States. The nativist message of Tenskwatawa, the Shawnee Prophet, and his brother Tecumseh found widespread support. Their call to resist white encroachment resonated most clearly in what later became Illinois, Michigan, and Wisconsin, among Chippewas, Potawatomis, and Winnebagos, who could predict that their territory would soon be threatened.

The nativists were spurred into action by the Treaty of Fort Wayne (1809), which turned over 2.5 million acres to the United States. Tecumseh met with William Henry Harrison, governor of the Indiana Territory, to request that the treaty be annulled. Failing that, the Indian leader went south to seek support from the Creeks, Cherokees, and Choctaws. He found allies among militant factions of Creeks and Seminoles, called the Red Sticks (from their war clubs). The Red Sticks opposed the accommodationists among their own people who sold land to the United States and adopted Anglo-American ways of life. Tecumseh's effort to create a pan-Indian movement throughout the trans-Appalachian west ultimately failed, however, because by 1811, large white populations in Tennessee, Kentucky, and Ohio formed a barrier between north and south.

In November 1811, William Henry Harrison decided to cut short Tecumseh's efforts for unity. The governor did not believe the Indian leader's assurance that whites were "unnecessarily alarmed at his measures—that they really meant nothing but peace." Harrison led a force against Prophetstown (Tippecanoe), the village that Tenskwatawa had founded several years before. Before Harrison struck, the Prophet attacked the encamped soldiers at night, but suffered casualties and withdrew. Harrison also lost men, but burned the town and claimed victory in what became known as the Battle of Tippecanoe.

The War of 1812 Begins

When news of the battle reached Washington, many officials interpreted it as evidence that a British-Indian alliance already existed. The outcome, they mistakenly believed, showed that the British were weak, incapable of sustaining their allies. "War Hawks" in Congress, including the newly elected Speaker of the House Henry Clay of Kentucky and Representative John C. Calhoun of South Carolina, advocated preparations for war. By April 1812, President Madison agreed. The Federalists opposed conflict with Great Britain in part to obstruct administration policy, in part for commercial interests. The Republicans were divided. Opponents claimed that Madison intended to wage war for territorial expansion in Canada and Florida.

Congress authorized a 25,000-man regular army and borrowing $11 million. Still, the nation was ill-prepared when Madison issued his war message on June 1. Military funding would prove difficult because the charter of the national bank had been allowed to expire in 1811 due to politics and state banking interests, leaving state banks but no central agency as a source of loans. Lack of federal taxes beyond import duties, which fell sharply when the British blockaded the Atlantic coast, further

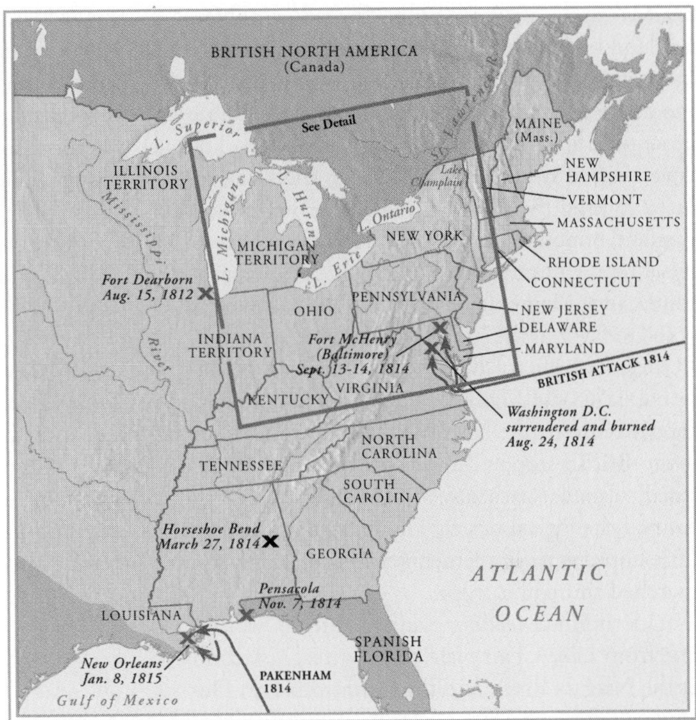

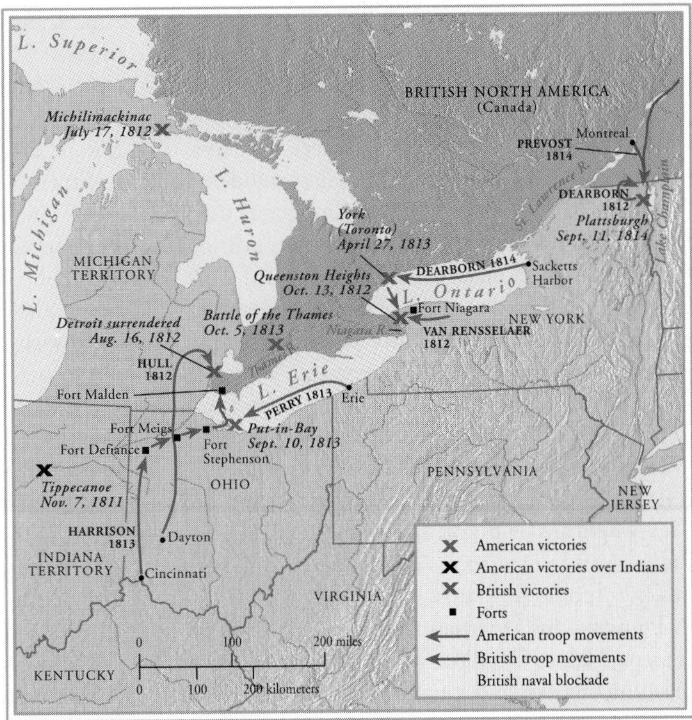

MAP 8.2 | THE WAR OF 1812

limited the country's resources. The failure of New England leaders to provide their share of funds—indeed merchants' provisioning of the enemy and the desire of some New Englanders for a separate peace—severely hampered the war effort. The governors of Massachusetts and Connecticut refused to send their militia. Not everyone in New England opposed the war, however, for the majority of representatives from Vermont, New Hampshire, and Maine (still part of Massachusetts) voted in favor of the June 1812 declaration of war.

Despite military deficiencies and lack of national unity, the Madison administration pushed forward into battle. Madison offered an armistice if the British stopped impressment, but they refused. Canada, with only 5,000 regular soldiers, seemed the logical target. The redcoats there had little hope for reinforcements as long as Napoleon marched through Europe.

U.S. military leaders planned three advances, one from Lake Champlain to Montreal, a second at the Niagara River, and the third from Fort Detroit east through Upper Canada. The Americans moved first in the west. General William Hull received orders to lead about 2,000 troops against Fort Malden, opposite Detroit, under command of British General Isaac Brock and reinforced by Tecumseh and his men. Hull dawdled long enough to allow more British soldiers to arrive. He failed to take Fort Malden and surrendered Detroit. The British and Native Americans then took control of much of the region by capturing Fort Michilimackinac, to the north, and Fort Dearborn, at the present site of Chicago. Another blow came for the United States in October, when the army lost the Battle of Queenston, opposite Fort Niagara, after the New York militia refused to leave American soil to assist the regular troops. William Henry Harrison, commissioned a general, reinforced Fort Wayne against Indian attack. The Americans held Fort Harrison (Terre Haute, Indiana) and other points along a line from Sandusky, Ohio, to St. Louis.

During this frustrating campaign against Canada, James Madison stood for reelection. Heading the Federalist ticket was DeWitt Clinton, a New York Republican and nephew of the vice president. Clinton tried to gain support from both political parties by advocating peace to the Federalists while telling the Republicans that Madison had failed to prosecute the war hard enough. The president won by an electoral tally of 128 to 89; he obtained substantial Republican majorities in the House and Senate.

In contrast to the army's failures in 1812, the tiny U.S. fleet had surprising success against the mighty Royal Navy. The *Constitution* sank the British *Guerrière* in August; two months later the *United States,* captained by Stephen Decatur, took the *Macedonian;* in December the *Constitution* destroyed the *Java.* Although British ships also won some rounds, the American defeats of an enemy considered master of the seas greatly bolstered public opinion.

Victories and Losses, 1813–1814

On land, however, 1813 began with another disaster for the Americans, as the British and Native Americans killed and captured nearly an entire force of 900 troops at Frenchtown, south of Detroit. The United States managed to hold Fort Meigs and Fort Stephenson in northern Ohio. But to destroy British control of Lake Erie and territory to the west, the army needed naval support. The United States began building ships at Presque Isle, Pennsylvania (now Erie), and on September 10, 1813, Oliver Hazard Perry defeated the British squadron at Put-in-Bay. This naval victory cleared the way for General Harrison to attack Fort Malden, from which the British and Indians hastily retreated toward Niagara. The Americans caught up with them at Moraviantown on October 5, winning a decisive victory known as the Battle of the Thames. To the east, the U.S. Army had burned York (Toronto), the capital of Upper Canada. But the Americans met defeat in an offensive against Montreal and lost Fort Niagara.

In the Mississippi Territory, the nativist Red Sticks waged civil war against Creek leaders who accommodated Anglo-American demands for land. The fratricidal conflict became a war against the United States in July 1813 when 180 American militia struck a much smaller group of Red Sticks. The Red Sticks, with 4,000 warriors but lacking adequate arms, faced overwhelming odds against the combined forces of U.S. troops, accommodationist Creeks, and Cherokee allies. Three armies entered Red Stick territory, destroying homes and dispersing families. The turning point came in March 1814, when General Andrew Jackson, with 3,000 militia and Indian allies, defeated 1,000 Red Sticks in the Battle of Horseshoe Bend, killing 800. The surviving militants escaped to Florida, where they joined nativist Seminoles and continued to fight.

In the summer of 1814, the British turned greater attention to the war in America, having defeated Napoleon in April. They sent 10,000 experienced redcoats to Canada; the American naval victory on Lake Champlain in September cut short the British invasion. Britain also sent forces to Chesapeake Bay, where in August they attacked the nearly defenseless Washington, D.C. Redcoats burned the Capitol and the president's mansion, shortly after the Madisons fled. The president and Mrs. Madison saved official documents and the Gilbert Stuart portrait of George Washington. The enemy promptly left the Capital, and the U.S. government returned.

The British then assaulted Baltimore. Despite heavy bombardment of Fort McHenry by the Royal Navy, the redcoats failed to take the city. James Monroe, who was by then secretary of war as well as secretary of state, took credit for Baltimore's stand. Francis Scott Key memorialized the scene of flaming rockets and exploding bombs in his poem "The Star Spangled Banner," which was later set to the tune of a popular English song and, in the early twentieth century, became the national anthem. The British sailed south to the Gulf Coast, intending to block off the Mississippi River. In late 1814, Andrew Jackson captured Pensacola, Florida, then organized the defense of New Orleans.

The Hartford Convention

Over the course of the war, sentiment had grown in New England for secession. The Massachusetts governor secretly contacted the British about a separate peace. In late 1814, a group of Federalists organized the Hartford Convention to find a more moderate course. The convention issued a report supporting the right of states to declare federal laws unconstitutional and arguing that states should be responsible for their own defense. The Hartford delegates called for significant amendments to the Constitution: removal of the three-fifths clause; a two-thirds majority in Congress to declare war and admit new states; a one-term limit on the president; and prohibition of naturalized citizens—who were largely Republican—from federal positions. These proposals, calculated to damage Republican power bases in the south and west and among new immigrants in the cities, fell on deaf ears when news of the peace treaty arrived from Europe.

The Treaty of Ghent

Peace came as both the British and the United States recognized that the end of the twenty-year struggle in Europe eliminated the rationale for war in America. The defeat of Napoleon removed Britain's need to regulate neutral trade and impress seamen. Both sides could also see that they had little hope of victory. Britain might continue its blockade and smother U.S. commerce, but to what purpose? Conquest of the former colonies, now expanded into the west, would require huge expenditures of manpower and funds. Victory at New Orleans would plug the Mississippi, but in late 1814 success was still uncertain.

Madison authorized John Quincy Adams, Albert Gallatin, Henry Clay, and two others, to meet the British peace delegation at Ghent, Belgium, in August 1814. After several months of stalemate, the negotiators agreed on Christmas Eve, 1814, to return to the status quo at the outbreak of war.

The British dropped their demands for part of Maine and an independent Indian territory north of the Ohio River, while the Americans stopped insisting that the British renounce impressment, which had ceased.

CONCLUSION

With its simple provision to reinstate the *status quo ante bellum,* the Treaty of Ghent might appear to make the War of 1812 meaningless. The losses of lives and dollars seem for nothing. Yet most Americans celebrated the peace, knowing that they had withstood Britain's attempt to treat them as colonials. A second generation of Americans had proven that they could survive a struggle with what was probably the world's most powerful nation. In addition, the United States had defeated Tecumseh's pan-Indian movement in the west, effectively ending Native American power east of the Mississippi.

Much had changed from 1800 to 1814. The Federalists transformed themselves from the architects of the national government in the 1790s to advocates of narrow sectional interests in 1814. Thomas Jefferson and James Madison, who had upheld states' rights, moved in the opposite direction during their administrations. Without denying their commitment to limited government, a skeleton military, low taxes, and republican principles, they expanded "the empire of liberty" by purchasing Louisiana and forcing Native Americans from their lands. Jefferson and Madison used every means short of armed conflict to protect commerce, then went to war when all else failed. In purchasing Louisiana, Jefferson relaxed his philosophy of strict interpretation of the Constitution in hope that the additional territory would extend the life of his agrarian republic. Madison facilitated the growth of nationalism by exacting respect from Great Britain. With the Atlantic world at peace once again, residents from Maine to Louisiana concentrated on making money and building their communities, all with a greater sense that they belonged to an American nation.

Recommended Readings

Brant, Irving. *James Madison.* 6 vols. (1941–61). Excellent, detailed biography of the fourth president.

Coles, Harry L. *The War of 1812* (1965). A readable one-volume study.

Dowd, Gregory Evans. *A Spirited Resistance: The North American Indian Struggle for Unity, 1745–1815* (1992). Demonstrates the significance of religion in Native American resistance.

Horsman, Reginald. *The Causes of the War of 1812* (1961). A good discussion of the circumstances leading to war.

McCoy, Drew R. *The Elusive Republic: Political Economy in Jeffersonian America* (1980). Insightful exploration of Jeffersonian politics and thought.

Malone, Dumas. *Jefferson and His Time.* 6 vols. (1948–81). The benchmark biography of Thomas Jefferson.

Moulton, Gary E., ed. *The Journals of the Lewis and Clark Expedition.* 7 vols. (1983–91). Most comprehensive edition of manuscript maps and journals.

Nash, Gary B. *Forging Freedom: The Formation of Philadelphia's Black Community, 1720–1840* (1988). Insightful study of the challenges of freedom for one community of African Americans in the North.

Smelser, Marshall. *The Democratic Republic, 1801–1815* (1992). A useful, lively overview of the period.

American Journey Online and InfoTrac College Edition

Visit the source collections at www.americanjourney.psmedia.com and infotrac.thomsonlearning.com and use the Search function with the following key terms to explore documents, images, audio and video clips, articles, and commentary related to the material in this chapter.

Thomas Jefferson
Louisiana Purchase
Lewis and Clark
Marbury v. Madison
Aaron Burr
Tecumseh
Tenskwatawa
Second Great Awakening

PASSAGES

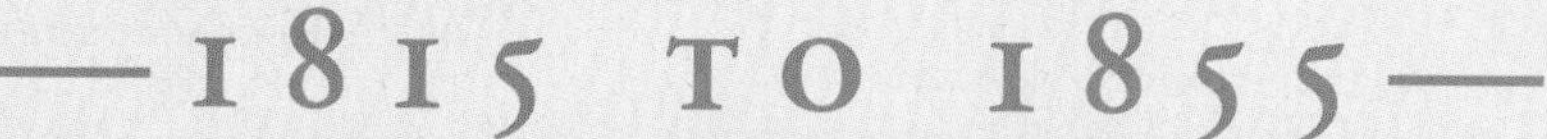

THE UNITED STATES redefined itself during the forty years after 1815. The boundaries of the nation, the character of its population, the nature of its economy, and the religious beliefs of its people all took new shape. Some of the changes confirmed what the architects of the young nation had expected several decades before; other changes proved to be surprises and the bitterest of disappointments. The speed and scale of transformation astonished everyone.

In 1815, the young United States held only eighteen states, with Louisiana standing exposed at the western boundary, Florida in the hands of the Spanish, and an unsettled line between Canada and the United States. The western half of the continent remained only vaguely known to Anglo-Americans and seemed too far away to be of importance any time soon. Even within the country's sketchy borders, American Indians populated large and rich areas in both the north and the south.

Four decades later, the continental boundaries of the nation had expanded beyond recognition. Florida had come into the Union from Spain. War with Mexico had brought in vast territories from Texas to California. Negotiation with Great Britain had defined the northern boundary from Maine to Oregon. Military and economic pressure on the American Indian nations had driven them across the Mississippi River. A new state entered the Union about every two and a half years; by the end of the 1850s thirty-three states—including two on the Pacific coast—claimed a place in the nation.

The population exploded. The number of Americans grew from 8.4 million in 1815 to 31.4 million by the end of the 1850s. Nearly 4 million of those people were held in slavery, whereas 3 million people had crossed the Atlantic from Europe in a mixture of hope and desperation. People spread out across the expanse of the burgeoning country, establishing farms and towns far from the older cities of the east. About half the population of an average town moved every ten years. By the end of the period the United States claimed 5 million more people than England and the new country boasted eight cities of more than 150,000 inhabitants—more than any other country in the world.

Large changes altered the scale of life, tying people together as few could have imagined in 1815. Steamboats transformed water transportation in the 1810s, canals boomed in the 1820s, and railroads arrived in the 1830s. The United States claimed over 35,000 miles of railroad track by the end of the era. In the 1840s, the first telegraph wires carried information from one city to another in a clatter of keys; by the late 1850s, telegraph wires stretched across the Atlantic Ocean. Novels sold tens of thousands of copies in a few months. Newspapers, confined to just a few major cities in 1815, became staples of American life in the 1830s and 1840s, read and published in hundreds of communities of every size. Daguerreotypes and colorful lithographs decorated homes that had been empty of pictures a generation earlier.

The United States became integrated ever more tightly into the international economy. The capacity of ships arriving in American ports doubled in the 1830s, doubled again in the 1840s, and then again in the 1850s. American vessels plied the Atlantic with cargoes of cotton and wheat for England and Europe. Clipper ships sailed around South America and into the Pacific, carrying prospectors and immigrants along with tea. The United States, anxious about European intervention in Latin America and the Caribbean, claimed the hemisphere as a place under its jurisdiction and protection.

(The Granger Collection, New York)

Americans created lodges, clubs, and societies of every sort. Baptists, Methodists, and Presbyterians vied with one another for converts. Reform groups emerged to stamp out alcohol and war, to encourage education and humane treatment of the unfortunate, to improve diet and health, and to bring the end of slavery. Women accounted for many members of these organizations, lending their energy and intelligence to activities beyond the home. Political parties mobilized nearly all adult white men, sweeping them up as Democrats, Whigs, Free Soilers, Know Nothings, and Republicans. Men swore allegiance to their party, expressing their passions and beliefs in slogans, songs, and parades. On election days, as many as eight out of ten eligible voters went to the polls, publicly proclaiming their support for their candidates.

The expansion of the United States was the expansion of the largest and most powerful slave society in the modern world. Slavery grew stronger with each passing decade, embracing an ever larger part of the continent to the south and west, holding more people within its bonds, accounting for a larger share of the nation's exports. As the years passed, the discussions in the churches, the reform organizations, and the political parties increasingly turned to sectional conflict. Rivalry and distrust between the North and the South infected everything in the public life of the country.

The years between 1815 and 1855, then, did not witness a smooth passage through an "industrial revolution" or "growth of the common man" or "westward expansion." Rather, these years marked a passage filled with rapids and countercurrents and waterfalls. Panics and depressions, internal and external wars, massive migration and immigration, freedom and slavery—all came tumultuously.

For additional information and resources pertaining to this period in American history, please visit the American Passages Web Site at:

http://ayersbrief.wadworth.com

1815	1820	1825	1830	1835

Politics & Diplomacy

1815: Battle of New Orleans
1816: Monroe elected president; "Era of Good Feelings" begins
Clay calls for "American System"
Indiana admitted to the Union
1817: Mississippi admitted to the Union
1818: Jackson invades Florida
Illinois admitted to the Union
1819: Transcontinental (or Adams-Onís) treaty with Spain
Alabama admitted to the Union
1820: Missouri Compromise
Monroe elected president
Maine admitted to the Union
1821: Missouri admitted to the Union
1822: Denmark Vesey Rebellion, Charleston
1823: Monroe Doctrine announced

1824: Contested election of John Quincy Adams
1828: Tariff of Abominations
Calhoun's *Exposition*
Election of Jackson
1829: David Walker's *Appeal*
Mexico tries to abolish slavery in Texas
1830: Indian Removal Act
Antimasonic party holds first national party convention
1831: Nat Turner's rebellion
Garrison's *The Liberator*
Jackson reorganizes cabinet, Van Buren over Calhoun

1832: Bank War begins
Nullification Crisis
Virginia debates over slavery
Jackson reelected
1833: Force Bill against South Carolina
Compromise Tariff
Slavery abolished in British Empire
1834: Whig party organized
1835: Arkansas admitted to the Union
Revolution breaks out in Texas
Abolitionists' postal campaign
War against Seminoles and runaway slaves in Florida
1836: Congress imposes gag rule
Texas Republic established; Battle of the Alamo

Social & Cultural Events

1816: American Colonization Society founded
American Bible Society founded
1819: Auburn penitentiary established
1824: Lafayette's visit
American Sunday School Union founded

1825: American Tract Society founded
1829: David Walker's *Appeal*
1830: *Book of Mormon*
Finney's revivals begin in Rochester
1831: Garrison's *The Liberator*
Mormons migrate from New York to Ohio
1833: Formation of American Anti-slavery Society

1837: Grimké sisters lecture to mixed audiences
Horace Mann becomes first secretary of Massachusetts State Board of Education
Ralph Waldo Emerson, "The American Scholar"
1839: Daguerreotypes introduced to the United States

Economics & Technology

1815: *Enterprise* first steamboat from New Orleans to Pittsburgh
1816: Second Bank of the United States chartered
1817: Mississippi admitted to the Union
1818: Erie Canal begun
National Road completed
1819: *Dartmouth College Case* and *McCulloch v. Maryland*
Financial panic and depression

1824: *Gibbons v. Ogden*
1825: Completion of Erie Canal
1828: Tariff of Abominations
1831: John Bull begins railroad operation
1832: Bank War begins
1833: Compromise Tariff
1834: National Trades Union formed
Cyrus McCormick patents reaper

1837: Financial panic
Charles River Bridge v. Warren Bridge decision
1839: Depression worsens
Daguerreotypes introduced to the United States

1840 1845 1850 1855

1838: John Quincy Adams successfully defeats attempt to annex Texas
1840: Congress passes Independent Treasury Act
Harrison elected president
Frederick Douglass escapes from slavery
American Anti-slavery Society splits
James G. Birney runs for president as candidate for Liberty party
1841: Harrison dies; John Tyler becomes president
Amistad case heard before the Supreme Court
1844: James K. Polk claims the United States' claim to "all Oregon"

1845: Texas and Florida admitted to the Union
1846: Mexican War begins; Stephen Kearny occupies Santa Fe; Zachary Taylor takes Monterey
Border between Canada and United States established at 49th parallel
Wilmot Proviso ignites sectional conflict
Bear Flag Republic in California proclaimed by John C. Frémont
1847: Taylor defeats Santa Anna at Buena Vista; Winfield Scott captures Vera Cruz and Mexico City
1848: Treaty of Guadalupe Hidalgo
Attempts to buy Cuba from Spain
Free Soil party runs Van Buren for president
Seneca Falls Convention
Zachary Taylor elected president

1849: California seeks admission to Union
1850: Nashville Convention attempts to unify South
Fugitive Slave Law
Taylor dies; Millard Fillmore becomes president
Compromise of 1850
1851: Maine adopts prohibition
Women's rights convention in Akron, Ohio
Indiana state constitution excludes free blacks
1852: Franklin Pierce elected president
1853: Gadsden Purchase
1854: Know-Nothings win unexpected victories
Whig party collapses
Republican party founded
Kansas-Nebraska Act
Ostend Manifesto encourages acquisition of Cuba

1840: Washingtonian temperance movement emerges
1841: Brook Farm founded
P. T. Barnum opens the American Museum
Amistad case heard before the Supreme Court
1842: Edgar Allan Poe, "The Murders in the Rue Morgue"
1844: Methodist Episcopal church divides over slavery
Edgar Allan Poe, "The Raven"

1846: Hiram Powers completes statue *The Greek Slave*
1847: Mormons reach Great Salt Lake Valley
1848: Seneca Falls Convention
Oneida Community established
Mormons settle in Great Basin

1850: Nathaniel Hawthorne, *The Scarlet Letter*
1851: Herman Melville, *Moby Dick*
Maine adopts prohibition
Women's rights convention in Akron, Ohio
1852: Harriet Beecher Stowe, *Uncle Tom's Cabin*
1854: Henry David Thoreau, *Walden*

1840: Congress passes Independent Treasury Act
1841: California sees arrival of first wagon train
Oregon fever
1843: Oregon sees arrival of first wagon trains
1844: Baltimore-Washington telegraph line
Samuel F. B. Morse patents the telegraph

1848: Gold discovered in California
Regular steamship trips between Liverpool and New York City
1849: "Forty-Niners" race to California
Cotton prices invigorate South

1854: High-point of immigration railroad reaches Mississippi River

Chapter 9

Exploded Boundaries, 1815–1826

THE, SUDDEN CLIMAX OF THE WAR OF 1812 surprised everyone. Ever since the nation's beginning, even the leaders of the United States had wondered whether a large and lightly governed republic could long endure. Miraculously, the new country did not lose the war. Indeed, upon the war's unexpected end the United States entered upon a period of economic growth and territorial expansion no one could have foreseen. Settlers pushed west in remarkable numbers. Throughout the country, steamboats, canals, and turnpikes tied the countryside to the cities and the cities to one another.

Such rapid growth did not come without a cost. An economic depression suddenly ground the economy to a halt, political crisis emerged, and slaves staged a revolt. Many Americans worried that the virtuous time of the Revolution had passed and a time of selfishness had taken its place. Only a resolute determination to redefine the family and to spread the word of God, many believed, would save America.

The Aftermath of War

The United States had little reason to celebrate as 1815 began. Washington lay in ruins. Rumor had it that delegates from the Hartford Convention would soon arrive in the Capital threatening to remove New England from the Union unless Congress revised the Constitution. People lost faith in President James Madison and other leaders.

War's End

Throughout the summer and fall of 1814 American and British delegations in the Belgian city of Ghent labored to construct a peace. After months of deadlock, the two delegations agreed simply to end the war and restore the previous borders between U.S. and British territories. Both sides, relieved to be rid of the conflict, quickly adopted the agreement.

http://ayersbrief.wadsworth.com

CHRONOLOGY

1815 Battle of New Orleans

Enterprise first steamboat from New Orleans to Pittsburgh

1816 Monroe elected president; "Era of Good Feelings" begins

Clay calls for "American System"

Second Bank of the United States chartered

Indiana admitted to the Union

American Colonization Society founded

American Bible Society founded

1817 Mississippi admitted to the Union

1818 Jackson invades Florida

Erie Canal begun

Illinois admitted to the Union

National Road completed

1819 Transcontinental (or Adams-Onís) Treaty with Spain

Dartmouth College Case and *McCulloch v. Maryland*

Financial panic and depression

Alabama admitted to the Union

Auburn penitentiary established

1820 Missouri Compromise

Monroe elected president

Maine admitted to the Union

1821 Missouri admitted to the Union

1822 Denmark Vesey Rebellion, Charleston

1823 Monroe Doctrine announced

1824 Contested election of John Quincy Adams

Lafayette's visit

Gibbons v. Ogden

American Sunday School Union founded

1825 Completion of Erie Canal

American Tract Society founded

Though the treaty was signed in December, bad weather in the Atlantic delayed until February the ship bringing news of the peace negotiations between the Americans and British. In the meantime, British forces planned to attack Mobile, seize control of the coast and the rivers, then move against New Orleans.

Such a plan posed a serious threat to the United States. New Orleans, distant and disconnected from the cities of the east coast, lay vulnerable to invasion. Once the British established a foothold there, troops could move up the Mississippi River. Moreover, a British invasion threatened to bring free and enslaved African Americans, French and Spanish settlers, Native Americans, and even pirates into the conflict throughout the Gulf territories.

The commander in charge of the American forces, Andrew Jackson, was especially sensitive to the dangers settlers faced on the Gulf Coast. Jackson, a Tennessee militia leader, had capped a tumultuous career by defeating and then enforcing harsh terms on Creek Indians in the early spring of 1814. Jackson pushed the Creeks into ceding 23 million acres of territory to the United States. Jackson's soldiers shoved the Creeks into the less productive lands of northeastern Alabama, while reserving the fertile black belt for white farmers.

The surprising victory of the United States over Britain in 1815 catapulted Andrew Jackson to prominence and bolstered the confidence of the young republic. (The Granger Collection, New York)

Jackson prepared to continue the war against other groups of Creeks who had fled to Spanish West Florida. After a victory over the British at Mobile, Jackson raced to New Orleans to fight yet more British troops. The American general got there first, in December of 1814.

A series of attacks by the British damaged the American forces but did not take New Orleans. The British general in charge, Sir Edward Pakenham, unleashed a frontal assault on January 8, 1815. Jackson's troops, dug in behind earthworks, fired directly into the charging British ranks; wave after wave of the onslaught fell as American troops took turns firing and reloading. In less than an hour it was over: Pakenham and two of his generals lay dead, along with over 2,000 casualties. The Americans suffered only thirteen dead and a few dozen wounded or missing. Nearly a month later, word of Jackson's remarkable success reached the nation's Capital. Nine days later news of the Treaty of Ghent, signed two weeks before the Battle of New Orleans, arrived in Washington.

The Era of Good Feelings

The United States now boasted a new sense of integrity and identity. President Madison announced that the Constitution had proven itself able to "bear the trials of adverse as well as prosperous circumstances." The northern borders of the United States took on greater solidity. The

Rush-Bagot Treaty of 1817 between the British and the United States calmed conflict on the Great Lakes, while the Convention of 1818 fixed the border with Canada at the 49th parallel.

The War of 1812 suggested to some that the federal government might play a constructive role in American society. Leading members of the Republican party began to view the central government more favorably. Henry Clay of Kentucky and John C. Calhoun of South Carolina urged Congress and the president to encourage the growth of enterprise by creating roads, canals, a strong navy, and a national bank. In their eyes, the war with Great Britain had shown the dangers of a sprawling American nation, its resources scattered, its defenses thin. Although these nationalists called their vision the "American System," representatives from New England objected to projects that seemed so expensive and threatening to local power. Outgoing President James Madison, unwilling to support all of Clay's and Calhoun's ambitious plans, did decide to support a national bank.

The man who succeeded Madison to the presidency, James Monroe, faced a brief challenge within his party in 1816 but won the national election easily. Monroe and his wife set a new tone for the presidency, with greater emphasis on etiquette, style, and entertaining. They had the Executive Mansion painted a brilliant white to cover the smoke stains from its burning during the war with England; it became known as the "White House." After his election, Monroe toured the Northeast, including New England. A journalist there, impressed, talked of a budding "Era of Good Feelings," an era without party rancor—a strong contrast to the bitter conflict of earlier decades.

Adopting John C. Calhoun's ideas for encouraging commerce and industry, Monroe urged Congress to use protective tariffs to protect American manufacturing, to build roads to tie the newly expanded markets and farms together, and to connect the abundant rivers and lakes in the United States with a system of canals. Monroe hoped his plan would be supported by a broad and nonpartisan consensus. The emerging Era of Good Feelings, Monroe assumed, would let the nation move forward without political strife or bitterness.

Native Peoples of the South

Relations with American Indians demanded considerable attention in the years following the peace with England. By this time, the American Indians of the southeast had lived in contact with European culture for more than two centuries. They had long combined their ancient practices with newer ones, especially commercial hunting. Expeditions covered ever-expanding territory to kill enough animals to satisfy the white trading partners upon whose goods the American Indians increasingly depended. Indians' clothing reflected the combination of cultures, as they combined moccasins with woolen breeches, imported cloth turbans, and jewelry made of melted silver coins. The intermingling worked both ways, for many English and Scots traders adopted parts of Indian dress and language and married into native families. African Americans, too, often took refuge with the Creeks and Seminoles, so that by 1815 mixed ancestry was common among the people of the southeast.

The removal of the British troops dealt a strong blow to the hopes of the natives of the Gulf Coast. Alliances with the British had been an effective way to hold back the white Americans. Now that alliance disappeared and the United States quickly sought to exert firm control over the eastern half of the continent. Andrew Jackson was placed in charge of negotiating with the Indians. He used heavy-handed treaties to force them from their former lands. Many of the natives resisted the removal, objecting that the treaties extracted by Jackson had been signed by men who had no authority to make such concessions. Although the various native peoples often fought with one another, whites insisted on lumping these diverse people into groups that could be more easily dealt with. Jackson and other officials left the Indians little choice but to accept bribes and annual grants of money in return for their lands.

American Society for Improving Indian Tribes, *The Blessings of Civilization* 1824

In this address to Congress, a prestigious religious group argues that the American Indians have suffered for generations at the hands of the United States. The only way to atone for these "national sins," the commissioners argue, is to educate the Indian people in the ways of white Americans. The document shows the good will that many white Americans held toward the Indians and the limitations of their understanding of the Indians' own desires.

. . . The history of our intercourse with Indians, from the first settlement of this country, contains many facts honorable to the character of our ancestors, and of our nation—many, also, too many, which are blots on this character; and which, in reflecting on them, cannot fail to fill us with regret, and with concern, lest the Lord of nations, who holds in his hand the scales of equal and everlasting justice, should in his wrath say to us, "As ye have done unto these Indians, so will I requite you." We here allude to the neglect with which these aboriginal tribes have been treated in regard to their civil, moral, and religious improvement—to the manner in which we have, in many, if not most instances, come into possession of their lands, and of their peltry: also, to the provocations we have given, in so many instances, to those cruel, desolating, and exterminating wars, which have been successively waged against them; and to the corrupting vices, and fatal diseases, which have been introduced among them, by wicked and unprincipled white people. These acts can be viewed in no other light, than as national sins, aggravated by our knowledge, and their ignorance; our strength and skill in war, and their weakness—by our treacherous abuse of their unsuspicious simplicity, and, especially, by the light and privileges of Christianity, which we enjoy, and of which they are destitute. . . .

. . . It *is* desirable that our Indians should receive such an education as has been mentioned, we conceive, because the civilized is preferable to the savage state; because the Bible, and the religion therein revealed to us, with its ordinances, are blessings of infinite and everlasting value and which the Indians do not now enjoy. It is also desirable as an act of common humanity. The progress of the white population, in the territories which were lately the hunting grounds of the Indians, is rapid, and probably will continue and increase. Their game, on which they principally depend for subsistence, is diminishing, and is already gone from those tribes who remain among us. . . . There is no place on the earth to which they can migrate, and live in the savage and hunter state. The Indian tribes must, therefore, be *progressively civilized,* or *successively* perish.

SOURCE American Board of Commissioners for Foreign Missions, Memorial to the Senate and the House of Representatives, in American Society for Improving Indian Tribes, *First Annual Report,* 1824, pp. 66–68.

As soon as Jackson managed to secure lands from the Creeks, Cherokees, and Chickasaws, white settlers rushed into the territories. Such incursions occurred across millions of acres in North Carolina, Kentucky, and Tennessee as well as in Alabama, Mississippi, and Georgia. The U.S. government made it easy for white settlers to buy land and sold about a million acres a year throughout the next decade. Not surprisingly, tensions steadily mounted between the ancient residents of the land and those who now claimed it.

Although tens of thousands of American Indians continued to live in the southeast, their position grew less tenable each year as white settlers moved onto their hunting lands. The Indians strove to adapt to white ways while maintaining their identity; the Cherokees, in particular, won praise for their "civilized" customs. One Cherokee, Sequoyah, devised an alphabet in his people's language in 1821. No matter what accommodations they made, however, the American Indians suffered repeated conflicts with whites who considered themselves the rightful owners of the land.

The Spanish in Florida

Like the American Indians, the Spanish who remained in Florida after 1815 had become vulnerable. Without the assistance of the British, they found it nearly impossible to resist American incursions into their territory. White Americans, for their part, felt they had a right, even an obligation, to drive the Spanish from the mainland. To make relations even more volatile, sixty miles from the southern border of the United States stood the so-called "Negro Fort," occupied by runaway slaves and their Indian allies. In the spring of 1816, Jackson warned the Spanish commandant of Pensacola that the stronghold was "occupied by upwards of two hundred and fifty negros many of whom have been enticed away from the service of their master." The fugitives would "not be tolerated by our government," Jackson warned, "and if not put down by Spanish Authority will compel us in self Defence to destroy them." Spain was eager, in fact, to be rid of the fort as well, but did not have the military power to overthrow it. The Spanish feared, correctly, that Jackson would use the refuge as an excuse to invade Florida. Indeed, the Americans sent an expedition against the fort; a projectile hit a powder magazine, killing 270 of the men, women, and children inside.

In 1818, Jackson's forces also punished groups of Seminoles, who, with their Creek allies, had launched raids of white settlers in south Georgia and then fled into Florida. The American soldiers burned a Seminole town, only to see their foes retaliate by attacking a boat of soldiers, women, and children on the Apalachicola River, killing all but a few on board. Jackson proceeded to invade Spanish territory. Some in Congress wanted to punish Jackson for what they considered his unauthorized attack, but the congressional hearings on Jackson's behavior in the war had little effect except to make Jackson suspicious of the men in power in Washington.

Meanwhile, American and Spanish officials negotiated. The U.S. delegation was led by John Quincy Adams, son of the former president. With Jackson's military victories giving force to his words, Adams held out until the Spanish, in return for 5 million dollars in compensation of private claims, ceded to the United States all territories east of the Mississippi River. In this, the Adams-Onís Treaty of 1819, the Spanish kept the vast territory from Texas to present-day California, while the United States claimed a northern border that ran unbroken to Oregon and the Pacific Ocean.

THE TIDES OF TRADE

The end of the Napoleonic Wars in 1815 unleashed the economies of Europe and the countries that dealt with them, including the United States. American prosperity grew as the population boomed, as people moved across the expanse of the continent, and as transportation leaped forward. Slavery expanded along with free labor, farms along with factories, the East along with the South and the West.

Corduroy roads, while offering some relief from mud and stones, proved poor competition with newer kinds of transportation such as canals and steamboats. (The Granger Collection, New York)

Banks, Corporations, and Law

Because far too little cash spread across the vast landscape, much business within the American country rested on nothing more than trust and promises. Credit relations became tangled and fragile. Throughout the years before and during the War of 1812, states chartered banks to help alleviate the problems caused by a shortage of cash. More than 400 such banks had been founded by 1818, issuing notes that served as currency in cash-starved areas where inflation raged.

Many influential men supported a new national bank. Advocates of the bank argued that the notes of state banks varied far too much in soundness and value, making the economic system dangerously unstable. The expanding country's economic system needed a central institution to coordinate the flow of money. Accordingly, in 1816 Congress chartered the Second Bank of the United States. Based in Philadelphia, it was authorized to establish branches wherever it wished. The new national bank was an amalgam of public and private enterprise: the federal government deposited its funds in the bank and appointed a fifth of the directors, but the bank ran as a private business. For the privilege of being the only such institution authorized to operate on a national basis, the bank handled, without fees, the funds of the federal treasury.

The courts encouraged the growth of business in the years after the peace of 1815. They increasingly favored market forces over custom and stability, shifting the advantage from farmers and landowners to developers. Those who wanted to dam rivers for factories or build roads enjoyed increasing precedence over those threatened by floods, fires, or disruption caused by development. The courts assumed that the public good from the growth of business outweighed the stability favored by older notions of justice. Because many people bitterly protested this shift in emphasis, state legislatures sometimes sought to curb the power of business interests.

The Supreme Court under Chief Justice John Marshall issued a number of important decisions that weakened the power of the states to constrain economic development. One decision of 1819 made bankruptcy laws more uniform across the country; another, *Dartmouth College v. Woodward,* sheltered corporations from legislative interference; yet another 1819 ruling, *McCulloch v. Maryland,* established the constitutionality of the Bank of the United States and protected it from state taxation. A fourth case in this period, *Gibbons v. Ogden* (1824), limited the rights of states to interfere in commerce with either special favors and monopolies or restrictive laws. In this new legal environment, business flourished.

The Erie Canal, connecting the Hudson River with Lake Erie, demanded a monumental engineering effort. It soon paid its way, however, as shippers and farmers rushed to use the new waterway. (The Granger Collection, New York)

Roads and Canals

Americans threw themselves into a frenzy of road and turnpike building after 1815. Investors, states, and even the federal government built thousands of miles of private roads—turnpikes—charging tolls to offset the roads' notoriously high maintenance costs. Some road builders laid logs side-by-side to provide a durable surface, though these so-called "corduroy roads" took a heavy toll on horse, wagon, and rider and wore out quickly besides. In 1818, the U.S. government opened the "National Road," connecting the Potomac River at Cumberland, Maryland, with Wheeling, [West] Virginia, on the Ohio River. The road was the best that technology could provide at the time, with excellent bridges and a relatively smooth stone surface. The road attracted so much business, however, that traffic jams slowed movement to a crawl and the road quickly fell into poor condition. Even on good roads, it often cost more to move bulky items such as corn or wheat than the products could bring at market.

Businesses and state governments began to plan dependable canals with controllable locks and a steady flow of water. Fortunately for New York, a flat passage broke through the Appalachian Mountains within the state's borders. New Yorkers believed that a canal through this area, connecting the Hudson River to Lake Erie, would far surpass any other kind of transportation. Such a canal would be ten times longer than any other canal then in existence: 364 miles through swamps and solid rock.

The mayor of New York City and future governor of the state, De Witt Clinton, became the foremost advocate of the canal. People scoffed at the money thrown away in "Clinton's Big Ditch." But the largely untrained engineers learned as they went along. Aqueducts had to span rivers and gorges, aqueducts tight and strong enough to withstand the weight of the water and the boats they carried. Locks had to be constructed of heavy timbers and even heavier stone. Thousands of laborers, many of them foreign-born, moved with the canal. Year after year, the canal edged toward Lake Erie; by 1819, the canal stretched for seventy-five miles. As soon as workers completed a segment, boats crowded upon its waters, the tolls they paid financing the portions yet unfinished.

Steamboats

Canals reached only a limited part of the vast North American continent. Rivers offered faster and cheaper travel, but their limitations were obvious as well. The rivers could be dangerously fast in some seasons and so slow as to be impassable in others. They often froze for months in the winter. Strong currents ran in only one direction. Those who wanted to transport goods northward had to push their boats against the current, sometimes with poles, sometimes by dragging the boats with ropes as the crews walked along the shore. Others simply sold their craft for scrap in New Orleans and walked back to Ohio or Illinois.

Not surprisingly, people dreamed of using steam engines to drive riverboats. Robert Fulton's steamboats had traversed the quieter waters of the Northeast since 1807, but he did not manage to build one for the rigors of the Mississippi until 1811. The War of 1812 slowed development of the steamboats, but innovation resumed with the war's end. As soon as Jackson won New Orleans in 1815, the *Enterprise* churned its way upriver from Louisiana all the way to Louisville, Kentucky. Dozens of other craft soon joined, competing with one another. In 1817, the journey from New Orleans to Louisville took twenty-five days; in 1819, fourteen days. Though the steamboats showed a dangerous propensity to explode, run aground, and slam into submerged obstacles, no one thought of going back to the old way of travel.

The increasing speed and frequency of the steamboats encouraged the growth of villages and towns along the rivers. Huge stacks of wood carted in from the countryside appeared wherever the steamboats regularly stopped for fuel; new stores sold the goods transported on the river. The populations of Louisville, Pittsburgh, and Cincinnati doubled or more than doubled between 1815 and 1825.

The Growth of the Plantation South

The demand for cotton in England took off after 1815. Cotton clothes were cheaper, easier to create, and more comfortable in warm weather than those made from wool or linen. No place in the world was as prepared to supply the burgeoning demand for cotton as the American South. Small farmers as well as planters from the older states of the southern seaboard saw opportunity in the new states of Alabama and Mississippi. Many white farmers also moved to western Tennessee and parts of Louisiana. The steamboat and the cotton gin gave southern planters powerful new tools, while slaves could clear and cultivate land for new plantations far more quickly than would have been otherwise possible.

The movement west followed the geographic and political contours of the areas recently acquired from the American Indians. The first settlements began along the rivers that made it possible to transport cotton to market and in those places where the Creeks and other Indians exercised no claims. The new plantation districts were disconnected from one another, centering on Montgomery in Alabama, Jackson in Mississippi, and Memphis in Tennessee. Small farmers occupied the land farthest from the rivers, supporting themselves with hunting and foraging as well as with growing small amounts of cotton. Young lawyers and editors headed out for the Southwest as well.

"The *Alabama Feaver* rages here with great violence and has *carried off* vast numbers of our Citizens," wrote one North Carolina planter in 1817. The fever proved contagious, "for as soon as one neighbour visits another who has just returned from the Alabama he immediately discovers the same symptoms." Even established men in the older states put their plantations up for sale; others saw the new states as a place for their grown children to get a fresh start. The combined population of Alabama, Mississippi, and Louisiana more than tripled between 1810 and 1820.

Some ambitious young men from northern states moved to the new cotton lands, the place in the United States, it seemed, where the greatest fortunes could be made in the shortest amount of time. But most of the new residents came from

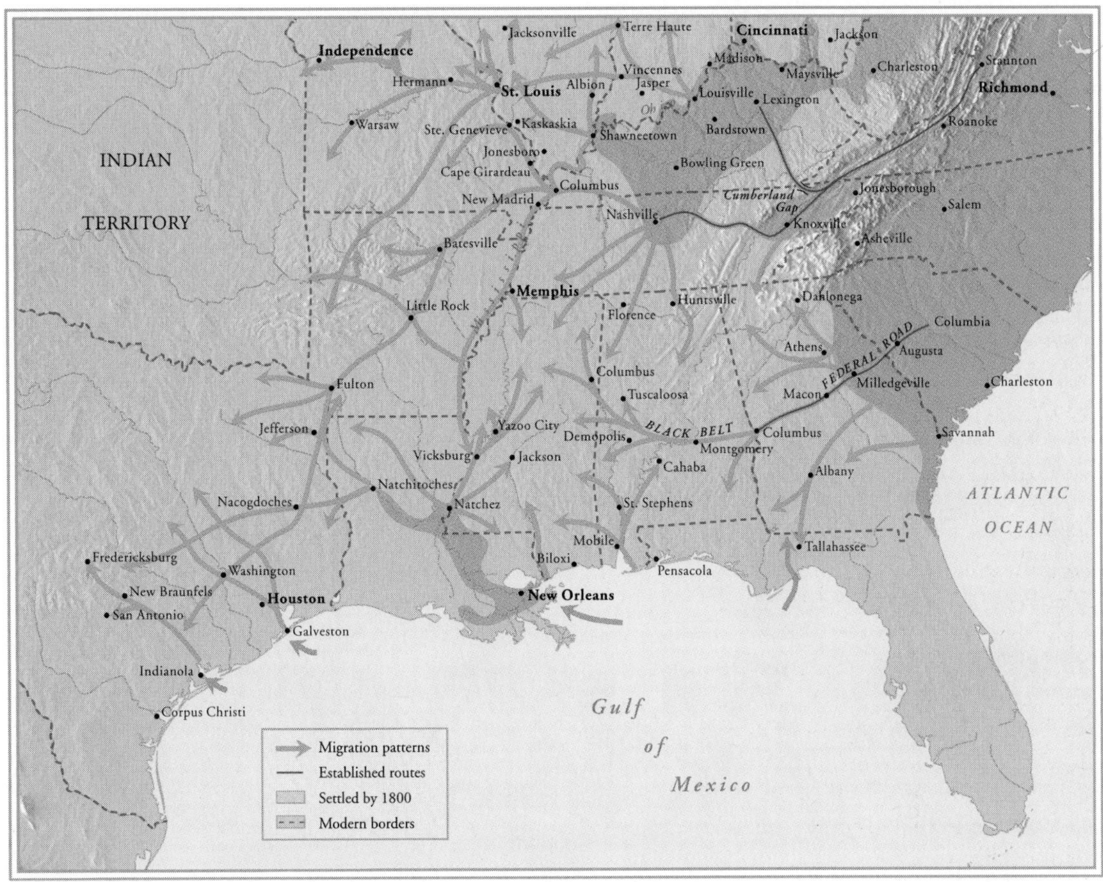

MAP 9.1 | THE PATHS OF SOUTHERN MIGRATION

older plantation states. Young southern men were especially eager to move and make their mark. Their wives, mothers, and daughters were often much less enthusiastic about migrating to Mississippi or Alabama, for it meant being removed from kin. The lure of the Southwest overrode concerns husbands may have felt for their wives' opinions, however, for the new states offered a chance at the independence they considered synonymous with manliness. They sought to build a world as much as possible like those of Virginia or Carolina, only more prosperous.

The expansion of the cotton kingdom broadened and deepened the slave trade. Many planters in the East took advantage of the opportunity to sell slaves "down south." Hundreds of thousands of slaves endured forcible migration to the new states of the Southwest in the 1810s and 1820s; some moved in groups along with their owners to new plantations, but many were sold as individuals to slave traders in the east, who then shipped or marched them to slave markets in New Orleans, Mobile, and other cities to the southwest. The families of many enslaved African Americans were broken apart.

The new plantations concentrated on cotton at the expense of everything else. The finest plantations clung to the rivers, for water offered the only way to get the ever-expanding cotton crop to market. Flatboats carried the bulky product to

The rapid spread of cotton plantations to the west fueled the domestic slave trade. This coffle of slaves marched from Virginia to Tennessee. (Abby Aldrich Rockefeller Elk Center, Williamsburg, VA)

barges waiting at the docks of Natchez and Vicksburg on the Mississippi or to ships waiting in the bays of Mobile and New Orleans. Food and other provisions for the plantations came down the rivers from the new farms and cities to the north. A new national economy knitted together the enormous expanse of the young United States.

Emergence of the Northwest

The area west of the Appalachians, north of the Ohio, and east of the Mississippi—the "Northwest"—was growing at an even faster pace than the Southwest. The 280,000 white settlers of 1810 in Ohio, Indiana, and Illinois grew to

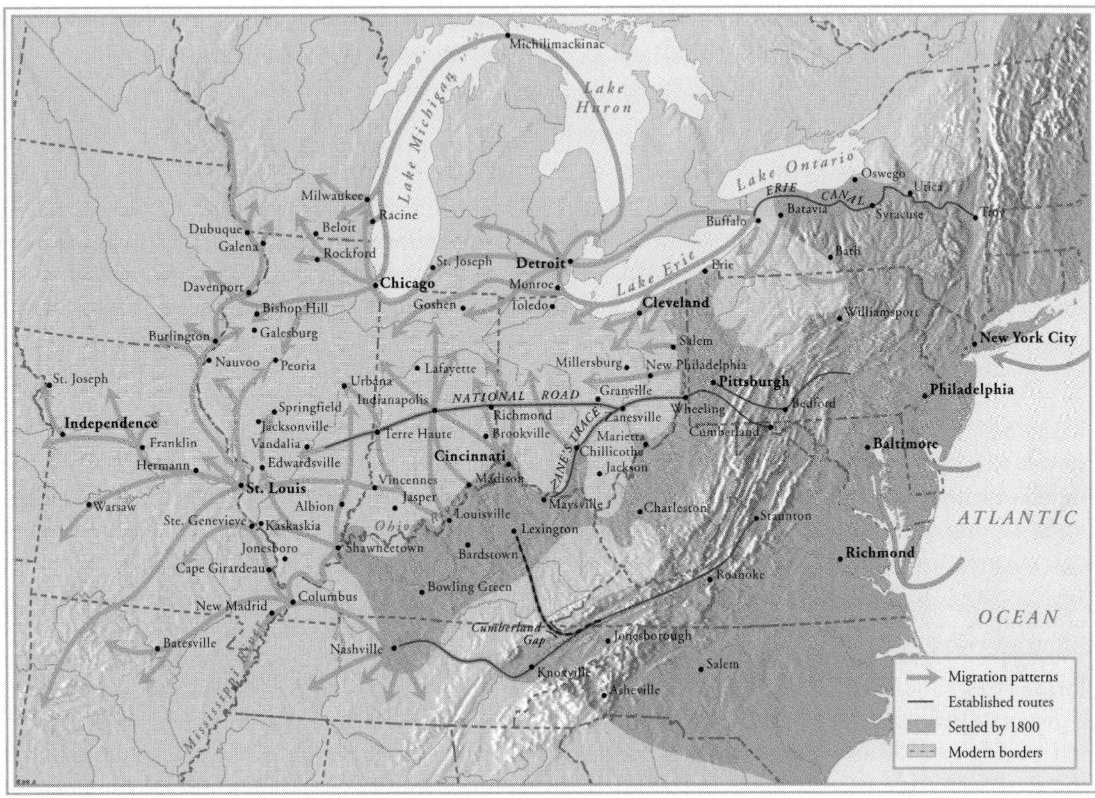

MAP 9.2 | THE PATHS OF NORTHERN MIGRATION

784,000 ten years later. Many of the settlers to the Northwest came from the states of the upper South; large parts of southern Ohio, Indiana, and Illinois were settled by people from Virginia, Kentucky, Tennessee, and North Carolina. Some southern migrants to the North professed themselves eager to move out of states with slavery, whereas others merely followed the easiest routes to good land. People from New England and New York filled the towns and farms of the northern parts of the new states of the Northwest.

As in the South, young people dominated migration to the Northwest. As in the Southwest, too, settlers to the Northwest did not move in a simple westward wave, but rather flowed up the rivers and spread from there, sometimes back towards the East. People often emigrated in groups. "We are seldom out of sight, as we travel on this grand track towards the Ohio," one traveller noted, "of family groups behind, and before us, some with a view to a particular spot, close to a brother perhaps, or a friend who has gone before." Family farms clustered closer together in the Northwest than in the Southwest because the absence of a large slave workforce meant that landholdings remained relatively small.

As in the South, white settlement in the Northwest was made possible by the subjugation of the native peoples. After the War of 1812, the U.S. government quickly established a series of forts throughout the Northwest to intimidate American Indians and to make sure that the British and Canadians did not regain a foothold. The growing numbers of white farmers made it difficult for Native Americans to hunt for a living. President Monroe exulted in the "rapid and gigantic" spread of white settlers into the Northwest, an expansion the "rights of nature demand and nothing can prevent." Whites who moved to the Northwest confronted only scattered remnants of native peoples, sometimes begging from homesteaders.

Most white settlers proved dissatisfied with the first land they claimed, for about two out of three migrants moved again within a few years. Rumors always circulated about richer land a bit farther west, about opportunity just over the horizon. Many people who had moved once found it easy to move again. Those who remained in a community became its "leading citizens," consolidating land into larger farms, setting up grist mills and sawmills, running for office, establishing the small towns that served as county seats and trading centers. In many cases, storekeepers were among the first to arrive and among those whose fortunes flourished best. Storekeepers became the bankers and wholesalers of their communities, often buying considerable amounts of land along the way.

Farm and Factory in the Northeast

While the economies of the West and the South were being transformed by settlers and slaves, the economy of the East underwent its own fundamental change. Since the colonial years, people outside the major cities had made in their own homes much of what they needed. This local production grew stronger when trade dried up during the war with England; 1815, in fact, saw an all-time peak in household manufacturing. Local blacksmiths, tailors, cobblers, and other artisans supplied what families could not produce for themselves, while local gristmills and sawmills processed crops and lumber.

Farms averaged a little over a hundred acres, about half occupied by wood lots for fuel and timber. Forests often dominated the farms of younger families whereas mature families proudly claimed large areas of cultivation, the products of years of labor. Farm families cleared their fields at spring thaw, manuring, plowing, and planting as soon as danger of frost passed. Livestock and poultry needed constant attention; sheep had to be washed and sheared and geese plucked in the spring. Farm families reaped flax in June, enjoyed a brief respite in August, and then pushed hard for the fall harvest. In winter, men and boys cut wood while women and girls spun thread and wove cloth for clothes. The garden and dairy were the responsibility of women and girls, the cash crops the responsibility of men.

After 1815, the farms in many parts of New England, New York, and Pennsylvania would be tied ever more tightly into the economies of the towns and cities. Farm families produced more cash crops and bought more things with money rather than through barter. Women worked in their homes to produce palm hats, portions of shoes, or articles of clothing that merchants from nearby cities gathered and had assembled in workshops. With so many young men leaving New England for the west, many communities found themselves with considerable numbers of young women who might never marry as well as older women who could not count on the support of sons. Piecework offered these women a chance to contribute to the economies of their households. It was important to everyone in their families that those wage-earning women did not have to leave home to earn those wages.

The expanded cash economy thus overlapped with and conflicted with an older, more self-contained economy. Families sought opportunity in new jobs and new markets even as they feared that the increasingly dense networks of trade would depress the value of their crops and entice young people from the farm. Although it would be generations before cities and factories dominated the economies of the North, in the meantime, farms, towns, and small factories grew ever more interconnected.

The textile industry of New England stood as the most dramatic example of industrial growth. The cost of cotton clothing fell faster than the cost for any other product as machinery and cheaper cotton lowered the price. Francis Cabot Lowell of Boston designed a power loom in 1813. The same year, Lowell and a partner, Nathan Appleton, spent over $400,000 to open the first factory in the United States that could integrate all the steps of making cloth under a single roof: the Boston Manufacturing Company, in Waltham, Massachusetts, where a waterfall with a ten-foot drop offered free power. Unlike earlier factories, it used unskilled labor and machines even for weaving, the most expensive part of the process. Lowell and Appleton recruited young New England farm women and girls as operatives. Young females had experience in producing yarn and cloth at home and they would work hard for low wages. As Appleton put it, the young women supplied "a fund of labor, well educated and virtuous" for the factory.

The operatives, considering millwork a three- or four-year commitment before they married and began families of their own, worked fourteen hours a day, six days a week. They agreed to stay with the mill for at least twelve months or to be put on a blacklist that would prevent them from getting a job elsewhere. The factory was unlike anything the young women had ever confronted: "You cannot think how odd everything seemed," one mill girl recalled; even those who had spun and woven for years could not be prepared for the "frightful" sight of "so many bands, and wheels, and springs in constant motion."

The social and economic ground for industrialization had been broken in the northeast. Mills, most of them small, grew up along the streams of Connecticut and the Delaware Valley of Pennsylvania and New Jersey, turning out not only textiles but also metal and wood products. These mills, like their bigger and more visible counterparts in Lowell, depended on low wages paid to workers without many other options. Many potential workers, competitors, and outside observers worried about the effects of the factories, even as investors and other supporters saw in the new buildings the hope for a richer and more productive American society.

The Price of Expansion

The prosperity of the immediate postwar years faltered badly in 1819. The enlarged scale of the new American economy entangled a far larger number of people than had ever been caught in economic hard times before. Meanwhile, the enlarged boundaries of the American nation brought troubles of their own as the North and the South fought over new territories in the West. Looking out over the world, political leaders declared the determination of the United States to control its entire hemisphere.

The Panic of 1819

A series of events in 1819 abroad and at home conspired to bring a sudden halt to some of the growth in the economy of the United States. Cotton lands in the southeast saw prices skyrocket as world demand for cotton cloth increased every year. Prices for southern cotton rose to such an extent that in 1818 and 1819 British manufacturers turned to cotton from other sources, especially India. The price of American cotton tumbled, along with the price of the land that produced it. And cotton was not the only crop whose price rapidly declined: the price of tobacco plummeted from 40 cents a pound to 4 cents, wheat fell from $2.41 a bushel to 88 cents. State banks built on inflated, even fraudulent, credit wavered and then crashed. The Panic of 1819 had begun.

The panic proved a sudden and sobering reminder of just how complicated and interdependent the economy of the nation was becoming. The cities were hit the hardest. About half a million workers lost their jobs as business ground to a halt. Wherever they could, families who had moved to towns and cities returned to the countryside to live with relatives. Things were not much safer in the country, however, where the failure of banks meant that apparently prosperous farmers saw household goods, farm animals, and slaves sold in humiliating auctions.

Many people, including congressmen, began to call for the revocation of the charter of the Second Bank of the United States. States had chafed throughout the two years of the bank's life at what they considered its dictatorial power. Several states tried to limit that power by levying extremely high taxes on the branches of the Bank of the United States in their states, but it was at this point that the Supreme Court ruled in *McCulloch v. Maryland* that the laws of the federal government "form the supreme law of the land."

Despite the panic, James Monroe was reelected to the presidency in 1820. The Federalist party, fatally crippled by its opposition to the War of 1812 and its support of the Hartford Convention, offered no effective opposition. Neither did Monroe face an organized contest from others within his own Republican party. He received every electoral vote but one. Most Americans seemed to blame someone other than President Monroe for the Panic of 1819 and the lingering hard times that followed it. The Era of Good Feelings somehow managed to survive in the White House—though, it turned out, not in the halls of Congress.

The Missouri Compromise

The recent admission of the new states of the Southwest and Northwest had left a precarious balance in the Senate between slave states and free. The Missouri territory posed a special challenge. Slavery had quickly spread in Missouri, stretching along the richest river lands. If Missouri were admitted with slavery—as its territorial legislature had decreed—then the slave states would hold a majority in the Senate. The three-fifths clause of the Constitution, northerners complained, gave the slave states twenty more members of Congress and twenty more electors for the presidency than they would have if only white population were counted. The South seemed to be getting extra representation unfairly.

The debates over slavery in Missouri in 1819 and 1820 were not debates between fervent abolitionists in the North and fervent proslavery advocates in the South. Instead, white northerners and southerners of all political persuasions agreed that as many blacks as possible should be shipped to Africa. White Americans who could agree on little else about slavery did agree that blacks and whites could not live together in the United States once slavery had ended. That was the message of the American Colonization Society, founded in 1816 and based in Washington, D.C. The society bought land in Africa—naming the new country "Liberia"—and sent about 12,000 African Americans there over the next fifty years.

In the meantime, slavery caused problems for the political system. A New York congressman, James Tallmadge, Jr., introduced an amendment to the bill that would admit Missouri as a state only if Missouri admitted no more slaves and if those slaves in the territory were freed when their children became twenty-five years old. More than eighty of the North's congressmen supported the Tallmadge amendment and only ten opposed it. In the Senate, though, the slave states prevailed by two votes. A deadlocked Congress adjourned in March of 1819 to meet again in December.

During the months in between politicians worked behind the scenes. The Union now seemed in danger of breaking apart from within. Simmering northern resentment, held in check for decades, was suddenly announced, even celebrated. Southerners felt betrayed. In their eyes, slavery was a thing they had inherited, an institution that would fade away naturally if left alone. White southerners thought northerners irresponsible and unrealistic to attack slavery as the Tallmadge amendment did.

In northern states, where anti-slavery societies had been relatively sedate, people suddenly announced the depth of their distaste for slavery. Furious meetings erupted in towns and cities across the North, turning out petitions and resolutions in large numbers. Slavery, these petitions thundered, was a blot on the nation, a violation of the spirit of Christianity, an abomination that must not spread into places it had not already ruined.

After weeks of debate, a compromise led by Henry Clay emerged from the Senate: Missouri, with no restriction on slavery, should be admitted to the Union at the same time as Maine, thereby ensuring the balance between slave and free states. Slavery would be prohibited in all the lands acquired in the Louisiana Purchase north of the southern border of Missouri at 36° 30′ latitude. Such a provision excluded the Arkansas territory, where slavery was already established, but closed to slavery the vast expanses of the Louisiana Territory—the future states of Iowa, Minnesota, Montana, Wyoming, Colorado, Idaho, the Dakotas, Nebraska, and Kansas. Any slaves who escaped to the free states would be returned.

The debate broke out again when the Missouri constitutional convention not only authorized slavery but decreed that the state legislature could never emancipate slaves without the consent of their masters; the proposed constitution also pronounced that free blacks would never be permitted to enter the new state. The national House of Representatives refused to admit Missouri under this document and the denunciation by both sides began again where it had paused. Finally, in early 1821, Henry Clay managed to fix a majority in the House in favor of a bill that would admit Missouri as long as the new state promised to pass no law barring the entry of a citizen from any other state. Exhausted, Congress ratified the law.

In a real sense, the debates over slavery in Missouri created "the North" and "the South," uniting the new states of the Northwest with the states of New England, New York, and Pennsylvania as they had not been united earlier, forging a tighter alliance between the new states of the Southwest and Virginia, the Carolinas, and Georgia. To the North, the South seemed greedy and corrupt; to the South, the North seemed greedy and hypocritical. The country became polarized as never before.

Vesey's Revolt

An event in 1822 in Charleston, South Carolina, forced white Americans, North and South, to pay greater attention to the people who lived under slavery's dominion. A free black man named Denmark Vesey had closely followed in the papers the debates over the Missouri controversy. What he read there reinforced what he had seen in the Bible and the documents of the American Revolution: slavery was immoral. Vesey, who had bought his freedom twenty years earlier, stood as a commanding presence among the African American people of the low country. He had several wives and many children whose bondage tormented him. A skilled carpenter and preacher, Vesey traveled up and down the coast and into the interior, berating those blacks who accepted racial insult. Many African Americans were attracted to him; most were afraid to oppose him regardless.

Vesey drew not only upon his own strengths, but upon those of a powerful ally, a man known as Gullah Jack. This man, an Angolan, had arrived in South Carolina near the turn of the century. Gullah Jack still looked very much the part of the conjurer he was, with huge whiskers, tiny arms, and unusual gestures. Like Vesey, he hated slavery. The two men found their most eager audience among the artisans and house slaves of Charleston who had the greatest amount of freedom. They found it relatively easy to meet with slaves receptive to their message. Allies in charge of stables and stores gave Vesey access to horses and weapons.

Vesey planned to launch an attack on white Charleston at midnight on a Saturday, when slaves from the countryside came to the city to sell produce. The conspirators hoped to seize the city's poorly protected guardhouse, stores, and roads before the whites could gather themselves in opposition. House slaves would kill their white owners. Once Charleston was secure, the rebels, Vesey planned, would sail to Haiti, where Toussaint L'Ouverture had staged a black rebellion decades earlier and where slavery had been abolished. But a house servant alerted Charleston whites to the danger only two days before the revolt planned for June 16, 1822. The governor ordered out five military companies, and Vesey called off the attack. Over the next two months, white authorities hanged thirty-five alleged conspirators and banished thirty-seven more from the state. Denmark Vesey was one of those killed.

Though many details remained murky, white South Carolinians believed that they had, by the narrowest of margins, avoided an unimaginable rebellion. The rebels came not from the ranks of the slaves living under the most brutal conditions but from among those most trusted by their owners. South Carolinians, and white southerners in general, blamed Vesey's Rebellion on the agitation against slavery by northern congressmen in the Missouri debate. "The events of 1822," a leading South Carolinian observed, "will long be remembered, as amongst the choicest fruits of the agitation of that question in Congress."

The Monroe Doctrine

Throughout the first and second decades of the nineteenth century, one struggle after another disrupted Latin America. Seeing Spain vulnerable in Europe and abroad, leaders in the colonies of the Western Hemisphere pushed ahead with their long-simmering plans for national independence. By 1822, Chile, Mexico, and the Portuguese colony of Brazil had all gained their independence.

Neither the United States nor Great Britain wanted to see France fill the vacuum left by Spain. A French or Russian empire would pose a threat much greater than any posed by the fading Spanish regime. Accordingly, in March of 1822, President Monroe urged Congress to recognize the new republics of Latin America. Throughout the next year, as the French army invaded Spain, the U.S. minister in England received a proposal that the United States and England jointly declare that neither country would annex any part of the tottering empire of Spain, nor permit any other power to do so. Monroe wanted to make the joint declaration, but Secretary of State John Quincy Adams persuaded him that it would be more fitting and dignified for the United States to declare its policy independently. Adams' policy was directed more against outside intervention in Latin America than in favor of the new republics, which he considered weak and unlikely to endure an attack by a major power.

In December of 1823, the president used his annual message to Congress to announce what would eventually become known as the Monroe Doctrine: "[T]he American continents, by the free and independent conditions which they have assumed and maintained, are henceforth not to be considered as subjects for future colonisation by any European power." The United States, for its part, would not interfere with Europe or its American dependencies. The Russians and Spanish denounced the American policy as "arrogant," but tolerated it because the European powers, exhausted by wars among themselves, had little desire to expand their involvement on the other side of the world. The leaders of the Latin American revolts welcomed the warning to the European powers, but were less certain about the United States' own intentions toward Latin America. The Monroe Doctrine, after all, did not say that the United States would not interfere in the Western Hemisphere, only that it would not permit European countries to do so.

THE SWIRL OF PUBLIC LIFE

Two events of 1824 threw into sharp relief the accomplishments and dangers of the emerging nation. The first event was the thirteen-month tour of the United States by one of the heroes of the American Revolution: the Marquis de Lafayette. The second event was the presidential election of 1824. Whereas Lafayette's visit tied the country together with bonds of memory and celebration, the election showed that Americans had become far more divided than had seemed possible only four years earlier.

Lafayette's Return

Lafayette sailed into New York and was met, fittingly enough, with a steamboat. He spent tumultuous and tearful days in New York, where old comrades and young admirers poured out to see the living embodiment of the sacrifices and bravery of the Revolutionary War. Then Lafayette set out to see the rest of the United States. He went first to New England, then down the coast to Philadelphia, Baltimore, Washington, Charleston, and then New Orleans. From there, he went up the Mississippi and on to Nashville. Everywhere he traveled, the hero met with booming guns, torchlight parades, thousands of children dressed in the colors of France, banquet after banquet, speech after speech. Some moments stood out: when the general cried, alone, at the grave of Washington at Mount Vernon, and when he traveled to Monticello to meet with Jefferson. Congress, knowing that the marquis was in serious financial difficulties, presented him with a gift of $200,000 (an enormous sum at the time). Slaves, hearing of the patriot's opposition to slavery, lined the roads wherever he went to cheer him on.

Lafayette was admired for his selflessness at the time of the American Revolution, for putting the cause of liberty before his own self-interest, for putting himself at risk in the pursuit of freedom. Such a posture of noble self-sacrifice was what Americans valued most in their public men and what they expected of those to whom power was given. In Lafayette, they could celebrate the best in themselves.

The Election of 1824

Many people felt, on the other hand, that they saw the worst of the country in the presidential election going on while Lafayette toured the country. Few eligible voters had bothered to cast a ballot four years earlier when James Monroe had won the presidency without opposition. But politicians and observers expected a more interesting contest in 1824. Many thought the next president would be William Crawford, secretary of the treasury. Others focused on John Quincy Adams, secretary of state. Others looked to John C. Calhoun of South Carolina, an impressive secretary of war and advocate of a strong government. Yet others placed their bets on Henry Clay of Kentucky, Speaker of the House of Representatives for many years. Finally, Andrew Jackson of Tennessee hoped to parlay his military fame into the presidency.

Several of these men realized they did not command sufficient national support to win the election outright. They hoped, however, to prevail if the election went into the House of Representatives. Cliques spread rumors and alliances of convenience flourished. Openly partisan newspapers sang the praises of their man and published lacerating rumors about his opponents. Local and state politicians worked feverishly in taverns, caucuses, and newspaper offices. Many American voters seemed disenchanted with the crass politicking, though, and relatively few voted in 1824. Jackson's popular vote nearly equaled that of Adams and Crawford combined, but the election was thrown into the House of Representatives because no candidate received a majority in the electoral college. The House could choose among the top three candidates: Jackson, Adams, and Crawford.

Since his fourth-place finish put him out of the running, Clay, the Speaker of the House, sought to strike the best deal he could with the other candidates. Considering Jackson unworthy of the post and a potential military despot, he discussed his future with Adams. When the vote came to the House of Representatives in early 1825, Adams won the presidency—taking the three states Clay had won in the electoral college. Two weeks later, Henry Clay received the appointment of secretary of state. Throughout the muddy little city of Washington, people speculated about the promises the upright John Quincy Adams had made to win the presidency (even though he had offered a secretary post to Andrew Jackson as well).

Adams wanted a stronger national government, internal improvements, and a tariff to protect American industry. But he could not mobilize support for his positions. He refused to use patronage to persuade or coerce people to go along with his plans. His administration bogged down into factionalism and paralysis, always with the shadow of his supposed "corrupt bargain" with Clay darkening his reputation.

New York politicians sought to harness ambition into useful and organized forms in the 1820s. Aaron Burr converted a simple patriotic club in New York City, the Society of Saint Tammany, into the beginnings of a major political machine. De Witt Clinton invented the "spoils system," in which it became the expectation that an incoming officeholder would remove those appointed by his predecessor and put his own supporters in their place. Martin Van Buren, a young lawyer and politician from New York, combined the city machine and the spoils system into a powerful statewide organization. He used newspapers in Albany and New York City to spread the word of the party to the fifty small newspapers he controlled throughout the state, which also published vast numbers of hand bills, posters, and ballots at election time. His goal was to combine party unity with personal advancement for party members.

Martin Van Buren opposed John Quincy Adams in the presidential contest of 1824 because Adams' nationally sponsored canals, roads, education, and other services would cut into the power of state government. Partly for this reason, Van Buren cast his lot with Andrew Jackson, who shared Van Buren's preference for localized power. As the next presidential election came closer, Van Buren, now a senator, worked ever more energetically for Jackson.

CHARACTER DEVELOPMENT

For generations before 1815, Americans had relied on authority and reputation to keep their families and communities stable. Young men and women remained in their parents' households well into their twenties. Workingmen served for years as apprentices and journeymen to master artisans, gradually working toward independence. Men and women carefully cultivated their reputations. Churches encouraged deference to the authority of God and institution.

The decade after 1815 saw a new emphasis on what people called "character." In a society so mobile, so disconnected from traditional sources of stability and identity, people felt the need for new ways of ensuring appropriate behavior. Americans looked to new kinds of institutions that could better deal with people cut off from older forms of social stability. They turned first to families, imparting to them primary responsibility for creating virtuous children and husbands.

Women at Home and Beyond

Women had long been recognized as the foundation of a good family. Women directly produced a large portion of the food farm families consumed, while town-dwelling families depended on women for running the household. During the era of the Revolution and early republic, women had been encouraged to raise virtuous children befitting a nation of free people. Churches had long depended on women as the source of spiritual energy and admirable role models.

Women became central in yet another way during the decades following 1815. As Americans looked about them, they became concerned that little seemed to be holding their society together. Men and women married at younger ages and left home far earlier than their parents had. The opening of land in the West undermined one of the principal forms of control exercised by fathers in earlier generations: the promise of passing on the family farm to sons who stayed at home.

The new economy, too, caused concern for many. Increasingly, men and women seemed pulled away from a sole focus on the family farm or family artisan shop. Men found new opportunities in town, often working for wages for a number of employers rather than serving for many years with one master. Middle-class women, too, saw their lives change. Bakeries, butcher shops, clothiers, and candlemakers began to offer, more easily and cheaply, some of the things that women had long labored to produce at home. Schools and academies became more common. Young women from poorer backgrounds came into cities looking for jobs as maids and laundresses, taking away some of the household burden for women well-off enough to hire them. Families in towns and cities had fewer children with each passing decade. Women's lives remained hard, as each birth threatened serious illness or death, but those lives began to change in important ways.

Ministers, journalists, and other opinion makers began to articulate an ideal of what has been called "domesticity." Families should seize the opportunities provided by the new situations, they said, and help lessen some of the costs created by the new order. Women could focus on nurturing their children in spirit and mind as well as in body. Women would become the moral center of the household, the guardians of good thoughts, clean living, and a sense of safety for children and husbands. Whereas the world beyond the household seemed increasingly threatening and disorienting, women could make the home a place of refuge and renewal.

Many middle-class women welcomed this message and this mission. In a time when public life made almost no provisions for female participation and when women found virtually no well-paying jobs open to them, the elevation of the home promised an elevation of women's role. Men believed what they said: they thought women naturally better than themselves, more moral and feeling, more intuitive and spiritual. Men worried about the coarseness and callousness of the tumultuous marketplace. Middle-class fathers wanted their children shielded from the hard world as long as possible.

Domesticity asked something of men as well. If the home were to be a haven, men would have

Depictions such as this portrait of Catherine Wheeler Hardy and her daughter celebrated the quiet domestic space shared by children and presided over by the mother. (Jeremiah Pearson Hardy, "Catherine Wheeler Hardy and Her Daughter Anne Eliza Hardy" 1842. Museum of Fine Arts, Boston, M. and M. Karolik Collection)

to make a greater investment in those homes than had their fathers. Men needed to respect the feelings of their wives more. Fathers were expected to spend more time with their children, providing a firm male model to accompany the softer nurture of their wives.

Such models of domesticity did not emerge overnight, of course. The early 1820s saw only the beginnings of a crusade to make all American homes fit this ideal. The effort began in towns and cities, making only gradual inroads into the countryside. It was stronger in the Northeast than in the South and West. Working-class families could not afford this idealized model. Women who had to work for others all day had little time to devote to their own families. Women who did wage work in their own homes mingled the market and the household in a way the creators of the domestic ideal deplored. Men who could not be certain of their next day's wages could not afford to keep children out of the workforce into their late teens. Slave families struggled to stay together in any way they could and could only imagine what it might be like to live in the homes held up as ideal. Nevertheless, that ideal was celebrated and elaborated with each passing year.

Stirrings of Reform

The same Americans who promoted the Christian, middle-class home as their ideal looked to other institutions and reforms in the early 1820s to help remake American society. They sought to extend the ideals of character, self-control, and education to those who seemed to fall beyond the good effects of family and household.

The Panic of 1819 and its aftermath made a deep impression on many town and city dwellers. Wherever they looked in those years, they saw hungry children, desperate fathers, and distraught mothers. They noticed increasing numbers of women selling themselves on the city streets. They worried over the many young men and women who seemed adrift in this rootless new society.

Activist people in the Northeast sought to counter these problems. Churches launched an ambitious drive to put Bibles in every American home, distributing a million Bibles each year. The American Sunday School Union, formed in 1824, wrote and published materials for children to be used in Sunday schools. Those schools, while based in churches, taught reading and writing as well as religion. They put the churches at the center of community life, giving children beyond the reach of traditional schooling a chance to learn some of the skills and attitudes necessary for spiritual and economic success. The American Tract Society, created in 1825, produced millions of short inspirational pamphlets to reach those who might not set foot in a church or pick up a Bible. The new organizations prided themselves on being national in reach, knitting Americans together with a common faith. They preached nothing controversial, claiming only to spread the good news of the Protestant Christian faith.

Another reform movement of these years took a different kind of strategy. Although the idea of the penitentiary had been discussed in Europe and the United States for several decades, support for that institution grew quickly after 1819. In a penitentiary, unlike a common jail, criminals would be locked in individual cells, alone with their conscience and the Bible. There, reflecting on their crimes, they would become "penitent" and would emerge as better people.

The most prominent penitentiaries were built in New York and Pennsylvania between 1819 and 1829. Reformers argued over whether prisoners should be isolated at all times, the Philadelphia model, or whether they might be allowed to work together in silence, as they did at Auburn in New York. In either case, Americans were proud of their penitentiaries, holding them up as examples of what the enlightened new nation could do. Almost every state in the nation soon built its own penitentiary.

Asylums for the deaf and blind, for the insane, for orphans, and for the poor also began to appear in the 1820s, replacing more informal kinds of care. Each institution placed its faith in strict order, in moral teaching, and in faith in the inherent good of human nature. The results were not immediately apparent, but the hope endured.

Reformers launched one other crusade in the 1810s and 1820s. Many people, religious and otherwise, saw alcohol as the scourge of American life. Men drank at work, farmers routinely turned their grain into whiskey, and rum was a major part of New England commerce. Everyone knew the costs of such drinking, and groups around the country mobilized locally to be more "temperant" in their use of ardent spirits.

The temperance movement slowly stewed until 1825, when Lyman Beecher, a prominent minister, delivered and then published six stirring sermons. Beecher argued that temperance was not enough, that only complete abstinence would remove the stain of alcohol from the United States. Drinkers must make a total and immediate break with their addiction. The next year supporters of abstinence formed the American Temperance Society and adopted the strategies of the American Bible Society, spreading the crusade among the Protestant churches of the country. Thousands joined, women as well as men, foreshadowing a flood of activity over the next century.

CONCLUSION

The United States saw enormous economic change between 1815 and 1826. As embargo and war ended, new states in both the Southwest and the Northwest pushed into the national and international economies. Cotton flowed out of Alabama and Mississippi in ever-growing amounts while food flowed from Indiana and Illinois. Banks proliferated with the expanding population. The major ports along the east coast grew as they had never grown before. New factory buildings went up along the streams and rivers of Massachusetts, Connecticut, Rhode Island, and Pennsylvania, producing by water power what hands had made only a few years earlier. Turnpikes and roads covered the country in an increasingly dense network. Coming on the heels of the Treaty of Ghent, such change seemed to mark the beginning of a new kind of security and prosperity for the United States.

The completion of the Erie Canal in 1825 demonstrated that Americans could accomplish great things. Soon after De Witt Clinton ceremoniously poured water from Lake Erie into the Atlantic, thousands of boats were traveling along the canal between Buffalo and New York City, sending a surge of prosperity along its route.

Accompanying this rapid expansion of boundaries of every sort, however, grew considerable anxiety that American society threatened to spin out of control. People worried that many Americans had moved beyond the influence of church, family, school, or employer. The centrifugal forces of the society threatened to pull it apart. No sooner had the postwar boom begun than some Americans began to suggest ways to contain the consequences of change. They offered political compromise, reform societies, and new ideals of the home as ways to counteract what they saw as chaos.

RECOMMENDED READINGS

Cashin, Joan E. *A Family Venture: Men and Women on the Southern Frontier* (1991). Tells the story of the southwestern migration in a compelling way.

Dangerfield, George. *The Awakening of American Nationalism, 1815–1828* (1965). A classic interpretation of the postwar era.

Davis, David Brion. *The Problem of Slavery in the Age of Revolution, 1770–1823* (1975). Gives a magisterial overview of the international struggles with slavery.

Freehling, William W. *The Road to Disunion: The Secessionists at Bay, 1776–1854* (1990). Portrays the drama of sectional conflict throughout this era.

Horwitz, Morton J. *The Transformation of American Law, 1780–1860* (1977). A strong and controversial argument about the law and commerce.

Mathews, Jean. *Toward a New Society: American Thought and Culture, 1800–1830* (1990). A subtle interpretation of cultural history of this period.

May, Ernest. *The Making of the Monroe Doctrine* (1976). A solid overview.

Rohrbough, Malcolm J. *The Trans-Appalachian Frontier: People, Societies, and Institutions, 1775–1850* (1978). Tells this complex story well.

Sellers, Charles G. *The Market Revolution: Jacksonian America, 1815–1846* (1991). Offers a stirring portrayal of the period with economic change at the center.

Sheriff, Carol. *The Artificial River: The Erie Canal and the Paradox of Progress, 1817–1862* (1996). A compelling account of the canal's origins, building, and effects.

American Journey Online and InfoTrac College Edition

Visit the source collections at www.americanjourney.psmedia.com and infotrac.thomsonlearning.com and use the Search function with the following key terms to explore documents, images, audio and video clips, articles, and commentary related to the material in this chapter.

James Monroe
Monroe Doctrine
Henry Clay
Missouri Compromise
Erie Canal

Chapter 10

The Years of Andrew Jackson, 1827–1836

TUMULTUOUS CHANGE came to the United States in the years Andrew Jackson served as president. Elections became broad public events. Voters and leaders hotly debated and contested the role of government in American life. Religious revivals swept up entire communities. Working people created labor unions and abolitionists launched a bold crusade against slavery.

Growing democracy was not the full story of these years, however. The people of the Creek, Choctaw, Cherokee, Seminole, Sac, and Fox nations were driven from their homes. A crisis threatened to ignite a military struggle between South Carolina and the federal government. The revolt of Nat Turner and debates over slavery in Virginia unleashed a proslavery reaction throughout much of the South. The defeat of Mexico in Texas opened a vast new territory. Few decades in American history witnessed more sweeping changes.

The Transformation of American Politics

John Quincy Adams had been elected in a fractious election that cast politics in a poor light. The squabbling of leading men over votes in the electoral college seemed clear evidence that the age of the revolutionary leaders had passed. As people called for a more democratic kind of politics, states across the Union lowered property requirements for voting and made judges elected rather than appointed officials. Voters seemed restless, hungry for someone to give direction and force to public life. Such a man emerged, along with a new kind of politics.

www http://ayersbrief.wadsworth.com

CHRONOLOGY

1828 Tariff of Abominations

Calhoun's *Exposition*

Election of Jackson

1829 David Walker's *Appeal*

Mexico tries to abolish slavery in Texas

1830 Indian Removal Act

The Book of Mormon

Finney's revivals begin in Rochester

1831 Nat Turner's rebellion

Garrison's *The Liberator*

Anti-Masonic party holds first national party convention

Jackson reorganizes cabinet, Van Buren over Calhoun

Mormons migrate from New York to Ohio

1832 Bank War begins

Virginia debates over slavery

Jackson reelected

1833 Formation of American Anti-slavery Society

Force Bill against South Carolina

Compromise Tariff

Slavery abolished in British Empire

Nullification Crisis

1834 Whig party organized

National Trades Union formed

1835 Arkansas admitted to the Union

Revolution breaks out in Texas

Abolitionists' postal campaign

War against Seminoles and runaway slaves in Florida

1836 Congress imposes gag rule

Texas Republic established; Battle of the Alamo

Treaty of New Echota

Election of Martin Van Buren

The Adams Twilight

The second half of John Quincy Adams' administration proved unhappy and unproductive. The "corrupt bargain," in which Henry Clay allegedly conspired to hand the presidency to Adams, still hung over the White House in 1827. In the eyes of many, Adams had proven himself unfit for office. The president's elite education made him a symbol of "aristocracy." Adams' many and diverse opponents organized against him and his policies almost from the beginning of his administration. It soon became clear that the president would be able to accomplish little of his ambitious agenda of internal improvements, a national university, and western exploration, ideals that might have won support in earlier years.

Supporters of Andrew Jackson of Tennessee, John C. Calhoun of South Carolina, and William Crawford of Georgia gradually joined forces in anticipation of the election of 1828. The struggle, Calhoun wrote to Jackson, was between "*power* and *liberty.*" The champion of power had had his turn, Adams' opponents believed; now it was time for the champions of liberty to step forward. After some jockeying, Andrew Jackson emerged as the man to challenge Adams.

Adams' supporters warned of the dangers of electing a raw and rough "military chieftain" to the presidency. Jackson's opponents distributed a handbill marked with eighteen coffins, each one representing a man Jackson had supposedly killed in a duel or ordered executed under his military command. The most incendiary charge, however, was that Jackson had married a woman married to another man. The facts of the case were unclear—it appears that Rachel Jackson was a religious woman, trapped in a bad marriage, who thought she had received a divorce when she married Jackson—but the anti-Jackson forces made the most of any suspicions to the contrary.

Anti-Masons

Charges of conspiracy and corruption raged throughout American politics in the 1820s. Some of the suspicions seemed confirmed by events in New York. As the economy of that state prospered, so did fraternal organizations of every sort. The Ancient Order of Masons did especially well. The Masons' exclusive society, surrounded by elaborate ritual and strict secrecy, many non-Masons felt, contradicted American ideals of democracy and openness. Since Masons were obliged to show business or political preference to a brother over "any other person in the same circumstances," some of those outside the order feared that Masons might win undue influence.

Suspicion of the Masons exploded when a brother named William Morgan turned against the order and decided to publish its secret rituals. Local Masonic leaders used their influence with county officials to harass and jail Morgan, who was later kidnapped. He disappeared; many said he had been murdered. The investigation soon stalled, however. Despite twenty trials and three special prosecutors, only a few convictions resulted. Fury against the Masons soon spread from New York to the rest of the country.

By 1827, nearly a hundred "Morgan committees" had met and formed in New York and began to spread across the entire northern half of the country. The movement gathered around it much of the anger and many of the anxieties of people who resented the growing power of merchants, manufacturers, lawyers, and a new class of professional politicians. Within two years, the "Anti-Masons" had established more than a hundred newspapers. They held public meetings and launched lobbying campaigns. Unlike earlier reform organizations, the Anti-Masons thrived on controversy. They devoted themselves to mobilizing people against a powerful entrenched force. They succeeded: Masonry lost more than half its members and created virtually no new lodges for the next fifteen years.

Birth of the Democrats

Even while the struggle over the Masons unfolded, Senator Martin Van Buren of New York was building a political coalition behind Andrew Jackson. Van Buren traveled throughout the United States, hammering out a new coalition of ambitious state politicians willing to back Jackson. The members of the coalition called themselves "Democratic Republicans," eventually to be shortened to "Democrats." Their candidates did extremely well in the off-year congressional elections of 1827, exploiting people's disapproval of the ineffectual Adams administration.

Throughout 1827 and 1828, Van Buren and the other party leaders organized voters. Although Jackson himself was a prominent Mason, Van Buren adopted techniques not unlike those pioneered by the Anti-Masons. Using every strategy at their disposal—bonfires, speeches, barbecues, parades, professional writers, and the first campaign song—these Jacksonians claimed that they had found a true man of the people to strip the office from the aristocratic Adams. The National Republicans, as Adams supporters became known, sniffed at what they considered the unseemly display that diverted attention from real issues, but they could not deny the power of the new methods to win voters' attention.

Voting turnout in 1828 doubled that of the 1824 election. Politicians at every level and on both sides made sure voters went to the polls. Jackson won easily over Adams, capturing the critical mid-Atlantic states and all the states of the South except Louisiana and Kentucky. The election proved bittersweet for Jackson, though, for his wife died soon afterward. Jackson blamed the slanderers of the other party for Rachel's death, for she had fallen ill after seeing an editorial denouncing her.

The People's President

Andrew Jackson, still dressed in black in mourning for Rachel, traveled by steamboat from Nashville to Washington in the winter of 1829 to begin his presidency. Ensconced in a hotel suite, Jackson assembled his cabinet, balancing North, South, and West. Van Buren, to no one's surprise, became secretary of state. Vice President Calhoun chafed at the appointment but could do little to change it; he and his wing of the party had to satisfy themselves with the appointment of one of their number as secretary of the treasury. The most controversial appointment, however, proved volatile for reasons that had little to do with political partisanship. Jackson chose an old Tennessee associate, John Eaton, as his secretary of war.

Andrew Jackson of Tennessee seemed to many people an inspiring leader. Others, however, saw him as a "military chieftain" dangerous with the power of the presidency. (1942.8.34 (587)/PA; Sully, Thomas, Andrew Jackson, Andrew W. Meelon Collection © 1998 Board of Trustees, National Gallery of Art, Washington, 1845, oil on canvas, .518 × .438 (20 318 × 17 114); framed; .749 × .666 (29 1/2 × 26 1/4))

Eaton, a widower in middle age, had married Peggy O'Neal Timberlake, an attractive and witty twenty-nine-year-old daughter of a well-known innkeeper in Washington. She was rumored to have driven her last husband to suicide, forcing him to defraud the government to pay debts she had run up. She was also rumored to have had sex with Eaton before their marriage. Eaton had asked Jackson's opinion of the marriage beforehand, receiving the old general's blessing. Jackson, in a gesture of friendship and support as the gossip flew, offered Eaton the cabinet position, apparently hoping he would decline. Unfortunately for Jackson, Eaton accepted. The decision electrified Washington.

Despite his rambunctious youth, Jackson disdained official Washington's fondness for strong drink, endless banquets, and overheated social life. He preferred instead to attend the city's churches. Jackson considered himself an outsider determined to reform Washington, to make the city worthy of the nation it was supposed to serve.

As the inauguration day of March 4 neared, Washington's population doubled as men who considered themselves important in General Jackson's election arrived in the city. They drank all the whiskey the city had to offer, slept five to a bed, and generally offended the more genteel residents of the capital. At the inauguration, 30,000 people crowded in to see the new president. After Jackson's brief address, members of the excited audience followed him back to the White House. They surged into the White House, spilling barrels of orange punch, standing with muddy boots on expensive chairs to get a better look at the proceedings, smashing thousands of dollars worth of china. Jackson, literally suffocated by admirers and disgusted by the scene, climbed out a rear window and went for a steak at his boardinghouse.

Jackson Takes Charge

Many people in Washington were as appalled at the events that followed the inauguration as they were with the inauguration itself. As the new administration got under way, Jackson and his advisors cleaned house in the federal government, removing those officials whose competence, honesty, or loyalty to Jackson and the Democrats were suspect. Although such a policy had become established practice in several major states, Jackson was the first president to make such sweeping changes on the federal level. He envisioned himself purging an arrogant bureaucracy of corruption. Some of the incumbents clearly deserved to lose their jobs, having served jail terms, embezzled funds, or succumbed to drink, but others were guilty only of being active partisans for the other side in the recent election.

Jackson removed about 900 of 10,000 men from their offices. One Jackson supporter unwisely announced to the Senate that the Jacksonians saw "nothing wrong in the rule that to the victors belong the spoils of the enemy." This proclamation gave an enduring notoriety to what from then on would be called the "spoils system." Jackson further infuriated opponents by appointing partisan newspaper editors to important posts. One key appointment, the collector of the Port of New York, did indeed prove disastrous, as the man eventually fled the United States with $1.2 million of the people's money. Yet over the course of Jackson's two terms he replaced only about 10 percent of all officeholders, not many more than his predecessors had.

The festering conflict within the administration over the so-called "Eaton affair" proved just how important matters of symbolism could be. The wives of the other cabinet members refused to be in the same room with Peggy Eaton. But Jackson would not be swayed in his support for John and Peggy Eaton. The new cabinet found itself bitterly divided between pro-Eaton and anti-Eaton factions. Jackson labored to mend fences, trying to find evidence to prove Mrs. Eaton's virtue. Nothing proved effective, though, and Jackson decided that the real villain of the story was Vice President Calhoun and his unbending wife Floride. By contrast, Martin Van Buren, a widower, cemented his friendship with the president by treating Mrs. Eaton with ostentatious respect. Jackson, embittered by the refusal of his other advisors to stand by Mrs. Eaton, largely abandoned his official cabinet and relied instead on an informal group of advisors, his so-called "kitchen cabinet."

STRUGGLES OVER SLAVERY

The years around 1830 saw several issues surrounding slavery come to a head. Southern states sought to define the limits of federal power. Feeling themselves neglected and abused by northern interests, South Carolina leaders tried to secure greater autonomy. At the same time, free blacks in both the North and South worked to replace the colonization movement with a campaign to create freedom for African Americans in America. Even as these public struggles unfolded, the largest slave revolt in the history of the United States erupted in Virginia. Combined, these events demonstrated that slavery and the issues on which it touched would bedevil the confident and boisterous young country.

Nullification

Before the election of 1828, Martin Van Buren and other Democrats had sought to broaden support for Jackson, by passing a tariff favorable to the economic interests of New Englanders and westerners. After elaborate deal making, the Democrats enacted a major tariff. But it came with a high cost: Southerners were furious with what they called this "tariff of abominations," for it raised the price they would have to pay for manufactured items and threatened markets abroad for southern cotton. John C. Calhoun feared not only that the tariff would bleed his state of South Carolina dry economically but that it would set a precedent for anti-slavery forces who might gain control of the federal government at some future date.

Accordingly, in the summer and early fall of 1828, a few months before he would become Jackson's vice president, Calhoun sought to find a principled way to reconcile his national ambitions and his local concerns. Rather than argue only against the tariff itself, Calhoun asserted the general rights of individual states within the Union. He insisted that interests had become so diverse in the United States that laws appropriate for one state or section might well harm another. Rather than merely letting the majority run roughshod over the minority, Calhoun believed, it made more sense to let a state "nullify" a national law within its own borders. Such nullification was constitutional, he said, because the federal system did not locate sovereignty in any one place, but rather divided it among the states and the nation. Should three-fourths of the states agree that a law must apply to all the country and amend the constitution, then that clear majority could overrule the nullification. The document in which Calhoun laid out his ideas, the *South Carolina Exposition and Protest* appeared in December of 1828; the pamphlet was published anonymously because it was too politically dangerous for the vice president of the United States to be publicly on record for nullification.

As Calhoun's position in the Jackson administration deteriorated and white South Carolinians grew increasingly angry at their helplessness in the face of the tariff, Calhoun remained silent in public on the issue. Meanwhile, the pressure built. In early 1830 Calhoun's handpicked spokesman, Senator Robert Hayne of South Carolina, engaged in a debate with Massachusetts Senator Daniel Webster over the power of the federal government. The debate was the first clear conflict between the states' rights argument and the defense of what Webster called "liberty and Union, now and forever, one and inseparable." Calhoun, whose position as vice president made him the presiding head of the Senate, could only watch from the podium. Most observers agreed that Daniel Webster dominated the debate; the Massachusetts senator's fame sky-rocketed. Calhoun could not remain in the background much longer; he would have to make his position known.

Calhoun's declaration of principles came at a celebration of Thomas Jefferson's birthday at the Indian Queen Hotel in Washington. President Jackson, Vice President Calhoun, and Secretary of State Van Buren were all present. Van Buren urged the president to make clear his own position on nullification and states' rights. As the officeholders went around the table, one toast after another proclaiming the rights of the states, Jackson became ever more steely. When it was his turn, the president stood, lifted his glass, and—staring at Calhoun—pronounced words filled with a meaning obvious to those present: "Our Federal Union—it must be preserved." Van Buren climbed on a chair to see how Calhoun would respond to this rebuke. "The Union—next to our liberty the most dear," he retorted, his glass trembling, "may we all remember that it can only be preserved by respecting the rights of the states and distributing equally the benefits and burdens of the Union." There was no going back.

South Carolina planters watched with growing alarm as the newspapers told of the success of British abolitionists in ending slavery in the British West Indies—the place from which many white South Carolina families had come generations earlier. White Carolinians felt they could display no weakness on the slavery issue. Throughout the state, raucous crowds gathered to call for a fight against the federal government on the tariff.

When the toasts at the Indian Queen Hotel revealed that President Jackson had no sympathy for the nullificationist position, the leaders of the movement in South Carolina were surprised and disappointed. After all, Jackson, like them, was a planter and slaveholder. Although he supported the rights of the states when only their own welfare seemed to be at stake, Jackson considered the tariff to be for the good of the nation as a whole. The South Carolina challenge would limit the power of the U.S. government to make law for the country in matters that transcended state boundaries. Jackson did not believe the United States could afford to permit such divisiveness to impair its strength in the world of nations.

Free Blacks and African American Abolitionism

Even as the white leaders of South Carolina struggled to define the extent of their powers within the Union, free blacks and slaves struggled to define their freedom. Communities of several thousand free blacks had emerged in every major northern city, establishing their own churches, newspapers, schools, and lodges.

Even more numerous were free African Americans in the upper South slave states. Although free blacks in the upper South were scattered throughout smaller towns and rural areas, they generally tended to gather in cities as they did in the North. The cities strung along the Atlantic and Gulf coasts—Norfolk, Savannah, Charleston, Mobile, and New Orleans—all contained several thousand free blacks.

Free African Americans stayed in the South to be closer to family members held in slavery and because, ironically, southern cities held out greater economic opportunity than the North. Because whites deemed many jobs "nigger work," black Southerners dominated some fields of labor. Black men constituted most of the barbers and teamsters, for example, while black women found work as laundresses and domestics. Free blacks in the South had to be careful, making sure that local officials kept records of their freedom, but they could acquire property and educate their children.

Free blacks throughout the country debated the merits of leaving the United States altogether. The colonization movement struggled in the 1820s; few black Americans were willing to be shipped to a place they had never seen. African Americans came to see in colonization an attack on their hard-won accomplishments in the United States. Rather than spending moral energy and money on removing black people, they argued, Americans should work instead to make the United States a fairer place.

David Walker proved to be an important figure in this movement. Walker had lived in Charleston at the time of Denmark Vesey's conspiracy. After the suppression of Vesey, Walker moved to Boston and established a used-clothing store. Walker did well in the business, bought a home, joined the African Methodist church, and gave his support to *Freedom's Journal,* an anticolonization paper published by black people in Boston and New York City.

In 1829 Walker released his *Appeal to the Colored Citizens of the World.* He called for black spiritual self-renewal, starting with African Americans' recognition of just how angry they were with their lot in the United States. They needed to channel that anger with God's love, Walker urged, making a group effort to end slavery immediately. He did not call for violence but for black Americans to be full Americans in both government and economy.

The *Appeal* created panic and repression as it spread throughout the South. Southern whites worried at this evidence of invisible networks of communication and resistance among the slaves, free blacks, and, perhaps, sympathetic whites in their midst. Events in Virginia bore out their worst suspicions.

The Crisis of Slavery in Virginia

Nat Turner was a field hand, born in 1800. Well known even in his youth for his intellectual abilities and his effectiveness as a preacher, on Sundays Turner traveled throughout the countryside around Southampton County, Virginia, coming to know most of the slaves and free black people who lived there. Praying and fasting, Turner saw visions: drops of blood that formed hieroglyphics on leaves, black shadows across the white moon. These things, he became certain, foretold a slave revolt. Turner chose to build his revolt around a

Nat Turner launched the largest slave revolt in the history of the United States, assembling a devoted band of lieutenants who kept secret the plans of the revolt. (The Granger Collection, New York)

small group of select lieutenants rather than to risk spreading the word broadly. Their plan was to begin the rebellion on their own and then attract compatriots along the way.

On August 22, 1831, Turner and his band began their revolt. They moved from one isolated farmhouse to the next, killing all the whites they found inside and gathering horses and weapons. As the night went on, Turner's men had killed about seventy people. By morning, word had rushed to Richmond of the unimaginable events in Southampton. Whites huddled together in Jerusalem, the county seat, and troops arrived to put down the revolt. Blacks, hundreds of miles away from Southhampton, many of whom had no connection with the rebellion, were killed by infuriated and frightened whites. Turner's troops were all captured or killed, but he managed to escape and to hide in the woods of the county for two months. Once captured, Turner narrated a remarkable "confession" in which he told of his visions and prophecies. At his hanging in November, he showed no signs of remorse.

White Southerners saw in Nat Turner their worst nightmares. Here was a literate slave, allowed to travel on his own, allowed to spread his own interpretation of the Bible to dissatisfied slaves. The crackdown was not long in coming, as delegates to the state assembly gathered in Richmond a month after Turner's execution. In a series of remarkable debates, these white Virginians openly admitted the debilitating effect of slavery on Virginia. They worried that slavery kept the economy from developing as it did in the North. Petitions flowed into Richmond urging the legislators to take a decisive step to rid Virginia of slavery. Defenders of slavery warned that the debates might result in more revolts. Enslaved Virginians were not an "ignorant herd of Africans," one delegate warned, but an "active, intelligent class, watching and weighing every movement of the Legislature."

Some delegates urged that the state purchase all slaves born after 1840 and colonize them in Africa or sell them to plantations farther south. Others argued that the Virginia economy would collapse without slavery, that slaves born before the date of freedom would revolt, that property rights guaranteed in the Constitution made it ridiculous to talk about taking slaves from their owners. Others went much further, arguing that slavery was not wrong at all but rather God's plan for civilizing Africans. The lawmakers, starkly divided, ultimately decided that it was "inexpedient" to take any step at all against slavery at that time, that it would be left for subsequent legislatures to begin

DAVID WALKER, *APPEAL . . . TO THE COLORED CITIZENS OF THE WORLD* 1829

David Walker, a free black man, argues with Thomas Jefferson's assertion that slavery in the United States was more benign and beneficial than in ancient Greece and Rome, places to which educated Americans looked for the measure of true civilization. In Walker's eyes, the connection between the ancients and modern whites shows a strain of cruelty that runs throughout the history of western culture. He attacks the un-Christian behavior of slavetraders and slaveholders even as he looks to God for ultimate judgment.

I have been for years troubling the pages of historians to find out what our fathers have done to the *white Christians of America,* to merit such condign punishment as they have inflicted on them, and do continue to inflict on us their children. But I must aver, that my researches have hitherto been to no effect. I have therefore come to the immovable conclusion, that they (Americans) have, and do continue to punish us for nothing else, but for enriching them and their country. For I cannot conceive of any thing else. Nor will I ever believe otherwise until the Lord shall convince me. . . .

The whites have always been an unjust, jealous, unmerciful, avaricious and blood thirsty set of beings, always seeking after power and authority.—We view them all over the confederacy of Greece, where they were first known to be any thing, (in consequence of education) we see them there, cutting each other's throats—trying to subject each other to wretchedness and misery, to effect which they used all kinds of deceitful, unfair and unmerciful means. We view them next in Rome, where the spirit of tyranny and deceit raged still higher.—We view them in Gaul, Spain and in Britain—in fine, we view them all over Europe, together with what were scattered about in Asia and Africa, as heathens, and we see them acting more like devils than accountable men. But some may ask, did not the blacks of Africa, and the mulattoes of Asia, go on in the same ways as did the whites of Europe? I answer no—they never were half so avaricious, deceitful and unmerciful as the whites, according to their knowledge. . . .

SOURCE David Walker, *Appeal, in Four Articles; Together with a Preamble to the Colored Citizens of the World.* . . . (Boston: September 28, 1829. 3d ed. Boston: D. Walker).

the process that would free Virginia from slavery. In the meantime, they passed harsher laws to limit the movement and gathering of free blacks and slaves.

REVIVAL AND REFORM

The power and influence of Protestant churches surged to a new level in the Jacksonian era. Revivals pulled in scores of new members, firing them with the desire to remake their lives. Many of those who experienced the spiritual rebirth of the revivals sought ways to demonstrate their faith and their hope for America. A radical new movement against slavery gathered force with stunning speed. At the same time, other Americans sought purer forms of religion, listening to prophets who spoke of new churches and new possibilities.

Revivalism

Since the late eighteenth century, revivals led by the major Protestant denominations had periodically inflamed the United States. In those revivals, people who had never declared their faith in Jesus Christ or who had fallen away from the church made public expressions of their faith. Thousands of people gathered to pray and hear ministers tell them of God's love and forgiveness. Learning of these gifts, and aware of their own sinfulness, men and women sometimes fell to the ground as if stricken. Others cried and screamed. The churches that devoted themselves to spreading the Gospel—known as "evangelical" churches because they sought to bring others the evangel, or "good news," of the Scripture—periodically experienced revivals or "awakenings" when numbers of people expressed or renewed their faith. This revivalism burst out again in the mid-1820s.

Many ministers and churches across the country were swept up in the awakening, but one man embodied its new and aggressive spirit: Charles Grandison Finney. Finney, a young attorney from Utica, New York, suddenly found himself struck with the power of God's love. "An overwhelming sense" of his wickedness brought Finney to his knees. "I wept aloud like a child [and] the Holy Spirit descended upon me in a manner that seemed to go through me body and soul," he recalled. Finney spread the word of the Bible in the plain and straightforward language of everyday life. He told people to seek out salvation, to throw themselves open to the mercy of Jesus.

Finney found in the young cities of western New York a receptive audience among young men and among women of every age. The churches, these people believed, had grown cold in the hands of the established ministry. They wanted a Christianity of activity, of spreading the word any way they could.

The revivals took on a new scale and urgency in 1830 as they ignited Rochester. Like other rapidly growing towns and cities along the Erie Canal, Rochester was ripe for revival. Many people worried that husbands and wives, workers and employers, rich and poor, were drifting apart. Politics appeared a morass of selfishness; alcohol seemed to drown hopes of social progress and family happiness; men seemed more concerned with their businesses, lodges, and politics than with their souls. When Finney came to town in 1830, he was met by a populace hungry for something to stir them up.

Women's prayer groups met daily and traveled from home to home in efforts to bring the word of Jesus. Women pleaded with their husbands to listen to the Reverend Finney. Employers made it clear to the men who worked under them that it would be noticed whether or not they attended the revival. These efforts transformed Rochester, bringing hundreds of people into the church who had not come before.

Such a powerful revival seemed evidence to many people that America could be changed by faith. As they watched saloons shut down, families brought together, and shops and stores closed while the revival was in progress, it appeared that the way was being prepared for God's kingdom on earth. If the United States could be adequately reformed, these people believed, the day of redemption could be hastened. Such faith bred a demand for immediate reforms. When the means of change lay only a prayer away, delay seemed a rejection of God's love.

Abolitionism

Religious ferment stirred some evangelicals to take immediate steps toward improving American society. Although the great majority of white Northerners (and Southerners) thought Christians should seek holiness mainly in their own hearts, others were equally certain that society itself could and should be changed. To many, slavery seemed the place to start.

William Lloyd Garrison was a key person in the emergence of the new anti-slavery movement. Garrison had been abandoned as an infant by his sea captain father and apprenticed to masters in one craft after another. At twelve, he found himself working in a print shop. At twenty-two, he became the editor of the first newspaper dedicated to the prohibition of alcohol. Believing in the necessity of ending slavery as well as drunkenness, Garrison joined the colonization movement and soon became editor of its paper as well.

In the late 1820s Garrison attended anticolonizationist meetings held by African Americans in eastern cities. Experiencing a mounting desire for a more aggressive antislavery crusade, he sought out financial supporters and a partner to launch a paper of his own: *The Liberator.* It called for the immediate start toward emancipation. "I *will* be as harsh as truth," Garrison announced, "and as uncompromising as justice. On this subject, I do not wish to think, speak, or write, with moderation. . . . I am in earnest—I will not equivocate—I will not excuse—I will not retreat a single inch—AND I WILL BE HEARD." He was.

Two hundred anti-slavery societies emerged in the early thirties. Some northern church members argued that it was the duty of good Christians to cast out slaveholders and to use the enormous power of the church as a force for freedom. These "immediatists" called for slaveholders to free their slaves immediately, hire them as free workers, and help repay the former slaves for their years of unpaid toil. These early abolitionists hoped to convert the slaveholders by persuasion and prayer, not by law and force.

William Lloyd Garrison played a key role in persuading many Northern whites that slavery was morally wrong and should be brought to an immediate end. (The Granger Collection, New York)

The American Anti-slavery Society formed in Philadelphia in 1833. Looking to the example of Great Britain, the members of the society expected American church leaders to take the lead against American slavery. The North would have to be converted before it could expect the South to follow. To convert the North, anti-slavery organizations held out the prospect of a free South, where 2 million freed slaves would constitute an "immense market" for the products of Northern "mechanics and manufacturers." These abolitionists expected the former slaves to remain in the South; they spoke little of the competition the freedpeople might provide to the workers of the North. Similarly, the anti-slavery people believed a free South would prosper, with planters and free whites flourishing as they had never flourished before.

Far more than any other organizations in the United States at this time, the anti-slavery cause brought together male and female, black and white, patrician and working class, Quaker and Unitarian, Baptist and Methodist, radical and moderate, and political and anti-political people. Each of these groups had its own vision of how the abolitionists should spend their energies and influence.

The anti-slavery societies used pamphlets, leaflets, and other literature as their major weapons. Rapid innovations in printing lowered the cost of producing such materials. The postal campaign reached its peak in 1834 and 1835, when a million pieces went out through the mail, much of it to the South. That literature, white Southerners furiously protested, virtually invited slaves to follow Nat Turner's example. Georgia slaveholders offered a $12,000 reward for the capture of wealthy merchant Arthur Tappan, who, along with his brother Lewis, funded much of the postal campaign against slavery.

The pamphlets infuriated people in much of the North as well. In 1835 mobs destroyed the homes of African Americans, pelted anti-slavery speakers, and dragged William Lloyd Garrison himself through the streets of Boston at the end of a rope. The leaders of that mob announced that they had assaulted Garrison "to assure our brethren of the South that we cherish rational and correct notions on the subject of slavery." Many white Northerners believed the abolitionists to be hypocrites. Antislavery speakers risked a mob every time they spoke; abolitionists' churches were blown up and their school buildings dragged into swamps.

Denunciation and harassment only made the abolitionists more certain of the need for their efforts. The 200 anti-slavery societies of 1835 grew to over 500 in 1836. The reformers flooded Congress with petitions calling for the end of slavery in the District of Columbia. The acceptance of these petitions by the House, Southerners argued, besmirched slaveholders' honor and threatened to incite slaves to rebellion. Congress sought to avoid conflict by merely tabling the petitions, but the compromise pleased no one. Over the next decade, Northerners of even a mild anti-slavery bent chafed at this "gag rule." Former President John Quincy Adams, now a Congressman, led their fight to be heard.

The Birth of Mormonism

Like so many American families of these years, that of Joseph Smith could not find a secure place. His father dreamed of bringing his family out of poverty, moving them from one community to another. Young Joseph, like hundreds of other people in upstate New York, looked for treasure rumored to have been buried long ago in the mountains; he watched with concern for his soul, too, as revivals came and went without his conversion. Smith reported that he felt the presence of an angel, however, who told him "that God had work for me to do, and that my name should be for good and evil among all nations, kindreds, and tongues. He said there was a book deposited, written upon gold plates, giving an account of the former inhabitants of this continent, and the source from which they sprang. He also said that, the fullness of the everlasting Gospel was contained in it." Smith claimed that the angel directed him to the location of the sacred writings.

In 1827, Smith began to transcribe what he had found; sitting in a tent divided by a partition, he read the plates to an assistant on the other side. *The Book of Mormon* took shape, telling of a promised land reserved for the righteous. North America, the book said, had been visited by Jesus in the distant past but the people had lost their way and fallen into disputation. Those people had been cursed by God for their sins and marked with dark skins; their descendants were the American Indians.

Joseph Smith and several followers traveled throughout New York selling copies of what they called the "Gold Bible." They were met with hostility, but they slowly gathered converts to their Church of Jesus Christ of the Latter-Day Saints.

Many of the new members were poor, but others had considerable resources. The most important converts were two brothers, Brigham and Joseph Young. As the movement gathered momentum, hundreds of people joined the church. The faithful moved first to Ohio and then to what Smith believed to be the original Eden: Missouri. But other settlers made no secret of their disapproval of the Mormons, who were constantly harassed by non-Mormons who feared the growing number of converts and the local economic power that came from the church members' pooled resources and hard work.

POLITICAL TURMOIL

Andrew Jackson made fervent enemies as well as devoted followers throughout his presidency. Politics quickened in preparation for the election of 1832 as voters and leaders mobilized in opposition or support. Jackson, furious at any resistance, lashed out. The nation had not seen such political conflict for decades, as citizens debated issues of the economy, states' rights, and morality.

Taking Sides

In September 1831, the first national political convention in U.S. history met in Baltimore. It was convened by the Anti-Masons, who were concerned with the state of American politics in general, not merely with the threat posed by the Masons. They attracted an impressive list of ambitious and accomplished young men to their convention, including many who believed the Jackson White House was too pro-Southern and too callous with the American Indians. The Anti-Masons found little appeal in John Quincy Adams' National Republicans, for that party seemed to be stuck in the past and hapless against the strong Jacksonian Democrats. The Anti-Masons promised to become a powerful third party, a wild card in an already tumultuous American politics.

The Jacksonians held their own convention the following spring. Jackson, fed up with the controversy over Peggy Eaton and alienated from Calhoun, early in 1831 asked all the members of his cabinet to resign. When the president reconstituted the cabinet, he replaced pro-Calhoun men with men more to his own liking. Van Buren was nominated to be the new minister to Great Britain. Calhoun, in a final act of revenge, cast the Senate vote that rejected Van Buren's appointment. Van Buren and Jackson got the last laugh when the convention of 1832 filled the vice presidential slot with Van Buren and removed Calhoun from the ticket.

The radicals in South Carolina, their last connection to the presidency broken, reacted with fury when Jackson signed another high tariff in 1832. Advocates of nullification won control of the South Carolina legislature and oversaw the election of a state convention. Such a convention, Calhoun and his allies declared, could nullify the U.S. Constitution because state conventions had been elected before the first national Constitutional Convention and authorized delegates to write a national document in the first place. The South Carolina convention announced that the federal tariffs passed in 1828 and 1832 were null, without force in South Carolina; South Carolina would secede if the U.S. government turned to arms to enforce the tariff. Calhoun resigned the vice presidency and became senator from South Carolina.

The Bank War

Despite the tariffs intended to serve their interests, most people in the Northeast felt they had received little from Andrew Jackson's first term. They viewed him as a defender of the backward South and West against the East. The fate of the Second Bank of the United States stood as the key issue in this regard. It was the job of Nicholas Biddle, the bank's president, to make sure that state banks kept plenty of metal currency—specie—on hand with which to pay the national bank when asked to do so. Such rules kept the state banks from inflating the currency with paper money unsupported by gold or silver. When the economy fell into trouble, on the other hand, the Bank of the United States would lessen its demands on the state banks, preventing panics and deflation.

Although businessmen appreciated this role of the bank, many other Americans distrusted it. In their eyes, this largely private institution enjoyed far too much power. Why should privileged stockholders in the bank, they asked, profit from the business of the federal government? Why should the national notes be allowed to depress the value of state notes?

For many voters, the whole business of banking seemed suspect, with its paper money, its profits seemingly without labor, its government-supported monopolies, its apparent speculation with public money. Andrew Jackson shared these feelings of mistrust. As a young man, he had lost a considerable amount of money to a speculator, and nothing he saw as president changed his mind about those who dealt in the mysteries of currency. He disliked monopoly, he disliked paper money, and he disliked the Bank of the United States.

The issue came to a head in 1832 as Henry Clay and other National Republicans, joined by South Carolina nullifiers such as Calhoun, sought to use the bank as a way to defeat Jackson for the presidency. A few months before the election in the fall, the bank's supporters steered its application for rechartering through Congress. Jackson vetoed the recharter, proclaiming that the bank was "unauthorized by the constitution, subversive of the rights of the States, and dangerous to the liberties of the people."

Jackson's opponents, in turn, saw the president, not the bank, as the usurper of American rights. Henry Clay and other opponents argued that his action posed a far greater threat to the American people than did the bank. If the president could force his way into the lawmaking process, the division of powers laid out in the Constitution would be violated and the Union would risk falling under despotic rule.

Jackson on the Offensive

The election of 1832 turned around these broad issues. Jackson portrayed himself as the champion of the common man fighting against a bloated aristocracy of privilege and monopoly. Clay, the candidate of the National Republicans, portrayed himself as the defender of the Union against an arrogant and power-hungry president, a man who had shown a disregard for morality and justice in his dealing with the American Indians and the spoils system as well as with the bank. William Wirt, the candidate of the Anti-Masons, declared himself the opponent of conspiracies, corruptions, and subversions larger and more insidious than the bank, all the more dangerous for not being clearly defined.

Despite the challenges on the bank and by the Anti-Masons, Jackson won by a considerable margin. Emboldened by his majority at the polls, the president went on the offensive. Before the bank could deploy its enormous financial resources to gather the two-thirds' majority necessary to override his earlier veto, Jackson moved all federal funds from the Bank of the United States to state banks. After others resisted, a newly appointed secretary of the treasury followed Jackson's plan and put the government deposits in seven state banks. Congressmen of both parties denounced Jackson's move. Biddle and his bank's supporters fought on for two more years, but without the government's deposits they had little leverage. Jackson's lieutenants efficiently mobilized the votes they needed in Congress to prevent the renewal of the bank's charter.

Even as the bank war raised one set of questions about the separation of powers, the nullification crisis brought another constitutional crisis to a climax. Nullification, Jackson had announced soon after his reelection, would not be tolerated. Disunion was treason, he warned, and would be treated as such; Congress passed a "Force Bill" to permit him to use military power to keep South Carolina in line. Recent opponents of Jackson such as Henry Clay and Daniel Webster were pleased—and surprised—at Jackson's nationalism.

Southerners in other states were caught in a difficult position, disapproving of South Carolina's radicalism but distrustful of the Force Bill.

On the same day it passed the Force Bill, Congress offered a compromise on the tariff: it would be slowly but steadily lowered over the next decade, giving northern manufacturers time to adapt. South Carolina, secretly relieved, declared itself the victor and accepted the compromise tariff; in a final display of states' rights defiance, though, the Carolinians nullified the Force Bill. Jackson ignored them, recognizing the emptiness of the gesture.

Those opposed to Jackson soon began to call themselves "Whigs." Like their British namesakes, the American Whigs saw themselves as the counterbalance to otherwise unchecked monarchical power—in this case "King Andrew I." The men who moved into the Whigs—former National Republicans, former Anti-Masons, and even former Democrats—shared little at first except their opposition to Jackson and his use of power. As the fight against Jackson continued, however, they would find more common ground.

Working People

Not everyone prospered during the 1820s and 1830s. Since prices and rents rose much more quickly than wages, urban working people found themselves falling behind. For generations, artisans and others who worked with their hands prided themselves on their contribution to America. These working men and women felt their contributions slighted in the new economy, however, their labor was no longer bringing the recognition and rewards it deserved.

To defend their rights, workers formed unions. After a failed strike for a ten-hour day by journeymen carpenters in Philadelphia in 1827, artisans pooled their efforts in the Mechanics' Union of Trade Associations, the first citywide federation of workingmen's groups. Members of fifteen different trades joined. In the early 1830s, trades' associations appeared in New York, Boston, Baltimore, Washington, and Louisville. By the mid-1830s, between 100,000 and 300,000 men and women belonged to unions.

A number of labor and political leaders, recognizing the power of such numbers, sought to mobilize the organized workers into politics. Although union members generally liked Andrew Jackson's blows against monopoly, they thought he pulled up short in his attack on privilege. They sought to push the political system into doing more to protect working people. Some unions became deeply engaged in politics and put forward their own candidates. In 1834, at the movement's high point, workers formed the National Trades Union to "unite and harmonize the efforts of all the productive classes of our country." It appeared that a self-conscious urban working class might become a potent factor in American political life.

THE INDIAN PEOPLES AND THE MEXICAN NATION

The most important "foreign relations" of Andrew Jackson's administration were with the native peoples of North America. The American Indians held immense areas of the South and the West when Jackson took office, land that many whites wanted and demanded. The southwestern border of the United States remained dangerously ambiguous as well. Mexico governed its Texas province loosely and many white Americans coveted that land. Both of these situations would undergo explosive change under Andrew Jackson.

Jackson and the American Indians

Andrew Jackson had announced, and acted upon, his attitudes toward the Indians years before he took office as president. The steady pressing of white population onto the rich lands of the

Cherokee, Chickasaw, Creeks, Seminoles, and Choctaws, he thought, left the people of those nations with two choices. If they could adapt themselves to agriculture and law, they might remain where they were, protected by the laws they pledged to obey; if they could not adapt, they would have to leave. Their only other choice, Jackson thought, was extinction.

White people had mixed feelings about the Indians. Americans of European descent considered the Indians admirable in many ways, dignified and free, able to learn and prosper. Not a few "white" and "black" families were proud to claim some Indian ancestry. Many white Americans, including some in Congress, had long contributed time and money to the Indians, helping to build and staff schools, sending seed and agricultural implements to ease the transition to farming.

By the late 1820s, the "civilized tribes" had adapted themselves to the dominant society. Many of the tribes were led by chiefs of mixed descent, leaders who lived in cabins, houses, and even mansions. The children of the Indian leaders and others went to schools established by white missionaries, who persuaded a considerable number of Indians to convert to Christianity. The Cherokees published a newspaper that included articles in both their own language and English.

Despite these adaptations, the Indians of the Southeast showed no desire to leave the land on which they lived. In their view, they had already given up more land than they should have. "We would not receive money for land in which our fathers and friends are buried," they declared. Most whites, especially those who lived nearby, bristled at the continuing presence of the native inhabitants. Many white people longed to banish the American Indians to land on the other side of the Mississippi River.

In 1827, the Cherokees held a national convention and drew up a written constitution. They desired both to declare their sovereignty over their lands and to show whites just how devoted they were to American values. But the new constitution, U.S. courts ruled, violated the law of both the nation and the state of Georgia, which petitioned the federal government to remove the Cherokees. An already volatile situation worsened when gold was discovered on the Indian lands and white prospectors rushed in. The Georgia legislature declared the Cherokees' laws null and void, placing Georgia law into effect instead. The Cherokees suddenly found themselves even more vulnerable than before.

Jackson told the Indians that he could do nothing to stop their mistreatment except to move them beyond the Mississippi River, where, he promised, they would be safe. The Indians and their supporters responded bitterly to such claims, arguing that the rights of the Constitution should certainly extend to people who had lived in North America since time immemorial. But the Jacksonians quickly pushed through the Indian Removal Act of 1830. Two Supreme Court decisions in favor of the Cherokees, in 1830 and in 1832, proved to be without effect, since they depended on the federal government to implement them and Jackson had no intention of doing anything of the sort.

In the face of the impending removal, most of the Indian peoples split into pro-assimilation, "progressive" factions and anti-assimilation, "conservative" factions. Missionaries and federal agents dealt primarily with the progressives, but many other Indians resisted, often by moving far into the backwoods. Many thousands of each nation remained behind, either those who had passed into white or black society through marriage or those who lived outside areas of heavy settlement.

Agents, some of mixed blood, swindled the Indians as they prepared for the removal. The Choctaws, the first to move, underwent horrific experiences, suffering greatly and dying in large numbers as they traveled in the worst winter on record with completely inadequate supplies. The Creeks, too, confronted frauds and assaults. The Indians who moved sold whatever they could not take with them, usually at a great loss. Wagons and carts carried the old and the sick, while women and children drove livestock along the trail. Some of the migrants used steamboats to travel up or down the Mississippi River and then to Oklahoma along the Arkansas or Red River, while others proceeded overland.

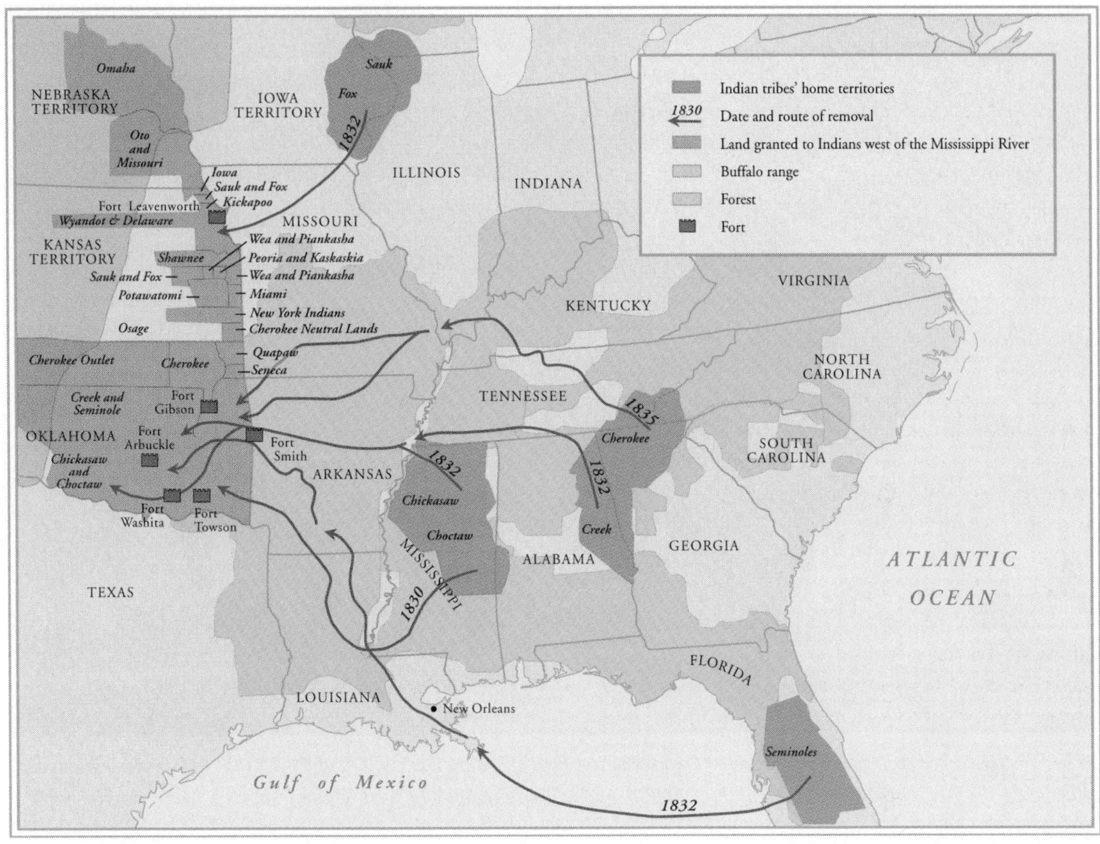

Map 10.1 | The Removal of the American Indians

The Cherokee removal was the most prolonged. After years of negotiating, the government struck a bargain with a small and unrepresentative number of the Cherokee in the Treaty of New Echota in 1836. Although groups of several hundred at a time left, 17,000 refused to leave by the deadline. General Winfield Scott then led 7,000 troops against them, driving people from their homes empty-handed, marching them to stockades and shipping them out by rail and water. About a quarter of all eastern Cherokees died in what they called "The Trail of Tears."

The Seminoles fought against removal as long as they could. Led by Osceola, the son of an English trader and the husband of an escaped slave, the Seminoles tried to break the will of the whites by killing soldiers and civilians and by burning their crops and homes. The Second Seminole War launched by the federal government to remove the 5,000 Indians began in 1836 and dragged on for six years. About 36,000 U.S. soldiers fought and 1,500 died; many more suffered debilitating disease. The federal government spent $20 million in the fight, even though few white people wanted to settle on the Seminoles' land. The United States captured Osceola only by deception at a supposed peace conference. He died in captivity a few months later, after which some Seminoles finally migrated to Oklahoma. But most of the Seminole people, able to use the swampy landscape to hide, were never driven out of Florida.

Fighting also erupted in the Illinois Territory between white settlers and the Sac and Fox Indians. These people, under the leadership of Black

The Cherokee called their forced migration to Oklahoma the Trail of Tears. About 4,000 of the 15,000 Indians forced to move died along the way, as did over 25,000 of the 100,000 southeastern Indians who were driven from their homes in these years. (Woolaroc Museum, Barrtlesville, Oklahoma)

Hawk, saw their lands along the Mississippi River taken over by whites in 1832. The whites burned the Indians' huts and plowed under their fields. In retaliation, the Sac and Fox destroyed white settlements. A large contingent of volunteers, regular troops, and allied Indians set out after Black Hawk and his people. Eventually, the whites outnumbered Black Hawk and overran his camp. Taken prisoner, Black Hawk refused to repent, telling his captors that he "has done nothing for which an Indian ought to be ashamed. He has fought for his countrymen, the squaws and papooses, against white men who came, year after year, to cheat them and take away their land." Black Hawk's words and deeds attracted considerable sympathy among whites in the East. Andrew Jackson met with Black Hawk and pardoned him; the chief's autobiography became a best-seller. The United States, using its defeat of the Sac as an example, found it much easier to induce the other Indians of the Old Northwest to cede 190 million acres for $70 million.

Conflict with Mexico

Speculators and settlers from the United States continually moved into Mexican Texas in the 1820s and 1830s. The Mexican officials, seeking the end of slavery in Mexico, wanted settlers but did not want the slaves white settlers often brought with them. The key leader in the American migration was Stephen F. Austin, a Virginia-born entrepreneur. Throughout the 1820s, Austin, negotiating with the changing Mexican governments, oversaw the arrival and settlement of hundreds of Americans. Although the Mexican laws on slavery shifted repeatedly, most of the American settlers argued that they had to have slaves if Texas were to develop as they and as Mexican leaders hoped. The Americans, with the tacit approval of local officials, improvised laws and took advantage of loopholes to keep slavery in fact if not in name.

American settlers and the Mexican government came into increasing conflict, as provincial officials attempted to collect tariffs and slow immigration into the district. Austin and the other Americans petitioned the Mexican government to let them become a separate Mexican state under its own administration, but they were rebuffed when Antonio López de Santa Anna took control of the government. In Santa Anna's eyes, the Texans were clearly inviting an expansionist United States to take this province away from Mexico; he sent in troops to meet the threat. In 1835, a convention of Texans voted to fight against Santa Anna.

Volunteers and money flowed into Texas from throughout the United States, where people had been watching the events in that area with great interest. Southern states in particular sent hundreds of men. Nevertheless, they were greatly outnumbered by the Mexicans. As the Mexican army sought to occupy San Antonio, 188 rebels—including Davy Crockett of Tennessee—took refuge in the Mission of the Alamo. Most of the people inside were American, but they were joined by *tejanos,* Mexicans of the province who allied themselves with the revolt for independence. The defenders of the Alamo held out against 3,000 Mexican soldiers for nearly two weeks, until the Mexicans finally stormed the mission and killed all inside except three white women, two white children, and an African American slave. After the Alamo, support for the rebellion grew rapidly in the United States, and "Remember the Alamo" became the rallying cry.

Santa Anna seemed on the verge of victory until Sam Houston, the general of the American forces, attacked a much larger Mexican force at San Jacinto in April of 1836. Rushing toward the entrenched Mexicans, the Texans overran the artillery and breastworks, winning a decisive battle in only eighteen minutes. Santa Anna himself was captured a day later. As a prisoner, he signed treaties removing Mexican troops from Texas, granting Texas its independence, and recognizing the Rio Grande as the boundary. The Mexican Congress, when it heard of this capitulation, announced that it would not be bound by these terms.

Texans and many Americans elsewhere urged the U.S. government to annex the new republic before it could be retaken by the Mexicans. That plea unleashed a heated and protracted debate between Southerners, who saw Texas as a vast new

The defeat of Santa Anna at San Jacinto brought the fight for Texas independence to a sudden and surprising culmination. (Archives & Information Services Division-Texas State Library. Photo by Eric Beggs)

empire, and Northerners, especially abolitionists, who opposed annexation because it would lead to slavery's expansion. The fate of Texas would be a key political issue for the next decade.

CONCLUSION

The vague and uncertain America of the 1810s and early 1820s became clearer under Andrew Jackson. No longer would politics be a matter of remote personalities in Washington, for now a two-party system mobilized voters. No longer would slavery be a matter beyond debate, for the nullification crisis, Walker's *Appeal,* Turner's revolt, and the emergence of an abolitionist movement made slavery a burning issue. The aggressive young churches of the Second Great Awakening ensured that the Protestant faith became a matter of public action and testimony. After bitter debate and resistance, the power of the American Indians of the eastern United States had been broken and their people removed. The public culture of the United States had become polarized over matters both public and private.

RECOMMENDED READINGS

Feller, Daniel. *The Jacksonian Promise: America, 1815–1840* (1995). Offers a recent, upbeat overview.

Freehling, Allison Goodyear. *Drift Toward Dissolution: The Virginia Slavery Debate of 1831–1832* (1982). A useful interpretation of the crisis in Virginia.

Freehling, William. *Prelude to Civil War: The Nullification Crisis in South Carolina, 1816–1836* (1966). The standard account of the subject.

Johnson, Paul. *A Shopkeeper's Millennium: Society and Revivals in Rochester, New York, 1815–1837* (1978). Tells the story of revivals in an exciting way.

Laurie, Bruce. *Artisans into Workers: Labor in Nineteenth-Century America* (1989). An excellent synthesis of this complicated history.

Roediger, David R. *The Wages of Whiteness: Race and the Making of the American Working Class* (1991). Boldly interprets the uses the white working class made of the notion of "race."

Walters, Ronald. *American Reformers, 1815–1860* (1996). An updated version of a fine analytical synthesis.

Watson, Harry L. *Liberty and Power: The Politics of Jacksonian America* (1990). A helpful and balanced interpretation of a subject that has been much debated by scholars.

Weber, David J. *The Mexican Frontier, 1821–1846: The American Southwest Under Mexico* (1982). The complex history of this region before war brought it into the United States.

Wiebe, Robert H. *The Opening of American Society: From the Adoption of the Constitution to the Eve of Disunion* (1984). Surveys this entire era.

AMERICAN JOURNEY ONLINE AND INFOTRAC COLLEGE EDITION

Visit the source collections at www.americanjourney.psmedia.com and infotrac.thomsonlearning.com and use the Search function with the following key terms to explore documents, images, audio and video clips, articles, and commentary related to the material in this chapter.

Andrew Jackson
Free Blacks
Abolitionism
Indian Removal Act
The Book of Mormon
Nat Turner
Texas Republic
Battle of the Alamo

Chapter 11

Panic and Boom, 1837–1845

IN 1837 the largest financial panic and depression the nation had ever experienced descended on the United States, with broad and immediate effects. The hard times shaped reform, literature, politics, slavery, westward migration, and foreign policy. Not surprisingly, these years of economic trouble also saw political turmoil and deep involvement by many aggrieved groups.

These hard years also saw the flowering of the reform spirit. Men and women energetically championed public education, abstinence from alcohol, anti-slavery, and a host of other improvements to American life. The popular press burgeoned, along with art, photography, and literature. A few leading thinkers articulated a bold and distinctive American philosophy, one that bore the marks of its tumultuous time.

Depression and Invention

The late 1830s and early 1840s produced a surprising mixture of bad and good economic news. The economy fell into prolonged depression, but at the same time, the creative energies of the American economy persisted. Courts and legislatures fostered an environment favorable to business while inventors and investors plunged ahead. To use a metaphor from the most important innovation of the time, the American economy kept one hand on the brake and the other on the throttle.

www http://ayersbrief.wadsworth.com

CHRONOLOGY

1837	Financial panic
	Charles River Bridge v. Warren Bridge decision
	Grimké sisters lecture to mixed audiences
	Elijah P. Lovejoy murdered in Alton, Illinois
	Horace Mann becomes first secretary of Massachusetts State Board of Education
	Ralph Waldo Emerson, "The American Scholar"
1838	John Quincy Adams successfully defeats attempt to annex Texas
1839	Depression worsens
	Daguerreotypes introduced to the United States
1840	Congress passes Independent Treasury Act
	Harrison elected president
	Frederick Douglass escapes from slavery
	American Anti-slavery Society splits
	Washingtonian temperance movement emerges
	James G. Birney runs for president as candidate for Liberty party
1841	Harrison dies; John Tyler becomes president
	Brook Farm founded
	California sees arrival of first wagon train
	Oregon fever
	P. T. Barnum opens the American Museum
	Amistad case heard before the Supreme Court
1842	Edgar Allan Poe, "The Murders in the Rue Morgue"
1843	Oregon sees arrival of first wagon trains
1844	Methodist Episcopal church divides over slavery
	James K. Polk claims the United States' claim to "all Oregon"
	Baltimore-Washington telegraph line
	Samuel F. B. Morse patents the telegraph
	Edgar Allan Poe, "The Raven"
1845	Texas and Florida admitted to the Union
	Baptist church divides over slavery

Panic and Depression

Andrew Jackson sought to leave a comfortable legacy to his hand-picked successor, Martin Van Buren, but even the inauguration ceremony in March 1837 accentuated the great disparities between the two men. Whereas Jackson's gaunt figure symbolized his sacrifices on the frontier and battlefield, Van Buren seemed the plump embodiment of a life spent in political office. Whereas Van Buren's inaugural speech inspired little enthusiasm in the crowd of 20,000, the mere sight of ex-President Jackson roused great cheers. Though Van Buren had been a principal architect of the so-called "spoils system," he replaced few officeholders on the lower levels of government and made few changes in Jackson's cabinet. The new president seemed content to carry on Jackson's work.

Within weeks of Van Buren's inauguration the American economy hit stormy waters. An unprecedented amount of silver poured into American banks in the mid-1830s, fueling rapid and sometimes dangerous investment. England demanded repayment of loans in specie just at the time that prices for American cotton declined because of record production. As a result, a major New Orleans cotton firm failed when it could not make its payments to British banks. That firm's failure, in turn, led to the closure of a number of banks that had loaned it money.

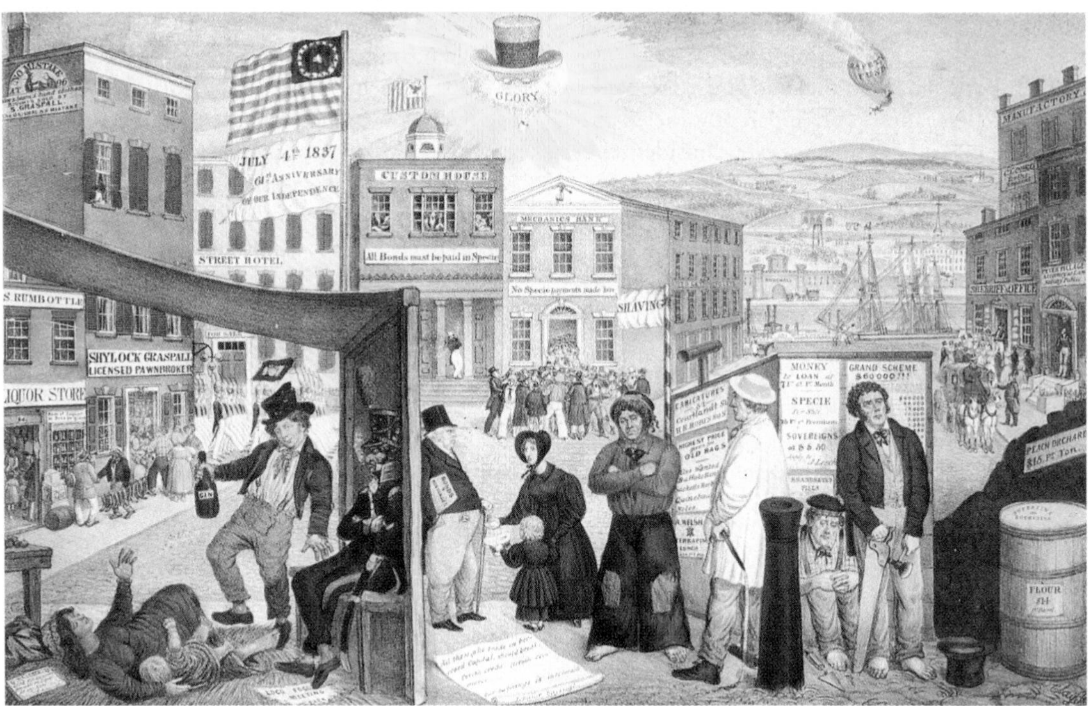

The irony of a Fourth of July celebration during hard times fills this cartoon, in which symbols of poverty and decay pile on one another. (Museum of the City of New York)

Despite the role of international trade in bringing on the crisis, many people blamed the problems on Jackson's banking policy, especially of accepting only specie, not paper money, for the purchase of public lands. They looked to Van Buren to lead the repeal of this strategy, but Jackson made it clear to Van Buren that he did not want to see his work undone. Delegations of merchants came to the White House to plead with Van Buren, but to no avail. A "run" began on the banks; customers withdrew a million dollars in specie in only two days in early May. The Panic of 1837 had begun. Soon it spread to every city of the country, to every region.

The panic quickly affected working people as well as the rich. Jobs dried up and many urban families had no idea of where they would get their next meal. In New York City, a poster warned that "Bread, Meat, Rent, Fuel—Their Prices Must Come Down. The Voice of the People Shall be Heard, and Will Prevail." Thousands of people gathered for a public meeting in the freezing weather. Told that a nearby warehouse held 50,000 barrels of flour, the protesters stormed the building; they took what they could and broke open hundreds of barrels more. The riots continued for days until the police managed to regain order.

The Panic of 1837 was followed by a better year in 1838, then by another panic in 1839. In the wake of that second panic, the stagnation of the economy spread more deeply and more widely, not ending until 1843. Labor unions weakened as workers grew afraid to risk their jobs. States' plans to finance canals, roads, and other public projects crashed. Several states defaulted on the bonds with which they intended to finance those improvements, leading furious European investors to shun American investments. Governors and legislators found themselves under attack from voters angry that the states had permitted themselves to go so far into debt.

Van Buren admitted that allowing state banks to hold federal funds had apparently fueled the speculation, but he would not even consider reinstating a national bank. Instead, he proposed what came to be known as the Sub-Treasury Plan or the Independent Treasury Plan. In that system, public funds would be disbursed by the secretary of the treasury as the economy seemed to dictate and banks would be kept out of the picture. It would be two more years before the plan passed, but by then it could do neither the country nor Martin Van Buren much good. The Whigs quickly won state-level offices and looked forward to harvesting more.

The Charles River Bridge Case

Even as the panic unfolded, some of the questions raised by the economic changes of the early 1830s worked their way through the American court system. The Charles River Bridge of Boston, for example, had been granted a franchise by the state legislature. The owners of the bridge charged a toll for everyone who crossed. As the population of Boston and Charlestown grew rapidly, so did the traffic and the tolls on the bridge. The bridge, which cost about $70,000 to build and improve, was bringing in $30,000 a year by the late 1820s. Another bridge also chartered by the state, the Warren Bridge, went up across the Charles, only 260 feet away. No sooner was the new bridge built than the traffic on the older bridge declined by more than half. The managers of the Charles River Bridge sued in court, claiming that their original charter implied a monopoly that the state had violated by building a competing bridge. Throughout the 1830s, the case proceeded to the U.S. Supreme Court and was heard in 1837.

The chief justice of the Supreme Court, Roger B. Taney, shared the Jacksonian animosity against monopolies. His decision regarding the *Charles River Bridge* case held that a state charter did not imply monopoly. Should old charters be permitted to hinder modern improvements, the country "would be obliged to stand still." The charters had perhaps been necessary in the past, he admitted, but by the 1830s such props no longer seemed necessary. Taney's decision in the *Charles River Bridge* reflected a growing consensus among Democrats and Whigs that older forms of economic privilege had to make way for innovation and investment.

Railroads

By the 1830s Americans had devised several means for dealing with the vast spaces of their continent. Thousands of miles of canals cut across the East while steamboats plied the waters of the North and South. Such means of transport, while cheap and dependable, remained relatively slow and limited in their reach. Inland cities longed for fast overland connections with the outside world and they knew of experiments with railroads in England and the United States over the last decade. When New Jersey sponsored a bold rail and canal connection between New York and Philadelphia in 1831, it ordered a custom-built locomotive from an English company—the *John Bull.* The railroad became an immediate success, carrying over 100,000 passengers in 1834.

American companies emulated and improved upon the English designs. By 1841, ten American railroad shops had sprung into existence. Those shops soon began changing the English designs, making the engines more powerful and the rails cheaper. Railroad companies quickly grew into some of the largest and most complex American businesses, employing hundreds of people and pioneering in management as well as engineering.

Railroads almost immediately became the key form of transportation in the United States. By 1840, American companies and states had built 3,300 miles of track; by 1850, the country claimed nearly 9,000 miles of railroad. The trains created whole new industries to serve them, as iron, coal, and steel burgeoned with the railroads' demand. The railroads consumed prodigious amounts of wood for their ties, trestles, and boil-

This locomotive in New York State, like its other early counterparts, pulled passenger cars based on old-fashioned carriages. The technology evolved quickly in the 1840s, however, and the United States played an important role in that evolution. (Collection of the Albany Institute of History & Art)

ers. They gave farmers quick and certain access to markets, and towns prospered or died depending on their rail connection.

Telegraph poles marched alongside the railroads, speeding the flow of information just as the railroads sped the flow of people and goods. Like the locomotive, the telegraph was the product of inventors in several different countries but received a major impetus from America. Samuel F. B. Morse patented his version of the electronic telegraph in 1840. Morse struggled with the invention for more than ten years, devising the code of dots and dashes that bears his name as well as ways to make the current travel farther. He finally received support from Congress in 1843, which invested $30,000 to run an experimental line from Washington to Baltimore. Following its success, the telegraph spread across the country with great speed.

CULTURAL FERMENT

A hunger for social—and self—improvement animated many Americans in the 1830s. People were fired by revivals and reform organizations. Some took practical routes to progress, focusing their efforts on schools and alcohol, whereas others explored philosophy and literature. Some used the new printing machinery of the age for entertainment, whereas others turn the fight against social evils. Each kind of cultural change amplified the others.

Public Schools

Many Americans had become dissatisfied with the way young people were schooled in the United States. No state had a statewide school system and local districts ran their own affairs, often wretchedly. The rich attended private schools or employed tutors, whereas the parents of poorer children had to sign oaths declaring themselves "paupers" before their children could benefit from charity schools. Parents from the middle classes, charged a fee according to the number of children they had, sent their offspring to schools often taught by untrained teachers. Hundreds of districts, especially in the South, created no schools at all. Many American children never went to school in the 1820s and 1830s and those who did often attended for only a short time.

Reformers argued that unequal and inadequate education would not suffice in America, a country dependent upon informed democracy. These reformers wanted free schools. Taxes and other state support would make it possible for all children to go to public schools. The rich would be more likely to send their children to such schools, reformers reasoned, if their tax dollars were supporting them; the poor would be more likely to send their children if they were not stigmatized as paupers. Buildings and teachers could be improved with the increased support.

A Massachusetts lawyer and Whig politician, Horace Mann, worked relentlessly to make rich citizens, especially manufacturers, see that a tax in support of schools was a wise investment. Think how much better workers would be, he argued, if they could read and calculate. Think to what good use women could be put as teachers, he argued, instilling their virtues of cooperation and peacefulness. Mann gradually persuaded influential people in Massachusetts of the practicability of common schools. In 1837, he became the first secretary of the Massachusetts Board of Education.

When Mann took over, many schools were in session for only a couple of months a year. He transformed that system during his tenure. The minimum school year stretched to six months, buildings and teacher training improved significantly, and teachers' pay increased by more than half.

Women teachers became common in the Northeast. Oberlin College in Ohio admitted women in 1837, making it the first coeducational institution in the country. Females attended new "normal schools" that provided teacher training; they read educational journals, underwent professional supervision, and taught with uniform textbooks. These standards spread throughout the North and the West in the 1840s and 1850s, as did McGuffey's Readers. These books, which sold an astonishing 9 million copies between 1836 and 1850, blended Christian piety and the virtues of hard work. Though each book aimed at a specific grade, the underlying message was always the same: "God has given you minds which are capable of indefinite improvement."

Transcendentalism

Leading thinkers saw the possibilities of improvement everywhere. Several of those thinkers came out of Unitarianism, a form of liberal Christianity especially strong in New England. Unitarianism encouraged people to emphasize feeling rather than doctrine. Several young people raised within the Unitarian church took these ideas further than their elders intended, rejecting much Christian doctrine. A belief in the literal truth of the Bible, these youthful critics argued, trapped religion in the past. Better to appeal directly to the heart from the very beginning. These thinkers wanted religion to transcend churches and denominations.

Women played an active role in this effort, with Margaret Fuller becoming especially important. Fuller had grown up in the Unitarian church in Cambridge, Massachusetts, receiving a fine education. But she felt herself adrift, full of "unemployed force," after her male classmates went on to college. She read widely and taught school with two other important figures in the revolt against Unitarianism: Elizabeth Peabody and Bronson Alcott. These three, like Horace Mann, believed that children were innately good and that education should be designed to let that goodness flourish. They argued that school, like church, should not be permitted to get in the way of people's natural connection with nature and with one another.

They soon took their lead from Ralph Waldo Emerson. Emerson had grown up around Concord, Massachusetts. Though descended from a distinguished ministerial family, he was raised by a widowed mother and forced to work his way through Harvard College. Uncomfortable as a minister and dissatisfied as a schoolteacher, Emerson set out for Europe. There he met exciting English intellectuals whose stirring ideas were to influence him deeply: Samuel Coleridge, Thomas Carlyle, and William Wordsworth. These writers provided Emerson with a perspective far removed from the cool Unitarianism on which he had been raised. Emerson perceived humankind as deeply tied to nature, filled with its rhythms and longings. He published such ideas in his first book,

Nature (1836), a work that gained him considerable attention from the like-minded young people of New England.

But it was Emerson's address before the Phi Beta Kappa initiates at Harvard in 1837 that announced his arrival to a larger audience. Emerson worried over the state of the nation after the Panic of 1837. The panic directly touched one of Emerson's friends in Concord, Henry David Thoreau, who graduated from Harvard in the panic year and could find no decent job. Emerson, older than Thoreau, had finally achieved some economic security in the summer of 1837 thanks to an inheritance, but he was well aware of the difficulties facing even the Phi Beta Kappa graduates of Harvard during August of that hard year.

Emerson titled his speech "The American Scholar." He argued that the scholar should be a man of action, a man of nature, a man of risk and endeavor. Books and poetry held tremendous power, Emerson admitted, but it was in activity, in striving, that the American scholar became truly American. It was time to set the teachings of Europe aside long enough to find America's own voice, Emerson told the graduates.

Emerson developed these ideas throughout the late 1830s, enjoying growing fame and influence through public lectures. Railroads made it feasible for the first time for speakers to cover a large amount of territory. Public speaking generally paid much better than any kind of writing. The growth of newspapers and other printing facilitated advertising, getting word of the lectures out beforehand and spreading summaries of the lectures to those unable to attend. People flocked to the lectures. In the lecture hall, Emerson exulted, "everything is admissible, philosophy, ethics, divinity, criticism, poetry, humor, fun, mimicry, anecdotes, jokes, ventriloquism. . . ."

Emerson's home in Concord became the gathering place for a group who came to be called the Transcendentalists, who sought to "transcend" the mundane into the mystical knowledge that every human possessed if he or she would listen to it. Margaret Fuller became the editor of the *Dial,* the Transcendentalist magazine, while Elizabeth Peabody opened a bookstore catering to the interests of the group. Bronson Alcott and about eighty others founded Brook Farm, one of the many utopian communities that tried to get off the ground in the 1830s and 1840s. Brook Farm put people to work in the fields in the morning and on their books in the afternoon. The community produced both crops and an impressive weekly newspaper. Its schools stood as examples of enlightened education. The experiment failed economically after a few years, but for a while Brook Farm offered the possibility of combining intellectual excitement, physical work, and social responsibility in a way the Transcendentalists craved.

Since the Transcendentalists believed that people should establish a close connection to nature, Henry David Thoreau decided to conduct an "experiment in human ecology." He wanted to see—and show—how a modern man could live in harmony with nature. In 1845, he built an isolated house in the woods near Walden Pond, carefully calculating the cost of nails and other supplies and keeping a thoughtful journal. He strove to be self-sufficient and self-contained. The experiment proved important for the book Thoreau eventually published about his experience, *Walden: Life in the Woods* (1854).

Art and Popular Culture

The Transcendentalists were not alone in their craving for intensity. American painters found an increasing audience for their works in the 1830s. The United States had never been very receptive to figurative art. Wealthy people bought portraits, but most other Americans had no pictures at all in their homes. Talented young painters born in the United States generally had to travel to Europe for their training and often for their livings as well. This began to change, however, as Americans developed more of a taste for painting.

Thomas Cole was the key figure in the emergence of American painting. Though born in England, he came to the Ohio frontier as a small child. Cole taught himself to paint but went to England and Italy to perfect his art. He returned to the village of Catskill in New York to paint the Hudson River Valley in the late 1830s and early 1840s. Soon, other painters, such as Asher Durand and Frederick Church, joined Cole in their fascination with the stirring American landscape, creating what became known as the Hudson River School.

Cole also turned to richly symbolic allegorical painting. His journey to Europe had struck him by its contrasts, "both the ruined towers that tell of outrage, and the gorgeous temples that speak of ostentation." He believed America, by contrast, "to be the abode of virtue." He embodied his notions of the cycles of civilization and personal life in two powerful allegorical series, *The Course of Empire* and *The Voyage of Life*. Engravings of these series became popular fixtures in American homes.

Other important artists followed their own paths through the American landscape. George Catlin spent much of the 1830s living among the American Indians of the Great Plains, making hundreds of drawings and paintings. In Catlin's paintings Easterners thought they might catch the last glimpse of a disappearing people. Audiences could also view vanishing wildlife in the remarkable watercolors of John James Audubon. Audubon, born in Haiti and educated in France, settled on the Kentucky frontier as a merchant after he married. He loved the American wilderness too much to stay in his shop, though, and he launched out on daunting journeys to record the environment and appearance of the birds of the young nation. After ten years of work Audubon produced *The Birds of America, from Original Drawings, with 435 Plates Showing 1,065 Figures* in four immense volumes, completing the project in 1838.

The most famous artistic production of antebellum America was a statue: Hiram Powers' *The Greek Slave,* completed in 1846. Powers grew up in the raw country of Ohio but moved to Italy as he prospered. There, Powers sculpted his statue of a nude young woman bound in chains. The young woman represented, Powers said, a Greek girl captured by the Turks in the Greco-Turkish war. As such, she represented Christianity and whiteness, unbowed by the evil and darkness surrounding her. Powers sought, and received, the endorsement of a group of American clergymen, removing any qualms audiences might have. *The Greek Slave* served as the model for hundreds of miniature copies that appeared in the drawing rooms of the finest homes.

The same drawing rooms also contained a novelty of the age: daguerreotypes. This form of photography developed in France but arrived in

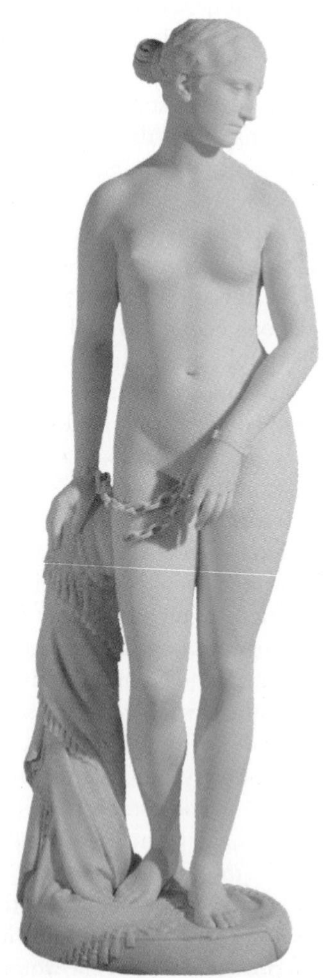

Hiram Power's The Greek Slave *became an American sensation, attracting large crowds and many imitators.* (The Newark Museum/Art Resource, NY)

the United States soon after its creation. Within a few years, more than eighty young photographers practiced their craft in New York City alone. This early photography was cumbersome and required long periods of stillness before the camera, but the American people hurried to studios to have their portraits done.

Engravings based on paintings and photographs soon filled the publications coming off the presses. For the first time, illustrations could be produced cheaply. Not only did the abolitionists and other reformers use these techniques to great effect, but so did a religious movement, the Millerites, who believed that signs in the Bible foretold the Day of Judgment in 1844. To spread the word, they published 4 million pieces of literature.

Seeing the opportunity afforded by this emergence of a popular audience for print, American writers worked hard to fill the hunger. One especially gifted author, Edgar Allan Poe, skillfully navigated between the market and his art. Poe wrote short stories, the kind of writing most in demand, but he brought to the form a kind of self-consciousness few had demonstrated before. Poe tapped into a widespread fascination with the occult, seances, and ghosts, filling his work with ruins, shadows, and legends. Works such as "The Murders in the Rue Morgue" marked the first appearance of the detective story. Throughout the hard decade of the 1840s Poe published stories such as "The Masque of the Red Death," "The Pit and the Pendulum," and "The Tell-Tale Heart" and poetry such as "The Raven." Plagued by ill health, however, Poe did not survive the decade.

A very different kind of entrepreneur, P. T. Barnum, a Connecticut storekeeper turned newspaper editor turned purveyor of popular entertainment, opened his American Museum in New York in 1841. Barnum displayed oddities that strained the limits of belief but that could not be completely disproved. Unlike earlier museums, Barnum's museum frankly offered entertainment, including magicians and midgets such as the famous Tom Thumb. The fact that the "curiosities" were often attacked as fakes by scientists did not seem to deter visitors: Barnum's American Museum flourished for the next twenty years.

The Washingtonians

Americans had long waged campaigns against intemperance, but in the depression years of the late 1830s and early 1840s the fight against drink took on a new urgency. Whereas earlier temperance movements had mainly enlisted those who were already opposed to alcohol, the new movement marked an effort by drinkers to reform themselves. Earlier attempts at temperance had often pitted middle- and upper-class reformers against members of the working class, but the new movement grew among people in the lower ranks of American society. Older reform attempts had been largely the efforts of men, but now women became active. The Washingtonian movement, named in honor of George Washington, gave these efforts great force and visibility.

The Washingtonians began in Baltimore in 1840, when six drinkers pledged to one another to quit drinking and to persuade other drinkers to do the same. Word of the new movement quickly spread up the eastern seaboard, and by 1843 the Washingtonians claimed millions of adherents. Partly as a result of the new organization, Americans' consumption of alcohol plummeted in the 1840s.

"Martha Washington" societies, for women only, grew rapidly, challenging the men's movement both in size and in fervor. These female temperance advocates were not well-to-do ladies stooping to help the fallen, but rather the wives of artisans and small businessmen. They helped families in distress to get back on their feet. They also provided a new edge to the temperance crusade, reminding men that drunkenness was more often than not a male failing and that it was the wives and children of drunkards who suffered most from their neglect, cruelty, and even violence.

Abolitionism

By the late 1830s the American Anti-slavery Society claimed over a quarter of a million members. The same lecture circuits that carried general-interest speakers such as Ralph Waldo Emerson also carried abolitionists. The first female abolitionist speakers—the Grimké sisters, Angelina and Sarah—were prize recruits into the anti-slavery ranks, for they were the daughters of a prominent South Carolina slave-owning planter. By telling New England audiences of their own experiences with slavery, the Grimkés held a credibility that white northern abolitionists could not match. In 1837, the Grimkés decided to exert their power in a new forum by lecturing to mixed audiences of men and women. Although some people strenuously objected to such an elevation of women in the public sphere, the Grimkés spoke to over 40,000 people in nine months in 1837 and 1838.

As it grew stronger, the anti-slavery cause met with more determined opposition. When abolitionist Elijah P. Lovejoy offended readers of his religious paper in St. Louis—denouncing a local judge who prevented the trial of a mob who had burned a black man alive—citizens of Alton, Illinois, invited Lovejoy to move to their town. Alton prided itself on being a progressive place, but soon some prominent members of the community, angered at Lovejoy's paper for its dissemination of "the highly odious doctrines of modern Abolitionism," held a public meeting demanding that he quit printing such ideas. Lovejoy only intensified his attacks on slavery. Mobs destroyed two of Lovejoy's presses, but he persisted. In November, a mob killed Lovejoy and shattered his press.

Abolitionists debated the proper response to such opposition. William Lloyd Garrison counseled his allies to offer no resistance to violence. He and his supporters renounced all allegiance to the established parties and churches, which had long since shown themselves tolerant of slavery. Other abolitionists, by contrast, used whatever means they could to bring slavery to an end, including political parties.

The differences among the abolitionists came to a head at the annual meeting of the American Anti-slavery Society in 1839. They differed most visibly in their attitudes toward the role of women. Women constituted perhaps half of all members of the anti-slavery organizations, but some male abolitionists sought to keep females in a subordinate role. Unable to resolve their differences, the abolitionists split. The more conservative group, based in New York, created the Liberty party to run a candidate for president in the upcoming election of 1840. Garrison's organization maintained a more radical stance on the role of women and the strategies through which abolition should be pursued.

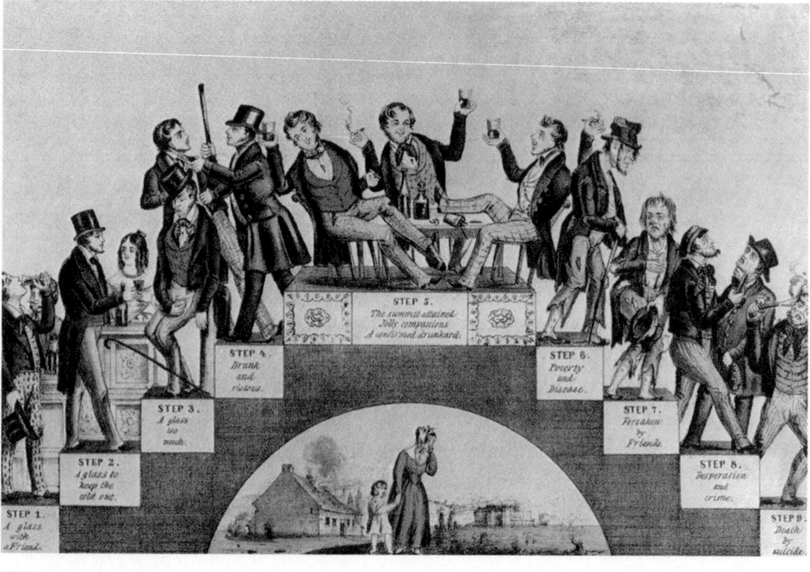

Temperance advocates called for total abstinence from drink, demonstrating in illustrations such as this that the very first drink could lead to crime and even suicide. (From the Collections of the Library of Congress)

Whatever their differences, abolitionists barraged Congress with petitions demanding that slavery be ended in the District of Columbia. Former President John Quincy Adams, now a congressman from Massachusetts, used all his parliamentary skill to fight the gag rule that prevented Congress from recognizing anti-slavery petitions; he finally succeeded in getting it overthrown in 1845. Adams also successfully defended Africans who had seized a slave ship bound for Cuba, the *Amistad,* and landed in Connecticut. Supported by a large network of abolitionists, Adams took the case before the U.S. Supreme Court and won not only the acquittal of the Africans for murdering the ship's captain but their freedom as well.

Black anti-slavery speakers greatly strengthened the anti-slavery cause. Speakers such as Henry Brown, Henry Bibb, Solomon Northup, Sojourner Truth, Harriet Tubman, and Ellen Craft electrified audiences. Slavery, they made clear, was nothing like the benign institution portrayed by its defenders.

Although white abolitionists valued the contributions of their black compatriots, they urged black speakers not to make too much of a fuss when confronted with the insults and indignities faced by black people in the North. African American abolitionists chafed under the restrictions they faced from fellow reformers and enemies alike; they demanded greater rights for northern as well as southern blacks. Their experiences showed the extent to which race was a national problem.

One of the most remarkable Americans of the nineteenth century burst into visibility in the early 1840s. Frederick Douglass had grown up in Maryland. Like other places in the upper South, Maryland's economy was diversifying in the 1830s and 1840s as commerce intensified and railroads spread. Douglass learned to read from his mistress, though it was against the law for her to teach him. He carried with him a copy of *Webster's Spelling Book* and *The Columbian Orator,* a book of speeches, including a slave's persuasive argument with his master to set him free.

Sent to Baltimore by his owner, Douglass worked in the shipyards, continued to read widely, and plotted his freedom. After several attempts at escape, Douglass finally borrowed the papers of a free black sailor and rode a train to freedom. Douglass found himself in New York City, alone and without any notion of what he should do. A runaway slave might be hunted down by a slavecatcher for a reward. Fortunately for Douglass, he met a black man who introduced the young runaway to the New York Anti-slavery Society. After white abolitionists saw the skill with which he spoke, they sent Douglass to travel throughout the North with William Lloyd Garrison.

One of the most influential and famous Americans of the nineteenth century, Frederick Douglass fought tirelessly against slavery and in favor of a wide range of social reforms. (The Granger Collection, New York)

THE SLAVE SOUTH

The South was an integral part of the United States throughout these years. Southern cotton drove much of the economy, southern politicians held much of the power, and southern concerns guided much foreign policy. The South was a prosperous place for white people, whose average per capita incomes compared favorably with those of northern whites. Thanks to the rapid expansion of newspapers and the telegraph, white Southerners took part in all the national conversations about race, slavery, and politics. The growing connections between the regions, in fact, emphasized the differences between the North and the South. As people in each region read the hard words those across the Mason-Dixon line frequently said about them, their distrust of one another grew. As increasing numbers of people such as Frederick Douglass escaped to the North, Northerners became ever more aware of their region's complicity in perpetuating slavery. Even as the two societies developed along similar lines, their single profound difference became ever more potent.

African Americans and the South

By the 1830s, slavery had spread over an enormous area stretching from Maryland to Texas. The decade had seen the domestic slave trade grow at a feverish rate, for the new planters of Mississippi, Alabama, and Louisiana eagerly imported slaves to clear land and plant cotton. By the time of the Panic of 1837, Alabama, Mississippi, and Louisiana grew more than half the nation's cotton. American slavery became ever more diverse as it expanded. Enslaved people

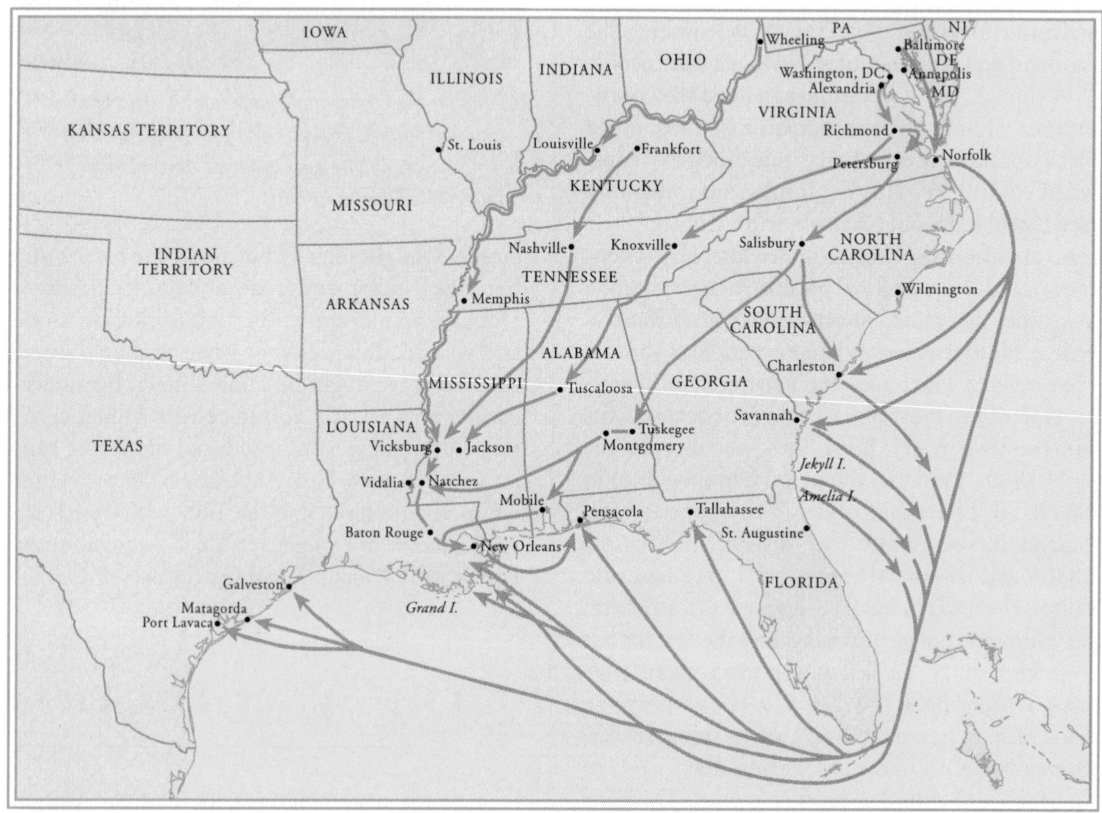

MAP 11.1 | PATHS OF THE SLAVE TRADE

worked in hemp, wheat, rice, corn, sugar, and tobacco fields as well as cotton. They worked with livestock and racehorses, practiced carpentry and blacksmithing, and labored on the docks of New Orleans, Mobile, and Memphis and in the shipyards of Baltimore. Some slaves lived where their families had dwelled for generations; others cleared new land along the Mississippi frontier. Some knew the white people among whom they lived quite well; others belonged to absolute strangers. Some worked in large groups of black people; others worked alone or beside whites.

Southern culture mixed English, African, Scots-Irish, Caribbean, French, Indian, and Hispanic sources into a rich and complex blend. Language, food, music, and religion took on new shapes as black and white cultures interacted. In the meantime, African Americans prided themselves on the stories, songs, and dances they knew to be particularly their own, on the styles of the baskets, quilts, and clothes they sewed, or the way they carried themselves. Black culture remained distinct and vibrant even as it influenced the larger American culture.

African American families tended to rely on a broader range of kin than did white families. Grandparents, aunts, and uncles often played significant roles in child rearing in black families. When people of actual blood relation were unavailable, southern slaves created "fictive kin," friends and neighbors given honorary titles of "brother" or "aunt" and treated as such. These arrangements permitted slave families considerable resiliency and variety.

Enslaved Americans generally lived in a relatively small community of others. About a quarter of all held in slavery lived on farms with fewer than nine slaves, whereas another quarter lived on the 3 percent of southern plantations that held more than fifty slaves. The remaining half lived on plantations with somewhere between ten and forty-nine bondspeople. African Americans often found wives or husbands on nearby farms, visiting one another on evenings and weekends.

Plantations and Farms

White slaveowners in the American South tended to live on the same plantation as their slaves, but wealthier whites put day-to-day control of their plantations in the hands of professional overseers. These overseers were often ambitious young men of middling background who used the overseer position as a stepping stone to their own plantation. Slaves could and did appeal to the owner if they thought the overseer unfair. Since a master might indeed trust a well-known slave more than a new overseer, the position involved tact as well as brute force.

On larger plantations, where slaves often worked in groups called gangs, trusted male slaves served as "drivers." Such drivers tended to be especially strong and skilled, commanding respect from whites as well as blacks. Although whites held the ultimate threat of force, they much preferred to keep the work moving smoothly, with as little trouble as possible. The driver could help both sides, protecting fellow slaves from abuse and assuring that the work got done efficiently. Drivers frequently found themselves caught between the two competing sets of demands, however, and slaves often resented or even hated drivers.

Chart 11.1 African Americans in the Slave States, 1860

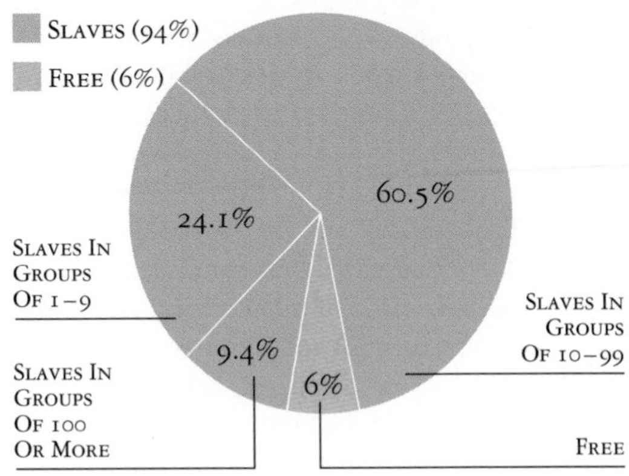

About three out of four enslaved people worked mainly in the fields. Almost all of them went to the fields during the peak times. Women, who worked in the fields alongside men, also served in the house as cooks and domestics. Slaves were well known for controlling the pace of work, reporting their tools broken or "lost" when they were forced to work too fast or too long. They traditionally had Sundays to garden for themselves, do their domestic chores, or hunt.

Slaves' lives were by no means simple. Lines of power often became complicated and tangled on plantations and farms, with masters, mistresses, sons, overseers, and drivers claiming authority. Slaves tended to work at several different jobs over the course of the year. Some slaves were respected as purveyors of healing or religious knowledge from Africa; some slaves were admired for their musical ability; others won recognition for their ability to read and preach the Gospel. These abilities did not always correspond with the opinions of whites, who frequently underestimated the abilities and character of the people among whom they lived.

Whites told themselves that they provided, "their people" a better life than they would have known in Africa. Indeed, southern masters explained the justice of slavery to themselves and to the North by stressing their Christian stewardship for the slaves. As one clergyman wrote to his fellow slaveholders in the early 1840s, slaves "were placed under our control . . . not exclusively for our benefit but theirs also."

Throughout the 1830s and 1840s, southern slaveholders and ministers prided themselves on their Christian mission to the slaves. Most masters would not permit their slaves to learn to read, but they did arrange to have Bible selections read to their slaves. Although many slaves eagerly accepted the Gospel in the white-dominated churches, others resented the obvious and shallow uses the masters made of the sermons, telling the slaves to accept their lot and to refrain from stealing food. Such slaves displayed their deepest religious feelings only in their own worship, in the secret meetings in brush arbors and cabins in the slave quarters. There, they prayed to be free and to be united in heaven with those they loved.

Largely oblivious to the lives their slaves led beyond their sight, masters pointed to the physical condition of the slaves as evidence of their concern for "their people." Compared with slaves in other places in the hemisphere, it was true, those of the American South were relatively well-fed and free of disease. They had limited and monotonous diets, but generally consumed enough nutrients. Slaves received ineffective or dangerous health care, their houses were small and drafty, and their clothing was limited to a few rough garments per year, but none of these conditions endangered slaves' physical survival. Slaves in the United States, working in relatively healthy settings and benefiting from a balanced ratio between men and women, generally lived longer than their counterparts elsewhere in the hemisphere.

On the other hand, many slaveowners did not refrain from having their slaves whipped on small provocation, branded, shackled, or locked up in sweltering enclosures; slave women suffered sexual abuse. Partly because expectant mothers were often kept in the fields until the last minute, about a third of all black babies died before they reached their first birthday. American slavery, whatever ameliorating features it might have had, compared to slavery elsewhere was a harsh institution.

The Politics of the White South

In the South as in the North, the Whigs portrayed themselves as the party of progress and prosperity. The lawyers, editors, and merchants who set up shop in the hamlets and towns of the South proved receptive to such views. The young men who followed such professions eagerly joined organizations such as the Masons, temperance groups, and political parties. They prided themselves on their broad views of national issues. In their eyes, only the Whigs reflected such enlightened perspectives. The large planters on the richest lands were also attracted to the Whigs. The Whigs drew, too, on the farmers in the mountains of the Upper South, men determined to develop connections to outside markets.

The Democrats, on the other hand, found their strongest supporters among the middling farmers and planters of the South. These men tended to be resentful of the taxes on their lands and slaves. They admired the Democrats' aggressive approach to removing the American Indians and to expanding in the West. Southerners distrustful of Northerners and of commerce found the minimal-government pronouncements of the Democrats appealing.

In the South both the Whigs and the Democrats declared themselves the friends of southern slavery, but they differed in their emphases. The Democrats pledged that they would protect slavery by extending the power of the government as little as possible. The Whigs, on the other hand, argued that the best way to protect slavery was for the South to build strong economic and political bridges to the North even as they put a Southerner in the White House.

The Challenge of the West

Americans of every sort kept their eyes to the west. Railroads, telegraphs, canals, and roads strained in that direction; population restlessly flowed there. But thoughtful people recognized that the lack of borders and limits posed threats as well as potential. When everything seemed possible, people placed few checks on their appetites. Every boundary was contested, every obstacle attacked.

The Election of 1840

The Whigs should have faced an easy contest in 1840. Much of the nation remained mired in depression. Van Buren offered little effective leadership during the economic crisis and many people held him to blame for the hard times. But the Whigs were not as strong as they might have been. Their party had been built piece by piece in the 1830s in reaction to Andrew Jackson. As a result, the party was a crazy-quilt of interests and factions. In 1836, the party had even permitted three candidates to run against Van Buren because no one man could command the party's full allegiance. Party leaders vowed that they would not let the same thing happen in 1840.

The Whigs were determined to find the one man who stood for the common beliefs that unified Whigs beneath their surface differences. Those beliefs turned around faith in commerce, self-control, Protestantism, learning, and self-improvement. Most important, the Whigs wanted to make an active response to the depression plaguing the nation by putting money in circulation, building internal improvements, and strengthening banks. The trick was to find a candidate who embodied their beliefs without appearing to be "aristocratic" or hungry for power.

The Whigs found such a man in William Henry Harrison. Harrison had made his name as a general—most notably in his defeat of an Indian confederacy in the Battle of Tippecanoe in 1811—and later served in the House of Representatives and in the Senate. He had won fame without gathering many political liabilities and was identified with no particular position.

The Whigs sought to balance their ticket with Senator John Tyler of Virginia. Tyler shared few beliefs with his fellow Whigs, but his embrace of slavery helped mollify Southerners. Moreover, his name made a nice pairing in the phrase that soon became famous: "Tippecanoe and Tyler, Too." One Whig warned that the combination of Harrison and Tyler had "rhyme, but no reason in it."

The Democrats were relieved that the Whigs had nominated Harrison. Democrats considered the old general a nonentity; one reporter commented sarcastically that if Harrison were merely given some hard cider and a small pension he would contentedly sit out the rest of his days in a log cabin. (He actually lived in a mansion and was a rich man.) The sarcasm backfired, though,

ALEXIS DE TOCQUEVILLE, *DEMOCRACY IN AMERICA* 1840

A young French nobleman, Tocqueville came to the United States to observe democracy in action. In the great book from which this selection is drawn, the sympathetic Tocqueville notes a central paradox of American life; all except slaves are free in virtually every facet of their lives and yet that freedom does not seem to bring happiness. Instead, it generates constant anxiety and a ceaseless yearning, as few seem able to grasp all that they can see.

. . .

In America I saw the freest and most enlightened men, placed in the happiest circumstances which the world affords; it seemed to me as if a cloud habitually hung upon their brow, and I thought them serious and almost sad even in their pleasures.

. . .

A native of the United States clings to this world's goods as if he were certain never to die; and he is so hasty in grasping at all within his reach, that one would suppose he was constantly afraid of not living long enough to enjoy them. He clutches everything, he holds nothing fast, but soon loosens his grasp to pursue fresh gratifications.

In the United States a man builds a house to spend his latter years in it, and he sells it before the roof is on; he plants a garden, and lets it [rents] just as the trees are coming into bearing; he brings a field into tillage, and leaves other men to gather the crops; he embraces a profession, and gives it up; he settles in a place, which he soon afterward leaves, to carry his changeable longings elsewhere. If his private affairs leave him any leisure, he instantly plunges into the vortex of politics; and if at the end of a year of unremitting labor he finds he has a few days' vacation, his eager curiosity whirls him over the vast extent of the United States, and he will travel fifteen hundred miles in a few days, to shake off his happiness. Death at length overtakes him, but it is before he is weary of his bootless chase of that complete felicity which is for ever on the wing.

Among democratic nations men easily attain a certain equality of conditions; they can never attain the equality they desire. It perpetually retires from before them, yet without hiding itself from their sight, and in retiring draws them on. At every moment they think they are about to grasp it; it escapes at every moment from their hold. They are near enough to see its charms, but too far off to enjoy them; and before they have fully tasted its delights, they die. . . .

SOURCE Alexis de Tocqueville, *Democracy in America,* Vol. II (Boston: C. C. Little & J. Brown, 1841), Second Book, Ch. 13.

for many Americans saw log cabins and home-brewed cider as evidence of American virtue and self-reliance. The Whigs, long frustrated at their reputation as snobs and elitists, seized on hard cider and log cabins as symbols of their party's loyalty to the common American.

All over the country, Whig speakers displayed paintings, signs, flags, and models of log cabins while freely dispensing cider to thirsty crowds. Harrison himself went out on the campaign trail, the first presidential candidate to do so. A new kind of American political style was being forged. For the first time, women became prominent at these rallies, encouraging their husbands, fathers, and suitors with smiles and waving kerchiefs. The Whigs embraced causes many women supported, such as temperance and allegiance to the church.

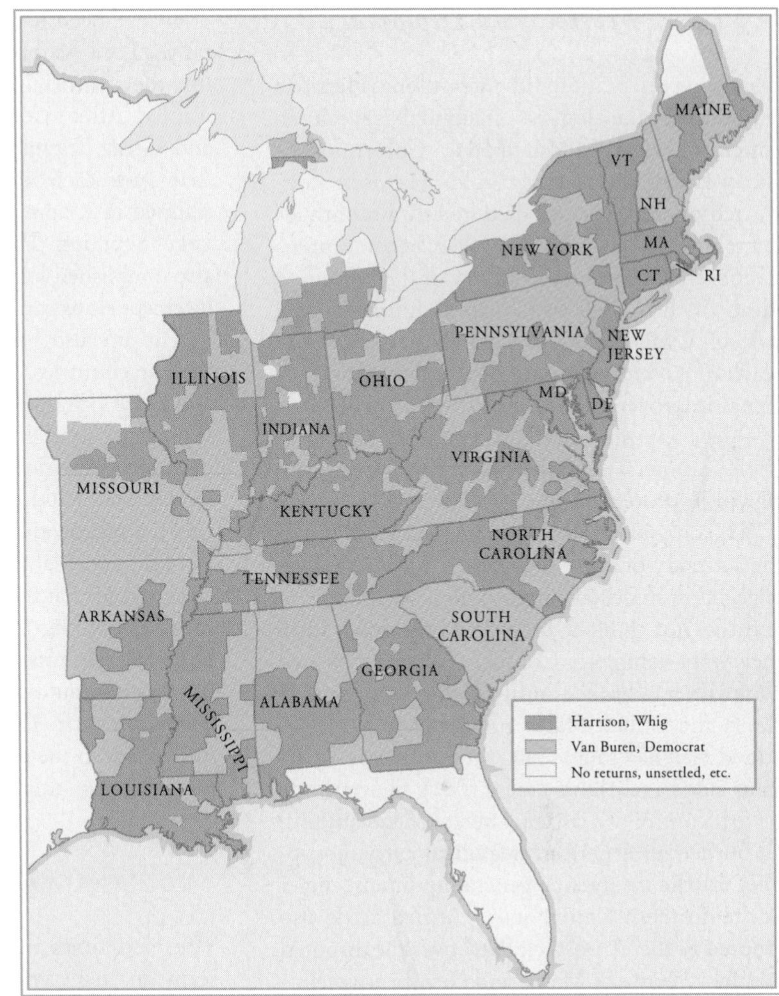

MAP 11.2 | THE ELECTION OF 1840

The Democrats had no idea of how to respond to the hard cider and log cabin campaign. Martin Van Buren proved an easy target for a Whig campaign that emphasized homespun values. The president's portly figure and penchant for silk vests and doeskin gloves made the Democrats' long-standing claims of representing the common man look hypocritical. Andrew Jackson himself came out to campaign, firing the same charges against the Whigs that had worked so well in the past, charges of elitism, hostility to slavery, and softness on the bank issue. Even these charges failed. Harrison won nineteen of the twenty-six states, bringing about half a million new voters to the Whigs. Voter turnout surged to a level almost unimaginable just a decade earlier: Eight of every ten eligible voters went to the polls. After 1840, elections would demand the combination of active campaigning, the search for potent symbols, and boisterous public displays that had proven so successful in that year.

Tyler, Webster, and Diplomacy

The Whig celebration did not last long. Harrison expounded the longest inaugural speech in American history in March 1841. Unfortunately, the weather was bitterly cold; Harrison contracted pneumonia and died exactly a month after taking office. John Tyler had become president even though he shared few of the prevailing ideals of the Whigs in Congress. Efforts on the part of Whig leaders to expand the power and reach of government with tariffs, banks, and internal improvements proved fruitless in the face of Tyler's opposition. All but one of the members of the cabinet Tyler inherited from Harrison resigned in protest.

The only member to stay on, Daniel Webster, the secretary of state, did so only because he was engaged in important negotiations with England and did not think it proper to step down until they were complete. Conflicts between the two countries had broken out over the boundary between the United States and Canada. In 1837, armed men had fought along the border as Americans aided a rebel movement trying to overthrow British control of Canada; later, a Canadian militia burned an American steamboat carrying supplies for the insurgents, generating intense anger in the northern United States. Armed battle also erupted in the "Aroostock War" over the disputed boundary between Maine and New Brunswick.

Conflict had long been building between the British and the Americans, too, over the African slave trade. Great Britain insisted that its vessels be permitted to search American ships off the coast of Africa to prevent the transportation of slaves to British colonies. Americans resented the intrusion in its affairs and refused. The issue threatened to explode in 1841, when American slaves seized the slaving ship the *Creole,* which was taking them from Virginia to New Orleans. The slaves steered the vessel to the Bahamas and claimed their freedom under British law. Much to the anger of southern whites, the British gave sanctuary to the slaves.

Daniel Webster met with the British representative, Lord Ashburton, to settle these issues before they flamed up into a war that neither nation wanted. After extensive debate, the United States and Great Britain decided on a new boundary that gave each about half of what they had claimed in Maine and in the area to the west of Lake Superior. The Webster-Ashburton Treaty also established joint American-British patrols to intercept ships carrying slaves from Africa.

Oregon also had troubled relations between the two countries. In the 1820s the United States and Great Britain had signed treaties with Russia, setting the southern boundary of Russia's claims in North America at 54°40′. As a result, the United States and Britain shared the Oregon Territory, a vast region covering present-day Oregon, Washington, Idaho, and British Columbia. Both sides agreed that the 49th parallel would be a reasonable dividing line. Depending on where the boundary line was drawn, either the British or the Americans would possess Puget Sound, a coveted deepwater port. The British let the issue remain unresolved in the early 1840s so that other, more pressing issues might be settled.

The "Wests"

The hard times in the East made moving west seem an increasingly attractive option. Horace Greeley, the most influential newspaper editor of the day, warned people looking for a job in the midst of the depression not to come to the city but rather to "go to the Great West." To people in New England, migration to the West in the 1840s often meant migration to the lands of the northern plains and surrounding the Great Lakes. To people from Virginia and Kentucky, migration to the West might mean heading to the free states of Ohio, Indiana, or Illinois or, more often, to Mississippi, Louisiana, and Texas. For people from the cities of the East, the destination might be a booming new city such as Indianapolis, Chicago, or Detroit.

One "West" that captured the imagination of Americans in these years lay in Oregon and California, word of whose beauty and wealth had slowly filtered east throughout the preceding decade. Although many people considered it nothing less than suicide to attempt to cross the Rockies and what was considered "The Great American Desert," a growing stream of families decided to take the chance. Most of those who moved to the Pacific coast gathered in northern Missouri or southern Iowa. They set out in early May across undulating plains, with water and firewood easy to find, their wagons pulled by oxen. The settlers gradually ascended to Fort Laramie, at the edge of the Rockies. By July, they had reached the Continental Divide, the point at which rivers on one side flowed to the east and those on the other flowed to the west. On the trail for more than three months by this point, the settlers had covered two-thirds of the distance of their journey.

From the Divide, the settlers heading to California split off from those going to Oregon. Both faced enormous difficulties in the remainder of their trip. They raced the weather, for early mountain snowstorms could be deadly. Some of the mountainous areas were so steep that wagons had to be dragged up one side and let down the other with ropes, chains, and pulleys. Finally, by October, 2,000 miles and six months after they had left Missouri or Iowa, the settlers crossed one last ridge and looked down on the sparkling valleys of Sacramento or the Willamette River.

Migration to the Pacific began slowly, with only a few dozen families making the treacherous journey between 1840 and 1842. The numbers mounted between 1843 and 1845, when over 5,000 people passed through Utah on their way to Oregon and California. Throughout the 1840s, the great majority of migrants chose Oregon over California as their destination. Oregon came to seem a respectable place for literate and upright Protestant families to settle whereas California seemed a gamble, attractive mainly to single men willing to take their chances in a boom economy that could go bust.

Manifest Destiny

In 1842, the Great United States Exploring Expedition returned from a journey of 87,780 nautical miles. It had circumnavigated the globe, located Antarctica, and explored the Pacific coast. The captain of the expedition reported that Oregon was a treasure trove of "forests, furs, and fisheries." If the United States did not use its military to occupy the territory all the way to the 54°40′ boundary, it would be risking much more than the Oregon territory itself. California might throw off the light Mexican rule under which it rested and join with an independent Oregon to create a nation "that is destined to control the destinies of the Pacific." The Tyler administration sought to downplay this report, not wanting to disrupt negotiations still pending on the boundary of Maine and Wisconsin.

The forces of expansion proved too strong for the administration to contain, however. In 1845, newspaper editor John Louis O'Sullivan announced that it was the "manifest destiny"—the clear and unavoidable fate—of the United States "to overspread the continent allotted by Providence for the free development of our yearly multiplying millions." In other words, God intended white Americans to fill in every corner of the continent, pushing aside American Indians, Mexicans, English, or anyone else.

The Democrats in Congress and President Tyler supported this expansion, focusing first on Texas. If the United States did not quickly annex Texas, Democrats believed, it might fall under the sway of the British and become not only a barrier to further American migration but also a bastion of anti-slavery. If, by contrast, the United States acted quickly, Texas could attract not only slaveholders and their slaves but also emancipated slaves, keeping them away from the North and the other attractive lands such as California and Oregon. Midwestern Democrats, for their part, agreed that expansion was essential to the American future. The country simply could not afford to have major ports and potential markets sealed off. These Democrats had their eye on Oregon.

James K. Polk, a former governor of Tennessee, got the Democratic nomination for president after an acrimonious convention and nine ballots. The Democrats appealed to both Northerners and Southerners with a program of aggressive expansion, attempting to counter fears of slavery's growth not by rejecting Texas but by embracing Oregon.

The Election of 1844

In 1844, the Whigs nominated Henry Clay for president on a program explicitly opposed to expansion. The apparently clear-cut choice between Clay and Polk soon became complicated, however. Clay announced that he would not oppose Texas annexation if it could be done peacefully and by consensus. Such a strategy backfired, attracting few advocates of expansion but alienating anti-slavery people in the North.

Meanwhile, the early 1840s witnessed bloody battles over religion. A growing stream of immigrants from Ireland, the great majority of them Catholic, flowed into northern cities. In Protestant eyes, the Roman Catholic church posed a direct threat to American institutions. That church's hierarchy was undemocratic, critics charged. In 1844 the largest anti-Catholic riot of antebellum America broke out in Philadelphia; several Catholic churches burned to the ground while authorities stood by. Because the Democrats proved far more sympathetic to the Irish than did the largely Protestant Whigs, the political differences between the parties now became inflamed with ethnic conflict.

Slavery, too, became an even more explosive issue in the early 1840s. In 1844 the Methodist church divided over slavery and the Baptists split the following year. Southern church leaders were angry that many of their northern brethren refused to believe that American slavery was part of God's plan. Five hundred thousand Southerners formed the Methodist Episcopal Church, South, while Baptists from nine southern states created the Southern Baptist Convention.

The conflicts over slavery exerted immediate political consequences. The abolitionist Liberty party won 62,000 voters in 1844. In New York, in fact, the Liberty party's strong showing took enough votes from Clay to give the state to Polk. And those electoral votes proved the difference in the national election, as Polk won the presidency by the narrowest of margins.

Even before Polk took office the Senate voted to annex Texas, an independent republic since 1836, as soon as Texas consented. Texas gave its approval in the fall of 1845 and won its vote in Washington at the end of that year. The Democrats sought to quiet concerns among Northerners by also annexing Oregon. Though some Americans clamored for all of Oregon to its northernmost boundary with Russian territory, chanting "Fifty-four Forty or Fight," neither the United States nor the British proved eager to fight. The boundary was soon set at the 49th parallel, an extension of the northern U.S. boundary from the east.

CONCLUSION

The years between 1837 and 1845 bore the imprint of the largest economic depression in the nation's history up to that time. The depression upset what had appeared to be a Democratic stranglehold on the presidency, making Martin Van Buren appear ineffectual. Widespread dissatisfaction with the Democrats' handling of the economy laid the foundation for the remarkable Whig victory of 1840, when William Henry Harrison—and Tyler, too—campaigned under the banner of the log cabin and cider. The depression also drove settlers to the West and drove politicians to focus the energies and anxieties of the country on faraway opportunities and dangers.

In a seeming paradox, these same years witnessed American culture at its most ebullient. Painters, philosophers, and poets spoke in a confident new American vernacular. Reformers pushed hard for improvements in education, temperance, anti-slavery, and much else. Popular culture such as novels, magazines, and Barnum's museum attracted thousands of people. Many Americans focused so much on the future that they often refused to acknowledge the immediate problems surrounding them.

Recommended Readings

Genovese, Eugene. *Roll, Jordan, Roll: The World the Slaves Made* (1974). Stands as the most powerful portrayal of American slavery.

Kaestle, Carl F. *Pillars of the Republic: Common Schools and American Society, 1780–1860* (1983). The most thorough and balanced account of education reform.

Kolchin, Peter. *American Slavery, 1619–1877* (1993). Offers a nuanced synthesis of much of the recent work.

Perry, Lewis. *Boats Against the Current: American Culture Between Revolution and Modernity, 1820–1860* (1993). A stimulating interpretation.

Rose, Anne C. *Voices of the Marketplace: American Thought and Culture, 1830–1860* (1995). Gives a compelling interpretation of cultural history.

Stevenson, Brenda E. *Life in Black and White: Family and Community in the Slave South* (1996). Paints a potent picture of both white and black Southerners.

Thornton, J. Mills, III. *Politics and Power in a Slave Society: Alabama, 1800–1860* (1978). Conveys the way democracy and slavery interacted in the South.

Unruh, John I. *The Plains Across: Overland Emigrants and the Trans-Mississippi West, 1840–1860* (1979). Tells this story with memorable detail.

Vance, James E., Jr. *The North American Railroad* (1995). Shows how the railroad developed in Europe and the United States.

American Journey Online and InfoTrac College Edition

Visit the source collections at www.americanjourney.psmedia.com and infotrac.thomsonlearning.com and use the Search function with the following key terms to explore documents, images, audio and video clips, articles, and commentary related to the material in this chapter.

Frederick Douglass
Harriet Tubman
Manifest Destiny
fugitive slave
abolition
Amistad
Temperance movement
Transcendentalism
Grimké

Chapter 12

Expansion and Reaction, 1846–1854

THE YEARS OF territorial expansion, population growth, and prosperity that accompanied victory in the Mexican War also proved to be years of unprecedented danger and foreboding for the United States. Heightened expectations of a transcontinental empire led to political conflict. Massive immigration from Europe fueled social conflict. Literature took on a more pessimistic tone. Female activists dicovered that progress for women would come only as a result of prolonged effort. The attempt to open the West to settlement divided Southerners and Northerners. The stopgap compromise on slavery satisfied neither side.

War with Mexico

Mexico had been a major concern for generations. Throughout the 1820s American leaders had struggled with the promise and danger posed by the annexation of Texas; throughout the 1830s and 1840s Americans had aided Texans in their fight against the Mexican army. The United States longed for the territories Mexico controlled in western North America, but Mexico pledged to keep those lands. No one could be sure that the United States could defeat Mexico in a large-scale war. But the United States seemed determined to find out.

The United States at War

The Mexican government had never recognized the independence of Texas, which Texans claimed as a result of their defeat of Santa Anna in 1836. President James K. Polk made matters worse by insisting that the border between Texas and Mexico lay at the Rio Grande, not at the Nueces River farther north. Even before the formal annexation of Texas took effect in 1845, Polk ordered American troops under the command of General Zachary Taylor to cross the Nueces.

Polk had his eyes not only on the border with Texas but on larger prizes still: the sale of California and New Mexico. Polk ordered John C. Frémont, leading an army expedition to map rivers within U.S. borders, to California. Frémont proceeded to support the "Bear Flag Rebellion," an armed struggle by American settlers against the Mexican government. Disrupted, the Mexican provinces might be sacrificed more easily and more cheaply to the United States.

CHRONOLOGY

1846 Mexican War begins; Stephen Kearny occupies Santa Fe; Zachary Taylor takes Monterey

Border between Canada and United States established at 49th parallel

Wilmot Proviso ignites sectional conflict

Bear Flag Republic in California proclaimed

Hiram Powers completes statue *The Greek Slave*

1847 Taylor defeats Santa Anna at Buena Vista; Winfield Scott captures Vera Cruz and Mexico City

Mormons reach Great Salt Lake Valley

1848 Gold discovered in California

Treaty of Guadalupe Hidalgo

Attempts to buy Cuba from Spain

Free Soil party runs Van Buren for president

Zachary Taylor elected president

Seneca Falls Convention

Oneida community established

Regular steamship trips between Liverpool and New York City

Mormons settle in Great Basin

1849 California seeks admission to Union

"Forty-Niners" race to California

Cotton prices invigorate South

Cholera epidemic returns

1850 Nashville Convention attempts to unify South

Fugitive Slave Law

Taylor dies; Millard Fillmore becomes president

Compromise of 1850

Nathaniel Hawthorne, *The Scarlet Letter*

First land-grant railroad: Illinois Central

John C. Calhoun dies

1851 Herman Melville, *Moby Dick*

Maine adopts prohibition

Woman's rights convention in Akron, Ohio

Indiana state constitution excludes free blacks

1852 Franklin Pierce elected president

Harriet Beecher Stowe, *Uncle Tom's Cabin*

Daniel Webster and Henry Clay die

1853 Gadsden Purchase

Nativism increases

1854 Know-Nothings win unexpected victories

Whig party collapses

Republican party founded

Kansas-Nebraska Act

Ostend Manifesto encourages acquisition of Cuba

Henry David Thoreau, *Walden*

High-point of immigration

Railroad reaches Mississippi River

The president prepared for war in Texas, seizing on a skirmish between Mexican and American troops north of the Rio Grande as a convenient excuse. He declared that Mexico had started a war when it "invaded our territory and shed American blood on the American soil." Even though northern Whigs continually denounced the war and its motives, Whig congressmen believed they had to support appropriations for the soldiers in the field.

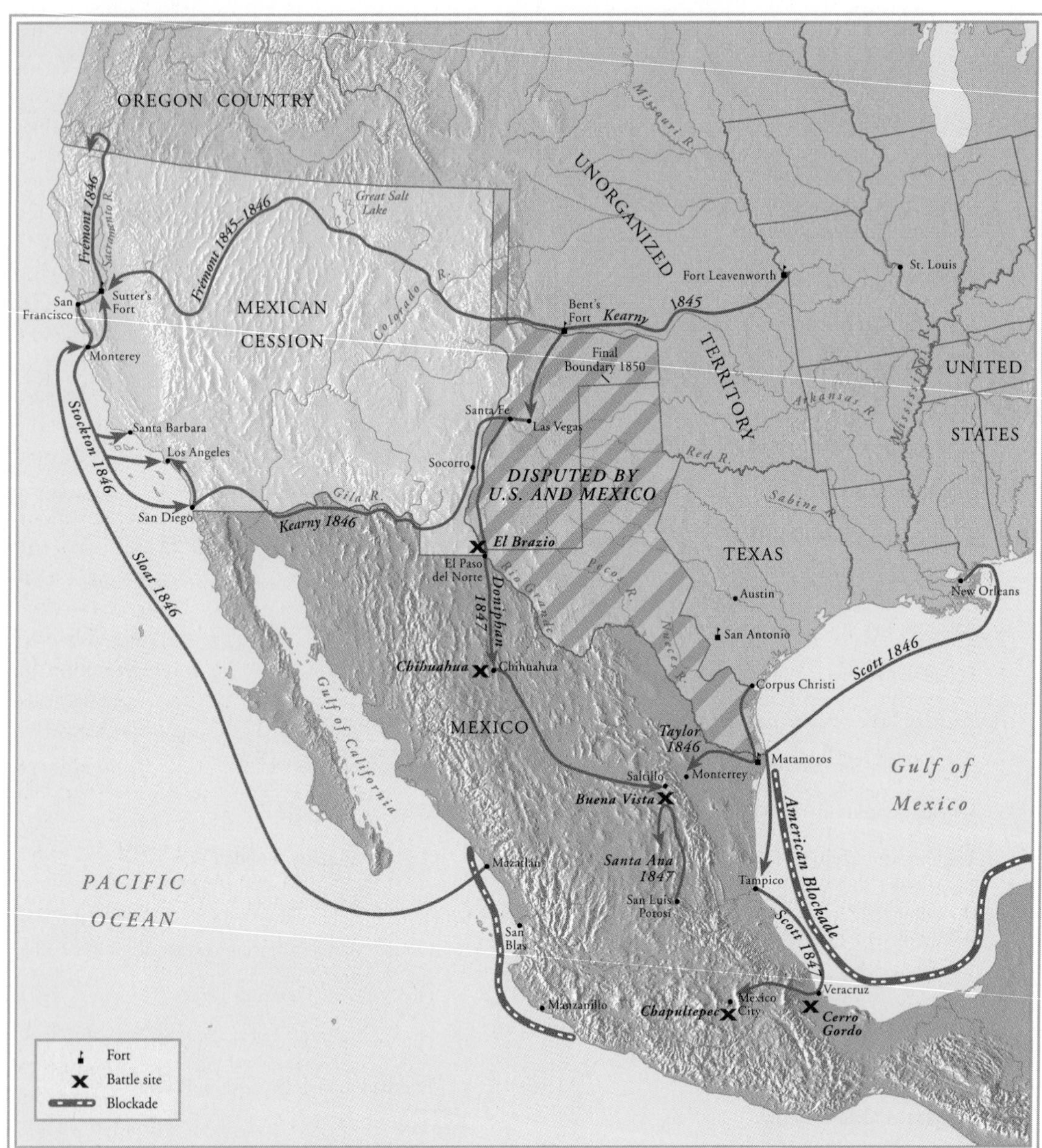

MAP 12.1 | THE MEXICAN WAR

American troops under the leadership of Colonel Stephen Kearney took Santa Fe in New Mexico with no casualties late in the summer of 1846. California proved to be a greater struggle, partly because Mexican settlers there put up more of a fight and partly because Frémont seemed to provoke fights where resistance might not otherwise have appeared. In any case, the American forces won control of California a few months after they had taken New Mexico. The United States Army, under Zachary Taylor and Winfield Scott, achieved a series of victories in Mexico itself in 1846 and 1847, including an impressive amphibious landing at Vera Cruz by Scott's forces that ended in the conquest of Mexico City and "the halls of Montezuma."

Though the Mexicans outnumbered the Americans, the U.S. forces enjoyed impressive leadership from their officer corps. The Mexican War familiarized Americans with names like Ulysses S. Grant, Jefferson Davis, and Robert E. Lee. Though it lost a high proportion of its men—about 14,000 of the 105,000 who fought—the United States Army proved remarkably effective. Nevertheless, Polk distrusted his two leading generals—Taylor and Scott—suspecting, correctly, that they might capitalize on their military success to seek the presidency.

The Consequences of War

Many Northerners worried about the expansion of slavery that might accompany victory over Mexico. To put such concerns to rest, David Wilmot, a Pennsylvania Democrat in favor of the war, made a bold move: when a bill to appropriate additional funds for American troops in Mexico came before Congress in 1846, Wilmot offered a "proviso," a condition, that declared that slavery could not be established in any territory the United States might win from Mexico as a result of the war. This proviso became a central topic of debate in the heated battle over slavery. The Wilmot Proviso went down to defeat and the war proceeded, but from 1846 on the opponents of slavery increasingly distrusted Polk and southern political leaders.

Henry David Thoreau protested the war with Mexico. As he wrote in his essay "On Civil Disobedience," Thoreau considered the Mexican War "the work of comparatively few individuals using the government as their tool." Thoreau decided to signal his disgust with the American government by refusing to pay his taxes. He spent only one night in jail before his friends paid his taxes for him, but Thoreau's essay proved influential later in American history when protesters looked for inspiration and justification.

The war with Mexico limped to an end in late 1847 and the beginning of 1848. American troops controlled Mexico City, the Gulf Coast, and all the northern provinces claimed by the United States, but the Mexican government refused to settle on terms of peace. President James K. Polk, General Winfield Scott, and peace commissioner Nicholas Trist bickered over the treaty. Northerners and Southerners viewed one another with undisguised distrust and distaste. Some Americans urged Polk to lay claim to all of the conquered country while others insisted that the United States should seize no territory at all from the war. Trist, on his own in Mexico, finally signed a treaty in Guadalupe Hidalgo that brought the negotiations to an end in February 1848.

Mexico, for $15 million and the abandonment of American claims against the Mexican government and its people, agreed to sell California, New Mexico, and all of Texas above the Rio Grande. When the treaty finally appeared before Congress for ratification the following month, many doubted that it would pass. The various cliques, however, swallowed their disagreements long enough to ratify the treaty in March. A prominent newspaper pronounced the treaty "a peace which every one will be glad of, but no one will be proud of." The Mexicans signed the treaty in May and the war finally closed.

War and Politics

James K. Polk did not seek reelection in 1848. The Democrats, scrambling to find someone to unite the northern and southern branches of the party, decided on Lewis Cass of Michigan. Cass, a rather colorless man except for his red wig, spoke for the majority of northern Democrats who sympathized with white Southerners in their determination to keep black people enslaved. He called for "popular sovereignty," for people in the territories to make up their own policies on slavery. Anti-slavery Democrats walked out of the Democratic convention and called their own convention in New York; there, they nominated Martin Van Buren for the presidency.

Abolitionists who had supported the Liberty party exulted at a candidate who might win a substantial number of votes. Anti-slavery "Conscience Whigs" also threw their support behind Van Buren. These various groups forged a working alliance for the election of 1848, declaring their solidarity behind the name of the Free Soil party and its stirring motto: "Free soil, free speech, free labor, and free men."

The mainstream Whigs found themselves in an awkward spot, for they had fervently opposed the Mexican War but now sought to capitalize on the popularity of General Zachary Taylor. Nevertheless, Taylor had several advantages as a candidate. He had no troubling political past. Though he was a slaveholding planter, he had opposed the war with Mexico before he had been sent there to lead American troops. Just what he thought about anything was quite unclear.

Taylor won the election in the electoral college, but the popular vote revealed little consensus. Taylor won eight slave states and seven free ones, while Cass won eight free states and seven slaveholding ones. Although Van Buren came in second in several important states, he did not win enough votes to cement the identity of the new Free Soil party, which did elect twelve men to Congress. The election had not clarified the issues that concerned most voters.

AMERICANS ON THE MOVE

Americans moved in massive numbers in the years around 1850. As the economy lifted, transportation developed, boundaries became settled, and gold beckoned, people flooded to the states of the old Northwest and the old Southwest as well as to Texas, Oregon, and California. The suffering of Ireland and political conflict within Germany drove millions across the Atlantic, filling the cities and farms of the East.

Rails, Sails, and Steam

The late 1840s and early 1850s saw the emergence of the fastest-growing rail lines and the fastest ships in the world. Private investors poured tens of millions of dollars into rail expansion. The federal government aided railroads with free surveys and vast grants of land. The major cities of the eastern seaboard competed against one another to attract as many rail lines as possible. Owners of mines and factories subsidized new railroads, as did Wall Street speculators and investors from Great Britain.

Railroads proved more important for some parts of the country than for others. Railroads flourished in New England and New York, where the density of population and manufacturing permitted the new technology to work most efficiently. Midwestern states such as Ohio, Illinois, and Indiana also showed themselves well-suited to the railroads. Chicago had no railroads at all in 1850 but by 1860 twelve lines converged in the city. Three of those lines stretched from Chicago all the way to New York City; a trip that had taken ten days before the railroad now took only a day and a half.

Rural areas as well as cities immediately felt the effects of the railroad. Farmers now found it profitable to ship their produce to a city a hundred miles away. Farmers specialized, becoming dairymen, vegetable growers, and fruit producers. Corn, wheat, hogs, and cattle flowed out of Ohio, Illinois, Indiana, and Wisconsin. The older farms of New England, New York, and Pennsylvania turned to specialty products such as cheese, maple sugar, vegetables, and cranberries. These products rode the railroad tracks to market, tying countryside and city together.

In the South, railroad building trailed off in the 1840s and did not pick up again until the late 1850s. The South relied instead on the steamboats that plied the Mississippi and other major rivers. The riverboats grew in size, number, and ornateness throughout the period. The 1850s marked the glory days of these riverboats, with cotton bales stacked on every square inch of deck.

Graceful and fast, American clipper ships raced around South America and across the Pacific. (The Granger Collection, New York)

Elsewhere, packet steamships carried mail, freight, and passengers up and down the eastern seaboard and over the Great Lakes. Beginning in 1848, Americans could count on regular steam travel between New York and Liverpool, England. These innovations in transportation, exciting as they were, came at a steep cost. "I never open a newspaper that does not contain some account of disasters and loss of life," one diarist observed.

Clipper ships enjoyed a brief but stirring heyday in the late forties and early fifties. Clippers used narrow hulls and towering sails to attain speeds that have yet to be reached by any other sailing vessels of their size. They sailed from New York to San Francisco, all the way around South America, in less than a hundred days. Although they were to be displaced after 1855 by uglier and more efficient steamships, for a few exciting years the clipper ships thrived on the high prices, small cargoes, long voyages, and desperate speed fueled by remarkable discoveries in California.

The Gold Rush

The natives of California had long known of the gold hidden in the rocks and creeks of that vast territory. White American settlers, too, had found gold deposits in the early 1840s. But it was a discovery in January of 1848 that changed everything.

In 1839, John Sutter had emigrated from Switzerland to the area that became Sacramento, where he established a large fort, trading post, and wheat farm. Sutter hired a carpenter named James Marshall to build a mill on the American River. While working on the project, Marshall happened to notice "something shining in the bottom of the ditch." He realized that the nugget, about half the size of a pea, was gold. Sutter, Marshall, and the other men on the place tried to keep the find a secret, but word leaked to San Francisco. There, sailors abandoned their ships and clerks left their shops to look for gold along the American River. By the end of 1848, such men had gathered nuggets and dust worth about $6 million.

Back east, people remained calm, even skeptical, about the discovery until 230 ounces of almost pure gold went on display in Washington. The Gold Rush began: "The coming of the Messiah, or the dawn of the Millennium could not have excited anything like the interest," one newspaper marvelled. By the end of 1849, over 700 ships carrying over 45,000 easterners sailed to California. Some of the ships went around South America;

Ships filled the harbor of the small town of San Francisco as "Forty-Niners" descended on nearby gold fields. (The Granger Collection, New York)

others transported their passengers to the Isthmus of Panama, which they crossed by foot and canoe.

About 55,000 settlers followed the overland trails cut across the continent. Some traveled alongside the continuing stream of settlers to Oregon, others followed trails directly to the gold fields from destinations as far south as Mexico. Whether they went by sea or land, the participants in the Gold Rush were quite different from other immigrants to the West. The "Forty-Niners" tended to be either single men or groups of men from the same locality. Most of the men who flooded into California had little interest in settling there permanently. They intended to find their share of the gold and move on. Once in California, men of all classes, colors, and nations worked feverishly alongside one another in the streams and mountainsides. Disease and miserable living conditions hounded them, sending thousands to their deaths.

When some Chinese men returned home from California flush with American riches and stories of the "Golden Mountain," the fever spread in Asia. About 70 percent of the Chinese immigrants came from Guangdong Province, where many peasants and artisans had become impoverished and desperate enough to launch the dangerous journey. Young men, in particular, thought California might offer a way to attain the wealth they needed to acquire a farm and a wife back in China. Migrants could buy tickets from brokers on credit, with high interest. Upon their arrival in California, the Chinese immigrants discovered that they had to borrow yet more money from Chinese merchants in San Francisco to be transported to the gold fields. The miners worked continuously in hopes of paying off that debt, but the costs seemed worth the potential reward.

California held out hope for African Americans, too. Most of the black migrants to California left from the coastal cities of New England. California beckoned with the promise of an American West where color really might not matter so much. Although abolitionists, black and white, warned that even California might not be safe for black migrants, several thousand African Americans decided to take the chance.

Whatever their race, few miners discovered a fortune. The average miner in 1848 found about an ounce of gold a day, worth around $20, or about twenty times what a laborer back east made with a daily wage. As the number of competing miners skyrocketed over the next few years, however, the average take declined until it reached about $6 a day in 1852. Mining became more mechanized, and soon the biggest profits went to companies that assaulted the river beds and ravines with battalions of workers, explosives, and crushing mills.

Although miners of every background went bust, California as a whole flourished. Towns appeared wherever people gathered to look for the gold. Men who tired of mining turned to farming instead, or teaching school, or building houses. San Francisco was the big winner: by 1850, it had grown into a brash and booming city of 35,000 diverse residents.

The Mormons' Great Migration

A different kind of westward movement was already in full force as the California Gold Rush got underway. These migrants were members of the Church of Jesus Christ of Latter-day Saints, or Mormons. In the face of relentless persecution Joseph Smith, the founder of the church, had led his flock to Illinois. There they established the

Persecuted in Illinois in the 1840s, the Mormons launched a mass migration to the Great Salt Lake in the state they called "Deseret." (Mormon Panorama Eighteen/*Crossing the Mississippi on the Ice,* by C .C. A Christensen © Courtesy Museum of Art, Brigham Young University)

town of Nauvoo, which by the mid-1840s had become the largest city in Illinois. But conflict erupted when Smith decreed that polygamy was God's will, that men within the church would marry several wives. When Smith ordered the destruction of a Mormon newspaper that opposed the new practice, the paper's owners signed warrants for his arrest. A mob of non-Mormons broke into the jail where Smith was being held and killed both him and his brother.

The Mormons turned to one of their elders, Brigham Young, to lead them in this time of trial. Young decided to move to a place beyond the reach of the Mormons' many enemies. Young knew about the Great Salt Lake, a place cut off from the east by mountains and from the west and south by deserts. The Mormons abandoned Nauvoo in the spring of 1846. In a well-coordinated migration, 15,000 Mormons moved in stages to the Great Salt Lake. When they first arrived, in 1847, the valley presented a daunting picture of rock and sagebrush but the settlers irrigated the land, turning it into a thriving community.

When frosts, insects, and drought ruined much of the crops in the spring of 1848, Young announced that the Mormons would pool their labor and their resources even more than before. They designed an ambitious city with wide streets surrounding a temple that would "surpass in grandeur of design and gorgeousness of decoration all edifices the world has yet seen." Young concentrated control of the city and its farms in his own hands and in those of his fellow church leaders.

As some non-Mormons settled at the Great Salt Lake, Young decided that a form of government other than the church must be established. He oversaw the creation of a state called "Deseret," a Mormon term meaning "honeybee." The Mormons began a successful campaign to attract new converts from Europe, Asia, and Latin America. In 1849, the residents of Deseret petitioned Congress for admission into the Union as a new state.

The High Tide of Immigration

Even as Americans moved west, a vast immigration from Ireland surged into the eastern United States. Irish immigration was not new; about a million people had left Ireland for the United States between 1815 and 1844. But the situation in Ireland changed much for the worse beginning in 1845, when a blight struck healthy potato fields, turning the leaves black almost overnight and filling the air with "a sickly odor of decay." This, the Great Potato Famine, which would last for nearly a decade, destroyed the basic food for most of the Irish people. Over a million people died; another 1.8 million fled to North America. In all, about a fourth of the island's population departed, with more people leaving in the eleven years after 1845 than in the preceding 250 years combined.

The Irish emigrants tended to be young, single, poor, unskilled, and Catholic; they came over in the dead of winter and with virtually no money or property. Although some Irish immigrants spread throughout North America, most congre-

CHART 12.1 IMMIGRATION TO THE UNITED STATES, 1820–1860

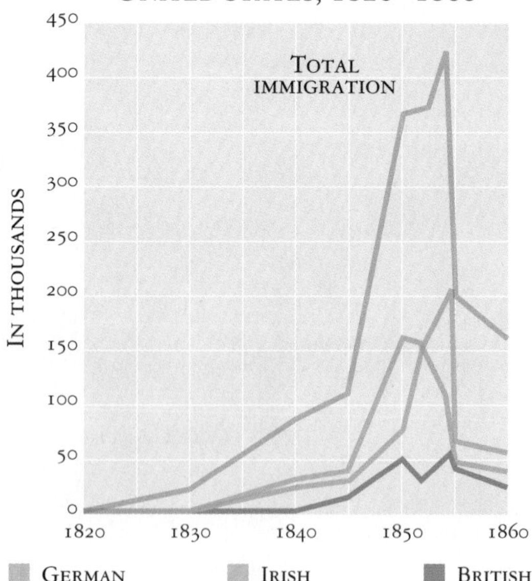

gated in the cities of the North and Midwest. They lived from day to day on whatever money they could earn. Most men worked on docks, others in canal and railroad construction; women worked as domestics and as unskilled laborers in textile mills. Desperately poor and widely despised, the Irish figured prominently in arrest reports and on penitentiary rolls.

The high tide of Irish immigration occurred simultaneously with the peak of German immigration. Over a million Germans came to America between 1846 and 1854, many of them dislocated by a failed revolution in Germany in 1848. The Germans tended to be farmers who brought some property with them and established farms in the Midwest. The Germans, more than the Irish, were divided by wealth, generation, politics, regional background, and religion. Combined, the Irish and German immigrants accounted for almost 15 percent of the entire population of the United States.

In the eyes of many white Protestants, the new arrivals appeared impossible to assimilate. The immigrants threatened to drive down wages because they were willing to work for so little. They also threatened to thwart enforced temperance. That movement gained momentum in 1851, when Maine became the first state to enact statewide prohibition of alcohol. The immigrants often received the right to vote in state and local elections soon after they landed and they voted heavily against prohibition.

In the face of such challenges to their values and power, "native Americans" organized against the immigrants. The most powerful manifestation of nativism appeared in New York City in 1849, when Charles Allen founded the Order of the Star Spangled Banner. Its membership was restricted to

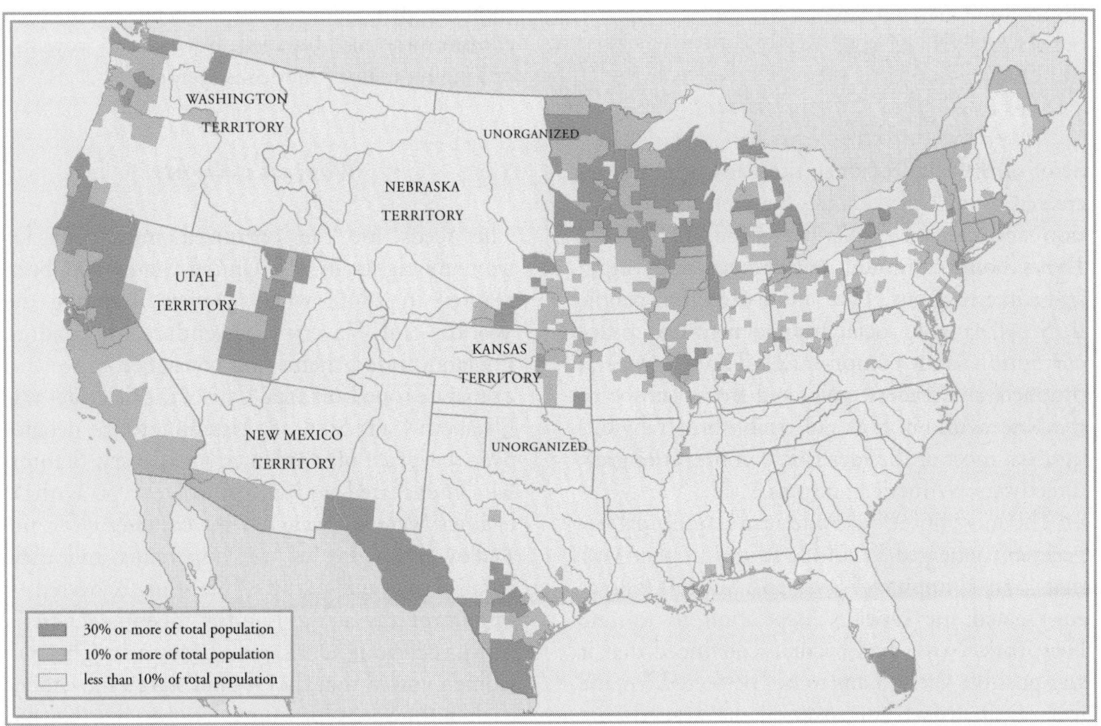

Map 12.2 | Foreign-Born Population, 1840–1860

native-born white Protestants sworn to secrecy. When asked about the order by outsiders, members were instructed to say "I know nothing"—and thus they became popularly known as the "Know-Nothings." The order grew slowly at first, but it drew on deeply held and deepening prejudices.

ACTION AND REFLECTION

The late 1840s and early 1850s, though relatively peaceful and prosperous, led a number of people to protest the drift of American life. Some became so disenchanted that they established utopian communities where they could experiment with alternative ways of organizing labor, power, and sexuality. Others launched a crusade for women's rights. Yet others wrote novels and poetry that reflected on American life.

Perfect Communities

Most of the hundred or so utopian communities created in the United States between the Revolution and the Civil War were founded in the 1840s. Some communities were secular in origin and some religious. They all insisted that people truly dedicated to social improvement had to flee corruption and compromise. Though several prophets and leaders emigrated from Europe to the New World in hopes of establishing religious utopias, most of the idealistic communities grew directly from American origins.

The most notorious American communal experiment emerged in 1848. It was in that year that John Humphrey Noyes and his 250 followers created the Oneida Association in upstate New York. Noyes had become convinced that it was possible for humans to be "perfected," made free of sin. Most controversial, he argued that people in a state of perfection should not be bound by conventional monogamous marriages; all belonged to one another sexually in "complex marriage." He gathered a small group of disciples around him who put such beliefs into action, practicing birth control by having males withdraw during intercourse.

Oneida experimented not only with sex but also with economic cooperation. Everyone performed the full range of labor. The women of the group cut their hair, wore pantaloons rather than skirts, and played sports with their male compatriots. Unlike other utopian communities, Oneida focused its energies on manufacturing rather than farming. The community produced an improved and profitable steel animal trap. Later, Oneida transformed itself into a profitable business corporation specializing in silverware.

The utopian communities testified to the freedom the United States offered. People took advantage of the isolation offered by the enormous space of the young country to experiment with communities based on religious, sexual, or philosophical principles. The proliferation of such communities also testified, however, to how full of longing many Americans seemed.

Woman's Rights

The seeds for the organized movement for woman's rights in the United States had been planted in 1840, when women attending the World's Anti-Slavery Convention in London, England, found themselves consigned to seats in a separate roped-off area. One of the delegates was Elizabeth Cady Stanton. Listening to the debates over the place of women in antislavery, Stanton felt "humiliated and chagrined, except as these feelings were outweighed by contempt for the shallow reasoning of the opponents and their comical pose and gestures." Stanton discovered an important ally at the London meeting: Lucretia Mott, a devout Quaker and feminist. The two women vowed that they would start a movement back in the States for woman's rights, but they did not soon find the opportunity they sought. Stanton devoted her time to raising her family in

Boston. In 1847, she moved with her family to Seneca Falls, New York.

While living in Seneca Falls, Stanton grew frustrated with the narrowness of life in a small town and the limitations placed on women there. Meeting with Lucretia Mott again, Stanton told her friend how miserable she had become. The two women joined with three of Mott's Quaker friends to plan a convention in July in Seneca Falls, although only Mott had had any experience in organizing a reform meeting. Stanton recalled that they "felt as helpless as if they had been suddenly asked to construct a steam engine."

Casting about for a way to express their grievances most effectively, they decided to model their "Declaration of Rights and Sentiments" on the Declaration of Independence. It began with a ringing statement: "The history of mankind is a history of repeated injuries and usurpations on the part of man toward woman, having in direct object the establishment of an absolute tyranny over her." The Declaration demanded the right to vote and insisted on women's full equality with men in every sphere of life, including property rights, education, employment, divorce, and in court. The organizers worried about how many people might attend the meeting—held in an obscure town during a busy season for farmers—but over a hundred people came, including a considerable number of men. Of those men the most prominent was Frederick Douglass. Douglass' newspaper, the *North Star,* was one of the few papers to give the convention a positive notice.

The organizers of the Seneca Falls Convention succeeded in their major role: getting Americans to talk about woman's rights. Word of the Declaration spread among the many women's groups working in other reform organizations. Stanton, Mott, and their allies determined that they would hold a convention each year to keep the momentum going.

At the Akron meeting in 1851 a black woman spoke. She had escaped slavery in New York in 1827 and supported her family by working as a domestic. In 1843, she had a vision in which she was commanded to carry the word of God; she renamed herself "Sojourner Truth." In Akron, Truth celebrated women. "I have plowed and reaped and husked and chopped and mowed, and can any man do more than that?" she asked.

Elizabeth Cady Stanton, one of the founders of the woman's rights movement, about the time of the Seneca Falls Convention of 1848. (Women's Rights National Historical Park, Courtesy of Seneca Falls Historical Society)

The campaign for woman's rights developed a complex relationship to abolition and to African Americans. The movement might offer a rare opportunity for women such as Sojourner Truth to be heard, but white woman's rights advocates generally phrased their demands for equal rights in terms of education and refinement that neglected black women and their needs.

Not all activist women, moreover, dedicated themselves to woman's rights. More conservative

"Declaration of Sentiments" of the Woman Suffrage Movement 1848

Sixty-eight women and thirty-two men signed this declaration, produced at Seneca Falls in 1848. Modeled on the Declaration of Independence, this document provided a touchstone for the woman's movement throughout the rest of the century and beyond.

The history of mankind is a history of repeated injuries and usurpations on the part of man toward woman, having in direct object the establishment of an absolute tyranny over her. To prove this, let facts be submitted to a candid world.

He has never permitted her to exercise her inalienable right to the elective franchise.

He has compelled her to submit to laws, in the formation of which she had no voice.

He has withheld from her rights which are given to the most ignorant and degraded men—both natives and foreigners.

Having deprived her of this first right of a citizen, the elective franchise, thereby leaving her without representation in the halls of legislation, he has oppressed her on all sides.

He has made her, if married, in the eye of the law, civilly dead.

He has taken from her all right in property, even to the wages she earns.

He has made her, morally, an irresponsible being, as she can commit many crimes with impunity, provided they be done in the presence of her husband. In the covenant of marriage, she is compelled to promise obedience to her husband, he becoming, to all intents and purposes, her master—the law giving him power to deprive her of her liberty, and to administer chastisement.

women devoted their energies to acquiring public funds for orphanages, shelters for "fallen" women, and the poor, using their connections to important men in state legislatures, on city boards, and in prosperous businesses to raise money and garner support. They asked for laws to criminalize seduction and to change property laws, to oppose Indian removal, restrict slavery, and stop the sale of liquor. They often proved successful and effective with these indirect means and saw little need for agitating for the vote for women.

Hawthorne, Melville, and Whitman

Whereas the 1830s and 1840s had been the time of transcendentalism, the 1850s saw American writers grappling with themes very much attuned to their time and place. Nathaniel Hawthorne's *The Scarlet Letter* and Herman Melville's *Moby Dick* were ironic, dark, and complex allegories, but Walt Whitman's *Leaves of Grass* evoked a determinedly hopeful vision. All three captured a key part of the American mood in the 1850s.

He has so framed the laws of divorce, as to what shall be the proper causes, and in case of separation, to whom the guardianship of the children shall be given, as to be wholly regardless of the happiness of women—the law, in all cases, going upon a false supposition of the supremacy of man, and giving all power into his hands.

After depriving her of all rights as a married woman, if single, and the owner of property, he has taxed her to support a government which recognizes her only when her property can be made profitable to it.

He has monopolized nearly all the profitable employments, and from those she is permitted to follow, she receives but a scanty remuneration. He closes against her all the avenues to wealth and distinction which he considers most honorable to himself. As a teacher of theology, medicine, or law, she is not known.

He has denied her the facilities for obtaining a thorough education, all colleges being closed against her.

He allows her in church, as well as state, but a subordinate position, claiming apostolic authority for her exclusion from the ministry, and, with some exceptions, from any public participation in the affairs of the church.

He has created a false public sentiment by giving to the world a different code of morals for men and women, by which moral delinquencies which exclude women from society, are not only tolerated, but deemed of little account in man.

He has usurped the prerogative of Jehovah himself, claiming it as his right to assign for her a sphere of action, when that belongs to her conscience and to her God.

He has endeavored, in every way that he could, to destroy her confidence in her own powers, to lessen her self-respect, and to make her willing to lead a dependent and abject life.

Now, in view of this entire disfranchisement of one-half the people of this country, their social and religious degradation—in view of the unjust laws above mentioned, and because women do feel themselves aggrieved, oppressed, and fraudulently deprived of their most sacred rights, we insist that they have immediate admission to all the rights and privileges which belong to them as citizens of the United States.

SOURCE Elizabeth Cady Stanton, et al., *History of Woman Suffrage,* Vol. 1 (Rochester, N.Y.: Fowler & Wells, 1889), 58–59.

Nathaniel Hawthorne's father died at sea and left his family to do the best it could with limited resources. Hawthorne went to Bowdoin College and then returned to his mother's home and set up as a writer. Quiet and ambitious, he did not marry until he was thirty-eight years old. He read almost indiscriminately, gulping down popular crime fiction as well as the latest literary products of Europe. Though he himself was not morose, Hawthorne was fascinated by the lingering consequences of sin. He turned to the history of New England as the setting for his best work, finding there an allegory for the struggles of his own age.

Hawthorne became an active supporter of the Democratic party. He wrote for the Democratic papers and won a job in the Salem customs house. Hawthorne's political experiences in the late 1840s embittered him, however, for his Whig opponents not only sought to remove Hawthorne from his post but also charged him with corruption. It was at this point that Hawthorne wrote *The Scarlet Letter,* a symbolic story about revenge and its costs. Though set in the colonial era, the novel opened with a biting portrayal of the Salem customs house and its petty (Whig) politicians. The novel propelled Hawthorne into literary fame.

After the arrival of Hawthorne's long-delayed prosperity, he and his family moved to Lenox, Massachusetts. There he met a younger writer, one who admired Hawthorne for his willingness to write complicated stories of guilt. The young author was Herman Melville. He had left school at the age of fifteen, tried his hand at writing, but, in need of work that paid better and more certainly, went to sea. His experiences gave him the subjects for most of his writing. His first two books, *Typee* and *Omoo,* adventure stories of the sea, did quite well. But Melville was not satisfied to write such books; he envisioned nothing less than an American epic.

Melville's masterpiece, about a ship captain's search for the great white whale "Moby Dick," created a peculiarly American idiom: part Old Testament, part adventure story, part how-to book, part encyclopedia. Good and evil swirled together in *Moby Dick.* Unlike *The Scarlet Letter, Moby Dick,* published in 1852, did not do well on the market. Melville, disenchanted, made his work more cynical and biting. His novel *The Confidence-Man,* published six years after *Moby Dick,* dwelt on the swindling, corruption, and self-deception that seemed at the heart of the United States in the 1850s. Few people at the time noticed Melville's bold experiments and he gradually fell silent.

Walt Whitman also labored on an epic work, *Leaves of Grass,* throughout the early 1850s. The collection of poems reflected America at mid-century in all its diversity, roughness, innocence, and exuberance. This poetry included everything and everyone, speaking in a language stripped of classical allusion and pretension. As Whitman wrote in the preface to this book, anyone who would be a poet in the mid-nineteenth century must "flood himself with the immediate age."

Whitman took the raucous city of New York as his subject. For him, cities were frontiers, full of democracy and possibility. Whitman participated fully in the life of the city, writing as a partisan Democratic journalist, running a shop, working as a building contractor, spending days in the public library, moving from one editing job to another, attending boisterous political meetings—all the while jotting notes for a new kind of epic poetry taking shape in his head.

As he invented a poetical style to match his kaleidoscopic vision of American life, Walt Whitman also invented an image of himself as the poet who would take in and express everything. Both his life and his poem would be "A Song of Myself." Whitman's book was literally self-made; in 1855 he set some of the type and hired friends—printers of legal work—to publish the book for him.

Leaves of Grass came out to no public recognition whatsoever. Whitman sent a few copies to people he admired, however, including Emerson. The reply could not have been more heartening: "I find it the most extraordinary piece of wit and wisdom that America has yet contributed." But most readers of the book, including several leading literary figures who read it on Emerson's recommendation, considered it vulgar, even obscene, shapeless, and crude. The hopeful words of *Leaves of Grass* soon became lost in years when a darker vision of the United States prevailed.

RACE, SLAVERY, AND POLITICS

The decade of the 1850s began with many signs of change and progress. The economy kicked into high gear. People flooded to the recently acquired territories of California and Oregon as well as to the upper and lower Mississippi region. Clipper ships, steamships, and railroads expanded their reach. Abolitionists, perfectionists, and feminists worked for the improvement of American society. Despite the generally positive turn of events, however, a persistent undercurrent of fear and anxiety wore at even the most privileged Americans.

The Crisis of 1850

Some of Americans' anxiety emanated from the new golden land of California, where lawlessness became rampant. The men who had left everything back east or in Europe to come to the goldfields showed little respect for the property rights—and even lives—of the Mexicans, Indians, or white men who were there before. In the eyes of many, anarchy threatened if California could not form a government quickly. A territorial convention created such a government in 1849, helping to restore order, but one of the provisions of the new constitution created great disorder of another kind back in the United States. The new constitution declared that "neither slavery nor involuntary servitude . . . shall ever be tolerated in this state."

This straightforward statement exacerbated conflicts that had been brewing in Washington ever since the Wilmot Proviso three years earlier. White Southerners of both parties considered the admission of a free California a grave threat to their own status in the Union, giving the Senate a free-labor majority. John C. Calhoun, the most vocal and extreme spokesman for the South, urged his fellow white Southerners to band together. If they did not cooperate, Calhoun argued, they would be overwhelmed by the numbers and the energy of the free states of the North and the West. Southern congressmen talked of commercial boycotts, even of secession.

Southern Whigs had put Zachary Taylor forward for the presidency in 1848 assuming that, as a Southerner himself, he would support the expansion of slavery. To their disbelief and disgust, Taylor urged that California be admitted as it wished to be admitted, without slavery. But Taylor's support of the proposed California constitution unleashed a bitter debate in Congress. White Southerners argued that to deny the South an equal representation in the Senate was to risk war between North and South. To give in on California was to lose the sectional balance on which their very safety rested. The most aggressive white Southerners wanted to go on the offensive before Northerners in Congress had time to act; in late 1849, they called a convention of the southern states, to meet in Nashville in June of 1850.

A fabled session of Congress occurred as a result. In January 1850, the three most famous legislators of the first half of the nineteenth century—John C. Calhoun, Henry Clay, and Daniel Webster—assumed leading roles in the great national drama. Calhoun played the role of the protagonist, delivering fiery warnings and denunciations on behalf of the white South; Clay reprised the role of the Great Compromiser that had made him famous in the Missouri controversy; Webster played the role of the conciliator, persuading the angry North to accept, in the name of the Union, the South's demand for respect. Clay and Webster rehearsed their lines in a private meeting before Clay presented his bill to Congress.

Clay's bold plan addressed in one inclusive "omnibus" bill all the issues tearing at the United States on the slavery issue. Balance the territory issue, he suggested, with other concerns that angered people about slavery. Leave slavery in the District of Columbia, but abolish the slave trade there. Provide a stronger law to capture fugitive slaves in the North, but announce that Congress had no power to regulate the slave trade among the states. Admit California as a free state, but leave undetermined the place of slavery in the other territories won from Mexico. Advocates on both sides hoped the compromise would buy time for passions to cool.

Clay made his plea with his characteristic eloquence and power. The eloquence appeared to be to little effect, however, for the same bitter arguments went on for months after Clay's speech. In March, Calhoun, too ill to speak himself, wrote an address in which he conceded nothing; three days later, Webster claimed to speak "not as a Massachusetts man, nor as a northern man, but as an American." Webster found himself widely denounced in the North as a traitor, buckling under to the slave mongerers. Moreover, President Zachary Taylor, like Clay and Webster a Whig, refused to support their compromise. William Seward of New York denounced the compromise as "radically wrong and essentially vicious."

The Nashville Convention of southern states, meanwhile, turned out to be ineffective, since six states sent no representatives and the representatives who did come disagreed on the proper course of action. The convention took no stand on the pending compromise; they waited to see its provisions.

The omnibus bill appeared doomed. A series of unanticipated events, however, aided the compromise. Both Calhoun and Taylor died a few months apart. Millard Fillmore was now president, and Fillmore supported the omnibus bill. Clay and Webster faded from view as younger, less prominent, members of Congress steered the various components of the compromise through committees and votes. The compromisers were led by Stephen A. Douglas, a promising young Democrat of Illinois. The majority of northern and southern senators and representatives tenaciously voted against one another, but each part of the compromise passed because a small group of conciliatory congressmen from each side worked together. By September the various components of the compromise of 1850 had become law.

The problem of slavery, of course, would not go away merely because of a political compromise. The fugitive slave component of the Compromise of 1850 proved especially troubling. The Fugitive Slave Act directly implicated white Northerners and insulted them with blatantly unjust provisions. The commissioners who decided the fate of black Americans accused of being runaway slaves, for example, received ten dollars if an accused fugitive were returned to his or her master but only five dollars if freed. Marshals and sheriffs could force bystanders to aid in the capture of an accused fugitive; if bystanders refused, they faced a substantial fine or even jail term. The alleged runaway could not even testify in his or her own defense or call witnesses. Perhaps most horrifying of all was this provision: no matter how many years before slaves had escaped, no matter how settled or respectable they had become, they could be captured and sent back into bondage.

Most northern whites offered no opposition and most of the two or three hundred alleged fugitives prosecuted under the law were ruled to be runaways and sent south. But abolitionists raged at the Fugitive Slave Law and they were not alone. Many Northerners were furious. Armed opposition to the slave catchers immediately arose in cities across the North; mobs broke into jails to free ex-slaves; one slaveowner who came north to claim his property was shot. The Fugitive Slave Law, far from calming the conflict between North and South, made it more bitter.

The White North and African Americans

The years surrounding the crisis of 1850, ironically, were also the years in which black minstrel shows reached their peak of popularity. The traveling troupes of minstrels offered the strange ritual of white men in blackface simultaneously ridiculing and paying homage to the creativity of African American culture. Although white people of all classes and backgrounds attended the minstrel shows, the quick-paced, humorous, and flashy skits and songs held special appeal for members of the white working class. Over the preceding decades, those workers had seen the value of their skills eroded by mechanization. In their eyes, the minstrel shows offered both a comforting dramatization of their own racial superiority and a way to associate imaginatively with carefree and fun-loving "black" people.

White Northerners revealed their ambivalences about African Americans in other ways as well. Whites who argued that the new territory of the West must be free soil frequently insisted on the exclusion of free blacks. Whites in cities associated black people with poverty and crime. A considerable majority of northern whites showed little interest in attending anti-slavery rallies.

Harriet Beecher Stowe's *Uncle Tom's Cabin* helped change white attitudes toward African Americans. Stowe had been writing throughout her life, but had not not become prominent. In 1849, her infant son died of cholera in Cincinnati; the next year she moved back to New England. There, people talked angrily of the new Fugitive Slave Law. "You don't know how my heart burns within me at the blindness and obtuseness of good people on so very simple a point of morality as this," she wrote to her brother Henry Ward Beecher.

Stowe put her objections to the law and its effects into a story printed serially in a moderate anti-slavery newspaper. Stowe based her portrayals of black people on the African Americans she had known in Cincinnati, where they worked for her as domestic servants. They told Stowe of the terrors of being sold south to Louisiana, of their vulnerability to sexual exploitation. Stowe also drew on firsthand narratives of escape. She switched the usual roles of the freedom narratives, however, making a woman—Eliza—the active heroine and a man—Uncle Tom—the one left behind to endure slavery. The love of a mother for her children drove the story. The image of Eliza crossing the partially frozen Ohio River, baby in her arms, grew into one of the most powerful and familiar scenes of American culture.

The novel sold 300,000 copies in 1852 alone and became the subject of the most popular play in American history. Readers and theatergoers were shocked at stories of cruelty, violence, and sexual abuse. Stowe used techniques commonly found in domestic novels—the sanctity of the family, the power of religion, the triumph of endurance—to show that black people had the same feelings as white people.

This book not only helped mobilize the white North's opinions on slavery, but it also proved an immediate and persistent bestseller. (The Bettmann Archive)

That *Uncle Tom's Cabin* and minstrel shows reached their peak of popularity at the same time gives some idea of the confusion and ambivalence with which white Northerners viewed African Americans in the early 1850s. Stowe's story was based on an anti-slavery message, but thousands of whites laughed at other whites in blackface. Only events could force Northerners to decide what they really thought.

The Know-Nothings

Franklin Pierce, the Democratic candidate for president in 1852, was a Northerner friendly to the white South. Pierce's opponent—Winfield Scott—proved to be less impressive despite his fame as a general in the war with Mexico. The death of Henry Clay in 1850 and Daniel Webster in 1852 left the Whigs adrift and directionless. Pierce crushed Scott in every state except four. "General opinion seems to be that the Whig party is dead and will soon be decomposed into its original elements," one diarist commented in the wake of the election.

Many influential Whigs took the 1852 election as a sign that the Democrats would always succeed by appealing to the lowest common denominator. The real, substantive issues that had originally shaped the two parties—banks, the tariff, and internal improvements—no longer distinguished them from one another. Neither did slavery and sectional issues sharply define the two parties, for each tried to appease both the North and the South. Even the broader cultural orientation of the two parties had blurred in 1852, as the Whigs appealed to the burgeoning foreign-born vote and Protestant nativists grew disgusted with the Whigs.

The Know-Nothings, growing steadily since their emergence in 1849, moved into politics in 1854, but in a way few expected. They did not announce their candidates beforehand, but rather wrote them in on the ballots, taking incumbents by complete surprise. The Know-Nothings won virtually all the seats in the Massachusetts legislature with this strategy. By 1855, they dominated New England and displaced the Whigs as the major opponents to the Democrats through the Middle Atlantic states, in much of the South, and in California.

No one in the major parties had anticipated such a turn of events. The Whigs, after all, had long attracted the nativists, fervent Protestants, and temperance advocates to which the Know-Nothings now appealed. But these disgruntled voters proved extremely receptive to the Know-Nothing appeal. The Know-Nothings, unlike the Whigs, left control of the party close to the grassroots. They offered a revitalized political party, one more receptive than the Whigs to the desires of its constituents and one that would attack problems rather than compromise on them. Many rural districts voted heavily for the Know-Nothings as a way to get back at the cities that had dominated the major parties for so long. For such reasons, the Know-Nothings made strong showings in the South as well as the North.

The appearance of the Know-Nothings reflected a deep-seated change in the American political system. The party system began disintegrating at the local and state level, with the Whigs fading in some states as early as 1852 and in others not until three years later. Voters defected from the Whigs to both the Know-Nothing and Free Soil parties.

Dreams of Expansion

The same forces of commerce and transportation that tied together the vastly expanded United States in the late 1840s and early 1850s pulled Americans into world affairs. American ships set out not only for Liverpool, but also for South America, Asia, Australia, New Zealand, and Tahiti. The ships carried lumber and hides, tea and silks, missionaries and scientists. American whaling ships patrolled the South Pacific, stopping for fuel and food at islands scattered over a vast territory. Some entrepreneurs even rushed to mine mountains of bird droppings piled up on remote Pacific islands. The droppings, called guano, offered a nitrogen-rich fertilizer much in demand on the farms and plantations of the eastern United States. American traders eager to break into the Asian market appeared in Japanese ports.

These exchanges in far-off ports often depended on the Hawaiian Islands as way stations. On a single day in 1852, for example, 131 whaling ships and eighteen merchant ships were tied up in Honolulu. Such trade came at a horrifying cost to the native population because of disease. Over the seventy-five years since the first contact with outsiders in the late eighteenth century, the Hawaiian population had declined from about 300,000 residents to only about 73,000. Around 2,000 foreigners lived in Hawaii by the early 1850s, a good many of them Americans. Though politicians and editors talked of annexing the islands for the United States, opposition on the islands and in Washington postponed any action.

Some well-placed Americans gazed at yet more Mexican territory with covetous eyes, urging the Pierce administration to acquire Baja California and other parts of northern Mexico. Mexico was not interested, though. Proponents of expansion had to settle for much less than they had wanted: after long wrangling, in 1853 the United States paid $15 million for a strip of Mexico to use as a route for a southern transcontinental railroad. This was the Gadsden Purchase, named for the American diplomat who negotiated it. The purchase defined the final borders of the continental United States.

Cuba seemed the most obvious place for further expansion. Many Americans believed that Cuba should be part of the United States. Cuba was rich and growing, its slave trade flourishing even after the slave trade to the United States had ended. Abolitionists and others talked of freeing Cuba both from slavery and from the Spanish, whereas white Southerners talked of adding this jewel to the slave empire.

The United States offered to buy Cuba from Spain in 1848, but met a rude rebuff. Franklin Pierce, pressured by the Southerners in his party and in his cabinet, in the early 1850s renewed the effort to "detach" Cuba from Spain. American diplomats in Europe created a furor when they clumsily wrote the "Ostend Manifesto," a statement of the policy they wanted the administration to follow: gain Cuba one way or the other. When the "manifesto" was leaked to the press, the Pierce administration was widely vilified. Pierce publicly renounced any intention of taking over Cuba. The movement to expand the United States into the Caribbean came to a temporary halt.

The Kansas-Nebraska Act

As the Cuban episode revealed, Franklin Pierce proved to be an ineffectual president. The best hope for the Democrats, Stephen A. Douglas determined, was to deflect attention to the West. Douglas called for two kinds of action: organizing the territories of the West, especially the Kansas and Nebraska area, and building a railroad across the continent to bind together the expanded United States. The two actions were interrelated, for the railroad could not be built through unorganized territory. Partly to get southern votes for the territorial organization and partly because he believed that slavery would not survive in the northern territories, Douglas wrote a bill invalidating the Missouri Compromise line. He proposed that the people of the new territories decide for themselves whether or not their states would permit slaves and slaveholders. Adopting the phrase, "popular sovereignty," Douglas put it forward in the Kansas-Nebraska Bill.

Douglas' plan unleashed political and sectional resentments that had been bottled up by prior compromises. Six prominent Free Soil senators, including Salmon P. Chase, Charles Sumner, and Joshua Giddings, denounced the plan as a plot by a "Slave Power" to make Nebraska a "dreary region of despotism, inhabited by masters and slaves."

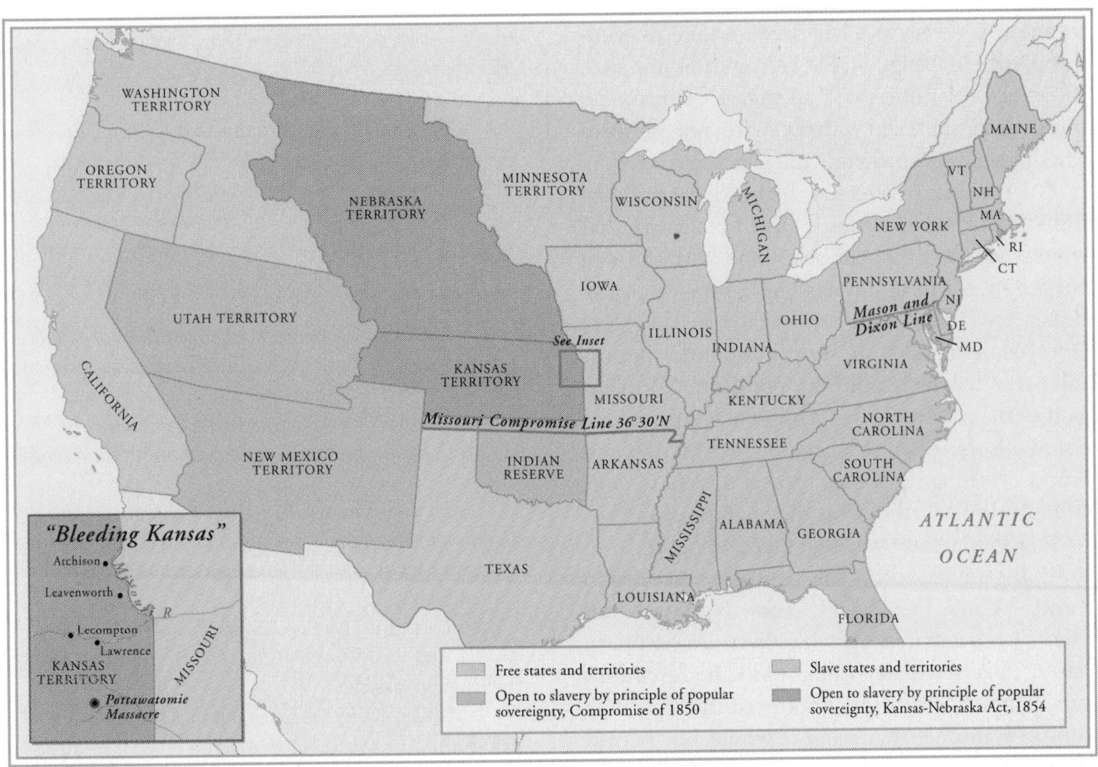

MAP 12.3 | KANSAS-NEBRASKA AND SLAVERY

Northern ministers publicly protested the pending legislation, while newspapers throughout the North scornfully attacked the proposal. Despite the widespread opposition, however, the opponents of the Kansas-Nebraska Bill could not coordinate their efforts sufficiently to stop its passage.

The fight over Kansas-Nebraska inflamed northern resentment as never before. Many Northerners determined that they could no longer trust Southerners to keep a bargain and that Northerners were no longer obligated to enforce the Fugitive Slave Act because the Kansas-Nebraska Act had nullified the Compromise of 1850. Attempts to arrest and extradite Anthony Burns, a fugitive slave in Boston, created such a turmoil that the mayor called out 1,500 militia to line the streets along the route between the courthouse and the ship that was to take Burns back to slavery in Virginia.

The Kansas-Nebraska Act sparked a chain reaction. It divided the Democratic party across the North; it upset the fragile balance of power between North and South in Congress; it provided a set of common concerns and language to unite disgruntled Northern Whigs, Free Soilers, and abolitionists. The Know-Nothings took advantage of the widespread disillusionment with the two major parties to work along lines apparently unrelated to slavery.

Over the next two years the northern political system churned as voters looked for a party that would reflect their concerns and also have a chance of winning power. The Know-Nothings began to fade almost as quickly as they had emerged. They came to seem just another political party led by ambitious politicians. Violent gangs that terrorized immigrants under the Know-Nothing banner alienated many voters and Know-Nothing legislators proved unable to control or punish Catholics as they had promised.

In 1854, a party was founded in Wisconsin to unite disgruntled voters. The new party appealed to former Whigs, Free Soilers, Know-Nothings, and even Democrats fed up with their pro-Southern party. This new party called itself the "Republican" party. Its platform announced that "no man can own another man" and it would not permit slavery in the territories or in new states.

CONCLUSION

The late 1840s and early 1850s saw the United States energized by victory over Mexico and the acquisition of vast new territories, by railroads and clipper ships, by westward migration, and by the arrival of millions of immigrants. As northern family farms spread during the good times, however, so did southern slavery. The gold of the West brought not only wealth but also lawlessness. The cities of the Atlantic coast seemed full to overflowing with immigrants from Ireland and Germany, whereas the cities of the Pacific burgeoned with immigrants from China and restless men from back east. Politicians seemed helpless in the face of these changes. Each political compromise only seemed to make things worse. The parties that had held the country together for a quarter of a century began to buckle under the stress.

RECOMMENDED READINGS

Anbinder, Tyler. *Nativism and Slavery: The Northern Know-Nothings and the Politics of the 1850s* (1992). Provides a full and balanced account.

Fellman, Michael. *The Unbounded Frame: Freedom and Community in Nineteenth-Century American Utopianism* (1973). A helpful overview of perfectionist communities.

Griffith, Elisabeth. *In Her Own Right: The Life of Elizabeth Cady Stanton* (1984). The compelling story of this crucial leader of the woman suffrage movement.

Hedrick, Joan D. *Harriet Beecher Stowe: A Life* (1994). A detailed portrait of the author of *Uncle Tom's Cabin.*

Hietala, Thomas R. *Manifest Design: Anxious Aggrandizement in Late Jacksonian America* (1985). Ties the war with Mexico into the larger patterns of life in the United States.

Lott, Eric. *Love and Theft: Blackface Minstrelsy and the American Working Class* (1993). An original and challenging analysis.

Miller, Kerby A. *Emigrants and Exiles: Ireland and the Irish Exodus to North America* (1985). A full account of the origins and impact of this migration.

Potter, David M. *The Impending Crisis: 1848–1861* (1976). A superb overview of American politics from the wake of the Mexican War to the outbreak of the Civil War.

Reynolds, David S. *Beneath the American Renaissance: The Subversive Imagination in the Age of Emerson and Melville* (1988). A brilliant exploration of the "classic" era of American literature.

Rohrbough, Malcolm J. *Days of Gold: The California Gold Rush and the American Nation* (1997). Offers a fresh and exciting account of its subject.

AMERICAN JOURNEY ONLINE AND INFOTRAC COLLEGE EDITION

Visit the source collections at www.americanjourney.psmedia.com and infotrac.thomsonlearning.com and use the Search function with the following key terms to explore documents, images, audio and video clips, articles, and commentary related to the material in this chapter.

Elizabeth Cady Stanton
Sojourner Truth
Zachary Taylor
Nathaniel Hawthorne
William Lloyd Garrison
Walt Whitman
Uncle Tom's Cabin
Harriet Beecher Stowe
Mormons
Seneca Falls Convention
Gold Rush
Herman Melville
Fugitive Slave Law
Know-Nothings
Kansas-Nebraska Act

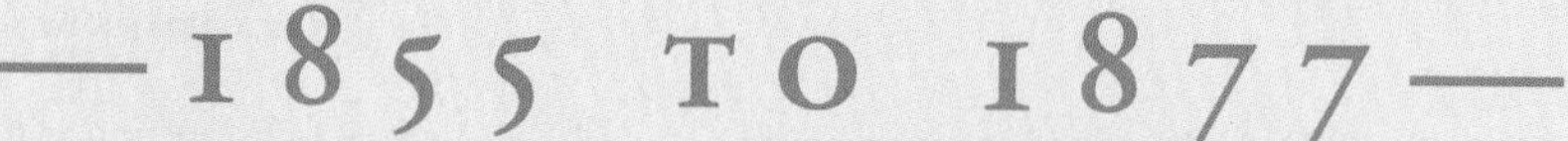

—1855 to 1877—

PASSAGES

Americans of the 1850s had no idea that the Civil War awaited them. They could not imagine that a vast war, larger than any Europe had known, could overwhelm the new republic. New farms and plantations, after all, spread rapidly in expectation of more boom years like the 1850s. Villages and workshops spread throughout the North while cities, fed by millions of immigrants from Europe, grew rapidly at harbors and along railroads and rivers. In the South, cotton and slavery created a per capita income for white Southerners higher than that of any country in Europe except England. Slavery, it was clear, would not collapse of its own contradictions any time soon; the institution had never been more profitable. Telegraphs, newspapers, steamboats, and railroads tied the North and South together more tightly every year.

The two sections viewed each other as aggressive and expansionist, intent on making the nation all one thing or another. The North claimed that the slaveholder South would destroy the best government on earth rather than accept the results of a fair election. The white South claimed that the arrogant and greedy North would destroy the nation rather than acknowledge what the Constitution had established. Both sides were filled with righteous rage, accepting violence to gain the upper hand, whether that involved capturing fugitive slaves or applauding John Brown's failed insurrection. Americans could not stop the momentum they had themselves created. Despite desperate efforts at compromise and delay, the war came.

Once the war could no longer be avoided, most people threw themselves into the conflict alongside their neighbors, whatever doubts they had held before. Confident that the war would be brief, young men on both sides enlisted to teach their enemies a lesson. Both the North and the South proved excellent at war. They innovated freely and successfully, fought relentlessly, discovered effective generals, and mobilized women as well as men. Indeed, the North's strengths and the South's strengths balanced so that the war went on for four years, killing 630,000 people, a proportion of the population equivalent to 5 million people in the United States today and a number larger than the country was ever to sacrifice in another war.

Throughout the conflict, from Lincoln's election to his death, the role of slavery remained both powerful and unclear. Lincoln announced that the war was for Union, not abolition. The Confederacy announced that the war was for independence, not merely slavery. Enslaved Americans in the South, however, forced slavery as an issue on both the Union and the Confederacy, risking their lives to flee to Union camps, undermining plantations and farms. Lincoln and much of the North came to see that ending slavery would end the Confederacy and help redeem the death and suffering. Two hundred thousand black men enlisted as soldiers and played a key role in bringing the Union victory.

The North and the South struggled with themselves even as they fought one another. The North broke apart along lines of class, ethnicity, party, and locale. By 1864, a considerable portion of the northern population wanted the war to end, with compromise if necessary. The opponents of Lincoln expected to overwhelm him in the election that fall and even Lincoln shared that expectation. The white South broke apart along lines of class, locale, and gender. Poor soldiers deserted; upcountry communities shielded deserters and resisted the Confederate government; impoverished white women rioted and resisted. Slaves rushed to the Union army at the first opportunity, every escape weakening the southern economy and Confederate morale.

Events on the battlefield, through 10,000 conflicts large and small, exerted their own logic and momentum. The Union army grew stronger as the Confederate army thinned and weakened. The victories of Grant and Sherman in 1864 destroyed the South's best hope of a negotiated peace. The relentless spread of the Union army throughout the South divided the Confederacy into smaller and smaller pieces, each helpless to aid the other. When Lee's army fell into defeat, the Confederate nation dissolved almost immediately.

Whatever Lincoln's plans for reuniting the nation, those plans ended at Ford's Theater in April of 1865. His successor, Andrew Johnson, took the most cautious route possible, limiting the scope of black freedom in every way he could. The white South's resolve, indeed, seemed greater than any power the Union wielded in the South. African Americans struggled to make their freedom real: they mobilized politically, founded churches and schools, and reconstituted families. They demanded rights as Americans and did all they could to secure those rights. Black Southerners found many white northern allies but many more white southern enemies who quickly turned to violence, as well as white Northerners who supported or tolerated the violence. The years of 1866 and 1867 were full of a promise and a terror no one could have imagined ten years before. In many ways, the Civil War had not yet ended; its consequences had hardly begun.

For the next decade, Reconstruction in the South gradually receded. The process left blacks with political rights in law because of the Fourteenth and Fifteenth Amendments, but with limited power. The presidency of Ulysses S. Grant was a disappointment because the hero of the war proved unable to provide effective leadership, sectional reconciliation, or honest government. An economic collapse in 1873 helped the Democrats restore the national political balance and hasten the end of Reconstruction. The disputed election between Rutherford B. Hayes and Samual J. Tilden in 1876 saw the abandonment of black Southerners to the rule of those who believed in white supremacy. The Civil War had preserved the Union and abolished slavery, but the unsettled problem of race cast a long shadow into the future.

For additional information and resources pertaining to this period in American history, please visit the American Passages Web Site at:

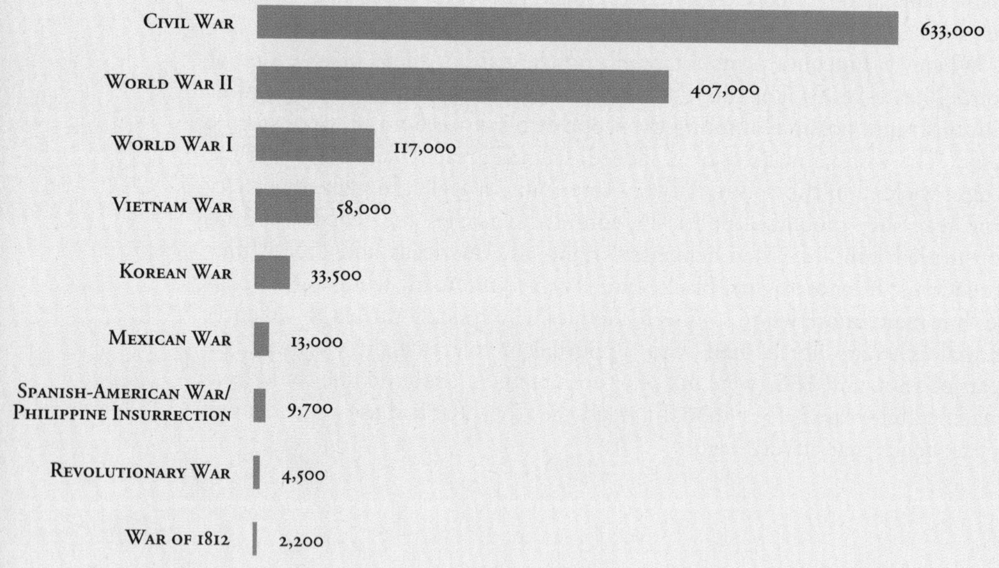

Winslow Homer's, Sunday Morning in Virginia, 1877. (Cincinnati Art Museum, John M. Emerey Fund. Acc 1924-247)

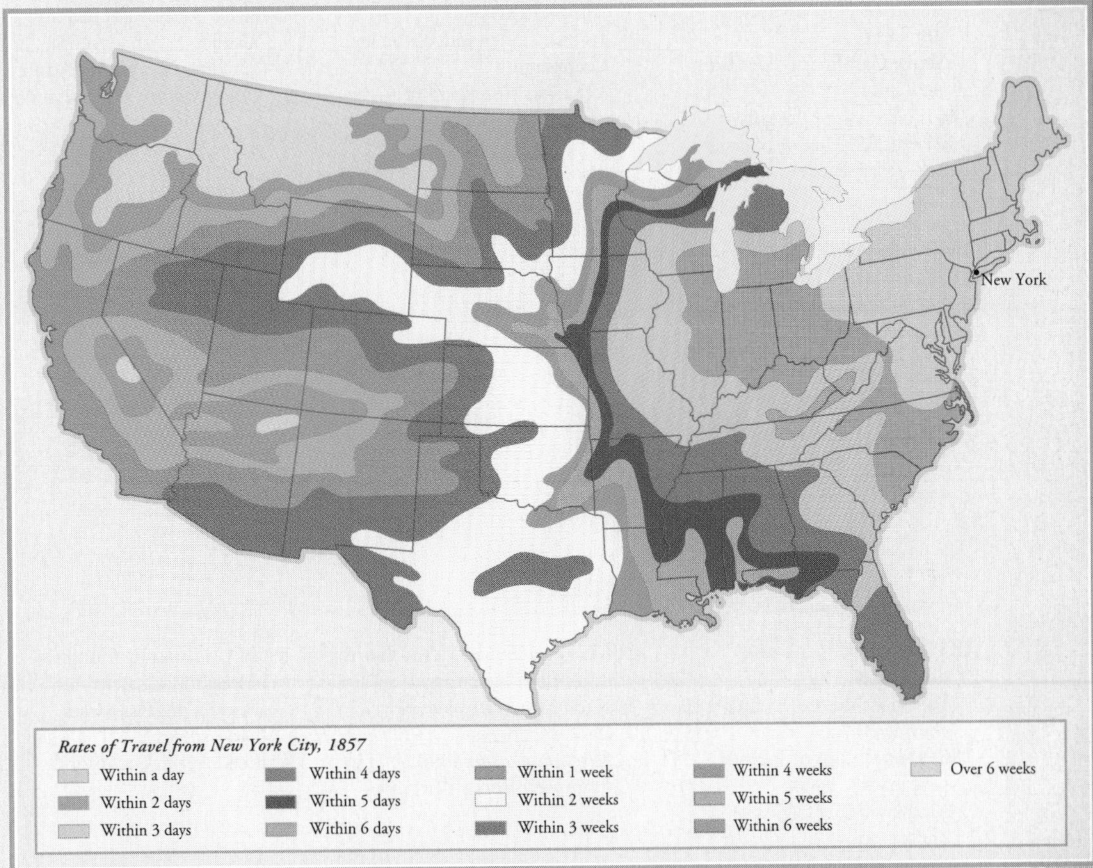

New York

Rates of Travel from New York City, 1857

Within a day
Within 2 days
Within 3 days
Within 4 days
Within 5 days
Within 6 days
Within 1 week
Within 2 weeks
Within 3 weeks
Within 4 weeks
Within 5 weeks
Within 6 weeks
Over 6 weeks

	1855	1861	1862	1863

POLITICS & DIPLOMACY

1855: Proslavery and free-soil forces clash in Kansas
Massachusetts desegregates public schools
1856: John Brown's raid in Kansas
James Buchanan elected president
Congressman Preston Brooks canes Senator Charles Sumner
1857: *Dred Scott* decision
Lecompton Constitution
Hinton R. Helper, *The Impending Crisis of the South*
1858: Lincoln-Douglas debates
1859: John Brown's raid on Harpers Ferry
Vicksburg convention calls for reopening of African slave trade
Kansas ratifies free-soil constitution
1860: Democratic convention divides
Abraham Lincoln elected president
South Carolina secedes from the Union
1861: Mississippi, Florida, Alabama, Georgia, Louisiana, and Texas secede
Montgomery Convention creates Confederate States of America
Lincoln inaugurated
Firing on and surrender of Fort Sumter
Arkansas, Tennessee, Virginia, and North Carolina secede
Confederate victory at Bull Run (Manassas)
Jefferson Davis elected president of Confederacy with six-year term
Union navy seizes Confederate commisioners Mason and Slidell from British ship *Trent*
1862: Confederates surrender Fort Donelson to Grant
Virginia v. Monitor in Hampton Roads, Virginia
Grant wins dramatic victory at Shiloh
New Orleans surrenders to Admiral Farragut
Jackson's Shenandoah Valley Campaign
Lee takes command of Army of Northern Virginia
Lee drives McClellan from Richmond in Seven Days' Battles
Confederate victory at Second Bull Run (Manassas)
Battle of Antietam (Sharpsburg)
First Emancipation Proclamation
Burnside replaces McClellan as commander of Army of the Potomac
Lee overwhelms Burnside at Fredericksburg
1863: Second Emancipation Proclamation
Culmination of Lee's victory over Hooker at Chancellorsville
Grant's successful campaign in Mississippi
Death of Stonewall Jackson
Union victory at Gettysburg
Vicksburg surrenders to Grant
Black troops fight at Fort Wagner, South Carolina
Lincoln's Gettysburg Address
Union victory at Chattanooga

SOCIAL & CULTURAL EVENTS

1857: Mass revivals
1858: Frederick Law Olmsted begins design for Central Park in New York City
1863: Lincoln's Gettysburg Address

ECONOMICS & TECHNOLOGY

1857: Financial panic and depression
Baltimore–St. Louis rail service completed
1861: Suspension of specie payments
Mathew Brady begins photography of Civil War
1862: Legal Tender Act in North authorizes "greenbacks"
Homestead Act passed by Union Congress
Virginia v. Monitor in Hampton Roads, Virginia
1863: Confederate Congress passes Impressment Act
Union Congress passes National Bank Act
Bread riot in Richmond

1864 1865 1866 1870 1871 1877

1864: Grant assumes command of all Union forces
Battle of the Wilderness in Virginia
Union victory at Cold Harbor
Sherman captures Atlanta
Lincoln reelected president
Beginning of Sherman's march from Atlanta to the Atlantic

1865: Congress passes Thirteenth Amendment, abolishing slavery
Congress creates Bureau of Refugees, Freedmen, and Abandoned Lands (Freedmen's Bureau)
Lincoln's second inauguration
Fall of Richmond to Union
Lee surrenders to Grant at Appomattox Court House
Lincoln assassinated; Andrew Johnson becomes president
Former Confederate states hold constitutional conventions through December; pass "black codes"
Thirteenth Amendment to Constitution ratified, abolishing slavery

1866: Congress passes Civil Rights Act and Freedmen's Bureau renewal over Johnson's veto
Riots in New Orleans and Memphis
Congress approves Fourteenth Amendment
Ku Klux Klan formed

1867: Congress passes Reconstruction Act and Tenure of Office Act
Johnson dismisses Secretary of War Stanton, triggering impeachment proceedings
First elections in South under Reconstruction Act
Passage of Reconstruction Act
Alaska purchase negotiations

1868: Andrew Johnson impeached and acquitted
U. S. Grant elected President

1869: Fifteenth Amendment passes Congress
Woman suffrage starts in Wyoming Territory

1870: Ku Klux Klan conducts terror raids in South

1871: Tweed Ring exposed in New York City

1872: Grant reelected

1873: Salary Grab and Credit Mobilier scandals

1874: Democrats gain in congressional elections

1875: Civil Rights Act passes Congress

1876: Hayes and Tilden in disputed election

1877: Hayes declared president after compromises settle election dispute

---

1865: First woman professor of astronomy appointed at Vassar College

1866: American Equal Rights Association founded to seek black and woman suffrage

1867: Horatio Alger begins publishing series of books for young boys

1868: Louisa May Alcott publishes *Little Women*

1869: Licensing of women lawyers begins
First intercollegiate football game played between Princeton and Rutgers

1870: First Greek letter sorority, Kappa Alpha Theta, founded

1871: Cable car invented

1872: American Public Health Association starts

1873: Mark Twain and Charles Dudley Warner publish *The Gilded Age*

1874: Women's Christian Temperance Union founded

1875: Smith and Wellesley College open to provide higher education for women

1876: Centennial Exposition in Philadelphia

1864: Confederate Congress assumes new powers of taxation, impressment of slaves
George Pullman invents sleeping car

1866: National Labor Union organized

1867: Patrons of Husbandry (Grange) founded

1868: First 8-hour day for federal workers

1869: Gold Corner scheme of Jay Gould and Jim Fisk
Transcontinental Railroad completed

1870: Standard Oil Company of Ohio organized

1871: Chicago fire burns center of city

1872: Adding machine invented

1873: Panic of 1873 starts depression

1874: Sale of typewriters begins
Tomkins Square riot of unemployed in New York City

1875: First dynamo for outdoor lighting constructed

1876: Heinz tomato ketchup marketed

1877: National railroad strike

Chapter 13

Broken Bonds, 1855–1861

THE UNITED STATES had never seemed stronger than at the beginning of 1855. The economy was booming, settlers pushed into the West, railroads spread at a relentless rate, and immigrants streamed into American farms and factories. Churches, schools, asylums, and reform organizations grew faster than ever.

But the signs of danger were not hard to see. The conflict between the North and the South grew more bitter with each passing political crisis. Every year brought a clash more divisive than the one before. The battle between North and South broke out in the Kansas territory, in the village of Harpers Ferry, and finally in the contest for president. The party system, weakened by nativism and loss of faith by voters, seemed powerless to stop the disintegration.

Sectional Conflict

Conflict between the North and the South had been a staple of American politics for decades before 1855. Territories proved a persistent problem, but Northerners and Southerners also argued over the tariff, nominees for high office, and religion. The arguments grew hot, but eventually calmed down until the next outbreak. Events of the late 1850s, however, broke the pattern. New crises came before the old ones could dissipate. The crises embroiled every political, economic, moral, and practical difference between the North and the South.

Bleeding Kansas

The Kansas-Nebraska Act declared that settlers would decide for themselves, in their "popular sovereignty," what kind of society they would create. But partisans from both the North and the South determined to fill the territory with settlers of their own political persuasion. "Come on, then, Gentlemen of the slave States," New York's Senator William H. Seward proclaimed soon after the Kansas-Nebraska Act passed. "We will engage in competition for the virgin soil of Kansas, and God give the victory to the side which is stronger in numbers as it is in right."

The Massachusetts Emigrant Aid Company announced that it planned to dispatch \$5 million and 20,000 settlers to Kansas to ensure that the

CHRONOLOGY

1855 Proslavery and free-soil forces clash in Kansas

Massachusetts desegregates public schools

1856 John Brown's raid in Kansas

James Buchanan elected president

Congressman Preston Brooks canes Senator Charles Sumner

1857 Financial panic and depression

Dred Scott decision

Lecompton Constitution

Baltimore–St. Louis rail service completed

Hinton R. Helper, *The Impending Crisis of the South*

Mass revivals

1858 Lincoln-Douglas debates

Frederick Law Olmsted begins design for Central Park in New York City

1859 John Brown's raid on Harpers Ferry

Vicksburg convention calls for reopening of African slave trade

Kansas ratifies free-soil constitution

1860 Democratic convention divides

Abraham Lincoln elected president

South Carolina secedes from the Union

1861 Mississippi, Florida, Alabama, Georgia, Louisiana, and Texas secede

Montgomery Convention creates Confederate States of America

Lincoln inaugurated

Firing on and surrender of Fort Sumter

embattled territory became a free state. Advocates of slavery in Kansas believed that the forces of abolition would overwhelm the territory before slaveholders could move there. The abolitionist press encouraged the impression that the anti-slavery settlers constituted a formidable foe.

Proslavery advocates in Missouri fought what they saw as Yankee invaders. On election day, they flooded across the border to vote in support of the proslavery candidates for the territorial legislature. This action by the "border ruffians," as the northern press quickly labeled them, was not necessary, for Southerners already accounted for six of every ten men settled in Kansas by 1855. In any case, the proslavery forces triumphed and took control of the territorial legislature in Lecompton. There, they passed a series of aggressive laws against free-soil advocates. Forbidding anti-slavery men to serve on juries or hold office, the legislature also decreed the death penalty for any person who assisted a fugitive slave.

Anti-slavery Kansans decided that their only recourse was to establish a rival government. They worked through the summer and fall of 1855 in Topeka to write a constitution of their own. Over the winter, the free-soil advocates "ratified" the constitution and elected their own legislature and governor. The free-soil delegates felt justified by the obvious injustice of their proslavery opponents.

Anti-slavery forces in New England and New York sent rifles to Kansas to arm what they saw as the side of righteousness. Southerners, in turn, organized an expedition to reinforce their comrades. Not surprisingly, this volatile situation soon exploded into violence. On May 21, 1856, a group of slave-state supporters marched into the free-soil stronghold of Lawrence, threw printing presses into the river, fired cannon at the Free State Hotel, and burned the hotel to the ground. Free-soilers labeled the episode the "sack of Lawrence."

At about the same time, in Washington, D.C., Representative Preston Brooks of South Carolina searched out Senator Charles Sumner of Massachusetts. Sumner had delivered a series of bitter speeches against slavery. Sumner attacked Brooks' relative and fellow South Carolinian, the elderly Senator Andrew P. Butler, for taking "the harlot, slavery" as his "mistress." Brooks, defending the honor of his family and his state, demonstrated his contempt for Sumner by striking him repeatedly about the head with a heavy rubber cane. Sumner, seated at a Senate desk screwed to the floor, ripped the chair from its moorings as he tried to rise. He did not return to his seat for two and a half years, the victim of shock. The empty seat became a symbol in the North of southern brutality; the incident became a symbol in the South of the only sort of response the arrogant North would respect.

The next day, an event back in Kansas intensified the conflict. The episode swirled around one John Brown, a free-soil emigrant to Kansas. Brown had been a supporter of abolitionism since 1834 and followed five of his sons to Kansas in 1855. There, he became furious at the proslavery forces. He accompanied a group of free-staters to defend Lawrence, but they heard of the hotel's destruction before they arrived. Brown persuaded four of his sons and a son-in-law, along with two other men, to exact revenge for the defeat. The band set out for Pottawatomie Creek. There, acting in the name of the "Army of the North," they took five men from three houses and split open their skulls. The men had been associated in some way with the territorial district court, but no one was, or is, sure of Brown's precise motives. He was never punished for the killings.

In the wake of the "sack of Lawrence," the caning of Sumner, and the "Pottawatomie Massacre"—exploding in just a three-day period in May of 1856—the territory became known as "Bleeding Kansas." A new governor finally helped quiet the conflict in September, but the legitimacy of the territorial government remained an issue of heated contention. The South won a hollow victory when it seized the first election for the

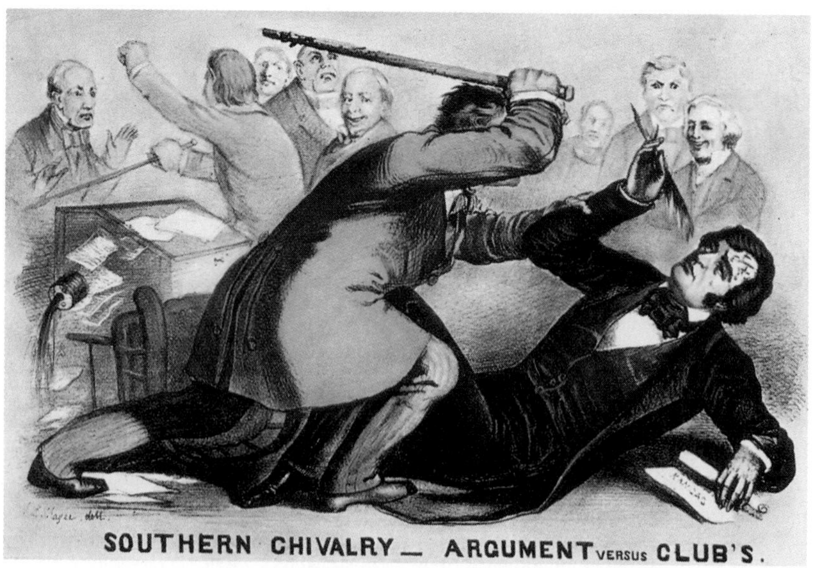

Preston Brooks' attack on Charles Sumner in the United States Senate electrified the nation in the spring of 1856. (The Granger Collection, New York)

territorial government in Kansas. That government would soon pass, but the symbolic value of Bleeding Kansas would long endure.

The Election of 1856

The events in Kansas proved a disaster for the Democrats. In one state after another, Democratic senators lost office in the off-year elections of 1854. To many Southerners, the Democrats seemed a mere tool of Stephen Douglas and his northern allies; to many Northerners, it seemed that Douglas' call for popular sovereignty was a cover for greedy slaveholders. President Franklin Pierce seemed incapable of leadership. The Democrats, needing someone who had not been tarnished by the events of the preceding two years, turned to James Buchanan to run in 1856. As minister to England, Buchanan had conveniently been out of the country during the entire Kansas mess.

The Know-Nothings alienated voters on both sides of the slavery issue by refusing to address the territorial problem directly. Southerners who had voted with the Know-Nothings had nowhere to turn but to the Democrats, but Northerners could devote their attention to the new Republican party. The Republicans bypassed their most outspoken anti-slavery men for the 1856 nomination and turned to John C. Frémont, famed as an explorer of the West. He had taken almost no public positions and had accumulated almost no political experience. The Republicans thought they had found just the sort of vague candidate who would give few potential voters a reason to vote against him.

The new Republican party was anti-slavery but not pro-black; Republicans avoided talking about race. What they did talk about was the goodness of the North: the North, they argued, was everything the South was not, a place where hardworking white men could build a life for their families free from the threat of arrogant, powerful, and greedy slaveholders.

The Republicans talked of the "Slave Power," a political conspiracy of the most powerful slaveholders. Republicans saw everything from the three-fifths clause to the bloodshed in Kansas as the fruit of the Slave Power. How else to explain the long list of southern victories at a time when the North grew more populous and wealthy? Kansas and the caning of Sumner showed that the Slave Power, a Cincinnati paper raged, "cannot tolerate free speech anywhere, and would stifle it in Washington with the bludgeon and the bowie-knife, as they are now trying to stifle it in Kansas."

Republicans attacked Catholics as well, repeating the charges that nativists had made for decades. Ironically, rumors that Frémont was a Catholic quickly surfaced and refused to subside. Moreover, Frémont refused to give direction to the national campaign. To make matters worse, Millard Fillmore, the former president, ran under the banner of the American party, as the Know-Nothings called themselves. Fillmore hoped that the three-way election would split the electorate so that the final decision would rest with the House, where he would appear as a compromise candidate.

On election day in 1856, 83 percent of the eligible voting men went to the polls, one of the highest turnouts of the era. Although Buchanan won all of the South except Maryland, he received only 45 percent of the popular vote in the country as a whole. A difference of a few thousand votes in a few states would have denied Buchanan the election. The Democrats had won, but were filled with anxiety; the Republicans had lost, but were filled with confidence. It was clear to everyone that the American political system was in flux and transition.

Observers of all political persuasions believed that James Buchanan had it within his power to strengthen the Democrats in both the North and the South. His party, after all, still controlled both houses of Congress. The Republicans, moreover, had drawn much of their power from the chaos in Kansas. Once Kansas had peacefully entered the Union as a free state under the banner of popular sovereignty, Democrats happily observed, no other territory awaited in which similar conflicts might be expected. Slavery, everyone seemed to

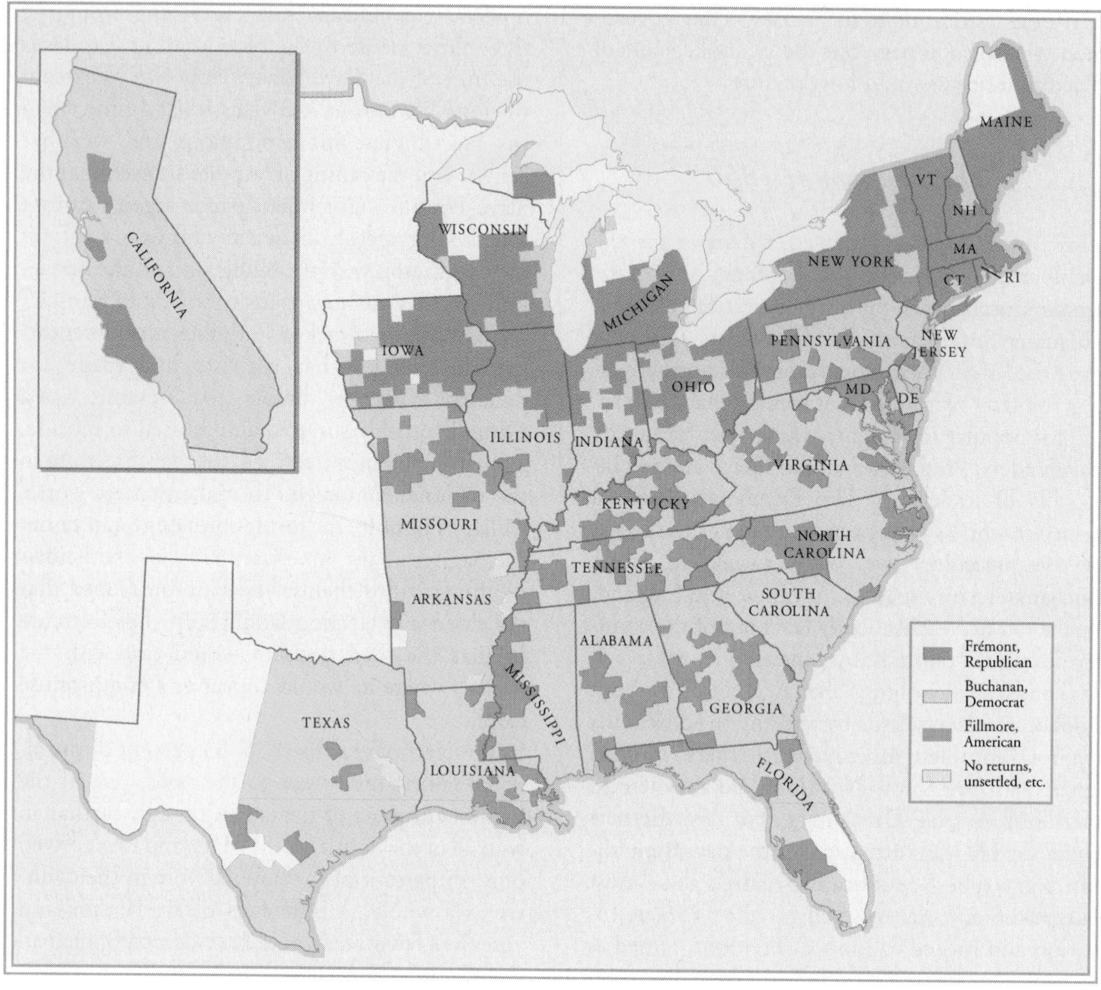

Map 13.1 | The Election of 1856

agree, had no chance in Oregon, Nebraska, Minnesota, Washington, Utah, or New Mexico. The territorial issue that had torn at the country since 1820 might finally die down.

Dred Scott

In his inaugural address, James Buchanan mentioned a case pending before the Supreme Court, the case of Dred Scott, a slave. That case had moved its way through various levels of courts for more than a decade. Scott, born in Virginia around 1800, had in the 1830s been taken by his master, an army surgeon named John Emerson, to territories far in the upper Midwest. Scott had married Harriet Robinson, the slave of a federal Indian agent. Dr. Emerson bought Harriet and thus owned the two daughters she bore with Scott. When Emerson died in 1843, Scott and his family became the property of Emerson's widow, who moved to St. Louis. In 1846 the Scotts petitioned for their freedom, claiming that their residence in the free territory entitled them to free status.

A long series of postponements and delays dragged the case on into the early 1850s, when the legal environment had become much more divided by political controversy over slavery. Democratic judges and lawyers worked to deny the Scotts their freedom on the grounds that such a precedent would undermine the right of Southerners to take slaves into the territories. A Republican lawyer agreed to carry the Scotts' case before the Supreme Court to counter the Democrats' aggressive claims. Unfortunately for the Republicans and the Scotts, five southern Democrats sat on the court, along with two northern Democrats, one northern Whig, and one northern Republican. Presiding was Chief Justice Roger B. Taney (pronounced "tawney"), an eighty-year-old Marylander first appointed to the court by Andrew Jackson in 1835.

The *Dred Scott* case came before the Supreme Court during the superheated months of 1856, when Kansas, the Brooks/Sumner affair, and the presidential election commanded the country's attention. Although the case could have been decided on relatively narrow grounds, the Democratic members of the Court wanted to issue a sweeping pronouncement that would settle once and for all the question of slavery in the territories. President-elect Buchanan pressured a fellow Pennsylvanian on the court to side with the Southerners. Two days after Buchanan took office in March of 1857, the court announced its decision in the *Dred Scott* case. It took Chief Justice Taney two hours to read the opinion.

Taney spent half his time denying that Scott had the right to bring a case in the first place. Black people, Taney decreed, could not become citizens of the United States because "they were not included, and were not intended to be included, under the word 'citizens' in the Constitution." Taney declared that at the time the Constitution was written, throughout the "civilized and enlightened portions of the world," members of the "negro African race" were held to be "altogether unfit to associate with the white race . . . and so far inferior, that they had no rights which the white man was bound to respect." Therefore,

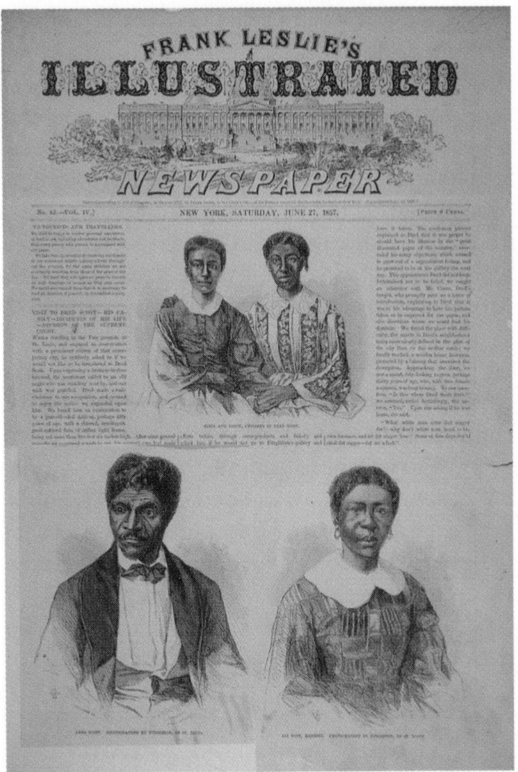
FRANK LESLIE'S
ILLUSTRATED
NEWSPAPER
NEW YORK, SATURDAY, JUNE 27, 1857.

The Dred Scott *case attracted the attention of the entire country in 1856. This northern newspaper depicted Scott and his family sympathetically, emphasizing family ties and the women of the family.* (The Granger Collection, New York)

Dred Scott had never been a citizen of Missouri and had no right to sue his mistress. Taney also decreed that Congress had never held a constitutional right to restrict slavery in the territories and that therefore the Missouri Compromise of 1820 was invalid. Two justices dissented from the majority's opinion, but the decision stood as the law of the land.

White Southerners exulted that they had been vindicated by the *Dred Scott* decision, that the Republicans' demand for territories free of slavery was simply unconstitutional. The Republicans, however, sneered at the decision, which they saw as one more corrupt act by the Slave Power Conspiracy. They reprinted the dissenting opinions in the *Dred Scott* case and denounced the decision in the state legislatures they controlled throughout the North. They argued that the Founding Fathers had never intended slavery to be a permanent part of the United States and merely tolerated bondage because they expected it to die of its own weight. If the *Dred Scott* decision were followed to its logical conclusion, they warned, the United States would reopen the slave trade with Africa and even extend slavery into northern states where it had been banned.

The Republicans thought the Court's audacious statement "the best thing that could have happened" to the Republican party. As an abolitionist newspaper put it, the "fiercer the insult, the bitterer the blow, the better." The Republicans expected the *Dred Scott* decision to make their party stronger. The Republicans needed to sweep the government in 1860, they argued, to clean out corruption and conspiracy from top to bottom.

Arguments over Slavery

Slavery had never been stronger in the United States than it was in 1857. The three and a half million slaves of the South extended over a vast territory stretching from Delaware to Texas. Theorists devised ever more elaborate and aggressive defenses of slavery, no longer depicting it merely as a necessary evil or an unfortunate inheritance from the English. Rather, they claimed, slavery was an instrument of God's will, a means of civilizing and Christianizing Africans otherwise lost to barbarism and heathenism. Southern physicians went to great lengths to prove that Africans and their descendants were physically and intellectually inferior to whites.

Some defenders of slavery argued that slavery was *better* than free labor, more humane and Christian. If the hypocritical and self-righteous men of the North would admit it, white Southerners argued, free labor exacted a great cost. Men, women, and children went hungry when unemployment, ill health, or old age struck. In the South, by contrast, slaveholders cared for their slaves even when those slaves had grown too old or feeble to work. The South's relative lack of schools, orphanages, asylums, and prisons, the defenders of the region insisted, testified not to backwardness but to a personalized society where individual responsibility replaced impersonal institutions.

Some white Southerners in the late 1850s argued for the expansion of American territory in Cuba or Central America, places where slavery could flourish. William Walker, a young Tennesseean, dreamed of personal glory and a new territory for slavery. After several attempts at "filibustering," small-scale military efforts, in Mexico, Walker took advantage of a civil war to gain power in Nicaragua in 1855 and 1856. But Central American leaders united against him, cholera wiped out his army, and the United States rejected his claims to legitimacy. White Southerners enthusiastically supported several attempts by Walker in the late 1850s to take Nicaragua, but he failed repeatedly.

Despite the agitation of a few editors and politicians for the reopening of the African slave trade, most white Southerners wanted above all to keep and protect what they had, not jeopardize slavery by brashly expanding it. Not only would a renewed slave trade with Africa ignite the opinion of the world against the South, but it would also drive down slave prices and create new problems of discipline and revolt. The white South prided itself on having created a stable and prosperous society during its two and a half centuries of slavery and did not want to endanger that society.

Moreover, the slave economy boomed in the late 1850s. Planters took advantage of improved cotton gins, river boats, railroads, and new kinds of seed to double, in the 1850s alone, their production of cotton. The claim of southern politicians that "Cotton is King" proved no empty boast. Even though northern factories and farms grew rapidly in the 1850s, cotton still accounted for fully half of all U.S. exports. Without cotton, many thousands of northern and British workers would have had no jobs.

The prosperity created by the cotton boom resonated throughout the southern economy. Southern cities grew quickly, attracting immigrants and businesses. Although the South could not keep up with the North, it actually did quite well by international standards. Considered as a separate economy, the South stood second in the world in the number of miles of railroad, sixth in cotton textile factories, and eighth in iron production. Slaves proved to be adaptable both to factories and cities. The number of slaves in cities declined in the 1850s mainly because the demand for slaves in the countryside was so strong.

The southern economy, then, was not weak or weakening in the 1850s. On the other hand, the South was not urbanizing or industrializing nearly as quickly as the North. The South did not create a large class of entrepreneurs or skilled workers, nor did the region invest much money in machinery to make its farms and plantations more efficient. The southern plantation economy, in effect, was too profitable for its own good. The short-term gains of the 1850s dissuaded wealthy Southerners from investing in businesses that held greater potential for long-term development.

Northerners considered the southern economy the mirror image of the North: sick rather than healthy, backward rather than dynamic. Critics of the South argued that slavery victimized not only slaves but also "poor whites." In the anti-slavery portrayal, the Slave Power's domination began at home, where haughty self-proclaimed aristocrats lorded over ignorant whites, bullying them into supporting parties and policies that worked against their own interests. Anti-slavery people charged that slaves degraded white labor in the South and substituted a cheap sense of racial superiority for actual accomplishment.

The most effective criticism of the South in this vein came from a Southerner: Hinton Rowan Helper, the son of a small slaveholding farmer in western North Carolina. In 1857, a northern press published Helper's book, *The Impending Crisis of the South,* which argued that the South's growth, prosperity, and cultural development were being held back by slavery. Helper deployed statistics from the census to prove his case, showing that land values, literacy levels, and manufacturing rates in the South were substantially lower than those in the North. He proposed that slaveholders be taxed to colonize all free blacks in Africa or Latin America.

CHART 13.1 EXTENT OF SLAVEHOLDING IN THE SOUTH POPULATION OF 7,981,000

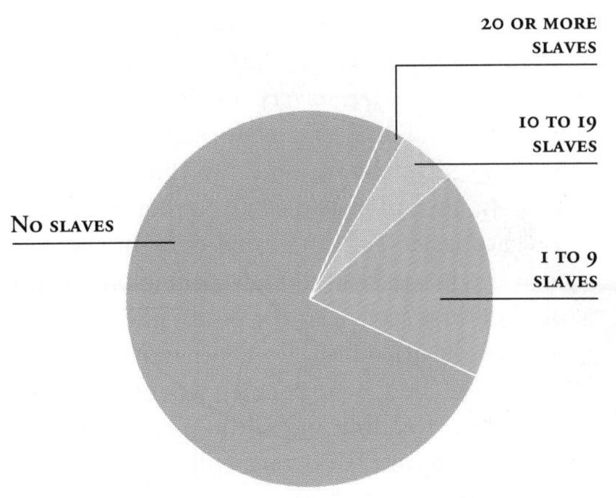

CHART 13.2 PATTERNS OF SLAVEHOLDING IN THE SOUTH, 1850 347,525 FAMILIES

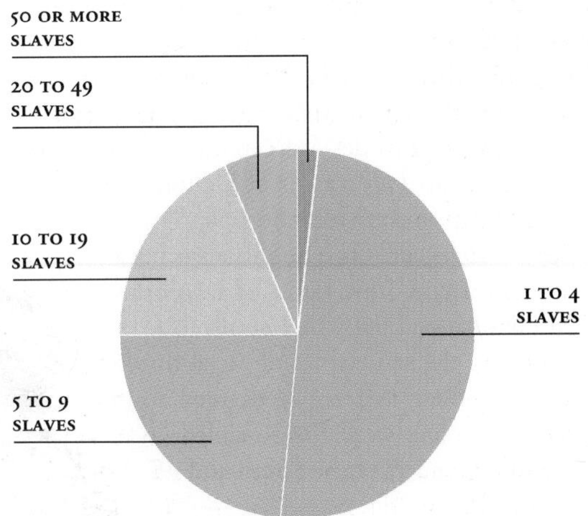

There is little indication that many southern whites agreed with Helper's assessment of their status. Most whites saw slavery as an avenue for their own advancement, not a hindrance. Many men and women bought a slave before they bought land. Slaveowners included women, shopkeepers, industrialists, lawyers, ministers, and even a few free blacks. No investment seemed to offer a more certain return than a slave, especially in the 1850s when slave prices rose rapidly. Although that rise in prices meant that a growing proportion of white people would be unable to afford a slave, most non-slaveholding whites apparently reconciled themselves to their situation or determined that they, too, would eventually join the slaveowning ranks.

Southern Solidarity and Differences

Politics reinforced the sense among southern white men that they lived in a fair and democratic society. Although many non-slaveholders in mountainous districts across the South voted against the large slaveholding districts, most southern white men voted in concert with the richest men in their immediate neighborhoods. In the eyes of the poorer men, their wealthy neighbors could act as spokesmen and brokers for the community in the state capital.

Southern whites identified themselves most of all as white people, tied to other whites by blood and heritage. Whites held black people in contempt despite their knowledge that many African Americans were more intelligent, hardworking, and Christian than many whites. To be white was to be the inheritor of all the accomplishments of the ancients, of Christendom, and the modern world. Such attitudes were reinforced at every level, from the daily rituals of life to the writings of leading thinkers from Europe. White Southerners railed against the Republicans because that party threatened this bond of race between the white North and the white South.

Despite the solidarities of racial thinking, important political differences divided Southerners. At one extreme were the so-called "fire-eaters," virulent defenders of the South and slavery. These men were diverse. Some lived in cities, others on plantations. Some, such as J. D. B. DeBow, wanted to make the South more industrial and modern, where as others rejected such development as a Yankee blight on the rural South. Whatever their differences, these men saw themselves as the voice of honesty. Men such as Robert Barnwell Rhett and Edmund Ruffin argued that the abolitionists and their Republican supporters intended to destroy the South. The only sane response, they believed, was to agitate the slavery issue constantly, to refuse to yield an inch in the territories or anywhere else. The fire-eaters were calling for secession as early as 1857.

At the other end of the political spectrum in the South were the former Whigs and Know-Nothings. They considered the Democrats, especially the fire-eaters, great threats to the future of the South and slavery. Former leaders of the Whigs and the nativist American party did their best to pull their allies into a new party opposed to the Democrats and attractive to a "thoughtful, sedate, constitution-abiding, conservative class of men." The many Unionists in the upper South, in cities, and even in some of the richest plantation districts felt drawn to this position. The editors of the former Whig and American papers warned voters that the Democrats would sell out the South in Kansas, that the Democrats talked a tough game but always ended up caving in to the North.

In the North, too, the major parties had to contend with activists on the fringes of respectable opinion. By 1857, the abolitionists had succeeded in making slavery detested throughout the North and had created much of the anti-southern energy that flowed into the Republican party. But abolitionists distrusted that party. The Republicans seemed interested only in the welfare of the white North. They denied any intention of ending slavery in the South and even resurrected talk of colonization, the movement the abolitionists had abandoned twenty-five years earlier. The Republicans, although better than the pro-southern Democrats, still dissatisfied the abolitionists.

JAMES D. B. DEBOW, "THE INTEREST IN SLAVERY OF THE SOUTHERN NON-SLAVEHOLDER," 1860

DeBow used his statistical expertise as a former superintendent of the United States Census to argue that the South was actually more democratic in property holding than the North and that slavery actually helped the non-slaveholding white Southerner in many ways.

[How does slavery benefit the non-slaveholding white man?]

1. The non-slaveholder of the South is assured that the remuneration afforded by his labor, over and above the expense of living, is larger than that which is afforded by the same labor in the free States.

2. The non-slaveholders, as a class, are not reduced by the necessity of our condition, as is the case in the free States, to find employment in crowded cities and come into competition in close and sickly workshops and factories, with remorseless and untiring machinery.

3. The non-slaveholder is not subjected to that competition with foreign pauper labor, which has degraded the free labor of the North and demoralized it to an extent which perhaps can never be estimated.

4. The non-slaveholder of the South preserves the status of the white man, and is not regarded as an inferior or a dependent.

5. The non-slaveholder knows that as soon as his savings will admit, he can become a slaveholder, and thus relieve his wife from the necessities of the kitchen and the laundry, and his children from the labors of the field.

6. The large slaveholders and proprietors of the South begin life in great part as non-slaveholders.

7. But should such fortune not be in reserve for the non-slaveholder, he will understand that by honesty and industry it may be realized to his children.

8. The sons of the non-slaveholder are and have always been among the leading and ruling spirits of the South; in industry as well as in politics.

9. Without the institution of slavery, the great staple products of the South would cease to be grown, and the immense annual results, which are distributed among every class of the community, and which give life to every branch of industry, would cease.

10. If emancipation be brought about as will undoubtedly be the case, unless the encroachments of the fanatical majorities of the North are resisted now the slaveholders, in the main, will escape the degrading equality which must result, by emigration, for which they would have the means, by disposing of their personal chattels: whilst the non-slaveholders, without these resources, would be compelled to remain and endure the degradation.

SOURCE "The Non-Slaveholders of the South," in DeBow and others, *The Interest in Slavery of the Southern Non-Slaveholder. The Right of Peaceful Secession. Slavery in the Bible.* (Charleston: Evans & Cogswell, 1860), pp. 3–5, 7–12.

A Society in Crisis

The American economy boomed in the mid-1850s. Not only did cotton do well, but so did the farms, factories, railroads, and cities of the North and West. People cheered the laying of a telegraphic cable all the way across the Atlantic Ocean, an incredible feat. Currier and Ives prints became the rage, brightening homes around the country with charming scenes of American life. The sale of newspapers, books, and magazines surged. Working people's organizations staged a comeback. Churches and schools spread with remarkable speed. The mileage of railroads tripled, to more than 30,000 miles.

But underlying this prosperity ran a deep current of unease. Some people worried that Americans were growing soft and self-indulgent. Others felt guilt that as the economy boomed, slavery became stronger. Others despaired at the state of American politics, which seemed in disarray. The conflict between the North and the South embodied all these anxieties, giving them concrete shape.

Financial Panic and Spiritual Revival

Late in the summer of 1857, people warned that there had been too much speculation recently, that companies and individuals had borrowed too much money. The end of the Crimean War in Europe seemed ominous for the United States, for now the countries of the Old World could turn their energies toward growing their own food, undermining the heavy demand for American farm products that had buoyed the economy for several years. When a major insurance company went under in 1857, a panic spread among New York banks, and railroad stocks plummeted along with western land values. Soon, banks and companies across the country began to fail.

Working people of all ranks lost their jobs. Not only unskilled laborers, domestics, and millworkers found themselves without work, but so did educated bookkeepers and clerks. Across the North, hundreds of thousands of people had no income and many were forced to rely on charity to feed and clothe themselves. Workers tried to organize, but employers shut down the mills and factories. As winter approached, many people wondered whether their families would survive through the cold months.

Southerners blamed northern financiers for bringing on the panic of 1857. Though the white and free black working people of southern cities suffered along with their counterparts to the North, white Southerners bragged that their region quickly recovered from the panic. They also bragged that their slaves, unlike white workers, never starved or went without a roof over their heads.

Throughout the country, the panic and depression of 1857 caused people to pause and take stock of their situation. Some said that the political system had betrayed the country, that selfish politicians had allowed banking to become too loose or the tariff too strict—or vice versa, since no one could be certain. Others warned that Americans had grown too rich and lazy for their own good, becoming too wrapped up in their material welfare at the expense of everything and everyone else.

A wave of religious revivals emerged in response to the panic. They lasted for over a year, sweeping back and forth across the country. Unlike earlier revivals, the religious spirit emerged not in rural districts but in the largest cities of the Northeast. Unlike earlier revivals, too, those of 1857 attracted a conspicuously large number of men as well as women. The revivals also witnessed the first active participation of denominations such as the Episcopalians and Unitarians. It seemed to many people, in fact, that the revivals were the most heartening and significant in American history, showing that the people in the forefront of modern America were trying to change their ways. And as people read their newspapers they saw plenty that needed to be changed—especially in Kansas.

The sudden financial panic of 1857 seemed to many Americans a sign of moral corruption and social decay. (© Corbis-Bettmann)

Kansas—Again

Most of the settlers who had arrived in Kansas in 1856 and 1857 were non-slaveholding migrants from the upper South. They did not appear eager to establish slavery in Kansas. An open election, therefore, would likely install a constitutional convention in favor of free soil at the time Kansas became a state. The proslavery legislature elected in the earliest days of the territory, however, still controlled Kansas in 1857. Free state advocates fought back, touring the North and raising money for the struggle against the Slave Power.

In November of 1857, the small band of proslavery delegates who still controlled the legislature proposed a new constitution. Kansas had to produce a constitution that the U.S. Congress would accept. The legislature provided that voters would choose between the constitution with slavery or without slavery. In either case, slaveowners already in Kansas would be permitted to keep their slaves. The Republicans portrayed the constitution as one more audacious act of the Slave Power, but in fact the "Lecompton Constitution" posed a serious problem for the Democrats. Northern members of the party could not support it without appearing too sympathetic to the South; they could not oppose it without alienating the southern Democrats that made up the bulk of the party's strength.

Stephen Douglas refused to endorse the Lecompton Constitution as a violation of popular sovereignty, but President Buchanan urged its adoption. He persuaded himself that the constitution was in fact a moderate compromise, letting Kansas enter the Union as a free state in the long run while protecting the slaveholders who were already there. Once Kansas was a state, he reasoned, its legislature could decide what to do with those slaves. Most northern voters saw the matter differently: though it was obvious that the great majority of Kansans wanted to enter the Union as a free state, those anti-slavery Kansans would be forced to accept slavery.

Republicans could hardly believe that Buchanan had handed them such an easy way to portray him as a tool of the South. And neither could Stephen Douglas, who recognized that Buchanan's actions would create enormous problems for the Democrats. The Democrats fought bitterly among themselves for months, Douglas denouncing the president and seeking to use the Senate to block the Lecompton Constitution, Buchanan using the powers of the presidency to mobilize senators against Douglas.

Moderate southern and northern Democrats warned that the South was destroying its only hope for continued success: a strong Democratic party in the North. When Kansas voters overwhelmingly rejected the Lecompton Constitution in 1858, they rejected Buchanan and the South as well. The Democrats suffered widespread defeat in the state elections that spring and lost control of the House. The prospects were not much better for the fall. Douglas himself faced a tough election battle and Buchanan did everything he could to destroy this rival in his own party. Running against a promising Republican candidate, Abraham Lincoln, Douglas needed all the help he could get.

The Lincoln-Douglas Debates

Abraham Lincoln was very much the underdog in the Illinois senatorial race of 1858. As a Whig in a heavily Democratic state, Lincoln had not found it easy to win or hold office in the 1840s and 1850s. He had lost repeatedly, occupying national office for all of two years: elected to the House of Representatives in 1846, Lincoln lasted only one term and was sent back to his law office in Springfield. There, Lincoln made a good living for himself and his family, drawing on his own abilities and the connections that came with his marriage to Mary Todd, a member of a prominent family. Lincoln's modest beginnings on the Kentucky and Illinois frontier lay comfortably in the past. Still, he longed for a major public office.

Though the short, portly, experienced, pragmatic, and famous Stephen Douglas seemed the opposite of the tall, thin, inexperienced, principled, and obscure Abraham Lincoln, the two men in fact shared a great deal. Douglas, too, had grown up poor. Douglas, although the most prominent Democrat in the country, was actually four years younger than Lincoln. Both Lincoln and Douglas shared their constituents' moderate positions on most national issues.

Illinois's population was composed of many New England migrants in the northern half of the state, upcountry southern migrants in the bottom half, and German and Irish immigrants in Chicago. Both the factories and the farms of Illinois prospered in the 1850s, as did abolitionists, Know-Nothings, Whigs, and southern-leaning Democrats. The Illinois senatorial election of 1858 promised to throw all these groups into contention. At stake was this question: could the Democrats survive as a national party, with Douglas as their leader, or were they doomed to become a party of the South?

Douglas traveled by private railroad car from Chicago to Springfield, the state capital and Lincoln's base. All along the way, Douglas gave speeches to thousands of people, telling them that he was the voice of experience, principled compromise, and popular sovereignty. He also told them that Lincoln held "monstrous revolutionary doctrines" of abolitionism. To Douglas' great annoyance, Lincoln followed the senator to rebut his arguments and charges, sometimes appearing in the crowd, sometimes arriving the next day. Douglas, though reluctant to give the relatively unknown Lincoln a share of attention, finally agreed to hold seven joint debates in the late summer and early fall.

Lincoln was far from an abolitionist, refusing to join the anti-slavery Liberty and Free Soil parties and staying with the Whigs longer than many of the men who became Republicans. He repeatedly brought up the *Dred Scott* decision from the previous year, however, arguing that it would permit slavery to spread into lands where Illinois men or their sons would otherwise migrate. Douglas offered what he saw as practical, commonsense responses to such charges, arguing that slavery would not spread anywhere the majority of the white population did not want it to. A far greater and more immediate threat, Douglas argued, was that the Republicans would force the South into desperate acts by dragging moral issues into political contexts. Let the sovereign white people of each state decide for themselves whether they would have slavery or not, Douglas counseled. Douglas did not defend slavery, but he declared that "I care more for the great principle of self-government, the right of the people to rule, than I do for all the negroes in Christendom."

Lincoln charged that Douglas' strategy merely postponed an inevitable reckoning between the slave states and the free states. He argued that "a house divided against itself cannot stand. . . . Either the opponents of slavery will arrest the further spread of it, . . . or its advocates will push it forward till it shall become alike lawful in all the States, old as well as new." Notwithstanding Douglas' efforts to dismiss the morality of slavery as beside the point, that morality repeatedly surfaced in the debates. Lincoln argued that he, not Douglas, was the one defending true self-government. Douglas' policy permitted the forces of slavery to grow stronger and more aggressive, while Lincoln's would place slavery on the path toward "ultimate extinction." It would likely be several generations before that extinction occurred, Lincoln believed, but the process could begin in 1858.

Lincoln made a distinction between different kinds of rights. African Americans, he thought, had economic rights, but he did not believe in social equality between blacks and whites. He would not grant black men the right to intermarry with whites, serve on juries, or vote, but he did believe that black people had the right not to be slaves. Lincoln took the offensive, making Douglas appear more of a defender of slavery than at heart he was.

The election was close, but the state legislature, which elected U.S. senators in these decades, went to the Democrats and they returned Douglas to Washington. Yet Lincoln had become identified as the spokesman for a principled yet restrained anti-slavery. All across the North, in fact, the Republicans made impressive gains in 1858. In every state, many people wanted the nation to find some compromise. But the political environment did not have a chance to calm in 1859, for it was then that John Brown returned to the national scene.

John Brown and Harpers Ferry

John Brown had become famous in the three years since he had burst into prominence in Bleeding Kansas in 1855. Anti-slavery people back east, assured by journalists that Brown had not personally killed anyone at Pottawatomie, admired the hard man for his firsthand opposition to slaveholders. Thus, as he toured New England in search of funds to carry on the cause, he found willing listeners and open hands. Anti-slavery advocates were eager to contribute to the fight against slavery in Kansas, not realizing they were contributing to a fight against slavery much closer to home.

Throughout 1857 and 1858, Brown planned for an attack on the federal arsenal at Harpers Ferry, Virginia. He had a thousand iron pikes forged to arm the slaves he believed would rise in rebellion once he and his men triggered the revolt. He tried to win the support of Frederick Douglass, who, while sympathetic, thought the plan doomed logistically. But Brown pressed on. One of his lieutenants moved to Harpers Ferry and even established a family there, preparing the way

The campaign launched by John Brown and twenty-one black and white allies in 1859 failed in its immediate aim of unleashing a rebellion of the enslaved but succeeded in heightening the moral and political debate over slavery. (© Corbis-Bettmann)

for the attack. In the meantime, Brown continued the fight against slavery in the West, freeing eleven slaves in Missouri, killing their master and leading them into Canada. Such exploits, though illegal, only heightened Brown's visibility and appeal in New England.

The assault on Harpers Ferry started in earnest in the summer of 1859, when Brown rented a farm seven miles away and assembled his men and munitions. To his disappointment, he could recruit only twenty-one men, five of them African Americans.

The raid began easily enough on Sunday, October 16, as Brown's men quickly seized the arsenal and a rifle-manufacturing plant. However, Brown and his men remained in the small armory building, waiting for word to spread among the slaves of Virginia that their day of liberation had come. The word spread instead among local whites, who quickly surrounded Brown's men, killing or capturing eight of them. Militia from Virginia and Maryland arrived the next day, followed soon after by federal troops. The troops rushed the armory. Ten of the abolitionist forces were killed, five (including Brown) wounded, and seven escaped. Brown was tried within two weeks and found guilty. He was sentenced to be hanged exactly a month later, on December 2.

The entire episode, from the raid to Brown's execution, took only about six weeks to unfold. Yet those six weeks saw opinion in both the North and the South change rapidly. Public opinion in the North and South, mixed at first, crystallized into sharply opposing viewpoints. Even those Northerners who were appalled at the violence were also appalled at the speed with which Brown was tried and condemned. Even those Southerners who read with reassurance early denunciations of Brown in the North were appalled when they realized that many Northerners refused to condemn the raid.

The rhetoric surrounding John Brown seemed almost cathartic, as both Northerners and Southerners said the worst they could imagine about the other. The many people of moderate sympathies on both sides watched, dismayed, as common ground eroded beneath their feet.

Brown had not set out to become a martyr. He fully expected to unleash a massive slave rebellion. Although his precise plans remain obscure, maps in his possession marked places where slaves outnumbered their masters and might overwhelm them with force. Brown wanted to play the role of Moses, leading the oppressed and chosen out of captivity. Once captured, however, Brown seemed to fit another role, that of Christ, selflessly dying for the salvation of others. No longer the Old Testament figure of blood and vengeance, Brown now appeared to many in the North as a New Testament figure of suffering and dignified sacrifice. Many Northerners came to believe that John Brown's body could be redeemed only with a return to the stern violence he had championed.

THE FIRST SECESSION

Everyone knew the election of 1860 held enormous meaning for the United States, but no one could be sure what that meaning might be. Would this be the election that brought everyone to their senses? Would the border states be able to control the election? Would northern voters suddenly realize the South meant what it said? The actual events proved far more threatening than most Americans had believed possible.

The Election of 1860

White Southerners automatically linked John Brown with the Republican party, though leading Republicans explicitly denied any connection. The Republicans, hoping to win support from the non-slaveholders in the South, arranged for the distribution of Hinton Helper's *Impending Crisis of the South.* The book had little effect in the South, however, and the Republicans realized that they would be a purely northern party. Not only had any southern base of support disappeared, but Harpers Ferry had made the Republicans far more attractive in the North than before.

The Democrats also felt the effects of Brown's raid. Meeting in Charleston in April 1860 to decide on their presidential nominee for the fall election, the northern Democrats nominated Stephen Douglas. The northern Democrats saw this as a compromise with the South. But southern Democrats demanded that the party explicitly support the rights of slaveholders to take their slaves into the territories. Northern Democrats could not afford to make that concession and still have a chance to win back home. The Southerners proved heedless of this plea, however, and walked out of the convention. Several weeks later, the Democrats met in Baltimore and nominated Douglas. Southerners, walking out once again, nominated John C. Breckinridge of Kentucky.

Before the Democratic convention met again in June, Unionists in both the North and the South tried to avert catastrophe by nominating a compromise candidate. Calling themselves the Constitutional Union party, they settled on John Bell of Tennessee. Many of these Unionists were former Whigs who no longer had a political home. They counted on the other candidates to create a deadlock that would have to be settled in the House of Representatives. There, the Unionists hoped, legislators would gratefully turn to their compromise candidate.

As the Democrats tore themselves apart, the Republicans met in Chicago. There, in efforts to put southern concerns at rest, the Republicans announced their belief in the right of each state to decide for itself whether it would have slavery. The Republicans cemented their appeal to voters unconcerned with the slavery issue by calling for protective tariffs, internal improvements, and free homesteads for anyone who would settle the West. The Republicans were much stronger than they had been only four years earlier. Party strategists calculated that they need only win Pennsylvania and one other state they had lost to the Democrats in 1856 to wrap up the election. The states they needed to take were Illinois, Indiana, or New Jersey—all of them on the border with the South and all of them far more moderate on the slavery question than states farther north. Thus, the Republicans turned to a moderate who was a favorite son of one of the crucial states: Abraham Lincoln of Illinois.

A certain air of unreality surrounded the election of 1860. People did not know that the way that they voted would bring on a civil war, or even secession. Although Stephen Douglas constantly warned of such a danger, both Breckinridge and Lincoln downplayed any such dire consequence. Ironically, all the years of conflict had persuaded both the North and the South that the other talked tougher than it would act. The parties staged loud and raucous political events that proved long on emotion and short on clearly defined positions. Lincoln said nothing and stayed close to home while his party leaders displayed split fence rails and touted his honesty.

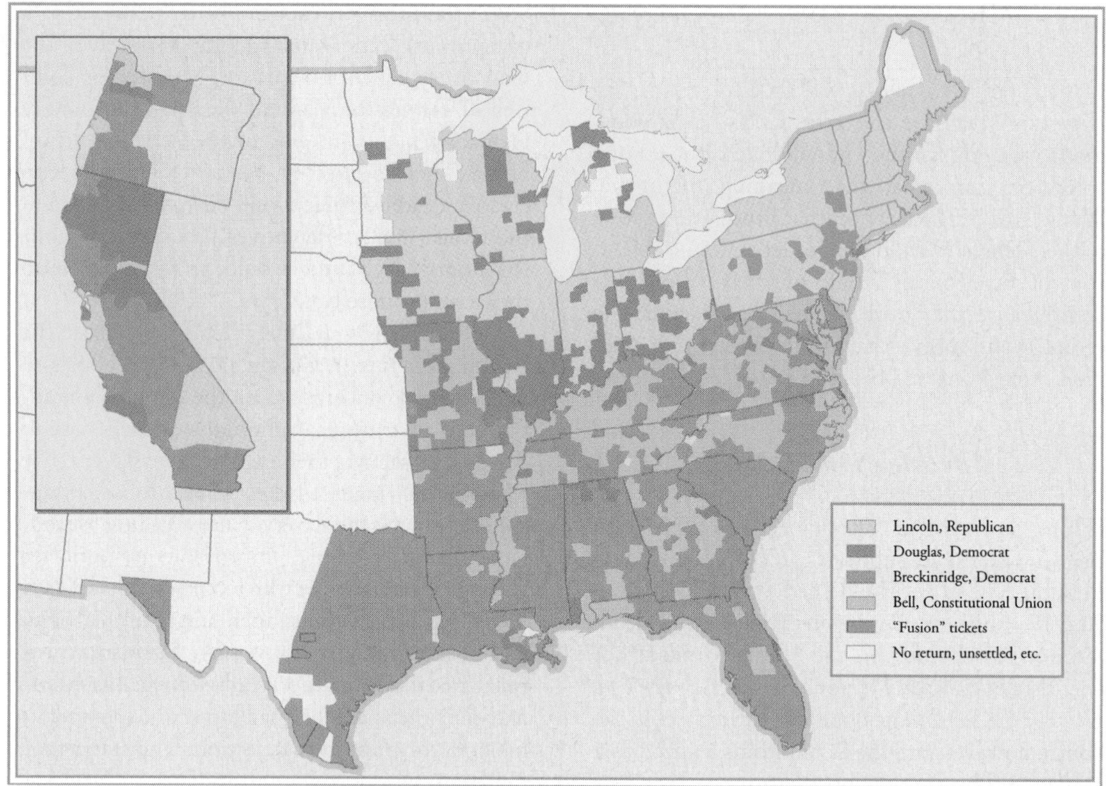

MAP 13.2 | THE ELECTION OF 1860

The election of 1860 was actually two separate elections, one in the North and one in the South. Lincoln made no attempt to explain himself to the South; Breckinridge made little attempt in the North. They never met face to face. Bell spoke mainly to the already converted. Douglas, speaking from New England to Alabama and everywhere in between, tried to warn people what could happen if they voted along sectional lines, but few were willing to believe their opponents would have the nerve to act on their threats.

On election day, November 6, Lincoln won in every northern state except New Jersey, which divided between Douglas and Lincoln. Douglas won outright only in Missouri. Breckinridge won all the South except the border states of Virginia, Tennessee, and Kentucky, which went with Bell. Even at this late stage of sectional division voters did not fit into easy categories. It was hardly a contest between a rural South and an industrial urban North, for northern cities tended to vote for compromise candidates, not for Lincoln. Similarly, over half of Southerners voted for Bell or Douglas, supporting the Union over the South.

Once the election returns were in, though, these complications seemed to evaporate. Even though Lincoln won only in the North, the election was not even close in the electoral college, where Lincoln won 180 electoral votes to Breckinridge's 72, Bell's 39, and Douglas' 12. In southern eyes, the North had arrogantly placed its own interests above those of the Union, insisting on electing a man who made no effort to win a single vote in the South. In northern eyes, the South was to blame, walking out of nominating conventions and talking of disunion. The election of 1860 completed what John Brown's raid had started: the estrangement of North and South.

The Quest for Southern Independence

The fire-eaters declared Abraham Lincoln's 1860 victory a sign that the North valued neither the Union nor the Constitution on which it was based. The South, they said, had every right, every incentive, to leave the Union. Although the Republicans claimed to work within the political system, Lincoln's supporters had violated an honored tradition of compromise.

Even though the Democrats still controlled Congress and the Supreme Court, Southerners believed that Lincoln would use the patronage of the federal government to install Republican officials throughout the South. Such officials could undermine slavery from within, eroding the authority of slaveowners. For years, Lincoln had talked of "a house" that had to be unified, of a nation that had to be all slave or all free. Would he not act to undermine slavery now that he was in power?

The nation's eyes turned to South Carolina. Influential men there, after all, had talked of secession since the nullification crisis nearly thirty years earlier. They believed that the same states that had created the Union could also dissolve that Union when it no longer served their purposes. The South Carolina legislature met on the day after Lincoln's election but did not secede immediately. Its members called for an election two months later to select delegates who would then decide the course the state should follow. In the meantime, they hoped, support for secession would grow.

States of the Deep South quickly lined up behind South Carolina. Carolina leaders, heartened by the response, seceded earlier than they had planned, on December 20. By February 1, Mississippi, Florida, Alabama, Georgia, Louisiana, and Texas had joined the secession movement. On February 4, delegates from these states met in Montgomery, Alabama, and created a provisional constitution, similar to that of the United States except in its explicit guarantee of slavery and states' rights. On February 18, the convention inaugurated a provisional president, Jefferson Davis of Mississippi, and vice president, Alexander H. Stephens of Georgia. Davis was a strong states' rights advocate but not a fervent secessionist. The states of the new Confederacy portrayed themselves as a calm and conservative people, not wild-eyed revolutionaries.

The advocates of secession knew they had to strike before Lincoln took office. Two bad things could happen if they waited to see what the new president did once in office. He might either attack the South by force or he might prove to be as moderate as he claimed to be. In the latter case, secessionists feared, white Southerners would let the moment pass.

Divisions over Secession

Many thousands of white Southerners resisted secession. Some argued that secession was treason. Others warned that the South was committing suicide. Others argued that the southern states should wait until they could cooperate with one another more formally and fully. By presenting a united front to the North, these "cooperationists" insisted, the South would not need to secede at all. The North, recognizing that the South really was not bluffing, would grant concessions protecting slavery forever.

The arguments against immediate secession appealed to a large portion of Southerners. Even in the southern states that rushed to secede in January of 1861, almost half of all votes went to delegates who had not supported immediate secession. The opposition to secession proved stronger still in the upper South. Upper-South moderates warned that their states would bear the brunt of any conflict between the lower South and the North. And voters listened: more than a month after the first seven states seceded, secession lost in Virginia by a two-to-one margin. The secessionists were stymied, too, in Tennessee, North Carolina, and Arkansas. The leaders of these border states believed they could bargain between the Gulf Confederacy and the North, winning the concessions the South wanted while maintaining the Union.

Northerners, too, remained quite divided at the beginning of 1861. Many recent immigrants viewed the conflict as none of their business. Northern Democrats called for conciliation with the South. Many black Northerners warned that a war for the Union alone did not deserve black support. A war to end bondage would be worth fighting, they argued, but in 1861 only the most aggressive white abolitionists spoke of such a cause.

People had plenty of opportunity to air their opinions, for events did not move quickly after Lincoln's election. After the first flush of secessionist victory at the beginning of 1861, people throughout the nation watched and waited to see what would happen when the new president officially assumed office on March 4. In the meantime, no one appeared to be in charge. James Buchanan, as lame-duck president, could not do much, and neither could the lame-duck Congress.

Most Republicans, including Lincoln, viewed the rhetoric and even the votes for southern secession as negotiating strategies rather than actual steps toward dissolving the Union. The Republicans showed no inclination to bargain with the South over what remained the key question: federal support for slavery in the territories. The tensions that had built up in the 1850s, Lincoln thought, could no longer be avoided. "The tug has to come," he argued, "and better now, than any time hereafter." If the North postponed action, Lincoln and other Republicans thought, the South would step up its efforts to gain new slave territories in the Caribbean and Central America, dragging the United States into war.

The Situation in Charleston

In the winter of 1861, the center of the conflict gradually shifted to two obscure forts in the harbor of Charleston, South Carolina. A Kentucky-born U.S. army officer, Major Robert Anderson, worried that secessionists would attack his small federal force at Fort Moultrie in Charleston. Determined to avoid a war, on December 26 Anderson moved his small garrison from Fort Moultrie to Fort Sumter, a facility occupying a safer position in the center of the Charleston harbor. When South Carolina guns drove away a ship President Buchanan had sent with supplies for Anderson and his men, Buchanan chose not to force the issue. Meanwhile, South Carolina troops strengthened their position around the Charleston harbor.

Men from both the North and the South worked frantically, but fruitlessly, to find a compromise during these weeks. Some urged the passage of a new constitutional amendment that would permit slavery forever; some urged the purchase of Cuba to permit slavery to expand; some urged that war be declared against another country to pull the United States together again. All the compromises were designed to placate the South. Abolitionists viewed such maneuvering with disgust and told their countrymen to let the South go. "If the Union can only be maintained by new concessions to the slaveholders," Frederick Douglass argued, "then . . . let the Union perish." Such views were not popular. Mobs attacked anti-slavery advocates throughout the North.

On February 11, Abraham Lincoln began a long and circuitous railway trip from Illinois to Washington, pausing frequently along the way to speak to well-wishers. At first, he played down the threat of secession—"Let it alone," he counseled, "and it will go down of itself." But as the train rolled on and the Confederate convention in Montgomery completed its provisional government, Lincoln became more wary. Warned of attempts on his life, Lincoln slipped into Washington under cover of darkness.

Lincoln Assumes Office

Lincoln assembled his government under the growing shadow of war. He sought to balance his cabinet with men of various backgrounds. The two most formidable cabinet members were Secretary of State William H. Seward, a moderate Republican, and Secretary of the Treasury Salmon P. Chase, a radical Republican inclined to take a harder line with the South. Fort Sumter stood as the most pressing issue facing the new administration. Any show of force to reclaim the fort from South Carolina, southern Unionists warned, and the secessionists would sweep border states such as Virginia into the Confederacy.

Lincoln, with Seward's advice, toned down the speech he delivered at his inauguration in March.

He told the South that he had no intention of disturbing slavery where it was already established, that he would not invade the region, that he would not attempt to fill offices with men repugnant to local sensibilities. But he also warned that secession was illegal. It was his duty to maintain the integrity of the federal government, and to do so he had to "hold, occupy, and possess" federal property in the states of the Confederacy, including Fort Sumter. Lincoln pleaded with his countrymen to move slowly, to let passions cool.

People heard in Lincoln's inaugural what they chose to hear. Republicans and Unionists in the South thought it a potent mixture of firmness and generosity. Skeptics, on the other hand, focused on the threat of coercion at Fort Sumter. If Lincoln attempted to use force of any kind, they warned, war would be the inevitable result. Lincoln did not plan on war; he was trying to buy time, hoping that compromisers in Washington would come up with a workable strategy.

The Crisis at Fort Sumter

But there was less time than Lincoln realized. On the very day after Lincoln's speech, Major Anderson reported to Washington that he would be out of food within four to six weeks. Lincoln finally decided that he had to act: he would send provisions but not military supplies to Fort Sumter. By doing so, Lincoln would maintain the balance he promised in his inaugural speech, keeping the fort but not using coercion unless attacked first.

The president recognized that this distinction would not matter to the Confederacy. Jefferson Davis and his government had decided a week earlier that any attempt to reprovision the fort

South Carolina troops fire cannon at the federal forces under the command of Major Robert Anderson. The shots opened the Civil War. (The Granger Collection, New York)

would be in and of itself an act of war. Davis believed that no foreign power would respect a country, especially one as new and tenuous as the Confederate States of America, if it allowed one of its major ports to be occupied by another country. The Union's resupply of the fort would mean they still controlled it.

The Confederate government decided that their commander in Charleston, P. G. T. Beauregard, should attack Fort Sumter before the relief expedition had a chance to arrive. On April 12, at 4:30 in the morning, Beauregard opened fire on the Union garrison. The shelling continued for thirty-three hours. Anderson held out for as long as he could, but when fire tore through the barracks and his ammunition ran low he decided the time for surrender had come. Northerners agreed that the events in South Carolina could not go unanswered. Southerners agreed that they would have no choice but to come to that state's aid if the North raised a hand against their fellow Southerners.

CONCLUSION

It was no accident that the slave states and free states experienced mounting animosity and distrust in the late 1850s. The rapid expansion of both the North and the South led people to focus their eyes on the West.

Watching the events of those years unfold, however, it is clear that the conflict could most certainly have taken other forms. Had Kansas been handled more adroitly by Buchanan and the Democrats, had Preston Brooks not caned Charles Sumner, had Chief Justice Taney not issued the *Dred Scott* decision, and had John Brown not given violence a martyr's sanction, the election of 1860 would not have become the watershed it did. This cascade of events washed the United States toward dissolution. Another cascade of events would soon push it into war.

RECOMMENDED READINGS

Crofts, Daniel W. *Old Southampton: Politics and Society in a Virginia County, 1834–1869* (1992). Provides a wonderfully detailed account of the way politics worked in communities.

Fehrenbacher, Don E. *The Dred Scott Case: Its Significance in American Law and Politics* (1978). The classic account of this complicated episode.

Finkelman, Paul, ed. *His Soul Goes Marching On: Responses to John Brown and the Harpers Ferry Raid* (1995). Contains fascinating articles about this much-interpreted event.

Foner, Eric. *Free Soil, Free Labor, Free Men: The Ideology of the Republican Party Before the Civil War* (1970). Masterfully demonstrates the power of free labor ideology.

Holt, Michael F. *The Political Crisis of the 1850s* (1978). Stresses the dynamics of the two-party system in bringing on the Civil War.

Morrison, Michael A. *Slavery and the American West: The Eclipse of Manifest Destiny and the Coming of the Civil War* (1997). A subtle and up-to-date survey of this critical topic.

Stampp, Kenneth. *America in 1857: A Nation on the Brink* (1990). Shows the advantages of examining the simultaneous processes and events of this period.

Wyatt-Brown, Bertram. *Southern Honor: Ethics and Behavior in the Old South* (1982). A bold and powerful interpretation of white southern culture.

Zarefsky, David. *Lincoln, Douglas, and Slavery: In the Crucible of Public Debate* (1990). Recasts our understanding of these famous political debates.

Visit the source collections at www.americanjourney.psmedia.com and infotrac.thomsonlearning.com and use the Search function with the following key terms to explore documents, images, audio and video clips, articles, and commentary related to the material in this chapter.

Dred Scott
Abraham Lincoln
Harpers Ferry
Fort Sumter
Lincoln-Douglas debates

Chapter 14

Descent into War, 1861–1862

AT THE BEGINNING OF 1861, Americans could not imagine anything like the war that soon consumed their nation. Events piled on one another in ways that no one could have predicted. The men who voted for Lincoln did not think the South would secede, the architects of secession did not think the North would resist, and neither side thought the other would or could fight for long. Events proved no more predictable once the war began. Last-minute reinforcements and retreats changed the outcome of battles; news from the battlefield shaped every political and diplomatic decision.

War Begins: April 1861 to July 1861

Neither the Union nor the Confederacy was ready for conflict in the spring of 1861. A number of states had yet to declare their loyalties and other states, communities, and families found themselves divided against themselves. In a matter of months, both the North and the South had to prepare for war.

Lincoln Calls for Troops

Two days after the Confederate flag went up over Fort Sumter on April 15, President Lincoln declared South Carolina in rebellion against the United States and called for 75,000 militiamen to help put the rebellion down. The president sought to appear restrained in his response. He still hoped that Unionists in southern states besides South Carolina would rally to the nation's defense if he showed that he was no extremist. Lincoln also acted cautiously because he had not received the approval of Congress, which would not convene until July.

Lincoln's attempt to blend firmness and conciliation failed. Southern states saw the call to the militia as an act of aggression against South Carolina and state sovereignty. The upper South states replied with defiance to Lincoln's requests for their troops. Virginia seceded two days later. Although many people in Virginia still clung to hopes of avoiding war, two delegates to every one voted for secession on April 17. These Virginians, like white Southerners of all inclinations and temperaments, refused to supply soldiers to confront another slave-holding state. Recognizing the importance of Virginia's addition to their ranks, the Confederacy immediately voted to move its capital to Richmond in May of 1861.

CHRONOLOGY

1861

April	15	Lincoln calls for 75,000 militia
April	17–May 20	Arkansas, Tennessee, Virginia, and North Carolina secede
May	29	Richmond becomes capital of Confederacy
July	21	Confederate victory at Bull Run (Manassas)
	25	Frémont takes command in the West
	27	McClellan takes command of Union forces near Washington
August	30	Frémont declares martial law, and frees slaves, in Missouri
September	6	Kentucky remains in the Union
November	1	McClellan assumes command of all Union armies
	6	Jefferson Davis elected president of Confederacy with six-year term
	7	Union capture of Port Royal, South Carolina
	8	Union navy seizes Confederate commisioners Mason and Slidell from British ship *Trent*
	19	Halleck replaces Frémont as Union commander in West
December	26	Union government releases Mason and Slidell
	30	Suspension of specie payments

1862

February	6	Union captures Fort Henry on Tennessee River
	16	Confederates surrender Fort Donelson to Grant
	22	Inauguration of Jefferson Davis
	25	Legal Tender Act in North authorizes "greenbacks"
		Confederates evacuate Nashville
	27	Confederate Congress authorizes martial law and suspends habeas corpus
March	8–9	*Virginia v. Monitor* in Hampton Roads, Virginia

The States Divide

Arkansas, Tennessee, and North Carolina quickly followed Virginia's example. The Oklahoma Territory, too, aligned itself with the Confederacy. There, leaders of the Five Civilized Tribes, slaveholders themselves, used the opportunity to fight against the U.S. government that had dispossessed them from their homes three decades earlier. The leaders of other Indian nations sided with the Union, however, and began to fight for control of the Indian Territory.

State leaders elsewhere frantically struggled with one another. In Maryland, rioters attacked Massachusetts troops as they marched through Baltimore two days after the secession of neighboring Virginia—spilling the first blood of the war when twelve civilians and four Union soldiers died in the gunfire. Maryland bitterly divided, the southern portion of the state sympathizing with the Confederacy, Baltimore and the western portion generally supporting the Union. Should the United States lose Maryland, the District of Columbia would be completely surrounded by Con-

Chronology

	17	McClellan begins move to James River Peninsula
April	5	McClellan begins siege of Yorktown
	6–7	Grant wins dramatic victory at Shiloh
	16	Confederacy passes Conscription Act
	25	New Orleans surrenders to Admiral Farragut
May	8–9	Jackson's Shenandoah Valley Campaign
	20	Homestead Act passed by Union Congress
	31	Lee takes command of Army of Northern Virginia
June	6	Confederates evacuate Memphis
	26	Lee drives McClellan from Richmond in Seven Days' Battles
July	11	Halleck appointed general-in-chief of Union armies
	12	Border states reject Lincoln plan for gradual emancipation
	17	Second Confiscation Act
	22	Cabinet hears Lincoln's draft of Emancipation Proclamation
August	3	Union decides to evacuate McClellan's troops from peninsula
	29–30	Confederate victory at Second Bull Run (Manassas)
September	4–6	Lee invades Maryland
	17	Battle of Antietam (Sharpsburg)
	22	First Emancipation Proclamation
October	3–4	Union victory at Corinth
November	7	Burnside replaces McClellan as commander of Army of the Potomac
		Republicans lose widely in mid-term elections in North
December	13	Lee overwhelms Burnside at Fredericksburg
	16–20	Crisis in Lincoln's cabinet
	27–29	Sherman defeated near Vicksburg

federate territory. Accordingly, Lincoln acted quickly to keep Maryland in line, jailing secession advocates and suspending the writ of habeas corpus so they could not be released.

Kentucky, after months of determined attempts to remain neutral, narrowly decided for the Union in September. Missouri officially remained in the Union but was ravaged from within for the next four years. Dissension took different form in the mountains of western Virginia. In June, delegates from fifty counties met in Wheeling to renounce the Virginia secession convention, begin the gradual abolition of slavery, and declare their loyalty to the Union. After a complicated series of conventions and elections, the state of West Virginia came into being in 1862 and joined the Union the following year.

As it turned out, the Union and the Confederacy divided about as evenly as possible. Virginia, Tennessee, North Carolina, and Arkansas, all of which went into the Confederacy, might well have decided to remain with the Union; had they done so, the Confederacy would have had little hope of sustaining a successful war against the North.

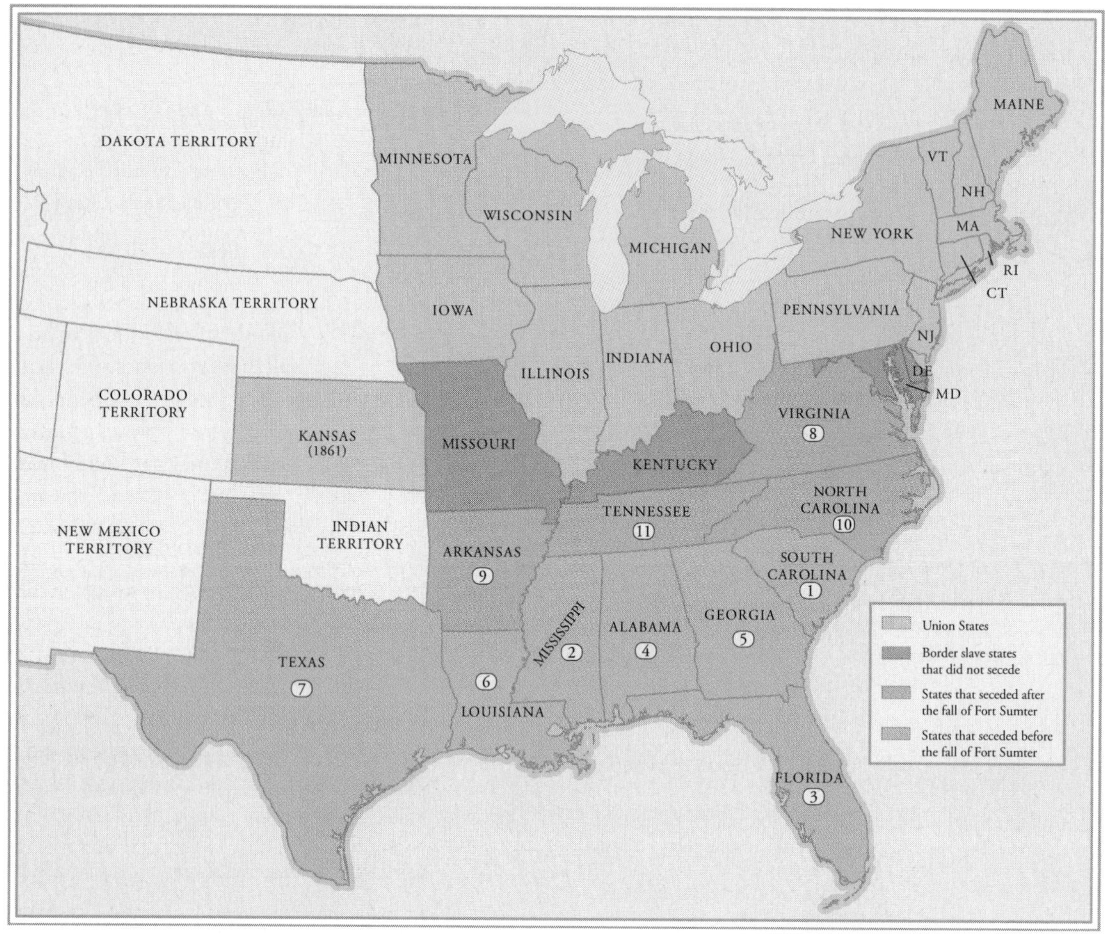

MAP 14.1 | THE COURSE OF SECESSION

Those states accounted for half of all manufacturing and half of all food production in the Confederacy. Maryland, Kentucky, and Missouri, on the other hand, might well have joined the Confederacy; had they done so, the Union cause would have been weakened, perhaps fatally. Kentucky and Missouri occupied crucial positions along the major rivers that led into the South. Even the dissidents balanced out. About 100,000 men from the border states that went with the Union ended up fighting for the Confederacy. About 90,000 men of the border states that went with the Confederacy ended up fighting for the Union.

Although Abraham Lincoln was criticized from every angle in these months, he managed to bring into the Union fold the states he had to win. Had he lost these struggles, he might well have failed in all the other struggles that awaited him.

The Numbers

Looking back, the cards seem heavily stacked in the North's favor. The Union, after all, had vastly greater industrial capacity, railroads, canals, food, draft animals, ships, and entrepreneurial talent,

all the things a mid-nineteenth-century war required. The Union could also claim four times as many white residents as the South. And although the 3.5 million enslaved people who lived in the Confederacy were extraordinarily valuable to the South, everyone recognized that the slaves could become equally valuable allies for the North.

Since the South acknowledged the North's advantages, many people then and since assumed that the Confederates must have been driven either by irrational rage or heedless bravery. Neither the Confederates nor the North, however, expected the secession crisis to turn into a full-fledged war, much less a four-year war. When Lincoln called for the 75,000 militia he called them for only ninety days' service. When southern boys and men rushed to enlist for the Confederacy in the spring of 1861, they assumed they would be back home in time to harvest their crops in the autumn.

Southerners considered themselves natural soldiers, caricaturing their new enemies as clerks and factory workers. Though the Union did have more city men and immigrants than the South, most Northerners, like Southerners, were young men raised on farms. Since both sides believed that their opponents were weak and divided, Northerners and Southerners thought the conflict would likely come to a swift, and peaceful, resolution. In such a struggle, sheer numbers did not seem nearly as important as they eventually became.

The Strategies

The military strategies of both sides sought to minimize actual fighting. The South saw itself as purely on the defensive; it would wait for northern armies to invade and then defeat them. The North, for its part, counted on what became known as the "Anaconda Plan," named after the snake of that name that slowly squeezes its prey to death. That plan depended on sending an overpowering force down the Mississippi River, dividing the South in two. At the same time, the Union navy would seal off the South from outside supplies. Ground troops and land battles would be kept to a minimum.

The Confederacy possessed considerable military advantages. It occupied an enormous area, larger than today's United Kingdom, France, Italy, and Spain combined. It possessed dozens of harbors and ports, connected by an excellent system of rivers and an adequate network of railroads. The Confederacy's long border with Mexico made it difficult to seal off outside supplies. The Confederacy could wage a defensive war, moving its troops internally from one point to another while the Union had to move around the perimeter. The many country roads of the South, known only to locals, would provide routes for Confederate surprise attacks or strategic retreats.

For a model of how such a defensive plan might work, Southerners looked to the American Revolution. Like the American colonies eighty years earlier, the Confederates did not have to win every battle nor conquer northern territory. Southerners thought they had only to keep fighting long enough for the North's political, economic, regional, and ethnic divisions to overwhelm its temporary unity. Indeed, the Confederacy enjoyed advantages the American colonies had not enjoyed. The new southern nation covered twice as much territory as the colonies and the North possessed nowhere near the military power of the British at the time of the Revolutionary War.

Leadership

There was also the matter of leadership. In 1861, many observers would have given the advantage to the Confederates in this regard. Abraham Lincoln, after all, had held public office for only two years before he assumed the presidency, and his only military service had been a brief battle against Indians. Jefferson Davis, by contrast, had distinguished himself in the war with Mexico. He had been secretary of war under Franklin Pierce and had served in the United States Senate. Davis,

unlike Lincoln, directed his forces' military strategy with the confidence born of firsthand knowledge and experience.

At the beginning of the war, too, it appeared that the South had the better generals. The southern leaders certainly had more experience: the average age of the Union generals in 1861 was thirty-eight; of Confederate generals, forty-seven. Robert E. Lee of Virginia had served as an engineer, an officer in the Mexican War in the 1840s, and superintendent of West Point in the late 1850s. He resigned his U.S. military commission and accepted command of Virginia's forces. Lee made the same tortured decision so many Southerners made when secession finally came: "With all my devotion to the Union and the feeling and loyalty of an American citizen, I have not been able to make up my mind to raise my hand against my relatives, my children, my home."

Neither the Union nor the Confederacy felt a need for a commanding general. Many lesser generals still had to be named quickly, however. Military experience and ability did not always prove to be the major considerations in these appointments. About a third of Union generals and half their Confederate counterparts had not been professional soldiers, though most had undergone some military training; overall, the North and the South placed roughly similar proportions of professional soldiers in command. Lincoln, forced to unify a people far more divided than the white population of the Confederacy, chose generals from the ranks of various constituencies he needed to appease: abolitionists, Democrats, Irish, and Germans.

Neither the Union nor the Confederacy enjoyed a clear advantage in civilian leadership. Both Lincoln and Davis assembled cabinets that balanced geography, political faction, personality, and expertise. The Confederates had to create a government from scratch, including the design of flags, stamps, and money. Davis ran through several secretaries of war and secretaries of state before finding the two men on whom he felt he could rely, James A. Seddon and Judah P. Benjamin, respectively.

The Union enjoyed a head start in such matters, but the Republicans had never been in federal power before and had many problems to iron out. Office-seekers besieged Washington at the very time Lincoln was trying to keep the South in the Union; he felt like an innkeeper, he said, faced with customers demanding rooms in one wing while he tried to put out a fire in another. Lincoln's cabinet ended up containing men whom he barely knew and upon whom he was not always sure he could rely.

The First Conflicts

Battles began before anyone was ready. On the day following Lincoln's call for troops in April, federal officers in charge of the arsenal at Harpers Ferry and the naval yard in Norfolk, Virginia, sought to destroy the weapons under their command before secessionists could seize them. Despite their efforts, Virginia troops managed to recover valuable gun-making machinery, artillery, and ships for the Confederate cause. A few weeks later, battles broke out along the B&O Railroad in what would become West Virginia, with Robert E. Lee, the new general for Virginia, leading an unsuccessful and embarrassing chase of troops under the command of George McClellan. Meanwhile, nearly four thousand Confederates, most of them from Texas, pushed into New Mexico. They hoped to win the mineral riches of Colorado and perhaps even California for the southern cause.

All these struggles showed both sides to be far from ready to fight a war in 1861. Not only were guns and uniforms scarce, but so were combat experience and even battlefield training. Even those men who had attended West Point had learned more about engineering than they had about tactical maneuvers. The United States Army contained only about 16,000 men, and most of them were scattered across the vast territory west of the Mississippi River. The militiamen who first responded to the calls of the Union and Confederacy had scarcely been trained at all.

Mobilization

Both sides took immediate steps to create new armies, organized within local communities and led by local men. The Confederate Congress authorized 400,000 volunteers in May of 1861. In its special session beginning in July of 1861, the Union Congress authorized 500,000 troops, each signing on for three years; 700,000 eventually enlisted under this law. Much mobilization took place on the local level. Prominent citizens often supplied uniforms, guns, and even food for the troops from their localities. Units elected their own officers. States competed to enlist the largest numbers of men. Local newspapers sought to make sure that state-level leaders dealt fairly with local troops and officers.

Some Northerners wondered whether the many divisions among classes, occupations, religions, and ethnic groups would hinder the Union war effort. Such doubters took heart at the response to the crisis of 1861. Both workingmen and wealthy men eagerly signed up. Members of ethnic groups took pride in forming their own units; the Irish and Germans supplied over 150,000 men each. Northerners congratulated themselves that patriotism and self-sacrifice had not been killed, as many feared, by the spirit of commerce so strong in the land.

Southerners, too, found reason to be proud in 1861. The leaders of the South had secretly worried that when push came to shove the nonslaveholders would not fight for a cause that many identified with the defense of slavery. But southern boys and men were activated by the same impulses that drove their northern counterparts: dreams of glory, youthful self-confidence, and a burning desire to impress family, friends, and young women with their bravery. At this point in the war, white Southerners talked less about slavery than they had before or than they would later. In their eyes, they fought to defend their farms and homes from "foreign" invaders.

Editors, politicians, and citizens of both the North and the South demanded that the conflict be wrapped up immediately. Confident of victory, they itched for the fight that would settle things once and for all.

The First Battle

Northerners soon grew impatient with the passive Anaconda Plan of cutting the South off from the outside. With so many men eagerly signing on to fight, Northerners thought they should get the war over with early, before the South had time to consolidate its forces. The Union already had 35,000 men poised in northern Virginia, about twenty-five miles away from a Confederate force of 20,000 under the command of P. G. T. Beauregard. Beauregard's troops protected an important rail junction at Manassas, along Bull Run (a "run" is a stream). Confederate and Union troops also watched one another warily in the Shenandoah Valley, about fifty miles to the west.

These troop deployments reflected a primary goal of each side in the early stages of the war: capturing the capital of their enemy. Union leaders thought that if they could win Richmond, the industrial, commercial, and administrative center of the South, the rest of the Confederacy would soon follow. Confederate leaders thought that if they could conquer the capital of the United States, forcing Lincoln and his cabinet to flee, European powers would recognize the Confederacy's sovereignty and legitimacy.

The officers of both the Union and the Confederacy had learned their strategy at West Point. These officers usually attempted to concentrate their force in hopes of overwhelming the enemy at the point of attack. The Union tried to take advantage of its greater numbers of men and resources; the Confederacy sought to use its interior lines, its knowledge of the Virginia landscape, and aggressive maneuvers to gain an advantage. Both sides knew what the other hoped and planned to do.

In the first major battle of the war, the South's advantages outweighed the North's. Both sides attempted to coordinate their troop movements near Washington and in the Shenandoah Valley. The valley had long served as a major corridor between the North and the South. If that corridor was left unprotected by the Union, Confederate forces could rush up the valley and capture Washington. But if too many troops protected the valley, the North would tie up men and resources that could be used more effectively elsewhere. The Confederacy employed cavalry, under the command of the flamboyant young colonel James E. B. (Jeb) Stuart, to move quickly up and down the valley, keeping the North off balance.

The Union, under the command of General Irvin McDowell, tried to concentrate most of its forces at Manassas by moving them from the valley. On July 21, the northern troops were finally ready to attack. Congressmen and other spectators drove their carriages out from Washington to "see the Rebels get whipped." Union troops flooded over the battlefield, fording the creeks, flanking the strongest points in the Confederate lines. The southern forces fell back to more defensible positions. When it looked as if the Confederates were to be routed, a southern general pointed out Thomas J. Jackson to his men, "There is Jackson standing like a stone wall! Rally behind the Virginians!" "Stonewall Jackson," until recently an undistinguished mathematics professor at the Virginia Military Institute, had been christened.

Early in the war, Thomas J. "Stonewall" Jackson was the most beloved Confederate leader, admired for his military daring and his devout religious belief. (The Granger Collection, New York)

The Confederate reinforcements that poured off the train at Manassas gave Beauregard a renewed spirit. The Union forces suffered confusion when the lack of a common uniform led some Northerners to mistake Confederates for their own troops. They began to pull back and then to run. Some civilian carriages got caught in the panicked flood of troops rushing back to Washington; the Confederates gleefully captured a congressman.

The South had claimed its first victory. Each side had engaged about 18,000 soldiers, making Bull Run by a considerable margin the largest battle ever waged in the United States up to that time. Both the North and the South lost about 600 men. Nevertheless, the humiliating rout confirmed the Confederate belief that one Rebel could whip ten Yankees.

Key parts of Confederate lore emerged from Bull Run as well: the rebel yell and the Confederate battle flag. The yell was not merely a scream or a roar, but a high wail, unnerving and strange. It served as the rallying cry for southern troops for the rest of the war. The first flag of the Confederacy, the "Stars and Bars," looked a great deal like that of the United States, leading to confusion in the heat of battle. After Bull Run, Beauregard designed a new flag—a square banner, red with a blue cross and white stars—to ensure that southern troops did not fire on one another. It was that battle flag, never the official flag of the Confederacy, that later generations came to consider synonymous with the South.

For the next two years, the Battle of Bull Run emboldened southern forces who fought in Virginia. The Confederacy, feeling itself invulnerable, fought aggressively, even recklessly, in the east. The Union fought cautiously, even tentatively, in Virginia. Neither side forgot this conflict even though they called it by different names. Northern forces generally named battles after physical features such as rivers and mountains; thus, they deemed this the Battle of Bull Run. Southerners usually named battles after nearby towns or villages; they called this one Manassas.

Women and War

Women had avidly studied the debates being waged in the newspapers. They had expressed their opinions in private conversation, in their letters, and in their diaries. Many had listened to the speeches on all sides. They had counseled their sons and husbands, sometimes urging their men on to join others of their community. They had worn cockades displaying their loyalties and had sung the latest songs. Once the speeches, songs, and toasts had come to an end and the fighting begun, women became even more active. Within two weeks of the war's beginning, women on the two sides had formed 20,000 aid societies. These societies devoted themselves to supplying the armies' needs, especially clothing and medical supplies. One such organization in Alabama provided, in just one month, "422 shirts, 551 pairs of drawers, 80 pairs of socks, 3 pairs of gloves, 6 boxes and one bale of hospital supplies, 128 pounds of tapioca, and a donation of $18 for hospital use."

With the first battles, women claimed positions as nurses even though men had served before as military nurses. Despite some initial grumbling by men, women converted themselves immediately into competent and devoted nurses. Dorothy Dix, long known as the champion of the mentally ill and other neglected people in the antebellum era, took matters in hand for the North. She became superintendent of nurses for the Union army, organizing 3,000 women who volunteered to serve. Concerned both about the effectiveness and propriety of women ministering to young male strangers, Dix decreed that she wanted only "plain" women, women over thirty, and women who would dress in brown and black.

Women's efforts soon became legendary. They labored until they could no longer stand, until their long dresses trailed blood from amputations and wounds. Kate Cumming and Phoebe Pember played leading roles in the Confederacy, and Clara Barton took her aid to the front lines of the Union and later founded the American Red Cross. Most

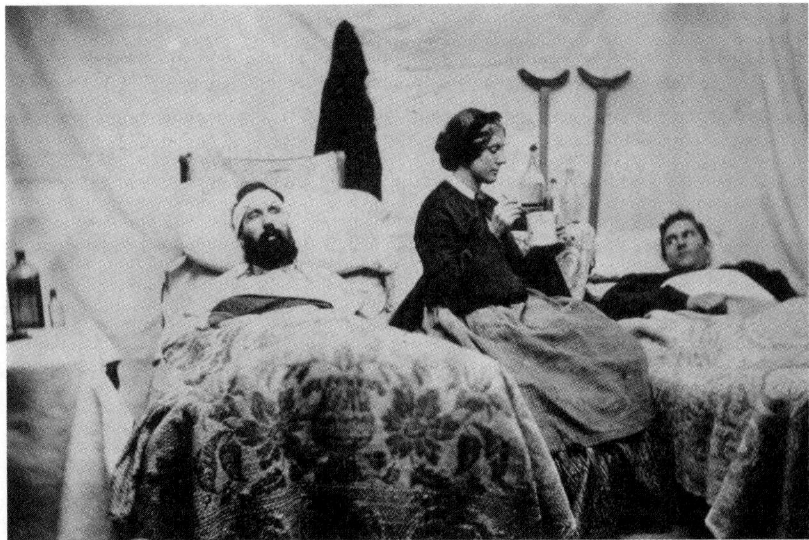

Women in both the North and South quickly stepped forward, sometimes against opposition, to save lives and relieve suffering. (© Corbis)

women stayed closer to home, working in factories or doing piecework in their households.

WAR TAKES COMMAND: AUGUST 1861 TO MARCH 1862

The war spread across the continent in the fall, winter, and spring of 1861–1862. Armies consolidated command and launched campaigns thousands of miles from headquarters. Governments transformed their economies, invented or reinvented navies, conducted diplomacy, and cemented the loyalties of those at home. Families steeled themselves for a war longer than they had been willing to imagine.

McClellan Assumes Control

The North, while embarrassed by Bull Run, took from that defeat a determination to fight more effectively. Volunteers flooded into recruitment offices. Lincoln removed the leaders responsible for that battle and replaced them with George B. McClellan. Although short of stature and only thirty-four years old, McClellan exuded great authority. He was known as the "young Napoleon." McClellan had distinguished himself in the Mexican War and had studied military tactics in Europe. Moreover, he had already frustrated Confederate forces with Robert E. Lee in western Virginia. He now threw himself into reorganizing and reenergizing the Union troops under his command.

The press lavished praise on the young general. Already inclined toward grandiose visions of his abilities, McClellan developed an exalted sense of himself. The cocky commander considered Lincoln an "idiot" and his cabinet incompetent "geese." McClellan ignored, avoided, and insulted those men at every opportunity. McClellan wanted to make his army perfectly prepared before he risked it, and his reputation, in battle against Confederates whose numbers his spies consistently exaggerated. Meanwhile, months dragged by. Lincoln and newspaper editors became furiously impatient but McClellan would not be moved.

The War in the West Begins

There was to be no waiting in the West. Four days after the battle at Bull Run, the Union installed a new commander in charge of the forces in Missouri: John C. Frémont, the "pathfinder of the West." Whereas the situation in Virginia unfolded slowly, the situation in Missouri burst into chaos in July and August of 1861. Guerrilla forces raged throughout the state. Confederate armies built up on the southern border, ready to attack in both the eastern and western parts of the state. Frémont decided that he had to protect the Mississippi River in the East and therefore left a weak force in the West. That force, outnumbered by the Confederates, staged a desperate attack, with terrible losses, at Wilson's Creek. As at Bull Run, the lack of a standard uniform color created deadly confusion. The northern units fell into ragged retreat, exposing Missouri to Rebel incursions.

With the army desperate for war materiel and supplies so far from Washington, contractors took advantage of the situation, selling substandard goods to the Union army at inflated prices. With the populace of Missouri so divided in its loyalties, Frémont did not know whom to trust. Frantic, he declared the entire state under martial law, decreed the death penalty for captured guerrillas, and seized the slaves and other property of all Confederate sympathizers. Slaveholders in the border states of Kentucky and Maryland threatened to throw their allegiances to the South if Lincoln did not overrule Frémont. The president, desperate to keep the border states within the Union, publicly reprimanded his general. When Frémont resisted, Lincoln felt that he had no choice but to remove Frémont from his post.

Events on the battlefield in the earliest stages of the war proved to be a poor guide to the long term. Although the North had been shaken by Bull Run and Missouri, it had lost neither Washington nor the border states. Although the South had apparently won at Bull Run, the Confederate forces, exhausted and bogged down in mud, had not taken advantage of the situation to attack the Union capital. Although slaveholders in the border states fumed at the Union government and military leaders, they remained in the Union. As a result, the South was deprived of a key strategic advantage: access to the Ohio River and a defensible border with the North. With the Union army able to move up and down the Ohio at will, the Confederates had to defend a vast, vague, and shifting border in Kentucky and Tennessee.

The war was not to be won by a decisive battle within a few months of the war's start. Instead, slower and less dramatic processes proved decisive. Armies and navies had to be built from scratch; economies had to be converted to wartime demands; households and families had to absorb growing sacrifices. These transformations began in earnest in the summer of 1861.

Paying for War

The Civil War, involving so many men over such an enormous territory, immediately became breathtakingly expensive. It was by no means clear how either side was going to pay. Although the Union and the Confederacy were, by any international standard, rich societies, neither had ever supported a large army or an active government. Taxes on imported goods and the sale of apparently endless public lands paid for what government there was. Ever since the Bank War of the 1830s the federal and state governments did little to manipulate the currency. As a result, when the war came, the men responsible for paying for it had only a few options—loans, new taxes, or the creation of paper money.

Loans met the least resistance in both the North and the South, but this borrowing could provide only a third of the cost of the war. Taxes proved even less effective. The Confederacy quickly decided that it had no choice but to turn to paper money. As soon as it could find adequate engravers and printing presses, the South began producing millions of dollars in the new currency. Catastrophic inflation began to grow as early as the winter of 1861–1862.

The situation was not quite as bad in the North, where taxes and bonds carried much more of the burden of financing the war, but the Union, too, was forced to issue paper money by the first winter of the war. People hoarded gold in anticipation of the deprivations a widened war would cause. New York banks felt they had no choice but to suspend specie payments in December of 1861. In February of 1862 the Union Congress reluctantly decided that it had no choice but to create paper money. The Legal Tender Act of that month permitted the treasury to release up to $10 million of the new currency, quickly dubbed "greenbacks."

The Confederate Homefront

Southerners watched helplessly as armies stripped their farms of food and livestock. They ministered to the bleeding young men dragged into their parlors and bedrooms. The residents of places where both Unionists and Confederates remained strong—such as Missouri and eastern Tennessee—became caught in internal civil wars that pitted roving gangs of thugs against one another. Governors received letters from women, their husbands and sons gone, who worried that they faced starvation if they did not get help soon.

Inflation ate away at the Confederacy like a cancer. The rapid rise in prices made currency worth less every day. Speculators could make money simply by buying up supplies and holding them while prices escalated. Farmers faced the temptation to grow cotton despite the needs of the armies. Cotton stored well and everyone knew that cotton would fetch a high price after the war, no matter who won. As a result, land and labor that could have grown food bent under the weight of cotton.

Confederate leaders worried that the plantations could not produce the food the armies so desperately needed if white men did not force the slaves to work. African Americans wanted to hunt, fish, or work for themselves and their own families rather than to labor for the white people. Plantation mistresses often discovered that slaves would not work when the master—and the whips and guns he wielded—no longer hung over the slaves. Accordingly, the Confederate Congress passed what became known as the "twenty negro law," exempting from the draft one white man on every plantation that had at least twenty slaves. That a government in such need of every available soldier felt compelled to write such laws revealed how central slavery remained even in the midst of war.

To many poorer Southerners, the law was another in a growing list of grievances. Resentment against wealthy men and women, mediated during peacetime by family ties, common church membership, careful manners, and democratic politics, quickly came to the surface in the context of war. Common people were quick to notice when plantation slaves labored over cotton rather than corn, when the well-to-do hoarded gold or dodged taxes. Wealthy young men sometimes entered the Confederate army as privates, but others considered an officer's commission their just due as gentlemen. Scions of plantation fortunes often did little to disguise their disgust or amusement at the speech or clothing of the poorer men alongside whom they fought. The poorer soldiers noticed, as did their wives.

Navies

The navies of the North and South had to adapt most quickly. Just as many battles, starting with Bull Run, broke out at rail junctions, so did the leaders on both sides recognize the centrality of ports and rivers. The North's Anaconda Plan depended on control of the waterways, stopping the shipment of the South's immensely valuable cotton crop, cutting the region off from importations of weapons and other manufactured goods, and dividing the Confederacy along the Mississippi River.

The Union enjoyed a great initial advantage in its number of ships, but many of those ships were scattered around the globe. It took months to bring them home. Moreover, most of the Union's vessels were deep-sea ships. With remarkable speed, however, the Union naval department built new craft and deployed them against the South. The skilled workers of the shipbuilding towns of the east coast produced hundreds of ships and boats.

The South had virtually no ships at the beginning of the war. The Confederacy immediately contracted with large shipbuilding companies in England. Jefferson Davis also authorized sailors to attack northern ships on the high seas and turn them in for a share of the booty. For a few months these "privateers" preyed on any unguarded ship they could find, but the Union navy quickly shut them down. The Confederates then used their naval officers to man ships that would attempt to sink rather than claim enemy ships. One intrepid officer, Raphael Semmes, escaped through the blockade in 1861 and seized eighteen Union ships before he was trapped at Gibraltar and forced to sell his ship and escape to England.

In the meantime, the North pushed its advantage. Larger ships began to blockade 189 harbors and ports from Virginia to Texas, patrolling 3,500 miles of coastline. Such enormous territory obviously proved difficult to control, especially because northern ships periodically had to travel to ports hundreds of miles away for supplies and fuel. When Union craft left for such journeys, southern blockade runners rushed into the unprotected ports. The Union navy decided to seize several southern ports for use as supply stations. The federal ships moved first in August, at Cape Hatteras in North Carolina, shelling the forts there and cutting off the supplies that dozens of blockade runners had brought into the Confederacy. The northern navy also took a station near Biloxi, Mississippi, from which they could patrol the Gulf of Mexico. The most valuable seizure, however, was Port Royal, South Carolina. Not only did that place offer an excellent harbor, but it stood midway between the major southern ports of Charleston and Savannah.

Diplomacy and the Trent Affair

On the day after the capture of Port Royal, a Union ship stopped a British mail packet, the *Trent,* as it traveled from Cuba to St. Thomas. The *Trent* carried James Mason and John Slidell, Confederate commissioners sailing to London and Paris to negotiate for the support of the British and French governments. The captain of the Union ship, Charles Wilkes, after firing two shots across the bow of the British vessel, boarded it and seized the Confederate emissaries. When Wilkes arrived in Boston to deposit Mason and Slidell in prison, he met with a hero's welcome. Congress ordered a medal struck in his honor.

The excitement began to wane, however, when people realized the possible repercussions of Wilkes' actions. Despite the growth of the Union navy, Great Britain still ruled the oceans. British newspapers and politicians called for war against the arrogant Americans. The *Trent* affair reflected the uneasy state of international relations created by the war. The Confederacy hoped that England or France, even both, would come to its aid. The importance of cotton in the international marketplace was such, Southerners argued, that the industrial powers of Europe could not long afford to allow the northern navy to enforce its blockade.

The situation in the winter of 1861–1862 proved more complicated than people had expected, however. International law did not offer a clear ruling on whether Captain Wilkes had acted legally. And neither did self-interest offer a clear guide to whether England should declare war on the United States or aid the Confederacy. The factories of Britain had stockpiled cotton in expectation of the war and did not clamor for intervention as Southerners had hoped. France and England watched one another warily, neither country eager to upset the fragile balance of power between themselves by taking the first step in America.

Public opinion within England and France divided, for it was by no means clear to most Europeans which side had the better claim to their sympathies. Lincoln repeatedly declared that the war was not a war to end slavery. That declaration, Lincoln believed, was necessary to cement the support of the border states, but it undercut the support of English and European abolitionists for the Union cause. The Confederates claimed to be fighting for self-determination, a cause with considerable appeal in Europe, but potential supporters often viewed southern slaveholding with disgust and distrust. Both the English and the French waited for events on the battlefields of North America to clarify issues.

The *Trent* affair, however, had to be settled at once. Its settlement came through diplomatic evasion and maneuvering. The U.S. officials decided that Wilkes had acted on his own, unauthorized by the government of the Union. Mason and Slidell were freed from prison and permitted to continue their journey. Although the Confederacy was jubilant at having "won," the underlying situation had not changed. Mason and Slidell found that though many powerful people elsewhere were sympathetic to the rebellious Southerners, they were unwilling to go to war against the United States.

The international situation remained tense and unsettled throughout the war. Leaders of both the North and the South could imagine situations in which England or France would intervene with weapons and supplies. Foreign intervention loomed as a fervent hope for the Confederacy and a great fear of the North.

The Rivers of the West

The Union felt starved for victories at the beginning of the hard winter of 1862. Northern troops remained bogged down in the eastern theater, but Union generals in the West moved aggressively. Deprived of control of the Ohio River when Kentucky sided with the Union, the Confederates under Albert Sidney Johnston desperately needed to stop the Union in the West. Troops under the command of Ulysses S. Grant, a relatively obscure general from Illinois, confronted a Confederate line of defense across southern Kentucky. Employing the Union's new river gunboats to great effect, Grant pushed down both the Tennessee and the Cumberland rivers across the Kentucky border into Tennessee.

Important Confederate forts stood on both these rivers, but Grant hoped to overwhelm them by combined attacks on water and land. He assaulted Fort Henry on the Tennessee River in early February, easily overcoming the fort's defenses with the big guns on his river craft. The Union now commanded a river that flowed all the way through Tennessee into northern Alabama. Grant sent his boats steaming back up the Tennessee River to the Cumberland while he marched his men overland to Fort Donelson. There, the Confederates fought desperately, destroying several of the gunboats. Despite the Confederacy's efforts, however, Grant pressed his advantage and overwhelmed southern troops that attempted to break out of the fort and retreat to nearby Nashville.

When the Confederate general in charge of the 13,000 troops who remained in the fort attempted to negotiate with Grant (an old friend) for their surrender, Grant brusquely responded: "No terms except an unconditional and immediate surrender can be accepted. I propose to move immediately upon your works." Grant's phrase soon echoed through northern newspapers, jokes, and even mildly risqué love letters. Grant's first two initials, northern newspapers crowed, actually stood for Unconditional Surrender. Within days, Union troops pushed into nearby Nashville, the capital of Tennessee, making it the first great conquest of the war.

Ulysses S. Grant distinguished himself in key battles in Tennessee and Mississippi in 1862. Many months and battles would pass, however, before Grant would assume command in the East. (The Granger Collection, New York)

The Monitor *and the* Virginia

Even as Grant's troops seized their victories on the rivers of Tennessee, the Union navy continued its relentless attack on the eastern seaboard of the Confederacy. A well-planned amphibious assault allowed the northern navy to consolidate its control of the North Carolina coast. The blockade steadily tightened.

Despite the Union's success, the southern navy had reason for hope in early 1862. Confederate Secretary of the Navy Stephen Mallory had created an effective and innovative department. Mallory sought to take advantage of recent developments in shipbuilding and naval warfare such as steam power, the screw propeller, and armor. The Confederacy eagerly experimented, too, with mines in their harbors.

Most important, the South examined the possibilities of iron-plated ships. In the years immediately preceding the Civil War, the French and British had been experimenting with such vessels but the United States remained far behind. The Confederacy began building an ironclad almost from the very beginning of the war, converting a

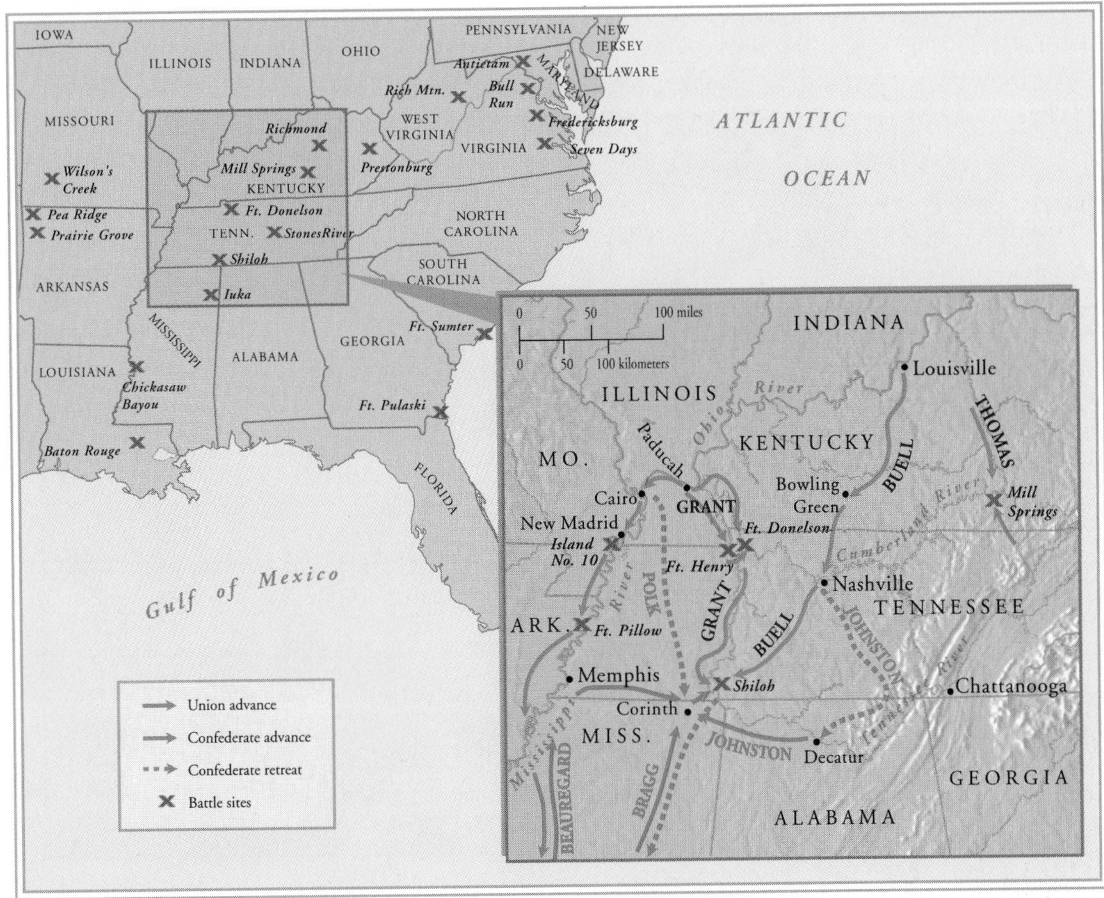

MAP 14.2 | THE CIVIL WAR IN THE WEST, 1861–1862

Union ship captured in Norfolk in April of 1861. They added walls of two-feet-thick solid oak, covered with four-inch-thick iron plate, and installed an iron ram on the front to rip through the wooden hulls of enemy ships. It carried ten heavy guns. The Confederacy changed the ship's name from the U.S.S. *Merrimack* to the C.S.S. *Virginia.*

The Union, for its part, hired a Swiss inventor to design a different kind of ironclad; his innovative plan called for a ship most of which would be submerged except for a rotating turret on top. It was by no means clear how such a craft might work in battle. No one was even sure it would stay afloat, much less fight effectively with its two guns. It was called the *Monitor.*

On March 8, 1862, the Confederates decided the time had come to unleash their new weapon. The *Virginia* attacked several Union ships occupying the harbor at Hampton Roads, Virginia. The ironclad overwhelmed two wooden ships and drove three others aground; their guns proved useless against the heavy iron sheathing.

In one of the more dramatic episodes of the young war, however, the Union happened to be sending its own ironclad to another Virginia port thirty miles away on the morning after the *Virginia* launched its attack. Hearing the sound of

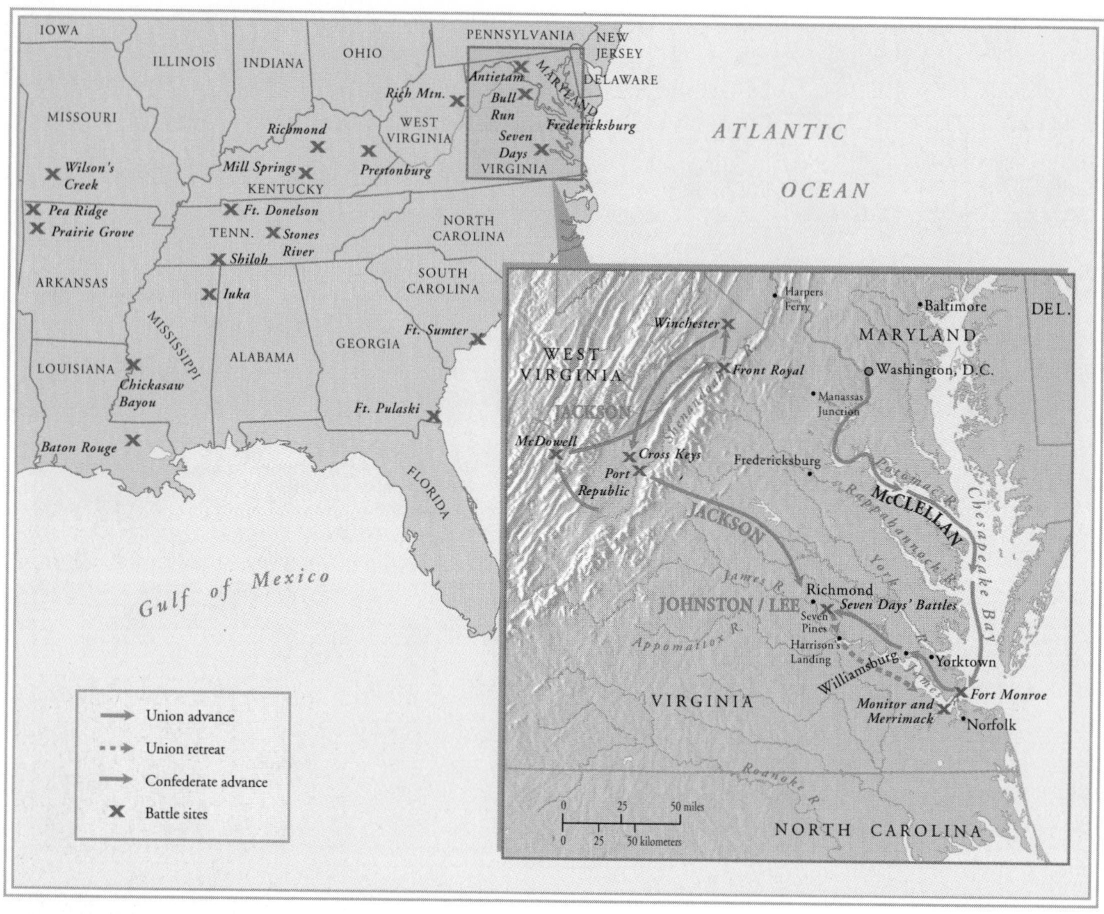

MAP 14.3 | THE CIVIL WAR IN THE EAST, SPRING 1862

the guns in Hampton Roads, the *Monitor* steamed down and arrived just in time. The two vessels pounded one another for hours. The imposing southern ironclad had been neutralized and the blockade would continue. Although neither iron ship actually won the battle of March 9, the advantages of the northern *Monitor* quickly became evident. Not only did that craft provide a much smaller target and a more maneuverable set of guns, but the *Monitor* required only half as much water in which to operate. The *Virginia* proved too big to retreat into rivers and too unwieldy for open seas. The Union began a crash campaign to build as many ironclads as possible, using the *Monitor* as its model.

THE UNION ON THE OFFENSIVE: MARCH TO SEPTEMBER 1862

The Union strategy had long pivoted around the effort to take Richmond. With apparently unlimited resources, Northerners expected to make quick work of Virginia. Although the Confederacy had put up a surprisingly effective campaign, the Union believed it would win the war in the spring and summer of 1862. As with all things in this war, however, events followed directions no one could foresee.

The Peninsular Campaign Begins

On the very day that the C.S.S. *Virginia* emerged at Hampton Roads, Abraham Lincoln gave his approval of General George McClellan's long-delayed plan to win the war in the East. Rather than fighting in northern Virginia, McClellan would attack on the peninsula between the James and York Rivers farther south, using the Chesapeake Bay as a supply route. By moving the war away from Washington, McClellan argued, he would lessen the threat to the nation's capital and find better roads from which to attack Richmond.

Four hundred watercraft of every description began transferring Union soldiers to the tip of the peninsula at Fort Monroe, about seventy miles from Richmond. The transfer of 100,000 men took weeks to unfold. McClellan required several more weeks to arrange them just so in preparation for what he expected to be his triumphant march into Richmond.

Shiloh

In the meantime, U. S. Grant and his fellow general William T. Sherman pushed their troops ever deeper into Tennessee. The Confederates had retreated to Corinth, Mississippi, where they regrouped and joined with other units. They planned to attack Grant to regain momentum if not the enormous territory and strategic rivers they had lost at Fort Henry and Fort Donelson. Grant established his own base of operations only twenty miles away, at Pittsburgh Landing, Tennessee. To the surprise of the Union, Johnston attacked the larger Union force at Shiloh Church on April 6.

In one of the bloodiest days of fighting in the war, the troops of Grant and William T. Sherman clashed with those of Albert Sidney Johnston and P. G. T. Beauregard. Johnston was killed and the Union forces seized a desperate, last-minute, and costly victory. ("The Hornet's Nest" by T. C. Lindsay. Cincinnati Historical Society)

The scattered woods and rough terrain around Shiloh turned the battle into a series of brutal fights among desperate groups of scattered men with little coordinated leadership. Johnston, killed leading an attack, was replaced by Beauregard, who succeeded in pushing the Union men back two miles. The Confederates' dominance proved short-lived, however, for 25,000 northern reinforcements arrived overnight. The Southerners received no new men. The next day saw Grant and his army regain the ground they had lost, driving the Confederates back to Corinth. Though the southern forces had been badly hurt, the northern forces were themselves too exhausted and shaken to pursue.

The carnage at Shiloh exceeded anything anyone had ever seen. The bloodiest battle in the hemisphere up to that point, Shiloh exacted a horrible toll: about 1,700 killed and 8,000 wounded on each side. About 2,000 of the wounded men in both the Union and the Confederacy forces would soon die. Newspapers and generals debated the outcome of the battle for months, trying to decide the hero and the loser, but it eventually became clear that the southern attempt to halt northern momentum in the Mississippi Valley had failed.

New Orleans

Yet another drama played itself out in New Orleans. There, a Union naval force under David Farragut determined to do what Confederates

Sarah Morgan, "Diary," March 1864

Sarah Morgan was a high-spirited teenager in Baton Rouge, Louisiana when the Civil War broke out, the daughter of a respected judge. Though she and her father supported the Union during the secession crisis, both invested their loyalty in the Confederacy once the Civil War began. This part of her diary, begun in 1862, records the grief that struck the hundreds of thousands of American families who lost sons, brothers, and fathers in the war. Despite her sense of helplessness, Morgan went on to write for a leading newspaper in South Carolina after the war.

March

Dead! dead! Both dead! O my brothers! what have we lived for except you? We who would so gladly have laid down our lives for yours, are left desolate to mourn over all we loved and hoped for, weak and helpless; while you, so strong, noble, and brave, have gone before us without a murmur. God knows best. But it is hard—O so hard! to give them up without a murmur!

considered impossible: overwhelm their largest city and largest port from the Gulf. Confederates recalled that the mighty British of 1815 had been unable to take New Orleans and fully expected the same fate to befall the Yankees. The city lay under the protection of two forts claiming 115 guns as well as a river blocked with logs and thick cables. So safe did they consider New Orleans that Confederate troops abandoned the city to fight at Shiloh, leaving the port protected only by militiamen.

Farragut had his own weapons, however: 20 mortar boats, 17 ships with 210 guns, and 15,000 soldiers. The Union navy pounded the forts for days with the mortars, unsuccessfully. Frustrated, on April 24 Farragut audaciously led his ships, single-file, past the forts and past Confederate ships that tried to ram the Union craft or set them on fire with flaming rafts. Once they had run this gauntlet, the Union ships had clear sailing right up to the docks of New Orleans. There, they confronted no resistance. Troops under the command of Benjamin Butler occupied New Orleans while Farragut continued to drive up the Mississippi River. He took Baton Rouge and Natchez, but Vicksburg held Farragut off. River boats coming from the north soon took Memphis as well, giving the Union control of all the Mississippi River except the area near Vicksburg. Northern forces used the river as a major supply route. Rather than a highway uniting the upper and lower South, the Mississippi became a chasm separating one half of the Confederacy from the other.

We cannot remember the day when our brothers were not all in all to us. What the boys would think; what the boys would say; what we would do when the boys came home, that has been our sole thought through life. A life time's hope wrecked in a moment—God help us! In our eyes, there is no one in the world quite so noble, quite so brave, quite so true as our brothers. And yet they are taken—and others useless to themselves and a curse to their families live on in safety, without fear of death. This is blasphemy. God knows best; I will not complain. But when I think of drunken, foolish, coarse Will Carter with horses and dogs his sole ambition, and drinking and gambling his idea of happiness, my heart swells within me. He lives, a torment to himself and a curse to others—he will live to a green old age as idle, as ignorant, as dissipated as he is now. . . .

If we had had any warning or preparation, this would not have been so unspeakably awful. But to shut ones eyes to all dangers and risks, and drown every rising fear with "God will send them back; I will not doubt his mercy," and then suddenly to learn that your faith has been presumption—and God wills that you shall undergo bitter affliction—it is a fearful awakening! What glory have we ever rendered to God that we should expect him to be so merciful to us? Are not all things His, and is He not infinitely more tender and compassionate than we deserve? . . .

Sewed to the paper that contained the last words we should hear of our dear brother, was a lock of hair grown long during his imprisonment. I think it was a noble, tender heart that remembered that one little deed of kindness, and a gentle, pitying hand that cut it from his head as he lay cold and stark in death. Good heart that loved our brave brother, kind hand that soothed his pain, you will not be forgotten by us!

SOURCE *The Civil War Diary of Sarah Morgan,* Charles East, ed. (Athens: University of Georgia Press, 1991), pp. 597–600.

The Confederate Draft

The end of April, then, seemed to promise the early end to the war that people had expected at its outbreak. Although many of the battles had been close that spring, they all seemed to turn out in favor of the North. The first year-long enlistments in the Confederate army were running out in April; many soldiers left for home. The Confederate Congress, fearful that its armies would be short of men as the Union stepped up its attacks, decided that it had no choice but to initiate a compulsory draft. All white men between the ages of eighteen and thirty-five were required to fight for three years. If men enlisted or reenlisted within the thirty days following passage of the law, they could choose the unit with which they fought.

Although the Confederacy eventually abolished substitution, in which men with enough money could pay a substitute to fight in their place, it still permitted men from many occupations to claim an exemption from military service. Governors appointed many men to positions in their state governments and militia so that they would be exempted from the draft. Within a few months, the Confederacy also exempted one white man for every twenty slaves he supervised in the twenty negro law. The draft, necessary though it was, divided Southerners more profoundly than anything else in the Civil War.

The Seven Days

"Every blow tells fearfully against the rebellion," a New York newspaper declared at the end of May. "It now requires no very far reaching prophet to predict the end of this struggle." From the viewpoint of the battlefields in Tennessee and Mississippi, the war did indeed seem to be nearing its end. And in Virginia George McClellan's troops, the pride of the Union and 100,000 strong, had pushed their way up the peninsula toward Richmond. By the end of May only five miles separated them from their destination.

Not that it would be easy for the Union troops to take Richmond. The river assaults that had worked so well two months earlier in Tennessee failed in Virginia. The Confederates were able to attack the river gunboats from the heights of Drewry's Bluff. Even the *Monitor* proved ineffectual when faced with an enemy one hundred feet above. Moreover, the Confederates had established imposing defenses around Richmond and concentrated many of their troops in the vicinity.

Defensive positioning proved more important in the American Civil War than in any prior conflict. Defenders gained their advantage from a new kind of weapon: the rifle. A rifle, unlike a musket, used a spiral groove in the barrel to put spin on a bullet, like a football pass, giving the bullet much greater stability and accuracy. A musket had been accurate at only about eighty yards but a rifle could hit a target at four times that distance. Although the benefits of rifling had long been recognized, it was not until the 1850s that a French inventor, Charles Minie, devised a way to make it possible for a rifled gun to fire without requiring the grooves to be cleaned. Although the rifles still had to be loaded from the end of the barrel, preventing even the most skillful soldiers from firing more than three times a minute, rifles nevertheless made it much more difficult for attacking troops to overwhelm a defense.

Lincoln and McClellan believed that Washington faced a direct threat from Confederate troops in the Shenandoah Valley under the command of the increasingly impressive Stonewall Jackson. For three months in the spring of 1862, Jackson maneuvered his men up and down the valley, creating the impression that his forces were larger than they were and that they could attack anywhere, any time. As a result, the Union divided its forces, depriving McClellan's invasion of tens of thousands of soldiers that would have otherwise been available for the assault on Richmond.

The Union and the Rebel forces tested one another around Richmond in May and June, inflicting heavy casualties in battles that settled nothing. Robert E. Lee replaced Joseph Johnston, wounded in battle, as general of the Confederate forces in Virginia. Lee quickly proved himself aggressive and daring. He almost immediately planned an attack against the larger force under McClellan's command. Lee sent out J. E. B. Stuart, his cavalry leader, who rode all the way around McClellan's troops, reconnoitering their position and stealing their supplies. Stuart reported that part of McClellan's troops were vulnerable to attack. Lee brought Jackson and his men to join in an assault. The resulting prolonged conflict around Richmond, which became known as the Seven Days' Battles, did not distinguish either side. The Confederates' offensive did not work as planned and Jackson failed to carry out his part of the assault. For the North's part, McClellan, though possessing far more troops than his opponents, believed himself outnumbered and sacrificed his advantage. Thirty thousand men had been killed and wounded.

Slavery Under Attack

By the summer of 1862 the war seemed to have reached a stalemate. Both the Union and the Confederacy believed a decisive battle could still win the war. The North took heart because Union ships controlled the coasts and rivers on the perimeter of the South even as Union troops pushed deep into Tennessee and Mississippi. The Confederacy took comfort because vast expanses of rich southern farmland and millions of productive slaves remained beyond the reach of Union control.

President Lincoln, while detesting slavery personally, feared that a campaign against bondage would divide the North. As the war dragged into its second year, however, even Northerners who did not oppose slavery on moral grounds could see that slavery offered the South a major advantage: slaves in the fields meant more white Southerners on the battlefields. More important, black Southerners themselves pressed slavery as a problem on the Union armies. Wherever those armies went, slaves fled to the Federals as refugees. The Union called the black people who made their way to the Union ranks "contrabands," a word usually used to describe smuggled goods. The term revealed the confusion among white Northerners about the status of the black people in their midst. Although some Union officers returned the slaves to their owners, other officers seized the opportunity to strike against slavery.

Northern leaders confronted such issues most directly near Port Royal, South Carolina. When the Union forces overran the Sea Islands along the coast in 1862, the relatively few whites who lived there fled, leaving behind 10,000 slaves. Almost immediately, various groups of Northerners began to vie for the opportunity to reshape southern society. The Sea Islands claimed some of the largest and richest plantations in the South, growing rare and expensive long-staple cotton. Union leaders felt it crucial that freed slaves prove they would work willingly and effectively. Female abolitionist schoolteachers journeyed down from New England, while men came from New York City and the Northwest to demonstrate that plantations run on the principles of free labor could be both productive and humane.

The former slaves valued the opportunity to learn to read and write and wanted land of their own, but they did not always appreciate lessons from the newcomer whites about religion and agriculture. Black people knew how to farm and knew their God. Not only in South Carolina, but wherever the Union army penetrated, officers and civilians sought to control black labor and rich land. Sometimes, federal officials decreed that the freed people could sign contracts with whomever they chose—but they had to sign contracts with someone. In other times and places, Union leaders permitted black people to take responsibility for some of the land they had worked as slaves. Some white Northerners proposed seizing land from former slaveholders to give to the former slaves.

General David Hunter, a man of abolitionist sympathies, took advantage of his position in Port Royal in the late spring of 1862 to organize a number of black military units and to declare slavery abolished in South Carolina, Georgia, and Florida. Lincoln revoked Hunter's proclamation, however. Lincoln did not envision the immediate emancipation decreed by Hunter, with no compensation to slaveholders and with former slaves living alongside their former masters. Lincoln thought that slavery must end gradually, with payments to the slaveholders for their loss of property. Ideally, Lincoln argued, the former slaves would be colonized beyond the borders of the United States, perhaps in Haiti or Liberia.

Lincoln also resisted those members of his party and his cabinet who thought that black men should be enlisted into the Union army. Such Republicans, often called "Radicals" for their support of black rights, passed laws that forbade northern commanders to return refugee slaves to their former masters, and they ended (albeit gradually and with compensation) slavery in the District of Columbia. Many northern Democrats bitterly opposed such expansion of the war's purposes and means, warning that abolition would only embitter and embolden the Confederates. Democrats sympathetic to the South, called "Copperheads" by their opponents, marched under the motto "The Constitution as it is and the Union as it was." They wanted slavery to remain in place so that the South would come back into the nation.

Lincoln sought to steer a course between the Radicals and the Copperheads. But in the summer of 1862 he moved closer to an assault on slavery. The Union army had strengthened its position in Kentucky and Missouri and it no longer appeared that the border states could effectively align themselves with the Confederates. Similarly, Lincoln came to see that the southern Unionists could not or would not organize effective opposition to the Confederacy from within. Lincoln decided that to win the war he would have to hit slavery.

On July 22, 1862, Lincoln and his cabinet authorized Federal military leaders to take whatever secessionist property they needed and to destroy any property that aided the Confederacy. That meant that Union officers could protect the black men and women who fled to northern camps, using them to work behind the lines. Lincoln decided to wait for a victory on the battlefield before announcing the most dramatic part of his plan: that as of January 1, 1863, he would declare all slaves in areas controlled by the Confederates free. Although this proclamation would free no slaves under Union control in the border states, it ruled out compromise that would end the war and bring the South back into the Union with slavery. Knowing that this announcement would unleash harsh criticism in the North, Lincoln wanted to wait until the North was flush with confidence before he announced this Preliminary Emancipation Proclamation. When and where that victory might occur, however, was by no means clear in July of 1862.

Second Manassas and Antietam

Confidence actually ran higher in the Confederacy than in the Union during the second summer of the war. The Union, after all, could draw little solace from McClellan's sluggish performance in the ferocious Seven Days' Battles outside of Richmond in June. Lincoln placed Henry Halleck, who advocated a more aggressive stance toward southern civilians and their slaves, in charge of all Union troops. The president put John Pope, who had been fighting in the West, in charge of the new Army of Virginia. McClellan still commanded troops, but his role had been restricted.

The new Union leaders decided to remove McClellan's troops from the peninsula of Virginia and consolidate them, under the joint command of Pope, with troops from the Shenandoah Valley. The forces began to move from the peninsula in August, creating a temporary opportunity for the Confederacy. Lee decided to attack Pope's troops while McClellan's were withdrawing. He hoped to occupy as much territory as possible, resting and resupplying his troops while complicating Union efforts to unify their forces.

Lee's plan worked better than he could have expected. Stonewall Jackson attacked Pope's men and pillaged a large federal supply depot at Manassas. Pope then fell under attack by James Longstreet's troops, who drove the new Yankee commander back into Washington. With McClellan no longer threatening Richmond and Pope posing no danger to northern Virginia, Lee decided to push into Maryland. He believed that large numbers of Marylanders would rush to the

Confederate cause. Lee had another audience in mind as well: England and France. In the wake of Union indecision and defeat in the summer of 1862, leaders in both countries were leaning toward recognition of the Confederacy. A major victory in northern territory, Lee felt certain, would prove that the South deserved the support of the major powers.

Lee acted so confidently because he knew he would face George McClellan again. On September 17, the two old adversaries fell into battle once more, this time at Antietam Creek, near Sharpsburg, Maryland. The Confederates had 35,000 men to McClellan's 72,000, but the Southerners held the defensive ground. The terrible battle ended in confusion and stalemate. More men were killed, wounded, or declared missing on this day than on any other day in the Civil War: 13,000 for the Confederacy and 12,000 for the Union. Lee had lost nearly a third of his army; McClellan, despite his numerical advantage, had been unable to shatter the enemy.

Neither side could be satisfied with the battle's outcome, but the North made the best of the situation. Lincoln decided that Antietam represented enough of a victory to justify his announcement of the Preliminary Emancipation Proclamation. The European powers decided that they would withhold their support for the Confederacy for the time being. The Confederacy decided that it would pull

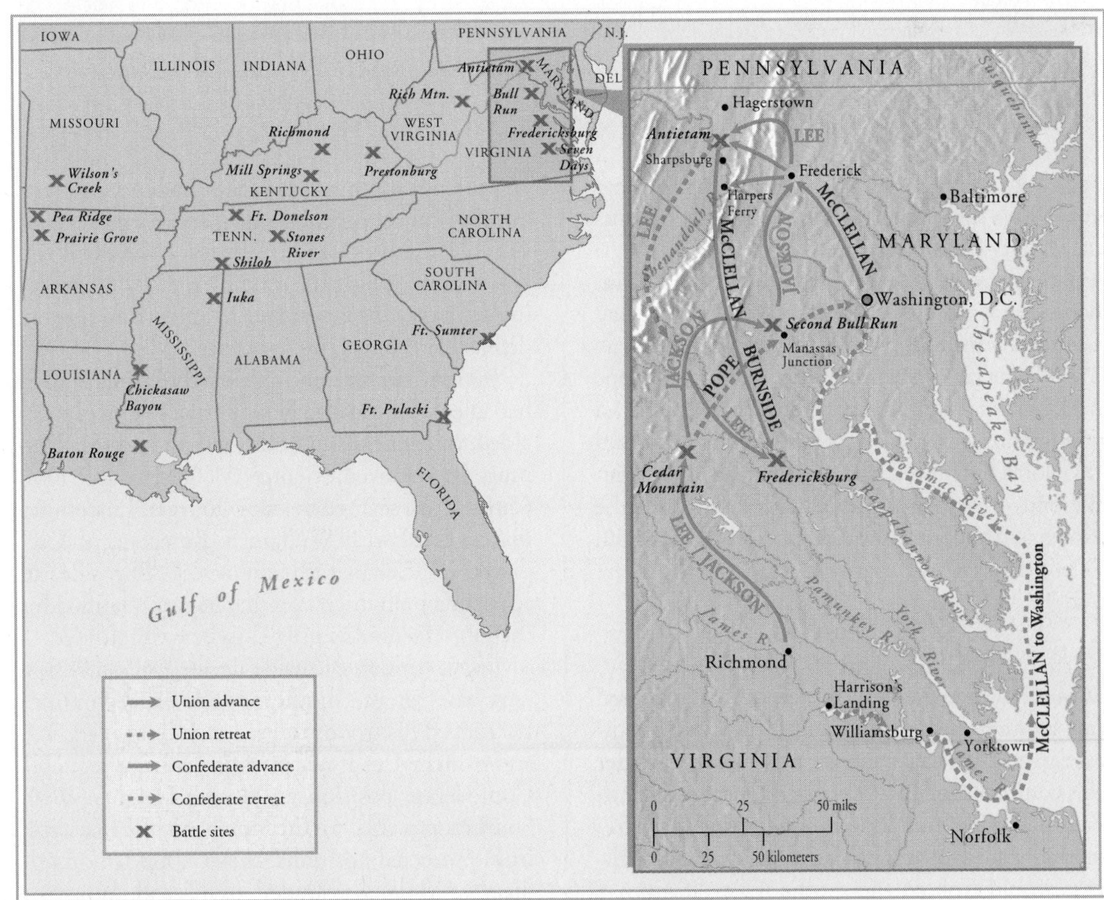

MAP 14.4 | THE CIVIL WAR IN THE EAST, SUMMER AND FALL 1862

The sunken road where Confederates battled Union soldiers on this Maryland battlefield became known as "Bloody Lane." Bodies piled up six deep on the bloodiest single day of the Civil War. (From the Tharpe collection of American Military Art)

back into Virginia to fight another day. Things could have turned out very differently at this juncture. Had McClellan destroyed Lee's army, the Confederacy might have given up its claims for independence before slavery had been ended. Had Lee merely held his ground in Virginia after driving McClellan away from Richmond and Pope back into Washington, on the other hand, England and France might have offered mediation—and the North might well have accepted, again without the end of slavery. As it was, however, both the North and the South would fight again and again.

Stalemate

While Northerners and Southerners slaughtered one another in Maryland with little clear advantage gained by either side, Southern forces under the command of Braxton Bragg pushed far into Kentucky, determined to regain ground lost early in the war. Confederates believed that Kentuckians would rush to the southern flag if given a chance. But Kentuckians had little confidence that the Confederates could prevail in Kentucky and did not want to risk all they had in support of a losing cause. Although the Confederates never suffered sharp defeat in Kentucky, they had too few men to occupy the state. Rather than risk losing his army, Bragg pulled his men into a more defensible position in Tennessee.

By the summer and fall of 1862, many men had died to little apparent purpose. Lincoln decided that generals in both the East and the West must be removed; George McClellan and Don Carlos Buell seemed too slow to react. Lincoln replaced Buell with William S. Rosecrans and replaced McClellan with Ambrose E. Burnside, an appealing man uncertain that he was qualified for the job. His doubts proved to be well founded.

In November, Burnside decided to establish a new base for yet another assault on Richmond. He moved his troops to Fredericksburg, Virginia, and launched an attack on a virtually impregnable Confederate position at Marye's Heights. With Southerners able to fire down on them at will from protected positions, over 12,000 Union soldiers were killed, wounded, or missing. At battle's end, both armies remained where they had been at the battle's beginning.

The North fell into mourning, humiliation, and anger at this sacrifice. Officers as well as enlisted men made no secret of their loss of faith in Burnside. In Tennessee, Rosecrans felt that he had to move against Bragg to demonstrate Union resolve and power. The two armies clashed on the last day of 1862 at Stones River near Murfreesboro. The two sides, losing about a third of their men each, fought to a virtual draw.

The winter of 1862–1863 saw the North and the South precariously balanced, both against one another and within their own societies. On the battlefield, the South had made impressive showings at Fredericksburg and at Second Manassas, but the northern army had held Kentucky and Maryland. The Confederacy still possessed Vicksburg, but Grant and Sherman were planning ways to take the city. Slaves ran to Union armies at every chance. The Preliminary Emancipation Proclamation had given the Union effort a new purpose and new credibility with liberals in Europe, but Lincoln faced mounting criticism within his own party and a growing threat from disgruntled Democrats. The North needed victories.

CONCLUSION

The bloody sacrifice without decisive victory of the Seven Days and Antietam fed disillusionment on both sides. The governments in both the North and the South found themselves the objects of bitter criticism. Military officers squabbled among themselves and with civilian leaders. The only thing people could agree on was that the war would not end soon.

The preceding year and a half had seen events and changes no one could have predicted. Eighteen months after Lincoln had begun his journey to Washington to become president, war had become a way of life. The boundaries between the Union and the Confederacy had been firmly drawn. The governments of both sides had begun to function effectively. The first volunteer units of both armies had been mobilized. Both the South and the North had claimed military victories. The Confederacy recalled the battle at Manassas with pride, whereas the Union took comfort in the steady success of its navy. The first international crisis, the *Trent* affair, had passed without dragging a major European power into the conflict. But in late 1862 both the North and the South felt that their cause must be clarified and given greater purpose.

RECOMMENDED READINGS

Boritt, Gabor. *Why the Civil War Came* (1996). A useful overview of recent thinking on this much-debated historical topic.

Crofts, Daniel W. *Reluctant Confederates: Upper South Unionists in the Secession Crisis* (1989). Analyzes the crucial border states with keen insight.

Jones, Howard. *The Union in Peril: The Crisis over British Intervention in the Civil War* (1992). Provides a fresh interpretation of a critical episode.

McPherson, James M. *Battle Cry of Freedom: The Civil War Era* (1988). The fullest one-volume account of the Civil War.

Paludan, Phillip Shaw. *A People's Contest: The Union and the Civil War, 1861–1865* (1988). Paints a portrait of the North during war.

Parish, Peter J. *The American Civil War* (1975). An elegant synthesis.

Royster, Charles. *The Destructive War: William Tecumseh Sherman, Stonewall Jackson, and the Americans* (1991). An original and disturbing meditation on war.

Simpson, Brooks D. *America's Civil War* (1996). A fine brief interpretation with a useful bibliography.

Thomas, Emory M. *The Confederate Nation, 1861–1865* (1979). The standard account.

American Journey Online and InfoTrac College Edition

Visit the source collections at www.americanjourney.psmedia.com and infotrac.thomsonlearning.com and use the Search function with the following key terms to explore documents, images, audio and video clips, articles, and commentary related to the material in this chapter.

George B. McClellan
Robert E. Lee
Civil War women
Stonewall Jackson
Antietam
Vicksburg

Chapter 15

Blood and Freedom, 1863–1867

The Civil War enveloped the entire nation, homefront and battlefield alike. The outcome of a battle could win an election or trigger a riot, while events at home affected the leaders' decisions of when and where to fight. In the North, the strong political opposition to Abraham Lincoln and his policies exerted a constant pressure on his policies and his conduct of the war. In the South, slaves abandoned plantations and white families' hardships led soldiers to rethink their loyalties.

People at War: Spring 1863

Both Northerners and Southerners expected the spring of 1863 to bring the climax of the Civil War. Much had been decided, organized, and mobilized over the preceding two years. The generals and the battlefields determined the outcome of battles, but perhaps the wives, slaves, workers, bureaucrats, draft dodgers, and politicians behind the lines would determine the outcome of the war.

Life in the Field

Soldiers eventually got used to the miseries of sleeping on the ground, poorly cooked food, driving rain, and endless mud. They learned to adapt to gambling, drinking, cursing, and prostitution, either by succumbing to the temptations or by steeling their resolve against them. They could toughen themselves to the intermittent mails and the arrival of bad news from home. Over time, veterans could even learn to absorb the deaths of men with whom they had shared so much.

But the most stalwart of soldiers could not adapt to the constant threat of diseases such as diarrhea, dysentery, typhoid, malaria, measles, diphtheria, and scarlet fever. As bloody as the battles were, disease killed twice as many men as died from the guns of the enemy. Many doctors of the Civil War era used the same instruments of surgery on soldier after soldier, unwittingly spreading disease. After every battle, screams filled the night as surgeons sawed off legs and arms, feet and hands, in often vain hopes of stopping gangrene.

www http://ayersbrief.wadsworth.com

Chronology

1863	
January	Second Emancipation Proclamation
March	Union Congress passes Conscription Act
	Confederate Congress passes Impressment Act
April	Bread riot in Richmond
May	Culmination of Lee's victory over Hooker at Chancellorsville
June	Lee's army crosses Potomac
July	Union victory at Gettysburg
	Vicksburg surrenders to Grant
	Port Hudson surrenders to Union
	Lee retreats across Potomac into Virginia
	New York City draft riots
	Black troops fight at Fort Wagner, South Carolina
October	Grant assumes control of Union forces in West
November	Lincoln's Gettysburg Address
	Union victory at Chattanooga
1864	
March	Grant assumes command of all Union forces
May	Battle of the Wilderness in Virginia
July	Union failure at Battle of the Crater near Petersburg
September	Sherman captures Atlanta
	Sheridan's victories in Shenandoah Valley
November	Lincoln reelected president
	Beginning of Sherman's march from Atlanta to the Atlantic
1865	
February	Columbia, South Carolina, burned; Confederates evacuate Charleston
March	Congress creates Bureau of Refugees, Freedmen, and Abandoned Lands (Freedmen's Bureau)
	Lincoln's second inauguration
	Confederate army authorizes recruitment of slaves into army
April	Fall of Richmond to Union
	Lee surrenders to Grant at Appomattox Court House
	Lincoln assassinated
May	Jefferson Davis captured
	Former Confederate states hold constitutional conventions through December; pass "black codes"
	African Americans hold conventions in South
December	Thirteenth Amendment to Constitution ratified, abolishing slavery
1866	
February	Johnson vetoes Freedmen's Bureau Bill
April	Congress passes Civil Rights Act and Freedmen's Bureau renewal over Johnson's veto
May	Riots in New Orleans and Memphis
June	Congress approves Fourteenth Amendment
	Ku Klux Klan formed
1867	
March	Congress passes Reconstruction Act and Tenure of Office Act
	Constitutional conventions in southern states
August	Johnson dismisses Secretary of War Stanton, triggering impeachment proceedings
	First elections in South under Reconstruction Act

Purposes

The North fought for ideals of union and democracy; the South fought for ideals of self-determination. But soldiers acted courageously not only because they believed in the official political purposes for which they were fighting, but also because they wanted to be admired by the people at home, because they wanted to do their part for their comrades, because they wanted to bring the war to a quicker end, and because they grew to hate the enemy.

Many men fought alongside their brothers, uncles, cousins. A steady stream of letters flowed back and forth between the units and the families and neighbors back home. Gossip, praise, and condemnation flourished. Any soldier who planned to return home knew that his deeds in the war would live with him the rest of his life. As a result, even fearful or halfhearted soldiers might throw themselves into battle to demonstrate their courage.

Whereas about three-fifths of Civil War soldiers were over twenty-one at the age of enlistment, the largest single group of soldiers was eighteen. For those who passed the birthdays of their late teens or early twenties on the battlefields, the transition to manhood became inseparable from the war. To be manly meant more than the simple ability to inflict violence on the enemy. It meant pride, responsibility, loyalty, and obedience. Every battle became a test of manhood, which had to be proven every time it was challenged under fire.

Courage developed, too, out of hatred. People on both sides spread the worst stories and rumors about one another. Newspapers printed exaggerated or fabricated atrocity reports about the enemy. The longer the war went on, the more people felt they had to hate one another to justify so much bloodshed.

The sermons men heard in the camps told them they were fighting on the side of the right. The Old Testament afforded rich imagery and compelling stories of violence inflicted for good causes. Many Americans believed that God enacted His will directly in human affairs. As the war ground on, the leaders, the soldiers, and the civilians of both sides came to feel that events were more than the product of human decision or even courage. Surely, they told themselves, so much suffering and sacrifice had to be for a larger purpose.

The Problems of the Confederate Government

Convinced that greedy merchants were holding supplies of flour until prices rose even higher, in the spring of 1863 poor women in Richmond broke open the stores of merchants accused of hoarding the precious staple, taking what they needed. The threat of being arrested and the promise of free supplies broke up the riot, but similar events occurred in several other southern cities. No one could tell when even larger riots might erupt again.

The rioters were not the only ones who took what they needed. Confederate officers in the field forced reluctant farmers to accept whatever prices the army offered, in an increasingly worthless currency. In the spring of 1863, the Confederate government attempted to curb the worst abuses of this practice in the Impressment Act. If a farmer did not think the prices he or she received were fair, the case could be appealed before local authorities. In practice, however, this cumbersome system failed. Farmers hid their produce from officers and resented it when they were forced to sell.

The southern government could not afford to lose civilian support. Although the absence of political parties originally appeared to be a sign of the South's consensus, that absence eventually undermined what original consensus the Confederacy had enjoyed. Jefferson Davis, without a party mechanism to discipline those who spoke out against him, could not remove enemies from office. Davis' own vice president, Alexander Stephens, became a persistent and outspoken critic of the Confederate president, actively undermining support for Davis and even allying with avowed enemies of Davis and his policies.

The Confederate government faced a fundamental dilemma. The whole point of secession had been to move political power closer to localities, protecting slavery in particular and self-determination in general. The government of the Confederacy, however, had to centralize power. If the armies were to be fed and clothed, if diplomats were to make a plausible case for the Confederacy's nationhood, if soldiers were to be mobilized, then the Confederate government had to exercise greater power than its creators had expected or intended. Jefferson Davis continually struggled with this tension. For every Southerner who considered Davis too weak, another considered the president dangerously powerful.

The Northern Homefront

In the North, the war heightened the strong differences between the Democrats and the Republicans. The Democrats won significant victories in congressional elections in the fall and winter of 1862, testifying to the depth and breadth of the opposition to Lincoln and his conduct of the war. Wealthy businessmen were eager to reestablish trade with their former southern partners, whereas Irish immigrants wanted to end the risk of the draft and competition from freed slaves. Many citizens of Ohio, Indiana, and Illinois, whose families had come from the South, wanted to renew the southern connections that had been broken by the war.

Black men had called for their inclusion in the U.S. Army from the beginning of the war. In the spring of 1863, the U.S. Colored Troops were formed and over 180,000 African American men fought for the Union over the next two years.
(© Corbis-Bettmann)

The Union passed its Conscription Act in March of 1863 because disease, wounds, and desertion had depleted the ranks faster than they could be replaced. When drafted, a man could appear for duty, hire a substitute to fight in his place, or simply pay a fee of $300 directly to the government. State and federal governments often paid bounties—signing bonuses—to those who volunteered. More than a few men took the bounties and then promptly deserted and moved to another locality to claim another bounty.

The opposition to the Lincoln government raised crucial issues. With the North claiming to fight for liberty, what limitations on freedom of speech and protest could it enforce? A Democratic congressman from Ohio, Clement Vallandigham, tested those limits in the spring of 1863. Hating both secessionists and abolitionists, Vallandigham refused to obey a general's orders to stop criticizing the Lincoln administration. He was arrested, tried before a military court, and sentenced to imprisonment for the rest of the war. Lincoln was dismayed by these events. He commuted Vallandigham's sentence, sending him to the Confederates in Tennessee, hoping to make Vallandigham appear a southern sympathizer rather than a martyr to the cause of free speech. Vallandigham quickly escaped to Canada, however, where he continued his criticisms. Ohio Democrats defiantly nominated Vallandigham for governor in the elections to be held in the fall of 1863. If things continued to go badly for the Union, who knew what kind of success a critic of Lincoln might find?

African American Soldiers

Though northern civilian and military leaders remained deeply divided and ambivalent about black freedom, it became clear to everyone that black men could be of great value to the Union. In May 1863, the War Department created the Bureau of Colored Troops.

At first, black recruits found themselves restricted to noncombat roles and a lower rate of pay: ten dollars a month versus the thirteen dollars a month and three-fifty clothing allowance given white soldiers. Black men, though eager to serve, protested that they could not support their families on such amounts. African Americans knew, and coveted, the rights and privileges of other Americans. They wrote petitions and appealed to higher authorities, often in the language of the Declaration of Independence and the Constitution.

Confederate officials who expected black soldiers to make reluctant or cowed fighters soon discovered otherwise. In May of 1863 two black regiments stormed, seven times, a heavily fortified Confederate installation at Port Hudson, Louisiana. Soon thereafter, black soldiers found themselves on the other side of the barricades. At Milliken's Bend, Louisiana, they fought Confederates hand-to-hand. Northern newspapers echoed the words of praise from generals in the field: "No troops could be more determined or more daring."

African American men in the North rushed to the recruiting tables. Frederick Douglass, the leading spokesman for black Americans, celebrated the enlistments: "Once let the black man get upon his person the brass letters, *U.S.;* let him get an eagle on his button, and a musket on his shoulder, and bullets in his pocket, and there is no power on earth which can deny that he has earned the right to citizenship in the United States." From Rhode Island to Ohio, black troops prepared to head south.

The Battlefields of Summer: 1863

Everything seemed in place for a climactic culmination of the war in the summer of 1863. The Union had almost severed the western half of the Confederacy from the eastern; The Federal army had penetrated deep into Tennessee and stood on the threshold of Georgia. On the other hand, the Confederate army had toughened itself to its disadvantages and learned to make the most of the advantages it enjoyed.

Vicksburg and Chancellorsville

Union leaders needed all the help they could get in early 1863. Grant and Sherman remained frustrated in their goal of seizing Vicksburg; Rosecrans faced Bragg in Tennessee; Lee's army had yet to be decisively defeated despite the men, resources, and determination thrown into battle against him. Lee would face General Joseph Hooker, whom Lincoln had chosen to replace Ambrose Burnside. Throughout the spring, "Fighting Joe" Hooker energized his men and repaired some of the damage to morale and readiness inflicted at Fredericksburg. But no one knew if he would be able to handle Lee.

The Northern public was especially impatient with Grant and Sherman. Grant knew the delays threatened his command. Vicksburg, heavily fortified by both geography and the Confederates, seemed most vulnerable to attack from the southeast, but to get there Grant would have to find a way to move his men across the Mississippi River without landing them in swamps. Throughout the long wet winter, Grant had tried one experiment after another, including digging canals. Nothing worked.

Grant finally decided on a bold move: he would run a flotilla of gunboats and barges past Vicksburg under the cover of night to ferry his men across the Mississippi south of the city, where the land was better. The guns of Vicksburg stood

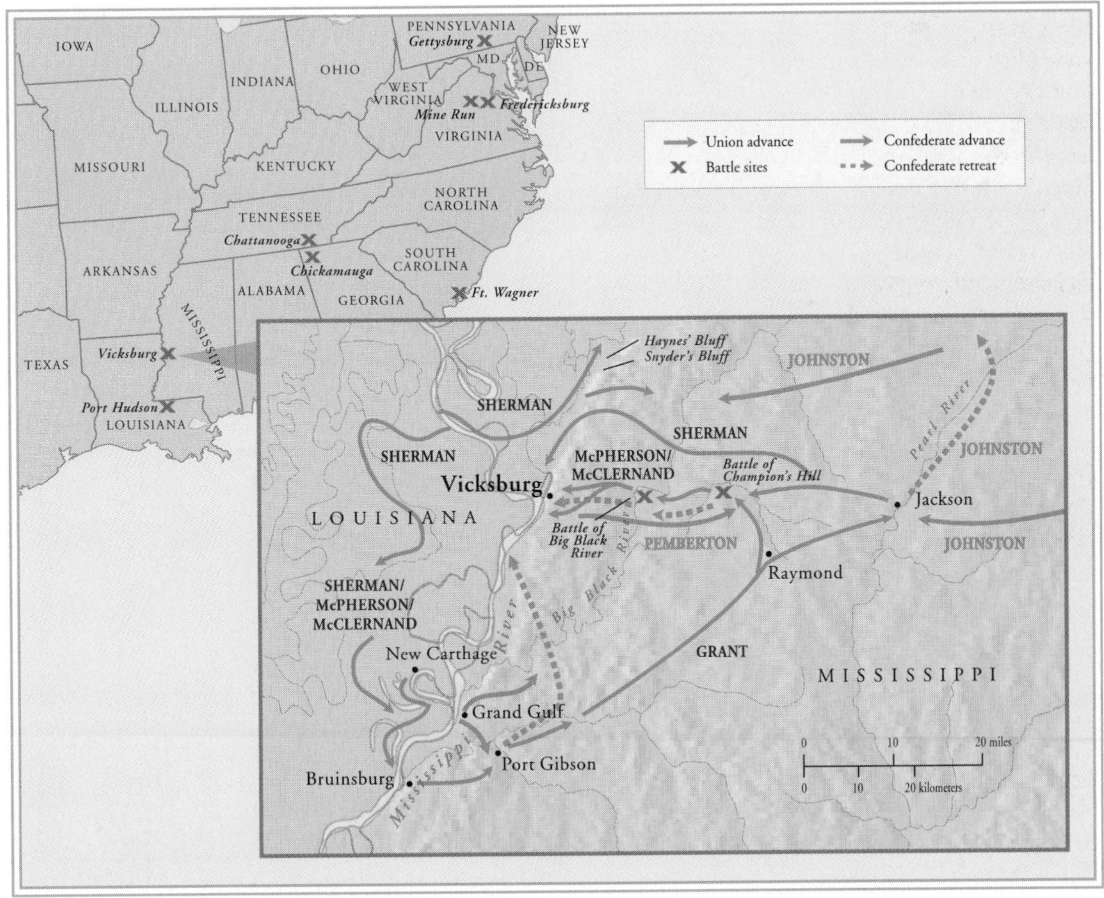

Map 15.1 | The Civil War, Summer 1863: Vicksburg

two hundred feet above the river, ready to fire down on any passing craft, but the Union men covered their boilers with sacks of grain and bales of cotton to protect them from the shelling. Most of the boats made it through. Grant had Sherman create a diversion, confusing the Confederates, and then ferried his entire army across the Mississippi. Grant's army remained vulnerable, cut off from his allies and his major supply base, but by late April he was finally where he wanted to be.

In the same week Grant made his landing near Vicksburg, Hooker began his attack on Lee, still based in Fredericksburg. Hooker commanded 130,000 men. Unlike Burnside, however, Hooker intended to outsmart Lee rather than try to overwhelm him with numbers. A large Union force would sweep around Lee and attack him from behind even as another force attacked from the front. To keep from being bottled up in Fredericksburg, Lee would have to emerge from his well-entrenched defensive position. Lee met this bold move with an even bolder one. He would divide his forces and send Stonewall Jackson to attack Hooker's men from the rear, outflanking Hooker's own flanking maneuver.

On May 2, Jackson assaulted Hooker's troops near Chancellorsville. The outnumbered Confederates defeated the surprised and indecisive Hooker, achieving a major victory. Southern jubilation, though, ended the very night of their tri-

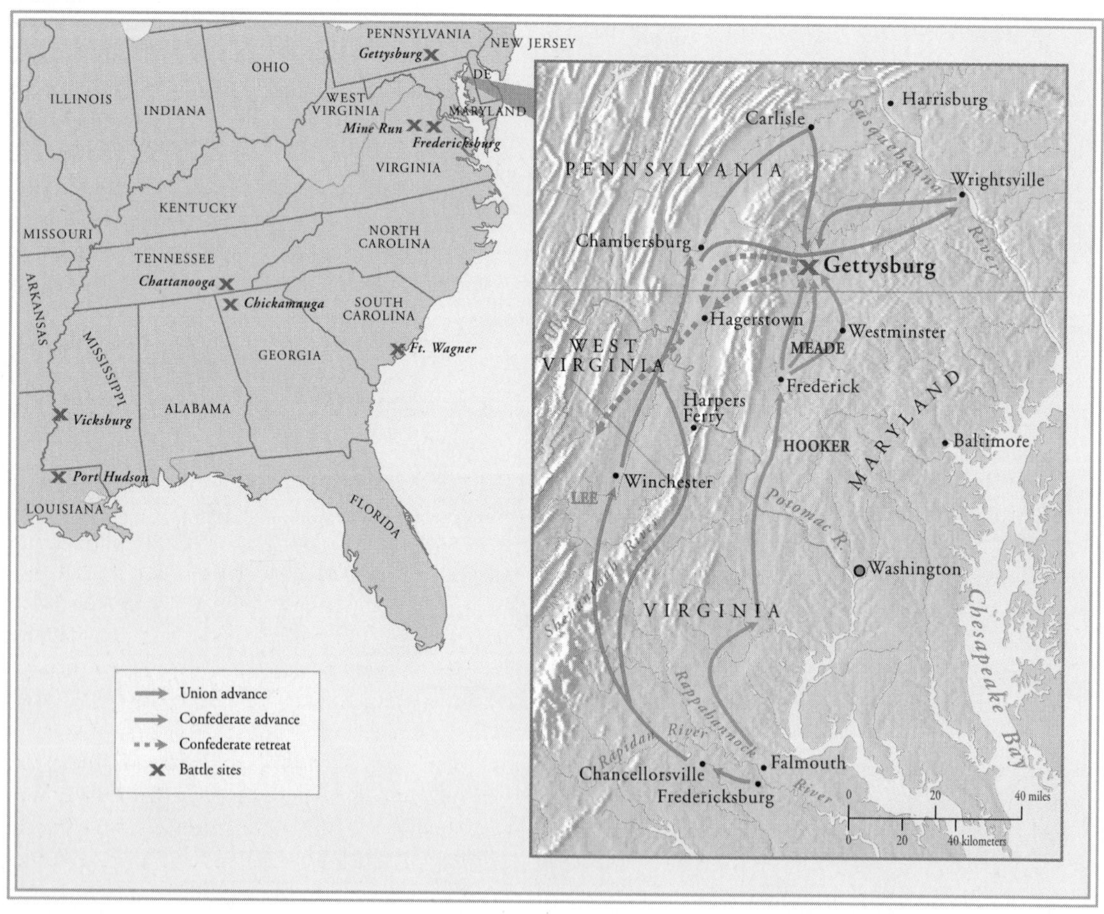

MAP 15.2 | THE CIVIL WAR, SUMMER 1863: VIRGINIA AND PENNSYLVANIA

umph, for nervous Confederate soldiers accidentally shot Stonewall Jackson while he surveyed the scene near the front lines. The surgeons removed his arm that evening and hoped that he might live.

While Jackson lay in his tent, fading in and out of consciousness, Lee managed to contain another assault on Fredericksburg and to push the Union troops away from their positions. The losses had once again been staggering, but Lee had overcome a larger opponent. After the last battles quieted, however, Jackson died. His death took with it Lee's most trusted general.

Gettysburg

Despite his victory at Chancellorsville, Lee recognized that the Confederacy was in trouble. Rosecrans still threatened to break through Tennessee into Georgia, Grant clawed his way closer to Vicksburg, and the Union blockade drew an ever tighter net around the coast. Some of his generals urged Lee to rush with his troops to Tennessee to defend the center of the Confederacy and pull Grant away from Vicksburg. But Lee decided that his most effective move would be to invade the North again, taking the pressure off Virginia and disheartening the Union. A successful strike into the North might even yet persuade Britain and France to recognize the Confederacy.

In early June, Lee began to move up through the Shenandoah Valley into southern Pennsylvania. Hooker seemed confused. When, after a minor dispute, Hooker offered his resignation to Lincoln, the president quickly accepted and put General George Meade in charge. Meade had to decide how best to stop the greatest threat the Confederate army had yet posed to the North. Washington and Baltimore lay in danger, along with the cities, towns, and farms of Pennsylvania. There, the Confederate troops enjoyed taking food and livestock from the rich land.

Although Lee and his men moved unchecked across the Potomac and deep into Pennsylvania, they found themselves in a dangerous situation. Lee had permitted Jeb Stuart's cavalry, his "eyes," to range widely from the main army; as a result, the Confederates had little idea where the Union army was or what moves it was making. For their part, Meade and his fellow officers decided to pursue Lee, but not too aggressively, looking for a likely time and place to confront the enemy.

On June 30, units from the Confederacy and the Union stumbled over one another at a small town neither side knew or cared much about: Gettysburg. On July 1, they began to struggle for the best defensive position near the town, fighting over the highest and most protected land. It appeared at first that the Southerners had the better of the first day's battle, but as the smoke cleared both sides could see that late in the day the Union army had consolidated itself on the most advantageous ground. Meade's men, after fierce fighting at the ends of their line, occupied a fishhook-shaped series of ridges and hills that permitted them to protect their flanks. The second day saw the Confederates slowly mobilize their forces for assaults on those positions and launch attacks late in the afternoon. The resulting battles in the peach orchard, the wheat field, Little Round Top, and the boulder-strewn area known as the Devil's Den proved horrific—with 35,000 men dead or wounded—but left the Union in control of the high ground.

Despite the Union's superior position, Lee decided on a frontal attack the next day. The Confederates hoped their artillery would soften the middle of the Union lines. The Confederates did not realize how little damage their guns had done until well-entrenched Union troops decimated waves of an attack led by George E. Pickett. Only a few southern men made it to the stone wall that protected the Northerners, and even those Confederates quickly fell. It proved a disastrous three days for the Confederacy, which lost 23,000 men through death or wounds, about a third of its entire force. While the Union lost similar numbers of men, it had more to lose. The Northerners and their new general had fought a defensive battle; the southern side, short on supplies and men, had gambled on an aggressive assault. The strategic and political consequences of the battle remained to be seen.

The next morning, a thousand miles away, Vicksburg surrendered to Ulysses S. Grant. Unlike

Gettysburg, where the battle had been fought in a place no one considered strategically important, Vicksburg held enormous tactical and psychological importance. It had been the symbol of Confederate doggedness and Union frustration. After six weeks of siege, after six weeks of near starvation behind the Confederate defenses, Vicksburg fell. The Mississippi River now divided the Confederacy while it tied the Union to the Gulf of Mexico.

Some Southerners, including Jefferson Davis, did not perceive Gettysburg as a defeat. In their eyes, Lee and his men had pushed deep into the Union, inflicted heavy losses, and damaged northern morale without being trapped there. Northerners at the time often agreed, pronouncing themselves more frustrated than satisfied with Meade, who had not destroyed Lee's army despite his greater numbers. During the Confederate retreat to Virginia the Southerners found themselves caught between a swollen Potomac River and pursuing Federal troops. Meade, his army exhausted and weakened, chose not to fight against the defenses Lee's men hurriedly put up against their pursuers. Meade could not know that the condition of the southern troops was even worse than his own. Fortunately for the Confederates, the river soon calmed enough that they were able to escape back into Virginia.

The New York City Draft Riots

On the very day that Lee struggled across the Potomac to safety, riots broke out in New York City. Northern working people held complicated feelings about the war. Many of those who labored in the North's factories, mines, farms, and railroads had come to the United States in the last few years. These people, mostly Irish and Germans, volunteered in large numbers to fight for the Union cause.

On the other hand, many of the immigrants viewed black Americans with dread and contempt. Urban labor organizations divided over Lincoln's election and over the response to secession. Many Irishmen, almost all of them Democrats, proclaimed that they had no quarrel with white Southerners and that they resented the federal government's draft. The obvious effect of inflation on the wages of workers created strong resentments as well. Working people sneered at those men who had enough money to hire substitutes to fight in their place. Three hundred dollars, after all, constituted half a year's wage for a working man.

Irish immigrants despaired at the losses among Irish-American units in the field. When their regiments were decimated at Fredericksburg, Gettysburg, and elsewhere, Irish people began to wonder if commanders valued their lives as highly as those of the native-born. When word came, just as the draft lottery was to take place in New York City on July 11, 1863, of the 23,000 men lost at Gettysburg, the fury of working people rose. On July 13, it exploded. Mobs began by assaulting draft officials, then turned their anger on any man who looked rich enough to have hired a substitute, then on pro-Lincoln newspapers and abolitionists' homes. They assaulted any African Americans they encountered on the streets.

The police struggled for three days to control the riot. Eventually, troops (including all-Irish units) rushed from the battlefields of Pennsylvania to aid the police. The troops fired into the rioters; over a hundred people died and another 300 were injured. The working people got some of what they wanted: more welfare relief, exemptions from the draft for those whose families would have no other means of support, and an exodus of black people who feared for their lives. Resistance to the draft and to blacks erupted, too, in the mining districts of Pennsylvania, in the immigrant sections of Chicago, and in the quarries of Vermont.

Ironically, a few days after the New York draft riots scores of black troops died during a bold nighttime assault on Fort Wagner near Charleston, South Carolina. Despite the bravery of the African Americans, the assault failed. The Confederates made a point of burying the African American soldiers in a mass grave along with their white officer, Robert Gould Shaw, intending to insult him and his memory. Instead, they elevated him to a northern martyr.

Chickamauga

After Gettysburg, Vicksburg, and the New York riots in July, events slowed until September, when Union General William Rosecrans left Chattanooga, near the Georgia border, and began moving toward Atlanta. His opponent, Braxton Bragg, hoped to entice Rosecrans into dividing his forces so that they could be cut off. The armies confronted one another at Chickamauga Creek—a Cherokee name meaning "river of death." The Confederates took advantage of Union mistakes on the heavily wooded battlefield, inflicting harrowing damage and driving Rosecrans back into Chattanooga. The Union troops were trapped there, the Confederates looming over them on Lookout Mountain and Missionary Ridge, with few routes of escape and limited supplies. The Northerners had gone from a position of apparent advantage to one of desperation.

Lincoln, judging Rosecrans "confused and stunned" by the battle at Chickamauga, used this opportunity to put Grant in charge of all Union armies between the Appalachian Mountains and the Mississippi River. In the fall of 1863, Grant traveled to Chattanooga, where Sherman joined him from Mississippi and Hooker came from Virginia.

The Gettysburg Address

The North's victories in the summer of 1863 aided Lincoln's popularity. The draft riots in New York City damaged the reputations of Democrats, whereas the bravery of black soldiers on the battlefields of Louisiana and South Carolina led white Northerners to rethink some of their prejudices. In the fall of 1863, the Republicans won major victories in Pennsylvania and Ohio. Lincoln determined to make the most of these heartening events.

When Lincoln received an invitation to speak at the dedication of the cemetery at Gettysburg on November 19, he saw it as a chance to impart a sense of direction and purpose to the Union cause. The event had not been planned with him in mind and the president was not even the featured speaker. Edward Everett, a scholar and famed lecturer, had been asked weeks before to give the main address. But Lincoln recognized that a battlefield offered the most effective backdrop for the things he wanted to say.

Burial crews had been laboring for weeks on the Gettysburg battlefield. Thousands of horse carcasses had been burned; thousands of human bodies had been hastily covered with a thin layer of soil. Pennsylvania purchased seventeen acres and hired a specialist in rural cemetery design to lay out the burial plots so that no state would be offended by the location or amount of space devoted to its fallen men. Only about a third of the reburials had taken place when Lincoln arrived; caskets remained stacked at the station.

Lincoln, contrary to legend, did not dash off his speech on the back of an envelope. He had reworked and polished it for several days. The "remarks," as the program put it, lasted three minutes. Lincoln used those minutes to maximum effect. He said virtually nothing about the details of the scene surrounding the 20,000 people at the ceremony. Neither did he mention slavery directly. Instead, he spoke of equality as the fundamental purpose of the war. He called for a "new birth of freedom."

Lincoln was attempting to shift the purpose of the war from Union for Union's sake to Union for freedom's sake. He sought to salvage something from the deaths of the 50,000 men at Gettysburg. Democratic newspapers rebuked Lincoln for his claim, arguing that white soldiers had "too much self-respect to declare that negroes were their equals." But other Northerners accepted Lincoln's exhortation as the definition of their purpose. They might not believe that blacks deserved to be included as full participants in a government of, by, and for "the people," but they did believe that the Union fought for liberty broadly conceived. As battles and years went by, the words of the Gettysburg Address would gain force and resonance.

Just four days after Lincoln's speech, Grant gave the North new reason to believe its ideals might triumph. On November 23, Grant's men overwhelmed the Confederates on Lookout Mountain outside Chattanooga; two days later, Union soldiers accomplished the improbable task of fighting their way up Missionary Ridge because Confederate artillery could not reach opponents coming up directly from below. The Union, now in control of Kentucky and Tennessee, had a wide and direct route into Georgia.

England and France finally determined in late 1863 that they would not try to intervene in the American war. The northern public, encouraged by events on the battlefield, supported Republican candidates in the congressional elections of 1863 more vigorously than had seemed possible just a few months before.

THE WINTER OF DISCONTENT: 1863–1864

The battles of the summer had been horrific. Both sides held their victories close to their hearts and brooded over their losses. The resolve and fury of summertime faded into the bitterness and bickering of winter. As the cycle rolled around again, people steeled themselves for a final push.

Politics North and South

Lincoln hoped to end the war as soon as possible, using persuasion as well as fighting to entice white Southerners back into the national fold. In early December 1863, Lincoln issued his proclamation of amnesty and reconstruction. To those who would take an oath of loyalty to the Union, Lincoln promised a full pardon and the return of all property other than slaves. Though he excluded Confederate leaders and high officers from this offer, Lincoln tried to include as many white southern men as possible. As soon as 10 percent of the number of voters in 1860 had sworn their loyalty to the Union, he decreed, the Southerners could begin forming new state governments. Education and apprenticeship programs would aid former slaves in the transition to full freedom. He did not provide for African- American participation in the new governments of the South.

Abolitionists and their allies attacked Lincoln's reconstruction plan as far too lenient to the rebel masters and not helpful enough for the former slaves. In the Wade-Davis bill of February 1864, Republican congressmen attempted to institute more stringent demands on former Confederates and offer more help to former slaves. They wanted to use the power of the national government to enforce a standard set of laws across the South. They feared that too weak a plan of reconstruction would permit former slaveowners and Confederates to negate much of what the war might win. Congressmen and Secretary of the Treasury Salmon P. Chase worked behind the scenes in opposition to Lincoln's plan.

Although Jefferson Davis did not have to worry about his own reelection in late 1863—the Confederacy had established the presidential term at six years—he did have to worry about congressional elections. They did not go well: 41 of the new 106 representatives expressly opposed Davis and his policies, while he held only a slight majority in the Senate. Just as northern Democrats called for compromise and peace, so did some Southerners. When Davis took a hands-off policy, he was criticized for doing too little. When he tried to assert more control, he found himself called "despotic" by his own vice president. The Confederacy stumbled through the winter and into the spring of 1864, desperately watching for signs that the North might be losing heart.

Prisons

Early in the Civil War, both sides had exchanged prisoners of war rather than spend men and resources maintaining prisons. Such arrangements worked well enough into 1863, but then things began to break down. The Confederates decreed that any former slave captured would be executed or re-enslaved, not taken prisoner. The Union, as a matter of principle, refused to participate in any exchanges so long as this policy remained in effect. Prisoners began piling up on both sides and stories of mistreatment became more frequent and more horrifying.

Northerners who heard of the Confederate camp at Andersonville, Georgia, became livid. The camp was built early in 1864 when the Confederates decided to move prisoners from Richmond. Not only would prisoners be less likely to be rescued by northern troops farther south, but they could more easily be supplied by railroad away from the heavy fighting in Virginia. The camp, built for 10,000 men, soon became overcrowded; it held 33,000 by August. Gangs of northern soldiers controlled daily life within the prison, routinely beating and robbing new arrivals. Of the 45,000 men eventually held at Andersonville, 13,000 died. Even higher proportions died at smaller camps in North Carolina. Although Confederates held in northern prisons were better supplied, even there, death rates reached as high as 24 percent. Overall, about 16 percent of northern soldiers died in prison, 12 percent of Southerners. Many in the North criticized Lincoln for refusing to reinstitute exchanges, but Lincoln would not sacrifice the former slaves. Moreover, he knew that exchanges helped the soldier-starved Confederacy more than they did the North.

Union Resolve

In March 1864 Lincoln gave new direction and purpose to the Union effort by putting Ulysses S. Grant in charge of all northern forces. Grant and Lincoln agreed that the Union had to use its superiority in materiel, manpower, and navy to attack the Confederacy on every front at once, forcing the South to decide what territory it would sacrifice. While Grant would fight in Virginia, he left William T. Sherman in charge in Chattanooga. Sherman would attack the young railroad center of Atlanta, cutting the Gulf South off from the Upper South. The loss of Atlanta would chop the Confederacy into pieces too small to resist the northern army.

In retrospect, the events of 1864 may appear anticlimactic. The Confederates seemed to face overwhelming odds. Yet Southerners recognized that everything turned around holding the Northerners off until the presidential election in the North. If the Southerners could inflict enough damage on the Union army, Northerners might elect someone willing to bring the war to an end through compromise. The Confederates knew, too, that the three-year terms of the most experienced veterans in the Union army expired in 1864. More than half of those veterans chose to leave the army even though the war was not over. They would be replaced with younger, less seasoned soldiers. The Confederates also realized that Grant, new to his command, would be confronting Robert E. Lee, who was fighting with an experienced army. All things considered, it was by no means clear in 1864 that the Union would win Virginia or the war.

African Americans played an increasingly large role in Union plans, for over 180,000 black soldiers enlisted just when the North needed them most. By the spring of 1864, the means of recruitment, training, and pay for these soldiers had become well established. The Confederates, however, refused to recognize the same rules of warfare for black soldiers that they acknowledged for whites. In April of 1864, at Fort Pillow in western Tennessee, Confederate cavalry under the command of Nathan Bedford Forrest shot down black Union soldiers who attempted to surrender.

With the election clock running, Grant set out in May 1864 to destroy Lee's army. The Battle of the Wilderness near Chancellorsville saw brutal fighting and horrible losses. Fire in the tangled woods trapped wounded men, burning them alive. Grant lost more men than Hooker had in the battle of the previous year, but whereas Hooker treated such losses as a decisive defeat, Grant pushed on.

Map 15.3 | The Civil War, 1864–1865

The two armies fought again and again over the next two months in the fields of Virginia. The Confederates turned the Union army back to the east of Richmond and rushed up the Shenandoah Valley to threaten Washington itself. The North repulsed the invasion and dispatched Philip Sheridan to the valley to make sure the Confederates did not regroup. With the Confederates pinned down in Petersburg, near Richmond, Pennsylvania coal miners volunteered to tunnel under the fortifications and plant explosives. Throughout July, they dug; finally, at the end of the month, they detonated a charge and blew an enormous crater in the Confederate lines. The attack that followed the explosion, however, failed. Union soldiers piled into the crater, where the rallying Confederates trapped them.

Fortunately for Lincoln, things were going better farther south. Throughout June and July, Sherman pushed relentlessly through north Georgia toward Atlanta. By the end of July, the southern army had fallen back into Atlanta, preparing to defend it from siege. It seemed only a matter of time before the Union triumphed. But how much time?

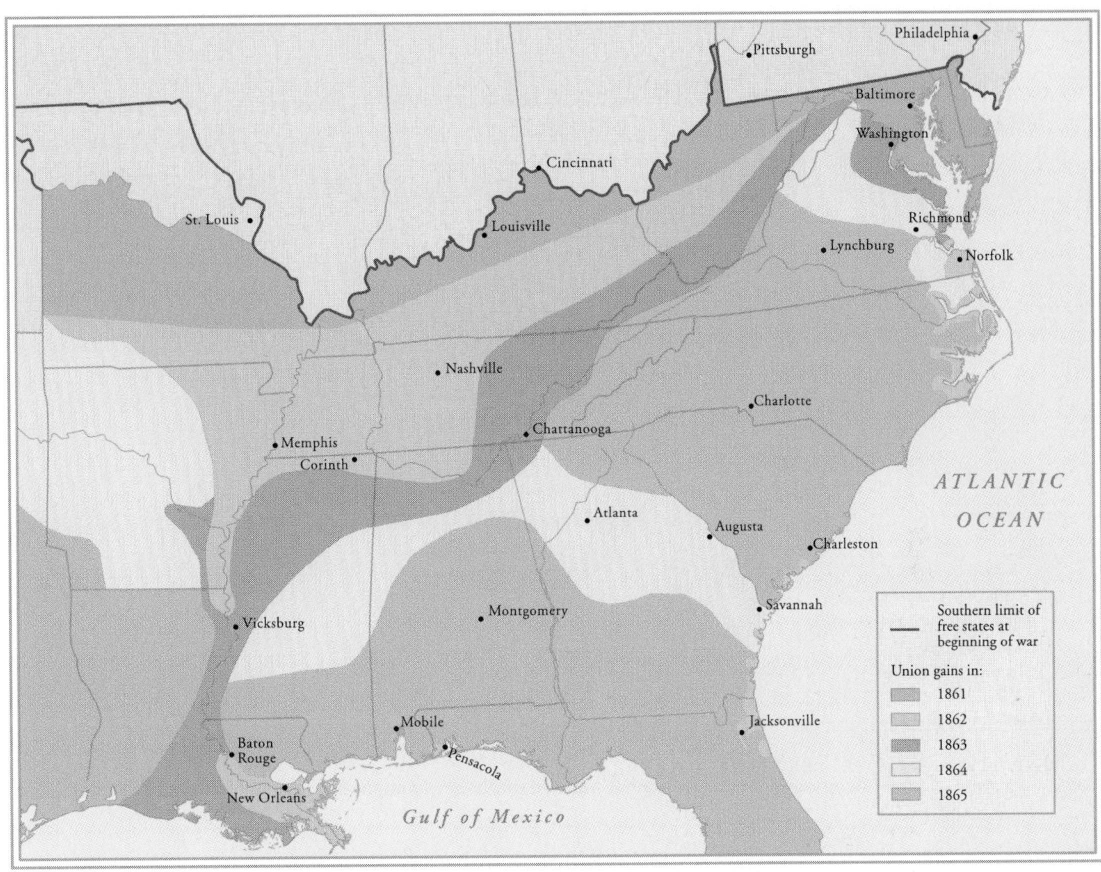

MAP 15.4 | CONQUEST OF THE SOUTH

The Northern Election of 1864

The president had to fight off challenges even within his own party. Some Republicans considered Lincoln too radical; others considered him too cautious. Through adroit use of patronage, however, Lincoln managed to win renomination in June. The Republican party tried to broaden its appeal to Democrats by nominating Andrew Johnson, a former Democrat, to the vice presidency.

In the meantime, the Democrats confidently moved forward. They knew that in the eyes of his critics, Lincoln had caused the war, trampled on constitutional rights, consolidated too much power, and refused to end the war when he had a chance. The Democrats intended to take full advantage of such criticisms, especially by nominating George McClellan as their candidate. McClellan demonstrated that a person could oppose Lincoln's political purposes of the war without being a coward or traitor. McClellan and the Democrats portrayed themselves as the truly national party, for they were determined to restore the United States to its prewar unity and grandeur. McClellan said he would end the war if the South would reenter the Union—bringing slavery with it. It was a bargain that appealed to many in the North.

Just when it appeared that the Democrats would unseat Lincoln, however, news from the

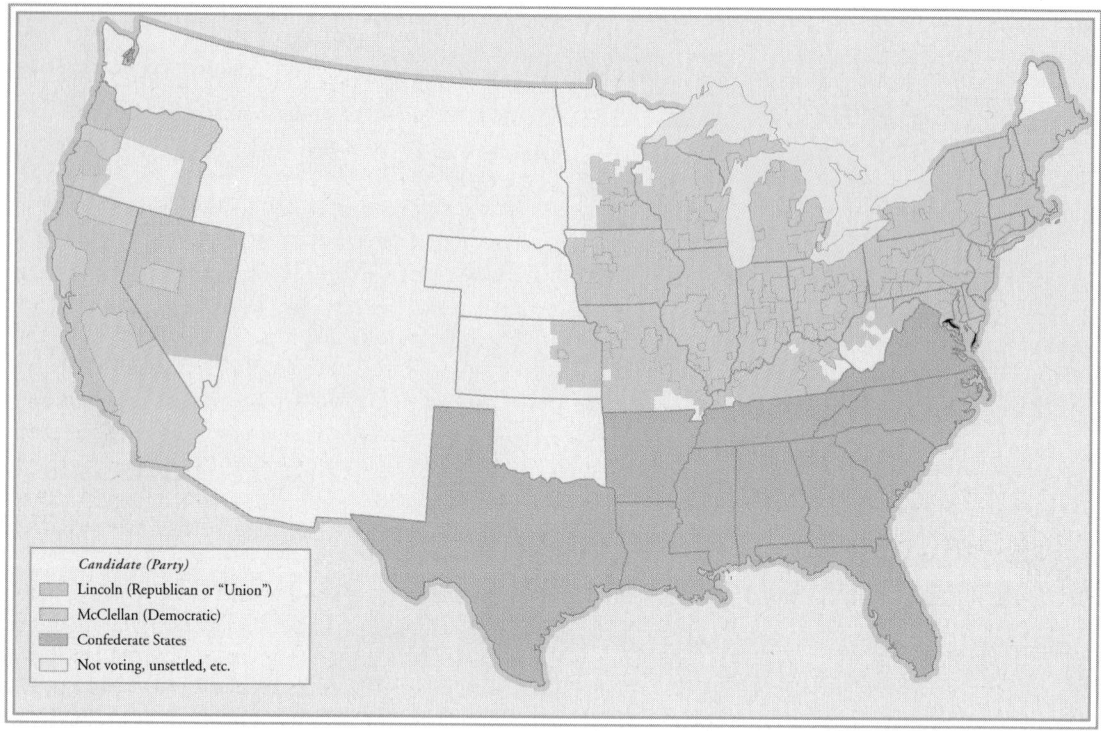

MAP 15.5 | THE ELECTION OF 1864

battlefield changed everything. Sherman swung around Atlanta and began destroying the railroads that made the small city an important junction. The Confederates, afraid they would be encircled and trapped within the city, set much of Atlanta on fire and abandoned it. Sherman and his army marched into the city on September 2. Two weeks later, Sheridan attacked the Confederates in the Shenandoah Valley, systematically destroying the valley's ability to support the southern army again.

Even with these military victories, Lincoln won only 55 percent of the popular vote. He did much better in the electoral college, sweeping every state except three. The Republicans also elected heavy majorities to both houses of Congress.

The March to the Sea

A week after Lincoln's election Sherman decided to set out across Georgia, provisioning his army along the way, taking the war to the southern people themselves. Such a march would be as much a demonstration of northern power as a military maneuver. The triumphant army of 60,000 made its way across the state throughout the fall of 1864. Large numbers of deserters from both sides, fugitive slaves, and outlaws took advantage of the situation to inflict widespread destruction and panic. Sherman arrived at Savannah on December 21. "I beg to present to you, as a Christmas gift, the city of Savannah," Sherman buoyantly telegraphed Lincoln.

This picture, taken four days before his assassination, shows the toll four years of war had taken on the 56-year-old president. (The Granger Collection, New York)

FROM WAR TO RECONSTRUCTION: 1865–1867

As the war ground to a halt in early 1865, Americans had to wonder if they remembered how to share a country with their former enemies. They had to wonder, too, how different the country would be with African Americans no longer as slaves. Of all the changes the United States had ever seen, emancipation stood as the most profound.

War's Climax

Events moved quickly at the beginning of 1865. In January, Sherman issued Special Field Order 15, which reserved land in coastal South Carolina, Georgia, and Florida for former slaves. Those who settled on the land would receive forty-acre plots. Four days later, the Republicans in Congress passed the Thirteenth Amendment, abolishing slavery forever. At the beginning of February, Sherman's troops began to march north into the Carolinas. Columbia, South Carolina, burned to the ground. Growing numbers of Confederate soldiers deserted from their armies. Lincoln met with Confederate officials to try to bring the war to an end, offering slaveowners compensation for their freed slaves if the Southerners would immediately cease the war. Jefferson Davis refused.

At the beginning of March, Lincoln was inaugurated for his second term. Rather than gloating at the impending victory on the battlefield, Lincoln called for his fellow citizens to "bind up the nation's wounds." That same month, Congress created the Bureau of Refugees, Freedmen, and Abandoned Lands to ease the transition from slavery to freedom. Nine days later, the Confederate government, after hotly debating whether to recruit slaves to fight as soldiers if their owners agreed, finally decided to do so after Lee, desperate for men, supported the measure.

Appomattox and Assassination

The Confederates' slave recruitment law did not have time to convert slaves to soldiers, however, for Grant soon began his final assault on Confederate troops in Virginia. Petersburg fell on April 2, Richmond the next day. Lee hoped to lead his army to the train station at Appomattox Court House to resupply them, but on April 9 Grant intercepted Lee's men just short of their destination. Lee, with nowhere else to go and no ally to come to his aid, surrendered.

A number of Confederate armies had yet to surrender, and Jefferson Davis had yet to be captured, but it was clear that the war had ended. The Southerners began to straggle home. Two days later, Lincoln addressed a Washington audience about what would come next for the freedmen. He admitted that Northerners differed "as to the mode, manner, and means of Reconstruction" and that the white South was "disorganized and discordant."

Lincoln did not live to take part in the planning, for he was assassinated on April 14 by John Wilkes Booth, a failed actor and southern sympathizer. Booth attacked Lincoln while the president sat with Mrs. Lincoln at Ford's Theater in Washington, shooting him in the back of the head and then leaping to the stage. Lincoln never recovered consciousness; he died early the next morning. After a long and frantic search, Booth was captured and killed in a burning barn.

The Costs and Consequences of the War

The North lost almost 365,000 men to death and disease in the Civil War, and the South lost 260,000. Another 277,000 Northerners were wounded, along with 195,000 Southerners. Black Americans lost 37,000 men in the Union army and another 10,000 men, women, and children in the contraband camps. Widows and orphans, black and white, northern and southern, faced decades of struggling without a male breadwinner. Many people found their emotional lives shattered by the war. Alcohol, drug abuse, crime, and violence became widespread problems.

The southern economy fell to its knees. Major southern cities had been reduced to ash. Railroads had been ripped from the ground, engines and cars burned. Fields had grown up in weeds and brush. Farm values fell by half. Livestock, tools, barns, and fences had been stolen or destroyed by the armies of both sides. Just as damaging in the long run, lines of credit had been severed. Before emancipation, planters had used slaves as collateral for loans. Now, without that basis, few people outside the South were willing to loan money to planters or other investors.

The Civil War did not mark a sudden turn in the northern economy, but it did accelerate processes already well underway. The nationalization of markets, the accumulation of wealth, and the dominance of larger manufacturing firms all became more marked after 1865. Greenbacks, bonds, and a national banking system regularized the flow of capital and spurred the growth of business. The Republicans passed the Department of Agriculture Act, the Morrill College Land Grant

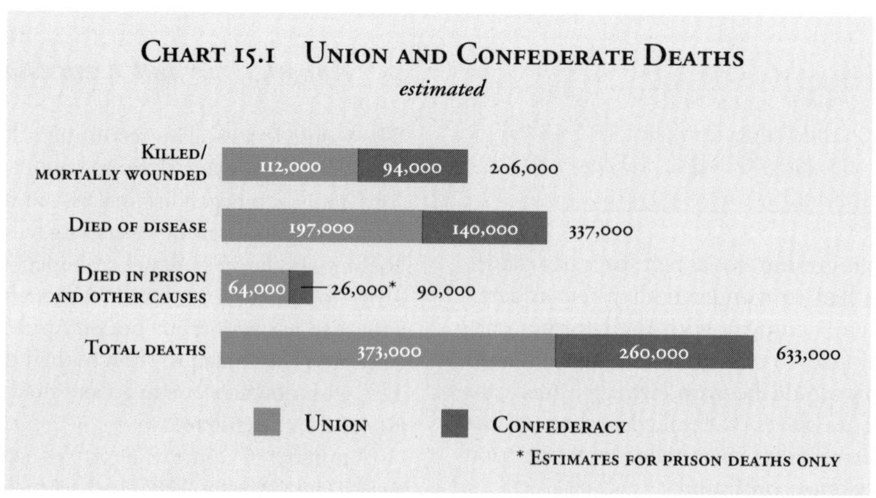

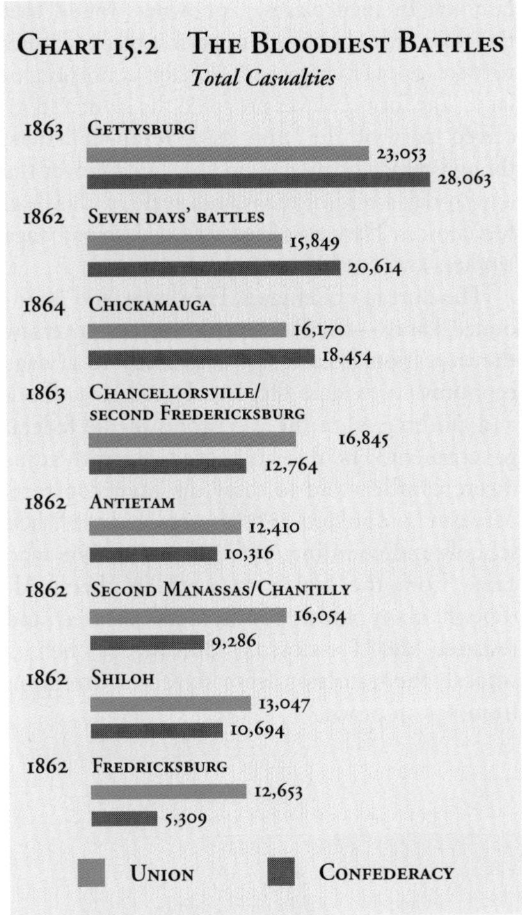

Act, the Homestead Act, and the Union Pacific Railroad Act, all using the power of the federal government to encourage settlement of the West, strengthen public education, and spur economic development. Despite the prosperity in the North, the hundreds of thousands of veterans faced many dislocations and readjustments as they returned to the farms, factories, and shops they had left months or years before.

Emancipation and the South

As the battles ground to a halt, slaves became former slaves. Some, especially the young, greeted freedom confidently, whereas others, especially the elderly, could not help but be wary of anything so strange, no matter how long and how much they had prayed for it. Some seized their freedom at the first opportunity, taking their families to Union camps or joining the army. Others celebrated when the Yankees came to their plantations, only to find that their owners and white neighbors retaliated when the soldiers left. Others bided their time. Some refused to believe the stories of freedom at all until their master or mistress called them together to announce that they were indeed no longer slaves.

Upon hearing the news, the freed people gathered to discuss their options. For many, the highest priority was to reunite their families. Such people set off on journeys in desperate efforts to find a husband, wife, child, or parent sold away in earlier years. For others, sheer survival was the highest priority. Freedom came in the late spring, barely in time to get crops in the ground. Some former slaves argued that their best bet was to stay where they were for the time being. They had heard rumors that the government would award them land. Between July and September of 1865, however, those dreams died. Union officers promised land to former slaves in Virginia, Louisiana, Mississippi, and South Carolina, but then Washington revoked the promises. The land would be returned to its former owners.

Former slaveowners also responded in many different ways. Some fled to Latin America. Others tried to keep as much of slavery as they could by whipping and chaining workers to keep them from leaving. Still others offered to let former slaves stay in their cabins and work for wages.

African Americans had no choice but to compromise with white landowners. At first, in the spring of 1865, planters insisted that the former slaves work as they had worked before emancipation, in "gangs." In return for their work, they would receive a portion of the crop, shared among all the workers. Many black people chafed at this arrangement, preferring to work as individuals or

After four years of war, little remained in the besieged cities of the Confederacy. (© Corbis-Bettmann)

families. In such places, landowners found that they had little choice but to permit black families to take primary responsibility for a portion of land. The former slaves provided the labor and received part of the crop as a result. Planters, though reluctant to give up any control over the day-to-day work on their land, realized they had few choices. They possessed little cash to pay wage workers and no alternative labor.

The Bureau of Refugees, Freedmen, and Abandoned Lands—the Freedmen's Bureau—oversaw the transition from a slave economy to a wage economy. Its agents dispensed medicine, food, and clothing from the vast stores of the federal government. The Bureau created courts to adjudicate conflicts and to draw up labor contracts between landholders and laborers. It established schools and coordinated female volunteers who came from the North to teach in them. Although many white Southerners resented and resisted the Freedmen's Bureau, it helped smooth the transition from slavery to freedom, from war to peace.

Black Southerners took advantage of the presence of Union troops to leave the farms and plantations on which they had been held. Many set out to find family members. (Worthwind Picture Archives)

Black Mobilization

Black Southerners mourned the loss of Abraham Lincoln. Without his leadership, former slaves rightly worried, the forces of reaction might overwhelm their freedom. Southerners of both races watched to see what Andrew Johnson might do.

Throughout the South, former slaves and former free blacks gathered in conventions to announce their vision of the new order. They wanted, above all else, equality before the law and the opportunity to vote. They did not demand confiscation of land nor did they speak extensively of economic concerns in general. Let us have our basic rights before the courts and at the ballot box, they said, and we will take care of ourselves. Such concerns and confidence reflected the perspective of the conventions' leadership: former free blacks, skilled artisans, ministers, and teachers. The great mass of southern blacks found their concerns neglected.

"Letter to the Union Convention, 1865,"

Black Citizens of Tennessee

In this petition by black Tennesseans to their white Unionist counterparts in the waning days of the Civil War, the themes of the Gettysburg Address receive eloquent endorsement. The fifty-nine men who signed the petition articulated the highest ideals of the American nation. There is no record of a response.

[Nashville, Tenn., January 9, 1865]

To the Union Convention of Tennessee Assembled in the Capitol at Nashville, January 9th, 1865: . . .

We claim to be men belonging to the great human family, descended from one great God, who is the common Father of all, and who bestowed on all races and tribes the priceless right of freedom. Of this right, for no offence of ours, we have long been cruelly deprived, and the common voice of the wise and good of all countries, has remonstrated against our enslavement, as one of the greatest crimes in all history.

We claim freedom, as our natural right, and ask that in harmony and cooperation with the nation at large, you should cut up by the roots the system of slavery, which is not only a wrong to us, but the source of all the evil which at present afflicts the State. For slavery, corrupt itself, corrupted nearly all, also, around it, so that it has influenced nearly all the slave States to rebel against the Federal Government, in order to set up a government of pirates under which slavery might be perpetrated.

(continued)

. . .

Devoted as we are to the principles of justice, of love to all men, and of equal rights on which our Government is based, and which make it the hope of the world. We know the burdens of citizenship, and are ready to bear them. We know the duties of the good citizen, and are ready to perform them cheerfully, and would ask to be put in a position in which we can discharge them more effectually. We do not ask for the privilege of citizenship, wishing to shun the obligations imposed by it.

Near 200,000 of our brethren are to-day performing military duty in the ranks of the Union army. Thousands of them have already died in battle, or perished by a cruel martyrdom for the sake of the Union, and we are ready and willing to sacrifice more. . . .

This is a democracy—a government of the people. It should aim to make every man, without regard to the color of his skin, the amount of his wealth, or the character of his religious faith, feel personally interested in its welfare. Every man who lives under the Government should feel that it is his property, his treasure, the bulwark and defense of himself and his family, his pearl of great price, which he must preserve, protect, and defend faithfully at all times, on all occasions, in every possible manner.

This is not a Democratic Government if a numerous, law-abiding, industrious, and useful class of citizens, born and bred on the soil, are to be treated as aliens and enemies, as an inferior degraded class, who must have no voice in the Government which they support, protect and defend, with all their heart, soul, mind, and body, both in peace and war. . . .

One other matter we would urge on your honorable body. At present we can have only partial protection from the courts. The testimony of twenty of the most intelligent, honorable, colored loyalists cannot convict a white traitor of a treasonable action. A white rebel might sell powder and lead to a rebel soldier in the presence of twenty colored soldiers, and yet their evidence would be worthless so far as the courts are concerned, and the rebel would escape. A colored man may have served for years faithfully in

Black Southerners agreed on the centrality of two institutions, however: the church and the school. At the very moment of freedom, they began to form their own churches. For generations, African Americans had been forced to worship alongside whites. For many ex-slaves, one of their first acts of freedom was to form their own churches. People who owned virtually nothing somehow built churches across the South. Those churches often served as schools as well.

Andrew Johnson

In the meantime, events in Washington undermined the efforts of black Southerners to build a new world for themselves. Andrew Johnson wanted to attract moderates from both the North and the South to a party that would change as little as possible. Johnson had been selected to run for the vice presidency because he was a Southerner who had remained true to the Union. As a result, both Northerners and Southerners distrusted Johnson. A longtime Democrat before the crisis of the Union, Johnson maintained a limited, Jacksonian view of government. The new president's well-known disdain for the wealthy planters of the South appealed to equally disdainful Republicans in Washington. Unlike them, however, Johnson held little sympathy for black people. Johnson saw himself pursuing Lincoln's highest goal: reuniting the Union. He believed the army, and yet his testimony in court would be rejected, while that of a white man who had served in the rebel army would be received. . . .

There have been white traitors in multitudes in Tennessee, but where we ask, is the black traitor? Can you forget how the colored man has fought at Fort Morgan, at Milliken's Bend, at Fort Pillow, before Petersburg, and your own city of Nashville?

When has the colored citizen, in this rebellion been tried and found wanting?. . .

In this great and fearful struggle of the nation with a wicked rebellion, we are anxious to perform the full measure of our duty both as citizens and soldiers to the Union cause we consecrate ourselves, and our families with all that we have on earth. Our souls burn with love for the great government of freedom and equal rights. Our white brethren have no cause for distrust as regards our fidelity, for neither death nor life, nor angels, nor principalities, nor powers, nor things present, nor things to come, nor height, nor depth, nor any other creature, shall be able to separate us from the love of the Union.

Praying that the great God, who is the common Father of us all, by whose help the land must be delivered from present evil, and before whom we must all stand at last to be judged by the rule of eternal justice, and not by passion and prejudice, may enlighten your minds and enable you to act with wisdom, justice, and magnanimity, we remain your faithful friends in all the perils and dangers which threaten our beloved country.

[59 signatures]

And many other colored citizens of Nashville.

SOURCE *Free at Last: A Documentary History of Slavery, Freedom, and the Civil War.* Ira Berlin, et al., eds. (New York: New Press, 1992) pp. 497–505.

that reunification should start by winning the support of white Southerners.

Johnson could hardly have been placed in a more difficult position. Congress was not in session at the time of Lincoln's death and would not be for seven months, so Johnson used the opportunity to implement his vision of reunion. In what became known as "Presidential Reconstruction," Johnson offered amnesty to former Confederates who would take an oath of loyalty to the Union, restoring their political and civil rights and immunizing them against the seizure of their property or prosecution for treason. Johnson's plans for political reunion made no provisions at all for black voting. Indeed, his plan threatened to return the South to even greater national power than it had held before because the entire African American population would now be considered when the number of representatives was calculated, not merely as three-fifths of a people as before the war.

White Southerners could hardly believe their good fortune. The state conventions elected in 1865 flaunted their opinions of the North. Some refused to fly the American flag, some refused to ratify the Thirteenth Amendment, some even refused to admit that secession had been illegal. Former Confederates filled important posts in state governments. Georgia elected Alexander H. Stephens, the ex-vice president of the aborted nation, to Congress.

The North erupted in outrage when the new state governments enacted the so-called "black

Andrew Johnson attempted to forge a new alliance between white Northerners and white Southerners, callously abandoning black Southerners in the process. (© Corbis-Bettmann)

codes," laws for the control of the former slaves. The southern white legislatures granted only the barest minimum of rights to black people: the right to marry, to hold property, to sue and be sued. Most of the laws decreed what African Americans could not do: move from one job to another, own or rent land, practice certain occupations. When the members of Congress convened in December of 1865, they reacted as many of their constituents did—with fury. To Northerners, even those inclined to deal leniently with the South, the former Confederates seemed to deny all the war had decided. And many Northerners blamed Johnson.

Johnson and the Radicals

It was not that most Northerners, even most Republicans, wanted the kind of policies promoted by Radicals such as Thaddeus Stevens, who called for land to be seized from wealthy planters and given to the former slaves, or of Charles Sumner, who wanted immediate and universal suffrage for blacks. But neither did they want the sort of capitulation that Johnson had tolerated. Moderates tried to devise plans that would be acceptable to both sides.

The moderates sought to continue the Freedmen's Bureau. The Bureau was understaffed and underfunded—only about 900 agents covered the entire South—but it offered some measure of hope for former slaves. The Bureau saw itself as a mediator between blacks and whites. It insisted on the innovation of formal contracts between laborer and landlord. Although these contracts infuriated southern white men, the Freedmen's Bureau ended up supporting landowners as often as black laborers. The moderates also attempted to institute a Civil Rights bill to define American citizenship for all those born in the United States, thereby including blacks. Citizenship would bring with it equal protection under the laws, though the bill said nothing about black voting.

Republicans supported the Freedmen's Bureau and Civil Rights bills as the starting place for rebuilding the nation. But Johnson vetoed both bills, claiming that they violated the rights of the states and of white Southerners who had been excluded from the decision-making. Republicans closed ranks to override Johnson's veto.

To prevent any future erosion of black rights, the Republicans proposed the Fourteenth Amendment, which, as eventually ratified, guaranteed citizenship to all American-born people and equal protection under the law for those citizens. The amendment decreed that any state that abridged the voting rights of any male inhabitants who were twenty-one and citizens would suffer a proportionate reduction in its congressional representation. Johnson urged the southern states to refuse to ratify the amendment, advice they promptly followed.

Throughout the second half of 1866 the North watched, appalled, as much that the Civil War had been fought for seemed to be brushed aside in the South. Not only did the southern men who met in the state conventions refuse to accept the relatively mild Fourteenth Amendment, but they made clear their determination to fight back in every way they could against further attempts to remake the South. The spring of that year saw riots in Memphis and New Orleans in which policemen and other whites brutally assaulted and killed black people with little or no provocation.

It was in 1866, too, that the Ku Klux Klan appeared. Founded in Tennessee, the Ku Klux Klan dedicated itself to maintaining white supremacy. The Klan dressed in costumes designed to overawe the former slaves, hiding behind their anonymity to avoid retaliation. The Klan became in effect a military wing of the Democratic party, devoting much of its energy to warning and killing white and black men who dared associate with the Republicans.

Johnson toured the country in the fall of 1866 to denounce the Republicans and their policies. The tour was a disaster. The voters rejected both Johnson and the Democrats, as the governorship and legislature of every northern state came under the control of the Republicans. The Republicans felt they held a mandate to push harder than they had before. They had only a few months, however, until their term ended in March, to decide what to do. They bitterly disagreed over the vote, land distribution, the courts, and education. Some wanted to put the South under military control for the indefinite future while others sought to return things to civilian control as soon as possible. Finally, on March 2, 1867, as time was running out on the session, they passed the Reconstruction Act.

The Reconstruction Act

The Reconstruction Act placed the South under military rule. All the southern states except Tennessee, which had been readmitted to the Union after it ratified the Fourteenth Amendment, were put in five military districts. Once order had been instituted, then the states would proceed to elect conventions to draw up new constitutions. The constitutions written by those conventions had to accept the Fourteenth Amendment and provide for universal manhood suffrage. Once a majority of the state's citizens and both houses of the national Congress had approved the new constitution, the state could be readmitted to the Union.

To ensure that Andrew Johnson did not undermine this plan—which soon became known as "Radical Reconstruction"—Congress sought to curb the president's power. With no threat of his veto after the 1866 elections, the Republicans could do much as they wanted. Congress decreed that it could call itself into special session. There, it limited the president's authority as commander-in-chief of the army and, in the Tenure of Office Act, prevented him from removing officials who had been confirmed by the Senate.

Johnson, characteristically, did not quietly accept such restrictions of his power. When he intentionally violated the Tenure of Office Act by removing Secretary of War Edwin Stanton in the summer of 1867, many in Congress decided that Johnson warranted impeachment. Matters stewed throughout the fall, while the first elections under the Reconstruction Act took place in the South.

Reconstruction Begins

After word of the Reconstruction Act circulated in the spring and summer, both black men and white claimed leadership roles within the Republican party. Black Northerners came to the South, looking for appointive and elective office. Ambitious black Southerners, many of whom had been free and relatively prosperous before the Civil War, put themselves forward as the natural leaders of the race. Such men became the backbone of the Republican party in black-belt districts.

White Southerners sneered at white Northerners who supported the Republican cause. They called them "carpetbaggers." These men, according to the insulting name, were supposedly so

The Ku Klux Klan emerged in 1866, devoting itself to the maintenance of white supremacy in all its forms. (The Granger Collection, New York)

devoid of connections and property in their northern homes that they could throw everything they had into a carpetbag—a cheap suitcase—and head south as soon as they read of the opportunities created by Radical Reconstruction. The majority of white Northerners who became Republican leaders in the South, however, had in fact moved to the region months or years before Reconstruction began. Many had been well educated in the North before the war and many held property in the South. Like white Southerners, however, the northern-born Republicans found the postwar South a difficult place in which to prosper. Black people were no more inclined to work for low wages for white Northerners than for anyone else, and southern whites often went out of their way to avoid doing business with the Yankees. As a result, when Reconstruction began, a considerable number of Northerners took up the Republican cause as a way to build a political career in the South.

White southern Republicans, labeled "scalawags" by their enemies, risked being called traitors to their race and region. Few white Republicans emerged in the plantation districts, because they endured ostracism, resistance, and violence. In the upcountry districts, however, former Whigs and Unionists asserted themselves against the planters and Confederates. The Republican party became strong in the mountains of east Tennessee, western North Carolina, eastern Kentucky, north Alabama, and northern Georgia. Many whites in these districts, though unwilling to join with low country African Americans or their white leaders, struck alliances of convenience with them. Black voters and white voters generally wanted and needed different things. Blacks, largely propertyless, called for an activist government to provide schools, orphanages, and hospitals. Most whites, on the other hand, owned land and called mainly for lower taxes.

Throughout the South, most whites watched, livid, as the Republicans mobilized black voters in enormous numbers in the fall of 1867. While many white Democrats boycotted the elections, the Republicans swept into the constitutional delegate positions. Although many black men voted, African American delegates made up only a relatively small part of the convention's delegates. They held the majority in South Carolina and Louisiana, but much smaller proportions elsewhere. About half of the 265 African Americans elected as delegates to the state conventions had been free before the war, and most were ministers, artisans, farmers, and teachers. Over the next two years, these delegates would meet to write new, much more democratic, constitutions for their states.

At the very moment of the success of the southern Republicans, however, ominous signs came from the North. Republicans were dismayed at the election returns in the North in 1867, for the Democrats' power surged from coast to coast. Many white voters thought that the Radicals had gone too far in their concern with black rights and wanted officeholders to devote their energies to problems closer to home. The Republicans in Washington heard the message. They began scaling back their support for any further advances in Reconstruction.

CONCLUSION

The Civil War changed the United States more deeply than any other event in the nineteenth century. The conflict brought the deaths of over 625,000 soldiers. It saw bitter rioting in the streets and the first assassination of a president. It brought a major shift in the balance of power among the regions and an expansion of the federal government. Most important, the war brought what few Americans could have imagined at the end of 1860: the immediate emancipation of 4 million enslaved people.

Freedom emerged from the war through a circuitous route. The war began as a war for Union. As the deaths mounted and African Americans seized freedom at every opportunity, abolitionists and Republicans increasingly insisted that the war become a war to end slavery. Many white Northerners supported emancipation because it seemed the best way to end the war. Abraham Lincoln worked desperately to keep the support of both the advocates and foes of emancipation, knowing that moving too quickly would shatter the fragile support that kept him in office. The New York City draft riots and the close elections of 1863 demonstrated that many Northerners resisted the continuation of the war and its embrace of black freedom. Only Union success on the battlefield in late 1864 permitted Lincoln's reelection. His assassination made an already confused situation far more so, ending slavery and restoring the Union without a blueprint and without leadership.

The end of the fighting saw the conflict shift in the South, as people struggled to determine what freedom would mean. For black Southerners, the goal was autonomy and respect. For white Northerners, the goal was to reconstruct the South in an idealized image of the North. For white Southerners, the goal was the reassertion of the power they had held before the war, especially power over the black people in their midst. Such goals could not be reconciled. The era of Reconstruction would be devoted to the struggle among them.

RECOMMENDED READINGS

Berlin, Ira, Fields, Barbara J., Miller, Steven F., Reidy, Joseph P., and Rowland, Leslie S., eds. *Freedom* (1985–). A fascinating multivolume documentary collection.

Donald, David. *Lincoln* (1995). Stands as the most elegant biography.

Faust, Drew Gilpin. *Mothers of Invention: Women of the Slaveholding South in the American Civil War* (1995). Offers a challenging and interesting interpretation.

Fellman, Michael. *Inside War: The Guerilla Conflict in Missouri During the American Civil War* (1989). Makes palpable the internal struggles in the border areas.

Foner, Eric. *Reconstruction: America's Unfinished Revolution, 1863–1877* (1988). A magisterial interpretation of the struggle over black freedom.

Gallagher, Gary W. *The Confederate War: How Popular Will, Nationalism, and Military Strategy Could Not Stave Off Defeat* (1997). Explores why the Confederacy could fight as long as it did.

Harris, William C. *With Charity for All: Lincoln and the Restoration of the Union* (1997). Offers a fresh assessment of Lincoln's attitudes toward the white South.

Hattaway, Herman, and Jones, Archer. *How the North Won: A Military History of the Civil War* (1983). Authoritatively describes strategy and tactics.

Litwack, Leon. *Been in the Storm So Long: The Aftermath of Slavery* (1979). Beautifully evokes the conflicting emotions and motives surrounding freedom.

Roark, James L. *Masters Without Slaves: Southern Planters in the Civil War and Reconstruction* (1978). Describes the war from the perspective of those who lost the most in southern defeat.

Rose, Willie Lee. *Rehearsal for Reconstruction: The Port Royal Experiment* (1964). A classic account of the first efforts to create northern policy toward the freed people.

AMERICAN JOURNEY ONLINE AND INFOTRAC COLLEGE EDITION

Visit the source collections at www.americanjourney.psmedia.com and infotrac.thomsonlearning.com and use the Search function with the following key terms to explore documents, images, audio and video clips, articles, and commentary related to the material in this chapter.

Ulysses S. Grant
African American soldiers
Vicksburg
Gettysburg Address
Appomattox
Emancipation

Chapter 16

Reconstruction Abandoned, 1867–1877

After 1867 the nation continued to struggle over the gains that black Americans had earned during the Civil War. The battle was fought with the greatest intensity in the South. There, whites sought to recapture as many of the features of slavery as they could. Violence, brutality, election fraud, and economic intimidation ended the experiment in multiracial politics known as Reconstruction.

Racial prejudice was at the heart of the problem, but other circumstances hastened the abandonment of Reconstruction. Settlement of the West claimed the energies of many people. In the mid-1870s, an economic depression made civil rights seem less relevant. White Americans worried that the national government was becoming too powerful, and they reverted to traditional beliefs in localism and state rights. For many in the North, the hum of industry, the spread of railroads, the rise of cities, all seemed more in tune with an era of progress than preserving the rights of former slaves. Slowly, painfully, the nation retreated from the principles for which the Civil War had been fought. In 1877 an informal sectional compromise sealed the return to white rule in the South.

Outside the political arena, industrialization transformed the economy. The completion of the two transcontinental railroads in 1869 symbolized the rapid pace of technological change. Four years later, however, the Panic of 1873 demonstrated that progress did not always move forward along an unbroken path.

A Period of Unrest

The waning of Reconstruction left African Americans and Indians further removed from the mainstream of society. As the drive to expand freedom for black Americans stalled, white dominance in the South hardened. Military defeat of the Indians confined them to reservations. Women found that their future remained subject to the wishes of a male-dominated nation. After the upheaval of the Civil War, the 1870s were a time to pause and reflect.

The Impeachment of Andrew Johnson

As President Andrew Johnson sought to block the Radical Reconstruction program, sentiment to

CHRONOLOGY

1867 Alaska purchase treaty signed

1868 Andrew Johnson impeached and then acquitted

Purchase of Alaska completed

Ulysses S. Grant wins presidency

1869 Ulysses S. Grant inaugurated as president

Transcontinental railroads link up

Licensing of women lawyers begins

Fifteenth Amendment passes Congress

"Gold Corner" scheme of Jay Gould and Jim Fisk

Woman suffrage enacted in Wyoming Territory

1870 Santo Domingo annexation treaty defeated

Ku Klux Klan terror raids in the South

First Greek letter sorority (Kappa Alpha Theta) founded

1871 Ku Klux Klan Act passes Congress

Tweed Ring exposed in New York City

Chicago fire burns three and a half miles of the city

1872 Liberal Republican movement challenges Grant

Grant wins reelection over Horace Greeley

1873 Panic of 1873 starts economic depression

Salary Grab and Crédit Mobilier scandals

Mark Twain and Charles Dudley Warner publish *The Gilded Age*

1874 Women's Christian Temperance Union founded

Democrats make substantial gains in the congressional elections

Sale of typewriters begins

Chautauqua movement for summer education starts

1875 Civil Rights Act passes Congress

Smith College and Wellesley College open to provide higher education for women

1876 Custer defeated at Little Big Horn

Heinz tomato ketchup is marketed

Centennial Exposition opens in Philadelphia

Tilden and Hayes are candidates in presidential election that remains contested as year ends

1877 Hayes declared winner of the presidency after series of compromises settles disputes

Reconstruction comes to an end

impeach him grew among Republicans in Congress. The Republicans could do little until December 1867, when Congress reassembled. By that time, impeachment efforts had faltered. After the Senate refused to accept Johnson's dismissal of Secretary of War Edwin M. Stanton in January 1868, Johnson replaced him anyway—an act of defiance that Republicans claimed was a clear breach of the Tenure of Office Act (see Chapter 15).

Emboldened by Johnson's action, the solidly Republican House voted for his impeachment and brought eleven charges against him. The trial got underway in March. Two months later the Senate failed to produce a two-thirds vote to convict the president.

The impeachment attempt failed for several reasons. Moderate Republicans feared that if a president were impeached and convicted on political grounds a bad precedent would be set. Johnson temporarily eased obstructive tactics, and the approach of the 1868 election also made ousting him seem less urgent.

Although he was acquitted, Johnson did not become more conciliatory. His intransigence encouraged southern whites and contributed to the resistance against African American equality that marked the 1870s.

The Purchase of Alaska

In March 1867, the Russian minister to the United States hinted to Secretary of State William H. Seward that the tsarist government in St. Petersburg would respond favorably to an American offer to purchase Alaska. The Russians knew that they could not defend their northern possession against the British in Canada. The Russian diplomat and Seward worked out a treaty that was signed on March 30, 1867. The United States paid $7,200,000 for Alaska. On April 9, the Senate gave its approval by a vote of thirty-seven to two.

Paying for the Alaska purchase required an appropriation from the House. The members did not take up the subject until July 1868, after the House had impeached the president. Faced with a *fait accompli* in that the occupation of the territory had occurred a year earlier, the House approved the money solidly on July 14, and the measure became law two weeks later.

The Election of 1868

The leading candidate for the Republican nomination was Ulysses S. Grant. His association with the Union victory gave him a popularity that transcended partisanship. In his letter of acceptance, Grant concluded with the phrase "let us

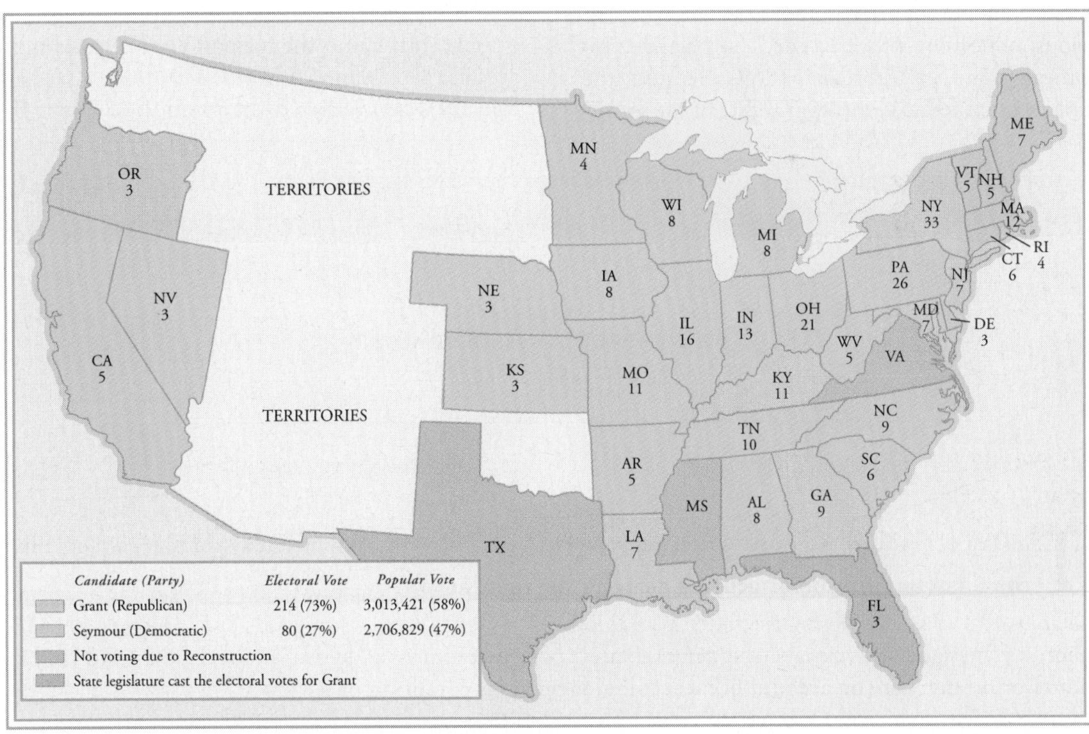

MAP 16.1 | THE ELECTION OF 1868

have peace" and that became the theme of his campaign. To run against Grant, the Democrats turned to the former governor of New York, Horatio Seymour. Along with his running mate, Frank Blair, Seymour made a campaign based on the philosophy of white supremacy. When the votes were counted, Grant had 53 percent and Seymour had 47 percent. In the electoral college, however, Grant had a more secure margin of 214 electoral votes to 80. The relatively close result indicated that white voters were cooling toward Reconstruction.

The Fifteenth Amendment and Woman Suffrage

After the 1868 election Republicans pushed for adoption of the Fifteenth Amendment to the Constitution, which stated that the federal and state governments could not abridge the right of a citizen to vote "on account of race, color, or previous condition of servitude." Legislative approval came in February 1869. Because the amendment reduced the legal ability of the southern states to exclude African Americans from voting, Democrats attacked it as "a step toward centralization and consolidation."

The new amendment did not assure African Americans the right to hold office, nor did it address the restrictions that northern states imposed on the right of other males to vote. These limits included literacy tests and property qualifications. State legislatures outside the South endorsed the amendment promptly and it was ratified in 1870.

The Fifteenth Amendment ignored women. Some advocates of woman suffrage, such as Susan B. Anthony, opposed the amendment because it excluded women. She favored voting barriers for black and Asian men if women did not have the vote. Despite his earlier support for woman suffrage, Frederick Douglass now said that "this hour belongs to the negro," meaning black males. At a meeting of the Equal Rights Association in May 1869, differing views about the right strategy for achieving woman suffrage caused an open rift.

The split led to the formation of two distinct groups. The National Woman Suffrage Association (NWSA) reflected the position of Susan B.

THE FIFTEENTH AMENDMENT
1870

The last of the three Reconstruction amendments, the Fifteenth Amendment said that race or color could not be a reason for denying a citizen the right to vote.

Sect. 1. The right of citizens of the United States to vote shall not be denied or abridged by the United States or by any State on account of race, color, or previous condition of servitude.

Sect. 2. The Congress shall have the power to enforce this article by appropriate legislation.

Anthony and Elizabeth Cady Stanton who believed that the Fifteenth Amendment should not be supported until it included women. The American Woman Suffrage Association (AWSA), led by Lucy Stone and Alice Stone Blackwell, endorsed the amendment and focused its suffrage efforts on the states. The new territory of Wyoming granted women the right of suffrage in 1869. The discord between the two suffrage organizations lasted for two decades, however, and slowed the progress toward reform.

GRANT'S FIRST TERM

The new president intended to administer the government rather than promote new programs. His limited view of the presidency meant that Congress played a dominant role during his administration. As a result, the office of the presidency lost some of the authority it had acquired during the Civil War.

The new administration faced hard choices. Southern Republicans wanted help from Washington against resurgent Democrats. A growing number of northern party members questioned whether continuation of Reconstruction was wise or practical. Within the Republican ranks, party reformers wanted to limit the power of the leaders to dole out patronage. They wanted to adopt a merit system for appointing officials; this was referred to as "civil service reform." Party regulars hoped that Grant would side with them against the reformers.

At first Grant tried to avoid partisan battles. For example, in selecting his cabinet he did not follow the advice of influential Republicans but relied instead on men who shared his cautious governing style. Cabinet officers were given free rein in using merit rather than political connections to staff their departments.

In the South, the Democrats endeavored to split the Republicans. Playing down their dislike of black voters, they centered their arguments on whether former Confederates should be allowed to cast ballots. The elections in 1869 produced mixed results. Republicans did well in Mississippi and won narrowly in Texas while Democrats prevailed in Virginia and Tennessee. The latter outcomes foreshadowed an erosion of Republican electoral strength as the Democrats reestablished their power in the South.

A calm and composed President Grant on his inauguration, March 4, 1869. (Reproduced from the collections of the Library of Congress)

The Railroads Meet

Throughout the 1860s, two transcontinental railroads had been laying track across the country. The Union Pacific had built westward and the Central Pacific eastward. The competing lines faced significant obstacles. The Central Pacific had crossed the heights of the Sierra Nevada mountains through rocky gorges and treacherous rivers. Several thousand Chinese laborers toiled

The completion of the transcontinental railroad at Promontory, Utah, in 1869 symbolized the joining together of the nation's two coasts. As the presence of photographers indicates, it also became an important media event. (The Granger Collection, New York)

on sheer cliffs with picks and dynamite. On the Union Pacific side, more than 10,000 construction men, many of them Irish immigrants, laid track across Nebraska and Wyoming.

On May 10, 1869, the two rail lines met at Promontory, Utah. Engine 119 of the Union Pacific stood with its cowcatcher touching the cowcatcher of the Central Pacific's Engine No. 60. A gold spike was driven into the ground with a silver sledgehammer. The transcontinental lines had been built so quickly in part because of loans and subsidies from the federal government. The process by which the financing had occurred would soon become one of the more notorious scandals of the Grant presidency.

The completion of the first transcontinental railroad in 1869 ushered in a period of railroad construction in which the nation developed one of the best and most comprehensive transportation systems in the world. It meant that the opening of the entire West was now possible. Farmers pushed out on to the fertile plains of what had once been erroneously labeled "The Great American Desert." This rapid expansion raised anew the question of what should happen to the Native Americans who had been pushed westward before the Civil War and to the nomadic tribes of Plains Indians.

Grant's "Peace Policy"

In its relations with Native Americans, the Grant administration pursued what became known as the "peace policy." This approach had first taken shape in the years just before Grant took office. Instead of treating the entire West as a huge Indian reservation as had been the case before the Civil War, the government would allocate areas to the tribes. These "reservations" would become places where Native Americans could be instructed about the cultural values and habits of white society, taught to grow crops, and paid a subsistence income until they were able to support themselves. Implementation of this program lagged, however, during 1868, and no reservations for peaceful tribes had yet been established when Grant became president.

The Peace Policy in Action

To supervise Indian policy, Grant named Jacob D. Cox as secretary of the interior. Cox, in turn, selected Ely Parker, a Seneca Indian, as commissioner of Indian affairs. The administration persuaded Congress to appropriate $2 million for Indian affairs and to set up a Board of Indian Commissioners to distribute the money.

The peace policy mixed kindness with coercion. If the Indians accepted the supervision of Christian church officials on the reservations, the government would leave them alone. Resistance to the peace policy, on the other hand, served as a reason for the U.S. Army to drive the Indians onto reservations. In its early months, the peace policy appeared to be a humane improvement over earlier practices. For the Indians, however, the new approach represented another assault on their traditional way of life. Moreover, it remained to be seen how the peace policy would fare in the face of economic and political pressures that continued white settlement generated.

An Era of Scandals

Scandals plagued the Grant administration. In the summer of 1869, two speculators, Jay Gould and Jim Fisk, sought to manipulate the market in gold. Their efforts caused a rise in the price of gold that produced financial turmoil on September 24, 1869, when investors who had contracted to sell gold at lower prices faced ruin. The government ordered the sale of its own gold supplies, and the crisis eased when the price returned to its normal level. The details of the controversy soon faded away but the administration was embarrassed by revelations that some members of Grant's family had aided Gould and Fisk in carrying out their plan. Some critics suggested that First Lady Julia Grant had participated. Even though Grant and his wife were not implicated, the episode raised serious doubts about the ethical standards of his presidency.

To this impression of corruption the Grant administration also added a sense of confusion and incompetence. In foreign policy, there was talk of confronting Spain in an attempt to acquire Cuba. Secretary of State Hamilton Fish forestalled that potential crisis. Grant also wanted to annex the Dominican Republic (Santo Domingo). A presidential agent negotiated an annexation treaty with Santo Domingo's rulers, and the pact was sent to the Senate. Grant pushed hard for approval of the treaty, but the Senate was suspicious of the president's goals and balked at endorsing what Grant had done with the treaty.

One diplomatic area in which Grant had some success was in the resolution of American claims for maritime losses against Great Britain over the *Alabama,* one of several Confederate merchant raiding ships that had been constructed in Great Britain during the Civil War. The *Alabama* had sunk numerous Union vessels. In 1871, Secretary of State Fish negotiated a treaty that led to an amicable settlement of the issue.

Grant and the Congress

Other issues troubled Grant's relations with Congress. Congressional Republicans split on a number of economic issues. The mainstream of the party now believed that a tariff policy to "protect" American industries against foreign competition would be in the best interests of the business community, workers, and the Republican party. A minority of party members viewed the protective policy as unwise. On the currency question, eastern Republicans favored the gold standard and what was known as "hard money"; western colleagues advocated an expansion of the money supply, government use of paper money or "greenbacks," and even some reliance on silver dollars as an alternative to gold.

Equally divisive was the issue of civil service. Calls for reform in the way government employees were selected intensified. Republicans who wanted to reduce the tariff, implement the civil service, and treat the South more leniently defected from the administration and formed what they called Liberal Republican alliances with Democrats in such states as West Virginia and Missouri. In the 1870s, "liberal" meant a person who favored a smaller government, lower tariffs, and an end to Reconstruction.

Grant and His Party

Faced with a series of challenges to his presidency during 1870, Grant displayed greater reliance on Republican leaders in Congress. These Republican regulars had little taste for civil service reform, lower tariffs, or an end to Reconstruction. The president's turn to traditional politicians alienated Liberal Republicans. The possibility of a split in the party increased.

The president's resolve to depend more on regular Republicans strengthened after the Senate defeated his treaty with Santo Domingo. Following this episode, Grant knew that he could not work with Republican opponents of his presidency or satisfy the clamor for milder Reconstruction policies, civil service reform, and a less active national government. The Democrats could always outbid him on those issues, and courting them would only weaken the Republicans further. Failure to maintain good relations with his own party would mean political disaster.

Toward the 1870 Elections

As a result, in 1870 Grant made conciliatory gestures toward the party mainstream. When Secretary of the Interior Jacob D. Cox complained about the practice of compelling government employees to make campaign contributions, Grant dismissed him. The president nominated his attorney general, Ebenezer R. Hoar, for the Supreme Court. When the Senate rejected him, Grant decided that Hoar too should leave the cabinet. To succeed him, he chose Amos T. Akerman, a southern Republican.

In the 1870 elections, the Grant administration aligned itself with Republicans who defended Congress and the White House. Officeholders who supported Liberal Republican candidates or Democrats were removed. Despite these actions, the fall elections produced a setback for the president and his party. Liberal Republicans won in West Virginia and Missouri. Nationwide, the Democrats gained forty-one seats in the House of Representatives. The Republicans retained control, however. The Democrats also gained six seats in the Senate, although the Republicans still held a decisive edge in that chamber as well.

The Ku Klux Klan in the South

By the summer of 1870, reports reached Washington of growing violence in the South. Roving bands of whites calling themselves the Ku Klux Klan (see Chapter 15) were responsible for the attacks. Throughout the South the Klan repressed any challenge to white dominance.

A cartoon attacks the Ku Klux Klan and the "white leagues" of the South for their terrorist tactics toward the African American population. The result for the freed slaves is a condition that is "worse than slavery." (The Granger Collection, New York)

The Klan and its offshoots, such as the Knights of the White Camellia and the White Brotherhood, acted as paramilitary agents of the Democratic party. In Tennessee a black Republican was beaten after he won an election for justice of the peace. His assailants told him "that they didn't dispute I was a very good fellow . . . but they did not intend any nigger to hold office in the United States."

The Klan would stop at nothing to eliminate its opponents. Leaders of the Republican party were hunted and killed. In an incident in Alabama, in October 1870, four blacks died in a Klan attack on an election meeting. A "negro chase" in South Carolina left thirteen blacks dead.

The Klansmen rode in white robes and hoods; their aim, they said, was to frighten their racial foes. The disguises also hid their identity. Throughout 1870, a wave of shootings and brutality swept across the South.

The Government and the Klan

During the 1870 election, the Klan violence had a devastating impact on Republicans in the South. In North Carolina, Georgia, Florida, and Alabama, the Klan's terror tactics intimidated voters and demoralized the party's leadership. In county after county the night riders attacked and murdered local black leaders.

By 1871 the Republicans had less stomach for military intervention in the political affairs of the South. As an Illinois newspaper put it, "the negro is now a voter and a citizen. Let him hereafter take his chances in the battle of life." The Klan's violence, however, presented a challenge that could not be ignored. If violence could not be stopped, the Republican party in the South might simply vanish. As a result, Congress adopted legislation to curb election fraud, bribery, and coercion in elections. When these measures proved inadequate, the lawmakers passed the Ku Klux Klan Act of 1871. This legislation outlawed conspiracies to deprive voters of their civil rights and prohibited efforts to bar any citizen from holding public office. The government received expanded powers to deal with such actions through the use of federal district attorneys to override state laws and, as a last resort, through military force.

Breaking the Klan's Power

Events in the South renewed the Republicans' resolve to end the lawbreaking and violence that the Klan represented. Attorney General Akerman argued that the threat the Klan posed to democratic government amounted to war. Akerman and his solicitor general, Benjamin H. Bristow, were now part of the Department of Justice, which had been established in 1870, and they mobilized federal district attorneys and U.S. marshals to enforce prosecutions against the Klan.

During 1871, the legal offensive against the Klan went forward. In state after state indictments came down against Klan leaders. Federal troops assisted the Justice Department's work in South Carolina. The Klan was discredited as a public agent in southern politics and its violence became more covert and less visible. Although the Klan prosecutions showed that effective federal action could force the southern states to comply with the rule of law, in the North sentiment for such stern measures was ebbing.

Scandals and Corruption: New York's Tweed Ring

The willingness to use national power that had marked the Reconstruction era receded in part because Americans increasingly believed that politics everywhere had become hopelessly corrupt. The most celebrated example of corruption in this period was the Tweed Ring, which dominated New York City during the late 1860s.

The leader of the ring was William Magear Tweed, Jr., who had risen through various city offices and by the early 1870s had won a seat in the state senate. He was closely identified with the Democratic party organization that met at a political clubhouse called Tammany Hall to plan electoral strategy. The expanding cities of the post–Civil War years offered politicians countless chances to profit from the allocation of lucrative contracts and official services. Tweed and his allies turned these new opportunities to their personal advantage.

"Boss" Tweed's power rested on the votes of the city's heavily Democratic population. Their votes were crucial if the party expected to carry the state in a presidential contest. Tammany Hall also made sure that city services and jobs were available to those who supported them at the polls. By the end of the 1860s, Tweed seemed to hold New York City's political destiny in his hands.

In fact, Tweed's moment at the top of New York politics was very brief. He came under assault from the *New York Times,* which devoted endless columns to exposing the misdeeds of the Democratic party and its leaders. More significant from a national perspective, a cartoonist named Thomas Nast used artistic skill to make

Tweed an object of derision. Nast's drawings depicted Tweed as the leader of a band of criminal freebooters, a money-grabbing scoundrel, a ludicrous caricature of an official in a democratic society.

In mid-1871, a resentful member of the Tweed Ring gave city account books to a reporter. The revelation of how much had been spent on city projects stunned the population. A courthouse that had been projected to cost $250,000 came to $13 million. Within a year, Tweed had been indicted and placed on trial. He escaped conviction in his first trial but was later retried and found guilty on 204 counts. He fled the country and took refuge in Spain. Arrested there when an official recognized him from a Nast cartoon, he returned to New York a broken man and died in 1878.

For many fearful Americans, Tweed's story symbolized the decline in ethical standards that they believed had followed the Civil War. They began to think that the expanded power of the state and the extension of the franchise to all white males and many freed slaves threatened the nation's political future. "We are in danger of going the way of all Republics," said one critic of the existing system. "First freedom, then glory; when that is past, Wealth, vice, corruption."

The Liberal Republican Challenge to Grant

Restoring "higher" ethical standards was the stated purpose of the Liberal Republicans, who sought a presidential candidate to run against President Grant in the 1872 election. Their political creed included ending Reconstruction and curbing the influence of political patronage through expanded use of the merit system. The leaders of the campaign were Senator Carl Schurz, a Missouri Republican, Edwin L. Godkin, editor of *The Nation,* and Charles Francis Adams, the son of former President John Quincy Adams.

Liberal Republicans believed in smaller government. Such Republican programs as the protective tariff appalled them. Most of all, they saw Reconstruction as a failed experiment in racial democracy. As Grant's one-time secretary of the interior, Jacob D. Cox, contended: "the South can only be governed through the part of the community that embodies the intelligence and the capital." In effect, black Americans in the South would have to look to whites in that region for protection of their rights and privileges.

The Liberal Republicans lacked a national candidate with the stature to challenge Grant. Although many party leaders were unhappy with the policies of the Grant administration, few were commanding political figures. Senator Carl Schurz had been born in Germany and therefore was ineligible under the Constitution. Other presidential hopefuls included Charles Francis Adams, Senator Lyman Trumbull of Illinois, and Horace Greeley, the editor of the New York *Tribune.*

In May 1872, the Liberal Republicans gathered in Cincinnati. The balloting revealed that the contest lay between the colorless Adams and the well-known and eccentric Greeley. Greeley won the nomination on the sixth ballot.

The sixty-one-year-old editor was an odd choice. He favored the protective tariff, which most reformers disliked, and was indifferent to civil service reform. Once a harsh critic of the South, he had mellowed and now favored ending Reconstruction. A lifetime of passions for such offbeat remedies as vegetarianism and the use of human manure in farming made him seem a political oddball in the eyes of many Americans. "That Grant is an Ass no man can deny," said one Liberal Republican, "but better an Ass than a mischievous idiot."

The 1872 Election

The Republican convention renominated Grant and chose Henry Wilson of Massachusetts to be his running mate. In its platform the party stressed the continuing problem of Reconstruction. The Republican appeal urged voters to preserve what had been achieved during the Civil War.

When the Democrats held their national convention in early July, they faced a dilemma. If they failed to nominate Greeley, they had no chance of

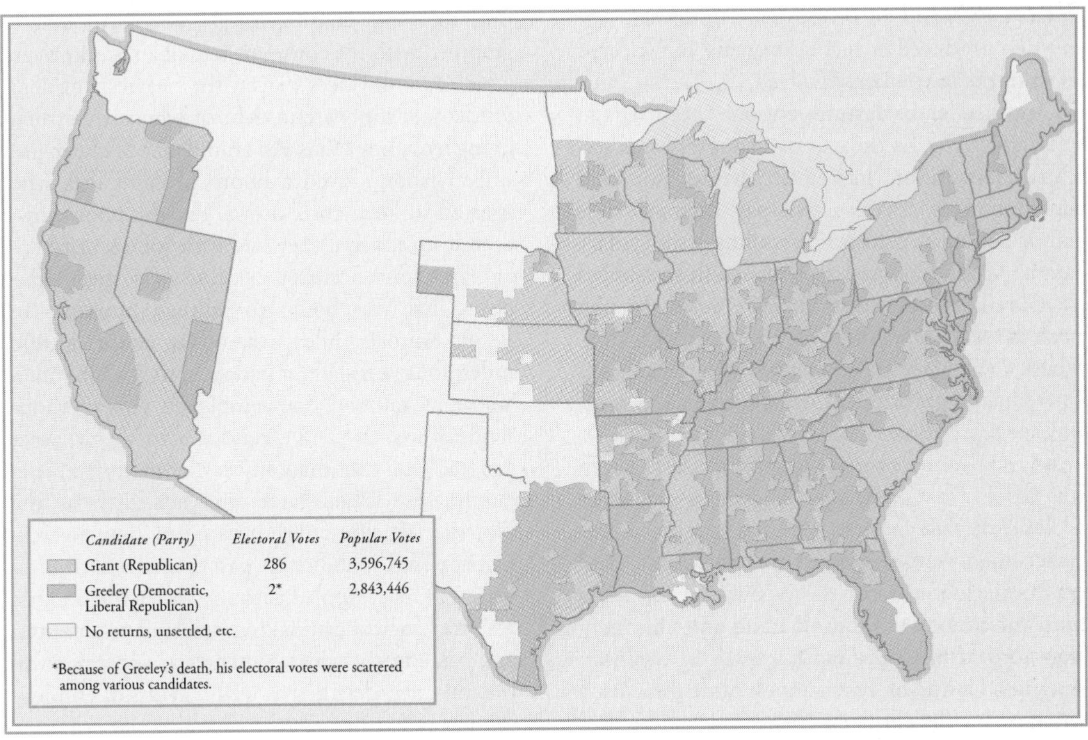

Map 16.2 | The Election of 1872

winning. Nominating him, however, would alienate southern voters. In the end the delegates accepted Greeley as their only alternative. The Liberal Republican-Democratic nominee made a vigorous campaign while Grant observed the tradition in which an incumbent president did not campaign actively.

The outcome was a decisive victory for Grant and his party. The president swamped Greeley in the popular vote and in the electoral tally. There were still enough Republicans in the South to enable Grant to carry all but five of the southern states. The election marked a low point for the Democrats.

Recurrent Scandals

As the excitement of the 1872 election died down, political attention turned to sensational allegations of corruption in Congress. The first scandal concerned the efforts of the Crédit Mobilier Company (named after a French company) to purchase influence with lawmakers during the late 1860s. The directors of the Union Pacific Railroad had established Crédit Mobilier to raise money to build the transcontinental line. By paying themselves to construct the railroad, the participants in the venture made large profits and the company's shareholders did as well. The only problem was that much of the money in effect came from the federal government through loans and guarantees.

To forestall a congressional probe into the company, Crédit Mobilier's managers gave leading Republicans in Congress a chance to buy shares in the company at prices well below their actual market value. When the lawmakers sold their shares, they pocketed the difference—the equivalent of a bribe. A newspaper broke the story in late 1872, and an investigation followed. The inquiry produced a few scapegoats but cleared most of the lawmakers involved.

Another embarrassing episode occurred in February 1873. At the end of a congressional session, a last-minute maneuver gave senators and representatives a retroactive pay increase. The public denounced the action, calling it the "Salary Grab." When Congress reconvened in December 1873, repeal of the salary increase sailed through both houses in a burst of political contrition. These two incidents generated widespread calls for reducing government expenditures and rooting out corruption.

Mark Twain captured the spirit of the times in his novel *The Gilded Age.* The main character, Colonel Beriah Sellers, was an engaging confidence man who embodied the boosterism and economic looseness of the postwar years, along with the healthy amount of fraud and chicanery that accompanied the rapid growth of business. In time, the title of Twain's book came to be used as a label for the entire era between the end of Reconstruction and the start of the twentieth century. "The Gilded Age" was, however, a richer and more complex time than the stereotype of corrupt politicians and fraudulent entrepreneurs that Twain portrayed.

THE PANIC OF 1873 AND ITS CONSEQUENCES

The sense of national crisis deepened in September 1873 when the banking house of Jay Cooke and Company failed. The disaster was triggered by the bank's inability to market the bonds of the Northern Pacific Railroad, in which it had invested heavily. An economic downturn ensued that rivaled similar panics that had occurred in 1819, 1837, and 1857.

A hallmark of the "Great Depression," as it was then called, was declining prices for agricultural products and manufactured goods. Americans grappled with the consequences of an economy in which falling prices placed the heaviest burdens on people who were in debt or who earned their living by selling labor. An abundance of cheap unskilled labor proved a boon for capitalists who wanted to keep costs down. For the poor, however, it meant that they had little job security.

The panic occurred because of a speculative post–Civil War boom in railroad building. In 1869, railroad mileage stood at about 47,000 miles; four years later it had risen to 70,268 miles. The new railroad lines employed tens of thousands of workers and extended across a far larger geographical area than any earlier manufacturing enterprises. When large railroads such as the Northern Pacific failed because of their overexpansion and inability to pay their debts, the resulting impact rippled through society. Economic activities such as car making, steel rail production, and passenger services, which were dependent on the rail lines, declined as well. Layoffs of employees and bankruptcies of businesses followed.

The Plight of the Unemployed

Americans who were thrown out of work during the 1870s had no system of unemployment insurance to fall back on. In some cities, up to a quarter of the labor force looked for work without success. The conventional wisdom held that natural forces had to operate to restore prosperity; any form of political intervention would be futile and dangerous. When President Grant proposed that the national government generate jobs through public works, the secretary of the treasury informed him: "It is not part of the business of government to find employment for people."

Those who were out of a job during the mid-1870s could not afford such a philosophical attitude. Laborers in the Northeast mounted a campaign calling for "Work or Bread" that included large public demonstrations in major cities. The marchers asked city and state governments to sponsor projects to create parks and construct streets, thereby providing work.

Labor unrest marked the first half of the decade. Numerous and prolonged strikes occurred in 1874 and 1875. In Pennsylvania the railroads used their control of police and strikebreakers to put down the "Long Strike" of coal miners and their supporters. Twenty alleged members of a secret society called the Molly Maguires were hanged.

Distress and Protest among the Farmers

In agricultural regions, the drop in farm prices also produced discontent. The resulting decline in income meant that debts on land and equipment were a greater burden on the hard-pressed farmers.

Farmers' protests were led by the Patrons of Husbandry, also known as the Grange. Created in 1867, the nonpartisan Grange focused on complaints about the high mortgages farmers owed, the prices they had to pay to middlemen such as the operators of grain elevators, and the discrimination that they suffered at the hands of railroads.

Regulating the Railroads

The answer to the railroads' power, the angry farmers argued, lay in using the power of state governments to force the railroads to end their discriminatory practices. That meant the creation of state railroad commissions with the power to establish equitable rates and prevent unfair treatment of those who shipped agricultural products. In 1870, Illinois adopted a new state constitution that mandated that the legislature "pass laws establishing maximum rates of charges for the transportation of passengers and freight." The legislature responded a year later, giving the Illinois Railroad Commission wide powers. Neighboring states such as Iowa, Minnesota, and Wisconsin followed suit in the next several years.

The pressure for regulatory legislation affected Congress in 1873–1874. An Iowa Republican introduced legislation in the House to establish a national railroad commission. The bill passed in the House, but the Senate never acted upon it. Federal legislation would not be enacted until 1887.

The decline in consumer prices and the burden of debt on farmers and businessmen in the South and West stimulated pressure for laws to put more money in circulation. That would make debts easier to pay. The Treasury Department's decision to end the coinage of silver in 1873 aroused particular ire among southern and western advocates of inflation; they called it the "Crime of 1873." Proponents contended that an overabundance of silver in the marketplace required the move to a gold standard. By coining silver into money at a price above its market levels, the government was in effect subsidizing American silver production and cheapening the currency. Opponents of the change, however, were suspicious of the dominance of eastern bankers over financial policy.

An effort to inject a modest amount of inflation into the economy came in 1875. A currency bill cleared both houses of Congress, providing some $64 million in additional money for the financial system. President Grant considered signing the bill, but he encountered economic conservatism among eastern Republicans. Their advice led him to veto the bill in April 1875, and Congress failed to override his action.

Women in the 1870s

Amid the male-dominated political scenes that marked this period, occasional episodes reminded the nation that women were not allowed to play a direct part in public life. Susan B. Anthony sought the opportunity to address the Liberal Republican and Republican national conventions in 1872, but without success. On election day she and fifteen other women registered and voted at their polling place in Rochester, New York. Anthony and the voting officials were arrested. Her trial in federal court led to a $100 fine, which she refused to pay. Rather than giving Anthony a reason for appealing the case to a higher court, authorities did not collect the fine against her.

Another champion of woman's rights was Victoria Claflin Woodhull. A faith healer and spiritualist from Ohio, she and her sister Tennessee Claflin came to New York, where in 1870 Victoria announced her candidacy for president of the United States. In 1872 she denounced one of the nation's leading ministers, Henry Ward Beecher, for having had an affair with a member of his congregation. The exposé led to one of the most sensational public trials of the nineteenth century. The proceedings ended in a hung jury, and Victoria Woodhull and her sister fled to England to escape from public outrage.

Overcoming Barriers to Equality

For women from the middle and upper classes the 1870s brought expanding educational opportunities. The number of women graduating from high school stood at nearly 9,000 in 1870, as compared with 7,000 men. Aware of these trends, state universities and private colleges opened their doors to women students in growing numbers. By 1872 nearly one hundred institutions of higher learning admitted women. Edward Clarke, a retired Harvard medical professor, warned in 1873 that when women expended their "limited energy" on higher education, they put their "female apparatus" at risk. Nevertheless, Cornell University began accepting women applicants in 1875.

One of the first female students at Cornell was M. Carey Thomas, who received her B.A. at Cornell in 1877. Five years later she received her Ph.D. at a German university. By the 1890s she had become the president of Bryn Mawr, a woman's college outside Philadelphia. Like other women in male-dominated institutions, she endured rudeness and indifference from her male colleagues. She later recalled that "it is a fiery ordeal to educate a lady by coeducation."

Obtaining an education did not ensure access to male-dominated professions, however. Myra Bradwell tried to become a lawyer in Illinois, but the state bar association rejected her application. She sued in federal court, and in 1873 the U.S. Supreme Court ruled that the law did not grant her the right to be admitted to the bar. That decision gave the Illinois legislature the authority to deny women the chance to practice law. In fact, in 1870 there were only five female lawyers in the entire country.

The Supreme Court also rebuffed efforts to secure woman suffrage through the courts. Virginia Minor, president of the Woman Suffrage Association in Missouri, tried to vote in the 1872 election, but the registrar of voters turned her away. She sued on the grounds that the action denied her her rights as a citizen. In the case of *Minor v. Happersett* (1875) the Supreme Court ruled unanimously that suffrage was not one of the rights of citizenship because "sex has never been made one of the elements of citizenship in the United States." To achieve the right to vote, women would have to amend the Constitution or obtain the right of suffrage from the states.

The Rise of Voluntary Associations

Blocked off from politics, women created a public space of their own through voluntary associations. Notable in this process were the efforts of black churchwomen, who established missionary societies to work both in the United States and abroad. Clubs and literary societies sprang up among white women as well. In New York City women created Sorosis, a club for women only, after the New York Press Club barred women from its membership. In 1873 delegates from local Sorosis clubs formed the Association for the Advancement of Women. The New England Woman's Club, located in Boston, succeeded in the early 1870s in changing local laws to allow women to serve on the School Committee. Later the club founded the Women's Education Association to expand educational opportunities for their sex.

Despite their inability to vote, women made their presence felt in public affairs in an unexpected way in 1873. Protests against the sale and use of alcohol erupted among women in New York, Ohio, and Michigan. Women marched in the streets and demanded that saloons and liquor dealers close their establishments. They also exhorted drunkards to reform. Middle-class women went down on their knees in front of bars and smashed barrels of liquor in public. The temperance movement was not limited to women, but the upsurge of activity among women gave the crusade a new militance.

The Woman's Christian Temperance Union

In August 1874 a group of temperance leaders assembled at Lake Chautauqua, New York, where they called for a national meeting that developed into the Woman's Christian Temperance Union. During the next five years temperance leagues and local organizations of the WCTU crusaded against intoxicating beverages. By the end of the 1870s a thousand unions had emerged, with an estimated 26,000 members. In 1879, Frances Willard became president of the Union. Under her leadership, the WCTU went beyond its original goal of temperance and ventured into broader areas of social reform such as woman suffrage and the treatment of children.

Women at Work

The 1870s also brought greater economic opportunities for women in sales and clerical work. The typewriter was developed in the early 1870s and young, college-educated women were an abundant source of skilled labor to operate the new machines. At the end of the decade women accounted for 40 percent of the total number of stenographers and typists in the country. The developments of the 1870s laid the foundation for the growth in numbers of female office workers during the rest of the nineteenth century.

As women became more involved in public life after the Civil War, they found outlets for their social concerns beyond the ballot box. One of the most important organizations was the Woman's Christian Temperance Union (WCTU). The artist evokes the imagery of the medieval Crusades to show women attacking the liquor industry and its political connections. (The Granger Collection, New York)

The most typical experience of American women, however, was toil. Black women in the South labored in the fields alongside their husbands who were tenant farmers or sharecroppers. In the growing cities, women worked in textile factories or became domestic servants. Many urban women took in boarders; their routine equalled that of a small hotel.

Middle-class women with domestic servants had some assistance, but they still did an incredible amount of work. Preparing food, doing laundry, keeping the house warm, and disposing of waste all required hand labor. Mary Mathews, a widowed teacher in the 1870s, "got up early every Monday morning and got my clothes all washed and boiled and in the rinsing water; then commenced my school at nine." Other days of the week passed in the same fashion for her and other women.

To assist women in performing these tasks, manuals about housework became popular in the 1870s, along with private cooking schools and college courses in home economics. Catherine Beecher collaborated with her famous sister, Harriet Beecher Stowe, in writing *The American Woman's Home* (1869). In this work, she argued "that family labor and care tend not only to good health, but to the *Highest culture of the mind.*" In the new coeducational colleges and universities, home economics programs offered instruction in operating kitchens and dining rooms in an efficient manner. Cooking schools appeared in large cities with a separate class for "plain cooks" and a "Ladies Class" for affluent women.

The ease with which divorces could be obtained in many states produced a movement to tighten the conditions under which marriages could be dissolved. Laws to limit the sale of birth control devices and restrict abortions reflected the same trend. The New York Society for the Suppression of Vice was formed in 1872 under the leadership of Anthony Comstock. It lobbied successfully for a national law barring obscene materials, including information about birth control and abortion, from the mails. Thus, while women had made some gains after the Civil War, they remained second-class citizens within the masculine political order of the Gilded Age.

POLITICS IN THE GILDED AGE

After the presidential election of 1872, the North's already weakened commitment to the continuation of Reconstruction ebbed more rapidly. The Grant administration was less willing to intervene in southern politics and the Justice Department prosecuted fewer individuals for violations of the Enforcement Acts against the Klan.

Northern support for Reconstruction had fallen away because the experiment in multiracial government appeared to have failed. Liberal Republicans and northern Democrats used racist propaganda against the political aspirations of southern blacks. White northerners found it easier to believe that the South would be better off when whites were once again dominant.

A damaging setback to African Americans' economic aspirations occurred with the failure of the Freedmen's Savings and Trust Company in Washington, D.C. Since its founding in 1865 the bank had managed the deposits of thousands of former slaves. It was supposed to provide lessons in thrift for its depositors. However, its managers sought larger returns by investing in speculative railroad projects. The Panic of 1873 caused huge losses, and the bank failed in the following year.

The Stigma of Corruption

Corruption among southern Republican governments became a favorite theme of critics of Reconstruction. There were some genuine instances of corruption, but these actions were far from widespread or typical. Moreover, the white governments that took over after Reconstruction also displayed lax political ethics and committed more serious misdeeds than their predecessors had. Nevertheless, the corruption issue gave the opponents of black political participation a perfect weapon which they exploited fully during the 1870s.

Although participation of African Americans in southern politics increased dramatically during Reconstruction, their role in the region's public life remained limited compared to whites. Sixteen blacks served in Congress during the period, most only briefly. Many more held offices in the state legislatures, but even there, numbers were comparatively modest. In 1868, for example, the Georgia legislature had 216 members, of whom only thirty-two were black. One black man, P. B. S. Pinchback, served as governor in Louisiana for a little more than a month. Six African Americans held the office of lieutenant governor in the states of Louisiana, Mississippi, and South Carolina.

Two blacks served in the U.S. Senate. Hiram Revels of Mississippi became the first African American to enter the Senate. His term began in 1870 but lasted only one year. From 1875 to 1881 Blanche K. Bruce represented Mississippi for a full term. Thus, by the 1870s blacks had begun to make their presence felt in politics, but the decline of Reconstruction made that trend a short-lived one.

The Resurgence of the Democrats

The changing political situation across the nation further diminished support for Reconstruction. Hard economic times arising from the Panic of 1873 worked against the Republicans. Discontented farmers wanted the government to inflate the currency and raise prices on their crops. Factory workers wanted to see more jobs become available. The fate of African Americans in the South became a secondary concern. Accordingly, angry voters turned to the Democrats in the 1874 congressional races. The party used the issue of Republican corruption to regain control of the House of Representatives for the first time in sixteen years. The Democrats also picked up ten Senate seats.

In the South, the resurgent Democrats "redeemed," as they called it, several states from Republican dominance. They began with Texas in 1873, then took back Arkansas. Louisiana experienced the emergence of the White League, which was determined that "the niggers shall not rule over us." In September open fighting erupted in New Orleans between armed Republicans and more than 3,000 White League partisans. President Grant sent in federal troops to restore calm. In Alabama the Democrats also relied on violence and murder to oust the Republicans. Some blacks who attempted to vote in the Barbour County election were shot; seven were killed and nearly seventy wounded.

The Democrats intended to use their control of the House of Representatives to roll back Reconstruction and also prevent any further expansion of black rights. During the lame-duck congressional session of 1874–1875, Republicans enacted a path-breaking civil rights law that gave black citizens the right to sue in federal courts when they confronted discrimination in public accommodations. The law involved an additional expansion of national power; it remained to be seen how the federal courts would rule when black plaintiffs sued to enforce their rights under the new civil rights statute.

Early in 1875 the Grant administration used troops to prevent occupation of the Louisiana state capitol and illegal seizure of the state government by the Democrats in the midst of an election dispute. The action drew widespread protests from many northern Democrats and a growing number of Republicans who argued in favor of allowing the white South to handle its own affairs. Meanwhile, the Democrats used more violence to overturn Republican rule in Mississippi. Without a national consensus behind civil rights and Reconstruction, the fate of black Americans lay in the hands of white southerners who were determined to keep African Americans in economic, political, and cultural subjection.

Why Reconstruction Failed

Reconstruction failed to change American race relations because it challenged long-standing racist arrangements in both the North and South. The Civil War had called these arrangements into question. African Americans had acted to expand their political role and become more than passive recipients of white oppression or largesse. Then the Panic of 1873, the scandals of the Grant presidency, and waning interest in black rights caused white Americans to back away from expansion of racial justice.

To help the freed slaves overcome the effects of slavery and racial bias would have involved an expansion of national governmental power to an extent that went beyond political beliefs of the nineteenth century. During the two decades that followed, black Americans experienced segregation and deepening oppression. The political gains of the Reconstruction era, especially the Fourteenth and Fifteenth Amendments remained unfulfilled promises.

THE END OF NATIVE AMERICAN RESISTANCE

While the United States was in the process of abridging its Civil War commitments to African Americans, the long struggle of Native Americans to resist white encroachment also ended. Indians' efforts to push back the wave of white encroachment failed, and after 1876 Native Americans lacked the power to determine their own destiny.

During the 1870s Easterners and new immigrants surged westward to the prairies. The newcomers competed with the Indians for space and resources. The amount of land devoted to wheat cultivation, for example, rose from nearly 21 million acres at the beginning of the decade to 62,545,000 in 1880.

The cattle industry exerted further pressure on the Indians in the late 1860s. Texans returning from the Civil War drove their herds north to markets in Kansas. These cattle and others in western territories such as Wyoming, the Dakotas, and Colorado occupied space on the prairies where Indians had traditionally pursued their nomadic hunting culture.

Annihilation of the Buffalo Herds

The systematic destruction of the buffalo herds dealt the most devastating blow to the Indians. In the societies of the Plains tribes, the meat of the bison supplied food, while the hides provided shelter and clothes. Removal of these resources was calamitous, but the cultural impact was even more severe. Buffalo represented the continuity of nature and the renewal of life cycles. Destruction of the buffalo ended the Indians' capacity to resist white incursions.

The decline of the buffalo herds began during the 1860s when drought, disease, and erosion shrank the animals' habitat. Then an expanding eastern market for buffalo robes and such products as pemmican (dried buffalo meat, berries, and fat) spurred intensive hunting of buffalo. As railroads penetrated the region, hunters could transport their products to customers with relative ease. The result was virtual extermination of the buffalo. More than *5 million* buffalo were slaughtered during the early 1870s. By the end of the nineteenth century only a few buffalo remained alive.

The opening of the West to white settlement in the 1870s produced the extermination of the huge buffalo herds that had roamed the prairies and sustained the Native American tribes. This picture shows some forty thousand hides piled up in a "hide yard" in Dodge City, Kansas. (Kansas State Historical Society)

A Last Stand for Custer and the Indians

During the mid-1870s, Native American tribes mounted a last, futile effort to stem the tide that was overwhelming their way of life. The renewed strife on the Plains occurred in spite of President Grant's peace policy. The churches' influence over the operation of Indian policy receded as corruption and politics again shaped the treatment of Native Americans. The tribes that retained their nomadic way of life confronted ever-increasing numbers of settlers and a hostile military.

Fighting erupted on the southern plains in 1874 when Comanches and Kiowas attacked wagon trains. A confrontation ensued between U.S. soldiers and Cheyennes, Kiowas, and Comanches that became known as the Red River War. The army did not win on the battlefield. Instead, the Indians' resistance collapsed because of lack of food and supplies.

In the North, the discovery of gold in the Black Hills of Dakota increased pressure on the Sioux to relinquish the area for white development. The Indians refused, and the U.S. government sent soldiers to protect the miners. The Indian leaders, Crazy Horse and Sitting Bull, rallied their followers to stop the army. Near what the Indians called the Greasy Grass (known to whites as the Little Big Horn), Colonel George Armstrong Custer led a force of 600 men. With a third of his detachment, he attacked more than 2,000 Sioux warriors. The result was the annihilation of Custer and his force on June 25, 1876. The Indian victory shocked the country, but it was only a momentary success. The army pursued the Indians during the months that followed, and by the end of the Grant administration, the only Indians who were able to fight actively against the army were the Apaches in the Southwest. The bad treatment that the Apaches received from the government produced sporadic clashes during the 1880s, and the army triumphed by the end of the decade.

One more tragic encounter, the Battle of Wounded Knee in 1890, lay ahead for the Plains Indians. For the most part the Grant presidency brought an end to the centuries of white–Indian warfare that had marked the history of the West in the United States.

THE ELECTION OF 1876

Several themes of late-nineteenth-century American life came together as the 1876 presidential election approached. The centennial of the Declaration of Independence offered citizens an opportunity to reflect on the nation's progress and the social issues that remained unresolved. The race question confronted leaders and citizens even as the passions and commitments of Reconstruction faded. The contest for the White House seemed unusually important as it would shape the direction of the country during the rest of the century.

The Continuing Shadow of Scandal

Toward the end of Grant's second term, political corruption continued to cast a shadow over the White House. Attention focused on the "Whiskey Ring" in the Treasury Department. The officials involved took kickbacks from liquor interests in return for not collecting federal excise taxes on whiskey. Grant had appointed a new secretary of the treasury, Benjamin H. Bristow. Grant said to Bristow: "Let no guilty man escape if it can be avoided." But when Bristow's probe discovered that the president's own secretary, Orville E. Babcock, had ties to a leader of the conspiracy, Grant allowed Babcock to avoid prosecution.

The final incident involved the secretary of war, W. W. Belknap. For some time Belknap's wife had been receiving regular cash gifts from a man who sold supplies to the army. When these financial ties were revealed, Belknap faced impeachment by a congressional committee. He resigned abruptly, and Grant accepted his hasty departure. The trail of scandal had now touched the White House, or so the president's critics argued. In the end, the most that could be laid at Grant's door was a too-trusting nature and bad judgment in some of his appointments.

Marking the Centennial

As the nation's one hundredth birthday neared, attention focused on the Centennial International Exhibition to be held in Philadelphia in May of 1876. On 285 acres of fairgrounds stood several hundred buildings and pavilions crammed with exhibits, specimens, and artifacts from thirty-seven nations. The fair opened on May 10 with 200,000 spectators, the entire Congress in attendance, and a welcoming address by President Grant. The crowd poured into the buildings to see what had been assembled as evidence of the advance of civilization in the United States.

For spectators the huge Corliss steam engine was a stellar attraction. Standing forty feet tall, it weighed 700 tons. Equally fascinating was the "harmonic telegraph" of Alexander Graham Bell, as the telephone was then called.

For all its technological marvels, the exhibition did not do justice to the complexity of American life in the 1870s. African Americans had almost no recognition at the fair. Native American cultures were depicted as "curiosities" consisting of totem poles, tepees, and trinkets. The Woman's Pavilion stressed homemaking. The exhibit evoked a protest from Elizabeth Cady Stanton and Susan B. Anthony. On July 4, 1876, they read a "Women's Declaration of Independence" that contrasted their aspirations with the traditional attitudes toward women expressed at the fair.

Nearly 10 million Americans came to the fair during its run, which ended on November 10. There they learned to eat bananas, and hot popcorn became a fad among city dwellers. Although the fair lost money, it contributed to a sense of national pride and confidence.

The Race for the White House

A key test of the nation's institutions occurred during the election of 1876. As the election year began, the Democrats were optimistic about their ability to regain power for the first time since 1860. The South would return to its usual Democratic allegiance; the Democrats could also capitalize on unhappiness with the difficult economic times in the North and Midwest.

To run as the Democratic candidate, the party selected the governor of New York, Samuel J. Tilden. Tilden had been an opponent of the Tweed Ring and was regarded as a political reformer. A corporate lawyer, he believed in the gold standard and governmental economy. His platform spoke of a "revival of Jeffersonian democracy" and called for "high standards of official morality."

Among the Republicans, there was some talk of a third term for President Grant. The scandals of his presidency, however, made him a political burden rather than an asset. The front-runner for the nomination was James G. Blaine of Maine, a former speaker of the House of Representatives. With the nomination seemingly in his grasp, Blaine encountered questions about his dealings with an Arkansas railroad while he was in the House. He answered the charges vigorously, but the episode raised problems about his ethics at a time when the party wanted to run a "clean" candidate against Tilden.

At the national convention Blaine took an early lead, but as the balloting continued, his candidacy lost momentum. Instead, the Republicans chose Governor Rutherford B. Hayes of Ohio as the nominee. Hayes had a good military record in the Civil War and there were no questions about his honesty. The Republicans chose William A. Wheeler of New York as their candidate for vice president.

In the campaign the Democrats stressed Republican corruption and Tilden's honesty. In response, the Republicans used the Reconstruction issue, as they had in the 1868 and 1872 contests. The rhetoric invoking the Civil War became known as "waving the bloody shirt," in memory of a Republican orator who had held up a blood-stained Union tunic and urged voters to remember the sacrifices of the Men in Blue. As one Republican put it, "Soldiers, every scar you have on your heroic bodies was given to you by a Democrat."

When the election results came in, it seemed at first that Tilden had won. With most of the South in his column, the Democratic candidate had also carried New York, Connecticut, and New Jersey. Preliminary counts indicated that Tilden had won 184 electoral votes, one short of the 185 needed for victory. Hayes, on the other hand, had 165 electoral votes. Yet three southern states—Louisiana, Florida, and South Carolina—and a disputed elector in Oregon were still in doubt. They might give Hayes the White House.

Republican operatives moved to contest the outcome in the three undecided states. Telegrams to party members called for evidence of intimidation of African American voters. Honest returns from these states, the Republicans argued, would show that Hayes had carried each one. The Republicans believed that they held a trump card. In the three states that they were contesting, the Republicans could rely on federal troops to safeguard state governments that were loyal to their cause. Otherwise, Democrats could simply occupy the state capitals and count the election returns their way.

The Constitution did not specify how a contested presidential election was to be decided. With each of the states in question sending in two sets of election returns, the House of Representatives had the responsibility for electing a president if no one won a majority in the electoral college. At the same time, the Senate had the constitutional duty to tabulate the electoral vote. With Republicans in control of the Senate and Democrats in control of the House, neither side could proceed without the support of the other.

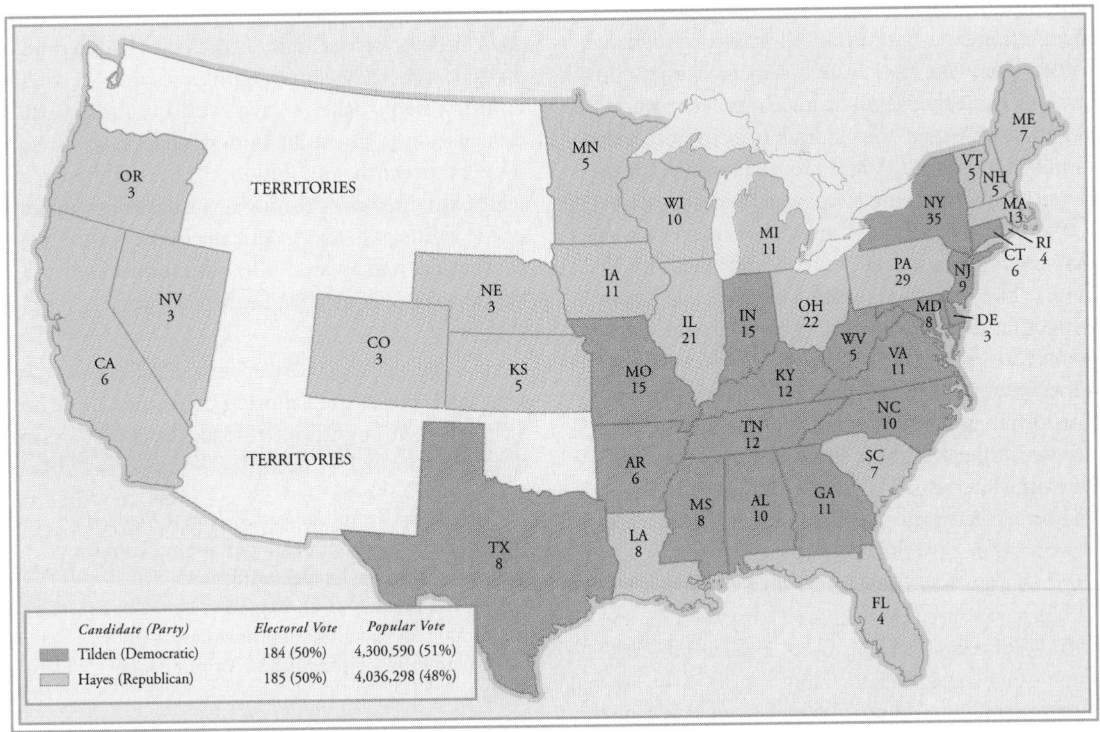

MAP 16.3 | THE ELECTION OF 1876

To resolve the crisis, Congress created an electoral commission of fifteen members, ten from the House and Senate and five from the Supreme Court. As originally conceived, the panel was to have seven Republicans, seven Democrats, and a politically independent Supreme Court justice named David Davis. Then Davis was elected to the U.S. Senate by the Illinois legislature with Democratic votes in a move to defeat a Republican incumbent. Their ploy won a Senate seat, but wounded Tilden's chances. Davis resigned from the commission and a Republican justice took his place. In a series of 8–7 votes along straight party lines, the electoral commission accepted the Republican returns from Louisiana, Florida, and South Carolina, allocated the single disputed Oregon electoral vote to Hayes as well, and declared that Hayes had received 185 electoral votes and Tilden 184.

Despite the electoral commission's decision, the Democratic House still had to declare Hayes the winner. With the March 4, 1877, inauguration date approaching, the Democrats postponed tallying the electoral vote in an effort either to make Tilden president after March 4 or to extract concessions from the Republicans. To prevent a crisis, negotiations began among leaders from both sides to put Hayes in the White House in return for the Republicans' agreement to end Reconstruction. The discussions were complex; they involved a variety of issues such as railroad subsidies for the South. The underlying issue, however, was Reconstruction. If Hayes became president, the South wanted assurances that Republican rule would not be maintained through federal military intervention. After much maneuvering, an unwritten understanding along these lines led Congress to decide on March 2, 1877, that Rutherford B. Hayes had been elected the president of the United States.

CONCLUSION

The events that led to Hayes' inauguration had great historical significance. Although Hayes did not withdraw federal troops from the South, neither did he use them to keep Republican governments in power. Nor did Hayes attempt to enforce Reconstruction in the courts. Whites regained control of the South's political institutions, while black southerners remained second-class citizens with limited political and economic rights.

Several powerful historical forces produced that sad result. Pervasive racism in both the North and the South labeled African Americans as unfit for self-government. Pursuing Reconstruction into the 1880s would have involved giving to the national government more power over the lives of individual Americans than would have been tolerated in that era. Weary of Reconstruction and its moral claims, the generation of white Americans who had fought the Civil War turned their attention to other national problems. In so doing, they condemned black citizens to continued segregation and oppression.

The Civil War and Reconstruction period did have a positive legacy. Slavery was abolished and the Union preserved. Black Americans had demonstrated that they could fight and die for their country, help make its laws, and function as full citizens when given an honest chance to do so. The Fourteenth and Fifteenth Amendments at least contained the promise of a further expansion of the rights of black Americans in the future. But the nation had missed a historic opportunity to create a more equitable, multiracial society.

RECOMMENDED READINGS

Bordin, Ruth. *Frances Willard: A Biography* (1986). A biography of the important leader of the Woman's Christian Temperance Union.

Du Bois, W. E. B. *Black Reconstruction in America* (1935). The first important revisionist study of Reconstruction by a distinguished African American historian and leader.

Foner, Eric. *Reconstruction: America's Unfinished Revolution, 1863–1877* (1988). An excellent treatment of the whole period, especially the decline of Reconstruction.

Hoogenboom, Ari. *Outlawing the Spoils: A History of the Civil Service Reform Movement, 1865–1883* (1961). Considers an important reform cause of the period.

Keller, Morton. *Affairs of State: Public Life in Late Nineteenth-Century America* (1977). Traces the changes that the Civil War and Reconstruction produced in how government and politics functioned.

McFeely, William S. *Grant: A Biography* (1981). A prize-winning biography that examines Grant's life from the perspective of the 1970s.

Sproat, John G. *"The Best Men": Liberal Reformers in the Gilded Age* (1968). A critical examination of the reformers who disliked the political system of the 1870s.

Summers, Mark Wahlgren. *The Era of Good Stealings* (1993). Uses the corruption issue of the 1870s to write the closest thing to a political history of the decade.

Woodward, C. Vann. *Reunion and Reaction: The Compromise of 1877 and the End of Reconstruction* (1951). Offers a provocative treatment of the disputed election of 1876.

American Journey Online and InfoTrac College Edition

Visit the source collections at www.americanjourney.psmedia.com and infotrac.thomsonlearning.com and use the Search function with the following key terms to explore documents, images, audio and video clips, articles, and commentary related to the material in this chapter.

Andrew Johnson
Suffrage
Temperance
Reconstruction
Crazy Horse
Sitting Bull
George Armstrong Custer
Transcontinental Railroad

Appendix

The Declaration of Independence

The Constitution of the United States of America

Admission of States

Population of the United States

Presidential Elections

Presidential Administrations

Justices of the U.S. Supreme Court

The Declaration of Independence

The Unanimous Declaration of the Thirteen United States of America

When in the Course of human events it becomes necessary for one people to dissolve the political bands which have connected them with another, and to assume among the Powers of the earth, the separate and equal station to which the Laws of Nature and of Nature's God entitle them, a decent respect to the opinions of mankind requires that they should declare the causes which impel them to the separation.

We hold these truths to be self-evident, that all men are created equal, that they are endowed by their Creator with certain unalienable Rights, that among these are Life, Liberty and the pursuit of Happiness. That to secure these rights, Governments are instituted among Men, deriving their just Powers from the consent of the governed. That whenever any Form of Government becomes destructive of these ends, it is the Right of the People to alter or to abolish it, and to institute new Government, laying its foundation on such principles and organizing its Powers in such form, as to them shall seem most likely to effect their Safety and Happiness. Prudence, indeed, will dictate that Governments long established should not be changed for light and transient causes; and accordingly all experience hath shewn, that mankind are more disposed to suffer, while evils are sufferable, than to right themselves by abolishing the forms to which they are accustomed. But when a long train of abuses and usurpations, pursuing invariably the same Object evinces a design to reduce them under absolute Despotism, it is their right, it is their duty, to throw off such Government, and to provide new Guards for their future security. Such has been the patient sufferance of these Colonies; and such is now the necessity which constrains them to alter their former Systems of Government. The history of the present King of Great Britain is a history of repeated injuries and usurpations, all having in direct object the establishment of an absolute Tyranny over these States. To prove this, let Facts be submitted to a candid world.

He has refused his Assent to Laws, the most wholesome and necessary for the public good.

He has forbidden his Governors to pass Laws of immediate and pressing importance, unless suspended in their operation till his Assent should be obtained; and when so suspended, he has utterly neglected to attend to them.

He has refused to pass other Laws for the accommodation of large districts of people, unless those people would relinquish the right of Representation in the Legislature, a right inestimable to them and formidable to tyrants only.

He has called together legislative bodies at places unusual, uncomfortable, and distant from the depository of their Public Records, for the sole Purpose of fatiguing them into compliance with his measures.

He has dissolved Representative Houses repeatedly, for opposing with manly firmness his invasions on the rights of the People.

He has refused for a long time, after such dissolutions, to cause others to be elected; whereby the Legislative Powers, incapable of Annihilation, have returned to the People at large for their exercise; the State remaining in the mean time exposed to all the dangers of invasion from without, and convulsions within.

He has endeavoured to prevent the Population of these States; for that purpose obstructing the Laws

---

Text is reprinted from the facsimile of the engrossed copy in the National Archives. The original spelling, capitalization, and punctuation have been retained. Paragraphing has been added.

for Naturalization of Foreigners; refusing to pass others to encourage their migrations hither, and raising the conditions of new Appropriations of Lands.

He has obstructed the Administration of Justice, by refusing his Assent to Laws for establishing Judiciary Powers.

He has made Judges dependent on his Will alone, for the tenure of their offices, and the amount and payment of their salaries.

He has erected a multitude of New Offices, and sent hither swarms of Officers to harass our People, and eat out their substance.

He has kept among us, in times of peace, Standing Armies without the Consent of our legislatures.

He has affected to render the Military independent of and superior to the Civil Power.

He has combined with others to subject us to a jurisdiction foreign to our constitution, and unacknowledged by our laws; giving his Assent to their Acts of pretended Legislation:

For Quartering large bodies of armed troops among us:

For protecting them, by a mock Trial, from Punishment for any Murders which they should commit on the Inhabitants of these States:

For cutting off our Trade with all parts of the world:

For imposing Taxes on us without our Consent:

For depriving us in many cases, of the benefits of Trial by Jury:

For transporting us beyond Seas to be tried for pretended offences:

For abolishing the free System of English Laws in a neighbouring Province, establishing therein an Arbitrary government, and enlarging its Boundaries so as to render it at once an example and fit instrument for introducing the same absolute rule into these Colonies:

For taking away our Charters, abolishing our most valuable Laws, and altering fundamentally the Forms of our Governments:

For suspending our own Legislatures, and declaring themselves invested with Power to legislate for us in all cases whatsoever.

He has abdicated Government here, by declaring us out of his Protection, and waging War against us.

He has plundered our seas, ravaged our Coasts, burnt our towns, and destroyed the lives of our people.

He is at this time transporting large Armies of foreign Mercenaries to compleat the works of death, desolation and tyranny, already begun with circumstances of Cruelty and perfidy scarcely paralleled in the most barbarous ages, and totally unworthy the Head of a civilized nation.

He has constrained our fellow Citizens taken Captive on the high Seas to bear Arms against their Country, to become the executioners of their friends and Brethren, or to fall themselves by their Hands.

He has excited domestic insurrections amongst us, and has endeavoured to bring on the inhabitants of our frontiers, the merciless Indian Savages, whose known rule of warfare, is an undistinguished destruction of all ages, sexes and conditions.

In every stage of these Oppressions We have Petitioned for Redress in the most humble terms: Our repeated Petitions have been answered only by repeated injury. A Prince, whose character is thus marked by every act which may define a Tyrant, is unfit to be the ruler of a free People.

Nor have We been wanting in attentions to our British brethren. We have warned them from time to time of attempts by their legislature to extend an unwarrantable jurisdiction over us. We have reminded them of the circumstances of our emigration and settlement here. We have appealed to their native justice and magnanimity, and we have conjured them by the ties of our common kindred to disavow thee usurpations, which, would inevitably interrupt our connections and correspondence. They too have been deaf to the voice of justice and of consanguinity. We must, therefore, acquiesce in the necessity, which denounces our Separation, and hold them, as we hold the rest of mankind, Enemies in War, in Peace Friends.

We, therefore, the Representatives of the United States of America, in General Congress, Assembled, appealing to the Supreme Judge of the world for the rectitude of our intentions, do, in the Name, and by Authority of the good People of these Colonies, solemnly publish and declare, That these United Colonies are, and of Right ought to be Free and Independent States; that they are

Absolved from all Allegiance to the British Crown, and that all political connection between them and the State of Great Britain, is and ought to be totally dissolved; and that, as Free and Independent States, they have full Power to levy War, conclude Peace, contract Alliances, establish Commerce, and to do all other Acts and Things which Independent States may of right do. And for the support of this Declaration, with a firm reliance on the protection of divine Providence, we mutually pledge to each other our Lives, our Fortunes and our sacred Honor.

The Constitution of the United States of America

We the People of the United States, in Order to form a more perfect Union, establish Justice, insure domestic Tranquility, provide for the common defence, promote the general Welfare, and secure the Blessings of Liberty to ourselves and our Posterity, do ordain and establish this Constitution for the United States of America.

Article I.

SECTION 1. All legislative Powers herein granted shall be vested in a Congress of the United States, which shall consist of a Senate and House of Representatives.

SECTION 2. The House of Representatives shall be composed of Members chosen every second Year by the People of the several States, and the Electors in each State shall have the Qualifications requisite for Electors of the most numerous Branch of the State Legislature.

No Person shall be a Representative who shall not have attained to the Age of twenty five Years, and been seven Years a Citizen of the United States, and who shall not, when elected, be an Inhabitant of that State in which he shall be chosen.

Representatives and direct Taxes[1] shall be apportioned among the several States which may be included within this Union, according to their respective Numbers, which shall be determined by adding to the whole Number of free Persons, including those bound to Service for a Term of Years, and excluding Indians not taxed, three fifths of all other Persons.[2] The actual Enumeration shall be made within three Years after the first Meeting of the Congress of the United States, and within every subsequent Term of ten Years, in such Manner as they shall by Law direct. The Number of Representatives shall not exceed one for every thirty Thousand, but each State shall have at Least one Representative; and until such enumeration shall be made, the State of New Hampshire shall be entitled to chuse three; Massachusetts eight; Rhode Island and Providence Plantations one; Connecticut five; New York six; New Jersey four; Pennsylvania eight; Delaware one; Maryland six; Virginia ten; North Carolina five; South Carolina five; and Georgia three.

When vacancies happen in the Representation from any State, the Executive Authority thereof shall issue Writs of Election to fill such Vacancies.

The House of Representatives shall chuse their Speaker and other Officers; and shall have the sole Power of Impeachment.

SECTION 3. The Senate of the United States shall be composed of two Senators from each State, chosen by the Legislature thereof, for six Years; and each Senator shall have one Vote.[3]

Immediately after they shall be assembled in Consequence of the first Election, they shall be divided as equally as may be into three Classes. The Seats of the Senators of the first Class shall be vacated at the Expiration of the second Year, of the second Class at the Expiration of the fourth Year, and of the third Class at the Expiration of the sixth Year, so that one third may be chosen every second Year; and if Vacancies happen by Resignation, or otherwise, during the Recess of the Legislature of any State, the Executive thereof may make temporary Appointments until

Text is from the engrossed copy in the National Archives. Original spelling, capitalization, and punctuation have been retained.

[1]Modified by the Sixteenth Amendment.

[2]Replaced by the Fourteenth Amendment.

[3]Superseded by the Seventeenth Amendment.

the next Meeting of the Legislature, which shall then fill such Vacancies.[4]

No Person shall be a Senator who shall not have attained to the Age of thirty Years, and been nine Years a Citizen of the United States, and who shall not, when elected, be an Inhabitant of that State for which he shall be chosen.

The Vice President of the United States shall be President of the Senate, but shall have no Vote, unless they be equally divided.

The Senate shall chuse their other Officers, and also a President pro tempore, in the Absence of the Vice President, or when he shall exercise the Office of President of the United States.

The Senate shall have the sole Power to try all Impeachments. When sitting for that Purpose, they shall be on Oath or Affirmation. When the President of the United States is tried, the Chief Justice shall preside: And no Person shall be convicted without the Concurrence of two thirds of the Members present.

Judgment in Cases of Impeachment shall not extend further than to removal from Office, and disqualification to hold and enjoy any Office of honor, Trust or Profit under the United States: but the Party convicted shall nevertheless be liable and subject to Indictment, Trial, Judgment and Punishment, according to Law.

SECTION 4. The Times, Places and Manner of holding Elections for Senators and Representatives, shall be prescribed in each State by the Legislature thereof, but the Congress may at any time by Law make or alter such Regulation, except as to the Places of chusing Senators.

The Congress shall assemble at least once in every Year, and such Meeting shall be on the first Monday in December, unless they shall by Law appoint a different Day.[5]

SECTION 5. Each House shall be the Judge of the Elections, Returns and Qualifications of its own Members, and a Majority of each shall constitute a Quorum to do Business; but a smaller Number may adjourn from day to day, and may be authorized to compel the Attendance of absent Members, in such Manner, and under such Penalties as each House may provide.

Each House may determine the Rules of its Proceedings, punish its Members for disorderly Behaviour, and, with the Concurrence of two thirds, expel a Member.

Each House shall keep a Journal of its Proceedings, and from time to time publish the same, excepting such Parts as may in their Judgment require Secrecy; and the Yeas and Nays of the Members of either House on any question shall, at the Desire of one fifth of those Present, be entered on the Journal.

Neither House, during the Session of Congress, shall, without the Consent of the other, adjourn for more than three days, nor to any other Place than that in which the two Houses shall be sitting.

SECTION 6. The Senators and Representatives shall receive a Compensation for their Services, to be ascertained by Law, and paid out of the Treasury of the United States. They shall in all Cases, except Treason, Felony and Breach of the Peace, be privileged from Arrest during their Attendance at the Session of their respective Houses, and in going to and returning from the same; and for any Speech or Debate in either House, they shall not be questioned in any other Place.

No Senator or Representative shall, during the Time for which he was elected, be appointed to any civil Office under the Authority of the United States, which shall have been created, or the Emoluments whereof shall have been encreased during such time; and no Person holding any Office under the United States, shall be a Member of either House during his Continuance in Office.

SECTION 7. All Bills for raising Revenue shall originate in the House of Representatives; but the Senate may propose or concur with Amendments as on other Bills.

Every Bill which shall have passed the House of Representatives and the Senate, shall, before it become a Law, be presented to the President of the United States; If he approve he shall sign it, but if not he shall return it, with his Objections to that House in which it shall have originated, who shall enter the Objections at large on their Journal, and

[4]Modified by the Seventeenth Amendment.

[5]Superseded by the Twentieth Amendment.

proceed to reconsider it. If after such Reconsideration two thirds of that House shall agree to pass the Bill, it shall be sent, together with the Objections, to the other House, by which it shall likewise be reconsidered, and if approved by two thirds of that House, it shall become a Law. But in all such Cases the Votes of both Houses shall be determined by yeas and Nays, and the Names of the Persons voting for and against the Bill shall be entered on the Journal of each House respectively. If any Bill shall not be returned by the President within ten Days (Sundays excepted) after it shall have been presented to him, the Same shall be a Law, in like Manner as if he had signed it, unless the Congress by their Adjournment prevent its Return, in which Case it shall not be a Law.

Every Order, Resolution, or Vote to which the Concurrence of the Senate and House of Representatives may be necessary (except on a question of Adjournment) shall be presented to the President of the United States; and before the Same shall take Effect, shall be approved by him, or being disapproved by him shall be repassed by two thirds of the Senate and House of Representatives, according to the Rules and Limitations prescribed in the Case of a Bill.

SECTION 8. The Congress shall have power To lay and collect Taxes, Duties, Imposts and Excises, to pay the Debts and provide for the common Defence and general Welfare of the United States; but all Duties, Imposts and Excises shall be uniform throughout the United States;

To borrow Money on the credit of the United States;

To regulate Commerce with foreign Nations, and among the several States, and with the Indian Tribes;

To establish an uniform Rule of Naturalization, and uniform Laws on the subject of Bankruptcies throughout the United States;

To coin Money, regulate the Value thereof, and of foreign Coin, and fix the Standard of Weights and Measures;

To provide for the Punishment of counterfeiting the Securities and current Coin of the United States;

To establish Post Offices and post Roads;

To promote the Progress of Science and useful Arts, by securing for limited Times to Authors and Inventors the exclusive Right to their respective Writings and Discoveries;

To constitute Tribunals inferior to the supreme Court;

To define and punish Piracies and Felonies committed on the high Seas, and Offences against the Law of Nations;

To declare War, grant Letters of Marque and Reprisal, and make Rules concerning Captures on Land and Water;

To raise and support Armies, but no Appropriation of Money to that Use shall be for a longer Term than two Years;

To provide and maintain a Navy;

To make Rules for the Government and Regulation of the land and naval Forces;

To provide for calling forth the Militia to execute the Laws of the Union, suppress Insurrections and repel Invasions;

To provide for organizing, arming, and disciplining, the Militia, and for governing such Part of them as may be employed in the Service of the United States, reserving to the States respectively, the Appointment of the Officers, and the Authority of training the Militia according to the discipline prescribed by Congress;

To exercise exclusive Legislation in all Cases whatsoever, over such District (not exceeding ten Miles square) as may, by Cession of particular States, and the Acceptance of Congress, become the Seat of the Government of the United States, and to exercise like Authority over all Places purchased by the Consent of the Legislature of the State in which the Same shall be, for the Erection of Forts, Magazines, Arsenals, dock-Yards, and other needful Buildings;—And

To make all Laws which shall be necessary and proper for carrying into Execution the foregoing Powers, and all other Powers vested by this Constitution in the Government of the United States, or in any Department or Officer thereof.

SECTION 9. The Migration or Importation of such Persons as any of the States now existing shall think proper to admit, shall not be prohibited by the Congress prior to the Year one thousand eight hundred and eight, but a Tax or duty may be imposed on such Importation, not exceeding ten dollars for each Person.

The Privilege of the Writ of Habeas Corpus shall not be suspended, unless when in Cases of Rebellion or Invasion the public Safety may require it.

No Bill of Attainder or ex post facto Law shall be passed.

No Capitation, or other direct, Tax shall be laid, unless in Proportion to the Census or Enumeration herein before directed to be taken.

No Tax or Duty shall be laid on Articles exported from any State.

No Preference shall be given by any Regulation of Commerce or Revenue to the Ports of one State over those of another: nor shall Vessels bound to, or from, one State, be obliged to enter, clear, or pay Duties in another.

No Money shall be drawn from the Treasury, but in Consequence of Appropriations made by Law, and a regular Statement and Account of the Receipts and Expenditures of all public Money shall be published from time to time.

No Title of Nobility shall be granted by the United States: And no Person holding any Office of Profit or Trust under them, shall, without the Consent of the Congress, accept of any present, Emolument, Office, or Title, of any kind whatever, from any King, Prince, or foreign State.

SECTION 10. No State shall enter into any Treaty, Alliance, or Confederation; grant Letters of Marque and Reprisal; coin Money; emit Bills of Credit; make any Thing but gold and silver Coin a Tender in Payment of Debts; pass any Bill of Attainder, ex post facto Law, or Law impairing the Obligation of Contracts, or grant any Title of Nobility.

No State shall, without the Consent of the Congress, lay any Imposts or Duties on Imports or Exports, except what may be absolutely necessary for executing its inspection Laws: and the net Produce of all Duties and Imposts, laid by any State on Imports or Exports, shall be for the Use of the Treasury of the United States; and all such Laws shall be subject to the Revision and Controul of the Congress.

No State shall, without the Consent of Congress, lay any Duty of Tonnage, keep Troops, or Ships of War in time of Peace, enter into any Agreement or Compact with another State, or with a foreign Power, or engage in War, unless actually invaded, or in such imminent Danger as will not admit of delay.

ARTICLE II.

SECTION 1. The executive Power shall be vested in a President of the United States of America. He shall hold his Office during the Term of four Years, and, together with the Vice President, chosen for the same Term, be elected, as follows:

Each State shall appoint, in such Manner as the Legislature thereof may direct, a Number of Electors, equal to the whole Number of Senators and Representatives to which the State may be entitled in the Congress: but no Senator or Representative, or Person holding an Office of Trust or Profit under the United States, shall be appointed an Elector.

The Electors shall meet in their respective States, and vote by Ballot for two Persons, of whom one at least shall not be an Inhabitant of the same State with themselves. And they shall make a List of all the Persons voted for, and of the Number of Votes for each; which List they shall sign and certify, and transmit sealed to the Seat of the Government of the United States, directed to the President of the Senate. The President of the Senate shall, in the Presence of the Senate and House of Representatives, open all the Certificates, and the Votes shall then be counted. The Person having the greatest Number of Votes shall be the President, if such Number be a Majority of the whole Number of Electors appointed; and if there be more than one who have such Majority, and have an equal Number of Votes, then the House of Representatives shall immediately chuse by Ballot one of them for President; and if no Person have a Majority, then from the five highest on the List the said House shall in like Manner chuse the President. But in chusing the President, the Votes shall be taken by States, the Representation from each State having one Vote; A quorum for this Purpose shall consist of a Member or Members from two thirds of the States, and a Majority of all the States shall be necessary to a Choice. In every Case, after the Choice of the President, the Person having the greatest Number of Votes of the Electors shall be the Vice President. But if there should remain two or more who have equal Votes, the Senate shall chuse from them by Ballot the Vice President.[6]

The Congress may determine the Time of chusing the Electors, and the Day on which they shall give their Votes; which Day shall be the same throughout the United States.

No Person except a natural born Citizen, or a Citizen of the United States, at the time of the Adoption of this Constitution, shall be eligible to the Office of President, neither shall any Person be eligible to that Office who shall not have attained to the Age of thirty five Years, and been fourteen Years a Resident within the United States.

In Case of the Removal of the President from Office, or of his Death, Resignation, or Inability to discharge the Powers and Duties of the said Office, the Same shall devolve on the Vice President, and the Congress may by Law provide for the Case of Removal, Death, Resignation or Inability, both of the President and Vice President, declaring what Officer shall then act as President, and such Officer shall act accordingly, until the Disability be removed, or a President shall be elected.[7]

The President shall, at stated Times, receive for his Services, a Compensation, which shall neither be encreased nor diminished during the Period for which he shall have been elected, and he shall not receive within that Period any other Emolument from the United States, or any of them.

Before he enters on the Execution of his Office, he shall take the following Oath or Affirmation:—"I do solemnly swear (or affirm) that I will faithfully execute the Office of President of the United States, and will to the best of my Ability, preserve, protect and defend the Constitution of the United States."

SECTION 2. The President shall be Commander in Chief of the Army and Navy of the United States, and of the Militia of the several States, when called into the actual Service of the United States; he may require the Opinion, in writing, of the principal Officer in each of the executive Departments, upon any Subject relating to the Duties of their respective Offices, and he shall have Power to grant Reprieves and Pardons for Offences against the United States, except in Cases of Impeachment.

He shall have Power, by and with the Advice and Consent of the Senate, to make Treaties, provided two thirds of the Senators present concur; and he shall nominate, and by and with the Advice and Consent of the Senate, shall appoint Ambassadors, other public Ministers and Consuls, Judges of the supreme Court, and all other Officers of the United States, whose Appointments are not herein otherwise provided for, and which shall be established by Law; but the Congress may by Law vest the Appointment of such inferior Officers, as they think proper, in the President alone, in the Courts of Law, or in the Heads of Departments.

The President shall have Power to fill up all Vacancies that may happen during the Recess of the Senate, by granting Commissions which shall expire at the End of their next Session.

SECTION 3. He shall from time to time give the Congress Information of the State of the Union, and recommend to their Consideration such Measures as he shall judge necessary and expedient; he may, on extraordinary Occasions, convene both Houses, or either of them, and in Case of Disagreement between them, with Respect to the Time of Adjournment, he may adjourn them to such Time as he shall think proper; he shall receive Ambassadors and other public Ministers; he shall take Care that the Laws be faithfully executed, and shall Commission all the Officers of the United States.

SECTION 4. The President, Vice President and all civil Officers of the United States, shall be removed from Office on Impeachment for, and Conviction of, Treason, Bribery, or other high Crimes and Misdemeanors.

ARTICLE III.

SECTION 1. The judicial Power of the United States, shall be vested in one supreme Court, and in such inferior Courts as the Congress may from time

[6]Superseded by the Twelfth Amendment.

[7]Modified by the Twenty-fifth Amendment.

to time ordain and establish. The Judges, both of the supreme and inferior Courts, shall hold their Offices during good Behaviour, and shall, at stated Times, receive for their Services, a Compensation, which shall not be diminished during their Continuance in Office.

SECTION 2. The judicial Power shall extend to all Cases, in Law and Equity, arising under this Constitution, the Laws of the United States, and Treaties made, or which shall be made, under their Authority;—to all Cases affecting Ambassadors, other public Ministers and Consuls;—to all Cases of admiralty and maritime Jurisdiction;—to Controversies to which the United States shall be a Party;—to Controversies between two or more States;—between a State and Citizens of another State[8]—between Citizens of different States,—between Citizens of the same State claiming Lands under Grants of different States, and between a State, or the Citizens thereof, and foreign States, Citizens or Subjects.

In all Cases affecting Ambassadors, other public Ministers and Consuls, and those in which a State shall be Party, the supreme Court shall have original Jurisdiction. In all the other Cases before mentioned, the supreme Court shall have appellate Jurisdiction, both as to Law and Fact, with such Exceptions, and under such Regulations as the Congress shall make.

The Trial of all Crimes, except in Cases of Impeachment, shall be by Jury; and such Trial shall be held in the State where the said Crimes shall have been committed; but when not committed within any State, the Trial shall be at such Place or Places as the Congress may by Law have directed.

SECTION 3. Treason against the United States, shall consist only in levying War against them, or in adhering to their Enemies, giving them Aid and Comfort. No Person shall be convicted of Treason unless on the Testimony of two Witnesses to the same overt Act, or on Confession in open Court.

The Congress shall have Power to declare the Punishment of Treason, but no Attainder of Treason shall work Corruption of Blood, or Forfeiture except during the Life of the Person attainted.

Article IV.

SECTION 1. Full Faith and Credit shall be given in each State to the public Acts, Records, and judicial Proceedings of every other State. And the Congress may by general Laws prescribe the Manner in which such Acts, Records and Proceedings shall be proved, and the Effect thereof.

SECTION 2. The Citizens of each State shall be entitled to all Privileges and Immunities of Citizens in the several States.

A Person charged in any State with Treason, Felony, or other Crime, who shall flee from Justice, and be found in another State, shall on Demand of the executive Authority of the State from which he fled, be delivered up, to be removed to the State having Jurisdiction of the Crime.

No Person held to Service or Labour in one State, under the Laws thereof, escaping into another, shall, in Consequence of any Law or Regulation therein, be discharged from such Service or Labour, but shall be delivered up on Claim of the Party to whom such Service or Labour may be due.

SECTION 3. New States may be admitted by the Congress into this Union; but no new State shall be formed or erected within the Jurisdiction of any other State, nor any State be formed by the Junction of two or more States, or Parts of States, without the Consent of the Legislatures of the States concerned as well as of the Congress.

The Congress shall have Power to dispose of and make all needful Rules and Regulations respecting the Territory or other Property belonging to the United States; and nothing in this Constitution shall be so construed as to Prejudice any Claims of the United States, or of any particular State.

SECTION 4. The United States shall guarantee to every State in this Union a Republican Form of Government, and shall protect each of them against Invasion; and on Application of the Legislature, or of the Executive (when the Legislature cannot be convened) against domestic Violence.

[8] Modified by the Eleventh Amendment.

Article V.

The Congress, whenever two thirds of both Houses shall deem it necessary, shall propose Amendments to this Constitution, or, on the Application of the Legislatures of two thirds of the several States, shall call a Convention for proposing Amendments, which, in either Case, shall be valid to all Intents and Purposes, as Part of this Constitution, when ratified by the Legislatures of three fourths of the several States, or by Conventions in three fourths thereof, as the one or the other Mode of Ratification may be proposed by the Congress; Provided that no Amendment which may be made prior to the Year One thousand eight hundred and eight shall in any Manner affect the first and fourth Clauses in the Ninth Section of the first Article; and that no State, without its Consent, shall be deprived of its equal Suffrage in the Senate.

Article VI.

All Debts contracted and Engagements entered into, before the Adoption of this Constitution, shall be as valid against the United States under this Constitution, as under the Confederation.

This Constitution, and the Laws of the United States which shall be made in Pursuance thereof; and all Treaties made, or which shall be made, under the Authority of the United States, shall be the supreme Law of the Land; and the Judges in every State shall be bound thereby, any Thing in the Constitution or Laws of any State to the Contrary notwithstanding.

The Senators and Representatives before mentioned, and the Members of the several State Legislatures, and all executive and judicial Officers, both of the United States and of the several States, shall be bound by Oath or Affirmation, to support this Constitution; but no religious Test shall ever be required as a Qualification to any Office or public Trust under the United States.

Article VII.

The Ratification of the Conventions of nine States, shall be sufficient for the Establishment of this Constitution between the States so ratifying the Same.

Done in Convention by the Unanimous Consent of the States present the Seventeenth Day of September in the Year of our Lord one thousand seven hundred and Eighty seven and of the Independence of the United States of America the Twelfth. In witness whereof We have hereunto subscribed our Names,

Articles in Addition to, and Amendment of, the Constitution of the United States of America, Proposed by Congress, and Ratified by the Legislatures of the Several States, Pursuant to the Fifth Article of the Original Constitution.

Amendment I[9]

Congress shall make no law respecting an establishment of religion, or prohibiting the free exercise thereof; or abridging the freedom of speech, or of the press; or the right of the people peaceably to assemble, and to petition the Government for a redress of grievances.

Amendment II

A well regulated Militia, being necessary to the security of a free State, the right of the people to keep and bear Arms shall not be infringed.

Amendment III

No Soldier shall, in time of peace, be quartered in any house, without the consent of the Owner, nor in time of war, but in a manner to be prescribed by law.

Amendment IV

The right of the people to be secure in their persons, houses, papers, and effects, against unreasonable searches and seizures, shall not be violated, and no Warrants shall issue, but upon probable cause, supported by Oath or affirmation, and particularly

[9]The first ten amendments were passed by Congress September 25, 1789. They were ratified by three-fourths of the states December 15, 1791.

describing the place to be searched, and the persons or things to be seized.

Amendment V

No person shall be held to answer for a capital or otherwise infamous crime, unless on a presentment or indictment of a Grand Jury, except in cases arising in the land or naval forces, or in the Militia, when in actual service in time of War or public danger; nor shall any person be subject for the same offence to be twice put in jeopardy of life or limb; nor shall be compelled in any criminal case to be a witness against himself, nor be deprived of life, liberty, or property, without due process of law; nor shall private property be taken for public use, without just compensation.

Amendment VI

In all criminal prosecutions, the accused shall enjoy the right to a speedy and public trial, by an impartial jury of the State and district wherein the crime shall have been committed, which district shall have been previously ascertained by law, and to be informed of the nature and cause of the accusation; to be confronted with the witnesses against him; to have compulsory process for obtaining witnesses in his favor, and to have the Assistance of Counsel for his defence.

Amendment VII

In suits at common law, where the value in controversy shall exceed twenty dollars, the right of trial by jury shall be preserved, and no fact tried by a jury, shall be otherwise reexamined in any Court of the United States, than according to the rules of the common law.

Amendment VIII

Excessive bail shall not be required, nor excessive fines imposed, nor cruel and unusual punishments inflicted.

Amendment IX

The enumeration in the Constitution, of certain rights, shall not be construed to deny or disparage others retained by the people.

Amendment X

The powers not delegated to the United States by the Constitution; nor prohibited by it to the States, are reserved to the States respectively, or to the people.

Amendment XI[10]

The Judicial power of the United States shall not be construed to extend to any suit in law or equity, commenced or prosecuted against one of the United States by Citizens of another State, or by Citizens or Subjects of any Foreign State.

Amendment XII[11]

The Electors shall meet in their respective States and vote by ballot for President and Vice-President, one of whom, at least, shall not be an inhabitant of the same State with themselves; they shall name in their ballots the person voted for as President, and in distinct ballots the person voted for as Vice-President, and they shall make distinct lists of all persons voted for as President, and of all persons voted for as Vice-President, and of the number of votes for each, which lists they shall sign and certify, and transmit sealed to the seat of the government of the United States, directed to the President of the Senate;—The President of the Senate shall, in the presence of the Senate and House of Representatives, open all the certificates and the votes shall then be counted;—The person having the greatest number of votes for President, shall be the President, if such number be a majority of the whole number of Electors appointed; and if no person have such majority, then from the persons having the high-

[10]Passed March 4, 1794. Ratified January 23, 1795.

[11]Passed December 9, 1803. Ratified June 15, 1804.

est numbers not exceeding three on the list of those voted for as President, the House of Representatives shall choose immediately, by ballot, the President. But in choosing the President, the votes shall be taken by states, the representation from each state having one vote; a quorum for this purpose shall consist of a member or members from two-thirds of the states, and a majority of all the states shall be necessary to a choice. And if the House of Representatives shall not choose a President whenever the right of choice shall devolve upon them, before the fourth day of March next following, then the Vice-President shall act as President, as in the case of the death or other constitutional disability of the President.—The person having the greatest number of votes as Vice-President, shall be the Vice-President, if such number be a majority of the whole number of Electors appointed, and if no person have a majority, then from the two highest numbers on the list, the Senate shall choose the Vice-President; a quorum for the purpose shall consist of two-thirds of the whole number of Senators, and a majority of the whole number shall be necessary to a choice. But no person constitutionally ineligible to the office of President shall be eligible to that of Vice-President of the United States.

Amendment XIII[12]

SECTION 1. Neither slavery nor involuntary servitude, except as a punishment for crime whereof the party shall have been duly convicted, shall exist within the United States, or any place subject to their jurisdiction.

SECTION 2. Congress shall have power to enforce this article by appropriate legislation.

Amendment XIV[13]

SECTION 1. All persons born or naturalized in the United States, and subject to the jurisdiction thereof, are citizens of the United States and of the State wherein they reside. No State shall make or enforce any law which shall abridge the privileges or immunities of citizens of the United States; nor shall any State deprive any person of life, liberty, or property, without due process of law; nor deny to any person within its jurisdiction the equal protection of the laws.

SECTION 2. Representatives shall be apportioned among the several States according to their respective numbers, counting the whole number of persons in each State, excluding Indians not taxed. But when the right to vote at any election for the choice of electors for President and Vice-President of the United States, Representatives in Congress, the Executive and Judicial officers of a State, or the members of the Legislature thereof, is denied to any of the male inhabitants of such State, being twenty-one years of age, and citizens of the United States, or in any way abridged, except for participation in rebellion, or other crime, the basis of representation therein shall be reduced in the proportion which the number of such male citizens shall bear to the whole number of male citizens twenty-one years of age in such State.

SECTION 3. No person shall be a Senator or Representative in Congress, or elector of President and Vice-President, or hold any office, civil or military, under the United States, or under any State, who, having previously taken an oath, as a member of Congress, or as an officer of the United States, or as a member of any State legislature, or as an executive or judicial officer of any State, to support the Constitution of the United States, shall have engaged in insurrection or rebellion against the same, or given aid or comfort to the enemies thereof. But Congress may by a vote of two-thirds of each House, remove such disability.

SECTION 4. The validity of the public debt of the United States, authorized by law, including debts incurred for payment of pensions and bounties for services in suppressing insurrection or rebellion, shall not be questioned. But neither the United States nor any State shall assume or pay any debt or obligation incurred in aid of insurrection or rebellion against the United States, or any claim for the loss or emancipation of any slave; but all such debts, obligations, and claims shall be held illegal and void.

---

[12]Passed January 31, 1865. Ratified December 6, 1865.

[13]Passed June 13, 1866. Ratified July 9, 1868.

SECTION 5. The Congress shall have the power to enforce, by appropriate legislation, the provisions of this article.

AMENDMENT XV[14]

SECTION 1. The right of citizens of the United States to vote shall not be denied or abridged by the United States or by any State on account of race, color, or previous conditions of servitude—

SECTION 2. The Congress shall have power to enforce this article by appropriate legislation.

AMENDMENT XVI

The Congress shall have power to lay and collect taxes on incomes, from whatever source derived, without apportionment among the several States, and without regard to any census or enumeration.

AMENDMENT XVII[15]

The Senate of the United States shall be composed of two Senators from each State, elected by the people thereof, for six years; and each Senator shall have one vote. The electors in each State shall have the qualifications requisite for electors of the most numerous branch of the State legislatures.

When vacancies happen in the representation of any State in the Senate, the executive authority of such State shall issue writs of election to fill such vacancies: *Provided,* That the legislature of any State may empower the executive thereof to make temporary appointments until the people fill the vacancies by election as the legislature may direct.

This amendment shall not be so construed as to affect the election or term of any Senator chosen before it becomes valid as part of the Constitution.

AMENDMENT XVIII[16]

SECTION 1. After one year from the ratification of this article the manufacture, sale, or transportation of intoxicating liquors within, the importation thereof into, or the exportation thereof from the United States and all territory subject to the jurisdiction thereof for beverage purposes is hereby prohibited.

SECTION 2. The Congress and the several States shall have concurrent power to enforce this article by appropriate legislation.

SECTION 3. This article shall be inoperative unless it shall have been ratified as an amendment to the Constitution by the legislatures of the several States, as provided in the Constitution, within seven years from the date of the submission hereof to the States by the Congress.

AMENDMENT XIX[17]

The right of citizens of the United States to vote shall not be denied or abridged by the United States or by any State on account of sex.

Congress shall have power to enforce this article by appropriate legislation.

AMENDMENT XX[18]

SECTION 1. The terms of the President and Vice-President shall end at noon on the 20th day of January, and the terms of Senators and Representatives at noon on the 3d day of January, of the years in which such terms would have ended if this article had not been ratified; and the terms of their successors shall then begin.

SECTION 2. The Congress shall assemble at least once in every year, and such meeting shall begin at noon on the 3d day of January, unless they shall by law appoint a different day.

SECTION 3. If, at the time fixed for the beginning of the term of the President, the President elect shall have died, the Vice-President elect shall become President. If a President shall not have been chosen before the time fixed for the beginning of his term, or if the President elect shall have failed to

[14]Passed February 26, 1869. Ratified February 2, 1870.

[15]Passed May 13, 1912. Ratified April 8, 1913.

[16]Passed December 18, 1917. Ratified January 16, 1919.

[17]Passed June 4, 1919. Ratified August 18, 1920.

[18]Passed March 2, 1932. Ratified January 23, 1933.

qualify, then the Vice-President elect shall act as President until a President shall have qualified; and the Congress may by law provide for the case wherein neither a President elect nor a Vice-President elect shall have qualified, declaring who shall then act as President, or the manner in which one who is to act shall be selected, and such person shall act accordingly until a President or Vice-President shall have qualified.

SECTION 4. The Congress may by law provide for the case of the death of any of the persons from whom the House of Representatives may choose a President whenever the right of choice shall have devolved upon them, and for the case of the death of any of the persons from whom the Senate may choose a Vice-President whenever the right of choice shall have devolved upon them.

SECTION 5. Sections 1 and 2 shall take effect on the 15th day of October following the ratification of this article.

SECTION 6. This article shall be inoperative unless it shall have been ratified as an amendment to the Constitution by the legislatures of three-fourths of the several States within seven years from the date of its submission.

AMENDMENT XXI[19]

SECTION 1. The eighteenth article of amendment to the Constitution of the United States is hereby repealed.

SECTION 2. The transportation or importation into any State, Territory, or possession of the United States for delivery or use therein of intoxicating liquors, in violation of the laws thereof, is hereby prohibited.

SECTION 3. This article shall be inoperative unless it shall have been ratified as an amendment to the Constitution by conventions in the several States, as provided in the Constitution, within seven years from the date of the submission hereof to the States by the Congress.

[19]Passed February 20, 1933. Ratified December 5, 1933.

AMENDMENT XXII[20]

No person shall be elected to the office of the President more than twice, and no person who has held the office of President, or acted as President, for more than two years of a term to which some other person was elected President shall be elected to the office of the President more than once.

But this Article shall not apply to any person holding the office of President when this Article was proposed by the Congress, and shall not prevent any person who may be holding the office of President, or acting as President, during the term within which this Article becomes operative from holding the office of President or acting as President during the remainder of such term.

AMENDMENT XXIII[21]

SECTION 1. The District constituting the seat of Government of the United States shall appoint in such manner as the Congress may direct:

A number of electors of President and Vice-President equal to the whole number of Senators and Representatives in Congress to which the District would be entitled if it were a State, but in no event more than the least populous State; they shall be in addition to those appointed by the States, but they shall be considered, for the purposes of the election of President and Vice President, to be electors appointed by the State; and they shall meet in the District and perform such duties as provided by the twelfth article of amendment.

SECTION 2. The Congress shall have power to enforce this article by appropriate legislation.

AMENDMENT XXIV[22]

SECTION 1. The right of citizens of the United States to vote in any primary or other election for President or Vice President, or for Senator or Representative in Congress, shall not be denied or abridged

[20]Passed March 12, 1947. Ratified March 1, 1951.

[21]Passed June 16, 1960. Ratified April 3, 1961.

[22]Passed August 27, 1962. Ratified January 23, 1964.

by the United States or any State by reason of failure to pay any poll tax or other tax.

SECTION 2. The Congress shall have power to enforce this article by appropriate legislation.

AMENDMENT XXV[23]

SECTION 1. In case of the removal of the President from office or of his death or resignation, the Vice-President shall become President.

SECTION 2. Whenever there is a vacancy in the office of the Vice-President, the President shall nominate a Vice-President who shall take office upon confirmation by a majority vote of both Houses of Congress.

SECTION 3. Whenever the President transmits to the President pro tempore of the Senate and the Speaker of the House of Representatives his written declaration that he is unable to discharge the powers and duties of his office, and until he transmits them a written declaration to the contrary, such powers and duties shall be discharged by the Vice-President as Acting President.

SECTION 4. Whenever the Vice-President and a majority of either the principal officers of the executive department or of such other body as Congress may by law provide, transmit to the President pro tempore of the Senate and the Speaker of the House of Representatives their written declaration that the President is unable to discharge the powers and duties of his office, the Vice President shall immediately assume the powers and duties of the office of Acting President

Thereafter, when the President transmits to the President pro tempore of the Senate and the Speaker of the House of Representatives his written declaration that no inability exists, he shall resume the powers and duties of his office unless the Vice-President and a majority of either the principal officers of the executive department or of such other body as Congress may by law provide, transmit within four days to the President pro tempore of the Senate and the Speaker of the House of Representatives their written declaration that the President is unable to discharge the powers and duties of his office. Thereupon Congress shall decide the issue, assembling within forty-eight hours for that purpose if not in session. If the Congress, within twenty-one days after receipt of the latter written declaration, or, if Congress is not in session, within twenty-one days after Congress is required to assemble, determines by two-thirds vote of both Houses that the President is unable to discharge the powers and duties of his office, the Vice-President shall continue to discharge the same as Acting President; otherwise, the President shall resume the powers and duties of his office.

AMENDMENT XXVI[24]

SECTION 1. The right of citizens of the United States, who are eighteen years of age or older, to vote shall not be denied or abridged by the United States or by any State on account of age.

SECTION 2. The Congress shall have power to enforce this article by appropriate legislation.

AMENDMENT XXVII[25]

No law, varying the compensation for the service of the Senators and Representatives, shall take effect, until an election of Representatives shall have intervened.

[23]Passed July 6, 1965. Ratified February 11, 1967.

[24]Passed March 23, 1971. Ratified July 5, 1971.

[25]Passed September 25, 1789. Ratified May 7, 1992.

Admission of States

Order of admission	State	Date of admission	Order of admission	State	Date of admission
1	Delaware	December 7, 1787	26	Michigan	January 26, 1837
2	Pennsylvania	December 12, 1787	27	Florida	March 3, 1845
3	New Jersey	December 18, 1787	28	Texas	December 29, 1845
4	Georgia	January 2, 1788	29	Iowa	December 28, 1846
5	Connecticut	January 9, 1788	30	Wisconsin	May 29, 1848
6	Massachusetts	February 6, 1788	31	California	September 9, 1850
7	Maryland	April 28, 1788	32	Minnesota	May 11, 1858
8	South Carolina	May 23, 1788	33	Oregon	February 14, 1859
9	New Hampshire	June 21, 1788	34	Kansas	January 29, 1861
10	Virginia	June 25, 1788	35	West Virginia	June 20, 1863
11	New York	July 26, 1788	36	Nevada	October 31, 1864
12	North Carolina	November 21, 1789	37	Nebraska	March 1, 1867
13	Rhode Island	May 29, 1790	38	Colorado	August 1, 1876
14	Vermont	March 4, 1791	39	North Dakota	November 2, 1889
15	Kentucky	June 1, 1792	40	South Dakota	November 2, 1889
16	Tennessee	June 1, 1796	41	Montana	November 8, 1889
17	Ohio	March 1, 1803	42	Washington	November 11, 1889
18	Louisiana	April 30, 1812	43	Idaho	July 3, 1890
19	Indiana	December 11, 1816	44	Wyoming	July 10, 1890
20	Mississippi	December 10, 1817	45	Utah	January 4, 1896
21	Illinois	December 3, 1818	46	Oklahoma	November 16, 1907
22	Alabama	December 14, 1819	47	New Mexico	January 6, 1912
23	Maine	March 15, 1820	48	Arizona	February 14, 1912
24	Missouri	August 10, 1821	49	Alaska	January 3, 1959
25	Arkansas	June 15, 1836	50	Hawaii	August 21, 1959

Population of the United States

Year	Total population	Number per square mile	Year	Total population	Number per square mile	Year	Total population	Number per square mile
1790	3,929	4.5	1808	6,838		1826	11,580	
1791	4,056		1809	7,031		1827	11,909	
1792	4,194		1810	7,224	4.3	1828	12,237	
1793	4,332		1811	7,460		1829	12,565	
1794	4,469		1812	7,700		1830	12,901	7.4
1795	4,607		1813	7,939		1831	13,321	
1796	4,745		1814	8,179		1832	13,742	
1797	4,883		1815	8,419		1833	14,162	
1798	5,021		1816	8,659		1834	14,582	
1799	5,159		1817	8,899		1835	15,003	
1800	5,297	6.1	1818	9,139		1836	15,423	
1801	5,486		1819	9,379		1837	15,843	
1802	5,679		1820	9,618	5.6	1838	16,264	
1803	5,872		1821	9,939		1839	16,684	
1804	5,065		1822	10,268		1840	17,120	9.8
1805	6,258		1823	10,596		1841	17,733	
1806	6,451		1824	10,924		1842	18,345	
1807	6,644		1825	11,252		1843	18,957	

Figures are from *Historical Statistics of the United States, Colonial Times to 1957* (1961), pp. 7, 8; *Statistical Abstract of the United States: 1974,* p. 5, Census Bureau for 1974 and 1975; and *Statistical Abstract of the United States: 1988,* p. 7.

Note: Population figures are in thousands. Density figures are for land area of continental United States.

POPULATION OF THE UNITED STATES, CONTINUED

Year	Total population	Number per square mile
1844	19,569	
1845	20,182	
1846	20,794	
1847	21,406	
1848	22,018	
1849	22,631	
1850	23,261	7.9
1851	24,086	
1852	24,911	
1853	25,736	
1854	26,561	
1855	27,386	
1856	28,212	
1857	29,037	
1858	29,862	
1859	30,687	
1860	31,513	10.6
1861	32,351	
1862	33,188	
1863	34,026	
1864	34,863	
1865	35,701	
1866	36,538	
1867	37,376	
1868	38,213	
1869	39,051	
1870	39,905	13.4
1871	40,938	
1872	41,972	
1873	43,006	
1874	44,040	
1875	45,073	
1876	46,107	
1877	47,141	
1878	48,174	
1879	49,208	
1880	50,262	16.9
1881	51,542	
1882	52,821	
1883	54,100	
1884	55,379	
1885	56,658	
1886	57,938	
1887	59,217	
1888	60,496	
1889	61,775	
1890	63,056	21.2
1891	64,361	
1892	65,666	
1893	66,970	
1894	68,275	
1895	69,580	

Year	Total population[1]	Number per square mile
1896	70,885	
1897	72,189	
1898	73,494	
1899	74,799	
1900	76,094	25.6
1901	77,585	
1902	79,160	
1903	80,632	
1904	82,165	
1905	83,820	
1906	85,437	
1907	87,000	
1908	88,709	
1909	90,492	
1910	92,407	31.0
1911	93,868	
1912	95,331	
1913	97,227	
1914	99,118	
1915	100,549	
1916	101,966	
1917	103,414	
1918	104,550	
1919	105,063	
1920	106,466	35.6
1921	108,541	
1922	110,055	
1923	111,950	
1924	114,113	
1925	115,832	
1926	117,399	
1927	119,038	
1928	120,501	
1929	121,700	
1930	122,775	41.2
1931	124,040	
1932	124,840	
1933	125,579	
1934	126,374	
1935	127,250	
1936	128,053	
1937	128,825	
1938	129,825	
1939	130,880	
1940	131,669	44.2
1941	133,894	
1942	135,361	
1943	137,250	
1944	138,916	
1945	140,468	
1946	141,936	
1947	144,698	

Year	Total population[1]	Number per square mile
1948	147,208	
1949	149,767	
1950	150,697	50.7
1951	154,878	
1952	157,553	
1953	160,184	
1954	163,026	
1955	165,931	
1956	168,903	
1957	171,984	
1958	174,882	
1959	177,830	
1960	178,464	60.1
1961	183,672	
1962	186,504	
1963	189,197	
1964	191,833	
1965	194,237	
1966	196,485	
1967	198,629	
1968	200,619	
1969	202,599	
1970	203,875	57.5[2]
1971	207,045	
1972	208,842	
1973	210,396	
1974	211,894	
1975	213,631	
1976	215,152	
1977	216,880	
1978	218,717	
1979	220,584	
1980	226,546	64.0
1981	230,138	
1982	232,520	
1983	234,799	
1984	237,001	
1985	239,283	
1986	241,596	
1987	234,773	
1988	245,051	
1989	247,350	
1990	250,122	
1991	254,521	
1992	245,908	
1993	257,908	
1994	261,875	
1995	263,434	
1996	266,096	
1997	267,901	
1998	269,501	
1999	272,700	
2000	281,400	

[1]Figures after 1940 represent total population including armed forces abroad, except in official census years.

[2]Figure includes Alaska and Hawaii.

PRESIDENTIAL ELECTIONS

Year	Number of states	Candidates[1]	Parties	Popular vote	Electoral vote	Percentage of popular vote[2]
1789	11	**George Washington**	No party designations		69	
		John Adams			34	
		Minor Candidates			35	
1792	15	**George Washington**	No party designations		132	
		John Adams			77	
		George Clinton			50	
		Minor Candidates			5	
1796	16	**John Adams**	Federalist		71	
		Thomas Jefferson	Democratic-Republican		68	
		Thomas Pinckney	Federalist		59	
		Aaron Burr	Democratic-Republican		30	
		Minor Candidates			48	
1800	16	**Thomas Jefferson**	Democratic-Republican		73	
		Aaron Burr	Democratic-Republican		73	
		John Adams	Federalist		65	
		Charles C. Pinckney	Federalist		64	
		John Jay	Federalist		1	
1804	17	**Thomas Jefferson**	Democratic-Republican		162	
		Charles C. Pinckney	Federalist		14	
1808	17	**James Madison**	Democratic-Republican		122	
		Charles C. Pinckney	Federalist		47	
		George Clinton	Democratic-Republican		6	
1812	18	**James Madison**	Democratic-Republican		128	
		DeWitt Clinton	Federalist		89	
1816	19	**James Monroe**	Democratic-Republican		183	
		Rufus King	Federalist		34	
1820	24	**James Monroe**	Democratic-Republican		231	
		John Quincy Adams	Independent Republican		1	
1824	24	**John Quincy Adams**	Democratic-Republican	108,740	84	30.5
		Andrew Jackson	Democratic-Republican	153,544	99	43.1
		William H. Crawford	Democratic-Republican	46,618	41	13.1
		Henry Clay	Democratic-Republican	47,136	37	13.2
1828	24	**Andrew Jackson**	Democratic	647,286	178	56.0
		John Quincy Adams	National Republican	508,064	83	44.0
1832	24	**Andrew Jackson**	Democratic	687,502	219	55.0
		Henry Clay	National Republican	530,189	49	42.4
		William Wirt	Anti-Masonic	33,108 (Wirt and Floyd combined)	7	
		John Floyd	National Republican		11	2.6

[1]Before the passage of the Twelfth Amendment in 1804, the Electoral College voted for two presidential candidates; the runner-up became vice president. Figures are from *Historical Statistics of the United States, Colonial Times to 1957* (1961), pp. 682–83; and the U.S. Department of Justice.

[2]Candidates receiving less than 1 percent of the popular vote have been omitted. For that reason the percentage of popular vote given for any election year may not total 100 percent.

Year	Number of states	Candidates[1]	Parties	Popular vote	Electoral vote	Percentage of popular vote[2]
1836	26	**Martin Van Buren**	Democratic	765,483	170	50.9
		William H. Harrison	Whig		73	
		Hugh L. White	Whig		26	
		Daniel Webster	Whig	739,795	14	
		W. P. Mangum	Whig		11	
1840	26	**William H. Harrison**	Whig	1,274,624	234	53.1
		Martin Van Buren	Democratic	1,127,781	60	46.9
1844	26	**James K. Polk**	Democratic	1,338,464	170	49.6
		Henry Clay	Whig	1,300,097	105	48.1
		James G. Birney	Liberty	62,300		2.3
1848	30	**Zachary Taylor**	Whig	1,360,967	163	47.4
		Lewis Cass	Democratic	1,222,342	127	42.5
		Martin Van Buren	Free Soil	291,263		10.1
1852	31	**Franklin Pierce**	Democratic	1,601,117	254	50.9
		Winfield Scott	Whig	1,385,453	42	44.1
		John P. Hale	Free Soil	155,825		5.0
1856	31	**James Buchanan**	Democratic	1,832,955	174	45.3
		John C. Frémont	Republican	1,339,932	114	33.1
		Millard Fillmore	American	871,731	8	21.6
1860	33	**Abraham Lincoln**	Republican	1,865,593	180	39.8
		Stephen A. Douglas	Democratic	1,382,713	12	29.5
		John C. Breckinridge	Democratic	848,356	72	18.1
		John Bell	Constitutional Union	592,906	39	12.6
1864	36	**Abraham Lincoln**	Republican	2,206,938	212	55.0
		George B. McClellan	Democratic	1,803,787	21	45.0
1868	37	**Ulysses S. Grant**	Republican	3,013,421	214	52.7
		Horatio Seymour	Democratic	2,706,829	80	47.3
1872	37	**Ulysses S. Grant**	Republican	3,596,745	286	55.6
		Horace Greeley	Democratic	2,843,446	[2]	43.9
1876	38	**Rutherford B. Hayes**	Republican	4,036,572	185	48.0
		Samuel J. Tilden	Democratic	4,284,020	184	51.0
1880	38	**James A. Garfield**	Republican	4,453,295	214	48.5
		Winfield S. Hancock	Democratic	4,414,082	155	48.1
		James B. Weaver	Greenback-Labor	308,578		3.4
1884	38	**Grover Cleveland**	Democratic	4,879,507	219	48.5
		James G. Blaine	Republican	4,850,293	182	48.2
		Benjamin F. Butler	Greenback-Labor	175,370		1.8
		John P. St. John	Prohibition	150,369		1.5
1888	38	**Benjamin Harrison**	Republican	5,477,129	233	47.9
		Grover Cleveland	Democratic	5,537,857	168	48.6
		Clinton B. Fisk	Prohibition	249,506		2.2
		Anson J. Streeter	Union Labor	146,935		1.3

[1]Candidates receiving less than 1 percent of the popular vote have been omitted. For that reason the percentage of popular vote given for any election year may not total 100 percent.

[2]Greeley died shortly after the election; the electors supporting him then divided their votes among minor candidates.

Year	Number of states	Candidates	Parties	Popular vote	Electoral vote	Percentage of popular vote[1]
1892	44	**Grover Cleveland**	Democratic	5,555,426	277	46.1
		Benjamin Harrison	Republican	5,182,690	145	43.0
		James B. Weaver	People's	1,029,846	22	8.5
		John Bidwell	Prohibition	264,133		2.2
1896	45	**William McKinley**	Republican	7,102,246	271	51.1
		William J. Bryan	Democratic	6,492,559	176	47.7
1900	45	**William McKinley**	Republican	7,218,491	292	51.7
		William J. Bryan	Democratic; Populist	6,356,734	155	45.5
		John C. Wooley	Prohibition	208,914		1.5
1904	45	**Theodore Roosevelt**	Republican	7,628,461	336	57.4
		Alton B. Parker	Democratic	5,084,223	140	37.6
		Eugene V. Debs	Socialist	402,283		3.0
		Silas C. Swallow	Prohibition	258,536		1.9
1908	46	**William H. Taft**	Republican	7,675,320	321	51.6
		William J. Bryan	Democratic	6,412,294	162	43.1
		Eugene V. Debs	Socialist	420,793		2.8
		Eugene W. Chafin	Prohibition	253,840		1.7
1912	48	**Woodrow Wilson**	Democratic	6,296,547	435	41.9
		Theodore Roosevelt	Progressive	4,118,571	88	27.4
		William H. Taft	Republican	3,486,720	8	23.2
		Eugene V. Debs	Socialist	900,672		6.0
		Eugene W. Chafin	Prohibition	206,275		1.4
1916	48	**Woodrow Wilson**	Democratic	9,127,695	277	49.4
		Charles E. Hughes	Republican	8,533,507	254	46.2
		A. L. Benson	Socialist	585,113		3.2
		J. Frank Hanly	Prohibition	220,506		1.2
1920	48	**Warren G. Harding**	Republican	16,143,407	404	60.4
		James M. Cox	Democratic	9,130,328	127	34.2
		Eugene V. Debs	Socialist	919,799		3.4
		P. P. Christensen	Farmer-Labor	265,411		1.0
1924	48	**Calvin Coolidge**	Republican	15,718,211	382	54.0
		John W. Davis	Democratic	8,385,283	136	28.8
		Robert M. La Follette	Progressive	4,831,289	13	16.6
1928	48	**Herbert C. Hoover**	Republican	21,391,993	444	58.2
		Alfred E. Smith	Democratic	15,016,169	87	40.9
1932	48	**Franklin D. Roosevelt**	Democratic	22,809,638	472	57.4
		Herbert C. Hoover	Republican	15,758,901	59	39.7
		Norman Thomas	Socialist	881,951		2.2

[1]Candidates receiving less than 1 percent of the popular vote have been omitted. For that reason the percentage of popular vote given for any election year may not total 100 percent.

Year	Number of states	Candidates	Parties	Popular vote	Electoral vote	Percentage of popular vote[1]
1936	48	**Franklin D. Roosevelt**	Democratic	27,752,869	523	60.8
		Alfred M. Landon	Republican	16,674,665	8	36.5
		William Lemke	Union	882,479		1.9
1940	48	**Franklin D. Roosevelt**	Democratic	27,307,819	449	54.8
		Wendell L. Willkie	Republican	22,321,018	82	44.8
1944	48	**Franklin D. Roosevelt**	Democratic	25,606,585	432	53.5
		Thomas E. Dewey	Republican	22,014,745	99	46.0
1948	48	**Harry S. Truman**	Democratic	24,105,812	303	49.5
		Thomas E. Dewey	Republican	21,970,065	189	45.1
		J. Strom Thurmond	States' Rights	1,169,063	39	2.4
		Henry A. Wallace	Progressive	1,157,172		2.4
1952	48	**Dwight D. Eisenhower**	Republican	33,936,234	442	55.1
		Adlai E. Stevenson	Democratic	27,314,992	89	44.4
1956	48	**Dwight D. Eisenhower**	Republican	35,590,472	457	57.6
		Adlai E. Stevenson	Democratic	26,022,752	73	42.1
1960	50	**John F. Kennedy**	Democratic	34,227,096	303	49.9
		Richard M. Nixon	Republican	34,108,546	219	49.6
1964	50	**Lyndon B. Johnson**	Democratic	43,126,506	486	61.1
		Barry M. Goldwater	Republican	27,176,799	52	38.5
1968	50	**Richard M. Nixon**	Republican	31,785,480	301	43.4
		Hubert H. Humphrey	Democratic	31,275,165	191	42.7
		George C. Wallace	American Independent	9,906,473	46	13.5
1972	50	**Richard M. Nixon**	Republican	47,169,911	520	60.7
		George S. McGovern	Democratic	29,170,383	17	37.5
1976	50	**Jimmy Carter**	Democratic	40,827,394	297	50.0
		Gerald R. Ford	Republican	39,145,977	240	47.9
1980	50	**Ronald W. Reagan**	Republican	43,899,248	489	50.8
		Jimmy Carter	Democratic	35,481,435	49	41.0
		John B. Anderson	Independent	5,719,437		6.6
		Ed Clark	Libertarian	920,859		1.0
1984	50	**Ronald W. Reagan**	Republican	54,281,858	525	59.2
		Walter F. Mondale	Democratic	37,457,215	13	40.8
1988	50	**George H. W. Bush**	Republican	47,917,341	426	54
		Michael Dukakis	Democratic	41,013,030	112	46
1992	50	**William Clinton**	Democratic	44,908,254	370	43.0
		George H. Bush	Republican	39,102,343	168	37.4
		Ross Perot	Independent	19,741,065		18.9
1996	50	**William Clinton**	Democratic	45,628,667	379	49.2
		Robert Dole	Republican	37,869,435	159	40.8
		Ross Perot	Reform	7,874,283	0	8.5
2000	50	**George W. Bush**	Republican	50,456,141	271	47.87
		Albert Gore	Democratic	50,996,039	266	48.38
		Ralph Nader	Green	2,882,807		2.73

[1]Candidates receiving less than 1 percent of the popular vote have been omitted. For that reason the percentage of popular vote given for any election year may not total 100 percent.

PRESIDENTIAL ADMINISTRATIONS

President	Vice President	Secretary of State	Secretary of Treasury	Secretary of War	Secretary of Navy	Postmaster General	Attorney General
George Washington 1789–1797	John Adams 1789–1797	Thomas Jefferson 1789–1794 Edmund Randolph 1794–1795 Timothy Pickering 1795–1797	Alexander Hamilton 1789–1795 Oliver Wolcott 1795–1797	Henry Knox 1789–1795 Timothy Pickering 1795–1796 James McHenry 1796–1797		Samuel Osgood 1789–1791 Timothy Pickering 1791–1795 Joseph Habersham 1795–1797	Edmund Randolph 1789–1794 William Bradford 1794–1795 Charles Lee 1795–1797
John Adams 1797–1801	Thomas Jefferson 1797–1801	Timothy Pickering 1797–1800 John Marshall 1800–1801	Oliver Wolcott 1797–1801 Samuel Dexter 1801	James McHenry 1797–1800 Samuel Dexter 1800–1801	Benjamin Stoddert 1798–1801	Joseph Habersham 1797–1801	Charles Lee 1797–1801
Thomas Jefferson 1801–1809	Aaron Burr 1801–1805 George Clinton 1805–1809	James Madison 1801–1809	Samuel Dexter 1801 Albert Gallatin 1801–1809	Henry Dearborn 1801–1809	Benjamin Stoddert 1801 Robert Smith 1801–1809	Joseph Habersham 1801 Gideon Granger 1801–1809	Levi Lincoln 1801–1805 John Breckinridge 1805–1807 Caesar Rodney 1807–1809
James Madison 1809–1817	George Clinton 1809–1813 Elbridge Gerry 1813–1817	Robert Smith 1809–1811 James Monroe 1811–1817	Albert Gallatin 1809–1814 George Campbell 1814 Alexander Dallas 1814–1816 William Crawford 1816–1817	William Eustis 1809–1813 John Armstrong 1813–1814 James Monroe 1814–1815 William Crawford 1815–1817	Paul Hamilton 1809–1813 William Jones 1813–1814 Benjamin Crowninshield 1814–1817	Gideon Granger 1809–1814 Return Meigs 1814–1817	Caesar Rodney 1809–1811 William Pinkney 1811–1814 Richard Rush 1814–1817
James Monroe 1817–1825	Daniel D. Tompkins 1817–1825	John Quincy Adams 1817–1825	William Crawford 1817–1825	George Graham 1817 John C. Calhoun 1817–1825	Benjamin Crowninshield 1817–1818 Smith Thompson 1818–1823 Samuel Southard 1823–1825	Return Meigs 1817–1823 John McLean 1823–1825	Richard Rush 1817 William Wirt 1817–1825
John Quincy Adams 1825–1829	John C. Calhoun 1825–1829	Henry Clay 1825–1829	Richard Rush 1825–1829	James Barbour 1825–1828 Peter B. Porter 1828–1829	Samuel Southard 1825–1829	John McLean 1825–1829	William Wirt 1825–1829
Andrew Jackson 1829–1837	John C. Calhoun 1829–1833 Martin Van Buren 1833–1837	Martin Van Buren 1829–1831 Edward Livingston 1831–1833 Louis McLane 1833–1834 John Forsyth 1834–1837	Samuel Ingham 1829–1831 Louis McLane 1831–1833 William Duane 1833 Roger B. Taney 1833–1834 Levi Woodbury 1834–1837	John H. Eaton 1829–1831 Lewis Cass 1831–1837 Benjamin Butler 1837	John Branch 1829–1831 Levi Woodbury 1831–1834 Mahlon Dickerson 1834–1837	William Barry 1829–1835 Amos Kendall 1835–1837	John M. Berrien 1829–1831 Roger B. Taney 1831–1833 Benjamin Butler 1833–1837
Martin Van Buren 1837–1841	Richard M. Johnson 1837–1841	John Forsyth 1837–1841	Levi Woodbury 1837–1841	Joel R. Poinsett 1837–1841	Mahlon Dickerson 1837–1838 James K. Paulding 1838–1841	Amos Kendall 1837–1840 John M. Niles 1840–1841	Benjamin Butler 1837–1838 Felix Grundy 1838–1840 Henry D. Gilpin 1840–1841

(continued)

President	Vice President	Secretary of State	Secretary of Treasury	Secretary of War
William H. Harrison 1841	John Tyler 1841	Daniel Webster 1841	Thomas Ewing 1841	John Bell 1841
John Tyler		Daniel Webster 1841–1845 Hugh S. Legaré 1843 Abel P. Upshur 1843–1844 John C. Calhoun 1844–1845	Thomas Ewing 1841 Walter Forward 1841–1843 John C. Spencer 1843–1844 George M. Bibb 1844–1845	John Bell 1841 John C. Spencer 1841–1843 James M. Porter 1843–1844 William Wilkins 1844–1845
James K. Polk 1845–1849	George M. Dallas 1845–1849	James Buchanan 1845–1849	Robert J. Walker 1845–1849	William L. Marcy 1845–1849
Zachary Taylor 1849–1850	Millard Fillmore 1849–1850	John M. Clayton 1849–1850	William M. Meredith 1849–1850	George W. Crawford 1849–1850
Millard Fillmore 1850–1853		Daniel Webster 1850–1852 Edward Everett 1852–1853	Thomas Corwin 1850–1853	Charles M. Conrad 1850–1853
Franklin Pierce 1853–1857	William R. King 1853–1857	William L. Marcy 1853–1857	James Guthrie 1853–1857	Jefferson Davis 1853–1857
James Buchanan 1857–1861	John C. Breckinridge 1857–1860	Lewis Cass 1857–1860 Jeremiah S. Black 1860–1861	Howell Cobb 1857–1860 Philip F. Thomas 1860–1861 John A. Dix 1861	John B. Floyd 1857–1861 Joseph Holt 1861
Abraham Lincoln 1861–1865	Hannibal Hamlin 1861–1865 Andrew Johnson 1865	William H. Seward 1861–1865	Salmon P. Chase 1861–1864 William P. Fessenden 1864–1865 Hugh McCulloch 1865	Simon Cameron 1861–1862 Edwin M. Stanton 1862–1865
Andrew Johnson 1865–1869		William H. Seward 1865–1869	Hugh McCulloch 1865–1869	Edwin M. Stanton 1865–1867 Ulysses S. Grant 1867–1868 John M. Schofield 1868–1869
Ulysses S. Grant 1869–1877	Schuyler Colfax 1869–1873 Henry Wilson 1873–1877	Elihu B. Washburne 1869 Hamilton Fish 1869–1877	George S. Boutwell 1869–1873 William A. Richardson 1873–1874 Benjamin H. Bristow 1874–1876 Lot M. Morrill 1876–1877	John A. Rawlins 1869 William T. Sherman 1869 William W. Belknap 1869–1876 Alphonso Taft 1876 James D. Cameron 1876–1877

Secretary of Navy	Postmaster General	Attorney General	Secretary of Interior
George E. Badger 1841	Francis Granger 1841	John J. Crittenden 1841	
George E. Badger 1841 Abel P. Upshur 1841–1843 David Henshaw 1843–1844 Thomas Gilmer 1844 John Y. Mason 1844–1845	Francis Granger 1841 Charles A. Wickliffe 1841–1845	John J. Crittenden 1841 Hugh S. Legaré 1841–1843 John Nelson 1843–1845	
George Bancroft 1845–1846 John Y. Mason 1846–1849	Cave Johnson 1845–1849	John Y. Mason 1845–1846 Nathan Clifford 1846–1848 Isaac Toucey 1848–1849	
William B. Preston 1849–1850	Jacob Collamer 1849–1850	Reverdy Johnson 1849–1850	Thomas Ewing 1849–1850
William A. Graham 1850–1852 John P. Kennedy 1852–1853	Nathan K. Hall 1850–1852 Sam D. Hubbard 1852–1853	John J. Crittenden 1850–1853	Thomas McKennan 1850 A. H. H. Stuart 1850–1853
James C. Dobbin 1853–1857	James Campbell 1853–1857	Caleb Cushing 1853–1857	Robert McClelland 1853–1857
Isaac Toucey 1857–1861	Aaron V. Brown 1857–1859 Joseph Holt 1859–1861 Horatio King 1861	Jeremiah S. Black 1857–1860 Edwin M. Stanton 1860–1861	Jacob Thompson 1857–1861
Gideon Welles 1861–1865	Horatio King 1861 Montgomery Blair 1861–1864 William Dennison 1864–1865	Edward Bates 1861–1864 James Speed 1864–1865	Caleb B. Smith 1861–1863 John P. Usher 1863–1865
Gideon Welles 1865–1869	William Dennison 1865–1866 Alexander Randall 1866–1869 William M. Evarts 1868–1869	James Speed 1865–1866 Henry Stanbery 1866–1868 O. H. Browning 1866–1869	John P. Usher 1865 James Harlan 1865–1866
Adolph E. Borie 1869 George M. Robeson 1869–1877	John A. J. Creswell 1869–1874 James W. Marshall 1874 Marshall Jewell 1874–1876 James N. Tyner 1876–1877	Ebenezer R. Hoar 1869–1870 Amos T. Akerman 1870–1871 G. H. Williams 1871–1875 Edwards Pierrepont 1875–1876 Alphonso Taft 1876–1877	Jacob D. Cox 1869–1870 Columbus Delano 1870–1875 Zachariah Chandler 1875–1877

President	Vice President	Secretary of State	Secretary of Treasury	Secretary of War	Secretary of Navy
Rutherford B. Hayes 1877–1881	William A. Wheeler 1877–1881	William M. Evarts 1877–1881	John Sherman 1877–1881	George W. McCrary 1877–1879 Alexander Ramsey 1879–1881	R. W. Thompson 1877–1881 Nathan Goff, Jr. 1881
James A. Garfield 1881	Chester A. Arthur 1881	James G. Blaine 1881	William Windom 1881	Robert T. Lincoln 1881	William H. Hunt 1881
Chester A. Arthur 1881–1885		F. T. Frelinghuysen 1881–1885	Charles J. Folger 1881–1884 Walter Q. Gresham 1884 Hugh McCulloch 1884–1885	Robert T. Lincoln 1881–1885	William E. Chandler 1881–1885
Grover Cleveland 1885–1889	T. A. Hendricks 1885	Thomas F. Bayard 1885–1889	Daniel Manning 1885–1887 Charles S. Fairchild 1887–1889	William C. Endicott 1885–1889	William C. Whitney 1885–1889
Benjamin Harrison 1889–1893	Levi P. Morton 1889–1893	James G. Blaine 1889–1892 John W. Foster 1892–1893	William Windom 1889–1891 Charles Foster 1892–1893	Redfield Procter 1889–1891 Stephen B. Elkins 1891–1893	Benjamin F. Tracy 1889–1893
Grover Cleveland 1893–1897	Adlai E. Stevenson 1893–1897	Walter Q. Gresham 1893–1895 Richard Olney 1895–1897	John G. Carlisle 1893–1897	Daniel S. Lamont 1893–1897	Hilary A. Herbert 1893–1897
William McKinley 1897–1901	Garret A. Hobart 1897–1899 Theodore Roosevelt 1901	John Sherman 1897–1898 William R. Day 1898 John Hay 1898–1901	Lyman J. Gage 1897–1901	Russell A. Alger 1897–1899 Elihu Root 1899–1901	John D. Long 1897–1901
Theodore Roosevelt 1901–1909	Charles Fairbanks 1905–1909	John Hay 1901–1905 Elihu Root 1905–1909 Robert Bacon 1909	Lyman J. Gage 1901–1902 Leslie M. Shaw 1902–1907 George B. Cortelyou 1907–1909	Elihu Root 1901–1904 William H. Taft 1904–1908 Luke E. Wright 1908–1909	John D. Long 1901–1902 William H. Moody 1902–1904 Paul Morton 1904–1905 Charles J. Bonaparte 1905–1906 Victor H. Metcalf 1906–1908 T. H. Newberry 1908–1909
William H. Taft 1909–1913	James S. Sherman 1909–1913	Philander C. Knox 1909–1913	Franklin MacVeagh 1909–1913	Jacob M. Dickinson 1909–1911 Henry L. Stimson 1911–1913	George von L. Meyer 1909–1913
Woodrow Wilson 1913–1921	Thomas R. Marshall 1913–1921	William J. Bryan 1913–1915 Robert Lansing 1915–1920 Bainbridge Colby 1920–1921	William G. McAdoo 1913–1918 Carter Glass 1918–1920 David F. Houston 1920–1921	Lindley M. Garrison 1913–1916 Newton D. Baker 1916–1921	Josephus Daniels 1913–1921

Postmaster General	Attorney General	Secretary of Interior	Secretary of Agriculture	Secretary of Commerce and Labor	
David M. Key 1877–1880 Horace Maynard 1880–1881	Charles Devens 1877–1881	Carl Schurz 1877–1881			
Thomas L. James 1881	Wayne MacVeagh 1881	S. J. Kirkwood 1881			
Thomas L. James 1881 Timothy O. Howe 1881–1883 Walter Q. Gresham 1883–1884 Frank Hatton 1884–1885	B. H. Brewster 1881–1885	Henry M. Teller 1881–1885			
William F. Vilas 1885–1888 Don M. Dickinson 1888–1889	A. H. Garland 1885–1889	L. Q. C. Lamar 1885–1888 William F. Vilas 1888–1889	Norman J. Colman 1889		
John Wanamaker 1889–1893	W. H. H. Miller 1889–1893	John W. Noble 1889–1893	Jeremiah M. Rusk 1889–1893		
Wilson S. Bissel 1893–1895 William L. Wilson 1895–1897	Richard Olney 1893–1895 Judson Harmon 1895–1897	Hoke Smith 1893–1896 David R. Francis 1896–1897	J. Sterling Morton 1893–1897		
James A. Gary 1897–1898 Charles E. Smith 1898–1901	Joseph McKenna 1897–1898 John W. Griggs 1898–1901 Philander C. Knox 1901	Cornelius N. Bliss 1897–1898 E. A. Hitchcock 1898–1901	James Wilson 1897–1901		
Charles E. Smith 1901–1902 Henry C. Payne 1902–1904 Robert J. Wynne 1904–1905 George B. Cortelyou 1905—1907 George von L. Meyer 1907–1909	Philander C. Knox 1901–1904 William H. Moody 1904–1906 Charles J. Bonaparte 1906–1909	E. A. Hitchcock 1901–1907 James R. Garfield 1907–1909	James Wilson 1901–1909	George B. Cortelyou 1903–1904 Victor H. Metcalf 1904–1906 Oscar S. Straus 1906–1909	
Frank H. Hitchcock 1909–1913	G. W. Wickersham 1909–1913	R. A. Ballinger 1909–1911 Walter L. Fisher 1911–1913	James Wilson 1909–1913	Charles Nagel 1909–1913	
				Secretary of Commerce	Secretary of Labor
Albert S. Burleson 1913–1921	J. C. McReynolds 1913–1914 T. W. Gregory 1914–1919 A. Mitchell Palmer 1919–1921	Franklin K. Lane 1913–1920 John B. Payne 1920–1921	David F. Houston 1913–1920 E. T. Meredith 1920–1921	W. C. Redfield 1913–1919 J. W. Alexander 1919–1921	William B. Wilson 1913–1921

President	Vice President	Secretary of State	Secretary of Treasury	Secretary of War	Secretary of Navy	Postmaster General	Attorney General
Warren G. Harding 1921–1923	Calvin Coolidge 1921–1923	Charles E. Hughes 1921–1923	Andrew W. Mellon 1921–1923	John W. Weeks 1921–1923	Edwin Denby 1921–1923	Will H. Hays 1921–1922 Hubert Work 1922–1923 Harry S. New 1923	H. M. Daugherty 1921–1923
Calvin Coolidge 1923–1929	Charles G. Dawes 1925–1929	Charles E. Hughes 1923–1925 Frank B. Kellogg 1925–1929	Andrew W. Mellon 1923–1929	John W. Weeks 1923–1925 Dwight F. Davis 1925–1929	Edwin Denby 1923–1924 Curtis D. Wilbur 1924–1929	Harry S. New 1923–1929	H. M. Daugherty 1923–1924 Harlan F. Stone 1924–1925 John G. Sargent 1925–1929
Herbert C. Hoover 1929–1933	Charles Curtis 1929–1933	Henry L. Stimson 1929–1933	Andrew W. Mellon 1929–1932 Ogden L. Mills 1932–1933	James W. Good 1929 Patrick J. Hurley 1929–1933	Charles F. Adams 1929–1933	Walter F. Brown 1929–1933	J. D. Mitchell 1929–1933
Franklin Delano Roosevelt 1933–1945	John Nance Garner 1933–1941 Henry A. Wallace 1941–1945 Harry S. Truman 1945	Cordell Hull 1933–1944 E. R. Stettinius, Jr. 1944–1945	William H. Woodin 1933–1934 Henry Morgenthau, Jr. 1934–1945	George H. Dern 1933–1936 Harry H. Woodring 1936–1940 Henry L. Stimson 1940–1945	Claude A. Swanson 1933–1940 Charles Edison 1940 Frank Knox 1940–1944 James V. Forrestal 1944–1945	James A. Farley 1933–1940 Frank C. Walker 1940–1945	H. S. Cummings 1933–1939 Frank Murphy 1939–1940 Robert Jackson 1940–1941 Francis Biddel 1941–1945
Harry S. Truman 1945–1953	Alben W. Barkley 1949–1953	James F. Byrnes 1945–1947 George C. Marshall 1947–1949 Dean G. Acheson 1949–1953	Fred M. Vinson 1945–1946 John W. Snyder 1946–1953	Robert P. Patterson 1945–1947 Kenneth C. Royall 1947	James V. Forrestal 1945–1947	R. E. Hannegan 1945–1947 Jesse M. Donaldson 1947–1953	Tom C. Clark 1945–1949 J. H. McGrat 1949–1952 James P. McGranery 1952–1953
				Secretary of Defense			
				James V. Forrestal 1947–1949 Louis A. Johnson 1949–1950 George C. Marshall 1950–1951 Robert A. Lovett 1951–1953			
Dwight D. Eisenhower 1953–1961	Richard M. Nixon 1953–1961	John Foster Dulles 1953–1959 Christian A. Herter 1957–1961	George M. Humphrey 1953–1957 Robert B. Anderson 1957–1961	Charles E. Wilson 1953–1957 Neil H. McElroy 1957–1961 Thomas S. Gates 1959–1961		A. E. Summerfield 1953–1961	H. Brownell, Jr. 1953–1957 William P. Rogers 1957–1961
John F. Kennedy 1961–1963	Lyndon B. Johnson 1961–1963	Dean Rusk 1961–1963	C. Douglas Dillon 1961–1963	Robert S. McNamara 1961–1963		J. Edward Day 1961–1963 John A. Gronouski 1961–1963	Robert F. Kennedy 1961–1963
Lyndon B. Johnson 1963–1969	Hubert H. Humphrey 1965–1969	Dean Rusk 1963–1969	C. Douglas Dillon 1963–1965 Henry H. Fowler 1965–1968 Joseph W. Barr 1968–1969	Robert S. McNamara 1963–1968 Clark M. Clifford 1968–1969		John A. Gronouski 1963–1965 Lawrence F. O'Brien 1965–1968 W. Marvin Watson 1968–1969	Robert F. Kennedy 1963–1965 N. deB. Katzenbach 1965–1967 Ramsey Clark 1967–1969

Secretary of Interior	Secretary of Agriculture	Secretary of Commerce	Secretary of Labor	Secretary of Health Education and Welfare	Secretary of Housing and Urban Development	Secretary of Transportation
Albert B. Fall 1921–1923 Huber Work 1923	Henry C. Wallace 1921–1923	Herbert C. Hoover 1921–1923	James J. Davis 1921–1923			
Hubert Work 1923–1928 Roy O. West 1928–1929	Henry C. Wallace 1923–1924 Howard M. Gore 1924–1925 W. J. Jardine 1925–1929	Herbert C. Hoover 1923–1928 William F. Whiting 1928–1929 Whiting 1925–1929	James J. Davis 1923–1929			
Ray L. Wilbur 1929–1933	Arthur M. Hyde 1929–1933 Roy D. Chapin 1932–1933	Robert P. Lamont 1929–1932 William N. Doak 1930–1933	James J. Davis 1929–1930			
Harold L. Ickes 1933–1945	Henry A. Wallace 1933–1940 Claude R. Wickard 1940–1945	Daniel C. Roper 1933–1939 Harry L. Hopkins v1939–1940 Jesse Jones 1940–1945 Henry A. Wallace 1945	Frances Perkins 1933–1945			
Harold L. Ickes 1945–1946 Julius A. Krug 1946–1949 Oscar L. Chapman 1949–1953	C. P. Anderson 1945–1948 C. F. Brannan 1948–1953	W. A. Harriman 1946–1948 Charles Sawyer 1948–1953	L. B. Schwellenbach 1945–1948 Maurice J. Tobin 1948–1953			
Douglas McKay 1953–1956 Fred Seaton 1956–1961	Ezra T. Benson 1953–1961	Sinclair Weeks 1953–1958 Lewis L. Strauss 1958–1961	Martin P. Durkin 1953 James P. Mitchell 1953–1961	Oveta Culp Hobby 1953–1955 Marion B. Folsom 1955–1958 Arthur S. Flemming 1958–1961		
Stewart L. Udall 1961–1963	Orville L. Freeman 1961–1963	Luther H. Hodges 1961–1963	Arthur J. Goldberg 1961–1963 W. Willard Wirtz 1962–1963	A. H. Ribicoff 1961–1962 Anthony J. Celebrezze 1962–1963		
Stewart L. Udall 1963–1969	Orville L. Freeman 1963–1969	Luther H. Hodges 1963–1965 John T. Connor 1965–1967 Alexander B. Trowbridge 1967–1968 C. R. Smith 1968–1969	W. Willard Wirtz 1963–1969	Anthony J. Celebrezze 1963–1965 John W. Gardner 1965–1968 Wilbur J. Cohen 1968–1969	Robert C. Weaver 1966–1968 Robert C. Wood 1968–1969	Alan S. Boyd 1966–1969

President	Vice President	Secretary of State	Secretary of Treasury	Secretary of Defense	Postmaster General[1]	Attorney General	Secretary of Interior	Secretary of Agriculture
Richard M. Nixon 1969–1974	Spiro T. Agnew 1969–1973 Gerald R. Ford 1973–1974	William P. Rogers 1969–1973 Henry A. Kissinger 1973–1974	David M. Kennedy 1969–1970 John B. Connally 1970–1972 George P. Schultz 1972–1974 William E. Simon 1974	Melvin R. Laird 1969–1973 Elliot L. Richardson 1973 James R. Schlesinger 1973–1974	Winton M. Blount 1969–1971	John M. Mitchell 1969–1972 Richard G. Kleindienst 1972–1973 Elliot L. Richardson 1973 William B. Saxbe 1974	Walter J. Hickel 1969–1971 Rogers C. B. Morton 1971–1974	Clifford M. Hardin 1969–1971 Earl L. Butz 1971–1974
Gerald R. Ford 1974–1977	Nelson A. Rockefeller 1974–1977	Henry A. Kissinger 1974–1977	William E. Simon 1974–1977	James R. Schlesinger 1974–1975 Donald H. Rumsfeld 1975–1977		William B. Saxbe 1974–1975 Edward H. Levi 1974–1975	Rogers C. B. Morton 1974–1976 Stanley K. Hathaway 1975 Thomas D. Kleppe 1975–1977	Earl L. Butz 1974–1977
Jimmy Carter 1977–1981	Walter F. Mondale 1977–1981	Cyrus R. Vance 1977–1980 Edmund S. Muskie 1980–1981	W. Michael Blumenthal 1977–1979 G. William Miller 1979–1981	Harold Brown 1977–1981		Griffin Bell 1977–1979 Benjamin R. Civiletti 1979–1981	Cecil D. Andrus 1977–1981	Robert Bergland 1977–1981
Ronald W. Reagan 1981–1989	George H. Bush 1981–1989	Alexander M. Haig, Jr. 1981–1982 George P. Shultz 1982–1989	Donald T. Regan 1981–1985 James A. Baker 1985–1988 Nicholas F. Brady 1988–1989	Caspar W. Weinberger 1981–1987 Frank C. Carlucci 1987–1989		William French Smith 1981–1985 Edwin Meese 1985–1988 Richard Thornburgh 1988–1989	James G. Watt 1981–1983 William P. Clark 1983–1985 Donald P. Hodel 1985–1989	John R. Block 1981–1986 Richard E. Lyng 1986–1989
George H. W. Bush 1989–1993	J. Danforth Quayle 1989–1993	James A. Baker 1989–1992 Lawrence S. Eagleburger 1992–1993	Nicholas F. Brady 1989–1993	Richard Cheney 1989–1993		Richard Thornburgh 1989–1990 William Barr 1990–1993	Manuel Lujan 1989–1993	Clayton Yeutter 1989–1990 Edwin Madigen 1990–1993
William Clinton 1993–2001	Albert Gore 1993–2001	Warren M. Christopher 1993–1996 Madeleine K. Albright 1997–2001	Lloyd Bentsen 1993–1994 Robert E. Rubin 1994–1999 Lawrence H. Summers 1999–2001	Les Aspin 1993–1994 William J. Perry 1994–1996 William S. Cohen 1997–2001		Janet Reno 1993–2001	Bruce Babbitt 1993–2001	Mike Espy 1993–1994 Dan Glickman 1995–2001
George W. Bush 2001–	Richard B. Cheney 2001–	Colin L. Powell 2001	Paul H. O'Neill 2001–	Donald H. Rumsfeld 2001–		John Ashcroft 2001–	Gale A. Norton 2001–	Ann M. Veneman 2001–

[1]On July 1, 1971, the Post Office became an independent agency. After that date, the Postmaster General was no longer a member of the Cabinet.

Secretary of Commerce	Secretary of Labor	Secretary of Health, Education and Welfare		Secretary of Housing and Urban Development	Secretary of Transportation	Secretary of Energy	Secretary of Veterans Affairs
Maurice H. Stans 1969–1972 Peter G. Peterson 1972 Frederick B. Dent 1972–1974	George P. Shultz 1969–1970 James D. Hodgson 1970–1973 Peter J. Brennan 1973–1974	Robert H. Finch 1969–1970 Elliot L. Richardson 1970–1973 Caspar W. Weinberger 1973–1974		George Romney 1969–1973 James T. Lynn 1973–1974	John A. Volpe 1969–1973 Claude S. Brinegar 1973–1974		
Frederick B. Dent 1974–1975 Rogers C. B. Morton 1975 Elliot L. Richardson 1975–1977	Peter J. Brennan 1974–1975 John T. Dunlop 1975–1976 W. J. Usery 1976–1977	Caspar W. Weinberger 1974–1975 Forrest D. Matthews 1975–1977		James T. Lynn 1974–1975 Carla A. Hills 1975–1977	Claude S. Brinegar 1974–1975 William T. Coleman 1975–1977		
Juanita Kreps 1977–1981	F. Ray Marshall 1977–1981	Joseph Califano 1977–1979 Patricia Roberts Harris 1979–1980		Patricia Roberts Harris 1977–1979 Moon Landrieu 1979–1981	Brock Adams 1977–1979 Neil E. Goldschmidt 1979–1981	James R. Schlesinger 1977–1979 Charles W. Duncan, Jr. 1979–1981	
		Secretary of Health and Human Services	Secretary of Education				
		Patricia Roberts Harris 1980–1981	Shirley M. Hufstedler 1980–1981				
Malcolm Baldridge 1981–1987 C. William Verity, Jr. 1987–1989	Raymond J. Donovan 1981–1985 William E. Brock 1985–1987 Ann Dore McLaughlin 1987–1989	Richard S. Schweiker 1981–1983 Margaret M. Heckler 1983–1985 Otis R. Bowen 1985–1989	Terrell H. Bell 1981–1985 William J. Bennett 1985–1988 Lauro Fred Cavazos 1988–1989	Samuel R. Pierce, Jr. 1981–1989	Drew Lewis 1981–1983 Elizabeth H. Dole 1983–1987 James H. Burnley 1987–1989	James B. Edwards 1981–1982 Donald P. Hodel 1982–1985 John S. Harrington 1985–1989	
Robert Mosbacher 1989–1993 Barbara Franklin 1991–1993	Elizabeth Dole 1989–1993 Lynn Martin 1993	Louis Sullivan 1989–1993	Lamar Alexander 1990–1993	Jack Kemp 1989–1993	Samuel Skinner 1989–1990 Andrew Card 1900–1993	James Watkins 1989–1993	Edward J. Derwinski 1989–1993
Ronald H. Brown 1993–1996 William M. Daley 1997–2000 Norman Y. Mineta 2000–2001	Robert B. Reich 1993–1996 Alexis M. Herman 1997–2001	Donna E. Shalala 1993–2001	Richard W. Riley 1993–2001	Henry G. Cisneros 1993–1996 Andrew M. Cuomo 1997–2001	Federico F. Peña 1993–1996 Rodney E. Slater 1997–2001	Hazel O'Leary 1993–1996 Federico F. Peña 1997–1998 Bill Richardson 1998–2001	Jesse Brown 1993–1997 Togo D. West, Jr.[2] 1998–2001
Donald L. Evans 2001–	Elaine L. Chao 2001–	Tommy G. Thompson 2001–	Roderick R. Paige 2001–	Melquiades R. Martinez 2001–	Norman Y. Mineta 2001–	Spencer Abraham 2001–	Anthony Principi 2001–

[2]Acting Secretary

Justices of the U.S. Supreme Court

Name	Term of Service	Years of Service	Appointed By
John Jay	1789–1795	5	Washington
John Rutledge	1789–1791	1	Washington
William Cushing	1789–1810	20	Washington
James Wilson	1789–1798	8	Washington
John Blair	1789–1796	6	Washington
Robert H. Harrison	1789–1790	—	Washington
James Iredell	1790–1799	9	Washington
Thomas Johnson	1791–1793	1	Washington
William Paterson	1793–1806	13	Washington
John Rutledge[1]	1795	—	Washington
Samuel Chase	1796–1811	15	Washington
Oliver Ellsworth	1796–1800	4	Washington
Bushrod Washington	1798–1829	31	J. Adams
Alfred Moore	1799–1804	4	J. Adams
John Marshall	1801–1835	34	J. Adams
William Johnson	1804–1834	30	Jefferson
H. Brockholst Livingston	1806–1823	16	Jefferson
Thomas Todd	1807–1826	18	Jefferson
Joseph Story	1811–1845	33	Madison
Gabriel Duval	1811–1835	24	Madison
Smith Thompson	1823–1843	20	Monroe
Robert Trimble	1826–1828	2	J. Q. Adams
John McLean	1829–1861	32	Jackson
Henry Baldwin	1830–1844	14	Jackson
James M. Wayne	1835–1867	32	Jackson
Roger B. Taney	1836–1864	28	Jackson
Philip P. Barbour	1836–1841	4	Jackson
John Catron	1837–1865	28	Van Buren
John McKinley	1837–1852	15	Van Buren
Peter V. Daniel	1841–1860	19	Van Buren
Samuel Nelson	1845–1872	27	Tyler
Levi Woodbury	1845–1851	5	Polk
Robert C. Grier	1846–1870	23	Polk
Benjamin R. Curtis	1851–1857	6	Fillmore
John A. Campbell	1853–1861	8	Pierce
Nathan Clifford	1858–1881	23	Buchanan
Noah H. Swayne	1862–1881	18	Lincoln
Samuel F. Miller	1862–1890	28	Lincoln
David Davis	1862–1877	14	Lincoln
Stephen J. Field	1863–1897	34	Lincoln
Salmon P. Chase	1864–1873	8	Lincoln
William Strong	1870–1880	10	Grant
Joseph P. Bradley	1870–1892	22	Grant
Ward Hunt	1873–1882	9	Grant
Morrison R. Waite	1874–1888	14	Grant
John M. Harlan	1877–1911	34	Hayes
William B. Woods	1880–1887	7	Hayes
Stanley Matthews	1881–1889	7	Garfield
Horace Gray	1882–1902	20	Arthur
Samuel Blatchford	1882–1893	11	Arthur
Lucius Q. C. Lamar	1888–1893	5	Cleveland
Melville W. Fuller	1888–1910	21	Cleveland
David J. Brewer	1890–1910	20	B. Harrison
Henry B. Brown	1890–1906	16	B. Harrison
George Shiras, Jr.	1892–1903	10	B. Harrison
Howell E. Jackson	1893–1895	2	B. Harrison
Edward D. White	1894–1910	16	Cleveland
Rufus W. Peckham	1895–1909	14	Cleveland
Joseph McKenna	1898–1925	26	McKinley
Oliver W. Holmes, Jr.	1902–1932	30	T. Roosevelt
William R. Day	1903–1922	19	T. Roosevelt
William H. Moody	1906–1910	3	T. Roosevelt
Horace H. Lurton	1910–1914	4	Taft
Charles E. Hughes	1910–1916	5	Taft
Willis Van Devanter	1911–1937	26	Taft
Joseph R. Lamar	1911–1916	5	Taft
Edward D. White	1910–1921	11	Taft
Mahlon Pitney	1912–1922	10	Taft
James C. McReynolds	1914–1941	26	Wilson
Louis D. Brandeis	1916–1939	22	Wilson
John H. Clarke	1916–1922	6	Wilson
William H. Taft	1921–1930	8	Harding
George Sutherland	1922–1938	15	Harding
Pierce Butler	1922–1939	16	Harding
Edward T. Sanford	1923–1930	7	Harding
Harlan F. Stone	1925–1941	16	Coolidge
Charles E. Hughes	1930–1941	11	Hoover
Owen J. Roberts	1930–1945	15	Hoover
Benjamin N. Cardozo	1932–1938	6	Hoover
Hugo L. Black	1937–1971	34	F. Roosevelt
Stanley F. Reed	1938–1957	19	F. Roosevelt
Felix Frankfurter	1939–1962	23	F. Roosevelt
William O. Douglas	1939–1975	36	F. Roosevelt
Frank Murphy	1940–1949	9	F. Roosevelt
Harlan F. Stone	1941–1946	5	F. Roosevelt
James F. Byrnes	1941–1942	1	F. Roosevelt
Robert H. Jackson	1941–1954	13	F. Roosevelt
Wiley B. Rutledge	1943–1949	6	F. Roosevelt
Harold H. Burton	1945–1958	13	Truman
Fred M. Vinson	1946–1953	7	Truman
Tom C. Clark	1949–1967	18	Truman
Sherman Minton	1949–1956	7	Truman
Earl Warren	1953–1969	16	Eisenhower
John Marshall Harlan	1955–1971	16	Eisenhower
William J. Brennan, Jr.	1956–1990	34	Eisenhower
Charles E. Whittaker	1957–1962	5	Eisenhower
Potter Stewart	1958–1981	23	Eisenhower
Byron R. White	1962–1993	31	Kennedy
Arthur J. Goldberg	1962–1965	3	Kennedy
Abe Fortas	1965–1969	4	Johnson
Thurgood Marshall	1967–1991	24	Johnson
Warren E. Burger	1969–1986	18	Nixon
Harry A. Blackmun	1970–1994	24	Nixon
Lewis F. Powell, Jr.	1971–1987	15	Nixon
William H. Rehnquist[2]	1971–	—	Nixon
John P. Stevens III	1975–	—	Ford
Sandra Day O'Connor	1981–	—	Reagan
Antonin Scalia	1986–	—	Reagan
Anthony M. Kennedy	1988–	—	Reagan
David Souter	1990–	—	Bush
Clarence Thomas	1991–	—	Bush
Ruth Bader Ginsburg	1993–	—	Clinton
Stephen G. Breyer	1994–	—	Clinton

Note: Chief Justices appear in bold type.

[1]Acting Chief Justice; Senate refused to confirm appointment.

[2]Chief Justice from 1986 on (Reagan administration).

Index